STRATEGIC MARKETING PROBLEMS

Cases and Comments

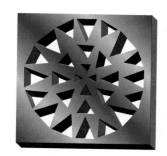

TENTH EDITION

Roger A. Kerin
Southern Methodist University

Robert A. Peterson
University of Texas at Austin

PEARSON

Prentice Hall

Upper Saddle River, New Jersey 07458

Library of Congress Cataloging-in-Publication Data

Kerin, Roger A.

    Strategic marketing problems: cases and comments / Roger A.
Kerin, Robert A. Peterson.— 10th ed.

      p.   cm.

    Includes bibliographical references and indexes.

    ISBN 0-13-142184-0

    1. Marketing—Decision making—Case studies. 2. Marketing—
Management—Case studies. I. Peterson, Robert A. (Robert Allen),
1944-II. Title.

HF5415.135.k47 2003

658.8'02—dc21

          2003044004

          CIP

Senior Editor: Wendy Craven
Editor-in-Chief: Jeff Shelstad
Assistant Editor: Melissa Pellerano
Executive Marketing Manager: Michelle O'Brien
Marketing Assistant: Amanda Fisher
Managing Editor (Production): Judy Leale
Production Editor: Virginia Somma
Production Assistant: Joe DeProspero
Buyer: Diane Peirano
Design Manager: Maria Lange
Designer: Steve Frim
Interior Design: Kim Nickisher
Cover Design: Kim Nickisher
Illustrator (Interior): Warren Fischbach
Manager, Print Production: Christy Mahon
Composition: Suzanne Duda
Printer/Binder: Courier Westford

Credits and acknowledgments borrowed from other sources and reproduced, with permission, in this textbook appear
on appropriate page within text.

Pearson Prentice Hall™ is a trademark of Pearson Education, Inc.
Pearson©is a registered trademark of Pearson p1c
Prentice Hall© is a registered trademark of Pearson Education, Inc.

Pearson Education LTD.
Pearson Education Singapore, Pte. Ltd
Pearson Education, Canada, Ltd
Pearson Education–Japan

Pearson Education Australia Pty, Limited
Pearson Education North Asia Ltds
Pearson Education de Mexico, S.A. de C.V.
Pearson Education Malaysia, Pte. Ltd

10 9 8 7 6 5 4 3 2 1
ISBN 0-13-142184-0

To Our Families

Contents

Preface

Decision making in marketing is first and foremost a skill. Like most skills, it requires tools and terminology. Like all skills, it is best learned through practice. This book is dedicated to the development of decision-making skills in marketing. Textual material introduces concepts and tools useful in structuring and solving marketing problems. Case studies describing actual marketing problems provide an opportunity for those concepts and tools to be employed in practice. In every case study, the decision maker must develop a strategy consistent with the underlying factors existing in the situation presented and must consider the implications of that strategy for the organization and its environment.

The tenth edition of *Strategic Marketing Problems: Cases and Comments* seeks a balance between marketing management content and process. The book consists of 10 chapters and 43 cases that feature contemporary marketing perspectives and practices.

Chapter 1, "Foundations of Strategic Marketing Management," provides an overview of the strategic marketing management process. The principal emphasis is on defining an organization's business, mission, and goals; identifying and framing organizational opportunities; formulating product-market strategies; budgeting; and controlling the marketing effort. The Appendix to Chapter 1 contains a marketing plan for an actual company, Paradise Kitchens®, Inc. The plan is annotated to focus attention on substantive elements of the plan as well a style and layout elements.

Chapter 2, "Financial Aspects of Marketing Management," reviews basic concepts from managerial accounting and managerial finance that are useful in marketing management. Primary emphasis is placed on such concepts as cost structure, relevant versus sunk costs, margins, contribution analysis, liquidity, discounted cash flow, operating leverage, and preparing *pro forma* income statements.

Chapter 3, "Marketing Decision Making and Case Analysis," introduces a systematic process for decision making and provides an overview of various aspects of case and decision analysis. Suggestions for preparing and presenting a case analysis are also provided. A sample case and written student analysis are presented in the Appendix at the end of the book. The student analysis illustrates the nature and scope of a written case presentation, including the qualitative and quantitative analyses essential to a good presentation.

Chapter 4, "Opportunity Analysis, Market Segmentation, and Market Targeting," focuses on the identification and evaluation of domestic and global marketing opportunities. Market segmentation, market targeting, and market potential and profitability concepts and applications are described in some depth.

Chapter 5, "Product and Service Strategy and Brand Management," focuses on the management of the organization's offering. New-offering development, life-cycle management, product or service positioning, branding decisions, brand equity, brand growth strategies, and brand valuation are emphasized.

Chapter 6, "Integrated Marketing Communication Strategy and Management," raises issues in the design, execution, and evaluation of an integrated communication mix. Decisions concerned with communications objectives, strategy, budgeting, programming, and effectiveness are addressed. In addition, sales management issues and the challenge of leveraging advertising and personal selling with marketing Web sites are highlighted.

Chapter 7, "Marketing Channel Strategy and Management," introduces a variety of considerations affecting channel selection and modification as well as trade relations. Specific decision areas covered include direct versus indirect distribution, dual distribution and multi-channel marketing, cost-benefit analysis of channel choice and management, and marketing channel conflict and coordination.

Chapter 8, "Pricing Strategy and Management," highlights concepts and applications in price determination and modification. Emphasis is placed on evaluating demand, cost, and competitive influences when selecting or modifying pricing strategies for products and services. Product-line pricing is also addressed.

Chapter 9, "Marketing Strategy Reformulation: The Control Process," focuses on the appraisal of marketing actions for the purpose of developing reformulation and recovery strategies. Considerations and techniques applicable to strategic and operations control in a marketing context are introduced.

Chapter 10, "Comprehensive Marketing Programs," raises issues in developing integrated marketing strategies. Emphasis is placed on marketing program decisions for new and existing products and services, including issues related to marketing-mix interactions, marketing program implementation, and marketing organization.

The case selection in this book reflects a broad overview of contemporary marketing problems and applications. One half of the cases are dated since 2000. Of the 43 cases included, 30 deal with consumer products and services and 13 have a business-to-business marketing orientation. Ten cases introduce marketing issues in the international arena. Marketing of services is addressed in four cases. One-half of the cases are new, revised, or updated for this edition, and many have spreadsheet applications embedded in the case analysis. All text and case material has been classroom tested.

The efforts of many people are reflected here. First, we thank those institutions and individuals who have kindly granted us permission to include their cases in this edition. The cases contribute significantly to the overall quality of the book, and each individual is prominently acknowledged in the Contents and at the bottom of the page on which the case begins. We specifically wish to thank the Harvard Business School, Stanford University, The University of Western Ontario, and Queen's University for granting permission to reproduce cases authored by their faculties. Second, we wish to thank our numerous collaborators, whose efforts made the difference between good cases and excellent cases. Third, we thank the adopters of the previous nine editions of the book for their many comments and suggestions for improvements. Finally, we wish to thank the numerous reviewers of this and previous editions for their conscientious and constructive reviews of our material. Naturally, we bear full responsibility for any errors of omission and commission in the final product.

Roger A. Kerin

Robert A. Peterson

CHAPTER 1

Foundations of Strategic Marketing Management

 The primary purpose of marketing is to create long-term and mutually beneficial exchange relationships between an entity and the publics (individuals and organizations) with which it interacts. Though this fundamental purpose of marketing is timeless, the manner in which organizations undertake it continues to evolve. No longer do marketing managers function solely to direct day-to-day operations; they must make strategic decisions as well. This elevation of marketing perspectives to a strategic position in organizations has resulted in expanded responsibilities for marketing managers. Increasingly, they find themselves involved in charting the direction of the organization and contributing to decisions that will create and sustain a competitive advantage and affect long-term organizational performance. According to a senior strategic-planning manager at General Electric:

> [T]he marketing manager is the most significant functional contributor to the strategic-planning process, with leadership roles in defining the business mission; analysis of the environmental, competitive, and business situations; developing objectives, goals, and strategies; and defining product, market distribution, and quality plans to implement the business's strategies. This involvement extends to the development of programs and operational plans that are fully linked with the strategic plan.[1]

The transition of the marketing manager from being only an implementer to being a maker of organization strategy has prompted the emergence of strategic marketing management as a course of study and practice. *Strategic marketing management* consists of five complex and interrelated analytical processes.

1. Defining the organization's business, mission, and goals
2. Identifying and framing organizational growth opportunities
3. Formulating product-market strategies
4. Budgeting marketing, financial, and production resources
5. Developing reformulation and recovery strategies

The remainder of this chapter discusses each of these processes and their relationships to one another.

■ DEFINING THE ORGANIZATION'S BUSINESS, MISSION, AND GOALS

The practice of strategic marketing management begins with a clearly stated business definition, mission, and set of goals or objectives. A business definition outlines the scope of a particular organization's operations. Its mission is a written statement of organizational purpose. Goals or objectives specify what an organization intends to achieve. Each plays an important role in describing the character of an organization and what it seeks to accomplish.

Business Definition

Determining what business an organization is in is neither obvious nor easy. In many instances, a single organization may operate several businesses, as is the case with large *Fortune* 500 companies. Defining each of these businesses is a necessary first step in strategic marketing management.

Contemporary strategic marketing perspectives indicate that an organization should define a business by the type of customers it wishes to serve, the particular needs of those customer groups it wishes to satisfy, and the means or technology by which the organization will satisfy these customer needs.[2] By defining a business from a customer or market perspective, an organization is appropriately viewed as a customer-satisfying endeavor, not a product-producing or service-delivery enterprise. Products and services are transient, as is often the technology or means used to produce or deliver them. Basic customer needs and customer groups are more enduring. For example, the means for delivering prerecorded music has undergone significant change over the past 25 years. During this period, the dominant prerecorded music technologies and products evolved from plastic records, to eight-track tapes, to cassettes, and most recently, to compact discs. By comparison, the principal consumer buying segment(s) and needs satisfied have varied little.

Much of the recent corporate restructuring and refocusing has resulted from senior company executives asking the question, "What business are we in?" The experience of *Encyclopaedia Britannica* is a case in point.[3] The venerable publishing company is best known for its comprehensive and authoritative 32-volume, leather-bound book reference series first printed in 1768. In the late 1990s, however, the company found itself in a precarious competitive environment. CD-ROMs and the Internet had become the study tools of choice for students, and Microsoft's Encarta CD-ROM and IBM's CD-ROM joint venture with *World Book* were attracting Britannica's core customers. The result? Book sales fell 83 percent between 1990 and 1997. Britannica's senior management was confident that the need for dependable and trustworthy information among curious and intelligent customers remained. However, the technology for satisfying these needs had changed. This realization prompted Britannica to redefine its business. According to a company official: "We're reinventing our business. We're not in the book business. We're in the information business." By early 2003, the company was on its way to becoming the premier information site on the Internet. Britannica's subscription service (www.eb.com) markets archival information to schools and public and business libraries. Its consumer Web site (www.britanica.com) is a source of information and search engine leading to some 150,000 Web sites selected by Britannica staffers for information quality and accuracy.

Business Mission

An organization's business mission complements its business definition. As a written statement, a mission underscores the scope of an organization's operations apparent in its business definition and reflects management's vision of what the organization seeks to do. Although there is no overall definition for all mission statements, most statements describe an organization's purpose with reference to its customers, products or services, markets, philosophy, and technology.[4] Some mission statements are generally stated, such as that for Saturn Corporation, a division of General Motors. Saturn's mission is to:

> Market vehicles developed and manufactured in the United States that are world leaders in quality, cost, and customer satisfaction through the integration of people, technology, and business systems and to transfer knowledge, technology, and experience throughout General Motors.

Others are more specifically written, like that for Hendison Electronics Corporation. Hendison Electronics Corporation aspires

> to serve the discriminating purchasers of home entertainment products who approach their purchase in a deliberate manner with heavy consideration of long-term benefits. We will emphasize home entertainment products with superior performance, style, reliability, and value that require representative display, professional selling, trained service, and brand acceptance—retailed through reputable electronic specialists to those consumers whom the company can most effectively service.

Mission statements also apply to not-for-profit organizations. For instance, the mission of the American Red Cross is

> to improve the quality of human life; to enhance self-reliance and concern for others; and to help people avoid, prepare for, and cope with emergencies.

A carefully crafted mission statement that succinctly conveys organizational purpose can provide numerous benefits to an organization, including focus to its marketing effort. It can (1) crystallize management's vision of the organization's long-term direction and character; (2) provide guidance in identifying, pursuing, and evaluating market and product opportunities; and (3) inspire and challenge employees to do those things that are valued by the organization and its customers. It also provides direction for setting business goals or objectives.

Business Goals

Goals or objectives convert the organization's mission into tangible actions and results that are to be achieved, often within a specific time frame. For example, the 3M Company emphasizes research and development and innovation in its business mission. This view is made tangible in one of the company's goals: 30 percent of 3M's annual revenues must come from company products that are less than four years old.[5]

Goals or objectives divide into three major categories: production, financial, and marketing. Production goals or objectives apply to the use of manufacturing and service capacity and to product and service quality. Financial goals or objectives focus on return on investment, return on sales, profit, cash flow, and shareholder wealth. Marketing goals or objectives emphasize market share, marketing productivity, sales volume, profit, customer satisfaction, and customer value creation. When production, financial, and marketing goals or objectives are combined, they represent a composite picture of organizational purpose within a specific time frame; accordingly, they must complement one another.

Goal or objective setting should be problem-centered and future-oriented. Because goals or objectives represent statements of what the organization wishes to achieve in a specific time frame, they implicitly arise from an understanding of the current situation. Therefore, managers need an appraisal of operations or a *situation analysis* to determine reasons for the gap between what was or is expected and what has happened or will happen. If performance has met expectations, the question arises as to future directions. If performance has not met expectations, managers must diagnose the reasons for this difference and enact a remedial program. Chapter 3 provides an expanded discussion on performing a situation analysis.

■ IDENTIFYING AND FRAMING ORGANIZATIONAL GROWTH OPPORTUNITIES

Once the character and direction of the organization have been outlined in its business definition, mission, and goals or objectives, the practice of strategic marketing management enters an entrepreneurial phase. Using business definition, mission, and goals as a guide, the search for and evaluation of organizational growth opportunities can begin.

Converting Environmental Opportunities into Organizational Opportunities

Three questions help marketing managers decide whether certain environmental opportunities represent viable organizational growth opportunities:

- What might we do?
- What do we do best?
- What must we do?

Each of these questions assists in identifying and framing organizational growth opportunities. They also highlight major concepts in strategic marketing management.

The *what might we do* question introduces the concept of *environmental opportunity*. Unmet or changing consumer needs, unsatisfied buyer groups, and new means or technology for delivering value to prospective buyers represent sources of environmental opportunities for organizations. In this regard, environmental opportunities are boundless. However, the mere presence of an environmental opportunity does not mean that an organizational growth opportunity exists. Two additional questions must be asked.

The *what do we do best* question introduces the concept of organizational capability, or distinctive competency. *Distinctive competency* describes an organization's unique strengths or qualities, including skills, technologies, or resources that distinguish it from other organizations.[6] In order for any of an organization's strengths or qualities to be considered truly distinctive and a source of competitive advantage, two criteria must be satisfied. First, the strength must be imperfectly imitable by competitors. That is, competitors cannot replicate a skill (such as the direct-marketing competency of Dell Computer) easily or without a sizable investment of time, effort, and money. Second, the strength should make a significant contribution to the benefits perceived by customers and, by doing so, provide superior value to them. For example, the ability to engage in technological innovation that is wanted and provides value to customers is a distinctive competency. Consider the Safety Razor Division of the Gillette Company.[7] Its distinctive competencies lie in three areas: (1) shaving technology and development, (2) high-volume manufacturing of precision metal and plastic products, and (3) marketing of mass-distributed consumer package goods. These competencies were responsible for the Mach 3 and Venus razor, which have sustained Gillette's dominance of the men's and women's wet-shaving market.

Finally, the *what must we do* question introduces the concept of success requirements in an industry or market. *Success requirements* are basic tasks that an organization must perform in a market or industry to compete successfully. These requirements are subtle in nature and often overlooked. For example, distribution and inventory control are critical success factors in the cosmetics industry. Firms competing in the personal computer industry recognize that the requirements for success include low-cost production capabilities, access to distribution channels, and continuous innovation in software development.

The linkage among environmental opportunity, distinctive competency, and success requirements will determine whether an organizational opportunity exists.

A clearly defined statement of success requirements serves as a device for matching an environmental opportunity with an organization's distinctive competencies. If *what must be done* is inconsistent with *what can be done* to capitalize on an environmental opportunity, an organizational growth opportunity will fail to materialize. Too often, organizations ignore this linkage and pursue seemingly lucrative environmental opportunities that are doomed from the start. Exxon Mobil Corporation learned this lesson painfully after investing $500 million in the office products market over a 10-year period only to see the venture fail. After the company abandoned this venture, a former Exxon Mobil executive summed up what had been learned: "Don't get involved where you don't have the skills. It's hard enough to make money at what you're good at."[8] By clearly establishing the linkages necessary for success before taking any action, an organization can minimize its risk of failure. An executive for L'eggs hosiery illustrates this point when specifying his new-venture criteria:

> [P]roducts that can be sold through food and drugstore outlets, are purchased by women, . . . can be easily and distinctly packaged, and comprise at least a $500 million retail market not already dominated by one or two major producers.[9]

When one considers L'eggs' past successes, it is apparent that whatever environmental opportunities are pursued will be consistent with what L'eggs does best, as illustrated by past achievements in markets whose success requirements are similar. An expanded discussion of these points is found in Chapter 4.

SWOT Analysis

SWOT analysis is a formal framework for identifying and framing organizational growth opportunities. SWOT is an acronym for an organization's *S*trengths and *W*eaknesses and external *O*pportunities and *T*hreats. It is an easy-to-use framework for focusing attention on the fact that an organizational growth opportunity results from a good fit between an organization's internal capabilities (apparent in its strengths and weaknesses) and its external environment reflected in the presence of environmental opportunities and threats. Many organizations also perform a SWOT analysis as part of their goal- or objective-setting process.

Exhibit 1.1 on page 6 displays a SWOT analysis framework depicting representative entries for internal strengths and weaknesses and external opportunities and threats. A strength is something that an organization is good at doing or some characteristic that gives the organization an important capability. Something an organization lacks or does poorly relative to other organizations is a weakness. Opportunities represent external developments or conditions in the environment that have favorable implications for the organization. Threats, on the other hand, pose dangers to the welfare of the organization.

A properly conducted SWOT analysis goes beyond the simple preparation of lists. Attention needs to be placed on evaluating strengths, weaknesses, opportunities, and threats and drawing conclusions about how each might affect the organization. The following questions might be asked once strengths, weaknesses, opportunities, and threats have been identified:

1. Which internal strengths represent distinctive competencies? Do these strengths compare favorably with what are believed to be market or industry success requirements? Looking at Exhibit 1.1, for example, does "proven innovation skill" strength represent a distinctive competency and a market success requirement?

2. Which internal weaknesses disqualify the organization from pursuing certain opportunities? Look again at Exhibit 1.1, and note that the organization acknowledges that it has a "weak distribution network and a subpar saleforce." How might

EXHIBIT 1.1

Sample SWOT Analysis Framework and Representative Examples

Selected Internal Factors	Representative		Selected External Factors	Representative	
	Strengths	Weaknesses		Opportunities	Threats
Management	Experienced management talent	Lack of management depth	Economic	Upturn in the business cycle; evidence of growing personal disposable income	Adverse shifts in foreign exchange rates
Marketing	Well thought of by buyers; effective advertising program	Weak distribution network; subpar sales force	Competition	Complacency among domestic competitors	Entry of lower-cost foreign competitors
Manufacturing	Available manufacturing capacity	Higher overall production costs relative to key competitors	Consumer trends	Unfulfilled customer needs on high and low end of product category suggesting a product line expansion possibility	Growing preference for private-label products
R&D	Proven innovation skills	Poor track record in bringing innovations to the marketplace	Technology	Patent protection of complementary technology ending	Newer substitute technologies imminent
Finance	Little debt relative to industry average	Weak cash flow position	Legal/ regulatory	Falling trade barriers in attractive foreign markets	Increased U.S. regulation of product-testing procedures and labeling
Offerings	Unique, high-quality products	Too narrow a product line	Industry/ market structure	New distribution channels evolving that reach a broader customer population	Low-entry barriers for new competitors

    this organizational weakness affect the opportunity described as "new distribution channels evolving that reach a broader customer population"?

3. Does a pattern emerge from the listing of strengths, weaknesses, opportunities, and threats? Inspection of Exhibit 1.1 reveals that low-entry barriers into the market/industry may contribute to the entry of lower-cost foreign competitors. This does not bode well for domestic competitors labeled as "complacent" and the organization's acknowledged high production costs.

■ FORMULATING PRODUCT-MARKET STRATEGIES

In practice, organizational opportunities frequently emerge from an organization's existing markets or from newly identified markets. Opportunities also arise for existing, improved, or new products and services. Matching products and markets to form product-market strategies is the subject of the next set of decision processes.

Product-market strategies consist of plans for matching an organization's existing or potential offerings with the needs of markets, informing markets that the offerings exist, having offerings available at the right time and place to facilitate exchange, and assigning prices to offerings. In short, a product-market strategy involves selecting specific markets and profitably reaching them through an integrated program called a *marketing mix.*

Exhibit 1.2 classifies product-market strategies according to the match between offerings and markets.[10] The operational implications and requirements of each strategy are briefly described in the following subsections.

Market-Penetration Strategy

A *market-penetration strategy* dictates that an organization seek to gain greater dominance in a market in which it already has an offering. This strategy involves attempts to increase present buyers' usage or consumption rates of the offering, attract buyers of competing offerings, or stimulate product trial among potential customers. The mix of marketing activities might include lower prices for the offerings, expanded distribution to provide wider coverage of an existing market, and heavier promotional efforts extolling the "unique" advantages of an organization's offering over competing offerings. For example, following the acquisition of Gatorade from Quaker Oats, PepsiCo has announced that it expects to increase Gatorade's 85 percent share of the sports drink market through broader distribution and more aggressive advertising.[11]

Several organizations have attempted to gain dominance by promoting more frequent and varied usage of their offering. For example, the Florida Orange Growers Association advocates drinking orange juice throughout the day rather than for breakfast only. Airlines stimulate usage through a variety of reduced-fare programs and various family-travel packages, designed to reach the primary traveler's spouse and children.

Marketing managers should consider a number of factors before adopting a penetration strategy. First, they must examine market growth. A penetration strategy is usually more effective in a growth market. Attempts to increase market share when volume is stable often result in aggressive retaliatory actions by competitors. Second, they must consider competitive reaction. Procter & Gamble implemented a penetration

EXHIBIT 1.2

Product-Market Strategies

		Markets	
		Existing	*New*
Offerings	*Existing*	Market penetration	Market development
	New	New offering development	Diversification

strategy for its Folgers coffee in selected East Coast cities, only to run head-on into an equally aggressive reaction from Kraft Foods' Maxwell House Division. According to one observer of the competitive situation:

> When Folger's mailed millions of coupons offering consumers 45 cents off on a one-pound can of coffee, Maxwell House countered with newspaper coupons of its own. When Folger's gave retailers 15 percent discounts from the list price . . . , Maxwell House met them head-on. [Maxwell House] let Folger's lead off with a TV blitz. . . . Then [Maxwell House] saturated the airwaves.[12]

The result of this struggle was no change in market share for either firm. Third, marketing managers must consider the capacity of the market to increase usage or consumption rates and the availability of new buyers. Both are particularly relevant when viewed from the perspective of the conversion costs involved in capturing buyers from competitors, stimulating usage, and attracting new users.

Market-Development Strategy

A *market-development strategy* dictates that an organization introduce its existing offerings to markets other than those it is currently serving. Examples include introducing existing products to different geographical areas (including international expansion) or different buying publics. For example, Harley-Davidson engaged in a market-development strategy when it entered Japan, Germany, Italy, and France. Lowe's, the home improvement chain, employed this strategy when it focused attention on attracting women shoppers to its stores.[13]

The mix of marketing activities used must often be varied to reach different markets with differing buying patterns and requirements. Reaching new markets often requires modification of the basic offering, different distribution outlets, or a change in sales effort and advertising.

Like the market-penetration strategy, market development involves a careful consideration of competitor strengths and weaknesses and competitor retaliation potential. Moreover, because the firm seeks new buyers, it must understand their number, motivation, and buying patterns in order to develop marketing activities successfully. Finally, the firm must consider its strengths, in terms of adaptability to new markets, in order to evaluate the potential success of the venture.

Market development in the international arena has grown in importance and usually takes one of four forms: (1) exporting, (2) licensing, (3) joint venture, or (4) direct investment.[14] Each option has advantages and disadvantages. Exporting involves marketing the same offering in another country either directly (through sales offices) or through intermediaries in a foreign country. Because this approach typically requires minimal capital investment and is easy to initiate, it is a popular option for developing foreign markets. Procter & Gamble, for instance, exports its deodorants, soaps, fragrances, shampoos, and other health and beauty products to Eastern Europe and Russia. Licensing is a contractual arrangement whereby one firm (licensee) is given the rights to patents, trademarks, know-how, and other intangible assets by its owner (licensor) in return for a royalty (usually 5 percent of gross sales) or a fee. For example, Cadbury Schweppes PLC, a London-based multinational firm, has licensed Hershey Foods to sell its candies in the United States for a fee of $300 million. Licensing provides a low-risk, quick, and capital-free entry into a foreign market. However, the licensor usually has no control over production and marketing by the licensee. A joint venture, often called a strategic alliance, involves investment by both a foreign firm and a local company to create a new entity in the host country. The two companies share ownership, control, and profits of the entity. Joint ventures are popular because one company may not have the necessary financial, technical, or managerial resources to enter a market alone. This approach also often ensures against trade barriers being imposed on the foreign firm by the government of the host company. Japanese companies frequently engage in joint ventures with American and European firms to gain access to foreign markets. A problem frequently arising from joint ventures is that the partners do not always agree on how the new entity should be run. Direct investment in a manufacturing and/or assembly facility in a foreign market is the most risky option and requires the greatest commitment. However, it brings the firm closer to its customers and may be the most profitable approach for developing foreign markets. For these reasons, direct investment must be evaluated closely in terms of benefits and costs. Direct investment often follows one of the three other approaches to foreign-market entry. For example, Mars, Inc. originally exported its M&Ms, Snickers, and Mars bars to Russia but recently opened a $200 million candy factory outside Moscow.

Product-Development Strategy

A *product-development strategy* dictates that the organization create new offerings for existing markets. The approach taken may be to develop totally new offerings (product innovation) to enhance the value to customers of existing offerings (product augmentation), or to broaden the existing line of offerings by adding different sizes, forms, flavors, and so forth (product line extension). Personal digital assistants, such as Palm Pilot, are an example of product innovation. Product augmentation can be achieved in numerous ways. One is to bundle complementary items or services with an existing offering. For example, programming services, application aids, and training programs for buyers enhance the value of personal computers. Another way is to improve the functional performance of the offering. Producers of facsimile machines have done this by improving print quality. Many types of product-line extensions are possible. Personal-care companies market deodorants in powder, spray, and liquid forms; Gatorade is sold in 18 flavors; and Frito-Lay offers its Lay's potato chips in a number of package sizes.

Companies successful at developing and commercializing new offerings lead their industries in sales growth and profitability. The likelihood of success is increased if the development effort results in offerings that satisfy a clearly understood buyer need. In the toy industry, for instance, these needs translate into products with three qualities: (1) lasting play value, (2) the ability to be shared with other children, and (3) the ability to stimulate a child's imagination.[15] Successful commercialization occurs when the offering can be communicated and delivered to a well-defined buyer group at a price it is willing and able to pay.

Important considerations in planning a product-development strategy concern the market size and volume necessary for the effort to be profitable, the magnitude and timing of competitive response, the impact of the new product on existing offerings, and the capacity (in terms of human and financial investment and technology) of the organization to deliver the offerings to the market(s). More importantly, successful new offerings must have a significant "point of difference" reflected in superior product or service characteristics that deliver unique and wanted benefits to consumers. Two examples from General Mills illustrate this view.[16] In 1995, the company introduced Fringos, a sweetened cereal flake about the size of a corn chip. Consumers were supposed to snack on them, but they didn't. The point of difference was not significant enough to get consumers to switch from competing snacks such as popcorn, potato chips, or tortilla chips. On the other hand, General Mills' Big G Milk 'n Cereal Bar, which combines cereal and a milk-based layer, has succeeded because it satisfies convenience-oriented consumers who desire to "eat and go."

The potential for cannibalism must be considered with a product-development strategy. *Cannibalism* occurs when sales of a new product or service come at the expense of sales of existing products or services already marketed by the firm. For example, it is estimated that 75 percent of Gillette's Mach 3 razor volume came from the company's other razors and shaving systems. Cannibalism of this degree is likely to occur in many product-development programs. The issue faced by the manager is whether it detracts from the overall profitability of the organization's total mix of offerings. At Gillette, the cannibalism rate for Mach 3 is viewed favorably since its gross profit margin is three times higher than the company's other razors.[17]

Diversification

Diversification involves the development or acquisition of offerings new to the organization and the introduction of those offerings to publics not previously served by the organization. Many firms have adopted this strategy in recent years to take advantage of perceived growth opportunities. Yet diversification is often a high-risk strategy because both the offerings (and often their underlying technology) and the public or market served are new to the organization.

Consider the following examples of failed diversification. Anheuser-Busch recorded 17 years of losses with its Eagle Snacks Division and incurred a $206 million write-off when the division was finally shut down. Singer's effort to develop a business-machines venture over a 10-year period was abandoned while still unprofitable. Gerber Products Company, which holds 70 percent of the U.S. baby-food market, has been mostly unsuccessful in diversifying into child-care centers, toys, furniture, and adult food and beverages. Coca-Cola's many attempts at diversification—acquiring wine companies, a movie studio, and a pasta manufacturer, and producing television game shows—have also proven to be largely unsuccessful. These examples highlight the importance of understanding the link between market success requirements and an organization's distinctive competency. In each of these cases, a bridge was not made between these two concepts and, thus, an organizational opportunity was not realized.[18]

Still, diversifications can be successful. Successful diversifications typically result from an organization's attempt to apply its distinctive competency in reaching new markets with new offerings. By relying on its marketing expertise and extensive distribution system, Procter & Gamble has had success with offerings ranging from cake mixes to disposable diapers to laundry detergents.

Strategy Selection

A recurrent issue in strategic marketing management is determining the consistency of product-market strategies with the organization's definition, mission and capabilities, market capacity and behavior, environmental forces, and competitive activities. Proper analysis of these factors depends on the availability and evaluation of relevant information. Information on markets should include data on size, buying behavior, and requirements. Information on environmental forces such as social, legal, political, demographic, and economic changes is necessary to determine the future viability of the organization's offerings and the markets served. In recent years, for example, organizations have had to alter or adapt their product-market strategies because of political actions (deregulation), social changes (increase in the number of employed women), economic fluctuations (income shifts and changes in disposable personal income), demographic trends (increasing racial and ethnic diversity), attitudes (value consciousness), technological advances (the growth of the Internet/World Wide Web), and population shifts (city to suburb and northern to southern United States)—to name just a few of the environmental changes. Competitive activities must be monitored to ascertain their existing or possible strategies and performance in satisfying buyer needs.

In practice, the strategy selection decision is based on an analysis of the costs and benefits of alternative strategies and their probabilities of success. For example, a manager may compare the costs and benefits involved in further penetrating an existing market to those associated with introducing the existing product to a new market. It is important to make a careful analysis of competitive structure; market growth, decline, or shifts; and opportunity costs (potential benefits not obtained). The product or ser-

EXHIBIT 1.3

Decision-Tree Format

Action	Response	Outcome

A_1 → R_1 → O_1
A_1 → R_2 → O_2
A_2 → R_1 → O_3
A_2 → R_2 → O_4

vice itself may dictate a strategy change. If the product has been purchased by all of the buyers it is going to attract in an existing market, opportunities for growth beyond replacement purchases are reduced. This situation would indicate a need to search out new buyers (markets) or to develop new products or services for present markets.

The probabilities of success of the various strategies must then be considered. A. T. Kearney, a management consulting firm, has provided rough probability estimates of success for each of the four basic strategies.[19] The probability of a successful diversification is 1 in 20. The probability of successfully introducing an existing product into a new market (market-development strategy) is 1 in 4. There is a 50–50 chance of success for a new product being introduced into an existing market (product-development strategy). Finally, minor modification of an offering directed toward its existing market (market-penetration strategy) has the highest probability of success.

A useful technique for gauging potential outcomes of alternative marketing strategies is to array possible actions, the response to these actions, and the outcomes in the form of a decision tree, so named because of the branching out of responses from action taken. This implies that for any action taken, certain responses can be anticipated, each with its own specific outcomes. Exhibit 1.3 shows a decision tree.

As an example, consider a situation in which a marketing manager must decide between a market-penetration strategy and a market-development strategy. Suppose the manager recognizes that competitors may react aggressively or passively to either strategy. This situation can be displayed vividly using the decision-tree scheme, as shown in Exhibit 1.4. This representation allows the manager to consider actions, responses, and outcomes simultaneously. The decision tree shows that the highest

EXHIBIT 1.4

Sample Decision Tree

Action	Response	Outcome

Market-penetration strategy → Aggressive competition → Estimated profit of $2 million
Market-penetration strategy → Passive competition → Estimated profit of $3 million
Market-development strategy → Aggressive competition → Estimated profit of $1 million
Market-development strategy → Passive competition → Estimated profit of $4 million

profits will result if a market-development strategy is enacted and competitors react passively. The manager must resolve the question of competitive reaction because an aggressive response will plunge the profit to $1 million, which is less than either outcome under the market-penetration strategy. The manager must rely on informed judgment to assess subjectively the likelihood of competitive response. Chapter 3 provides a more detailed description of decision analysis and its application.

The Marketing Mix

Matching offerings and markets requires recognition of the other marketing activities available to the marketing manager. Combined with the offering, these activities form the marketing mix.

A marketing mix typically encompasses activities controllable by the organization. These include the kind of product, service, or idea offered (product strategy), how it will be communicated to buyers (communication strategy), the method for distributing the offering to buyers (channel strategy), and the amount buyers will pay for the offering (price strategy). Each of these individual strategies is described later in this book. Here it is sufficient to note that each element of the marketing mix plays a role in stimulating a market's (buyers') willingness and ability to buy and creating customer value. For example, communications—personal selling, advertising, sales promotion, and public relations—informs and assures buyers that the offering will meet their needs. Marketing channels satisfy buyers' shopping patterns and purchase requirements in terms of point-of-purchase information and offering availability. Price represents the value or benefits provided by the offering.

The appropriate marketing mix for a product or service depends on the success requirements of the markets at which it is directed. The "rightness" of a product, communication, channel, or price strategy can be interpreted only in the context of markets served. Recognition of this fact has prompted the use of regional marketing, whereby different marketing mixes are employed to accommodate unique consumer preferences and competitive conditions in different geographical areas. For instance, Frito-Lay's Tostitos brand of tortilla chips is marketed as a specialty product sold mostly through delicatessens in some northeastern states. The brand's communication and price policies are not aggressive in these states because of fragmented competition. Tortilla chips in southwestern states are a commodity-type product sold by many competitors through supermarkets. The Tostitos brand is, therefore, supported in that geographic area by more aggressive price and communication programs. Firms that market products and services worldwide often "glocalize" their marketing mixes. That is, global decisions are made in such areas as product development, but decisions related to advertising, pricing, and distribution are arrived at by local (country-specific) marketing managers. A prime example of glocalization is found in the marketing of Swatch watches. In developed countries, Swatch watches are marketed as a fashion item; in less developed countries, the marketing mix emphasizes simple design, affordable cost, and functional qualities.

Internet/Web-based technologies have created another market setting, called the market*space*. Companies that succeed in the new marketspace deliver customer value through the interactive capabilities of these technologies, which allow for greater flexibility in managing marketing mix elements. For example, online sellers routinely adjust prices to changing environmental conditions, purchase situations, and purchase behaviors of online buyers. Also, interactive two-way Internet/Web-based capabilities in marketspace allow a customer to tell a seller exactly what his or her buying interests and requirements are, making possible the transformation of a product or service into a customized solution for the buyer. In addition, the purpose and role of marketing communications and marketing channels in this market setting change as described in Chapters 6 and 7, respectively.

In addition to being consistent with the needs of markets served, a marketing mix must be consistent with the organization's capacity, and the individual activities must complement one another. Several questions offer direction in evaluating an organization's marketing mix. First, is the marketing mix internally consistent? Do the individual activities complement one another to form a whole, as opposed to fragmented pieces? Does the mix fit the organization, the market, and the environment into which it will be introduced? Second, are buyers more sensitive to some marketing mix activities than to others? For example, are they more likely to respond favorably to a decrease in price or an increase in advertising? Third, what are the costs of performing marketing mix activities and the costs of attracting and retaining buyers? Do these costs exceed their benefits? Can the organization afford the marketing mix expenditures? Finally, is the marketing mix properly timed? For example, are communications scheduled to coincide with product availability? Is the entire marketing mix timely with respect to the buying cycle of consumers, competitor actions, and the ebb and flow of environmental forces?

Implementation of the marketing mix is as much an art as a science. Successful implementation requires an understanding of markets, environmental forces, organizational capacity, and marketing mix activities with a healthy respect for competitor reactions. These topics are raised again in Chapter 10. An example of an implementation with less than successful results is that of A&P's WEO (Where Economy Originates) program. Prior to implementing the program, A&P had watched its sales volume plateau with shrinking profits, while other supermarket chains continued to increase sales volume and profits. When the WEO program was initiated, it emphasized discount pricing (price strategy) with heavy promotional expenditures (communication strategy). The program increased sales volume by $800 million but produced a profit loss of over $50 million. In the words of one industry observer at the time:

> Its competitors are convinced that A&P's assault with WEO was doomed from the start. Too many of its stores are relics of a bygone era. Many are in poor locations [distribution strategy]. . . . They are just not big enough to support the tremendous volume that is necessary to make a discounting operation profitable [capacity] . . . stores lack shelf space for stocking general merchandise items, such as housewares and children's clothing [product strategy].[20]

The product-market strategy employed by A&P could be classified as a market-penetration strategy. Its implementation, however, could be questioned in terms of internal consistency, costs of the marketing mix activities, and fit with organizational capacity. Moreover, the retail grocery industry was plagued at the time by rising food costs, an environmental force that had a destructive effect on strategy success.

■ BUDGETING MARKETING, FINANCIAL, AND PRODUCTION RESOURCES

The fourth phase in the strategic marketing management process is budgeting. A budget is a formal, quantitative expression of an organization's planning and strategy initiatives expressed in financial terms. A well-prepared budget meshes and balances an organization's financial, production, and marketing resources so that overall organizational goals or objectives are attained.

An organization's master budget consists of two parts: (1) an operating budget and (2) a financial budget. The operating budget focuses on an organization's income statement. Since the operating budget projects future revenues and expenses, it is sometimes referred to as a *pro forma* income statement or profit plan. The financial budget focuses on the effect that the operating budget and other initiatives (such as capital expenditures) will have on the organization's cash position. For example, the master budget for AM General included an income statement that detailed revenues, expenses, and profit for its existing Hummer model. Its financial budget included the capital expenditure to manufacture the Hummer H2 model, exclusively distributed and marketed by General Motors in 2002.

In addition to the operating and financial budget, many organizations prepare supplemental special budgets, such as an advertising and sales budget, and related reports tied to the master budget. For example, a report showing how revenues, costs, and profits change under different marketing decisions and competitive and economic conditions is often prepared. As indicated, budgeting is more than an accounting function. It is an essential element of strategic marketing management.

A complete description of the budgetary process is beyond the scope of this section. However, Chapter 2, "Financial Aspects of Marketing Management," provides an overview of cost concepts and behavior. It also describes useful analytical tools for dealing with the financial dimensions of strategic marketing management, including cost-volume-profit analysis, discounted cash flow, and the preparation of *pro forma* income statements.

■ DEVELOPING REFORMULATION AND RECOVERY STRATEGIES

Reformulation and recovery strategies form the cornerstone of adaptive behavior in organizations. Strategies are rarely timeless. Changing markets, economic conditions, and competitive behavior require periodic, if not sudden, adjustments in strategy.

Marketing audit and control procedures are fundamental to the development of reformulation and recovery strategies. The *marketing audit* has been defined as follows:

> A marketing audit is a comprehensive, systematic, independent, and periodic examination of a company's—or business unit's—marketing environment, objectives, strategies and activities with a view of determining problem areas and opportunities and recommending a plan of action to improve the company's marketing performance.[21]

The audit process directs the manager's attention to both the strategic fit of the organization with its environment and the operational aspects of the marketing program. Strategic aspects of the marketing audit address the synoptic question, "Are we doing the right things?" Operational aspects address an equally synoptic question— "Are we doing things right?"

The distinction between strategic and operational perspectives, as well as the implementation of each, is examined in Chapter 9. Suffice it to say here that marketing audit and control procedures underlie the processes of defining the organization's business, mission, and goals or objectives, identifying external opportunities and threats and internal strengths and weaknesses, formulating product-market strategies and marketing mix activities, and budgeting resources. The intellectual process of developing reformulation and recovery strategies during the planning process serves two important purposes. First, it forces the manager to consider the "what if" questions. For example, "What if an unexpected environmental threat arises that renders a strategy obsolete?" or "What if competitive and market response to a strategy is inconsistent with what was originally expected?" Such questions focus the manager's attention on the sensitivity of results to assumptions made in the strategy-development process. Second, preplanning of reformulation and recovery strategies, or *contingency plans*, leads to a faster reaction time in implementing remedial action. Marshaling and reorienting resources is a time-consuming process itself without additional time lost in planning.

■ DRAFTING A MARKETING PLAN

A marketing plan embodies the strategic marketing management process. It is a formal, written document that describes the context and scope of an organization's marketing effort to achieve defined goals or objectives within a specific future time period. Marketing plans go by a variety of names depending on their particular focus. For example, there are business marketing plans, product marketing plans, and brand marketing plans. At Frito-Lay, Inc., for instance, a marketing plan is drafted for a particular business (snack chips), for a product class (potato chips, tortilla chips), and for specific brands (Lay's potato chips, Ruffles potato chips). Marketing plans also have a time dimension. Short-run marketing plans typically focus on a one-year period and are called annual marketing plans. Long-run marketing plans often have a three- to five-year planning horizon.

A formal, written marketing plan represents a distillation of and the attention and thought given the five interrelated analytical processes in this chapter. It is the tangible result of an intellectual effort. As a written document, a marketing plan also exhibits certain stylistic elements. Although there is no "generic" marketing plan that applies to all organizations and all situations, marketing plans follow a general format. The appendix at the end of this chapter provides an actual example of a condensed marketing plan for Paradise Kitchens®, Inc., a company that produces and markets a unique line of single-serve and microwaveable Southwestern/Mexican-style frozen chili products. This example illustrates both the substance and style of a five-year marketing plan.

■ MARKETING ETHICS AND SOCIAL RESPONSIBILITY

On a final note, it must be emphasized that matters of ethics and social responsibility permeate every aspect of the strategic marketing management process. Indeed, most marketing decisions involve some degree of moral judgment and reflect an organization's orientation toward the publics with which it interacts. Enlightened marketing executives no longer subscribe to the view that if an action is legal, then it is also ethical and socially responsible. These executives are sensitive to the fact that the marketplace is populated by individuals and groups with diverse value systems. Moreover, they recognize that their actions will be judged publicly by others with different values and interests.

Enlightened ethical and socially responsible decisions arise from the ability of marketers to discern the precise issues involved and their willingness to take action even when the outcome may negatively affect their standing in an organization or the company's financial interests. Although the moral foundations on which marketing decisions are made will vary among individuals and organizations, failure to recognize issues and take appropriate action is the least ethical and most socially irresponsible approach. A positive approach to ethical and socially responsible behavior is illustrated by Anheuser-Busch, which has spent almost $400 million since 1982 to promote responsible drinking of alcoholic beverages. Anheuser-Busch executives acknowledge the potential for alcohol abuse and are willing to forgo business generated by misuse of the company's products. These executives have discerned the issues and have recognized an ethical obligation to present and potential customers. They have also recognized the company's social responsibility to the general public by encouraging safe driving and responsible drinking habits.[22]

NOTES

1. Steve Harrell, strategic planner at General Electric, quoted in Philip Kotler, *Marketing Management*, 11th ed. (Upper Saddle River, NJ: Prentice Hall, 2003): 90.

2. Derek E. Abell, *Defining the Business: The Starting Point of Strategic Planning* (Upper Saddle River, NJ: Prentice Hall, 1980); Roger A. Kerin, Vijay Mahajan, and P. Rajan Varadarajan, *Contemporary Perspective on Strategic Market Planning* (Boston: Allyn and Bacon, 1990).

3. "Britannica.com Arrives, Belatedly," *Advertising Age* (May 10, 1999): 24; and "Britannica Gets Its Groove Back," *Business 2.0* (August 2002): 64–68.

4. Jeffrey Abrahams, *The Mission Statement Book*, Revised Edition (Berkeley, CA: Ten Speed Press, 1999).

5. Eric von Hippel, Stephan Thomke, and Mary Sonnack, "Creating Breakthroughs at 3M," *Harvard Business Review* (September–October 1999): 47–56.

6. Robert A. Pitts and David Lei, *Strategic Management: Building and Sustaining Competitive Advantage*, 3rd ed. (St. Paul, MN: West Publishing Company, 2003): 6.

7. "Gillette Safety Razor Division: The Blank Cassette Project," Harvard Business School case #9-574-058; Glenn Rifkin, "Mach 3: Anatomy of Gillette's Latest Global Launch," *Strategy & Business* (2nd quarter, 1999): 34–41; and "Gillette's Edge," *BRANDWEEK* (May 28, 2001): 5.

8. "Exxon's Flop in Field of Office Gear Shows Diversification Perils," *Wall Street Journal* (September 3, 1985): 1ff.

9. "Hanes Expands L'eggs to the Entire Family," *Business Week* (June 14, 1975): 57ff.

10. This classification is adapted from H. Igor Ansoff, *Corporate Strategy* (New York: McGraw-Hill, 1964): Chapter 6. For an extended discussion on product-market strategies, see Roger A. Kerin, Vijay Mahajan, and P. Rajan Varadarajan, *Contemporary Perspectives on Strategic Market Planning* (Boston: Allyn and Bacon, 1990): Chapter 6.

11. "PepsiCo Asks More of Gatorade Despite Its 85% Market Share," *Wall Street Journal* (June 11, 2002): B4.

12. H. Menzies, "Why Folger's Is Getting Creamed Back East," *Fortune* (July 17, 1978): 69.

13. "Lowe's Is Sprucing Up Its House," *Business Week* (June 3, 2002): 56.

14. Philip R. Cateora and John L. Graham, *International Marketing*, 11th ed. (Burr Ridge, IL: McGraw-Hill/Irwin, 2002): Chapter 11.

15. "Hasbro, Inc." in Eric N. Berkowitz, Roger A. Kerin, Steven N. Hartley, and William Rudelius, *Marketing*, 5th ed. (Chicago: Richard D. Irwin, 1997): 656–657.

16. Greg Burns, "Has General Mills Had Its Wheaties?" *Business Week* (May 8, 1995): 68–69; and Julie Forster, "The Lucky Charm of Steve Sanger," *Business Week* (March 26, 2001): 75–76.

17. "Gillette Co. Sees Strong Early Sales for Its New Razor," *Wall Street Journal* (July 17, 1998): B3.

18. Failed diversification attempts, along with advice on diversification, are detailed in Chris Zook with James Allen, *Profit from the Core* (Cambridge, MA: Harvard Business School Press, 2001).

19. These estimates were reported in "The Breakdown of U.S. Innovation," *Business Week* (February 16, 1976): 56ff.

20. Robert F. Hartley, *Marketing Mistakes*, 5th ed. (New York: John Wiley & Sons, 1992). Items in brackets added for illustrative purposes.

21. Philip Kotler, *Marketing Management*, 11th ed. (Upper Saddle River, NJ: Prentice Hall, 2003): 695–696.

22. "Our Commitment to Preventing Alcohol Abuse and Underage Drinking," www.beeresponsible.com.

A Sample Marketing Plan

Crafting a marketing plan is hard but satisfying work. When completed, a marketing plan serves as a roadmap that details the context and scope of marketing activities including, but not limited to, a mission statement, goals and objectives, a situation analysis, growth opportunities, target market(s) and marketing (mix) program, a budget, and an implementation schedule.

As a written document, the plan conveys in words the analysis, ideas, and aspirations of its author pertaining to a business, product, and/or brand marketing effort. How a marketing plan is written communicates not only the substance of the marketing effort but also the professionalism of the author. Writing style will not overcome limitations in substance. However, a poorly written marketing plan can detract from the perceived substance of the plan.

■ WRITING AND STYLE CONSIDERATIONS

Given the importance of a carefully crafted marketing plan, authors of marketing plans adhere to certain guidelines. The following writing and style guidelines generally apply:

- Use a direct, professional writing style. Use appropriate business and marketing terms without jargon. Present and future tenses with active voice are generally better than past tense and passive voice.

- Be positive and specific. At the same time, avoid superlatives ("terrific," "wonderful"). Specifics are better than glittering generalities. Use numbers for impact, justifying computations and projections with facts or reasonable quantitative assumptions where possible.

- Use bullet points for succinctness and emphasis. As with the list you are reading, bullets enable key points to be highlighted effectively and with great efficiency.

- Use "A-level" (the first level) and "B-level" (the second level) headings under major section headings to help readers make easy transitions from one topic to another. This also forces the writer to organize the plan more carefully. Use these headings liberally, at least once every 200 to 300 words.

- Use visuals where appropriate. Illustrations, graphs, and charts enable large amounts of information to be presented succinctly.

- Shoot for a plan 15 to 35 pages in length, not including financial projections and appendices. An uncomplicated small business may require only 15 pages, while a new business startup may require more than 35 pages.

- Use care in layout, design, and presentation. Laser or ink-jet printers give a more professional look than do dot matrix printers or typewriters. A bound report with a cover and clear title page adds professionalism.

■ SAMPLE FIVE-YEAR ANNOTATED MARKETING PLAN
   FOR PARADISE KITCHENS® INC.

The marketing plan that follows for Paradise Kitchens® Inc. is based on an actual plan developed by the company. The company was founded in 1989, and its products entered distribution in 1990. To protect proprietary information about the company, a number of details and certain data have been altered, but the basic logic of the plan has been preserved. Various appendices are omitted due to space limitations.

Notes in the margins next to the Paradise Kitchens® Inc. marketing plan fall into two categories:

1. *Substantive notes* elaborate on the rationale or significance of an element in the marketing plan.

2. *Writing style, format, and layout notes* explain the editorial or visual rationale for the element.

As you read the marketing plan, you might consider adding your own notes in the margins related to the discussion in the text. For example, you may wish to compare the application of SWOT analysis and reference to "points of difference" in the Paradise Kitchens® Inc. marketing plan with the discussion in Chapter 1. As you read additional chapters in the text, you may return to the marketing plan and insert additional notes pertaining to terminology used and techniques employed.

The Table of Contents provides quick access to the topics in the plan, usually organized by section and subsection headings.

Seen by many experts as the single most important element in the plan, the Executive Summary, with a maximum of two pages, "sells" the document to readers through its clarity and brevity.

The Company Description highlights the recent history and recent successes of the organization.

The Strategic Focus and Plan sets the strategic direction for the entire organization, a direction with which proposed actions of the marketing plan must be consistent. This section is not included in all marketing plans.

The Mission Statement focuses the activities of Paradise Kitchens for the stakeholder groups to be served.

FIVE-YEAR MARKETING PLAN
Paradise Kitchens®, Inc.

Table of Contents

1. Executive Summary

2. Company Description

Paradise Kitchens®, Inc. was started in 1989 by cofounders Randall F. Peters and Leah E. Peters to develop and market Howlin' Coyote® Chili, a unique line of single-serve and microwaveable Southwestern/Mexican style frozen chili products. The Howlin' Coyote® line of chili was introduced into the Minneapolis-St. Paul market in 1990. The line was subsequently expanded to Denver in 1992 and Phoenix in 1994.

To the Company's knowledge, Howlin' Coyote® is the only premium-quality, authentic Southwestern/Mexican style, frozen chili sold in U.S. grocery stores. Its high quality has gained fast, widespread acceptance in these markets. In fact, same-store sales doubled in the last year for which data are available. The Company believes the Howlin' Coyote® brand can be extended to other categories of Southwestern/Mexican food products.

Paradise Kitchens believes its high-quality, high-price strategy has proven successful. This marketing plan outlines how the Company will extend its geographic coverage from 3 markets to 20 markets by the year 2003.

3. Strategic Focus and Plan

This section covers three aspects of corporate strategy that influence the marketing plan: (1) the mission, (2) goals, and (3) core competence/sustainable competitive advantage of Paradise Kitchens.

MISSION

The mission and vision of Paradise Kitchens is to market lines of high-quality Southwestern/Mexican food products at premium prices that satisfy consumers in this fast-growing food segment while providing challenging career opportunities for employees and above-average returns to stockholders.

GOALS

For the coming five years Paradise Kitchens seeks to achieve the following goals:

- Nonfinancial goals
  1. To retain its present image as the highest-quality line of Southwestern/Mexican products in the food categories in which it competes.
  2. To enter 17 new metropolitan markets.
  3. To achieve national distribution in two convenience store or supermarket chains by 2001 and five by 2003.
  4. To add a new product line every third year.
  5. To be among the top three chili lines—regardless of packaging (frozen, canned) in one third of the metro markets in which it competes by 2001 and two thirds by 2003.

- Financial goals
  1. To obtain a real (inflation adjusted) growth in earnings per share of 8 percent per year over time.
  2. To obtain a return on equity of at least 20 percent.
  3. To have a public stock offering by the year 2001.

CORE COMPETENCY AND SUSTAINABLE COMPETITIVE ADVANTAGE

In terms of core competency, Paradise Kitchens seeks to achieve a unique ability (1) to provide distinctive, high-quality chilies and related products using Southwestern/Mexican recipes that appeal to and excite contemporary tastes for these products and (2) to deliver these products to the customer's table using effective manufacturing and distribution systems that maintain the Company's quality standards.

To translate these core competencies into a sustainable competitive advantage, the Company will work closely with key suppliers and distributors to build the relationships and alliances necessary to satisfy the high taste standards of our customers.

4. Situation Analysis

This situation analysis starts with a snapshot of the current environment in which Paradise Kitchens finds itself by providing a brief SWOT (strengths, weaknesses, opportunities, threats) analysis. After this overview, the analysis probes ever-finer levels of detail: industry, competitors, company, and consumers.

The Goals section sets both the financial and nonfinancial targets—where possible in quantitative terms—against which the company's performance will be measured.

Lists use parallel construction to improve readability—in this case a series of infinitives starting with "To . . ."

The Situation Analysis is a snapshot to answer the question, "Where are we now?"

The SWOT Analysis identifies strengths, weaknesses, opportunities, and threats to provide a solid foundation as a springboard to identify subsequent *actions* in the marketing plan.

SWOT ANALYSIS

Figure 1 shows the internal and external factors affecting the market opportunities for Paradise Kitchens. Stated briefly, this SWOT analysis highlights the great strides taken by the Company in the eight years since its products first appeared on grocers' shelves. In the Company's favor internally are its strengths of an experienced management team and board of directors, excellent acceptance of its lines in the three metropolitan markets in which it competes, and a strong manufacturing and distribution system to serve these limited markets. Favorable external factors (opportunities) include the increasing appeal of Southwestern/Mexican foods, the strength of the upscale market for the Company's products, and food-processing technological breakthroughs that make it easier for smaller food producers to compete.

Figure 1. SWOT Analysis for Paradise Kitchens

Internal Factor	Strengths	Weaknesses
Management	Experienced and entrepreneurial management and board	Small size can restrict options
Offerings	Unique, high-quality, high-price products	Many lower-quality, lower-price competitors
Marketing	Distribution in 3 markets with excellent acceptance	No national awareness or distribution
Personnel	Good workforce, though small; little turnover	Big gap if key employee leaves
Finance	Excellent growth in sales revenues	Limited resources may restrict growth opportunities when compared to giant competitors
Manufacturing	Sole supplier ensures high quality	Lack economies of scale of huge competitors
R&D	Continuing efforts to ensure quality in delivered products	

Each long table, graph, or photo is given a figure number and title. It then appears as soon as possible after the first reference in the text, accommodating necessary page breaks. This also avoids breaking long tables like this one in the middle. Short tables or graphs that are less than 1½ inches are often inserted in the text without figure numbers because they don't cause serious problems with page breaks.

Figure 1.   SWOT Analysis for Paradise Kitchens (continued)

External Factors	Opportunities	Threats
Consumer/Social	Upscale market, likely to be stable; Southwestern/Mexican food category is fast-growing segment	Premium price may limit access to mass markets
Competitive	Distinctive name and packaging in its markets	Not patentable; competitors can attempt to duplicate product
Technological	Technical breakthroughs enable smaller food producers to achieve many economies available to large competitors	
Economic	Consumer income is high; convenience important to U.S. households	Many households "eating out," and bringing prepared take-out into home
Legal/Regulatory	High U.S. Food & Drug Admin. standards eliminate fly-by-night competitors	

> The Industry Analysis section provides the backdrop for the subsequent, more detailed analysis of competition, the company, and the company's customers. Without an in-depth understanding of the industry, the remaining analysis may be misdirected.

> Even though relatively brief, this in-depth treatment of the Spicy Southwestern/Mexican food industry in the United States demonstrates to the plan's readers the company's understanding of the industry in which it competes. It gives readers confidence that the company thoroughly understands its own industry.

   Among unfavorable factors, the main weakness is the limited size of Paradise Kitchens relative to its competitors in terms of the depth of the management team, available financial resources, and national awareness and distribution of product lines. Threats include the danger that the Company's premium prices may limit access to mass markets and competition from the "eating-out" and "take-out" markets.

INDUSTRY ANALYSIS: TRENDS IN SPICY AND MEXICAN FOODS

   Total spice consumption increased 50 percent from 1985 to 1995, and consumption of spices jumped from an annual average of 2 pounds per American in 1988 to 2.7 pounds in 1994. Currently, Mexican food and ingredients are used in 64 percent of American households. Burritos, enchiladas, and taco dinner kits, which had insignificant numbers in 1981, reached between 4 percent and 11 percent of American households in 1996. Age Wave, Inc.'s *1998 Boomer Report* also stated that Baby Boomers consumed 84 percent more Mexican food in 1995 than they did in 1986.

According to *Grocery Marketing,* as the general population becomes more accustomed to different ethnic cuisines and styles of eating, spicy foods and unusual flavors are turning up on the dinner tables of middle America and the aisles of supermarkets, as well. As Baby Boomers grow older, their taste buds will become less sensitive, and they will want stronger-tasting foods. In addition to age, growth in population, incomes, and tastes in the American diet should continue to fuel the trend for spicy foods in the United States. Retail sales of fiery food could top $1.8 billion in the year 2000, according to *Packaged Facts,* up from $1 billion in 1994.

These trends reflect a generally more favorable attitude toward spicy foods on the part of Americans. The Southwestern/Mexican market includes the foods shown in Figure 2.

Figure 2.   Some Foods Included in the Southwestern/ Mexican Product Category 1996

Item	Percentage of Sales	Sales in Millions
Salsa	39	$624
Cheese/bean dips	13	208
Refried beans	9	144
Seasoning mix	8	128
Chilies	7	112
Taco shells	7	112
Dinner kits	5	80
Taco sauce	3	48
Enchilada sauce	2	32
Other	7	112
Total	100	$1,600

This summary of sales in the Southwestern/Mexican product category shows it is significant and provides a variety of future opportunities for Paradise Kitchens.

COMPETITORS IN SOUTHWESTERN/MEXICAN MARKET

The chili market represents $495 million in annual sales. The products fall primarily into two groups: canned chili (62 percent of sales) and dry chili (16 percent of sales). The remaining 22 percent of sales go to frozen chili products. Besides Howlin' Coyote®, Stouffers and Marie Callender's offer frozen chilies as part of their broad lines of frozen dinners and entrees. Major canned chili brands include Hormel, Wolf, Dennison, Stagg, Chili Man, Chili Magic, and Castleberry's. Their retail prices range from $.99 to $1.79.

As with the Industry Analysis, the Competitor Analysis demonstrates that the company has a realistic understanding of who its major competitors are and what their marketing strategies are. Again, a realistic assessment gives confidence to readers that subsequent marketing actions in the plan rest on a solid foundation.

Bluntly put, the major disadvantage of the segment's dominant product, canned chili, is that it does not taste very good. A taste test described in the October 1990 issue of *Consumer Reports* magazine ranked 26 canned chili products "poor" to "fair" in overall sensory quality. The study concluded, "Chili doesn't have to be hot to be good. But really good chili, hot or mild, doesn't come out of a can."

Dry mix brands include such familiar spice brands as Lawry's, McCormick, French's, and Durkee, along with smaller offerings such as Wick Fowler's and Carroll Shelby's. Their retail prices range from $.99 to $1.99. The *Consumer Reports* study was more favorable about dry chili mixes, ranking them from "fair" to "very good." The magazine recommended, "If you want good chili, make it with fresh ingredients and one of the seasoning mixes we tested." A major drawback of dry mixes is that they require the preparers to add their own meat, beans, and tomatoes and take more preparation time than canned or frozen chilies.

The *Consumer Reports* study did not include the frozen chili entrees from Stouffer's or Marie Callender's (Howlin' Coyote® was not yet on the market at the time of the test). However, it is fair to say that these products—consisting of ground beef, chili beans, and tomato sauce—are of average quality. Furthermore, they are not singled out for special marketing or promotional programs by their manufacturers. Marie Callender's (including cornbread) retails for $3.09, and Stouffer's retails for $2.99.

COMPANY ANALYSIS

The Company Analysis provides details of the company's strengths and marketing strategies that will enable it to achieve the mission and goals identified earlier.

The husband-and-wife team that cofounded Paradise Kitchens®, Inc. in 1989 has 44 years of experience between them in the food-processing business. Both have played key roles in the management of the Pillsbury Company. They are being advised by a highly seasoned group of business professionals who have extensive understanding of the requirements for new product development.

Currently, Howlin' Coyote® products compete in the chili and Mexican frozen entree segments of the Southwestern/Mexican food market. While the chili obviously competes as a stand-alone product, its exceptional quality means it can complement such dishes as burritos, nachos, and enchiladas and can be readily used as a smothering sauce for pasta, rice, or potatoes. This flexibility of use is relatively rare in the prepared food marketplace. With Howlin' Coyote®, Paradise Kitchens is broadening the position of frozen chili in a way that can lead to impressive market share for the new product category.

This "introductory over-view" sentence tells the reader the topics covered in the section—in this case customer characteristics and health and nutrition concerns. While this sentence may be omitted in short memos or plans, it helps readers see where the text is leading. These sentences are used throughout this plan.

The higher-level "A heading" of Customer Analysis has a more dom-inant typeface and position than the lower-level "B heading" of Customer Characteristics. These headings introduce the reader to the sequence and level of topics covered.

Satisfying customers and providing genuine value to them is why organizations exist in a market economy. This section addresses the question of "Who are the customers for Paradise Kitchens' products?"

The Company now uses a single outside producer with which it works closely to maintain the consistently high quality required in its products. The greater volume has increased production efficiencies, resulting in a steady decrease in the cost of goods sold.

CUSTOMER ANALYSIS

In terms of customer analysis, this section describes (1) the characteristics of customers expected to buy Howlin' Coyote® products and (2) health and nutrition concerns of Americans today.

Customer Characteristics. Demographically, chili products in general are purchased by consumers representing a broad range of socioeconomic backgrounds. Howlin' Coyote® chili is purchased chiefly by consumers who have achieved higher levels of education and whose income is $30,000 and higher. These consumers represent 57 percent of canned and dry mix chili users.

The household buying Howlin' Coyote® has one to three people in it. Among married couples, Howlin' Coyote® is predominantly bought by households in which both spouses work. While women are a majority of the buyers, single men represent a significant segment. Anecdotally, Howlin' Coyote® has heard from fathers of teenaged boys who say they keep a freezer stocked with the chili because the boys devour it.

Because the chili offers a quick way to make a tasty meal, the product's biggest users tend to be those most pressed for time. Howlin' Coyote®'s premium pricing also means that its purchasers are skewed toward the higher end of the income range. Buyers range in age from 25 to 55. Because consumers in the western United States have adopted spicy foods more readily than the rest of the country, Howlin' Coyote®'s initial marketing expansion efforts will be concentrated in that region.

This section demonstrates the company's insights into a major trend that has a potentially large impact.

Health and Nutrition Concerns. Coverage of food issues in the U.S. media is often erratic and occasionally alarmist. Because Americans are concerned about their diets, studies from organizations of widely varying credibility frequently receive significant attention from the major news organizations. For instance, a study of fat levels of movie popcorn was reported in all the major media. Similarly, studies on the healthfulness of Mexican food have received prominent "play" in print and broadcast reports. The high caloric levels of much Mexican and Southwestern-style food had been widely reported and often exaggerated.

Less certain is the link between these reports and consumer buying behavior. Most indications are that while Americans are well-versed in dietary matters, they are not significantly changing their eating patterns. The experience of other food manufacturers is that Americans expect certain foods to be high in calories and are not drawn to those that claim to be low-calorie versions. Low-fat frozen pizza was a flop. Therefore, while Howlin' Coyote® is already lower in calories, fat, and sodium than its competitors, those qualities are not being stressed in its promotions. Instead, in the space and time available for promotions, Howlin' Coyote®'s taste, convenience, and flexibility are stressed.

5. Product-Market Focus

This section describes the five-year marketing and product objectives for Paradise Kitchens and the target markets, points of difference, and positioning of its lines of Howlin' Coyote® chilies.

MARKETING AND PRODUCT OBJECTIVES

Howlin' Coyote®'s marketing intent is to take full advantage of its brand potential while building a base from which other revenue sources can be mined—both in and out of the retail grocery business. These are detailed in four areas below:

The chances of success for a new product are significantly increased if objectives are set for the product itself and if target market segments are identified for it. This section makes these explicit for Paradise Kitchens. The objectives also serve as the planned targets against which marketing activities are measured in program implementation and control.

- Current markets. Current markets will be grown by expanding brand and flavor distribution at the retail level. In addition, same-store sales will be grown by increasing consumer awareness and repeat purchases. With this increase in same-store sales, the more desirable broker/warehouse distribution channel will become available, increasing efficiency and saving costs.

- New markets. By the end of Year 5, the chili and salsa business will be expanded to a total of 20 metropolitan areas. This will represent 72 percent of U.S. food store sales.
- Food service. Food service sales will include chili products and smothering sauces. Sales are expected to reach $693,000 by the end of Year 3 and $1.5 million by the end of Year 5.
- New products. Howlin' Coyote®'s brand presence will be expanded at the retail level through the addition of new products in the frozen-foods section. This will be accomplished through new product concept screening in Year 1 to identify new potential products. These products will be brought to market in Years 2 and 3. Additionally, the brand may be licensed in select categories.

TARGET MARKETS

This section identifies the specific niches or target markets toward which the company's products are directed. When appropriate and when space permits, this section often includes a product-market matrix.

The primary target market for Howlin' Coyote® products is households with one to three people, where often both adults work, with household income typically above $30,000 per year. These households contain more experienced, adventurous consumers of Southwestern/Mexican food and want premium quality products.

POINTS OF DIFFERENCE

The "points of difference"—characteristics that make Howlin' Coyote® chilies unique relative to competitors—fall into three important areas:

An organization cannot grow by offering only "me-too products." The greatest single factor in a new product's failure is the lack of significant "points of difference" that set it apart from competitors' substitutes. This section makes these points of difference explicit.

- Unique taste and convenience. No known competitor offers a high-quality, "authentic" frozen chili in a range of flavors. And no existing chili has the same combination of quick preparation and home-style taste.
- Taste trends. The American palate is increasingly intrigued by hot spices, and Howlin' Coyote® brands offer more "kick" than most other prepared chilies.
- Premium packaging. Howlin' Coyote®'s high-value packaging graphics convey the unique, high-quality product contained inside and the product's nontraditional positioning.

A positioning strategy helps communicate the company's unique points of difference of its products to prospective customers in a simple, clear way. This section describes this positioning.

Everything that has gone before in the marketing plan sets the stage for the marketing mix actions covered in the marketing program.

This section describes in detail three key elements of the company's product strategy: the product line, its quality and how this is achieved, and its "cutting edge" packaging.

Using parallel structure, this bulleted list presents the product line efficiently and crisply.

POSITIONING

In the past chili products have been either convenient or tasty, but not both. Howlin' Coyote® pairs these two desirable characteristics to obtain a positioning in consumers' minds as very high-quality "authentic Southwestern/Mexican tasting" chilies that can be prepared easily and quickly.

6. Marketing Program

The four marketing mix elements of the Howlin' Coyote® chili marketing program are detailed below. Note that "chile" is the vegetable and "chili" is the dish.

PRODUCT STRATEGY

After first summarizing the product line, the approach to product quality and packaging is covered.

Product Line. Howlin' Coyote® chili, retailing for $2.99 for a 10- or 11.5-ounce serving, is available in five flavors. The five are:

- Green Chile Chili: braised extra-lean pork with fire-roasted green chilies, onions, tomato chunks, bold spices, and jalapeno peppers, based on a Southwestern favorite.
- Red Chile Chili: extra-lean cubed pork, deep-red acho chilies, and sweet onions; known as the "Texas Bowl of Red."
- Beef and Black Bean Chili: lean braised beef with black beans, tomato chunks, and Howlin' Coyote®'s own blend of red chilies and authentic spicing.
- Chicken Chunk Chili: hearty chunks of tender chicken, fire-roasted green chilies, black beans, pinto beans, diced onions, and zesty spices.
- Mean Bean Chili: vegetarian, with nine distinctive bean varieties and fire-roasted green chilies, tomato chunks, onion, and a robust blend of spices and rich red chilies.

Unique Product Quality. The flavoring systems of the Howlin' Coyote® chilies are proprietary. The products' tastiness is due to extra care lavished upon the ingredients during production. The ingredients used are of unusually high quality. Meats are low-fat cuts and are fresh, not frozen, to preserve cell structure and moistness. Chilies are fire-roasted for fresher taste, not the canned variety used by more mainstream products. Tomatoes and vegetables are select quality. No preservatives or artificial flavors are used.

Packaging. Reflecting the "cutting edge" marketing strategy of its producers, Howlin' Coyote® bucks conventional wisdom in packaging. It avoids placing predictable photographs of the product on its containers. (Head to any grocer's freezer and you will be hard-pressed to find a product that does not feature a heavily stylized photograph of the contents.) Instead, Howlin' Coyote®'s package shows a Southwestern motif that communicates the product's out-of-the-ordinary positioning. This approach signals the product's nontraditional qualities: "adventurous" eating with minimal fuss—a frozen meal for people who do not normally enjoy frozen meals.

PRICE STRATEGY

Howlin' Coyote® Chili is, at $2.99 for a 10- to 11.5-ounce package, priced comparably to the other frozen offerings and higher than the canned and dried chili varieties. However, the significant taste advantages it has over canned chilies and the convenience advantages over dried chilies justify this pricing strategy.

PROMOTION STRATEGY

Key promotion programs feature in-store demonstrations, recipes, and cents-off coupons.

In-Store Demonstrations. In-store demonstrations will be conducted to give consumers a chance to try Howlin' Coyote® products and learn about their unique qualities. Demos will be conducted regularly in all markets to increase awareness and trial purchases.

Recipes. Because the products' flexibility of use is a key selling point, recipes will be offered to consumers to stimulate use. The recipes will be given at all in-store demonstrations, on the back of packages, and through a mail-in recipe book offer. In addition, recipes will be included in coupons sent by direct-mail or free-standing inserts. For new markets, recipes will be included on in-pack coupon inserts.

Cents-Off Coupons. To generate trial and repeat purchase of Howlin' Coyote® products, coupons will be distributed in four ways:

- In Sunday newspaper inserts. Inserts are highly read and will help generate awareness. Coupled with in-store

---

This Price Strategy section makes the company's price point very clear, along with its price position relative to potential substitutes. When appropriate and when space permits, this section might contain a break-even analysis.

Elements of the Promotion Strategy are highlighted here with B-headings in terms of the three key promotional activities the company is emphasizing for its product line: in-store demonstrations, recipes featuring its Howlin' Coyote® chilies, and cents-off coupons.

Another bulleted list adds many details for the reader, including methods of gaining customer awareness, trial, and repeat purchases as Howlin' Coyote® enters new metropolitan areas.

demonstrations, this has been a very successful technique so far.

- In-pack coupons. Inside each box of Howlin' Coyote® chili will be coupons for $1 off two more packages of the chili. These coupons will be included for the first three months the product is shipped to a new market. Doing so encourages repeat purchases by new users.
- Direct-mail chili coupons. Those households that fit the Howlin' Coyote® demographics described above will be mailed coupons. This is likely to be an efficient promotion due to its greater audience selectivity.
- In-store demonstrations. Coupons will be passed out at in-store demonstrations to give an additional incentive to purchase.

The Distribution Strategy is described here in terms of both (1) the present method and (2) the new one to be used when the increased sales volume makes it feasible.

DISTRIBUTION STRATEGY

Howlin' Coyote® is distributed in its present markets through a food distributor. The distributor buys the product, warehouses it, and then resells and delivers it to grocery retailers on a store-by-store basis. This is typical for products that have moderate sales—compared with, say, staples like milk or bread. As sales grow, we will shift to a more efficient system using a broker who sells the products to retail chains and grocery wholesalers.

7. Financial Data and Projections

All the marketing mix decisions covered in the marketing program have both revenue and expense effects. These are summarized in this section of the marketing plan.

PAST SALES REVENUES

Historically, Howlin' Coyote® has had a steady increase in sales revenues since its introduction in 1990. In 1994, sales jumped, due largely to new promotion strategies. Sales have continued to rise during the last four years, but at a less dramatic rate. The trend in sales revenues appears in Figure 3.

Figure 3. Sales Revenues for Paradise Kitchens®, Inc.

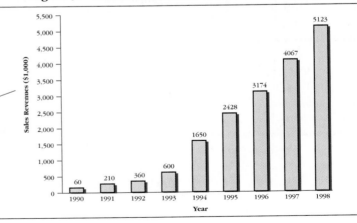

The graph shows more clearly the dramatic growth of sales revenue than data in a table would do.

Because this table is very short, it is woven into the text, rather than given a table number and title.

The Five-Year Financial Projections section starts with the judgment forecast of cases sold and the resulting net sales. Gross profit and then operating profit—critical for the company's survival—are projected. An actual plan often contains many pages of computer-generated spreadsheet projections, usually shown in an appendix to the plan.

FIVE-YEAR PROJECTIONS

Five-year financial projections for Paradise Kitchens appear below:

| Financial Element | Units | Actual 1998 | Projections | | | | |
			Year 1 1999	Year 2 2000	Year 3 2001	Year 4 2002	Year 5 2003
Cases sold	1,000	353	684	889	1,249	1,499	1,799
Net sales	$1,000	5,123	9,913	12,884	18,111	21,733	26,080
Gross profit	$1,000	2,545	4,820	6,527	8,831	10,597	12,717
Selling and general and admin. expenses	$1,000	2,206	3,835	3,621	6,026	7,231	8,678
Operating profit (loss)	$1,000	339	985	2,906	2,805	3,366	4,039

These projections reflect the continuing growth in number of cases sold (with 8 packages of Howlin' Coyote® chili per case) and increasing production and distribution economies of scale as sales volume increases.

The Implementation Plan shows how the company will turn plans into results. Gantt charts are often used to set deadlines and assign responsibilities for the many tactical marketing decisions needed to enter a new market.

The essence of Evaluation and Control is comparing actual sales with the targeted values set in the plan and taking appropriate actions. Note that the section briefly describes a contingency plan for alternative actions, depending on how successful the entry into a new market turns out to be.

Various appendices may appear at the end of the plan, depending on the purpose and audience for them. For example, detailed financial spreadsheets often appear in an appendix.

8. Implementation Plan

Introducing Howlin' Coyote® chilies to new metropolitan areas is a complex task and requires that creative promotional activities gain consumer awareness and initial trial among the target market households identified earlier. The anticipated rollout schedule to enter these metropolitan markets appears in Figure 4.

Figure 4. Rollout Schedule to Enter New U.S. Markets

Year	New Markets Added	Cumulative Markets	Cumulative Percentage of U.S. Market
Today (1998)	2	5	16
Year 1 (1999)	3	8	21
Year 2 (2000)	4	12	29
Year 3 (2001)	2	14	37
Year 4 (2002)	3	17	45
Year 5 (2003)	3	20	53

The diverse regional tastes in chili will be monitored carefully to assess whether minor modifications may be required in the chili recipes. For example, what is seen as "hot" in Boston may not be seen as "hot" in Dallas. As the rollout to new metropolitan areas continues, Paradise Kitchens will assess manufacturing and distribution trade-offs. This is important in determining whether to start new production with selected high-quality regional contract packers.

9. Evaluation and Control

Monthly sales targets in cases have been set for Howlin' Coyote® chili for each metropolitan area. Actual case sales will be compared with these targets and tactical marketing programs modified to reflect the unique sets of factors in each metropolitan area. The speed of the roll out program may increase or decrease, depending on Paradise Kitchens' performance in the successive metropolitan markets it enters. Similarly, as described above in the section on the implementation plan, Paradise Kitchens may elect to respond to variations in regional tastes by using contract packers, which will reduce transportation and warehousing costs but will require special efforts to monitor production quality.

10. Appendices

CHAPTER **2**

Financial Aspects of Marketing Management

 Marketing managers are accountable for the impact of their actions on profits. Therefore, they need a working knowledge of basic accounting and finance. This chapter provides an overview of several concepts from managerial accounting and managerial finance that are useful in marketing management: (1) variable and fixed costs, (2) relevant and sunk costs, (3) margins, (4) contribution analysis, (5) liquidity, (6) operating leverage, and (7) discounted cash flow. In addition, considerations when preparing *pro forma* income statements are described.

■ VARIABLE AND FIXED COSTS

An organization's costs divide into two broad categories: variable costs and fixed costs.

Variable Costs

Variable costs are expenses that are uniform per unit of output within a relevant time period (usually defined as a budget year); yet total variable costs fluctuate in direct proportion to the output volume of units produced. In other words, as volume increases, total variable costs increase.

Variable costs are divided into two categories, one of which is *cost of goods sold*. For a manufacturer or a provider of a service, cost of goods sold covers materials, labor, and factory overhead applied directly to production. For a reseller (wholesaler or retailer), cost of goods sold consists primarily of the cost of merchandise. The second category of variable costs consists of expenses that are not directly tied to production but that nevertheless vary directly with volume. Examples include sales commissions, discounts, and delivery expenses.

Fixed Costs

Fixed costs are expenses that do not fluctuate with output volume within a relevant time period (the budget year) but become progressively smaller per unit of output as volume increases. The decrease in per-unit fixed cost results from the increase in the number of output units over which fixed costs are allocated. Note, however, that no matter how large volume becomes, the absolute size of fixed costs remains unchanged.

Fixed costs divide into two categories: programmed costs and committed costs. *Programmed costs* result from attempts to generate sales volume. *Marketing expenditures are generally classified as programmed costs.* Examples include advertising, sales promotion, and sales salaries. *Committed costs* are those required to maintain the organization. They are usually nonmarketing expenditures such as rent and administrative and clerical salaries.

It is important to understand the concept of fixed cost. Remember that total fixed costs do not change during a budget year, regardless of changes in volume. Once fixed expenditures for a marketing program have been made, they remain the same whether or not the program causes unit volume to change.

Despite the clear-cut classification of costs into variable and fixed categories suggested here, cost classification is not always apparent in actual practice. Many times costs have a fixed and a variable component. For example, selling expenses often have a fixed component (such as salary) and a variable component (such as commissions or bonus) that are not always evident at first glance.

■ RELEVANT AND SUNK COSTS

Relevant Costs

Relevant costs are expenditures that (1) are expected to occur in the future as a result of some marketing action and (2) differ among marketing alternatives being considered. In short, relevant costs are future expenditures unique to the decision alternatives under consideration.

The concept of relevant cost can best be illustrated by an example. Suppose a manager considers adding a new product to the product mix. Relevant costs include potential expenditures for manufacturing and marketing the product, plus salary costs arising from the time sales personnel give to the new product at the expense of other products. If this additional product does not affect the salary costs of sales personnel, salaries are not a relevant cost.

As a general rule, opportunity costs are also relevant costs. Opportunity costs are the forgone benefits from an alternative not chosen.

Sunk Costs

Sunk costs are the direct opposite of relevant costs. Sunk costs are past expenditures for a given activity and are typically irrelevant in whole or in part to future decisions. In a marketing context, sunk costs include past research and development expenditures (including test marketing) and last year's advertising expense. These expenditures, although real, will neither recur in the future nor influence future expenditures. When marketing managers attempt to incorporate sunk costs into future decisions affecting new expenditures, they often fall prey to the *sunk cost fallacy*—that is, they attempt to recoup spent dollars by spending still more dollars in the future.

■ MARGINS

Another useful concept for marketing managers is that of *margin*, which refers to the difference between the selling price and the "cost" of a product or service. Margins are expressed on a total volume basis or on an individual unit basis, in dollar terms or as percentages. The three described here are gross, trade, and net profit margins.

Gross Margin

Gross margin, or gross profit, is the difference between total sales revenue and total cost of goods sold, or, on a per-unit basis, the difference between unit selling price and unit cost of goods sold. Gross margin may be expressed in dollar terms or as a percentage.

Total Gross Margin	Dollar Amount	Percentage
Net sales	$100	100%
Cost of goods sold	−40	−40
Gross profit margin	$60	60%
Unit Gross Margin		
Unit sales price	$1.00	100%
Unit cost of goods sold	−0.40	−40
Unit gross profit margin	$0.60	60%

Gross margin analysis is a useful tool because it implicitly includes unit selling prices of products or services, unit costs, and unit volume. A decrease in gross margin is of immediate concern to a marketing manager, because such a change has a direct impact on profits, providing that other expenditures remain unchanged. Changes in total gross margin should be examined in depth to determine whether the change was brought about by fluctuations in unit volume, changes in unit price or unit cost of goods sold, or a modification in the sales mix of the firm's products or services.

Trade Margin

Trade margin is the difference between unit sales price and unit cost at each level of a marketing channel (for example, manufacturer → wholesaler → retailer). A trade margin is frequently referred to as a *markup* or *mark-on* by channel members, and it is often expressed as a percentage.

Trade margins are occasionally confusing, since the margin percentage can be computed on the basis of cost or selling price. Consider the following example. Suppose a retailer purchases an item for $10 and sells it at a price of $20—that is, a $10 margin. What is the retailer's margin percentage?

Retailer margin as a percentage of cost is

$$\frac{\$10}{\$10} \times 100 = 100 \text{ percent}$$

Retailer margin as a percentage of selling price is

$$\frac{\$10}{\$20} \times 100 = 50 \text{ percent}$$

Differences in margin percentages show the importance of knowing the base (cost or selling price) on which the margin percentage is determined. *Trade margin percentages are usually determined on the basis of selling price*, but practices do vary among firms and industries.

Trade margins affect the pricing of individual items in two ways. First, suppose a wholesaler purchases an item for $2.00 and seeks to achieve a 30 percent margin on this item based on selling price. What would be the selling price?

$2.00 = 70$ percent of selling price

or

Selling price = $2.00/0.70 = $2.86

Second, suppose a manufacturer suggests a retail list price of $6.00 on an item for ultimate resale to the consumer. The item will be sold through retailers whose policy is to obtain a 40 percent margin based on selling price. For what price must the manufacturer sell the item to the retailer?

$$\frac{x}{\$6.00} = 40 \text{ percent of selling price}$$

where x is the retailer margin. Solving for x indicates that the retailer must obtain $2.40 for this item. Therefore, the manufacturer must set the price to the retailer at $3.60 ($6.00 - $2.40).

The manufacturer's problem of suggesting a price for ultimate resale to the consumer becomes more complex as the number of intermediaries between the manufacturer and the final consumer increases. This complexity can be illustrated by expanding the above example to include a wholesaler between the manufacturer and retailer. The retailer receives a 40 percent margin on the sales price. If the retailer must receive $2.40 per unit, the wholesaler must sell the item for $3.60 per unit. In order for the wholesaler to receive a 20 percent margin, for what price must the manufacturer sell the unit to the wholesaler?

$$\frac{x}{\$3.60} = 20 \text{ percent wholesaler margin on selling price}$$

where x is the wholesaler margin. Solving for x shows that the wholesaler's margin is $0.72 for this item. Therefore, the manufacturer must set the price to the wholesaler at $2.88.

This example shows that a manager must work backward from the ultimate price to the consumer through the marketing channel to arrive at a product's selling price. Assuming that the manufacturer's cost of goods sold is $2.00, we can calculate the following margins, which incidentally show the manufacturer's gross margin of 30.6 percent.

	Unit Cost of Goods Sold	Unit Selling Price	Gross Margin as a Percentage of Selling Price
Manufacturer	$2.00	$2.88	30.6%
Wholesaler	2.88	3.60	20.0
Retailer	3.60	6.00	40.0
Consumer	6.00		

Net Profit Margin (Before Taxes)

The last margin to be considered is the net profit margin before taxes. This margin is expressed as a dollar figure or a percentage. *Net profit margin* is the remainder after cost of goods sold, other variable costs, and fixed costs have been subtracted from sales revenue. The place of net profit margin in an organization's income statement is illustrated by the following:

	Dollar Amount	Percentage
Net sales	$100,000	100%
Cost of goods sold	−30,000	−30
Gross profit margin	$70,000	70%
Selling expenses	−20,000	−20
Fixed expenses	−40,000	−40
Net profit margin	$10,000	10%

Net profit margin dollars represent a major source of funding for the organization. As will be shown later, net profit influences the working capital position of the organization; hence, the dollar amount ultimately affects the organization's ability to pay its cost of goods sold plus its selling and administrative expenses. Furthermore, net profit also affects the organization's cash flow position.

■ CONTRIBUTION ANALYSIS

Contribution analysis is an important concept in marketing management. *Contribution* is the difference between total sales revenue and total variable costs, or, on a per-unit basis, the difference between unit selling price and unit variable cost. Contribution analysis is particularly useful in assessing relationships among costs, prices, and volumes of products and services.

Break-Even Analysis

Break-even analysis is one of the simplest applications of contribution analysis. *Break-even analysis* identifies the unit or dollar sales volume at which an organization neither makes a profit nor incurs a loss. Stated in equation form:

Total revenue = total variable costs + total fixed costs

Since break-even analysis identifies the level of sales volume at which total costs (fixed and variable) and total revenue are equal, it is a valuable tool for evaluating an organization's profit goals and assessing the riskiness of actions.

Break-even analysis requires three pieces of information: (1) an estimate of unit variable costs, (2) an estimate of the total dollar fixed costs to produce and market the product or service unit (note that only relevant costs apply), and (3) the selling price for each product or service unit.

The formula for determining the number of units required to break even is as follows:

$$\text{Unit break-even volume} = \frac{\text{total dollar fixed costs}}{\text{unit selling price} - \text{unit variable cost}}$$

The denominator in this formula (unit selling price minus unit variable costs) is called *contribution per unit*. Contribution per unit is the dollar amount that each unit sold "contributes" to the payment of fixed costs.

Consider the following example. A manufacturer plans to sell a product for $5.00. The unit variable costs are $2.00, and total fixed costs assigned to the product are $30,000. How many units must be sold to break even?

$$\text{Fixed costs} = \$30,000$$

$$\text{Contribution per unit} = \text{unit selling price} - \text{unit variable cost}$$

$$= \$5 - \$2 = \$3$$

$$\text{Unit break-even volume} = \$30,000/\$3 = 10,000 \text{ units}$$

This example shows that for every unit sold at $5.00, $2.00 is used to pay variable costs. The balance of $3.00 "contributes" to fixed costs.

A related question is what the manufacturer's dollar sales volume must be to break even. The manager need only multiply unit break-even volume by the unit selling price to determine the dollar break-even volume: 10,000 units × $5 = $50,000.

A manager can calculate a dollar break-even point directly without first computing unit break-even volume. First, the *contribution margin* must be determined from the formula:

$$\text{Contribution margin} = \frac{\text{unit selling price} - \text{unit variable cost}}{\text{unit selling price}}$$

Using the figures from our example, we find that the contribution margin is 60 percent:

$$\text{Contribution margin} = \frac{\$5 - \$2}{\$5} = 60 \text{ percent}$$

Then the dollar break-even point is computed as follows:

$$\text{Break-even dollar volume} = \frac{\text{total fixed costs}}{\text{contribution margin}} = \frac{\$30{,}000}{0.60} = \$50{,}000$$

In many cases it is useful to develop a graphic representation of a break-even analysis. Exhibit 2.1 provides a visual solution to the problem posed previously. The horizontal line at \$30,000 represents fixed costs. The upward-sloping line beginning at \$30,000 represents the total cost, which is equal to the sum of fixed plus variable costs. This line has a slope equal to \$2.00—each unit increase in volume results in a \$2.00 increase in the total cost. The upward-sloping line beginning at zero represents revenue and has a slope of \$5.00—each unit increase in sales produces a \$5.00 increase in revenue. The distance between the revenue line and the total cost line represents dollars of profit (above the break-even point) or loss (below the break-even point).

EXHIBIT 2.1

Break-Even Analysis Chart

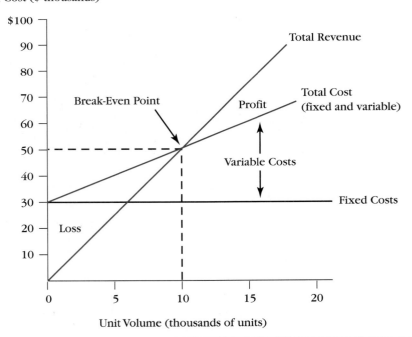

Unit Volume (thousands of units)

Sensitivity Analysis

Contribution analysis can be applied in a number of different ways, depending on the manager's needs. The following illustrations show how the break-even points in our example can be varied by changing selling price, variable costs, and fixed costs.

1. What would break-even volume be if fixed costs were increased to $40,000 while the selling price and variable costs remained unchanged?

Fixed costs = $40,000

Contribution per unit = $3

Unit break-even volume = $40,000/$3 = 13,333 units

Dollar break-even volume = $40,000/0.60 = $66,667

Note that the difference between the dollar break-even volume calculated from the contribution margin and the result of simply multiplying unit selling price by unit break-even volume (13,333 × $5 = $66,665) is due to rounding.

2. What would break-even volume be if selling price were dropped from $5.00 to $4.00 while fixed and variable costs remained unchanged?

Fixed costs = $30,000

Contribution per unit = $2

Unit break-even volume = $30,000/$2 = 15,000 units

Dollar break-even volume = $30,000/0.50 = $60,000

3. Finally, what would break-even volume be if the unit variable cost per unit were reduced to $1.50, selling price remained at $5.00, and fixed costs were $30,000?

Fixed costs = $30,000

Contribution per unit = $3.50

Unit break-even volume = $30,000/$3.50 = 8,571 units

Dollar break-even volume = $30,000/0.70 = $42,857

Contribution Analysis and Profit Impact

No manager is content to operate at the break-even point in unit or dollar sales volume. Profits are necessary for the continued operation of an organization. A modified break-even analysis is used to incorporate a profit goal.

To modify the break-even formula to incorporate a dollar profit goal, we need only regard the profit goal as an additional fixed cost, as follows:

$$\frac{\text{Unit volume to achieve}}{\text{dollar profit goal}} = \frac{\text{total dollar fixed costs} + \text{dollar profit goal}}{\text{contribution per unit}}$$

Suppose a firm has fixed costs of $200,000 budgeted for a product or service, the unit selling price is $25.00, and the unit variable costs are $10.00. How many units must be sold to achieve a dollar profit goal of $20,000?

Fixed costs + profit goal = $200,000 + $20,000 = $220,000

Contribution per unit = $25 – $10 = $15

Unit volume to achieve dollar profit goal = $220,000/$15

= 14,667 units

Many firms specify their profit goal as a percentage of sales rather than as a dollar amount ("Our profit goal is a 20 percent profit on sales"). This objective can be incorporated into the break-even formula by subtracting the profit goal from the contribution-per-unit. If the goal is to achieve a 20 percent profit on sales, each dollar of sales must "contribute" $0.20 to profit. In our example, each unit sold for $25.00 must contribute $5.00 to profit (.20 × $25.00). The break-even formula incorporating a percent profit on sales goal is as follows:

$$\text{Unit volume to achieve profit goal} = \frac{\text{total dollar fixed costs}}{\text{contribution per unit} - \text{unit profit goal}}$$

The unit volume break-even point to achieve a 20 percent profit goal is 20,000 units:

$$\text{Fixed costs} = \$200,000$$

$$\text{Contribution per unit} - \text{unit profit goal} = \$25 - \$10 - \$5 = \$10$$

$$\text{Unit volume to achieve profit goal} = \$200,000/\$10$$

$$= 20,000 \text{ units}$$

Contribution Analysis and Market Size

An important consideration in contribution analysis is the relationship of break-even unit or dollar volume to market size. Consider the situation in which a manager has conducted a break-even analysis and found the unit volume break-even point to be 50,000 units. This number has meaning only when compared with the potential size of the market segment sought. If the market potential is 100,000 units, the manager's product or service must capture 50 percent of the market sought to break even. An important question to be resolved is whether such a percentage can be achieved. A manager can assess the feasibility of a venture by comparing the break-even volume with market size and market-capture percentage.

Contribution Analysis and Performance Measurement

A second application of contribution analysis lies in performance measurement. For example, a marketing manager may wish to examine the performance of products. Consider an organization with two products, X and Y. A description of each product's financial performance follows:

	Product X (10,000 volume)	Product Y (20,000 volume)	Total (30,000 volume)
Unit price	$ 10	$ 3	
Sales revenue	100,000	60,000	$160,000
Unit variable cost	4	1.50	
Total variable cost	40,000	30,000	70,000
Unit contribution	6	1.50	
Total contribution	60,000	30,000	90,000
Fixed costs	45,000	10,000	55,000
Net profit	$ 15,000	$20,000	$ 35,000

The net profit figure shows that Product Y is more profitable than Product X. Product X is four times more profitable than Product Y on a unit-contribution basis, however, and generates twice the contribution dollars to overhead. The difference in profitability comes from the allocation of fixed costs to the products. In measuring performance, it is important to consider which products contribute most heavily to the organization's total fixed costs ($55,000 in this example) and then to total profit.

Should a manager look only at net profit, a decision might be made to drop Product X. Product Y would then have to cover total fixed costs, however. If the fixed costs remain at $55,000 and only Product Y is sold, this organization will experience a *net loss* of $25,000, assuming no change in Product Y volume.

Assessment of Cannibalization

A third application of contribution analysis is in the assessment of cannibalization effects. Cannibalization is the process by which one product or service sold by a firm gains a portion of its revenue by diverting sales from another product or service also sold by the firm. For example, sales of Brand X's new gel toothpaste may be at the expense of sales of Brand X's existing opaque white toothpaste. The problem facing a marketing manager is to assess the financial effect of cannibalization.

Consider the following data:

	Existing Opaque White Toothpaste	*New Gel Toothpaste*
Unit selling price	$1.00	$1.10
Unit variable costs	–0.20	–0.40
Unit contribution	$0.80	$0.70

The gel toothpaste can be sold at a slightly higher price, given its formulation and taste, but the variable costs are also higher. Hence, the gel toothpaste has a lower contribution per unit. Therefore, for every unit of the gel toothpaste sold instead of a unit of the opaque white toothpaste, the firm "loses" $0.10. Suppose further that the company expects to sell 1 million units of the new gel toothpaste in the first year after introduction and that, of that amount, 500,000 units will be diverted from the opaque white toothpaste, of which the company had expected to sell 1 million units. The task of the marketing manager is to determine how the introduction of the new gel toothpaste will affect Brand X's total contribution dollars.

One approach to assessing the financial impact of cannibalization is shown here:

1. Brand X expects to lose $0.10 for each unit diverted from the opaque white toothpaste to the gel toothpaste.

2. Given that 500,000 units will be cannibalized from the opaque white toothpaste, the total contribution *lost* is $50,000 ($0.10 × 500,000 units).

3. However, the new gel toothpaste will sell an additional 500,000 units at a contribution per unit of $0.70, which means that $350,000 ($0.70 × 500,000 units) in additional contribution will be generated.

4. Therefore, the net financial effect is a positive increase in contribution dollars of $300,000 ($350,000 – $50,000).

Another approach to assessing the cannibalization effect is as follows:

1. The opaque white toothpaste alone had been expected to sell 1 million units with a unit contribution of $0.80. Therefore, contribution dollars without the gel would equal $800,000 ($0.80 × 1,000,000 units).

2. The gel toothpaste is expected to sell 1 million units with a unit contribution of $0.70.

3. Given the cannibalism rate of 50 percent (that is, one-half of the gel's volume is diverted from the opaque white toothpaste), the combined contribution can be calculated as follows:

Product	Unit Volume	Unit Contribution	Contribution Dollars
Opaque white toothpaste	500,000	$0.80	$400,000
Gel toothpaste:			
Cannibalized volume	500,000	0.70	350,000
Incremental volume	500,000	0.70	350,000
Total	1,500,000		$1,100,000
Less original forecast volume for opaque white toothpaste	1,000,000	0.80	800,000
Total	+500,000		+$300,000

Both approaches arrive at the same conclusion: Brand X will benefit by $300,000 from the introduction of the gel toothpaste. The manager should use whichever approach he or she is more comfortable with in an analytic sense.

It should be emphasized, however, that the incremental fixed costs associated with advertising and sales promotion or any additions or changes in manufacturing capacity must be considered to complete the analysis. If the fixed costs approximate or exceed $300,000, the new product should be viewed in a very different light.

■ LIQUIDITY

Liquidity refers to an organization's ability to meet short-term (usually within a budget year) financial obligations. A key measure of an organization's liquidity position is its working capital. *Working capital* is the dollar value of an organization's *current assets* (such as cash, accounts receivable, prepaid expenses, inventory) *minus* the dollar value of *current liabilities* (such as short-term accounts payable for goods and services, income taxes).

A manager should be aware of the impact of marketing actions on working capital. Marketing expenditures precede sales volume; therefore, cash outlays for marketing efforts reduce current assets. If marketing expenditures cannot be met out of cash, accounts payable are incurred. In either case, working capital is reduced. In a positive vein, a marketing manager's creation of sales volume, with corresponding increases in net profit, contributes to working capital. Since the timing of marketing expenditures and sales volume is often lagged, a marketing manager must be wary of marketing efforts that unnecessarily deplete working capital and must assess the likelihood of potential sales, given a specified expenditure level.

■ OPERATING LEVERAGE

A financial concept closely akin to break-even analysis is operating leverage. *Operating leverage* refers to the extent to which fixed costs and variable costs are used in the production and marketing of products and services. Firms that have high total fixed costs relative to total variable costs are defined as having high operating leverage. Examples of firms with high operating leverage include airlines and heavy-equipment manufacturers. Firms with low total fixed costs relative to total variable costs are defined as having low operating leverage. Firms typically having low operating leverage include residential contractors and wholesale distributors.

The higher a firm's operating leverage, the faster its total profits will increase once sales exceed break-even volume. By the same token, however, those firms with

EXHIBIT 2.2

Effect of Operating Leverage on Profit

	Base Case		10% Increase in Sales		10% Decrease in Sales	
	High-Fixed-Cost Firm	High-Variable-Cost Firm	High-Fixed-Cost Firm	High-Variable-Cost Firm	High-Fixed-Cost Firm	High-Variable-Cost Firm
Sales	$100,000	$100,000	$110,000	$110,000	$90,000	$90,000
Variable costs	20,000	80,000	22,000	88,000	18,000	72,000
Fixed costs	80,000	20,000	80,000	20,000	80,000	20,000
Profit	$0	$0	$8,000	$2,000	($8,000)	($2,000)

high operating leverage will incur losses at a faster rate once sales volume falls below the break-even point.

Exhibit 2.2 illustrates the effect of operating leverage on profit. The base case shows two firms that have identical break-even sales volumes. The cost structures of the two firms differ, however, with one having high fixed and low variable costs and the other having low fixed and high variable costs. Note that when sales volume is increased 10 percent, the firm with high fixed and low variable costs achieves a much higher profit than the firm with low fixed and high variable costs. When sales volume declines, however, just the opposite is true. That is, the firm with high fixed and low variable costs incurs losses at a faster rate than the firm with high variable and low fixed costs once sales fall below the break-even point.

The message of operating leverage should be clear from this example. Firms with high operating leverage benefit more from sales gains than do firms with low operating leverage. At the same time, firms with high operating leverage are more sensitive to sales-volume declines, since losses will be incurred at a faster rate. Knowledge of a firm's cost structure will, therefore, prove valuable in assessing the gains and losses from changes in sales volume brought about by marketing efforts.

■ DISCOUNTED CASH FLOW

Another useful concept from finance is discounted cash flow. Discounted cash flow incorporates the theory of the time value of money, or present-value analysis. The idea behind the present value of money is that a dollar received next year is not equivalent to a dollar received today because the use of money has a value reflected by risk, inflation, and opportunity cost. To illustrate, if $500 can be invested today at 10 percent, $550 will be received a year later ($500 + 10% of $500). In other words, $550 to be received next year has a present value of $500 if 10 percent can be earned ($550/1.10 = $500). Following this line of reasoning, the estimated results of an investment (e.g., a business) can be stated as a cash equivalent at the present time (i.e., its present value). *Discounted cash flows* are future cash flows expressed in terms of their present value.

The discounted cash flow technique employs this reasoning by evaluating the present value of a business's net *cash flow* (cash inflows minus cash outflows). A simplified view of cash flow is "cash flow from operations," which is net income plus depreciation charges, because depreciation is a noncash charge against sales to determine net income. The present value of a stream of cash flows is obtained by selecting an interest or discount rate at which these flows are to be valued, or discounted, and the timing of each. The interest or discount rate is often defined by the opportunity *cost of capital*—the cost of earnings opportunities forgone by investing in a business with its attendant risk as opposed to investing in risk-free securities such as U.S. Treasury bills.

A simple application of discounted cash flow analysis illustrates the mechanics involved. Suppose, for example, that a firm is considering investing $105,000 in one of two businesses. The firm has forecast cash flows for each business over the next five years. The discount rate adopted by the firm is 15 percent. Given the discount rate of 15 percent, the cash flow when the investment is made is a negative $105,000 (no cash inflows, only outflows). The first-year cash flow for Business A is discounted by the factor $1/(1 + 0.15)^1$, or $25,000 \times 0.879 = \$21,700$. The second-year cash flow for Business A is discounted by the factor $1/(1 + 0.15)^2$, or $35,000 \times 0.756 = \$26,460$, and so forth. Exhibit 2.3 shows the complete analysis for Businesses A and B for the five-year planning horizon.

Three points are of particular interest. First, an important series of numbers is the *cumulative cash flow*. This series shows that the cumulative cash flows from Business B are greater than from Business A. Second, the *payback period* is two years for Business B, as opposed to about three years for Business A. In other words, Business B will recover its investment sooner than will Business A. Finally, the discounted cash flows incorporating the time value of money are clearly indicated. Business A will produce a higher cash flow in later years than will Business B. However, the present value of these cash flows, when discounted, is less than the value of the cash flows that Business B will produce.

From a decision-making perspective, both businesses produce a positive net present value. This is important given the decision rule when interpreting net present value: An investment should be accepted if the net present value is positive and rejected if it is negative. In which business should the firm invest its capital? Assuming that the firm wishes to create value for its shareholders, the option with the higher net present value (Business B) is preferred.

A valuable characteristic of present-value analysis is that the discount factors and discounted cash are additive. If the projected cash flows from an investment are equal over a specified time period, summing the discount factors for each of the time periods (say three years) and multiplying this figure by the annual cash flow estimate will give the present value.

EXHIBIT 2.3

Application of Discounted Cash Flow Analysis with a 15 Percent Discount Factor

| Year | Discount Factor | Business A | | | Business B | | |
		Cash Flow	Cumulative Cash Flow	Discounted Cash Flow	Cash Flow	Cumulative Cash Flow	Discounted Cash Flow
0	1.000	($105,000)	($105,000)	($105,000)	($105,000)	($105,000)	($105,000)
1	0.870	25,000	(80,000)	21,750	50,000	(55,000)	43,500
2	0.756	35,000	(45,000)	26,460	55,000	0	41,580
3	0.658	50,000	5,000	32,900	60,000	60,000	39,480
4	0.572	70,000	75,000	40,040	65,000	125,000	37,180
5	0.497	90,000	165,000	44,730	70,000	195,000	34,790
Totals				$ 60,880			$ 91,530

Suppose, for example, that a firm can expect a constant cash flow of $10 million per year for three years, and the discount rate is 15 percent. The present value of this cash flow can be computed as follows (in millions of dollars):

$$0.870 \times \$10 = \$8.70$$
$$0.756 \times \$10 = \$7.56$$
$$\underline{0.658 \times \$10 = \$6.58}$$
$$2.284 \times \$10 = \$22.84$$

Any basic finance textbook covers discounted cash flow in depth and should be consulted for further study. As a word of caution, the application of discounted cash flow analysis is deceptively simple. Determining appropriate discount rates and projecting future cash flows is not an easy task. Conservative estimates and the use of several "what if" scenarios will ensure that the discounted cash flow technique will highlight investment opportunities that create value for the firm and its shareholders.

■ PREPARING A PRO FORMA INCOME STATEMENT

Because marketing managers are accountable for the profit impact of their actions, they must translate their strategies and tactics into *pro forma*, or projected, income statements. A *pro forma* income statement displays projected revenues, budgeted expenses, and estimated net profit for an organization, product, or service during a specific planning period, usually a year. *Pro forma* income statements include a sales forecast and a listing of variable and fixed costs that can be programmed or committed.

Pro forma income statements can be prepared in different ways and reflect varying levels of specificity. Exhibit 2.4 shows a typical layout for a *pro forma* income statement consisting of six major categories or line items:

EXHIBIT 2.4

Pro Forma Income Statement for the 12-Month Period Ended December 31, 2002

Sales		$1,000,000
Cost of goods sold		500,000
Gross margin		$500,000
Marketing expenses		
Sales expenses	$170,000	
Advertising expenses	90,000	
Freight or delivery expenses	40,000	300,000
General and administrative expenses		
Administrative salaries	$120,000	
Depreciation on buildings and equipment	20,000	
Interest expense	5,000	
Property taxes and insurance	5,000	
Other administrative expenses	5,000	155,000
Net profit before (income) tax		$45,000

1. *Sales*—forecasted unit volume times unit selling price.

2. *Cost of goods sold*—costs incurred in buying or producing products and services. Generally speaking, these costs are constant per unit within certain volume ranges and vary with total unit volume.

3. *Gross margin* (sometimes called *gross profit*)—represents the remainder after cost of goods sold has been subtracted from sales.

4. *Marketing expenses*—generally, programmed expenses budgeted to produce sales. Advertising expenses are typically fixed. Sales expenses can be fixed, such as a salesperson's salary, or variable, such as sales commissions. Freight or delivery expenses are typically constant per unit and vary with total unit volume.

5. *General and administrative expenses*—generally, committed fixed costs for the planning period, which cannot be avoided if the organization is to operate. These costs are frequently called overhead.

6. *Net income before (income) taxes* (often called *net profit before taxes*)—the remainder after all costs have been subtracted from sales.

A *pro forma* income statement reflects a marketing manager's expectations (sales) given certain inputs (costs). This means that a manager must think specifically about customer response to strategies and tactics and focus attention on the organization's financial objectives of profitability and growth when preparing a *pro forma* income statement.

■ SUMMARY

This chapter provides an overview of basic accounting and financial concepts. A word of caution is necessary, however. Financial analysis of marketing actions is a necessary but insufficient criterion for justifying marketing programs. A careful analysis of other variables impinging on the decision at hand is required. Thus, judgment enters the picture. "Numbers" serve only to complement general marketing analysis skills and are not an end in themselves. In this regard, it is wise to consider some words of Albert Einstein: "Not everything that counts can be counted, and not everything that can be counted counts."

■ EXERCISES

1. Executives of Studio Recordings, Inc., produced the latest compact disc by the Starshine Sisters Band, titled *Sunshine/Moonshine*. The following cost information pertains to the new CD:

CD package and disc (direct material and labor)	$1.25/CD
Songwriters' royalties	$0.35/CD
Recording artists' royalties	$1.00/CD
Advertising and promotion	$275,000
Studio Recordings, Inc., overhead	$250,000
Selling price to CD distributor	$9.00

Calculate the following:

    a. Contribution per CD unit

    b. Break-even volume in CD units and dollars

    c. Net profit if 1 million CDs are sold

    d. Necessary CD unit volume to achieve a $200,000 profit

2. Video Concepts, Inc. (VCI) markets video equipment and film through a variety of retail outlets. Presently, VCI is faced with a decision as to whether it should obtain the distribution rights to an unreleased film entitled *Touch of Orange*. If this film is distributed by VCI directly to large retailers, VCI's investment in the project would be $150,000. VCI estimates the total market for the film to be 100,000 units. Other data available are as follows:

Cost of distribution rights for film	$125,000
Label design	5,000
Package design	10,000
Advertising	35,000
Reproduction of copies (per 1,000)	4,000
Manufacture of labels and packaging (per 1,000)	500
Royalties (per 1,000)	500

VCI's suggested retail price for the film is $20 per unit. The retailer's margin is 40 percent.

    a. What is VCI's unit contribution and contribution margin?

    b. What is the break-even point in units? In dollars?

    c. What share of the market would the film have to achieve to earn a 20 percent return on VCI's investment the first year?

3. The group product manager for ointments at American Therapeutic Corporation was reviewing price and promotion alternatives for two products: Rash-Away and Red-Away. Both products were designed to reduce skin irritation, but Red-Away was primarily a cosmetic treatment whereas Rash-Away also included a compound that eliminated the rash.

    The price and promotion alternatives recommended for the two products by their respective brand managers included the possibility of using additional promotion or a price reduction to stimulate sales volume. A volume, price, and cost summary for the two products follows:

	Rash-Away	*Red-Away*
Unit price	$2.00	$1.00
Unit variable costs	1.40	0.25
Unit contribution	$0.60	$0.75
Unit volume	1,000,000 units	1,500,000 units

    Both brand managers included a recommendation to either reduce price by 10 percent or invest an incremental $150,000 in advertising.

    a. What absolute increase in unit sales and dollar sales will be necessary to recoup the incremental increase in advertising expenditures for Rash-Away? For Red-Away?

    b. How many additional sales dollars must be produced to cover each $1.00 of incremental advertising for Rash-Away? For Red-Away?

    c. What absolute increase in unit sales and dollar sales will be necessary to maintain the level of total contribution dollars if the price of each product is reduced by 10 percent?

4. After spending $300,000 for research and development, chemists at Diversified Citrus Industries have developed a new breakfast drink. The drink, called Zap,

will provide the consumer with twice the amount of vitamin C currently available in breakfast drinks. Zap will be packaged in an eight-ounce can and will be introduced to the breakfast drink market, which is estimated to be equivalent to 21 million eight-ounce cans nationally.

One major management concern is the lack of funds available for marketing. Accordingly, management has decided to use newspapers (rather than television) to promote Zap in the introductory year and distribute Zap in major metropolitan areas that account for 65 percent of U.S. breakfast drink volume. Newspaper advertising will carry a coupon that will entitle the consumer to receive $0.20 off the price of the first can purchased. The retailer will receive the regular margin and be reimbursed for redeemed coupons by Diversified Citrus Industries. Past experience indicates that for every five cans sold during the introductory year, one coupon will be returned. The cost of the newspaper advertising campaign (excluding coupon returns) will be $250,000. Other fixed overhead costs are expected to be $90,000 per year.

Management has decided that the suggested retail price to the consumer for the eight-ounce can will be $0.50. The only unit variable costs for the product are $0.18 for materials and $0.06 for labor. The company intends to give retailers a margin of 20 percent off the suggested retail price and wholesalers a margin of 10 percent of the retailers' cost of the item.

    a. At what price will Diversified Citrus Industries be selling its product to wholesalers?

    b. What is the contribution per unit for Zap?

    c. What is the break-even unit volume in the first year?

    d. What is the first-year break-even share of market?

5. Video Concepts, Inc. (VCI) manufactures a line of videocassette recorders (VCRs) that are distributed to large retailers. The line consists of three models of VCRs. The following data are available regarding the models:

Model	VCR Selling Price per Unit	Variable Cost per Unit	Demand/Year (units)
Model LX1	$175	$100	2,000
Model LX2	250	125	1,000
Model LX3	300	140	500

VCI is considering the addition of a fourth model to its line of VCRs. This model would be sold to retailers for $375. The variable cost of this unit is $225. The demand for the new Model LX4 is estimated to be 300 units per year. Sixty percent of these unit sales of the new model is expected to come from other models already being manufactured by VCI (10 percent from Model LX1, 30 percent from Model LX2, and 60 percent from Model LX3). VCI will incur a fixed cost of $20,000 to add the new model to the line. Based on the preceding data, should VCI add the new Model LX4 to its line of VCRs? Why?

6. Max Leonard, vice president of Marketing for Dysk Computer, Inc., must decide whether to introduce a midpriced version of the firm's DC6900 personal computer product line—the DC6900-X. The DC6900-X would sell for $3,900, with unit variable costs of $1,800. Projections made by an independent marketing research firm indicate that the DC6900-X would achieve a sales volume of 500,000 units next year, in its first year of commercialization. One-half of the first year's volume would come from competitors' personal computers and market growth. However, a consumer research study indicates that 30 percent of the DC6900-X sales volume would come from the higher-priced

DC6900-Omega personal computer, which sells for $5,900 (with unit variable costs of $2,200). Another 20 percent of the DC6900-X sales volume would come from the economy-priced DC6900-Alpha personal computer, priced at $2,500 (with unit variable costs of $1,200). The DC6900-Omega unit volume is expected to be 400,000 units next year, and the DC6900-Alpha is expected to achieve a 600,000-unit sales level. The fixed costs of launching the DC6900-X have been forecast to be $2 million during the first year of commercialization. Should Mr. Leonard add the DC6900-X model to the line of personal computers? Why?

7. A sports nutrition company is examining whether a new high-performance sports drink should be added to its product line. A preliminary feasibility analysis indicated that the company would need to invest $17.5 million in a new manufacturing facility to produce and package the product. A financial analysis using sales and cost data supplied by marketing and production personnel indicated that the net cash flow (cash inflows minus cash outflows) would be $6.1 million in the first year of commercialization, $7.4 million in year 2, $7.0 million in year 3, and $5.5 million in year 4.

Senior company executives were undecided whether to move forward with the development of the new product. They requested that a discounted cash flow analysis be performed using two different discount rates: 20 percent and 15 percent.

a. Should the company proceed with development of the product if the discount rate is 20 percent? Why?

b. Does the decision to proceed with development of the product change if the discount rate is 15 percent? Why?

8. The annual planning process at Century Office Systems, Inc. had been arduous but produced a number of important marketing initiatives for the next year. Most notably, company executives had decided to restructure its product-marketing team into two separate groups: (1) Corporate Office Systems and (2) Home Office Systems. Angela Blake was assigned responsibility for the Home Office Systems group, which would market the company's word-processing hardware and software for home and office-at-home use by individuals. Her marketing plan, which included a sales forecast for next year of $25 million, was the result of a detailed market analysis and negotiations with individuals both inside and outside the company. Discussions with the sales director indicated that 40 percent of the company sales force would be dedicated to selling products of the Home Office Systems group. Sales representatives would receive a 15 percent commission on sales of home office systems. Under the new organizational structure, the Home Office Systems group would be charged with 40 percent of the budgeted sales force expenditure. The sales director's budget for salaries and fringe benefits of the sales force and non-commission selling costs for both the Corporate and Home Office Systems groups was $7.5 million.

The advertising and promotion budget contained three elements: trade magazine advertising, cooperative newspaper advertising with Century Office Systems, Inc. dealers, and sales promotion materials including product brochures, technical manuals, catalogs, and point-of-purchase displays. Trade magazine ads and sales promotion materials were to be developed by the company's advertising and public relations agency. Production and media placement costs were budgeted at $300,000. Cooperative advertising copy for both newspaper and radio use had budgeted production costs of $100,000. Century Office Systems, Inc.'s, cooperative advertising allowance policy stated that the company would allocate 5 percent of company sales to dealers to promote its office systems. Dealers always used their complete cooperative advertising allowances.

Meetings with manufacturing and operations personnel indicated that the direct costs of material and labor and direct factory overhead to produce the Home Office System product line represented 50 percent of sales. The accounting department would assign $600,000 in indirect manufacturing overhead (for example, depreciation, maintenance) to the product line and $300,000 for administrative overhead (clerical, telephone, office space, and so forth). Freight for the product line would average 8 percent of sales.

Blake's staff consisted of two product managers and a marketing assistant. Salaries and fringe benefits for Ms. Blake and her staff were $250,000 per year.

    a.   Prepare a *pro forma* income statement for the Home Office Systems group given the information provided.

    b.   Prepare a *pro forma* income statement for the Home Office Systems group given annual sales of only $20 million.

    c.   At what level of dollar sales will the Home Office Systems group break even?

CHAPTER 3

Marketing Decision Making and Case Analysis

 Skill in decision making is a prerequisite to being an effective marketing manager. Indeed, Nobel laureate Herbert Simon viewed managing and decision making as being one and the same.[1] Another management theorist, Peter Drucker, has said that the burden of decision making can be lessened and better decisions can result if a manager recognizes that "decision making is a rational and systematic process and that its organization is a definite sequence of steps, each of them in turn rational and systematic."[2]

One objective of this chapter is to introduce a systematic process for decision making; another is to introduce basic considerations in case analysis. Just as decision making and managing can be viewed as being identical in scope, so the decision-making process and case analysis go hand in hand. For this reason, many companies today use case studies when interviewing an applicant to assess his or her decision-making skill. They have found that the applicant's approach to the case demonstrates strategic thinking, analytical ability and judgment, along with a variety of communication skills, including listening, questioning, and dealing with confrontation.[3]

■ DECISION-MAKING PROCESS

Although no simple formula exists that can assure a correct solution to all problems at all times, use of a systematic decision-making process can increase the likelihood of arriving at better solutions. The decision-making process described here is called DECIDE:[4]

<u>D</u>efine the problem.

<u>E</u>numerate the decision factors.

<u>C</u>onsider relevant information.

<u>I</u>dentify the best alternative.

<u>D</u>evelop a plan for implementing the chosen alternative.

<u>E</u>valuate the decision and the decision process.

A definition and a discussion of the implications of each step follow.

Define the Problem

The philosopher John Dewey observed that "a problem well defined is half solved." What this statement means in a marketing setting is that a well-defined problem outlines the framework within which a solution can be derived. This framework includes the *objectives* of the decision maker, a recognition of *constraints*, and a clearly articulated *success measure*, or goal, for assessing progress toward solving the problem.

Consider the situation faced by El Nacho Foods, a marketer of Mexican foods. The company had positioned its line of Mexican foods as a high-quality brand and used advertising effectively to convey that message. Shortly after the company's introduction of frozen dinners, two of its competitors began cutting the price of their frozen dinner entrees. The firm lost market share and sales as a result of these price reductions; this loss led to reductions in the contribution dollars available for advertising and sales promotion. How might the problem be defined in this situation? One definition of the problem leads to the question: "Should we reduce our price?" A much better definition of the problem leads one to ask: "How can we maintain our quality brand image (objective) and regain our lost market share (success measure), given limited funds for advertising and sales promotion (constraint)?"

The first problem definition asks for a response to an immediate issue facing the company. It does not articulate the broader and more important considerations of competitive positioning. Hence, the problem statement fails to capture the significance of the issue raised. The second definition provides a broader perspective on the immediate issue posed and allows the manager greater latitude in seeking solutions.

In a case study, the analyst is frequently given alternative courses of action to consider. The narrow approach to case analysis is simply to compare these different options. Such an approach often leads to the selection of alternative A or alternative B without regard to the significance of the choice in the broader context of the situation facing the company or the decision maker.

Enumerate the Decision Factors

Two sets of decision factors must be enumerated in the decision-making process: (1) *alternative courses of action*, and (2) *uncertainties* in the competitive environment. Alternative courses of action are controllable decision factors because the decision maker has complete command of them. Alternatives are typically product-market strategies or changes in the various elements of the organization's marketing mix (described in Chapter 1). Uncertainties, on the other hand, are uncontrollable factors that the manager cannot influence. In a marketing context, they often include actions of competitors, market size, and buyer response to marketing action. Assumptions often have to be made concerning these factors. These assumptions need to be spelled out, particularly if they will influence the evaluation of alternative courses of action.

The experience of Cluett Peabody and Company, the maker of Arrow shirts, illustrates how the combination of an action and uncertainties can spell disaster. Arrow departed from its normal practice of selling classic men's shirts to offer a new line featuring bolder colors, busier patterns, and higher prices (action). The firm soon realized that men's tastes had changed to more conservative styles (environmental uncertainties). The result? The company posted a $4.5 million loss. According to the company president, "We tried to be exciting, and we really didn't look at the market."[5]

Case analysis provides an opportunity to relate alternatives to uncertainties, and these factors *must* be related if decision making is to be effective. No expected outcome, financial or otherwise, of a chosen course of action can realistically be considered apart from the environment into which it is introduced.

Consider Relevant Information

The third step in the decision-making process is the consideration of relevant information. *Relevant information*, like the relevant costs discussed in Chapter 2, consists of information that relates to the alternatives identified by the manager as being likely to affect future events. More specifically, relevant information might include characteristics of the industry or competitive environment, characteristics of the organization (such as competitive strengths and position), and characteristics of the alternatives themselves.

Identifying relevant information is difficult both for the practicing manager and for the case analyst. There is frequently an overabundance of facts, figures, and viewpoints available in any decision-making setting. In fact, it has been said that "The truly successful managers and leaders of the [twenty-first] century will . . . be characterized not by how they can access information, but how they can access the most relevant information and differentiate it from the exponentially multiplying masses of nonrelevant information."[6] Determining what matters and what does not is a skill that is best gained through experience. Analyzing many and varied cases is one way to develop this skill.

Two notes of caution are necessary. First, the case analyst must resist the temptation to consider *everything* in a case as "fact." Many cases, including actual marketing situations, contain conflicting data. Part of the task in any case analysis is to exercise judgment in assessing the validity of the data presented. Second, in many instances relevant information must be created. An example of creating relevant information is the blending together of several pieces of data, as in the calculation of a simple break-even point.

It should be clear at this point that even though the consideration of relevant information is the third step in the decision-making process, relevant information will also affect the two previous steps. As the manager or case analyst becomes more deeply involved in considering and evaluating information, the problem definition may be modified or the decision factors may change.[7]

Upon the conclusion of the first three steps, the manager or case analyst has completed a *situation analysis*. The situation analysis should produce an answer to the synoptic question, "Where are we now?" (Specific questions relating to situation analysis are found in Exhibit 3.4 later in this chapter.)

Identify the Best Alternative

Identifying the best alternative is the fourth step in the decision-making process. The selection of a course of action is not simply a matter of choosing Alternative A over other alternatives but, rather, of evaluating identified alternatives and the uncertainties apparent in the problem setting.

A framework for identifying the best alternative is *decision analysis*, which was introduced in Chapter 1. In its simplest form, decision analysis matches each alternative identified by the manager with the uncertainties existing in the environment and assigns a quantitative value to the outcome associated with each match. Managers implicitly use a decision tree and a payoff table to describe the relationship among alternatives, uncertainties, and potential outcomes. The use of decision analysis and the application of decision trees and payoff tables can be illustrated by referring back to the situation faced by El Nacho Foods.

Suppose that at the conclusion of Step 2 in the DECIDE process (that is, enumerating decision factors), El Nacho executives identified two alternatives: (1) reduce the price on frozen dinners, or (2) maintain the price. They also recognized two uncertainties: (1) Competitors could maintain the lower price, or (2) competitors

EXHIBIT 3.1

Decision Tree for El Nacho Foods

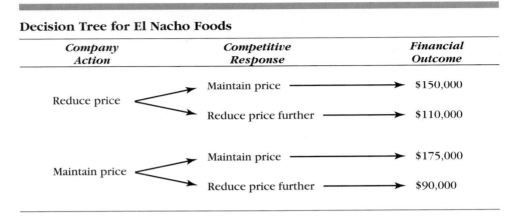

Company Action	Competitive Response	Financial Outcome
Reduce price	Maintain price	$150,000
	Reduce price further	$110,000
Maintain price	Maintain price	$175,000
	Reduce price further	$90,000

could reduce the price further. Suppose further that at the conclusion of Step 3 in the DECIDE process (considering relevant information), El Nacho executives examined the changes in market share and sales volume that would be brought about by the pricing actions. They also calculated the contribution per unit of frozen dinners for each alternative for each competitor response. They performed a contribution analysis because the problem was defined in terms of contribution to advertising and sales promotion in Step 1 of the DECIDE process (defining the problem).

Given two alternatives, two competitive responses, and a calculated contribution per unit for each combination, they identified four unique financial outcomes. These outcomes are displayed in the decision tree shown in Exhibit 3.1.

It is apparent from the decision tree that the largest contribution will be generated if El Nacho maintains its price on frozen dinners *and* competitors maintain their lower price. If El Nacho maintains its price and competitors reduce their price further, however, the lowest contribution among the four outcomes identified will be generated. The choice of an alternative obviously depends on the likelihood of occurrence of uncertainties in the environment.

A *payoff table* is a useful tool for displaying the alternatives, uncertainties, and outcomes facing a firm. In addition, a payoff table includes another dimension—management's subjective determination of the probability of the occurrence of an uncertainty. Suppose, for example, that El Nacho management believes that competitors are also operating with slim contribution margins and, hence, are most likely to maintain the lower price regardless of El Nacho's action. They believe that there is a 10 percent chance that competitors will reduce the price of frozen dinners even further.[8] Since only two uncertainties have been identified, the subjective probability of competitors' maintaining their price is 90 percent (note that the probabilities assigned to the uncertainties must total 1.0, or 100 percent). Given these probabilities, the payoff table for El Nacho Foods is shown in Exhibit 3.2.

The payoff table allows the manager or case analyst to compute the "expected monetary value" for each alternative. The expected monetary value is calculated by multiplying the outcome for each uncertainty by its probability of occurrence and then totaling across the uncertainties for each alternative. The expected monetary value of an alternative can be viewed as the value that would be obtained if the manager were to choose the same alternative many times under the same conditions.

The expected monetary value of the price-reduction alternative equals the probability that competitors will maintain prices, multiplied by the financial contribution if competitors maintain prices, plus the probability that competitors will further reduce

EXHIBIT 3.2

Payoff Table for El Nacho Foods

		Uncertainties	
		Competitors Maintain Price (Probability = 0.9)	Competitors Reduce Price (Probability = 0.1)
Alternatives	Reduce price	$150,000	$110,000
	Maintain price	$175,000	$90,000

prices, multiplied by the financial contribution if competitors further reduce prices. The calculation is

$$(0.9)(\$150,000) + (0.1)(\$110,000) = \$135,000 + \$11,000 = \$146,000$$

The expected monetary value of maintaining the price is

$$(0.9)(\$175,000) + (0.1)(\$90,000) = \$157,500 + \$9,000 = \$166,500$$

The higher average contribution of $166,500 for maintaining the price indicates that El Nacho's management should maintain the price. The contribution is higher because competitors are expected to maintain their prices nine times out of ten. Under the same conditions (same outcomes, same probability estimates), El Nacho would achieve an average contribution of $146,000 if the price-reduction alternative were chosen. A rational management would, therefore, select the price-maintenance alternative.

Familiarity with decision analysis is important for four reasons. First, decision analysis is a fundamental tool for considering "what if" situations. By organizing alternatives, uncertainties, and outcomes in this manner, a manager or case analyst becomes sensitive to the dynamic processes present in a competitive environment. Second, decision analysis forces the case analyst to quantify outcomes associated with specific actions. Third, decision analysis is useful in a variety of settings. For example, Warner-Lambert Canada, Ltd. applied decision analysis when deciding to manufacture and distribute Listerine throat lozenges in Canada; Ford Motor Company used decision analysis in deciding whether to produce its own tires, and Pillsbury used it in determining whether to switch from a box to a bag for a certain grocery product.[9] Fourth, an extension of decision analysis can be used in determining the value of "perfect" information.

Exhibit 3.3 on page 56 shows how the expected monetary value of "perfect" information (EMVPI) can be calculated using the El Nacho Foods example. Simply speaking, EMVPI is the difference between what El Nacho would achieve in contribution dollars if its management knew for certain what competitors would do and the average contribution dollars realized without such information. In other words, if El Nacho knew for certain that competitors would maintain their price, the "maintain price" alternative would be selected. If El Nacho management knew for certain that competitors would reduce their price, however, the "reduce price" alternative would be chosen. Assuming El Nacho management faced this decision 10 times and knew what competitor reaction would be each time, El Nacho management would make the appropriate decision each time. The result would be an expected monetary value of $168,500. The difference of $2,000 between $168,500 and $166,500 (the best alternative without such information) is viewed as the upper limit to pay for "perfect" information. EMVPI is a useful guide for determining how much money should be spent for marketing research information to identify the best alternative or course of action.

EXHIBIT 3.3

Decision Analysis and the Value of Information

		Payoff Table Uncertainties	
		Competitors Maintain Price (Probability = 0.9)	*Competitors Reduce Price (Probability = 0.1)*
Alternatives	A_1: Reduce price	$150,000	$110,000
	A_2: Maintain price	$175,000	$90,000

Calculation of Expected Monetary Value (EMV):

$EMV_{A_1} = 0.9(\$150,000) + 0.1(\$110,000) = \$146,000$

$EMV_{A_2} = 0.9(\$175,000) + 0.1(\$90,000) = \$166,500$

Calculation of Expected Monetary Value of Perfect Information (EMVPI):

$EMV_{certainty} = 0.9(\$175,000) + 0.1(\$110,000) = \$168,500$

$EMVPI = EMV_{certainty} - EMV_{best\ alternative}$

$EMVPI = \$168,500 - \$166,500 = \$2,000$

Develop a Plan for Implementing the Chosen Alternative

The selection of a course of action must be followed by development of a plan for its implementation. Simply deciding what to do will not make it happen. The execution phase is critical, and planning for it forces the case analyst to consider resource allocation and timing questions. For example, if a new product launch is recommended, it is important to consider how managerial, financial, and manufacturing resources will be allocated to this course of action. If a price reduction is recommended, it will be important to monitor whether the reduced prices are reaching the final consumer and not being absorbed by resellers in the marketing channel. Timing is crucial, since a marketing plan takes time to develop and implement.

As a final note, it is important to recognize that strategy formulation and implementation are not necessarily separate sequential processes. Rather, an interactive give-and-take occurs between formulation and implementation until the case analyst realizes that "what might be done can be done," given organizational strengths and market requirements. Another reading of the discussion on the marketing mix in Chapter 1 will highlight these points.

Evaluate the Decision and the Decision Process

The last step in the decision-making process is evaluating the decision made and the decision process itself. With respect to the decision itself, two questions should be asked. First, *Was a decision made?* This seemingly odd question addresses a common shortcoming of case analyses, whereby a case analyst does not make a decision but, rather, "talks about" the situation facing the organization.

The second question is, *Was the decision appropriate, given the situation identified in the case setting?* This question speaks to the issue of insufficient information on the one hand and the failure to consider and interpret information on the other. In many marketing cases, and indeed in some actual business situations, some of the information needed to make a decision is simply not available. When information is incomplete, assumptions must be made. A case analyst is often expected to make assumptions to fill in gaps, but such assumptions should be logically developed and articulated. Merely making assumptions to make the "solution" fit a preconceived notion of the correct answer is a death knell in case analysis and business practice.

The case analyst should constantly monitor how he or she applies the decision-making process. The mere fact that one's decision was right is not sufficient reason to think that the decision process was appropriate. For example, we have all found ourselves lost while trying to locate a home or business from an address. Eventually we somehow find it but are again at a loss when later asked to direct someone else to the same address. Analogously, the case analyst may arrive at the "correct" solution but be unable to outline (map) the process involved.

After completing a class discussion of a case, a written case assignment, or a group presentation, the case analyst should critically examine his or her performance by answering the following questions:

1. Did I define the problem adequately?
2. Did I identify all pertinent alternatives and uncertainties? Were my assumptions realistic?
3. Did I consider all information relevant to the case?
4. Did I recommend the appropriate course of action? If so, was my logic consistent with the recommendation? If not, were my assumptions different from the assumptions made by others? Did I overlook an important piece of information?
5. Did I consider how my recommendation could be implemented?

Honest answers to these questions will improve the chances of making better decisions in the future.

■ PREPARING AND PRESENTING A CASE ANALYSIS

How do I prepare and present a case? This question is voiced by virtually every student exposed to the case method for the first time. One of the most difficult tasks in preparing a case for presentation—or, more generally, resolving an actual marketing problem—is structuring your thinking process to address relevant forces confronting the organization in question. The previous discussion of the decision-making process should be of help in this regard. The remainder of this chapter provides some useful hints to assist you in preparing and presenting a marketing case.

Approaching the Case

On your first reading of a marketing case, you should concentrate on becoming acquainted with the situation in which the organization finds itself. This first reading should provide some insights into the problem requiring resolution, as well as background information on the environment and organization.

Then read the case again, paying particular attention to key facts and assumptions. At this point, you should determine the relevance and reliability of the quantitative data provided in the context of what you see as the issues or problems facing the organization. Valuable insights often arise from analyzing two or more bits of quantitative information concurrently. It is essential that extensive note taking occurs during the second reading. Working by writing is very important; simply highlighting statements or numbers in the case is not sufficient. Behavioral scientists estimate that the human mind can focus on only eight facts at a time and that our mental ability to link these facts in a meaningful way is limited without assistance.[10] Experienced analysts and managers always work out ideas on paper—whether they are working alone or in a group.

There are three pitfalls you should avoid during the second reading. First, *do not rush to a conclusion*. If you do so, information is likely to be overlooked or possibly distorted to fit a preconceived notion of the answer. Second, *do not "work the numbers"* until you understand their meaning and derivation. Third, *do not confuse supposition with fact*. Many statements are made in a case, such as "Our firm subscribes to the marketing concept." Is this a fact, based on an appraisal of the firm's actions and performance, or a supposition?

Formulating the Case Analysis

The previous remarks should provide some direction in approaching a marketing case. The marketing case analysis worksheet shown in Exhibit 3.4 provides a framework for organizing information. Four analytical categories are shown, with illustrative questions pertaining to each. You will find it useful to consider each analytical category when preparing a case.

Nature of the Industry, Market, and Buying Behavior   The first analytical category focuses on the organization's environment—the context in which the organization operates. Specific topics of interest include (1) an assessment of the structure, conduct, and performance of the industry and competition, and (2) an understanding of who the buyers are and why, where, when, how, what, and how much they buy.

The Organization   It is important to develop an understanding of the organization's financial, human, and material resources, its strengths and weaknesses, and the reasons for its success or failure. Of particular importance is an understanding of what the organization wishes to do. The "fit" between the organization and its environment

EXHIBIT 3.4

Marketing Case Analysis Worksheet

	Specific Points of Inquiry
Nature of the industry, market, and buyer behavior	1. What is the nature of industry structure, conduct, and performance? 2. Who are the competitors, and what are their strengths and weaknesses? 3. How do consumers buy in this industry or market? 4. Can the market be segmented? How? Can the segments be quantified? 5. What are the requirements for success in this industry?
The organization	1. What are the organization's mission, objectives, and distinctive competency? 2. What is its offering to the market? How can its past and present performance be characterized? What is its potential? 3. What is the situation in which the manager or organization finds itself? 4. What factors have contributed to the present situation?
A plan of action	1. What actions are available to the organization? 2. What are the costs and benefits of action in both qualitative and quantitative terms? 3. Is there a disparity between what the organization wants to do, should do, can do, and must do?
Potential outcomes	1. What will be the buyer, trade, and competitive response to each course of action? 2. How will each course of action satisfy buyer, trade, and organization requirements? 3. What is the potential profitability of each course of action? 4. Will the action enhance or reduce the organization's ability to compete in the future?

represents the first major link drawn in case analysis. This link is the essence of the situation analysis, since it is an interpretation of where the organization currently stands. A SWOT analysis like that described in Chapter 1 might be helpful in organizing your thoughts at this point.

A Plan of Action   You should be prepared to identify possible courses of action on the basis of the situation analysis. More often than not, several alternatives are possible, and each should be fully articulated. Each course of action typically has associated costs and revenues. These should be carefully calculated on the basis of realistic estimates of the magnitude of effort expected in their pursuit.

Potential Outcomes   Finally, the potential outcomes of all courses of action identified should be evaluated. On the basis of the appraisal of outcomes, one course of action or strategy should be recommended. The evaluation, however, must indicate not only why the recommendation was preferred, but also why other actions were dismissed.

Though it is always useful to consider each of the analytical categories just described, the method in which they are arranged may vary. There is no one way to analyze a case, just as there is no single correct way to attack a marketing problem. Just be sure to cover the bases.

Formulating the Case Analysis in Teams   Just as organizations now rely on teams to examine marketing issues, student teams are often assigned a case to analyze. A case analysis by a team will also consider the four analytical categories just discussed. However, a team-based case analysis introduces additional considerations that can affect the quality of a team experience and the analysis itself.

If the instructor asks you to form your own team, care should be taken in choosing team members. Forming teams on the basis of friendships is common but not always wise. Rather, try to create a balanced team where various skills complement one another (financial skills, oral presentation skills, writing skills, and so on). Seek out individuals who are committed and dependable.

The behavior of a team can also affect the quality of a case analysis. Care should be taken to avoid "groupthink"—the tendency for groups that work together over a period of time to produce poorly reasoned decisions. Groupthink is evident when social pressures and conflict avoidance overtake the desire to rigorously question analyses and alternatives in favor of seeking conformity and consensus. Common outcomes of groupthink are an incomplete survey of issues and alternatives, failure to consider the risks of the group's decision, failure to reappraise initially rejected alternatives, limited recognition and evaluation of case information, and failure to work out contingency plans due to overconfidence in the likelihood of success of a chosen course of action and the correctness of a decision.[11] Alfred Sloan, the legendary chairman of General Motors, was acutely aware of groupthink in his executive ranks. He was often heard to say, "I take it we are all in complete agreement on the decision here. Then I propose we postpone further discussion of the matter until our next meeting to give ourselves time to develop disagreement and perhaps gain some understanding of what the decision is all about."[12] Case study teams might do the same to avoid the pitfalls of groupthink.

Communicating the Case Analysis

Three means exist for communicating case analyses: (1) class discussion, (2) oral presentation, and (3) written report.

Class Discussion   Discussing case studies in the classroom setting can be an exciting experience, provided that each student actively prepares for and participates in the discussion. Preparation involves more than simply reading the case prior to the scheduled class period—the case should be carefully analyzed, using the four analytical categories described earlier. Four to five hours of preparation are usually required for each assigned case. The notes developed during the preparation should be brought to class.

Similarly, participation involves more than talking. Other students should be carefully watched and listened to during a class discussion. Attentiveness to the views of others is necessary in order to build on previous comments and analyses. Most class discussions follow a similar format. Class analysis begins with a discussion of the organization and its environment. This discussion is followed first by a discussion of the alternative courses of action and then by a consideration of possible implementation strategies. Knowing where the class is in the discussion is important both for organizing the multitude of ideas and analyses presented and for preparing remarks for the subsequent steps in the class discussion.

Immediately after the class discussion, you should prepare a short summary of the analysis developed in class. This summary, which should include the specific facts, ideas, analyses, and generalizations developed, will be useful in comparing and contrasting case situations.

Oral Presentation   An oral presentation of a case requires a slightly different set of skills. Usually, a group of three to five students conducts a rigorous analysis of a case and presents it to classmates. Role-playing may be featured: Class members may serve as an executive committee witnessing the presentation of a task force or project team.

A polished delivery is very important in oral presentations.[13] Thus, the group should rehearse its presentation, with group members seriously critiquing one another's performance. Oral presentations provide an opportunity to verbalize your analysis and recommendations and visually enhance your remarks with carefully crafted and informative transparencies, electronic slides, or other visual aids. At a minimum, slides or transparencies should cover each of the following areas:

1. An opening slide showing the "title" of the presentation and names of the presenters.

2. A slide that outlines the presentation (perhaps with presenters' names by each topic).

3. One or more slides detailing the key problems and strategic issues that management needs to address.

4. A series of slides covering your analysis of the company's situation or problem.

5. A series of slides containing your recommendations and the supporting arguments and reasoning for each recommendation—one slide for each recommendation and the associated reasoning has a lot of merit.

Remember that slides and transparencies help to communicate your ideas to the audience. They are not meant to substitute for the oral presentation. Slides and transparencies may be referred to but should *never* be read to the audience. Also keep in mind that too many graphics, images, colors, and transitions may divert the attention of the audience and disrupt the flow of the presentation. Finally, keep in mind that dazzling slides and transparencies will not hide a superficial or flawed case analysis from a perceptive audience.

Written Report   What you need to do to generate a written analysis of a case assignment is similar to what you should do to prepare for class discussion. The only difference is in the submission of the analysis; a written report should be carefully organized, legible (preferably typed), and grammatically correct.

There is no one correct approach to organizing a written case analysis. However, it is usually wise to think about the report as having three major sections: (1) identification of the strategic issues and problems, (2) analysis and evaluation, and (3) recommendations. The first section should contain a focused paragraph that defines the problem and specifies the constraints and options available to the organization. Material in the second section should provide a carefully developed assessment of the industry, market and buyer behavior, the organization, and the alternative courses of action. *Analysis and evaluation should represent the bulk of the written report.* This section should not contain a restatement of case information; it should contain an assessment of the facts, quantitative data, and management views. The last section should consist of a set of recommendations. These recommendations should be documented with references to the previous section and should be operational given the case situation. By all means, commit to a decision!

A case and a written student analysis of it are presented in the appendix at the end of the book. It is recommended that you carefully analyze the case before reading the student analysis.

NOTES

1. Herbert A. Simon, *The New Science of Management Decision* (New York: Harper & Row, 1960).

2. Peter Drucker, "How to Make a Business Decision," *Nation's Business* (April 1956): 38–39.

3. Melissa Raffoni, "Use Case Interviewing to Improve Your Hiring," *Harvard Management Update* (July 1999): 10.

4. DECIDE acronym copyright © by William Rudelius. Used with permission.

5. "Cluett Peabody & Co. Loses Shirt Trying to Jazz Up the Arrow Man," *Wall Street Journal* (July 28, 1988): 24.

6. Mark David Nevins and Stephen A. Stumpf, "21st-Century Leadership: Redefining Management Education," *Strategy & Business* (Third Quarter, 1999): 41–51.

7. Lawrence D. Gibson, "Defining Marketing Problems," *Marketing Research* (Spring 1998): 5–12.

8. An issue that frequently arises in developing these subjective probabilities is how to select them. One source is past experience, in the form of statistics such as A. T. Kearney's probabilities of success for alternative strategies, presented in Chapter 1. Alternatively, case information can be used to develop probability estimates. At the very least, when two possible uncertainties exist, a subjective probability of .5 can be assigned to each. This means that the two uncertainties have an equal chance of occurring. These probabilities can then be revised up or down, depending on case information.

9. These examples and a further reading on decision analysis can be found in Peter C. Bell, *Management Science/Operations Research: A Strategic Perspective* (Cincinnati, OH: South-Western Publishing, 1999): Chapter 3.

10. Amitai Etzioni, "Humble Decision Making," *Harvard Business Review* (July–August 1989): 122–126.

11. Max Bazerman, *Judgment in Managerial Decision Making*, 5th ed. (New York: John Wiley & Sons, 2001).

12. This quote appears in David A. Garvin and Michael A. Roberto, "What You Don't Know About Making Decisions," *Harvard Business Review* (September 2001): 108–116.

13. This discussion is based on material in Arthur A. Thompson, Jr. and A. J. Strickland, *Strategic Management: Concepts and Cases*, 12th ed. (Burr Ridge, IL: McGraw-Hill/Irwin, 2001): C12–C13.

CHAPTER **4**

Opportunity Analysis, Market Segmentation, and Market Targeting

 The development and implementation of marketing strategy are complicated and challenging tasks. At its pinnacle, marketing strategy involves the selection of markets and the development of programs to reach these markets. This process is carried out in a manner that simultaneously benefits both the markets selected (satisfying the needs or wants of buyers) and the organization (typically in dollar-profit terms).

Within this framework, a necessary first task is opportunity analysis, market segmentation, and market targeting. This chapter describes analytical concepts and tools that marketing managers find useful in performing opportunity analyses, segmenting markets, selecting market targets, and estimating market and sales potential.

■ OPPORTUNITY ANALYSIS

Opportunity analysis consists of three interrelated activities:

- Opportunity identification
- Opportunity-organization matching
- Opportunity evaluation

Opportunities arise from identifying new types or classes of buyers, uncovering unsatisfied needs of buyers, or creating new ways or means for satisfying buyer needs. Opportunity analysis focuses on finding markets that an organization can profitably serve.

The success of Reebok International, Ltd. illustrates a disciplined approach to *opportunity identification*. In 1981, Reebok had sales of $1.5 million and was known primarily for its high-quality custom running shoes. Consumer interest in running had plateaued, however, and new opportunities had to be identified for the company to grow. Over the next 20+ years, Reebok systematically pursued opportunities based on buyer types, buyer needs, and technological innovation as a means to satisfy the needs of buyers. Reebok identified buyer "performance-oriented" needs with a focus on specific athletic activities (such as tennis, basketball, golf, and track and field) and "nonathletic" needs with an emphasis on comfort and style for three types of buyers— men, women, and children. Technological innovation, most recently with the addition of computer chips and motion detectors, has met the needs of buyers interested in measuring their athletic performance. The result? Reebok now posts sales of $3 billion annually.[1]

Opportunity-organization matching determines whether an identified market opportunity is consistent with the definition of the organization's business, mission statement, and distinctive competencies. This determination usually involves an assessment of the organization's strengths and weaknesses and an identification of the success requirements for operating profitably in a market. A SWOT analysis like that described in Chapter 1 is often employed to assess the match between identified market opportunities and the organization.

For some companies, market opportunities that promise sizable sales and profit gains are not pursued because they do not conform to an organization's character. Starbucks is a case in point. The company has built a thriving business serving freshly brewed, specialty, gourmet coffee. However, the company refuses to use artifically flavored coffee despite its growth potential. According to company chairman Howard Schultz, "The largest growth segment in our category is artificially flavored coffee; it would give us maybe 40 percent incremental volume, but we won't do it." He adds, "It's not in our DNA."[2]

Opportunity evaluation typically has two distinct phases—qualitative and quantitative. The qualitative phase focuses on matching the attractiveness of an opportunity with the potential for uncovering a market niche. Attractiveness is dependent on (1) competitive activity; (2) buyer requirements; (3) market demand and supplier sources; (4) social, political, economic, and technological forces; and (5) organizational capabilities. Each of these factors in turn must be tied to its impact on the types of buyers sought, the needs of buyers, and the means for satisfying these needs. Exhibit 4.1 is an opportunity evaluation matrix containing illustrative questions useful in the qualitative analysis of a market opportunity. The quantitative phase yields estimates of market sales potential and sales forecasts. It also produces budgets for financial, human, marketing, and production resources, which are necessary to assess the profitability of a market opportunity.

Opportunity identification, matching, and evaluation are challenging assignments, because subjective factors play a large role and managerial insight and foresight are necessary. These activities are even more difficult in the global arena, where social and political forces and uncertainties related to organizational capabilities in unfamiliar economic environments assume a significant role.

■ WHAT IS A MARKET?

The fact that an opportunity has been identified does not necessarily imply that a market exists for the organization. Although definitions vary, a *market* may be considered to be the prospective buyers (individuals or organizations) willing and able to purchase the existing or potential offering (product or service) of an organization.

This definition of a market has several managerial implications. First, the definition focuses on buyers, not on products or services. People and organizations whose idiosyncrasies dictate whether and how products and services will be acquired, consumed, or used make up markets. Second, by highlighting the buyer's willingness and ability to purchase a product or service, this definition introduces the concept of *effective demand*. Even if buyers are willing to purchase a product or service, exchange cannot occur unless they are able to do so. Likewise, if buyers are able to purchase a product or service but are unwilling to do so, exchange will not occur. These relationships are important to grasp because a marketing strategist must ascertain the extent of effective demand for an offering in order to determine whether a market exists. To a large degree, the extent of effective demand will depend on the

EXHIBIT 4.1

Opportunity Evaluation Matrix: Attractiveness Criteria

Market Niche Criterion	Competitive Activity	Buyer Requirements	Demand/ Supply	Political, Technological, and Socioeconomic Forces	Organizational Capabilities
Buyer type	How many and which firms are competing for this user group?	What affects buyer willingness and ability to buy?	Do different buyer types have different levels of effective demand? How important are adequate sources of supply?	How sensitive are different buyers to these forces?	Can we gain access to buyers through marketing-mix variables? Can we supply these buyers?
Buyer needs	Which firms are satisfying which buyer needs?	Are there buyer needs that are not being satisfied? What are they?	Are buyer needs likely to be long term? Do we have or can we acquire resources to satisfy buyer needs?	How sensitive are buyer needs to these forces?	Which buyer needs can our organization satisfy?
Means for satisfying buyer needs	What are the strategies being employed to satisfy buyer needs?	Is the technology for satisfying buyer needs changing?	To what extent are the means for satisfying buyer needs affected by supply sources? Is the demand for the means for satisfying buyer needs changing?	How sensitive are the means for satisfying buyer needs to these forces?	Do we have the financial, human, technological, and marketing expertise to satisfy buyer needs?

marketing-mix activities of the organization. Third, use of the term *offering*, rather than *product* or *service*, expands the definition of what organizations provide for buyers. Products and services are not purchased for the sake of purchase; they are purchased for the values or benefits that buyers expect to derive from them. It is for this reason that the late Charles Revson of Revlon Cosmetics continually reiterated that his company did not sell cosmetics but, rather, hope. This expanded definition of an offering requires strategists to consider benefits provided by a product or service apart from its tangible nature.

Frequently, one hears or reads about the automobile market, the soft drink market, or the health care market. These terms can be misleading because each refers to a composite of multiple minimarkets. Viewing a market as composed of minimarkets allows a marketer to better gauge opportunities. Consider, for example, the "coffee market." Exhibit 4.2 on page 66 shows how the U.S. coffee market might be broken down into multiple markets by a marketing manager for Maxwell House or Folgers. With this breakdown, the manager can more effectively identify who is competing in the caffeinated versus the decaffeinated markets and how they are competing, monitor changes in sales volume for instant decaffeinated coffee, and appreciate differences between buyer taste preferences and competition in the South and in New England.

EXHIBIT 4.2

Market Structure for Coffee

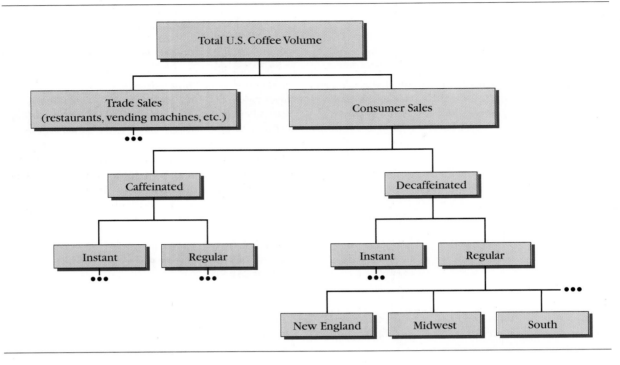

For these reasons, among others, regional marketing has become popular. For example, Folgers' management observed that vacuum brick-packs of coffee were relatively more popular than cans in the South. They repackaged their Folgers brand coffee for those markets and developed a new advertising campaign. Sales of Folgers coffee increased 32 percent in targeted markets.[3]

Finally, how a market is defined has a crucial effect on the concept of market share. *Market share* can be defined as the sales of a firm, product, or brand divided by the sales of the "market." Obviously, market definition is critical in calculating this percentage. For example, consider the market share of Brand X, an instant, decaffeinated coffee brand with annual sales of $1 billion. Depending on the definition of the market, the brand's share will range from 12.5 percent to 50 percent, as shown in the following table.

Market Definition	Dollar Sales	Brand X Sales	Market Share
U.S. coffee market	$8 billion	$1 billion	12.5%
U.S. decaffeinated coffee market	$4 billion	$1 billion	25.0%
U.S. instant decaffeinated coffee market	$2 billion	$1 billion	50.0%

■ MARKET SEGMENTATION

A useful technique for structuring markets is *market segmentation*—the breaking down or building up of potential buyers into groups. These groups are typically termed *market segments*. Each segment is thought of as possessing some sort of homogeneous characteristic relating to its purchasing or consumption behavior, which is ultimately reflected in its responsiveness to marketing programs. Market segmentation grew out of the recognition that, in general, an organization cannot be all things to all people.

Although the legendary Henry Ford is reputed to have said that buyers of his Ford automobiles could have any color they desired as long as it was black, most marketers today agree that such an undifferentiated marketing strategy is no longer appropriate. The idea that an organization can effectively apply one marketing strategy to satisfy all possible buyers is not viable in today's marketing environment.

At the other extreme, unless the organization is highly specialized and sells only to, say, one buyer, it is often not feasible to treat each potential buyer as unique. Thus, as one marketing authority has so aptly written, market segmentation "is a compromise between the ineffectiveness of treating all customers alike and the inefficiency of treating each one differently."[4]

Advances in information technology and flexible manufacturing and service delivery systems have made "segments of one" a reality in some settings. *Mass customization*—tailoring products and services to the tastes and preferences of individual buyers in high volumes and at a relatively low cost—combines the efficiencies of mass production and the effectiveness of designing offerings to a single buyer's unique wants.

Benefits of Market Segmentation

Segmentation offers three principal benefits with regard to the development of marketing strategy.[5] Market segmentation:

1. *Identifies opportunities for new product development.* The analysis of various segments of present and potential buyers can reveal one or more groups whose specific needs are not being well satisfied. These segments represent possible opportunities for new product development. Frito-Lay, Inc. is a case in point. The company identified two attitudinal and lifestyle market segments. "Indulgers" are consumers who know they should limit their fat consumption but cannot and those who simply don't care. This segment represents 47 percent of snack chip consumers who are heavy users of snack chips. The other 53 percent of consumers are "compromisers," who enjoy snacking but restrict their snack chip intake because of nutritional concerns. Frito-Lay, Inc. decided to invest heavily in the "compromiser" segment with new "better-for-you" products in the late 1990s. Baked Lay's low-fat potato crisps posted sales of $250 million in their first full year in the market. This success was followed by the WOW! snack chip line, which included Ruffles, Doritos, and Tostitos made with a low-fat, calorie-free cooking oil. This line recorded first-year sales of $350 million and was the most successful food introduction of the past decade.[6]

2. *Helps in the design of marketing programs that are most effective for reaching homogeneous groups of consumers.* In addition to product development, segmentation permits refinements in the pricing, advertising and promotion, and distribution elements of the marketing mix. For example, Procter & Gamble markets its Crest toothpaste with different advertising and promotion campaigns directed at six different market segments, including children, Hispanics, and senior citizens.[7]

3. *Improves the allocation of marketing resources.* Market segmentation also can provide guidance in directing marketing resources. All market segments are not necessarily equal in terms of an organization's ability to serve them effectively and profitably. As with any opportunity assessment, a company's strengths and capabilities relative to each identified segment's needs and

competitive situation must be considered. Returning to the athletic shoe "market" discussed earlier, consider how New Balance competes with the likes of Nike and Reebok, two performance-oriented shoe marketers. Instead of allocating resources to compete directly with Nike and Reebok in the "performance" segment, New Balance focuses on the baby boomer (40- to 58-year-old) nonathletic segment. It offers comfortable shoes for older men and women and spends its marketing resources networking with podiatrists, not athletes.[8]

Bases for Market Segmentation

Two broad types of variables are commonly used for market segmentation. Socioeconomic characteristics of consumers, such as gender, age, occupation, income, family life cycle, education, and geographic location make up one type. The other type consists of behavioral variables, including benefits sought from products and services, usage behavior, lifestyle, and attitudes. For industrial buyers, socioeconomic characteristics may include company size and location, and industry or customers served. Behavioral variables may include purchasing objectives and practices as well as product and service benefits. The appropriateness of any one or combination of variables in a specific situation will depend on whether or not a variable relates to purchasing, use, or consumption behavior and responsiveness to marketing programs.

The choice of variable(s) to use to segment a market often depends on insights into buyer behavior, provided by creative research. Segmentation of the cell phone market by Nokia illustrates this point. According to the director of America's brand marketing at Nokia, "Different people have different usage needs. Some people want and need all of the latest and most advanced data-related features and functions, while others are happy with basic voice connectivity. Even people with similar usage needs often have differing lifestyles representing various value sets. For example, some people have an active lifestyle in which sports and fitness play an important role, while for others arts, fashion and trends may be very important."[9]

Nokia's research on consumer usage, lifestyles, and individual preferences identified six market segments: "Basic" consumers who need voice connectivity and a durable style; "Expression" consumers who want to customize and personalize features; "Classic" consumers who prefer a traditional appearance and Web browser function; "Fashion" consumers who want a very small phone as a fashion item; "Premium" consumers who are interested in all technological and service features; and "Communicator" consumers who want to combine all of their communication devices (e.g., telephone, pager, PDA). The company subsequently developed and marketed cell phone models for each of these segments.

Requirements for Effective Market Segmentation

Ultimately, market segmentation is a means to an end: to identify and profile distinct groups of buyers who differ in their needs, preferences, and responsiveness to an organization's marketing programs. Effective market segmentation should provide answers to six fundamental buyer-related questions for each market segment:

1. Who are they?
2. What do they want to buy?
3. How do they want to buy?
4. When do they want to buy?
5. Where do they want to buy?
6. Why do they want to buy?

More often than not, the answers should be expressed in a narrative form documented with quantitative and qualitative research.

From a managerial perspective, effective market segmentation means that each segment identified and profiled satisfies four fundamental requirements.[10] Each market segment should be:

1. *Measurable*. The size and buying power of a market segment can be quantitatively determined.

2. *Differentiable*. A market segment is distinguishable from other segments and responds differently to different marketing programs.

3. *Accessible*. A segment can be effectively reached and served through an economically viable marketing program.

4. *Substantial*. A segment should be large enough in term of sales volume potential to cover the cost of the organization serving it and return a satisfactory profit.

■ OFFERING-MARKET MATRIX

A useful procedure for investigating markets is to construct an *offering-market matrix*. Such a matrix relates offerings to selected groups of buyers. Exhibit 4.3 shows an illustrative matrix for handheld calculators marketed by Texas Instruments, Casio, Citizen Business Machines, and Hewlett-Packard, among others. Four possible user

EXHIBIT 4.3

Offering-Market Matrix for Handheld Calculators

Offering Characteristics	Market Segments (User Groups)			
	Business	Scientific	Home	School
Simple (arithmetic operations only)				
Moderate (arithmetic operations, squares, and square roots)				
Complex (all of the above plus business, scientific, and statistical functions)				
Very complex (all of the above plus programmable features)				

groups (or market segments) are business, scientific, home, and school. Displaying offerings and user groups in this manner facilitates identification of competitors and their offerings and possible gaps in the calculator market reflected in empty cells in the matrix. Knowing where competitors are prominent provides a basis for determining whether a market opportunity exists. Identification of gaps in the market and knowledge of competitive activities in specific offering-market cells should assist the marketing manager in gauging the effective demand for an organization's offering and the likelihood of developing a profitable marketing program.

Consider, for instance, handheld calculator offerings for the large primary and secondary school market. Hewlett-Packard, a major competitor in the business and scientific segment, has concluded that an opportunity exists in the school market for *handheld computers*, including its iPaq handheld, which offers the same features as calculators plus programs for scientific data evaluation and graphing. Calendars and address lists are available as well. Does a market opportunity exist for Hewlett-Packard? A lot will depend on Texas Instruments' response since it dominates the school segment with offerings that capture 80 percent of the school market for handheld calculators.[11]

■ MARKET TARGETING

After a market has been segmented, it is necessary to select the segments(s) on which marketing efforts will be focused. *Market targeting* (or target marketing) is merely the specification of the segment(s) the organization wishes to pursue. Once the manager has selected the target market(s), the organization must decide which marketing strategies to employ.

For example, recognizing that Wal-Mart, Lowe's, and a host of regional competitors were targeting the home-improvement "do-it-yourselfer" segment for home repairs and remodeling, Home Depot decided to pursue the "professional" segment for growth alongside the "do-it-yourselfer" segment. This segment consisted of housing professionals, such as managers of major apartment and condominium complexes and hotel chains, and professional building contractors. Once decided, the company modified its merchandise assortment to meet the needs of the "professional" segment and broadened its services, including longer store hours, delivery, commercial credit, truck and equipment rental, and ordering via phone, fax, or the Internet.[12]

Two frequently used market targeting approaches are *differentiated marketing* and *concentrated marketing*. In a differentiated marketing approach, the organization simultaneously pursues several different market segments, usually with a unique marketing strategy for each. An example of this type of marketing is the strategy of Nokia following its segmentation research described earlier. Exhibit 4.4 shows Nokia's offering-market matrix in mid-2002 featuring nine different cell phone models designed for and marketed to six market segments.[13] Nokia's differential marketing approach, along with continued technological advancements, has contributed to its status as the world's leading cell phone manufacturer. As a rule, differentiated marketing is expensive to implement. Managing multiple products across multiple market segments increases marketing, inventory, administrative, and advertising and promotion costs as well as product development expenditures.

In a concentrated approach, the organization focuses on a single market segment. An extreme case would be one in which an organization marketed a single product offering to a single market segment. More commonly, an organization will offer one or more product lines to a single segment. For many years, Gerber proclaimed that "babies are our only business" and focused almost exclusively on baby foods. Gerber still offers baby foods, which is its primary business. However, today Gerber offers companion lines of baby skin care and health care products, baby care products such as bottles, pacifiers, and playthings, and insurance policies.[14] Through a concentrated

EXHIBIT 4.4

Nokia Offering-Market Matrix for Cell Phones Depicting a Differentiated Marketing Strategy (Featuring Mid-2002 Product Line Market Targets)

Offering Characteristics	Market Segments					
	BASIC	FASHION	EXPRESSION	CLASSIC	PREMIUM	COMMUNICATOR
	Teens needing voice connectivity; durability	"Very visible" buyers, not needing heavy use	Cool, young adults connecting with friends	Traditional, satisfying various business needs	Interested in latest technological and service features	All-in-one communicator
Youthful design and style, durable, easy to use, game feature	Model 5210					
Color covers, downloading ring tones, music, pictures		Model 5100 Model 3300				
Small size, very stylish, user friendly, Internet access			Model 8260 Model 8390			
Traditional style, Web browser, phone book and calendar				Model 6340		
MP3 player, messaging with keyboard, game platform, Internet access					Model 5310 Model 8890	
Digital camera, enhanced user interface, multimedia messaging, PDA						Model 7650

marketing approach, a company gains a strong knowledge of a segment's needs and can achieve a strong market position—Gerber commands a 70 percent market share in baby foods. Furthermore, concentrated marketing provides operating economics through specialization in manufacturing and marketing. However, concentrated marketing has risks. Specializing in one segment can limit a company's growth prospects, particularly if the segment size declines. Also, competitors might invade the segment.

■ MARKET SALES POTENTIAL AND PROFITABILITY

An essential activity in opportunity evaluation is the determination of market sales potential and profitability. Estimating a market's sales potential for offerings is a difficult task even for a seasoned marketing executive. Markets and offerings can be defined in numerous ways that can lead to different estimates of market size and dollar sales potential. This was illustrated earlier in the description of market structure and resulting market shares in the U.S. coffee industry. For innovative offerings or new markets, marketing analysts must often rely almost entirely on judgment and creativity when estimating market sales potential. Therefore, it is understandable that market sales potential estimates vary greatly for high-definition television (HDTV) and hybrid (gasoline- and battery-powered) automobiles. The underlying technology for both offerings is still evolving as is the physical form. In such dynamic settings, measures for identifying prospective market segments are uncertain.

Estimating Market Sales Potential

Market sales potential is a quantitative approximation of effective demand. Specifically, *market sales potential* is the maximum level of sales that might be available to all organizations serving a defined market in a specific time period given (1) the marketing-mix activities and effort of all organizations, and (2) a set of environmental conditions. As this definition indicates, market sales potential is not a fixed amount. Rather, it is a function of a number of factors, some of which are controllable and others not controllable by organizations. For instance, controllable marketing-mix activities and marketing-related expenditures of organizations can influence market sales potential. On the other hand, consumer disposable income, government regulations, and other social, economic, and political conditions are not controllable by organizations, but do affect market sales potential. These uncontrollable factors are particularly relevant in estimating market sales potential in developing countries. For example, U.S., European, and Japanese passenger car manufacturers have come to realize that automobile market sales potential in China, the world's most populous country, is affected by obstacles outside their control. In China, sudden government policy shifts toward foreign manufacturers are common. There are less than 1,000 auto distributorships in the entire country. China is a cash-based society, and consumers have little access to financing or credit, making buying a car a formidable proposition. The bicycle is the preferred mode of transportation, which is understandable because China has limited navigable roads for cars outside its major cities, where 80 percent of the population lives.[15]

Three variables are commonly considered when estimating market sales potential.[16] These include (1) the number of prospective buyers (*B*) who are willing and able to purchase an offering; (2) the quantity (*Q*) of an offering purchased by an average buyer in a specific time period, typically one calendar year; and (3) the price (*P*) of an average unit of the offering. Market sales potential is the product of these three variables:

Market sales potential = $B \times Q \times P$

Though simple, this expression contains the building blocks for developing a more complex formulation through what is called the *chain ratio method*, which involves multiplying a base number by several adjusting factors that are believed to influence market sales potential. An application of this method by Coca-Cola and Pepsi-Cola is shown in the following calculation of cola-flavored carbonated soft drink potential in a South American country:

Market sales potential for cola-flavored carbonated soft drinks in a country = Population aged 8 years and over × proportion of the population that consumes carbonated soft drinks on a daily basis × proportion of the population preferring cola-flavored carbonated soft drinks × the average number of carbonated soft drink occasions per day × the average amount consumed per consumption occasion (expressed in ounces) × 365 days in a calendar year × the average price per ounce of cola

The chain ratio method serves three important purposes. First, it yields a quantitative estimate of market sales potential. Second, it highlights factors that are controllable and not controllable by organizations. Clearly, a country's population aged 8 years and older is an uncontrollable factor. However, the other factors are controllable or can be influenced to some degree. For example, organizations can influence the proportion of a population that consumes carbonated soft drinks through primary demand advertising and the cost of cola drinks through pricing. If either of these two factors change, market sales potential changes, other things being equal. Finally, it affords a manager flexibility in estimating market sales potential for different buyer groups and different offerings. For example, by including another factor such as the proportion of the population preferring diet colas, the potential for this offering can be calculated.

Sales and Profit Forecasting

Sales and profit forecasting follow the estimation of market sales potential. A *sales forecast* is the level of sales a single organization expects to achieve based on a chosen marketing strategy and an assumed competitive environment. An organization's forecasted sales are typically some fraction of estimated market sales potential.

Forecasted sales reflect the size of the target market(s) chosen by the organization and the marketing mix chosen for these target market(s). Forecasted sales also reflect the assumed number of competitors and competitive intensity in the chosen target market(s). For example, suppose an organization's target market represents one-fourth of 1 million prospective buyers for a particular offering. The marketing channel chosen for the offering provides access to about three-fourths of these buyers and the communication program (advertising) reaches these same buyers. Suppose further that the average purchase rate is 20 units of an offering per year and the average offering unit price is $10.00. Using a version of the chain ratio method, forecasted sales might be calculated as follows:

Total estimated prospective buyers	1 million
times	
Target market (25% of total buyers)	× .25
times	
Distribution/Communication coverage (75% of target market)	× .75
times	
Annual purchase rate (20 units per year)	× 20
times	
Average offering unit price ($10.00)	× $10.00
Forecasted sales	$37.5 million

The $37.5 million sales forecast does not consider the number of competitors vying for the same market target nor does it consider competitive intensity. Therefore, this sales forecast should be adjusted downward to reflect these realities.

Forecasting sales, like estimating market sales potential, is not an easy task. Nevertheless, the task is central to opportunity evaluation and must be undertaken. For this reason, sales forecasting is addressed again in Chapter 5 in reference to product and service life cycles.

Finally, a *pro forma* income statement should be prepared showing forecasted sales, budgeted expenses, and estimated net profit (Chapter 2). When completed, the marketing analyst can review the identified opportunities and decide which can be most profitably pursued given organizational capabilities.

NOTES

1. The Reebok example is detailed in Roger A. Kerin, Eric. N. Berkowitz, Steven Hartley, and William Rudelius, *Marketing*, 7th ed. (Burr Ridge, IL: McGraw-Hill/Irwin, 2003): 239–242.

2. Terry Lefton, "Schultz' Caffeinated Crusade," *BRANDWEEK* (July 5, 1999): 20–25.

3. For additional examples of regional marketing, see S. McKenna, *The Complete Guide to Regional Marketing* (Homewood, IL: Richard D. Irwin, 1992).

4. Ben M. Enis, *Marketing Principles: The Management Process*, 2nd ed. (Pacific Palisades, CA: Goodyear, 1977): 241.

5. Orville C. Walker, Jr., Harper W. Boyd, Jr., John Mullins, and Jean-Claude Larréché, *Marketing Strategy: A Decision-Focused Approach* (Burr Ridge, IL: McGraw-Hill/Irwin, 2003): 152–153.

6. "Salting Away Big Profits," *U. S. News & World Report* (September 16, 1996): 71–72; and "American Marketing Association Edison Award Best New Products," *Marketing News* (March 29, 1999): special supplement.

7. "Make It Simple," *Business Week* (September 9, 1996): 96–104.

8. "Sneaker Company Tags Out-of-Breath Baby Boomers," *Wall Street Journal* (January 16, 1998): B1, B6.

9. "Nokia: A Phone for Every Segment," in Roger A. Kerin, et.al. *Marketing*, 7th ed (Burr Ridge, IL: McGraw-Hill/Irwin, 2003): 262–263.

10. Philip Kotler, *Marketing Management*, 11th ed. (Upper Saddle River, NJ: Prentice Hall, 2003): 286.

11. "Competition for Classrooms," *Dallas Morning News* (November 12, 2002): 1D, 6D.

12. Janice Revell, "Can Home Depot Get Its Groove Back?" *Fortune* (February 3, 2003): 110–112.

13. "Nokia Unveils Phones to Beat Gloom," CNN.com/World, March 12, 2002; "Battle of the Nordic Giants," *Newsweek* (November 11, 2002): E16–E19; and "Nokia: A Phone for Every Segment" (reference cited).

14. *www.gerber.com*, January 10, 2003.

15. Stephen M. Shaw and Feng Wang, "Moving Goods in China," *The McKinsey Quarterly* (Number 2, 2002): 28–34.

16. Portions of this discussion are based on Philip Kotler, *Marketing Management* (reference cited) Chapter 4.

Sorzal Distributors

Sorzal Distributors is an importer and distributor of a wide variety of South American and African artifacts. It is also a major source of southwestern Indian—especially Hopi and Navajo—authentic jewelry and pottery. Although the firm's headquarters is located in Phoenix, Arizona, there are currently branch offices in Los Angeles, Miami, and Boston.

Sorzal (named after the national bird of Honduras) originated as a trading post operation near Tucson, Arizona, in the early 1900s. Through a series of judicious decisions, the firm established itself as one of the more reputable dealers in authentic southwestern jewelry and pottery. Over the years, Sorzal gradually expanded its product line to include pre-Columbian artifacts from Peru and Venezuela (see Exhibit 1 on page 76) and tribal and burial artifacts from Africa. Through its careful verification of the authenticity of these South American and African artifacts, Sorzal developed a national reputation as one of the most respected importers of these types of artifacts.

In the mid-1990s, Sorzal further expanded its product line to include items that were replicas of authentic artifacts. For example, African fertility gods and masks were made by craftspeople who took great pains to produce these items so that only the truly knowledgeable buyer—a collector—would know that they were replicas. Sorzal now has native craftspeople in Central America, South America, Africa, and the southwestern United States who provide these items. Replicas account for only a small portion of total Sorzal sales; the company agreed to enter this business only at the prodding of the firm's clients, who desired an expanded line. The replicas have found most favor among gift buyers and individuals looking for decorative items.

Sorzal's gross sales are about $25 million and have increased at a relatively constant rate of 20 percent per year over the last decade, despite little price inflation. Myron Rangard, the firm's national sales manager, attributed the sales increase to the popularity of Sorzal's product line and to the expanded distribution of South American and African artifacts:

> For some reason, our South American and certainly our African artifacts have been gaining greater acceptance. Two of our department store customers featured examples of our African line in their Christmas catalogs last year. I personally think consumer tastes are changing from the modern and abstract to the more concrete, like our products.

Sorzal distributes its products exclusively through specialty dealers (including interior designers and decorators), firm-sponsored showings, and a few exclusive department stores. Often, the company is the sole supplier to its clients. Rangard recently expressed the reasons for this highly limited distribution:

> Our limited distribution has been dictated to us because of the nature of our product line. As acceptance grew, we expanded our distribution to specialty dealers and some exclusive department stores. Previously, we had to push our products through our

This case was prepared by Professors Roger A. Kerin, of the Edwin L. Cox School of Business, Southern Methodist University, and Robert A. Peterson, of The University of Texas at Austin, as a basis for class discussion and is not designed to illustrate effective or ineffective handling of an administrative situation. Names have been disguised. Copyright © 2003 by Roger A. Kerin and Robert A. Peterson. No part of this case may be reproduced without the written permission of the copyright holders.

EXHIBIT 1

Pre-Columbian Water Vessel from Peru

own showings. Furthermore, we just didn't have the product. These South American artifacts aren't always easy to get and the political situation in Africa is limiting our supply. Our perennial supply problem has become even more critical in recent years for several reasons. Not only must we search harder for new products, but the competition for authentic artifacts has increased tenfold. On top of this, we must now contend with governments not allowing exportation of certain artifacts because of their "national significance."

The problem of supply has forced Sorzal to add three new buyers in the last two years. Whereas Sorzal identified five major competitors a decade ago, there are 11 today. "Our bargaining position has eroded," noted David Olsen, Director of Procurement. "We have watched our gross margin slip in recent years due to aggressive competitive bidding by others."

"And competition at the retail level has increased also," injected Rangard. "Not only are some of our larger specialty and exclusive department store customers sending out their own buyers to deal directly with some of our Hopi, Navajo, and African suppliers, but also we are often faced with amateurs or fly-by-night competitors. These people move into a city and dump a bunch of inauthentic junk on the public at exorbitant prices. Such antics give the industry a bad name." Rangard acknowledged that high-quality, authentically made decorative items were also available on the Internet (see, for example, authenticafrica.com and novica.com).

A recent article in *Time* magazine supported Rangard's observation.[1] According to the article, which featured African artifacts:

> It's best to buy from a dealer you can trust since a growing number of fakes are turning up on the market. Throughout Africa, artisans in "craft centers" simply churn out copies of authentic items. And sometimes, "traditional" art is created in the absence of any tradition. In Kenya, for example, masks made by the Masai people sell for anywhere from $50 to $200. But the Masai have never carved masks. [According to an authority on African antiquities] "90% of what's coming into the U.S. are replicas or tourist art that's being made to look old."

In recent years, several mass-merchandise department store chains have begun to sell merchandise similar to that offered by Sorzal. Even though product quality was often mixed and most items were replicas, occasionally an authentic group of items was found in these stores, according to company sales representatives. Subsequent inquiries by both Rangard and Olsen revealed that other competing distributors had signed purchase contracts with these outlets. Moreover, the items were typically being sold at retail prices below those charged by Sorzal's dealers.

In early January 2003, Rangard was contacted by a mass-merchandise department store chain concerning the possibility of carrying a complete line of Sorzal products and particularly a full assortment of authentic items. The chain was currently selling a competitor's items but wished to add a more exclusive product line. A tentative contract submitted by the chain stated that it would buy at 10 percent below Sorzal's existing prices, and that its initial purchase would be for no less than $750,000. Depending on consumer acceptance, purchases were estimated to be at least $4 million annually. An important clause in the contract dealt with the supply of replicas. Inspection of this clause revealed that Sorzal would have to triple its replica production to satisfy the contractual obligation. Soon after Sorzal executives began discussing the contract, Sorzal's president, Andrew Smythe, mentioned that accepting the contract could have a dramatic effect on how Sorzal defined its business. Smythe added:

> The contract presents us with an opportunity to broaden our firm's position. The upside is that we have the potential to add $4 million in additional sales over and above our annual growth. On the other hand, do we want to commit such a large percent of our business to replicas? Is that the direction that the market is going? What effect will this contract have on our current dealers, and, I might add, our current customers?
>
> I want you both (Rangard and Olsen) to consider this contract in light of your respective functions and the company as a whole. Let's meet in a few days to discuss this matter again.

---

[1]"Looting Africa," *Time* (July 30, 2001): 49–52

Jones•Blair Company

In early January 1998, Alexander Barrett, President of Jones•Blair Company, slumped back in his chair as his senior management executives filed out of the conference room. "Another meeting and still no resolution," he thought. After two lengthy meetings, the executive group still had not decided where and how to deploy corporate marketing efforts among the various architectural paint coatings markets served by the company in the southwestern United States. He asked his secretary to schedule another meeting for next week.

■ THE U.S. PAINT INDUSTRY

The U.S. paint industry is divided into three broad segments: (1) architectural coatings, (2) original equipment manufacturing (OEM) coatings, and (3) special-purpose coatings. Architectural coatings consist of general-purpose paints, varnishes, and lacquers used on residential, commercial, and institutional structures, sold through wholesalers and retailers, and purchased by do-it-yourself consumers, painting contractors, and professional painters. Architectural coatings are commonly called *shelf goods* and account for 43 percent total industry dollar sales. OEM coatings are formulated to industrial buyer specifications and are applied to original equipment during manufacturing. These coatings are used for durable goods such as automobiles, trucks, transportation equipment, appliances, furniture and fixtures, metal containers and building products, and industrial machinery and equipment. OEM coatings represent 35 percent of total industry dollar sales. Special-purpose coatings are formulated for special applications or environmental conditions, such as extreme temperatures, exposure to chemicals, or corrosive conditions. These coatings are used for automotive and machinery refinishing, industrial construction and maintenance (including factories, equipment, utilities, and railroads), bridges, marine applications (ship and offshore facilities such as oil rigs), highway and traffic markings, aerosol and metallic paints, and roof paints. Special-purpose coatings account for 22 percent of total industry dollar sales.

The U.S. paint industry is generally considered to be a maturing industry. Industry sales in 1997 were estimated to be slightly over $13 billion. Average annual dollar sales growth was forecasted to approximate the general rate of inflation through 2000.

Outlook for Architectural Paint Coatings and Sundries

Industry sources estimated U.S. sales of architectural paint coatings and sundries (brushes, rollers, paint removers and thinners, etc.) to be $10 billion-plus in 1997.

The cooperation of Jones•Blair Company in the preparation of this case is gratefully acknowledged. This case was prepared by Professor Roger A. Kerin, Edwin L. Cox School of Business, Southern Methodist University, as a basis for class discussion and is not designed to illustrate effective or ineffective handling of an administrative situation. Certain names and selected market and sales data have been disguised and are not useful for research purposes. Copyright © 1998 by Roger A. Kerin. No part of this case may be reproduced without written permission of the copyright holder.

Architectural coatings are considered to be a mature market with long-term sales growth projected in the range of 1 to 2 percent per year. Demand for architectural coatings and sundries reflect the level of house redecorating, maintenance, and repair, as well as sales of existing homes, and to a lesser extent new home, commercial, and industrial construction. Industry sources also noted that the demand for architectural coatings and sundries is affected by two other factors. First, the architectural coating segment faced competition from alternative materials, such as aluminum and vinyl siding, interior wall coverings, and wood paneling. Second, paint companies had developed higher-quality products that reduced the amount of paint necessary per application and the frequency of repainting. Counteracting these factors, industry observers foresaw increasing demand for paint sundries due to a trend toward do-it-yourself painting by household consumers.

U.S. paint manufacturers are under growing pressure to reduce emissions of volatile organic compounds (VOCs) from paints and to limit the consumption of solvents. The Environmental Protection Agency (EPA) has proposed a three-step plan for the reduction of VOCs in architectural and industrial maintenance coatings. The first phase of the plan, which took effect in 1996, required a 25 percent reduction in VOC content from the base year of 1990. VOCs must be reduced by 35 percent (from the 1990 base year) in 2000 and 45 percent in the third phase in 2003. Compliance with EPA regulations has further eroded historically low profit margins in the paint industry.

Consolidation and Competition in the Architectural Coatings Segment

Slow sales growth, the necessity for ongoing research and development, and recent compliance with governmental regulations have fueled merger and acquisition activity in the U.S. paint industry since 1990. Companies seeking growth and a higher sales base to support increasing costs are making acquisitions. Companies that were unwilling or unable to make capital and research and development (R&D) commitments necessary to remain competitive sold their paint businesses. Industry sources estimate that the number of paint companies is currently 600, or about 40 percent fewer companies than in 1975. The number of paint companies is presently declining at a rate of 2 to 3 percent per year. Merger activity generally involved the purchase of small companies by larger firms to boost their specific market or geographic presence. Still, because of readily available technology and difference in paint formulations associated with regional climatic needs, a small number of regional paint manufacturers, such as Jones•Blair Company, have competed successfully against paint manufacturers that distribute their products nationally.

Major producers of paint for the architectural coatings segment include Sherwin-Williams, Benjamin Moore, the Glidden unit of Imperial Chemicals, PPG Industries, Valspar Corporation, Grow Group, and Pratt & Lambert. These producers account for upwards of 60 percent of sales in the architectural coatings segment. They market paint under their own brand names and for retailers under private, controlled, or store brand names. For example, Sherwin-Williams markets the Sherwin-Williams brand and produces paint for Sears.

About 50 percent of architectural coatings are sold under private, controlled, or store brands. Sears, Kmart, Wal-Mart, and Home Depot are major marketers of these brands. In addition, hardware store groups such as True Value and Ace Hardware market their own paint brands.

Specialty paint stores, lumberyards, and independent hardware stores that sell architectural paint and paint sundries have been able to compete in the paint business despite the presence of mass merchandisers (such as Sears) and home improvement centers (such as Lowe's and Home Depot). Industry sources estimate that specialty paint stores account for about 36 percent of paint and sundry sales; hardware and lumberyards account for 14 percent. Furthermore, specialty paint and hardware stores and lumberyards in nonmetropolitan areas have outdistanced mass merchandisers and home improvement centers as sources for paint and paint sundries. This is largely attributable to a lack of home improvement centers and mass-merchandiser distribution in these areas and paint store, hardware, and lumberyard customer relations and service. However, Wal-Mart has been an effective competitor in many nonmetropolitan areas.

Exhibit 1 shows store patronage by do-it-yourself painters and professional painters for 1994 and 1995. As indicated, home centers (including wholesale home centers) and

EXHIBIT 1

Store Patronage by Type of Buyer: Do-It-Yourselfer and Professional Painter

Where Do-It-Yourselfers Most Often Buy Paint and Sundries

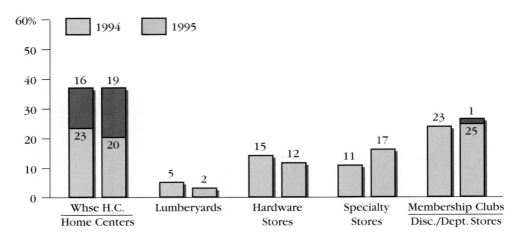

Where Professional Painters Purchased Majority of Paint/Varnish/Stain

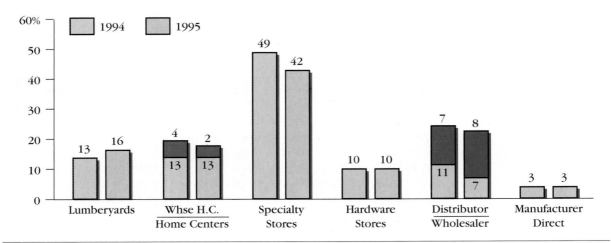

Source: Home Improvement Research Institute. Reprinted from *National Home Center News*, "10 Forces Reshaping the Retail Home Improvement Market," © 1996. Used with permission.

mass merchandisers (including membership clubs such as Sam's) represent the two most frequently patronized categories of retailers shopped by do-it-yourself painters for paint and sundry items. Specialty paint stores and lumberyards were the most frequently patronized retail stores by professional painters for paint products and sundry items.

Architectural Coatings Purchase Behavior

Approximately 50 percent of architectural coatings dollar sales are accounted for by do-it-yourselfer painters. Professional painter purchases account for 25 percent of dollar sales. The remainder of architectural coatings dollar sales result from government, export, and contractor sales.

Almost 60 percent of annual architectural coatings sales are for interior paints. Exterior paint represents 38 percent of sales. Lacquers and all other applications make up the balance of sales. Slightly less than one in four households purchase interior house paint in any given year. The percentage of households purchasing exterior house paint is considerably less than that for interior paint. The popularity of do-it-yourself painting, particularly for interior applications, has increased the paint and sundry item product line carried by retail outlets. Paint industry consumer research indicates that the average dollar paint purchase per purchase occasion is about $74.00. The average dollar sundry purchase per purchase occasion is about $12.00.

Recent research by the Home Improvement Research Institute indicates that do-it-yourself painters first choose a retail outlet for paint and paint sundries, then choose a paint brand. This research also identified four steps in the do-it-yourself decision process for home improvement products, including paint. The results of this research are summarized in Exhibit 2.

"Paint has become a commodity," commented Barrett. "Do-it-yourself purchasers all too often view paint as paint—a covering—and try to get the best price. But there

EXHIBIT 2

Consumer Buying Decision Process for Home Improvement Products

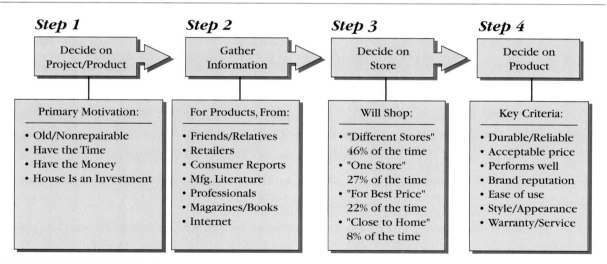

Source: Home Improvement Research Institute. Reprinted from *National Home Center News*, "10 Forces Reshaping the Retail Home Improvement Market," © 1996. Used with permission.

are a significant number of people who desire service as well in the form of information about application, color matching, surface preparation, and durability," he added. He conceded that "once paint is on the wall, you can't initially tell the difference between premium-priced and competitively priced paint."

"There is a difference between painting contractors and professional painters, however," he continued. "Pot and brush guys [professional painters] do seek out quality products, since their reputation is on the line and maintenance firms don't want to have to paint an office each time a mark appears on a wall. They want paint that is durable, washable, and will cover in a single coat. They also look to retailers who will go the extra mile to give them service. Many request and get credit from stores. They appreciate being able to get to stores early in the morning to pick up paint and supplies. They deal with stores that can mix large quantities of custom colors and expect to work with knowledgeable store employees who can give them what they want. It is not surprising to me that paint stores remain the preferred outlet for paint and sundries for professional painters. Contractors simply want a coating in many instances and strive for the lowest price, particularly on big jobs."

■ JONES•BLAIR COMPANY SERVICE AREA

Jones•Blair Company markets its paint and sundry items in over 50 countries in Texas, Oklahoma, New Mexico, and Louisiana from its plant and headquarters in Dallas, Texas. The eleven county Dallas–Fort Worth (DFW) metropolitan area is the major business and financial center in the company's southwestern service area.

Competition at the retail level has accelerated in recent years. Sears and Kmart have multiple outlets in DFW, as do Sherwin-Williams and Home Depot. Competition for retail selling space in paint stores, lumberyards, and hardware stores has also increased. "Our research indicates that 1,000 of these outlets now operate in the 50-county service area, and DFW houses 450 of them," noted Barrett. "When you consider that the typical lumberyard or hardware store gets 10 percent of its volume ($65,000) from paint and the typical paint store has annual sales of $400,000 with three brands, you can see that getting and keeping widespread distribution is a key success factor in this industry. Over 1,200 outlets were in operation in the area in 1990; about 600 were situated in the DFW area."

Competition at the paint manufacturing level has increased as well. The major change in competitive behavior has occurred among paint companies that sell to contractors serving the home construction industry. These companies have aggressively priced their products to capture a higher percentage of the home construction market. "Fortunately, these companies have not pursued the 400 or so professional painting firms in DFW and the 200 professional painters outside the DFW area or the do-it-yourselfer market as yet," said Barrett. "They have not been able to gain access to retail outlets, but they may buy their way in through free goods, promotional allowances, or whatever means are available to them in the future."

"We believe that mass merchandisers control 50 percent of the do-it-yourselfer paint market in the DFW metropolitan area. Price seems to be the attraction, but we can't quarrel with their quality," noted Barrett.

The estimated dollar volume of architectural paint and allied products sold in Jones•Blair's 50-county service area in 1997 was $80 million (excluding contractor sales). DFW was estimated to account for 60 percent of this figure, with the remaining volume being sold in other areas. Do-it-yourself household buyers were believed to account for 70 percent of non–contractor-related volume in DFW and 90 percent of non–contractor-related volume in other areas. A five-year summary of architectural paint and allied product sales in the Jones•Blair service area is shown in Exhibit 3.

EXHIBIT 3

Architectural Paint and Sundry Sales Volume, Excluding Contractor Sales (in Millions of Dollars)

Year	Total Dollar Sales	DFW Area Sales	Non-DFW Area Sales
1993	$75.7	$50.9	$24.8
1994	76.4	50.8	25.6
1995	77.6	50.5	27.1
1996	78.4	50.7	27.7
1997	80.0	48.0	32.0

■ JONES•BLAIR COMPANY

Jones•Blair Company is a privately held corporation that produces and markets architectural paint under the Jones•Blair brand name. In addition to producing a full line of architectural coatings, the company sells paint sundries (brushes, rollers, thinners, etc.) under the Jones•Blair name, even though these items are not manufactured by the company. The company also operates a very large OEM coatings division, which sells its products throughout the U.S. and worldwide.

Company architectural paint and allied products sales volume in 1997 was $12 million, and net profit before taxes was $1,140,000. Dollar sales had increased at an average annual rate of 4 percent per year over the past decade. Paint gallonage, however, had remained stable over the past five years. "We have been very successful in maintaining our margins even with increased research and development, material and labor costs, but I'm afraid we're approaching the threshold on our prices," Barrett said. "We are now the highest-priced paint in our service area." In 1997, paint cost-of-goods sold, including freight expenses, was 60 percent of net sales.

Distribution

The company distributes its products through 200 independent paint stores, lumber-yards, and hardware outlets. Forty percent of its outlets are located in the 11-county DFW area. The remaining outlets are situated in the other 39 counties in the service area. Jones•Blair sales are distributed evenly between DFW and non-DFW accounts. Exhibit 4 shows the account and sales volume distribution by size of dollar purchase per year.

EXHIBIT 4

Account and Sales Volume Percentage Distribution by Dollar Purchase per Year

Dollar Purchase/Year	Retail Accounts			Dollar Sales Volume		
	DFW	Non-DFW	Total	DFW	Non-DFW	Total
$50,000 +	7%	10%	17%	28%	28%	56%
$25,000–$50,000	14	20	34	13	13	26
Less than $25,000	19	30	49	9	9	18
Total	40%	60%	100%	50%	50%	100%

Retail outlets outside the DFW area with paint and sundry purchases exceeding $50,000 annually carry only the Jones•Blair product line. However, except for 14 outlets in DFW (those with purchases greater than $50,000 annually), which carry the Jones•Blair line exclusively, DFW retailers carry two or three lines, with Jones•Blair's line being premium priced. "Our experience to date shows that in our DFW outlets, the effect of multiple lines has been to cause a decline in gallonage volume. The non-DFW outlets, by comparison, have grown in gallonage volume. When you combine the two, you have stable gallonage volume," remarked Barrett.

Promotional Efforts for Architectural Coating Sales

Jones•Blair employs eight sales representatives. They are responsible for monitoring inventories of Jones•Blair paint and sundry items in each retail outlet, as well as for order taking, assisting in store display, and coordinating cooperative advertising programs. A recent survey of Jones•Blair paint dealers indicated that the sales representatives were well liked, helpful, professional, and knowledgeable about paint. Commenting on the survey findings, Barrett said, "Our reps are on a first-name basis with their customers. It is common for our reps to discuss business and family over coffee during a sales call, and some of our people even 'mind the store' when the proprietor has to run an errand or two." Sales representatives are paid a salary and a 1 percent commission on sales.

The company spends approximately 3 percent of net sales on advertising and sales promotion efforts. Approximately 55 percent of advertising and sales promotion dollars are allocated to cooperative advertising programs with retail accounts. The cooperative program, whereby Jones•Blair pays a portion of an account's media costs based on the dollar amount of paint purchased from Jones•Blair, applies to newspaper advertising and seasonal catalogs distributed in a retailer's immediate trade area. Exhibit 5 shows an example of a Jones•Blair Company cooperative print advertisement. The remainder of the advertising and sales promotion budget is spent on in-store displays, corporate brand advertising, outdoor signs, regional magazines, premiums, and advertising production costs. The company also established a corporate Web site (*www.jones-blair.com*) in early 1997. The Web site provides information on Jones•Blair OEM coatings and architectural coatings.

■ PLANNING MEETING

Senior management executives of Jones•Blair Company assembled again to consider the question of where and how to deploy corporate marketing efforts among the various architectural paint coatings markets served by the company. Barrett opened the meeting with a statement that it was absolutely necessary to resolve this question at the meeting in order for the tactical plan to be developed. The peak painting season was soon approaching and decisions had to be made.

Vice President of Advertising: Alex, I still believe that we must direct our efforts toward bolstering our presence in the DFW do-it-yourselfer market. I just received the results of our DFW consumer advertising awareness study. As you can see [Exhibit 6], awareness is related to paint purchase behavior. Industry research on paint purchase behavior indicates that a large number of do-it-yourselfers choose a store before selecting a brand. However, a brand name is also important to consumers because they do think about paint they have seen advertised when choosing a brand. This becomes very important in those stores carrying multiple brands. It seems to me that we need an awareness level of at least 30 percent among do-it-yourselfers to materially affect our sales.

EXHIBIT 5

Jones•Blair Company Print Advertisement

(DEALER IMPRINT)

Preliminary talks with our ad agency indicate that an increase of $350,000 in corporate brand advertising beyond what we are now spending, with an emphasis on television, will be necessary to achieve this awareness level. Furthermore, this television coverage will reach non-DFW consumers in some 15 counties as well.

Vice President of Operations: I don't agree. Advertising is not the way to go, and reference to the DFW area alone is too narrow a focus. We have to be competitive in the do-it-yourselfer paint market, period. Our shopper research program indicated that dealers will quickly back off from our brand when the customer appears price-

EXHIBIT 6

Percentage of DFW Population That Was Aware of Paint Brands and Purchased Paint in the Last 12 Months

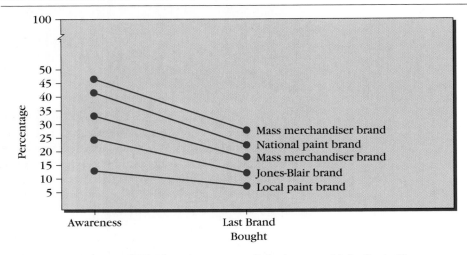

Awareness Question: "What brands come to mind when you think of paint?"

Last Brand Bought: "What paint brand did you purchase the last time you bought paint?"

Note: Sample size was $N = 400$. Percentages are subject to a 5 percent sampling error.

sensitive. We must cut our price by 20 percent on all paint products to achieve parity with national paint brands. Look here. In today's newspaper, we advertise a price-off special on our exterior paint, and our price is still noticeably higher than a mass merchandiser's everyday price. With both ads on the same page, a customer would have to be an idiot to patronize one of our dealers.

Vice President of Sales: Forget the DFW market. We ought to be putting our effort into non-DFW areas, where half of our sales and most of our dealers exist right now. I hate to admit it, but our sales representatives could be more aggressive. We have only added five new accounts in the last five years; our account penetration in non-DFW areas is only 16 percent. I'm partially at fault, but I'm ready to act. We should add one additional sales representative whose sole responsibility is to develop new retail account leads and presentations or call on professional painters to solicit their business through our dealers. I've figured the direct cost to keep one rep in the field at $60,000 per year, excluding commission.

Vice President of Finance: Everyone is proposing a change in our orientation. Let me be the devil's advocate and favor pursuing our current approach. We now sell to both the home owner and the professional painter in DFW and non-DFW markets through our dealers. We have been and will continue to be profitable by judiciously guarding our margins and controlling costs. Our contribution margin is 35 percent. Everyone suggests that increasing our costs will somehow result in greater sales volume. Let me remind you, Alex, we have said that it is our policy to recoup noncapital expenditures within a one-year time horizon. If we increase our advertising by an incremental amount of $350,000, then we had better see the incremental sales volume as well. The same goes for additional sales representatives and, I might add, any across-the-board cut in prices.

Mr. Barrett: We keep going over the same ground. All of you have valid arguments, but we must prioritize. Let's think about what's best for all of us.

Increased advertising seems reasonable, since national paint firms and mass merchandisers outspend us tenfold in absolute terms. You are right in saying people have to be aware of us before they will buy, or even consider, Jones•Blair. But I am not sure what advertising will do for us given that about 75 percent of the audience is not buying paint. Your reference to DFW as being our major market has been questioned by others. Can't we take that $350,000 of incremental advertising and apply it toward newspapers and catalogs in non-DFW areas?

The price cut is a more drastic action. We might have to do it just to keep our gallonage volume. It would appear from our sales representatives' forecast that gallonage demand for paint in our service area will not increase next year and we can't increase our prices this year. Any increases will have to come out of a competitor's hide. Moreover, since our costs are unlikely to decline, we must recoup gross profit dollars from an increase in volume. Is this possible?

The idea of hiring additional representatives has merit, but what do we do with them? Do they focus on the retail account side or on recruiting the professional painter? Our survey of retail outlets indicated that 70 percent of sales through our DFW dealers went to the professional painter, while 70 percent of our sales through our non-DFW outlets went to do-it-yourselfers. These figures are identical to the 1990 survey of retail outlets. Our contractor sales in DFW and other areas are minimal. We would need a 40 percent price cut to attract contractors, not to mention the increased costs, expertise, and headaches of competitive bidding for large jobs.

Now that I've had my say, let's think about your proposals again. We're not leaving until we agree on a course of action.

eBay's Globalization Strategy

In late April 2001 Matt Bannick walked back to his office on the eBay campus after a long meeting with company CEO Meg Whitman. Bannick and Whitman had spent a portion of their meeting that afternoon discussing the goals for eBay in terms of international growth. eBay had been continually increasing its international presence, launching or acquiring sites across the globe in pursuit of the company's original vision "to create the world's largest global trading community and to help people trade practically anything on earth." As eBay's senior vice president of international, Bannick had spearheaded company growth for the past six months. Most recently, on February 21, 2001, eBay announced the acquisition of iBazar, the leading Internet online trading site in France, Italy, Spain, the Netherlands, Belgium, and Portugal as well as having a presence in Sweden, Portugal, and Brazil.

As the world's leading online auction company, eBay already had a "footprint" throughout North America, Europe, and Asia/Pacific. Through its country-specific sites in the United States, Australia, Austria, Canada, France, Germany, Ireland, Italy, Japan, Korea, New Zealand, Switzerland, and the United Kingdom, eBay has presence in the countries making up about 90 percent of the worldwide e-commerce market. Users in any country in the world could access eBay through the U.S. site (and use U.S. currency), or any of the international sites to trade in local currencies. The acquisition of iBazar enabled eBay to be the market leader in six European countries, and solidified the company's position as the leading European online trading site. As Bannick put it, eBay was "delighted" with its expansion in Europe. Almost without exception, the company had successfully timed, executed, and rolled out local sites in the world's biggest e-commerce markets. This success in "glocalization"[1] primed the company to approach the next tier of markets: emerging markets with potential for growth. Near the top of the list was Latin America, and the acquisition of iBazar brought Latin America to the front of Bannick's mind.

Bannick took a quick detour to the local Whole Foods market near the campus to get a sandwich for lunch. He mentally reviewed some of the issues that he and Whitman had just discussed. eBay had issued a specific international growth plan: to compete in 10 international markets by the end of 2001, and to be in 25 countries by 2005. The company had already proven it was on track to exceed those goals. Now that eBay had a Brazilian presence in Latin America, was the timing right to pursue growth in the market? The company could grow through further acquisitions or

---

[1]This term grew out of the global strategies of firms like eBay, creating local presences throughout the globe. As *Red Herring* reported, "The canon among global strategists is that foreign outfits must try to look and feel like a local company—thus the buzzword 'glocalization.'" Mark Spiegler, "Glocalization: Easier Said Than Done," *Red Herring*, October 9, 2000.

---

organic growth. On the other hand, he and Meg had agreed that the most important goal right now for the international team was successful completion and execution of the recent acquisitions. Maybe the timing was better to hold onto iBazar, but hold off on any more activity in the region until a time when his team had more bandwidth to focus on this market. Finally, maybe even any position could be a distraction. Bannick and his team already had quite a bit on their plates. In the future, eBay could have another opportunity to go into Latin America through an acquisition or simply organic growth. Should the company now sell iBazar's Brazilian division to pull out entirely from Latin America and focus on eBay's core European and Asian markets?

As he waited for his sandwich to be prepared, Bannick jotted a quick list of considerations on the back of a napkin:

eBay's Global Expansion Aided by Flexible Entry Modes

- Organic growth: Adopted in the U.K., Canada, Austria, Ireland, New Zealand, and Switzerland. Also initiated in France and Italy, but these markets subsumed by the iBazar acquisition.
- Acquisition: Adopted in Germany, Korea, and now again with iBazar.
- Joint ventures: Adopted successfully in Australia; less successful in Japan.

Options for Latin America

- eBay could retain iBazar's Brazilian operation,
  - and consider growing organically from there (either within Brazil or also into other Latin American countries).
  - and grow its presence through acquisition. (The two main possibilities are MercadoLibre.com and deRemate.com.)
- eBay could dispose of iBazar's Brazilian operation,
  - selling it for cash and holding off on its pursuit of the Latin American market.
  - selling it for equity in a competitor (thus keeping a finger in the Latin American pie).
  - simply shutting it down.

A few minutes later Bannick picked up his sandwich and walked back to his office. He wanted to have a concrete recommendation before his next meeting with Whitman.

■ HISTORY OF eBAY

Pierre Omidyar (originally from France) and Jeff Skoll (originally from Canada) founded eBay in May 1996 with headquarters in San Jose, California. It was to be a place for "practically anybody to sell practically anything on earth." The company grew out of AuctionWeb, which Omidyar launched in September 1995. Omidyar had created AuctionWeb as an open marketplace that was a truly level playing field for all members of the community to discuss, compare, and ultimately trade computer items as well as collectibles. The Web site unexpectedly took off, reaching thousands of registered users in just two years. By January 1997, AuctionWeb—with 39,000 registered users—could not handle the large load of page views. To solve the system issues, Omidyar designed and wrote the code for an entirely new system: eBay (short for Echo Bay Technologies). In September 1997, the AuctionWeb platform was turned off and the eBay platform opened.

Launching eBay

By the time of the switch from AuctionWeb, eBay was the leading Internet auction site in the world. The new service was fully automated, topically arranged, intuitive and easy to use—see Exhibit 1. It operated 24 hours a day, seven days a week. eBay had developed a successful and thriving Web-based "community" for the buying and selling of personal items (e.g., antiques, coins, collectibles, etc.) in an auction format. As the company Web site put it:

> eBay provides buyers and sellers a place to socialize, to discuss topics of common interest and, ultimately, to conduct business in a compelling trading environment, thus fostering a large and growing commerce-oriented online community.

eBay fostered rapid growth through a "virtuous cycle (circle)." Sellers were attracted to eBay as a result of the large number of potential buyers, and buyers in turn were attracted to eBay by the broad selection of goods listed. Exhibit 2 charts eBay's growth in visitors and listings since August 1998. Exhibit 3 on page 92 shows eBay's auction listings by category.

EXHIBIT 1

Introduction to eBay "U.S." Web site (excerpted from eBay Web pages)

What does it cost?

- There's no charge to browse, bid on or buy items at eBay. But you do pay fees to list and sell items.
- When you list your item for sale at eBay, you pay a non-refundable insertion fee. Insertion fees vary by the type of listing you choose: Regular Listings, Reserve Price Auction Listings, or Dutch Auction Listings. The insertion fee is based upon the opening value of the items you list for sale. The opening value is the minimum bid multiplied by the quantity of items you offer. The maximum insertion fee for any Dutch Auction is $3.30 (insertion fees begin at $.30 for items under $10; reserve price fees range from $.50 to $1.00).
- At the end of a listing, you will be charged a final value fee based on the final sale price (final value) of your item: Examples of final value:
  - If an item sold for $25 or less, your final value fee is 5% of the final sale price.
  - If your item sold for more than $25, please follow the next steps: Take 5 percent of the first $25 of your final sale price. Calculate 2.5 percent out of the additional amount from $25.01 to $1,000. If your final value was more than $1,000, take that additional amount and calculate 1.25 percent of the remaining amount. Add the amounts together, from steps 1,2, and 3, and you have your final value fee!

Is trading on eBay safe?

- Instantly check the "reputation" or business practices of anyone at eBay.
- Every eBay user is covered, at no additional cost, by the eBay Fraud Protection Program.
- An escrow service can give you added security whether you're a buyer or seller in transactions involving expensive items.
- A dispute resolution service will work with buyers and sellers to help resolve disputes that may arise.

What do eBay local sites offer?

- Country- (or region-) specific categories and content
- The ability to trade in local currency (if applicable)
- The ability to search for items located within the city/region or country
- Unparalleled access to a worldwide community of traders, with over 300,000 new items listed every day and over 3 million items for sale at any one time. Local site sellers can list their item so it can be viewed from any eBay site and buyers can view items listed anywhere in the world.
- Local chat boards for eBay's local community

EXHIBIT 2

eBay Growth in Visitors and Listings—Media Metrix Traffic Trends

eBay has one of the highest levels of unique visitors each month among e-commerce companies. It is one of the top-ten sites on the Internet.

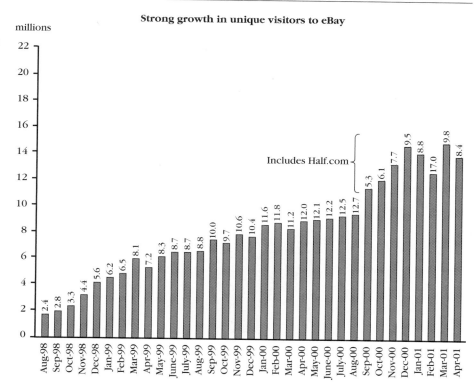

Strong growth in unique visitors to eBay

Includes Half.com

Note: Unique visitors as of September 2000 include Half.com.

Source: Media Metrix, Goldman Sachs Research.

Although listings are one of the many leading indicators we track, as listings reach scale, they will become less important. Auction and user growth will ultimately be better metrics, in the same way that orders and customers are more important than number of available SKUs for an e-tailer.

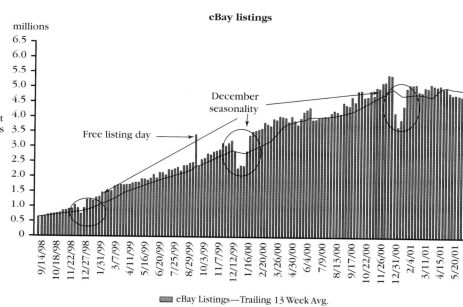

eBay listings

Free listing day

December seasonality

eBay Listings—Trailing 13 Week Avg.

Source: Goldman Sachs (May 31, 2001)

EXHIBIT 3

eBay Auction Listings By Category

Although eBay's roots are in auctioning collectibles, its listings are diversifying well beyond collectibles, which now account for only 26% of listings.

Auction listings By category as of May 21, 2001

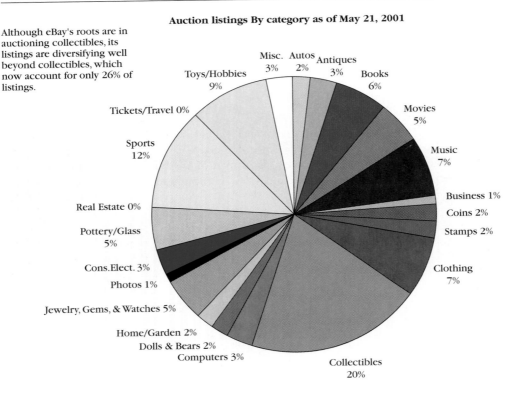

Source: Goldman Sachs (May 31, 2001)

Focus on Growth

From the company's inception, growth and market saturation were priorities from the management team. As Jeff Skoll put it:

> We knew that if we were going to have a shot at being the big one, we needed to move quickly. It's the virtuous cycle: the more posted items, the more people visiting the site; the more people visiting the site, the more posted items. People who are selling things like to go to where there are people who are buying, and people who are buying seek a broad selection of wares being sold.

The team brainstormed several major marketing strategies, deciding that an Initial Public Offering would provide not only great publicity, but also fuel growth. Skoll recalled, "Between the press and the road show, what better way to get 'free' publicity and national advertising? We were profitable, we had a service with paying customers, and we were on the Internet. We believed that if we could take the Company public, we would have a major first-mover advantage."

Omidyar and Skoll prepared the Company for IPO by strengthening the senior management team, including the following additions:

Jan. 1997	Michael Wilson—V.P. Product Development From the Well (Software Coy.)
Aug. 1997	Steve Westly—V.P. Business Development From Whowhere (Internet directory)
Nov. 1997	Gary Bengier—CFO From Vxtreme (Internet video products)
Feb. 1998	Meg Whitman—CEO From Hasbro/FTC
Aug. 1998	Brian Swette—Senior V.P. Marketing From Pepsi-Cola

In addition, the board of directors was strengthened with the addition of Robert Kagle (Benchmark Capital), Scott Cook (Intuit), and Howard Schultz (Starbucks). Benchmark was the sole venture capital investor in eBay—a $3 million investment in June 1997. Omidyar maintained his role as chairman of the board, and Skoll became vice president of strategic planning and analysis. On September 24, 1998, eBay completed its initial public offering (ticker symbol EBAY). The company raised $63 million by selling approximately 9 percent of its stock.

From its early days, eBay was often portrayed as a poster child of the new economy. It is widely recognized as the leading online auction company in the world with a demonstrated proven and profitable business model. The company's financial statement information is summarized in Exhibit 4 on page 94. Two other "poster child" companies of the new economy—Amazon.com and Yahoo!—have set up online auction sites to compete with eBay (as well as having non-auction based e-commerce sites).

Fueling Mega-Growth

To further propel eBay's growth, the management team considered various strategies—including vertical and geographic expansion—and various methods of execution. The team discussed a geographic strategy. The company would acquire, launch, or sponsor regional and city-specific auction sites in an effort to attract larger ticket items and items that were not easily transported (fragile goods, automobiles, etc.). The company first implemented its U.S. geographic expansion strategy with the early 1999 launch of eBay-LA, a city-specific site whose initial success reinforced the potential of this strategy.

In April 1999, eBay moved into the off-line auction market by acquiring Butterfield and Butterfield (Butterfields) a major San Francisco auction house. Butterfields was, at the time, the fourth largest "off-line" auction house in the country. eBay approached this move with care; for its first forays into non-organic expansion, the company was testing its ability to grow in leaps and bounds—and in new directions. As Michael Wilson, then vice president of engineering, put it, "We had spent quite a bit of time making sure the acquisition was aligned with our overall strategy; we didn't want to fall short on the execution." The acquisition not only fueled growth for the company—the additional 350 Butterfield employees virtually doubled the eBay roster—but also gained valuable assets for eBay. The acquisition brought eBay Butterfields' expertise and reputation in the fine arts (including popular eBay categories of decorative arts and celebrity memorabilia); furthermore, Butterfields had experience in transaction facilitation, especially in appraisal and the high-end market. (The combination of online and off-line activities meant eBay's financial statements became less comparable to other purely online e-commerce companies.)

While the company had built its reputation on an auction format for consumer-to-consumer trading, the eBay mission of helping "practically anybody sell practically anything" did not limit eBay to auctions. The company first approached the non-auction trading format by introducing a "fixed-price" option to its site. Sellers had the option

EXHIBIT 4

eBay Summary Financial Statement Information
($ Millions—December 31, Fiscal Year End)

Income Statement	1996	1997	1998	1999	2000
Net revenues	$ 0.372	$5.744	$47.352	$224.724	$431.424
Cost of net revenues	0.014	0.746	6.859	57.588	95.453
Gross profit	0.358	4.998	40.493	167.136	335.971
Operating expenses:					
Sales and marketing	0.032	1.730	19.841	95.956	166.767
Product development	0.028	0.831	4.606	23.785	55.863
General and administrative	0.045	0.950	9.080	43.055	73.027
Amortization and other	—	—	0.805	5.504	5.320
Total operating expenses	0.105	3.511	34.332	168.300	300.977
Income from operations	0.253	1.487	6.161	(1.164)	34.994
Interest and other income	0.001	0.059	0.908	23.422	46.337
Interest expense	—	(0.003)	(0.039)	(1.943)	(3.374)
Income before income taxes	0.254	1.543	7.030	20.315	77.957
Provision for income taxes	(0.106)	(0.669)	(4.632)	(9.385)	(32.725)
Net income	0.148	0.874	2.398	10.828	48.294
Balance Sheet	**1996**	**1997**	**1998**	**1999**	**2000**
Cash and cash equivalents		$3.723	$31.790	$219.679	$201.873
Short-term investments		—	40.401	181.086	354.166
Total assets		5.619	92.483	963.942	1,182.403
Total current liabilities		1.124	8.038	88.825	137.442
Long-term debt/leases		0.305	—	15.018	11.404
Stockholders' equity (SE)		1.015	84.445	852.467	1,013.760
Total Liabilities + SE		5.619	92.483	963.942	1,182.403
Operating Data					
Number of registered users at 12/31 (millions)	0.041	0.341	2.181	10.006	22.472
Number of items listed (in millions)	0.289	4.394	33.668	129.560	264.653
Gross merchandise sales (in millions)	$7	$95	$745	$2,805	$5,422

to list an item with a "buy it now" function; a buyer could agree to buy the item for the "buy it now" price, and avoid the auction format. Mike Harkey, general manager of music for eBay, described the rationale of the new format. "It's easier for the lister to present 'commodity items' in the fixed-price format, and it's easier for the buyer as well. With commodity items, for example, the buyer wants a good deal, but might not have the patience to wait a week or more for an auction to end." A few months before the introduction of the "buy it now" feature, eBay had acquired Half.com, a below-retail fixed-price trading Web site. As eBay's press release described: "Half.com offers people a fixed-price, online marketplace to buy and sell high quality, previously owned goods at discounted prices. Unlike auctions, where the selling price is based on bidding, the seller fixes the price for items at the time an item is listed."

Harkey explained that the acquisitions of Butterfields and Half.com, and the introduction of eBay-LA were all facets in the company's strategy to be the best online trading community, and to best serve the needs of the world's customers: "At first these elements might appear discrete. Over time, however, you'll see the distinctions blur as eBay grows and incorporates these elements into our global presence."

A member of eBay management summarized the company's growth strategy as following "growth initiatives along a series of dimensions: increasing the breadth and depth of products on the site; increasing the geographic presence of the brand locally and internationally; increasing the range of pricing formats through fixed price and auctions; and finally providing buyers and sellers with services to enhance the velocity and reduce the friction of trade."

In an important way, eBay was a global trading company from day zero. Its first "trading room" Web site was listed on the World Wide Web in 1997. For example, an individual auction in 1998 could have involved a United Kingdom buyer and an Australian seller for an item from the 1992 Summer Olympics in Barcelona, Spain. However, all eBay buyers and sellers at that time used a single trading platform that was expressed in U.S. dollars, used U.S. (Pacific daylight) time for auction closing, and was decidedly U.S.-centric in its appearance. Becoming a global player raised the challenge of having multiple trading rooms or platforms in which individual country currencies, times, merchandise, legal regulations, and customs, etc. were explicitly recognized, developed, and marketed.

■ GLOBALIZATION AND GLOCALIZATION—*SPRECHEN SIE eBAY?*

Establishing a truly global trading community was part of the eBay mission since the company's inception. Though management had an eye towards globalization since the beginning, the company exercised patience in plotting its international expansion. eBay launched officially in September 1997. It did not make its first global move until 1999. In February 1999, it entered the Australian market via a joint venture (with a "trading room") expressed in Australian dollars, using Australian east coast time for auction closings, and adding Australian-oriented classification of listings. The site went live in October 1999. In June 1999 it entered the German market by acquiring Alando.de, a German-based online auction company. Matt Bannick explained the delay in entering international markets as follows:

> The U.S. business was growing at a phenomenal pace, so we wanted to make sure we were taking care of our core domestic markets first. Also, the international e-commerce markets were very nascent. There weren't as many people online, and the market wasn't there yet. Third, we wanted to be in markets where we could be profitable in a short amount of time. Finally, it required a substantial amount of work to internationalize the code base.

In 1999, some international markets showed promising growth, and there was evidence that an international market was developing for the eBay service. The company believed that local sites would meet the needs of international customers in a meaningful way. Much as the users of local U.S. regional sites expressed positive reinforcement, international users valued sites that presented material in their native language, and according to their local customs and preferences. CEO Meg Whitman believed that eBay was uniquely qualified to compete globally: "We have a paradigm that works equally as well around the world as it does in the United States."

Even with the clear strategic value of international expansion, the company acknowledged many challenges in its global execution. The challenges included the aforementioned general demands of creating the new content in a new language, setting up international technical support, and meeting demand on the management "bandwidth." And, of course, each country had its own special needs, as well as different legislative and regulatory restrictions. An example that gained worldwide attention was the difference in the legality of items (such as firearms or Nazi memorabilia) allowed or not allowed to be traded in different countries. Given the challenges, eBay pursued expansion deliberately but carefully. Whitman commented that a deliberately slow pace meant that eBay wasn't always the first to any market, "We were not the first to virtually any global markets. . . ." But passing up on a first-mover advantage didn't appear to hurt eBay. As Whitman observed: ". . . but now we are the number-one player in all of them [except Japan]."

In addition to patience in plotting a move, eBay used simple logic in selecting the countries for expansion. Matt Bannick described eBay's thought process:

> We went into countries that made a lot of sense for us in terms of being able to generate in a reasonably short term the kind of revenue that we need to build and sustain a community. . . . Where do you put the individual country sites and where can you justify their presence? We looked at the countries that had the largest e-commerce potential, and where there was a reasonable culture of trading. You can go through a list of the top 20 e-commerce countries in the world, and realize that's where eBay has decided to go.

Exhibit 5 outlines the growth in eBay's international sites. Given the challenges of international growth and the country-specific demands in each market, the company pursued different market entry strategies for each of these inroads. There was also an element of opportunistic behavior by eBay as it reacted to opportunities presented to it, or challenges arising with new competitors.

Germany—the Acquisition Entry Mode

In June 1999, eBay acquired alando.de, the leading online trading company in Germany. Germany boasted approximately 10 million Internet users in 1999, and alando had created a strong relationship with its user base. The acquisition facilitated eBay's desire for speed to market, local know-how, and relevant traffic. eBay founder Pierre Omidyar explained, "The acquisition of alando.de accelerated eBay's vision of creating a passionate, vibrant, and loyal global trading community."

Interestingly, alando seemed to have purposely built itself from inception as an attractive eBay acquisition candidate. Bannick commented that the German site bore remarkable similarity to eBay, right down to the company values that eBay prominently listed on their site: "They'd essentially translated the eBay values into German. That's the degree to which they had gone to mirror eBay in what alando.de was trying to accomplish in Germany."

Even with the strong similarities between the sites, eBay did not immediately impose its brand after the acquisition. Instead, eBay followed a gradual phasing-in of the eBay logo and specifics. A few months after the acquisition, the eBay name appeared along with alando, calling the site an "eBay company." Within eighteen months, eBay was the sole brand on the site. It can be accessed by either (a) logging into *www.ebay.com* and clicking on the Germany Global Site, or (b) logging into *www.ebay.de*.

United Kingdom and Ireland—the "Greenfield" Entry Mode

Later that year, eBay moved directly into the United Kingdom. It launched the eBay UK site (a "trading room" using the pound as a trading currency and London time for auction closings) in October 1999. The development of a UK site illustrated Whitman's point of achieving market leadership, even without first mover advantage. When eBay launched eBayUK, the site was far smaller than QXL, then the UK's leading Internet trading site. eBay quickly overtook QXL and became the biggest site in the UK in terms of consumer sales and revenues. Furthermore, the site gave eBay a platform from which to launch other international sites. Ireland, for example, was a fairly simple

EXHIBIT 5

Summary Information on eBay's International Expansion

A. From Goldman Sachs (May 31, 2001)

Date Announced/ Launched	Country	Partner Versus Direct Entry
24-Feb-99	Australia and New Zealand	JV with PBL Online Ltd. (owns eCorp)
22-Jun-99	Germany	Acquisition of Alando.de
October-99	U.K.	Direct
17-Feb-00	Japan	JV with NEC (PC company which operates BIGGLOBE ISP)
10-Apr-00	Canada	Direct
4-Oct-00	France	Direct
18-Dec-01	Austria	Direct
8-Jan-01	Korea	Major stake in Internet Auction
15-Jan-01	Italy	Direct
21-Feb-01	France, Spain, Belgium, Italy, the Netherlands, Sweden, Portugal, and Brazil	Purchase of iBazar
29-Mar-01	Ireland, New Zealand, Switzerland	Direct

Source: Goldman Sachs Research, company reports.

B. From Morgan Stanley Dean Witter (April 20, 2001)

While the U.S. market still accounts for the lion's share of transactions, eBay's twelve international markets now combine for 15+% of total listings, a share we believe will rise gradually over time.

eBay International Fee Structure

Country	Launch Date	Listing Fees	Final Value Fees
U.K.	CH1:99	X	X
Canada	CQ4:00	X	X
Germany	CQ3:99	X	X
Australia	CQ4:99	X	X
Japan	CQ1:00		X
France*	CQ4:00		X
South Korea	CQ1:01	X	X
Austria	CQ4:00	X	X
Italy	CQ1:01		X
Ireland	CQ1:01	X	X
Switzerland	CQ1:01	X	X
New Zealand	CQ1:01	X	X

*eBay France charges Listing Fees for Automobiles and Real Estate Auctions.

(continued)

EXHIBIT 5 *(continued)*

eBay Site Listings by Country

Country	Listings	% of Total
U.S.	5,141,283	84
Germany	736,676	12
UK	121,211	2
Australia	15,025	0.20
Japan	3,954	0.10
France	3,169	0.10
Italy	2,543	0
Canada	2,541	0

Note: Listings are calculated as of 4/17/01; Listings in South Korea, Austria, Italy, Ireland, Switzerland, and New Zealand are not included.

Source: eBay.

outgrowth. Bannick explained, "To launch Ireland (in March 2001) we simply created an Irish home page with Irish content—and thus created an Irish presence. But it uses the Queen's English, and it uses much of the same functionality for help and for the community."

Australia—the Joint Venture Entry Mode

For eBay's development of a presence in Australia it followed yet a third entry strategy: a joint venture. eBay had neither a clear and attractive acquisition candidate in Australia, nor a deep knowledge of the Australian trading community. A partnership with the right team, however, could bring eBay knowledge of the market, traffic, and—ideally—savvy local management. In February 1999, eBay formed a joint venture partnership with PBL Online, a new economy holding company owned by the Australian Packer family, and the parent company of eCorp. The Packer family, including Kerry Packer and his son James, held dominant positions in television and magazines in Australia. ECorp had been set up to develop joint venture relationships with new economy companies with proven business models. They sought out a relationship with eBay, who had also been approached by several other Australian players seeking joint venture deals. ECorp's pitch for being chosen included leveraging of its own already substantial new economy skills in Australia, and its strong media presence. This would sizably reduce the management oversight required from eBay in San Jose for a new venture. As in the UK, eBay was not first to market. In late 1998, the John Fairfax media company had set up Sold.com, an online Australian auction company bearing much similarity to eBay.

eBay explained that Australia was already part of its community, through Australians' existing use of eBay. "Already thousands of Australians were avid eBay users—some making their living from selling on eBay while others had discovered a fun and entertaining Web site that allows them to pursue their collecting passions."[2] The combined presence enhanced the reach and scope of both partners in the JV, offering a strong Australian trading forum. "The new eBay Australia offered an irresistible combination for Australian traders: compelling local categories and listings, as well as access to a worldwide community of 5.6 million active buyers and sellers," said

---

[2]eBay Press Release, October 20, 1999.

Alison Deans, then managing director of eBay Australia & New Zealand. "No other Web site offers Australians such a vibrant local marketplace and worldwide reach."

Japan—Another Joint Venture Entry Mode

In early 2000, eBay pursued a second joint venture in its launch of eBay Japan. The company entered into a JV agreement with NEC and its BIGLOBE Internet service provider; bringing eBay both technology and an Internet presence. The Form 10k for 2000 of eBay noted:

> On February 17, 2000, eBay Japan Inc., a wholly owned subsidiary of eBay, entered into a shareholder and marketing services agreement with NEC Corporation. In accordance with the shareholder agreement, NEC acquired 30% of eBay Japan and eBay retained the remaining 70% interest of eBay Japan.
>
> In accordance with the marketing agreement, NEC provided marketing and services to eBay Japan in an effort to deliver a minimum level of confirmed registered users. As compensation for the marketing and other services performed by NEC, eBay Japan paid NEC an annual up-front fee of approximately $1.5 million. The first payment was made in April 2000, and additional payments will be payable on the anniversary of such date in each of the subsequent three years as long as the contract is in effect. If NEC is unable to deliver the minimum level of confirmed registered users, then eBay will have the right to repurchase shares of eBay Japan from NEC.

Like earlier eBay international trading rooms, the site was tailored to the local market: fully in Japanese, the site listed prices in yen and offered users over 800 merchandise categories, ranging from local favorites such as "Hello Kitty," Pokemon, and artisan pottery, to popular international categories including computers and electronics. eBay lauded the development as groundbreaking. Japan represented one of the biggest Internet markets outside the United States. "The launch of eBay Japan was a milestone in the company's international expansion," said Merle Okawara, president of eBay Japan.

The performance of the Japanese joint venture has, by all admissions, turned out to be lackluster, though Bannick did not attribute the poor performance to any problems with the joint venture. "The partnership made sense at the time. NEC had very good traffic through BIGLOBE, which was one of the biggest ISPs in the country. There were a whole host of issues [that explained eBay's underperformance in Japan]. One significant reason was that Yahoo! got there first. They got a lot of traffic and traction early on." (Yahoo! also subsequently became a major competitor in Australia. In February 2001 it acquired Sold.com—eBay's largest Australian online auction competitor—from John Fairfax.)

More Acquisitions—iBazar and Internet Auction Company

In early 2001, eBay completed two major acquisitions. It bought Europe's pioneering online auction site, iBazar, and South Korea's leading online auction site, Internet Auction Company. An eBay executive explained the relevance of the iBazar acquisition: "The deal brought eBay a strong position in Europe and was an important step toward realizing the company's goal of establishing one marketplace that spans Europe's borders, with the eventual aim of a panglobal site."[3] iBazar was the leading Internet auction site in France, Italy, Spain, the Netherlands, Belgium, and Portugal. It also had a presence in Sweden and Portugal as well as Brazil. eBay paid approximately $100 million in stock. The eBay press release stated:

> "This deal is a tremendous step forward for eBay," said Meg Whitman, president and CEO, eBay Inc. "In one strategic move we have increased our pan-European footprint,

---

[3] *Yahoo.com.* YahooFinance, 2001.

as well as the strength of our global trading community. Today we are much closer to realizing our dream of a marketplace where people anywhere on the planet can seamlessly trade almost anything."

Based in Paris, iBazar introduced online person-to-person trading in France when it launched in October 1998. Today, it features online marketplaces in eight countries: Belgium, Brazil, France, Italy, the Netherlands, Portugal, Spain, and Sweden. iBazar has a total of 2.4 million registered users, and during the fourth quarter of 2000, it reported more than 3.1 million listings and gross merchandise sales (GMS) of more than $95 million. Based on GMS and reach, iBazar is considered to have the leading sites in all of its markets except for Sweden.

The Industry Standard (February 22, 2001) noted that the $100 million price was "miniscule compared with iBazar's valuation in March 2000 when an Italian bank put in $19 million (at a valuation of over $500 million]. . . As hopes of an IPO crumbled for iBazar the firm has been said to be looking for a buyer for the last six months." As part of the acquisition, eBay acquired the "ebay.fr" domain name which had been held by the iBazar CEO.

The Korean acquisition reflected eBay's second entry into Asia, this time following a different strategy. This market entry was rapid. Instead of building a presence in a new continent, eBay gained controlling interest of a site that had excellent traction and success in the community. *AsiaWise* magazine noted that Internet Auction Company's important advantages went beyond a first mover advantage and "network effects." As the magazine put it: "There's another home-grown factor that also helped to make Internet Auction interesting to eBay: the Korean firm's 'escrow system.' The escrow system helps users to get around a fundamental sticking point in online auctions: trust . . . Auction's escrow system has helped Korean online users, reluctant to deal with strangers by tradition, gain confidence and assurance in online transactions, and has contributed to the Internet's penetration in the country."

■ I'D LIKE TO BUY THE WORLD A COKE. . . OR A CUCKOO CLOCK, OR A CD PLAYER

Having laid the groundwork in select international markets, a number of follow-on markets were easily addressed with organic growth. As Bannick said, a Canadian presence was essentially created de facto; Canadians were already online and tuned in to the U.S. site. Creating a Canadian site was as easy as creating a local site within the Unites States. Similarly, other existing country-specific sites facilitated simple roll-outs in new countries. To that point, in 2001 eBay launched country-specific sites in Ireland, New Zealand, and Switzerland. Bannick explained that launching some new sites could be almost "cookie cutter":

> It's the language that really creates the complexity and the cost. And once you get that, you can leverage it. So for example, with our German platform, we were able to do sites in Austria and Switzerland very easily, because we could use many of the same pages. So it was very easy. In a market like Switzerland you have maybe 5 million German speakers. Now, a separate country of 5 million people speaking a separate language wouldn't be interesting. Doing a Norwegian site, for example, would therefore be tough financially because you'd have to build and maintain a totally separate language.
>
> The new sites were part of eBay's strategy to leverage common languages and cultures in order to enter new international markets more quickly and efficiently with minimal investment in technology.

eBay also pointed out the advantage to customers: "Users can now more readily find locally listed items and other users who share the same language and culture. The improved local access would make browsing and buying more convenient.

Shipping was also be easier without the need to cross national borders. Although trading online will be done in currencies currently available on eBay, users could finalize payments amongst themselves in any currency they choose." In other words, more customers would be using eBay, and more trades would get done, so more money would flow to eBay's bottom line.

Though a handful of countries were natural markets for organic growth, eBay developed a reputation for growth by acquisition. Alex Aboitiz, vice president of strategic planning of MercadoLibre.com—a Latin American trading site—explained that making acquisitions made sense for eBay:

> eBay really moved away from a Greenfield strategy. . . They bought alando.de, they bought the Korean company [Internet Auction Company], then they bought iBazar. These acquisitions gave them a really strong position, in a short time. eBay was in a great position for these acquisitions: There's already a management team in place, so there's less drain on the management in San Jose. There's pressure [from the market] for growth, and growth through acquisition takes a lot less time than starting from scratch. And eBay [had] a lot of cash, and their shares [were still strong enough to easily] buy a company.

Expansion to Latin America—Do You Know the Way to Sao Paolo?

The acquisition of iBazar was driven by eBay's desire to dominate the European market. Serendipitously, iBazar also gave eBay entry into a new continent: South America. As Bannick explained, "Our thoughts and plans for Latin America were very much in the nascent stage." Even so, Bannick knew that the Latin American market was on eBay's list for eventual development. Brazil was already among the top twenty global e-commerce markets, and eBay was already in over half of them. The Latin American market—itself in a nascent stage—had shown rapid growth recently, with dramatic ongoing growth forecast over the next five years (see Exhibit 6 on pages 102-103). According to an IDC study, the Latin American Internet audience would grow by an average of 40 percent each year between now and 2005, resulting in an estimated 75-77 million Internet users in Latin America by 2005, up from just 15 million in 2000. A Boston Consulting Group (BCG) study estimated that the total value of e-auction transactions in Latin America had increased sixteen-fold in one year: from $12 million in 1999 to $192 million in 2000, with Brazil representing over half of the region's e-commerce activity.[4] Online trade specifically was expected to be worth $72 billion in Latin America by 2005, again largely dominated by Mexico and Brazil. The founder of DeRemate, one of the region's online trading sites, put it in first-person terms: "We have 300,000 registered users across the region. It took eBay slightly over a year to get to the 100,000 mark. It took us four months."

Challenges

Although the Brazil market was desirable (at some stage), and eBay now had an entrance thanks to iBazar, a domination of the market was hardly in hand. iBazar was not the strongest player in Brazil. It had no other presence in Latin America. Creating a major presence in Latin America would require effort and input. If Bannick and his team planned to grow organically from this acquisition, they would face many of the challenges of a greenfield entry.

Language would present a major challenge. iBazar's only Latin American presence was Brazil (using the Portuguese language). While iBazar did have knowledge of Spanish language—it controlled Spain's leading Web site—Spanish "Castilian" was quite different from "Spanish" spoken in most Latin American countries. Also history proved

---

[4]*Latin Venture Newsletter*, 2000.

that presence in Brazil did not always translate into success in the rest of the continent. Lokau.com was a Brazilian auction site that had expanded into Mexico. The company was unsuccessful and soon after closed its doors in Mexico and held on to a small share of the Brazilian market. Another issue would be the relatively limited scope of familiarity the Latin American market had with eBay and iBazar. Latin American consumers had a natural predilection to doing business with known commodities. As Alex Aboitiz of MercadoLibre put it, "eBay is such a known commodity in the United States it was part of their daily lives. It appeared on *Friends*. In Latin America, chances are the average person wouldn't know anything about eBay."

Furthermore, Latin America was likely not a region that would show sizable profitability any time soon. Even with rapid growth of Internet use, only a minority of Latin Americans had ready access to the Web. Less than half of Latin American consumers had telephone connections in 2000 (for example, 25 percent of Chileans, 23 percent of Argentines, 22 percent of Colombians, nearly 20 percent of Brazilians, as compared to 97 percent of U.S. consumers). Broadband adoption was even lower in Latin America. While 6 million Americans had broadband Internet access in 2000, in Argentina, Brazil, and Mexico combined, only 111,000 consumers had broadband.

Another challenge was defining exactly where "Latin America" started and stopped. Was it a geographic region or was it a community that shared some common Latin heritage? Under the later interpretation, the U.S. market itself potentially had a sizable Latin component. Indeed, both MercadoLibre and DeRemate had U.S.-focused trading rooms in U.S. dollars and U.S. time, but in Spanish language. One upside to having individual Latin American geographies ("trading sites") was the added value to the existing eBay North American community. A broadened product selection from an

EXHIBIT 6

Latin American Internet Penetration

E-commerce in Latin America is estimated to grow to $8 billion by 2003. The number of Internet users is expected to reach 43 million by 2003.

Internet in Latin America % of households

■ Can currently afford Internet access
□ Can afford Internet access with US ISP prices and flat telephone rates
▨ Can afford Internet access with PC leasing and flat telephone rates

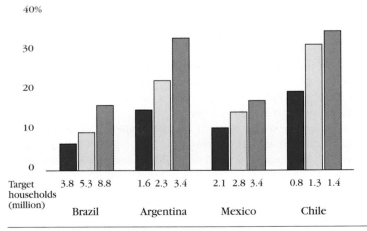

Source: The Boston Consulting Group.

EXHIBIT 6 *(continued)*

Country by Country Internet Penetration Data—Latin America

Brazil	1999	2000 (est.)	2001 (est.)	2004 (est.)
Population (000)	164,356	166,505	168,682	175,387
Population Growth (%)		1.3%	1.3%	1.3%
Internet Users (000)	3,508	6,087	9,413	20,845
Internet Penetration	2.13%	3.7%	5.6%	11.9%

Argentina				
Population (000)	33,072	33,504	33,942	35,291
Population Growth (%)		1.3%	1.3%	1.3%
Internet Users (000)	1,092	1,852	2,798	6,053
Internet Penetration	3.30%	5.5%	8.2%	17.2%

Mexico				
Population (000)	97,324	99,288	101,292	107,550
Population Growth (%)		2.0%	2.0%	2.0%
Internet Users (000)	681	1,449	2,755	7,094
Internet Penetration	0.70%	1.5%	2.7%	6.6%

Colombia				
Population (000)	38,082	38,580	39,085	40,639
Population Growth (%)		1.3%	1.3%	1.3%
Internet Users (000)	541	866	1,234	2,608
Internet Penetration	1.42%	2.24%	3.16%	6.42%

Venezuela				
Population (000)	24,052	24,367	24,685	25,666
Population Growth (%)		1.3%	1.3%	1.3%
Internet Users (000)	313	407	516	947
Internet Penetration	1.30%	1.67%	2.09%	3.69%

Chile				
Population (000)	15,025	15,176	15,328	15,795
Population Growth (%)		1.0%	1.0%	1.0%
Internet Users (000)	331	594	951	2,181
Internet Penetration	2.20%	3.91%	6.20%	13.81%

Other Latin America				
Population (000)	109,890	111,726	113,641	119,582
Population Growth (%)		1.7%	1.7%	1.7%
Internet Users (000)	880	1,246	1,735	4,075
Internet Penetration	0.80%	1.12%	1.53%	3.41%

Total Latin America				
Population (000)	481,801	489,146	496,655	519,910
Population Growth (%)		1.5%	1.5%	1.5%
Internet Users (000)	7,346	12,501	19,402	43,803
Internet Penetration	1.52%	2.56%	3.91%	8.43%

Source: Goldman Sachs.

area where many existing eBay users had a rich heritage and often some current family members residing was attractive to eBay.

Yet another challenge was the mind-set of thinking of Latin America as a "homogeneous" continent whereas in fact there were important differences across the individual countries. The two existing major auction companies in this area recognized these differences by having country-specific sites in many individual countries. Within two years of their founding, the two major Latin American auction companies had the following "separate" trading rooms (each with their own currency, time, etc.):

	Meracado.Libre	*DeRemate*
Argentina	Yes	Yes
Brazil	Yes	Yes
Chile	Yes	Yes
Colombia	Yes	Yes
Ecuador	Yes	—
Mexico	Yes	Yes
Peru	—	Yes
Puerto Rico	—	Yes
Spain	Yes	—
Uruguay	Yes	Yes
U.S.A.	Yes	Yes
Venezuela	Yes	Yes

Bannick strongly believed that Latin America had much heterogeneity. However, he wondered about the economic rationale followed by both MercadoLibre and De Remate in planting their flag in so many countries in their early days.

Finally, there was the eBay managerial bandwidth issue to consider. How much bandwidth would Brazil and Latin America require from eBay management? As Bannick explained:

> We'd just done two huge acquisitions in the last couple of months. The most important thing for me at the time was to make sure we executed in Korea and in Europe. It was the number one priority. So did we really want to take on Latin America? How much would that diffuse our management efforts in markets [like Korean and southern Europe] that are 10 to 20 times the size?

Growth Through Acquisition?

A possible option for eBay would be to acquire an existing Latin American player (in addition to iBazar's Brazilian site). An acquisition had several attractive features. eBay was clearly experienced with acquisitions, and had experienced success in recent European acquisitions. As Rajiv Dutta, eBay's chief financial officer told the *San Francisco Chronicle*, "In each country there are 'baby eBays' developing, and some of those may be quality acquisition targets." Historically eBay had pursued acquisition when an appropriate candidate existed in the target market, and/or when a potential threat existed in the target market. In Latin America, eBay had acquired the third of the four major players in the market. Any of the three remaining players—MercadoLibre, DeRemate, and Lokau—could be potential acquisitions. Bannick had carried out several informal conversations with the management teams at both MercadoLibre and DeRemate, though acquisition was never seriously discussed or proposed by either side. Alex Aboitiz of MercadoLibre explained that an acquisition could be ideal for both eBay and the acquired company:

These [potential target] companies were looking for strategic partners and eBay was clearly the partner of choice. Some of the companies were also running out of cash, and a cash infusion could save them. For eBay, this meant the price was right. Furthermore, a partnership would help eBay speed towards their goal of global growth. The expansion into Latin America would be facilitated by an experienced management team already in place.

■ DECISIONS

Matt Bannick picked up his sandwich and walked back to his office with his note-covered napkin in hand. He planned to put his thoughts on paper in a draft memo to Meg Whitman that covered several points, including:

- assessment of Latin America and a rough timeline for eBay's future in the region;
- his thoughts on how eBay should grow in the region, including in which countries and with whom; and
- for the immediate future—how to handle the Brazilian division of iBazar.

Camar Automotive Hoist

In September 2000, Mark Camar, President of Camar Automotive Hoist (CAH), had just finished reading a feasibility report on entering the European market in 2001. CAH manufactured surface automotive hoists, a product used by garages, service stations, and other repair shops to lift cars for servicing (Exhibit 1). The report, prepared by CAH's marketing manager, Pierre Gagnon, outlined the opportunities in the European Union and the entry options available.

Mark was not sure if CAH was ready for this move. While the company had been successful in expanding sales into the U.S. market, he wondered if this success could be repeated in Europe. He thought that, with more effort, sales could be increased in the United States. On the other hand, there were some positive aspects to the European idea. He began reviewing the information in preparation for the meeting the following day with Pierre.

■ CAMAR AUTOMOTIVE HOIST

Mark, a design engineer, had worked for eight years for the Canadian subsidiary of a U.S. automotive hoist manufacturer. During those years, he had spent considerable time designing an above-ground (or surface) automotive hoist. Although he was very enthusiastic about the unique aspects of the hoist, including a scissor lift and wheel alignment pads, senior management expressed no interest in the idea. In 1990, Mark left the company to start his own business with the express purpose of designing and manufacturing the hoist. He left with the good wishes of his previous employer, who had no objections to Mark's plans to start a new business.

Over the next three years, Mark obtained financing from a venture capital firm, opened a plant in Lachine, Quebec, and began manufacturing and marketing the hoist, called the Camar Lift (Exhibit 1).

From the beginning, Mark had taken considerable pride in the development and marketing of the Camar Lift. The original design included a scissor lift and a safety locking mechanism that allowed the hoist to be raised to any level and locked in place. As well, the scissor lift offered easy access for the mechanic to work on the raised vehicle. Because the hoist was fully hydraulic and had no chains or pulleys, it required little maintenance. Another key feature was the alignment turn plates that were an integral part of the lift. The turn plates meant that mechanics could accurately and easily perform wheel alignment jobs. Because it was a surface lift, it could be installed in a garage in less than a day.

Mark continually made improvements to the product, including adding more safety features. In fact, the Camar Lift was considered a leader in automotive lift safety. Safety was an important factor in the automotive hoist market. Although hoists seldom malfunctioned, when they did it often resulted in a serious accident.

This case was prepared by Professor Gordon H. G. McDougall, Wilfrid Laurier University, as the basis for class discussion rather than to illustrate either effective or ineffective handling of an administrative situation. Certain names and data have been disguised and are not useful for research purposes. Used by permission.

EXHIBIT 1

Examples of Automotive Hoists

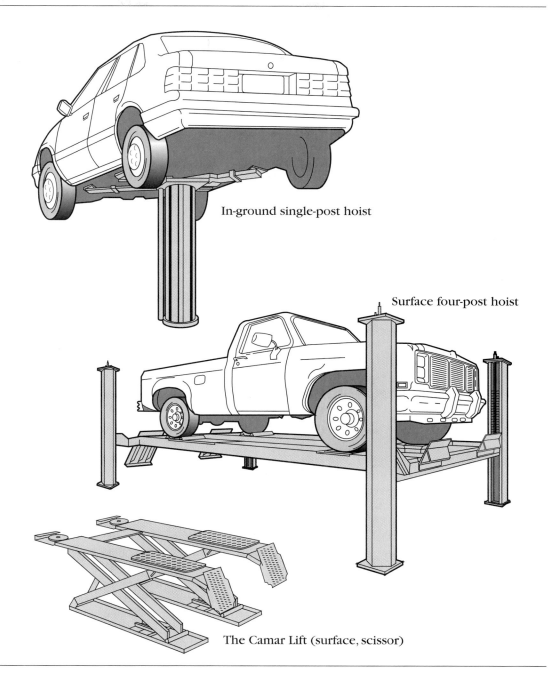

In-ground single-post hoist

Surface four-post hoist

The Camar Lift (surface, scissor)

The Camar Lift developed a reputation in the industry as the "Cadillac" of hoists; the unit was judged by many as superior to competitive offerings because of its design, the quality of the workmanship, the safety features, the ease of installation, and the five-year warranty. Mark held four patents on the Camar Lift, including the lifting mechanism on the scissor design and the safety locking mechanism. A number of versions of the product were designed that made the Camar Lift suitable

EXHIBIT 2

Camar Automotive Hoist—Selected Financial Statistics (1997–1999)

	1997	1998	1999
Sales	$6,218,000	$7,454,000	$9,708,000
Cost of Sales	4,540,000	5,541,000	6,990,000
Contribution	1,678,000	1,913,000	2,718,000
Marketing Expenses*	507,000	510,000	530,000
Administrative Expenses	810,000	820,000	840,000
Earnings Before Tax	361,000	583,000	1,348,000
Units Sold	723	847	1,054

Source: Company records

* Marketing expenses in 1999 included advertising ($70,000), four salespeople ($240,000), marketing manager, and three sales support staff ($220,000).

(depending on the model) for a variety of tasks, including rustproofing, muffler repairs, and general mechanical repairs.

In 1991, CAH sold 23 hoists and had sales of $172,500. During the early years, the majority of sales were to independent service stations and garages specializing in wheel alignment in the Quebec and Ontario market. Most of the units were sold by Pierre, who was hired in 1992 to handle the marketing side of the operation. In 1994, Pierre began using distributors to sell the hoist to a wider geographic market in Canada. In 1996, he signed an agreement with a large automotive wholesaler to represent CAH in the U.S. market. By 1999, the company had sold 1,054 hoists and had sales of $9,708,000 (Exhibit 2). In 1999, about 60 percent of sales were to the United States with the remaining 40 percent to the Canadian market.

■ INDUSTRY

Approximately 49,000 hoists were sold each year in North America. Hoists were typically purchased by any automotive outlet that serviced or repaired cars, including new-car dealers, used-car dealers, specialty shops (e.g., muffler repair, transmission repair, wheel alignment), chains (e.g., Firestone, Goodyear, Canadian Tire), and independent garages. It was estimated that new-car dealers purchased 30 percent of all units sold in a given year. In general, the specialty shops focused on one type of repair, such as mufflers or rust proofing, while "non-specialty" outlets handled a variety of repairs. While there was some crossover, in general CAH competed in the specialty shop segment and, in particular, those shops that dealt with wheel alignment. This included chains such as Firestone and Canadian Tire as well as new-car dealers (e.g., Ford) that devote a certain percentage of their lifts to the wheel alignment business and independent garages that specialized in wheel alignment.

The purpose of a hoist was to lift an automobile into a position where a mechanic or service person could easily work on the car. Because different repairs required different positions, a wide variety of hoists had been developed to meet specific needs. For example, a muffler repair shop required a hoist where the mechanic could gain easy access to the underside of the car. Similarly, a wheel alignment job required a hoist that offered a level platform where the wheels could be adjusted as well, providing easy access for the mechanic. Pierre estimated that 85 percent of CAH's sales were to the wheel alignment market in service centers like Firestone, Goodyear, and Canadian Tire, and independent garages that specialized in wheel alignment. About 15 percent of sales were made to customers who used the hoist for general mechanical repairs.

Firms purchasing hoists were part of an industry called the *automobile aftermarket*. This industry was involved in supplying parts and service for new and used cars and was worth more than $54 billion at retail in 1999 while servicing the approximately 14 million cars on the road in Canada. The industry was large and diverse; there were more than 4,000 new-car dealers in Canada, more than 400 Canadian Tire stores, more than 100 stores in each of the Firestone and Goodyear chains, and more than 220 stores in the Rust Check chain.

The purchase of an automotive hoist was often an important decision for the service station owner or dealer. Because the price of hoists ranged from $3,000 to $15,000, it was a capital expense for most businesses.

For the owner/operator of a new service center or car dealership, the decision involved determining what type of hoist was required and then what brand would best suit the company. Most new service centers or car dealerships had multiple bays for servicing cars. In these cases, the decision would involve what types of hoists were required (for example, inground, surface). Often more than one type of hoist was purchased, depending on the service center/dealership needs.

Experienced garage owners seeking a replacement hoist (the typical hoist had a useful life of 10 to 13 years) would usually determine what products were available and then make a decision. If the garage owners were also mechanics, they would probably be aware of two or three types of hoists but not very knowledgeable about the brands or products currently available. Garage owners or dealers who were not mechanics probably knew very little about hoists. The owners of car or service dealerships often bought the product that was recommended and/or approved by the parent company.

■ COMPETITION

Sixteen companies competed in the automotive lift market in North America: four Canadian and twelve U.S. firms. With the advent of the Free Trade Agreement in 1989, the duties on hoists between the two countries were phased out over a 10-year period; by 1999 exports and imports of hoists were duty-free. For Mark, the import duties had never played a part in any decisions—the fluctuating exchange rates between the two countries had a far greater impact on selling prices. In the past three years the Canadian dollar had fluctuated between $.65 and $.70 versus the U.S. dollar (e.g., CDN$1.00 buys US$.65) and forecast rates were expected to stay within this range.

A wide variety of hoists were manufactured in the industry. The two basic types of hoists were in-ground and surface. As the names imply, in-ground hoists required a pit to be dug "in-ground," where the piston that raised the hoist was installed. In-ground hoists were either single post or multiple post, were permanent, and obviously could not be moved. In-ground lifts constituted approximately 21 percent of total lift sales in 1999 (Exhibit 3). Surface lifts were installed on a flat surface, usually concrete. Surface lifts came in two basic types, post lift hoists and scissor hoists. Surface lifts, compared to in-ground lifts, were easier to install and could be moved if necessary. Surface lifts constituted 79 percent of total lift sales in 1999. Within each type of hoist (e.g., post lift surface hoists), there were numerous variations in terms of size, shape, and lifting capacity.

The industry was dominated by two large U.S. firms, AHV Lifts and Berne Manufacturing, who together held approximately 60 percent of the market. AHV Lifts, the

EXHIBIT 3

North American Automotive Lift Unit Sales, by Type (1997–1999)

	1997	*1998*	*1999*
In-ground			
Single post	5,885	5,772	5,518
Multiple post	4,812	6,625	5,075
Surface			
Two-post	27,019	28,757	28,923
Four-post	3,862	3,162	3,745
Scissor	2,170	2,258	2,316
Other	4,486	3,613	3,695
Total	48,234	50,187	49,272

Source: Company records

largest firm with approximately 40 percent of the market and annual sales of about $60 million, offered a complete line of hoists (that is, in-ground, surface) but focused primarily on the in-ground market and the two-post surface market. AHV Lifts was the only company that had its own direct salesforce; all other companies used (1) only wholesalers or (2) a combination of wholesalers and company salesforce. AHV Lifts offered standard hoists with few extra features and competed primarily on price. Berne Manufacturing, with a market share of approximately 20 percent, also competed in the in-ground and two-post surface markets. It used a combination of wholesalers and company salespeople and, like AHV Lifts, competed primarily on price.

Most of the remaining firms in the industry were companies that operated in a regional market (e.g., California, British Columbia) and/or that offered a limited product line (e.g., four-post surface hoist).

CAH had two competitors that manufactured scissor lifts. AHV Lift marketed a scissor hoist that had a different lifting mechanism and did not include the safety locking features of the Camar Lift. On average, the AHV scissor lift was sold for about 20 percent less than the Camar Lift. The second competitor, Mete Lift, was a small regional company with sales in California and Oregon. It had a design that was very similar to the Camar Lift but lacked some of its safety features. The Mete Lift, regarded as a well-manufactured product, sold for about 5 percent less than the Camar Lift.

■ MARKETING STRATEGY

As of early 2000, CAH had developed a reputation for a quality product backed by good service in the hoist lift market, primarily in the wheel alignment segment.

The distribution system employed by CAH reflected the need to engage in extensive personal selling. Three types of distributors were used: a company sales force, Canadian distributors, and a U.S. automotive wholesaler. The company sales force consisted of four salespeople and Pierre. Their main task was to service large "direct" accounts. The initial step was to get the Camar Lift approved by large chains and manufacturers, and then, having received the approval, to sell to individual dealers or operators. For example, if General Motors approved the hoist, then CAH could sell it to individual General Motors dealers. CAH sold directly to the individual dealers of a number of large accounts including General Motors, Ford, Chrysler, Petro-Canada, Firestone, and Goodyear. CAH had been successful in obtaining manufacturer approval from the big three automobile manufacturers in both Canada and the United States. As well, CAH had also received approval from service companies such as Canadian Tire and Goodyear. To date, CAH had not been rejected by any major account; however, in some cases, the approval process had taken more than four years.

In total, the company sales force generated about 25 percent of the unit sales each year. Sales to the large "direct" accounts in the United States went through CAH's U.S. wholesaler.

The Canadian distributors sold, installed, and serviced units across Canada. These distributors handled the Camar Lift and carried a line of noncompetitive automotive equipment products (for example, engine diagnostic equipment, wheel balancing equipment) and noncompetitive lifts. These distributors focused on the smaller chains and the independent service stations and garages.

The U.S. wholesaler sold a complete product line to service stations as well as manufacturing some equipment. The Camar Lift was one of five different types of lifts that the wholesaler sold. Although the wholesaler provided CAH with extensive distribution in the United States, the Camar Lift was a minor product within the wholesaler's total line. While Pierre did not have any actual figures, he thought that the Camar Lift probably accounted for less than 20 percent of the total lift sales of the U.S. wholesaler.

Both Mark and Pierre felt that the U.S. market had unrealized potential. With a population of 264 million people and more than 146 million registered vehicles, the U.S. market was almost 10 times the size of the Canadian market (population of 30 million, approximately 14 million vehicles). Pierre noted that the six New England states (population over 13 million); the three largest mid-Atlantic states (population over 38 million), and the three largest mid-Eastern states (population over 32 million) were all within a day's drive of the factory in Lachine. Mark and Pierre had considered setting up a sales office in New York to service these states, but they were concerned that the U.S. wholesaler would not be willing to relinquish any of its territory. They had also considered working more closely with the wholesaler to encourage it to "push" the Camar Lift. It appeared that the wholesaler's major objective was to sell a hoist, not necessarily the Camar Lift.

CAH distributed a catalogue-type package with products, uses, prices, and other required information for both distributors and users. In addition, CAH advertised in trade publications (for example, *AutoInc.*), and Pierre travelled to trade shows in Canada and the United States to promote the Camar Lift.

In 1999, Camar Lifts sold for an average retail price of $10,990 and CAH received, on average, $9,210 for each unit sold. This average reflected the mix of sales through the three distribution channels: (1) direct (where CAH received 100 percent of the selling price), (2) Canadian distributors (where CAH received 80 percent of the selling price) and (3) the U.S. wholesaler (where CAH received 78 percent of the selling price).

Both Mark and Pierre believed that the company's success to date was based on a strategy of offering a superior product that was primarily targeted to the needs of specific customers. The strategy stressed continual product improvements, quality workmanship, and service. Personal selling was a key aspect of the strategy; salespeople could show customers the benefits of the Camar Lift over competing products.

■ THE EUROPEAN MARKET

Against this background, Mark had been thinking of ways to continue the rapid growth of the company. One possibility that kept coming up was the promise and potential of the European market. The fact that Europe became a single market in

1993 suggested that it was an opportunity that should at least be explored. With this in mind, Mark asked Pierre to prepare a report on the possibility of CAH entering the European market. The highlights of Pierre's report follow.

History of the European Union

The European Union (EU) had its basis formed from the 1957 "Treaty of Rome," in which five countries decided it would be in their best interests to form an internal market. These countries were France, Spain, Italy, West Germany, and Luxembourg. By 1990, the EU consisted of 15 countries (the additional ten were Austria, Belgium, Denmark, Finland, Greece, Ireland, the Netherlands, Portugal, Sweden, and the United Kingdom) with a population of more than 376 million people. Virtually all barriers (physical, technical, and fiscal) in the European Community were scheduled to be removed for companies located within the EU. This allowed the free movement of goods, persons, services, and capital.

In the last 15 years, many North American and Japanese firms had established themselves in the EU. The reasoning for this was twofold. First, these companies regarded the community as an opportunity to increase global market share and profits. The market was attractive because of its sheer size and lack of internal barriers. Second, there was continuing concern that companies not established within the EU would have difficulty exporting to the EU due to changing standards and tariffs. To date, this concern has not materialized.

Market Potential

The key indicator of the potential market for the Camar Lift hoist was the number of passenger cars and commercial vehicles in use in a particular country. Four countries in Europe had more than 20 million vehicles in use, with Germany having the largest domestic fleet of 44 million vehicles followed in order by Italy, France, and the United Kingdom (Exhibit 4). The number of vehicles was an important indicator, since the more vehicles in use meant a greater number of service and repair facilities that needed vehicle hoists—potentially the Camar Lift.

An indicator of the future vehicle repair and service market was the number of new-vehicle registrations. The registration of new vehicles was important as this maintained the number of vehicles in use by replacing cars that had been retired. Again, Germany had the most new cars registered in 1997 and was followed in order by France, the United Kingdom, and Italy.

EXHIBIT 4

Number of Vehicles (1997) and Population (000s)

Country	Vehicles in Use (000s)		New Vehicle Registrations (000s)	Population (000s)
	Passenger	Small Commercial		
Germany	41,400	2,800	3,500	82,100
France	28,000	4,900	2,200	59,000
Italy	33,200	2,700	1,800	56,700
United Kingdom	23,500	4,000	2,200	59,100
Spain	15,300	2,800	1,000	39,200

Based primarily on the fact that a large domestic market was important for initial growth, the selection of a European country should be limited to the "Big Four" industrialized nations: Germany, France, the United Kingdom, or Italy. In an international survey, companies from North America and Europe ranked European countries on a scale of 1 to 100 on market potential and investment-site potential. The results showed that Germany was favored for both market potential and investment site opportunities, while France, the United Kingdom, and Spain placed second, third, and fourth respectively. Italy did not place in the top four in either market or investment-site potential. However, Italy had a large number of vehicles in use, had the fourth largest population in Europe, and was an acknowledged leader in car technology and production.

Little information was available on the competition within Europe. There was, as yet, no dominant manufacturer as was the case in North America. At this time, there was one firm in Germany that manufactured a scissor-type lift. The firm sold most of its units within the German market. The only other available information was that 22 firms in Italy manufactured vehicle lifts.

Investment Options

Pierre felt that CAH had three options for expansion into the European market: licensing, joint venture, or direct investment. The licensing option was a real possibility, as a French firm had expressed an interest in manufacturing the Camar Lift.

In June 2000, Pierre had attended a trade show in Detroit to promote the Camar Lift. At the show he met Phillipe Beaupre, the marketing manager for Bar Maisse, a French manufacturer of wheel alignment equipment. The firm, located in Chelles, France, sold a range of wheel alignment equipment throughout Europe. The best-selling product was an electronic modular aligner that enabled a mechanic to use a sophisticated computer system to align the wheels of a car. Phillipe was seeking a North American distributor for the modular aligner and other products manufactured by Bar Maisse.

At the show, Pierre and Phillipe had a casual conversation where both explained what their respective companies manufactured; they exchanged company brochures and business cards, and both went on to other exhibits. The next day, Phillipe sought out Pierre and asked if he might be interested in having Bar Maisse manufacture and market the Camar Lift in Europe. Phillipe felt the lift would complement Bar Maisse's product line and the licensing would be of mutual benefit to both parties. They agreed to pursue the idea. Upon his return to Lachine, Pierre told Mark about these discussions and they agreed to explore this possibility.

Pierre called a number of colleagues in the industry and asked them what they knew about Bar Maisse. About half had not heard of the company but those who had commented favorably on the quality of its products. One colleague, with European experience, knew the company well and said that Bar Maisse's management had integrity and would make a good partner. In July, Pierre sent a letter to Phillipe stating that CAH was interested in further discussions; he enclosed various company brochures including price lists and technical information on the Camar Lift. In late August, Phillipe responded, stating that Bar Maisse would like to enter a three-year licensing agreement with CAH to manufacture the Camar Lift in Europe. In exchange for the manufacturing rights, Bar Maisse was prepared to pay a royalty rate of 5 percent of gross sales. Pierre had not yet responded to this proposal.

A second possibility was a joint venture. Pierre had wondered if it might not be better for CAH to offer a counter proposal to Bar Maisse for a joint venture. He had not worked out any details, but Pierre felt that CAH would learn more about the European market and probably make more money if they were an active partner in Europe. Pierre's idea was a 50–50 proposal where the two parties shared the investment and the profits. He envisaged a situation where Bar Maisse would manufacture the Camar Lift in its plant with technical assistance from CAH. Pierre also thought that CAH could get involved in the marketing of the lift through the Bar Maisse distribution system. Further, he thought that the Camar Lift, with proper marketing, could gain a reasonable share of the European market. If that happened, Pierre felt that CAH was likely to make greater returns with a joint venture.

The third option was direct investment, where CAH would establish a manufacturing facility and set up a management group to market the lift. Pierre had contacted a business acquaintance who had recently been involved in manufacturing fabricated steel sheds in Germany. On the basis of discussions with his acquaintance, he estimated the costs involved in setting up a plant in Europe at (1) $250,000 for capital equipment (welding machines, cranes, other equipment); (2) $200,000 in incremental costs to set up the plant; and (3) carrying costs to cover $1,000,000 in inventory and accounts receivable. While the actual costs of renting a building for the factory would depend on the site location, he estimated that annual building rent including heat, light, and insurance would be about $80,000. Pierre recognized that these estimates were guidelines, but he felt that the estimates were probably within 20 percent of actual costs.

■ THE DECISION

As Mark considered the contents of the report, a number of thoughts crossed his mind. He began making notes concerning the European possibility and the future of the company:

- If CAH decided to enter Europe, Pierre would be the obvious choice to head up the "direct investment" option or the "joint venture" option. Mark felt that Pierre had been instrumental in the success of the company to date.

- While CAH had the financial resources to go ahead with the direct investment option, the joint venture would spread the risk (and the returns) over the two companies.

- CAH had built its reputation on designing and manufacturing a quality product. Regardless of the option, Mark wanted the firm's reputation to be maintained.

- Either the licensing agreement or the joint venture appeared to build on the two companies' strengths; Bar Maisse had knowledge of the market, and CAH had the product. What troubled Mark was whether this apparent synergy would work or whether Bar Maisse would seek to control the operation.

- It was difficult to estimate sales under any of the options. With the first two (licensing and joint venture), it would depend on the effort and expertise of Bar Maisse; with the third, it would depend on Pierre.

- CAH's sales in the U.S. market could be increased if the U.S. wholesaler would "push" the Camar Lift. Alternatively, the establishment of a sales office in New York to cover the eastern states could also increase sales.

As Mark reflected on the situation, he knew he should probably get additional information—but it wasn't obvious exactly what information would help him make a yes or no decision. He knew one thing for sure—he was going to keep this company on a fast growth track, and at tomorrow's meeting he and Pierre would decide how to do it.

Vector Marketing Corporation
Growth Drivers

Jim Stitt, CEO and president of ALCAS Corporation, Vector Marketing Corporation's parent corporation, glanced at his watch as he left the first staff meeting of 2003 and mentally calculated whether he had time to make a call to the "Vector Triad," Michael Lancellot, Al DiLeonardo, and Bruce Goodman, before his next appointment. "Growth. . . extraordinary growth," he murmured to no one in particular as he walked into his office, "that's the fundamental opportunity ALCAS has through Vector for the foreseeable future—the opportunity to grow revenues to at least $500 million annually in the next five years. How do we make sure that it happens. . . and that we ultimately get to $1 billion in annual revenues?"

The ALCAS corporate long-range planning team was scheduled to meet in the next six weeks, and Stitt had been pressing Lancellot, DiLeonardo, and Goodman to have a five-year marketing strategy for Vector ready to discuss at the meeting. When he arrived at his office, Stitt opened the "issues file" that he had compiled over the past few weeks and thought back to his conversation with the Vector Triad earlier in the day. He had told the Triad that there were three major issues that had to be addressed before the marketing strategy could be finalized:

- How to staff up the field sales organization to power the growth that all the executives felt was there.

- How to ensure that facilities, equipment, and people were in place to manufacture the volume of products projected for 2004 and 2005.

- How to identify the major growth driver for the second half of the decade and begin laying the groundwork for its implementation.

Each of the issues was important, but identifying the major growth driver for the second half of the decade and laying the groundwork for its implementation was considered the most important strategic issue facing the company and the one that needed the most effort to develop thoroughly. Stitt rose from his desk and walked down the hall to Erick Laine's office.

As Stitt left his office, Erick J. Laine, chairman of ALCAS Corporation, swiveled his chair around to look out his office window. His office overlooked the employees' parking lot, and Laine noticed that the first snow of 2003 was beginning to dust the vehicles. A smile spread across Laine's face as he recalled the company's achievements in 2002. ALCAS Corporation again experienced record revenues. Corporate revenues in 2001 had increased 37.5 percent over the year 2000, to $210 million, and in 2002 were just over $253 million. Employee profit-share bonuses would probably again be at peak levels for the seventh year in a row, and employee morale was high. Laine could hardly wait to see the detailed financials for 2002.

Laine reflected with satisfaction on the conversation he had just had with Jim Stitt. Stitt was correct, he thought. An opportunity for phenomenal revenue growth lay before the company. Exceptional growth had been underway for three years, but how to sustain it for the long term? In the past two years, the company had purchased more than $19 million in new equipment and added nearly three acres of manufacturing and distribution space just to meet increased demand.

As Laine contemplated the future of ALCAS Corporation and the nation's economy, he considered the effect that the Internet debacle of the last two years had on both the nation's economy and the stock market. He also reflected sadly on the September 11th tragedy the year before and the impact it had had on the economy and the market. He was grateful that ALCAS was a privately held company and, therefore, sheltered from the stock market's fluctuations, but what would the economy be like in the next few years, and what would the company's marketplace look like? The market for high-end durables, and even the consumer price index, had remained reasonably stable through all the turmoil in the last two years, but would this stability continue?[1] These were certainly headache-causing questions, but Laine believed that the answers held a wonderful future for the company.

■ ALCAS CORPORATION

Although in 2003 ALCAS Corporation was more than 50 years old, its roots went back yet another 50 years. In 1902, ALCOA, Aluminum Company of America, created the WearEver subsidiary to market aluminum cookware using in-home (non-store) demonstrations. In 1948, ALCOA and W. R. Case & Sons, then the country's leading cutlery producer, formed a joint venture to manufacture high-quality kitchen cutlery that would be marketed through ALCOA's WearEver subsidiary. The joint venture was incorporated as Alcas Cutlery Corporation (*Al* for ALCOA and *cas* for Case), and a manufacturing facility was established in Olean, a small city on the western edge of New York. In 1949, the first CUTCO cutlery was produced.

Case sold its 49 percent interest in Alcas Cutlery Corporation to ALCOA in 1972. Ten years later, in September 1982, ALCOA sold Alcas Cutlery Corporation through a leveraged buyout to a management team led by Erick Laine, then the president of Alcas Cutlery Corporation. Since 1982 the company has been a closely held private company. Company revenues at the time of the leveraged buyout were slightly less than $5 million.

After a period of aggressive growth and a series of reorganizations and acquisitions, Alcas Cutlery Corporation changed its name to ALCAS Corporation and morphed into a "family" consisting of five interrelated companies. As shown in Exhibit 1, ALCAS is now the parent holding company of CUTCO Cutlery Corporation, Vector Marketing Corporation, CUTCO International, and KA-BAR Knives, all of which are administratively headquartered in Olean, and all of which are profit centers. CUTCO Cutlery Corporation manufactures the cutlery that Vector Marketing Corporation markets in North America (the United States and Canada), and CUTCO International markets CUTCO products outside of North America.

KA-BAR Knives, a marketer of sport and utility knives established in 1898 under the name of Union Razor Company, was acquired by ALCAS in 1996. KA-BAR knives are marketed domestically through independent sales representatives and internationally by an in-house staff to direct marketers, wholesalers, and retailers. CUTCO

---

[1]Case writer's note: Consumer prices increased an average of 2.6 percent per year during the latter part of the 1990s and the early 2000s.

EXHIBIT 1

ALCAS Corporate Structure

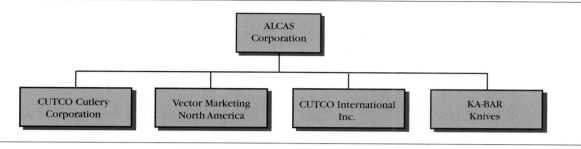

Source: Company records.

Cutlery Corporation manufactures 33 of the 63 KA-BAR knife products. The other 30 knife products are manufactured by a U.S. supplier and two suppliers located in Asia. Although KA-BAR knives vary widely in price, the best-selling ones are priced between $30 and $50.

By the end of 2002, ALCAS was the largest manufacturer of high-quality kitchen cutlery and accessories in North America. The corporate vision was to "become the largest, most respected and widely recognized cutlery company in the world. . . ." ALCAS presently employs more than 1,100 people at its Olean headquarters, an increase of more than 80 percent since 1997. (See Exhibit 2 on page 118 for a picture of the Olean headquarters.) Exhibit 3 on page 119 presents the revenues obtained by the various ALCAS entities during the period 1998–2002.

■ THE CUTCO PRODUCT LINE

The original CUTCO product line consisted of nine basic items, including a table knife and fork, a carving knife and fork, a butcher knife, and a spatula. (The CUTCO name was derived from a company once owned by ALCOA, *Co*oking *UT*ensil *CO*mpany.) On April 29, 1949, the first order of CUTCO cutlery—six knives, two forks, a spatula, and two storage trays—was shipped by automobile from Olean to New Kensington, Pennsylvania. The CUTCO product line has since grown to include more than 500 SKUs (stock-keeping units), nearly double that of a decade ago. Even so, the core of the product line still consists of ten basic knives that can be purchased individually or in various sets ranging from a two-item gift pack to the Homemaker Set Plus Eight, which consists of the ten basic knives and eight table knives displayed in a wooden block. Exhibit 4 on page 120 shows the Homemaker Set Plus Eight displayed in the wooden block. Retail prices in 2002 ranged from $22 for a vegetable peeler to $805 for a complete Homemaker Set Plus Eight. The company also offers a complementary line of accessory kitchen products, including various types of shears, potato masher, pizza cutter, turning fork, and cleaver, as well as pocket and hunting knives and garden pruner. In 2000–2001, the company introduced a five-piece set of flatware (teaspoon, dinner fork, table knife, soup spoon, salad fork) and a set of six serving pieces. A four-piece garden tool set was also introduced in 2000–2001. In 2002, the company added an ice cream scoop, a cheese knife, and a "bird's beak" paring knife. Despite these non-knife additions, "cutting edge" cutlery items still account for about 90 percent of sales.

EXHIBIT 2

ALCAS Corporate Headquarters

Source: Company files.

From the first product made, CUTCO cutlery was designed to be the finest cutlery in the world. Prices of CUTCO products are increased by an average of 5 percent every other year (e.g., 1995, 1997, 1999, 2001), primarily to offset one-half of rising labor and material costs. The other half is meant to be covered with improved efficiencies.

In addition to being known for its outstanding quality, CUTCO cutlery is instantly recognizable because of its exclusive and unique wedge-lock handle and the Double-D® knife blade grind. First introduced in 1952 and improved considerably in 1972, the (universal) wedge-lock handle is an ergonomically designed and scientifically contoured handle that creates a firm yet comfortable and safe grip by wedging the fingers apart across the handle while locking the thumb and fingers in place. Handles are made from thermo-resin material that will not chip, crack, fade, or absorb moisture and come in two colors—classic brown and pearl white. Every CUTCO product has a full lifetime ("forever") guarantee that includes free factory sharpening. If any product is found to be defective, it will be replaced at no cost to the customer.

EXHIBIT 3

ALCAS Consolidated Revenues, 1998–2002 ($ in Thousands)

	1998	1999	2000	2001	2002
Vector (direct sales)	$102,102	$106,733	$128,166	$182,764	$220,642
Vector (catalog/Internet)	9,386	10,662	11,089	11,705	13,535
CUTCO International	9,968	9,132	10,160	12,153	15,231
KA-BAR/Misc.	2,290	3,554	3,531	3,420	3,732
Total	$123,746	$130,081	$152,946	$210,042	$253,140

Source: Company records.

The Double-D® grind, which was added to certain knife blades in 1960, consists of three razor-sharp edges angled and recessed in such a fashion that a blade can cut forward, backward, and straight down without the cutting edges becoming worn through contact with plates, cutting boards, or countertops. Unlike the typical serrated knife blade, the Double-D® knife blade does not rip or tear what is being cut and can be resharpened (at the factory).

■ VECTOR MARKETING CORPORATION

CUTCO cutlery was marketed from 1949 through 1970 by a segment of the WearEver sales force. In 1970, the CUTCO sales force was merged with the rest of the WearEver cookware sales force and the two product lines marketed together for the next decade. In 1981, WearEver decided to convert its sales force into approximately 100 small, independent distributorships that would market the CUTCO product line. On January 1, 1982, Alcas Cutlery Corporation assumed responsibility for all CUTCO marketing activities.

During the next three years, several multi-state independent distributorships evolved through mergers and buyouts. In 1985, the company saw the need to have greater control over its sales efforts and took steps to create a nationwide in-house CUTCO sales and marketing infrastructure. It did so by first acquiring the largest independent distributor, Vector Marketing Corporation, which operated in the eastern United States. Vector Marketing Corporation became a wholly owned subsidiary of ALCAS. Shortly thereafter, ALCAS acquired a second independent distributorship, CWE Industries, which operated in the western part of the United States. The acquisition of BrekMar Corporation, which operated in the Midwest, and three southern-based distributorships followed, all of which were merged into Vector Marketing Corporation.

During a recent meeting of the board of directors, Erick Laine reflected back on the time when Vector Marketing Corporation was acquired in 1985. He remarked that:

> The addition of Vector Marketing was the most significant organizational move we made since we purchased Alcas Cutlery Corporation from ALCOA in 1982. Acquiring an in-house CUTCO marketing capability (Vector) gave us complete control over our major market. With that capability, marketing decisions relating to new office locations, expansion plans, rate of growth, and distribution methods were under the control of the company.

CUTCO cutlery has always been marketed through direct selling. This is viewed as a distinct advantage because it allows the quality and performance features of the

EXHIBIT 4

Homemaker Set Plus Eight

Source: Company files.

product to be explained and demonstrated directly to potential customers. Direct selling sets ALCAS apart from its major competitors, J. A. Henckels Zwillingswerk, Inc. ("Henckels"), Wusthof-Trident, and Chicago Cutlery.[2] These competitors have traditionally used department stores and mass merchandisers to market their products. Of the three major competitors, Henckels, a German company, is the largest, with U.S. retail sales approximating those of Vector. Although the "street price" of Henckels cutlery is typically 25 percent less than its list price, Vector and Henckels list prices are very similar for comparable items.

Vector Marketing Corporation Structure

Vector Marketing Corporation sales efforts are organized by geographic location. The United States consists of six geographic sales regions (Central, Midwest, Northeast, Eastern, Southwest, and Western). These six regions are respectively combined into two "companies"—Vector East (Midwest, Northeast, and Eastern regions) and Vector West (Central, Southwest, and Western regions). Each of these two "companies" is headed by a president. Canada is treated as a separate region and is headed by a sales manager.

The president of Vector East, Al DiLeonardo, the president of Vector West, Bruce Goodman, and the sales manager of Canada all report to the president/CEO of Vector Marketing Corporation, Michael Lancellot. Exhibit 5 contains an illustrative chart showing the Vector East sales organization.

Each of the six regions is headed by a regional sales manager, who in some cases is an executive vice president, and a regional sales director. Within each region are five

EXHIBIT 5

Vector East Sales Organization

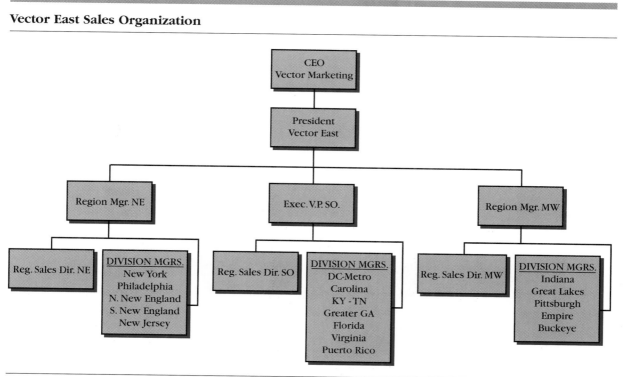

Source: Company records.

---

[2]Chicago Cutlery, a longtime U.S. competitor, discontinued its U.S. manufacturing operations in 2001.

to six divisions, and within these divisions are a total of approximately 250 district or permanent offices and another 280 "branch offices." Branch offices are summer offices that operate for about 17 weeks every summer. A district office operates throughout the year and typically is located in an area with a population base of at least 200,000 people.

The people actually selling CUTCO cutlery are independent contractors who effectively operate their own business. As such, these sales representatives are paid a commission on the products they sell. Although they are eligible for demonstration-based compensation, sales representatives usually move to a full sales commission compensation system that exceeds demonstration-based compensation soon after they start selling. None of the sales representatives receives a salary from the company.

What makes the sales representatives unique is that, for the most part, they are college students who sell CUTCO products during their summer vacations. As a consequence of this "summer selling season," a majority of Vector's sales occur in the May—August period each year. Fifty-five percent of the sales representatives are males. Each summer tens of thousands of college students are recruited to sell CUTCO products. Recruiting is done through a variety of methods, including newspaper advertisements, direct mailings, the Internet, and on-campus recruiting. The more than 1,600 sales representatives selling for an entire summer earn an average of $3,000. The average earnings of the top 250 sales representatives in a typical summer are in excess of $10,000, and the very top sales representatives can earn more than $20,000 for a summer of selling. Vector is structured to facilitate recruiting, training, and motivating college students to sell CUTCO products, and it does so very well.

Sales are made through in-home presentations in which sales representatives demonstrate the superiority of CUTCO cutlery by cutting food items as well as rope and leather. These presentations are prearranged through referrals and appointments and are considered to be a key to company success. As Marty Domitrovich, the president of Vector Training, frequently says,

> Selling yourself is paramount in any sales situation. I firmly believe that people buy from individuals they like, and there is no better way to make a solid impression than face to face. There is no substitute for the personal touch that comes from sitting across from someone in his or her home and allowing them to actually try your product. Personal, professional demonstrations sell CUTCO cutlery. Period.

Often a sales representative's first sale is made to his or her parents, relatives, or neighbors. Interestingly enough, about one in six sales are made each year to previous purchasers of CUTCO products. Because CUTCO products tend to "sell themselves" after people have seen a demonstration, there is relatively little need for a "hard sell" on the part of sales representatives. Training emphasizes appointment setting, demonstrations, order writing, and referrals. There is no "cold calling" or door-to-door selling.

Sales representatives typically meet with their Vector managers Monday evenings to discuss the prior week's activities and plan the current week's activities. During these meetings, the sales representatives turn in their sales orders and money collected from the prior week. The managers overnight the orders and money to Olean, where orders are approved and filled.

In 2002, Vector filled more than 1 million separate orders in the United States, up from 580,000 orders in 1999, with each order representing one direct sales customer. Products are shipped directly to customers within three to five weeks during the summer selling season, and within two to three weeks at other times. Both UPS and the U.S. Postal Service are used to deliver products. The projected operating margin of Vector in 2002 on direct sales was approximately 10.5 percent.[3]

---

[3]All operating margins are disguised, although the relationships among them are representative.

To motivate sales representatives, Vector employs a variety of promotional activities, events, and competitions. Not only are the sales representatives rewarded directly for the sales they make (through their commissions); they are also eligible to receive trophies, bonuses, trips, and even scholarships for achieving certain sales levels. Those sales representatives who are particularly successful have the additional opportunity to establish and manage one of the branch offices. Managing a branch office requires a dedicated and active program of recruiting and training throughout the preceding school year.

The particular direct-selling model that Vector uses differs from the direct-selling models used by virtually all other direct-selling firms. Only one other direct-selling company, the Southwestern Company in Nashville, Tennessee, uses college students as its primary sales force to market a variety of books and related educational materials during summer vacations. Even so, Vector and Southwestern possess very different marketing strategies. For example, whereas Vector trains small groups of sales representatives at district or branch offices, Southwestern simultaneously trains hundreds of sales representatives at its Nashville headquarters. Moreover, whereas Vector sales representatives use a referral system for sales leads, Southwestern sales representatives focus on door-to-door presentations. Finally, whereas Vector sales representatives typically sell in their home cities, Southwestern sales representatives typically are assigned to sell in a city away from their home.

Vector Catalog Sales

Because over 90 percent of Vector sales representatives only sell for one summer, the customers they create often lose contact with CUTCO products and the company. To maintain a continuing relationship with, and service to, these customers, Vector initiated a small catalog mailing in 1985. This catalog has since been expanded to 36 pages and is mailed to 4 million CUTCO customers as often as four times per year. Mailings are timed to occur in September through December so as not to conflict with the summer selling season. In 2002, catalog mailings generated more than 100,000 orders and almost $12 million in sales, with a corresponding operating margin of 15 percent.[4] If the customer of a current Vector sales representative makes a catalog purchase, the sales representative and the sales representative's manager receive a reduced commission. The sales representative will continue to receive commissions on catalog sales for as long as he or she maintains a very modest level of activity. If a sales representative is no longer actively selling for Vector, only the sales representative's manager receives a commission for a catalog purchase.

The Vector Customer

The company's most recent estimate is that more than 12 million customers have purchased CUTCO products since its inception in 1949. Many of the early customers' names were not captured, but since 1989, when Vector began systematically capturing and retaining customers' names and addresses, a database of more than 6 million customers has been constructed. The "typical" Vector customer is a married homeowner with one or more older children, relatively affluent, and holds a managerial or professional employment position. The average annual income of a typical customer is more than $50,000, and in certain geographic areas the average customer's annual income is in excess of $100,000. Most Vector customers have at least a bachelor's degree. Sixty percent are between 40 and 59 years of age. There is no discernible difference between Vector's direct-sales customers and customers who purchase from its catalogs. The typical customer enjoys reading, traveling, cooking, and gardening.

---

[4]All operating margins are disguised, although the relationships among them are representative.

■ INTERNATIONAL EXPANSION

International expansion began in 1990, with the establishment of Vector Marketing Canada, Ltd. By the end of 2001, Canadian sales accounted for about 4.2 percent of ALCAS corporate revenues. CUTCO Korea began as a subsidiary of ALCAS Corporation in 1992. For cultural reasons the standard Vector marketing approach was not very successful in Korea, but a change in the recruiting approach produced revenues of nearly $8 million in Korea in 1996. Due to a serious dip in the Asian economy, revenues declined to $2–$3 million in 1997–1998. By 2001 revenues had rebounded to $8.5 million and were estimated to be $13 million in 2002.

CUTCO International was created in 1994 to manage marketing efforts beyond North America, and CUTCO Korea was placed under its control that year. Australian and German sales organizations were established in 1996 under the direction of CUTCO International. The German operation was converted to an independently owned distributorship in 1999 due to accumulating losses. In 2001 the decision was made to discontinue the Australian operation because of losses experienced there. Other international entries included those in the United Kingdom and Costa Rica. The CUTCO International operating margin was about 2.5 percent.[5]

■ A NOTE ON DIRECT-SELLING

Direct selling is face-to-face selling away from a fixed business location. Therefore, it is a form of nonstore retailing. The direct-selling industry consists of numerous well-known firms such as AMWAY, Avon, Mary Kay Cosmetics, and Tupperware. At the same time, however, the industry itself is not well known, principally because it is "invisible." By definition, there are no physical stores and, because direct selling is essentially a push marketing strategy, direct-selling firms do very little advertising. Hence, there is less public awareness of most direct-selling firms than of major retailers. In addition, the majority of direct-selling firms are small, privately owned firms created and operated by entrepreneurs, many of whom often want a low public profile.

According to the Direct Selling Association, the direct-selling industry trade association, in 2000 (the most recent year for which data are available) industry sales in the United States were approximately $25.5 billion. This figure reflects an average annual growth rate of 5.2 percent over the preceding five years. (Globally, direct sales were estimated to be about $83.6 billion, with Japan accounting for slightly more than $25 billion.)

Virtually all direct sellers (99.8 percent) are independent contractors. Of the estimated 11 million direct sellers in the United States in 2000 (up from 8.5 million in 1996), 72 percent are women, and 77 percent are married. Seventy-two percent are 35 years of age or older. Only 10 percent work full time in direct selling, and one source estimated that nearly half earn less than $500 annually. A survey of direct sellers conducted for the Direct Selling Association in 1997 revealed that substantial numbers worked only to earn money for a particular purchase (such as a vacation), worked only because they liked and used a product or service themselves, or worked because they enjoyed the social aspect of direct selling.

Sixty-five percent of direct selling takes place in a residence. Over 70 percent of direct selling takes place on a one-to-one basis. The other major form of direct selling is the "party plan." Party plan selling represents a combination of group selling and

---

[5]All operating margins are disguised, although the relationships among them are representative.

entertainment. The Longaberger basket party, in which six to eight homemakers get together at the home of a hostess, is the quintessential example of party plan selling.

The most popular form of one-to-one direct selling is network or multilevel marketing. About 83 percent of all independent contractors selling one-to-one do so through a multilevel marketing program. Direct sellers in a multilevel marketing program are not only rewarded for the sales that they personally make. They are also rewarded for the sales that people they recruit make, and the sales of people in turn recruited by the individuals they recruited, and so on (i.e., their "downline" in multilevel marketing terms; hence, the notion of multi or many levels).

The Typical Direct-Selling Customer

Of the products and services marketed through direct selling, personal care and home-related products and services are among the most popular. Cosmetics, vitamins and dietary supplements, kitchenware, long-distance telephone services, and cleaning products are currently among the best-selling products and services in the direct-selling industry. Even so, virtually any product or service seems to be amendable to this mode of marketing. In Japan, for example, a large percentage of new automobiles is sold door-to-door.

Although estimates differ, a majority of the households in the United States have at one time or another purchased a product or service from a direct seller. This suggests that the typical direct-selling customer should have characteristics similar to people in general or at least people who shop retail stores. More specifically, direct-selling customers tend to be affluent females 35–54 years of age. Relative to the overall population in the United States, the typical direct-selling customer has somewhat more education and a larger household income.

Direct-Selling Web Sites

Although the majority of direct-selling firms have Web sites, and the Web accounted for about 5.5 percent of direct-selling sales dollars in 2000, most direct-selling Web sites are limited to providing customer service and contact information. During the past few years several large direct-selling firms experimented with marketing their products and services on the Web. For example, Avon, which claims to be the largest direct seller of cosmetics and personal care products, began marketing some of its products through several Internet retailers as well as on its own Web site. In fiscal 2002, approximately 20 percent of Avon's $6 billion in revenues were derived from Internet-related activities. Tupperware, which markets storage containers, kitchen aids, educational materials, and toys, launched an extensive Web site to market its products, facilitate party planning by its distributors, recruit new distributors, and provide distributor locations for customers. The company attempted to create the feel of a magazine by incorporating a recipe database and recipe exchange mechanism, information forum, and so forth on its Web site.

Alticor, the parent company of AMWAY, the largest direct seller of household, personal care, nutritional, and ancillary products, took a slightly different approach to Web-based marketing. It established a new company and the independent Web site Quixtar ("Quick-Star"), through which it intended to sell not only its own products but those of many other firms as well. In fiscal 2002, Quixtar reported revenues of $901 million, an increase of $150 million over fiscal 2001 revenues and about 20 percent of Alticor's worldwide revenues.

Although estimates vary dramatically, Census Bureau information indicates that about 45 percent of people 18 years of age or older in the United States have access to the Internet. By the end of 2002, the modal customer of a Web-based company in the United States was a male 35–54 years of age with an average income in excess of $50,000. The average shopper was estimated to spend about $54 online in 2002.

Nearly all college students have access to the Web and an e-mail address, whether through school or at home.

Even though only a small percentage of the consumers presently accessing the Web actually purchase anything, the number of consumers shopping on the Web is predicted to increase significantly in the next few years. Books, computer software and hardware, music, and travel seem to be the product and service categories from which consumers are most likely to make a purchase on the Web. Cutlery products can be found on the Web at a variety of sites. The entire CUTCO product line is displayed on *www.cutco.com*, although this site presently does not provide for online purchasing.

■ VECTOR INTERNET ACTIVITY

For the last four years, Michael Lancellot and the other executives at Vector and ALCAS have been grappling with the issue of what role the Internet should play in Vector marketing. During the period 1999–2002, Vector personnel worked on a strategy to use the Internet as a vehicle to recruit college students to be sales representatives, with the result that a major Web site *(www.workforstudents.com)* is currently being used. The number of applications received through this Web site has been very encouraging, and the Internet recruiting strategy as a whole appears to be very successful. Consequently, the company plans to expand its Internet recruiting efforts in the coming year.

For more than four years Vector has operated a customer-oriented Web site *(www.cutco.com)* focusing on customer service and product information. Within the past three years, Vector has, on a trial basis, offered selected catalog customers the opportunity to make their "catalog purchases" online using a Web site restricted to prior CUTCO purchasers *(www.cutco-online.com)*. In 2002, approximately 14,000 purchases of CUTCO products were made online, with corresponding revenues of $1.8 million and an operating margin of 20 percent.[6]

Vector service representatives report that they have received numerous requests from consumers who are not currently CUTCO product owners but who want to order CUTCO products online. Up to this point these consumers have been advised that they can only order from a sales representative. However, as Michael Lancellot has consistently maintained:

> We have a very important responsibility to make sure that we are meeting the needs of our customers. With a 50-year reputation for product quality and service, it is imperative that Vector meet customer expectations. One of these expectations is the ability to order CUTCO products online. However, while it is important that we meet the expectations of our customers, it is critically important that we protect the interest of our field sales organization.

Erick Laine agreed with Lancellot on the importance of meeting customer expectations, but he also cautioned that, "We certainly do not want to do anything with the Internet that would harm our direct-sales operation. We know that selling CUTCO products requires a personal demonstration and the hands-on opportunity to 'test drive' that only our field organization can provide."

■ GROWTH DRIVERS

In ALCAS corporate board and vector executive board meetings in the spring of 2002, there were general discussions of the major "growth drivers" of the business. The pur-

---

[6]All operating margins are disguised, although the relationships among them are representative.

pose of these discussions was primarily to gain an understanding of the dynamics of the very strong revenue growth that Vector had experienced in 2000 and 2001 and was projected to achieve in 2002.

As a vehicle to start the discussions, Erick Laine presented a chart listing "Key Growth Drivers" of the business in the past 20 years, starting in 1982, when Alcas Cutlery Corporation was purchased from ALCOA. Initially the CUTCO product, by virtue of its high performance, high quality, and exceptional demonstrability, constituted the major driver of the business.

Key Growth Drivers

Period	Major Driver
1982–1984	CUTCO Product
1985–1993	Vector College Recruiting Program/Geographic Growth
1994–1998	Investment in Recruiting and Training Program Enhancements
1999–2002	Investing in People/Investing in Structure

The introduction of the Vector College Recruiting Program was the second significant driver of the business. This recruiting program brought in college students who, by virtue of their intelligence, trainability, and ability to present themselves well, made outstanding sales representatives. The approaches used to recruit these college students generated many more recruits than any prior recruiting approach. Moreover, the fact that the recruits were college students resulted in a large number of candidates for management opportunities after graduation. The large number of managerial candidates in turn provided the management talent to open substantial numbers of new offices. New offices in turn fueled a high rate of geographic growth.

In 1994, the company decided to make major investments in money and energy to increase the effectiveness of the key elements of the Vector program. These investments went into activities such as enhancing the effectiveness of recruiting and training activities. Among the outcomes of these activities were the

- development of Internet recruiting approaches and mechanisms.
- assignment of a full-time manager to expand sales in fairs and shows. In the mid-1990s, Vector sales representatives attended less than 200 fairs and shows annually. In 2002 alone, they attended more than 700 fairs and shows.
- institution of a very solid and effective program for "field training"—an enhancement over the "classroom" training given every sales representative as he or she begins selling CUTCO products.

There was general agreement among the ALCAS board and Vector executive board members that the current major driver—investing in people/investing in structure—had provided the strongest revenue growth the company had experienced in the past 20 years. Significant investments in new leadership and building sales management structures spurred the strongest growth period in the history of the company and resulted in the development of what is clearly the strongest, most effective sales management organization the company has ever had. This driver was also believed to be able to increase revenues for the foreseeable future and would likely enable the company to achieve its $500 million annual revenue goal in the next five years. At the same time, though, since history had shown that growth drivers change over time, company executives believed that there would most likely need to be a new growth driver to take over in the second half of this decade, particularly since top management had set an informal goal of $1 billion in revenue by 2012. Both boards agreed to revisit the topic of growth drivers with the aim of making it a major focus for strategic planning sessions scheduled in September and November.

■ THE STRATEGIC PLANNING MEETINGS

In September 2002, and then again in November 2002, the combined ALCAS corporate board and Vector executive board devoted virtually all of two two-day strategic planning sessions to the topic of growth drivers. At the outset of the meetings it was generally acknowledged that it would be necessary to invest in and put into place at least one additional major growth driver in order to sustain the growth levels required to meet both the $500 million and $1 billion revenue goals that the company had set.

The two boards had met repeatedly in the prior months and together had identified a list of five candidate future growth drivers. Despite this identification, one individual in the meetings had continually argued that a "status quo strategy" should be seriously considered since, "after all, manufacturing can barely keep up with increased demand as it is, and the growth that we are naturally experiencing at the present time will be enough to carry the company to its goals. There are about 105 million households in the United States, of which more than 40 percent have incomes above $50,000, and nearly 15 million college students. Thus, both our potential market and our sales representative pool are sufficiently large to carry us without doing anything different. The risks associated with any of the proposed growth drivers are simply too great."

The five potential growth drivers identified were:

- Acquisitions
- Investment in recruiting approaches and recruiting structures
- Investment in expanding CUTCO brand recognition/preference
- Expansion into international markets
- Increased use of other sales channels

During the course of the four strategic planning meetings (two in September, two in November), comprehensive presentations were made of the pros and cons of each of the growth drivers under consideration. Considerable input from key officers was registered from these discussions.

Acquisitions

ALCAS Corporation has a very strong balance sheet, with cash reserves in excess of $20 million. With this level of cash reserves and a strong balance sheet, which would comfortably support borrowing from financial institutions, the prospect of acquisitions as a growth mechanism is very intriguing. Although none of the executives in attendance had tried to precisely tie down how much money would be required for an acquisition, there was some agreement that it would take a minimum of $10–$15 million to fund any meaningful acquisition.

Brent Driscoll (president of CUTCO Cutlery Corporation) and Jim Stitt in particular acknowledged that an appropriate acquisition of a company that provided increased cutlery manufacturing capacity might be an effective way of ensuring that the additional plant capacity needed for the growth expansion envisioned would be available in a timely fashion. Simultaneously, though, John Whelpley (vice president and chief administrative officer of Vector Marketing Corporation) and Peter Laine (executive vice president of finance and administration of ALCAS Corporation) expressed serious reservations about acquisitions as a major growth driver. Although both acknowledged that ALCAS had sizable cash reserves and ready access to additional cash to make acquisitions, they felt the real price of devoting much energy to acquisitions would be to dilute the focus on the company's core business, with the net effect being little or no additional net revenue growth.

Recruiting Approaches

Because the number of recruits is such an obvious driver of Vector's revenue growth, there was widespread agreement that additional investment and intensive efforts to improve the recruiting approaches could be a major growth driver. Vector is already very proactive in Internet recruiting, but it is conceivable there could be a substantial expansion of that activity and/or the application of new Internet technologies. It was agreed that an investment of at least $5–$10 million in technology and recruiting management infrastructure would be necessary to produce any measurable results.

Bruce Goodman, Al DiLeonardo, and Michael Lancellot all expressed considerable enthusiasm for the prospect of gaining additional growth through intensive energy and investment devoted to improving recruiting approaches and strategies. They reminded everyone present in the meetings that significant sales gains were made by implementing a variety of improved recruiting procedures during the mid-1990s and that with new technologies such as the Web now available at a much more sophisticated level, there could be additional gains made by investing in recruiting procedures and new technologies now.

CUTCO Brand Recognition

Marketing staff members present at the meetings pointed out that brand recognition is always a positive and, indeed, a necessary, component of consumer product sales. Over the past 20 years, and the past 15 years in particular, the CUTCO product line had grown substantially, not only in its brand recognition, but also in brand preference, with virtually no formal mass market advertising. One staff member offered the opinion that because brand preference was presently so high, it might be possible to dramatically increase current word-of-mouth brand recognition with relatively little additional expenditures and, subsequently, create significant revenue increases. For example, the staff member noted that annual public relations expenditures in the neighborhood of $1–$2 million might ultimately increase annual revenues by as much as $10–$20 million.

Creed Terry, Vector's executive vice president of marketing, spoke enthusiastically of the long-term sales benefits that could be gained through investments in creating more consumer exposure to the CUTCO brand. He reinforced the marketing staff member's opinion that because CUTCO already had significant brand recognition and preference, dramatic incremental increases in brand recognition could likely be gained without a great deal of extra investment.

International Expansion

Beginning with the entry into Canada in 1990 and then into Korea in 1992, ALCAS has periodically attempted to expand internationally. However, only Canada (which is now part of Vector Marketing Corporation) and Korea have been considered successful. Countries in which entries have been unsuccessful include the United Kingdom, Germany, Costa Rica, and Australia. Each country entry has been costly, with expenses averaging $10–$15 million per attempted entry. Because North American revenue growth has been especially strong in the past three to five years, ALCAS management has pulled back somewhat from its international activities, but still recognizes that there is a huge market potential in international markets.

Erick Laine and Mark George (president of CUTCO International) suggested the potential of reenergizing major international marketing efforts to capture a share of the consumer product market growth that is developing in Asian countries. Although they, like other ALCAS executives, realized that reengagement of aggressive international entries would take substantial financial resources (it is estimated that an expenditure of $10–$15 million per entry would still apply), and that it would require substantial investment of management personnel as well, they suggested the possibility of a strategic partner to take the CUTCO product line into China and Japan.

Other Sales Channels

Vector was presently utilizing both catalogs and the Web as supplementary channels to the direct-selling channel. The prospect that catalog and online revenues could be increased significantly was clearly evident, but not without the risk of some negative consequences for the conventional college student program. All of the executives present in the planning meetings were clearly aware of the potential of catalogs and the Web to generate higher profit margins than the direct-selling channel, and a wide-ranging discussion took place among the executives in which everyone participated. A key point of the discussion was the relatively minimal cost of expanding the two supplementary channels; an expenditure of $3 million was considered more than adequate to significantly increase both catalog and online revenues. However, as Jim Stitt noted at the conclusion of the meeting, "The cash expenditures required to obtain expanded catalog and Internet sales could be only a small portion of the total cost. If we don't do this right, the negative impact on our Vector sales force could be dramatic and result in lost sales far greater than any gains we could project from these two channels. Let's look at this very carefully."

Frito-Lay's® Dips

In late 1986, Ben Ball, Marketing Director, and Ann Mirabito, Product Manager, had just completed the planning review for the line of dips sold by Frito-Lay, Inc. Frito-Lay's® Dips were a highly profitable product line and had shown phenomenal sales growth in the past five years. Sales in 1985 were $87 million, compared with $30 million in 1981.

A major issue raised at the planning meeting was where and how Frito-Lay's® Dips could be developed further. Two different viewpoints were expressed. One view was that the dip line should be more aggressively promoted in its present market segment. This segment was broadly defined as the "chip dip" category. The other view was that Frito-Lay should also actively pursue the "vegetable dip" category. The company had recently introduced a shelf-stable, sour cream–based French onion dip nationally, and 1986 sales were forecasted to be $10 million. The new dip was the first sour cream–based dip introduced by Frito-Lay. Some executives felt that this dip could provide a bridge to the vegetable dip category, which could be further developed.

Frito-Lay executives had yet to decide how much emphasis to place on each category in 1987. Furthermore, expense budgets would need special consideration. More aggressive marketing would require higher marketing investment or at least a reallocation of funds, while at the same time the gross margin and profit contribution of dips would have to be preserved.

■ DIP CATEGORY

Dips are typically used as an appetizer, snack, or accompaniment to a meal. Dip popularity has risen in recent years as a result of the convenience of use, multiple uses, and "grazing" trends in the United States. Dips can be served along with chips, crackers, or raw vegetables.

The market for dips is highly fragmented and difficult to measure; however, upward of 80 percent of dip sales are accounted for by supermarkets. According to industry estimates, total dip retail dollar sales volume through supermarkets was $620 million in 1985. Two-thirds of this dollar volume was captured by prepared dips; the remaining one-third was accounted for by dip mixes for at-home preparation. About 55 percent of the prepared dips sold in supermarkets required refrigeration. The major competitors in this segment were Kraft, Borden, a large number of regional dairies, and numerous store brands. Refrigerated dip retail prices were typically in the range of $0.07 to $0.15 per ounce. About 45 percent of prepared dips were "shelf stable" (that is, they were packaged in metal cans and required no refrigeration). These dips could be displayed virtually anywhere in a supermarket, though they were typically located

This case was prepared by Jeanne Bertels, graduate student, under the supervision of Professor Roger A. Kerin, of the Edwin L. Cox School of Business, Southern Methodist University, as a basis for class discussion and is not designed to illustrate effective or ineffective handling of an administrative situation. The cooperation of Frito-Lay, Inc. is gratefully acknowledged. Selected financial and market data have been disguised or approximated and are not useful for research purposes. Copyright © 1986 by Roger A. Kerin. No part of this case may be reproduced without the written permission of the copyright holder.

near snack foods. Frito-Lay was the major competitor in shelf-stable dips, followed by regional chip manufacturers. Shelf-stable dip retail prices were in the range from $0.13 to $0.20 per ounce. By comparison, prices of dip mix were typically $0.09 per ounce (including the cost of a sour cream mixer or base).

Exhibit 1 shows a breakdown of the $620 million sales of dips in supermarkets by product type. Industry research indicates that dip dollar sales are growing at 10 percent per year, but this growth has come about because of price (inflationary) increases. No real growth is evident. Virtually all of the growth in 1984 and 1985 was accounted for by cheese-based dips, which captured market share from other dip flavors.

Flavor Popularity and Usage

Sour cream-based dips are the most popular flavor. Sour cream-based prepared dips and dip mixes account for about 50 percent of total dip sales. Cheese-based dips are the second most popular segment and account for about 25 percent of total dip sales. Bean and picante dips account for about 10 percent of total dip sales, and cream cheese-based dips account for the remaining 15 percent.

Dips are most frequently used with salty snacks, such as potato chips and corn chips. Whereas about 67 percent of total dip sales are linked to salty snack usage, virtually all bean and picante dips are consumed with salty snacks. One-fourth of cream cheese-based dip volume and 85 percent of cheese-based volume are linked with chip usage. Shelf-stable dips and many dip mixes are located adjacent to salty snack foods in supermarkets. Dry soup mixes are typically shelved with canned soups. Approximately 33 percent of all dip sales ($207 million) are linked to vegetable usage, and most of this volume is sold through supermarkets. Vegetable dips are located throughout supermarkets, in produce, soup mix, salad dressing, and snack sections, because they are viewed as a complementary as opposed to a primary product. Two brands—Libby's Dip Mixes and Bennett's Toppings/Dips—are located in the produce section, but each is sold only on a regional basis. Numerous local brands are also shelved in the produce section.

The popularity of Mexican food, including nachos, has fueled the growth of cheese-based dips in particular. New product introductions and accompanying market expenditures have also stimulated trial and acceptance of Mexican-style dips. For instance, Kraft, a major competitor in cheese dips, added Mexican flavors to both new and existing product lines in 1984. New products included Kraft Nacho Cheese Dip and Kraft Premium Jalapeno Cheese Dip. Kraft also added a Mexican zest to two of its popular products: Velveeta Mexican process cheese spread features jalapeno peppers, and Kraft Cheese Whiz is offered in variations of hot salsa and mild salsa. Kraft competes primarily in the refrigerated segment of the dip market. In late 1985, however, Kraft entered the shelf-stable market with Kraft Nacho Dip and Kraft Hot Nacho Dip.

Dip Substitutes

Even though the market for dips is large, it is estimated that about 20 percent of all dip volume consumed by households in the United States is homemade. In addition, many consumers use refrigerated salad dressings for dips, especially for vegetables. It is estimated that 35 percent of refrigerated salad dressing volume is used for dips. These refrigerated salad dressings are typically located in the produce section of supermarkets and include such brands as Marie's, Bob's Big Boy, Marzetti's, and Walden Farms, as well as a few local brands in different areas of the country. Market research indicates that refrigerated salad dressings sold in the produce section of supermarkets account for $67 million in retail sales annually. Retail sales of refrigerated salad dressings have been growing at a compound annual rate of 18 percent since 1978.

EXHIBIT 1

Estimated 1985 Supermarket Dip Sales at Retail Prices

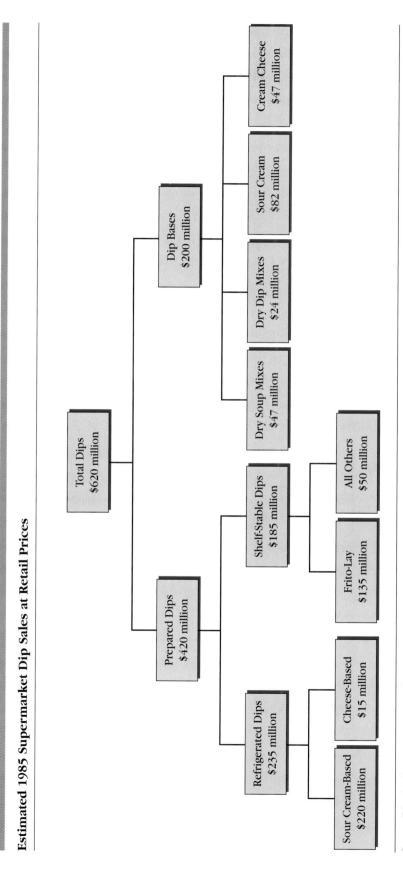

Source: Frito-Lay, Inc. company records.

Competitive Activity

Competitive activity in the dip market accelerated in 1984 and 1985. During these two years, numerous new products were introduced, and advertising expenditures increased. Industry sources estimated that dip competitors combined (excluding Frito-Lay) spent $58 million for consumer advertising alone in 1985. This figure was 25 percent higher than in 1984.

Equally noteworthy is the fact that large, well-financed companies began to aggressively pursue the dip market. For example, Campbell Soup introduced a nacho soup/dip and a line of vegetable dip mixes in 1985, and Lipton expanded its line of vegetable dip mixes and upgraded its packaging in 1985. According to Ann Mirabito, "These companies, coupled with Borden, Kraft, and regional chip manufacturers, have dramatically altered the competitive environment for chip dips in the past two years."

■ FRITO-LAY, INC.

Frito-Lay, Inc. is a division of PepsiCo, Inc., a New York–based diversified consumer goods and services firm. Other PepsiCo, Inc. divisions include Pizza Hut, Taco Bell, Pepsi Cola Bottling Group, Kentucky Fried Chicken, and PepsiCo Foods International. PepsiCo, Inc. recorded net sales of over $8 billion in 1985.

Frito-Lay is a nationally recognized leader in the manufacture and marketing of salty snack foods. The company's major salty snack products and brands include potato chips (Lay's®, O'Grady's®, Ruffles®, Delta Gold®), corn chips (Fritos®), tortilla chips (Doritos®, Tostitos®), cheese puffs (Cheetos®), and pretzels (Rold Gold®). Other well-known products include Baken-Ets® brand fried pork skins, Munchos® brand potato chips, and Funyuns® brand onion-flavored snacks. In addition, the company markets a line of nuts, peanut butter crackers, processed beef sticks, Grandma's® brand cookies and snack bars, and assorted other snacks. Frito-Lay's net sales in 1985 approached $3 billion.

Given the nature of its products, Frito-Lay competes primarily within what is termed the salty snack food segment of the snack food market. In 1985, Frito-Lay captured about 33 percent of the salty snack food tonnage sold in the United States.

The Dip Business

The first two dips introduced by Frito-Lay were Frito-Lay's® Jalapeno Bean Dip and Enchilada Bean Dip. These dips, marketed in the 1950s, were viewed as a logical complement to the company's Fritos® corn chips. A Picante Sauce Dip was introduced in 1978 to complement the newly introduced Tostitos® tortilla chips. These three dips were the only Frito-Lay dips sold until 1983.

Dip popularity accelerated extension of the dip product line in 1983. In late 1983 and early 1984, Frito-Lay introduced a number of cheese-based dips, including Mild Cheddar, Cheddar and Herb, Cheddar and Jalapeno, and Cheddar and Bacon, all of which were packaged in nine-ounce cans like the Mexican-style dips. According to Ben Ball, "Cheese dips were an extension of Frito-Lay's tortilla chip business and were a response to the Mexican food phenomenon sweeping the country." These new dips were shelf stable and were sold under the Frito-Lay's® brand name. Ball commented, "There was some discussion about whether or not we should use the Frito-Lay's® brand name with the cheese dips. However, we chose to stay with the Frito-Lay's® name to trade off the company's equity in salty snacks and capitalize on the company's strengths in marketing and distribution." The cheese dips, like their predecessors, were displayed in the salty snack section of supermarkets.

In 1986, Frito-Lay introduced its first sour cream-based, shelf-stable dip. This dip carried the Frito-Lay's® brand name and was displayed in the salty snack section of

EXHIBIT 2

Dollar Sales of Frito-Lay's® Dips (in Millions of Dollars)

Year	Mexican Dips	Cheese Dips	Sour Cream Dip	Total Dips
1986 (forecast)	$41	$48	$10	$99
1985	39	48	—	87
1984	40	55	—	95
1983	38	5	—	43
1982	35	—	—	35
1981	30	—	—	30

supermarkets. Its French onion flavor was viewed as an ideal accent for the company's potato chips. Industry data indicated that about 50 percent of salty snack volume sold in the United States was accounted for by potato chips. In addition, this onion dip was also deemed suitable as a vegetable dip.

Frito-Lay's dip sales for the period 1981–1985 are shown in Exhibit 2. Jalapeno Bean Dip and Picante Sauce Dip showed consistent, although slow growth in these years. Enchilada Bean Dip was dropped from the Mexican dip line in mid-1985 as a result of falling sales. Sales trends indicated that Mexican dips would show a 4 percent increase in sales in 1986. Cheese dips, by comparison, represented a huge success and outsold Mexican dips in their introductory year. Nevertheless, total dollar sales of dips declined in 1985, and forecasted 1986 sales of cheese dips would be unchanged from the previous year. Ann Mirabito attributed the decline to three factors. First, the novelty of shelf-stable cheese dips had passed. Mirabito commented, "We had good initial penetration for the products; however, with the passage of time, we settled down to a core group of customers." Second, she believed that increased competitive activity had played a part in slowing Frito-Lay's dip volume growth. Third, discontinuance of Enchilada Bean Dip had had an unexpected effect. It had been expected that consumers would switch to Frito-Lay's other Mexican dips. "They didn't, and we lost customers," Mirabito noted. Nevertheless, dips were a highly profitable product line. Exhibit 3 on page 136 shows the 1985 income statement for the dip product line.

Dip Distribution and Sales Effort

Frito-Lay distributes its products through 350,000 outlets nationwide. In 1985, 34,000 outlets were supermarkets, 47,000 were convenience stores, and 20,000 were nonfood outlets. The remainder of Frito-Lay's 350,000 outlets were small grocery stores, liquor stores, service stations, and a variety of institutional customers. The great majority of Frito-Lay's® Dips, however, are sold through supermarkets.

Frito-Lay's distribution system is organized around four geographical zones that cover the entire United States. Each zone contains distribution centers that inventory products for the Frito-Lay sales force, which is composed of over 10,000 individuals who make 400,000 sales and delivery calls during an average workday. Each Frito-Lay salesperson follows a specific, assigned route and is responsible for selling company products to present and potential customers on his or her route.

Frito-Lay uses a "front-door store delivery system," in which one person performs the sales and delivery functions. During a visit to a store, the driver/salesperson takes orders, unloads the product, stocks and arranges the shelves, and handles in-store merchandising. This sales and delivery system is particularly suited to the 270,000 nonchain outlets serviced by Frito-Lay. Experience has indicated, however, that sales calls on chain-store accounts, which include most supermarkets, virtually

EXHIBIT 3

Income Statement for Frito-Lay's® Dips, 1985 (in Thousand of Dollars)

	Mexican Dip	*Cheese Dip*	*Total Dip*
Net sales	$39,040	$48,296	$87,336
Gross margin	19,146	21,876	41,022
Marketing expense:			
Selling	8,798	11,044	19,842
Freight	1,464	1,825	3,289
Consumer advertising	60	87	147
Consumer and trade promotion	851	1,352	2,203
Total marketing expense	11,173	14,308	25,481
General and administrative overhead	2,781	3,791	6,572
Profit contribution	$5,192	$3,777	$8,969

Note: Selling and freight expenses are variable costs, consumer advertising and consumer and trade promotion are fixed costs budgeted annually, and general and administrative overhead expenses are fixed costs.

always require participation by a Frito-Lay Region or Division Manager. Such participation is necessary because chain-store snack buyers purchase for all outlets in the chain and approve in-store merchandising plans as well. Furthermore, the sales task and account servicing are more time-consuming and complex, although no less important, than those required for individual outlets (for example, "mom-and-pop" grocery stores and liquor stores).

Dip Marketing

Prior to 1983, the Frito-Lay's® Dips line was viewed as a nonpromoted profit producer. With the introduction of cheese dips in 1983, Frito-Lay began promoting dips, but virtually all marketing and promotion were directed toward retail-store snack food buyers in the form of trade-oriented promotions. In 1985, the emphasis shifted to consumer promotions such as product sampling and couponing to generate trial of the new products, and television and radio advertising was used for the first time since the 1950s. Frito-Lay's new product effort, coupled with increased competitive activity, resulted in further planned increases in consumer advertising and promotion in 1986. Exhibit 4 summarizes the advertising and merchandising expenditures for

EXHIBIT 4

Frito-Lay's® Dips Advertising and Merchandising Expenditures, 1983–1986

Year	*Consumer Advertising[a]*	*Consumer Promotion[b]*	*Trade Promotion[c]*	*Total*
1986	$1,170,000	$3,389,220	$169,290	$4,728,510
1985	147,045	1,459,050	744,101	2,350,196
1984	None	535,266	312,180	847,446
1983	None	22,322	425,478	447,800

[a] Television and radio advertising.

[b] Product sampling, cents-off coupons, etc.

[c] Trade discounts, advertising to store buyers, etc.

EXHIBIT 5

Frito-Lay's® Dips Consumer Promotion

dips for the period 1983–1986. Exhibit 5 illustrates a typical consumer promotion, and Exhibit 6 on page 138 shows a typical trade promotion. A Frito-Lay's® Dip television commercial is shown in Exhibit 7 on page 139.

Ann Mirabito provided the following rationale for the change in promotion emphasis:

> The phenomenal success of Frito-Lay's® Dips was due to two factors. First, we had the right products—cheese dips were novel, and our flavors were innovative. Second, we had the right merchandising location next to salty snacks. Prior to 1985, all of our advertising and merchandising spending was trade-oriented because our goal was to gain distribution in supermarkets and shelf space rapidly. Our consumer household penetration increased from 12 percent in 1983 to 20 percent in 1984, driven largely by placing cheese dips near salty snacks. In 1985, penetration flattened, indicating a need for consumer-pull marketing.

For the most part, dips were promoted jointly with Frito-Lay salty snacks, particularly Doritos® tortilla chips. According to Ben Ball, this approach was adopted because "dips are a complementary product." He added, "Growth occurred when our dips were displayed in conjunction with a natural carrier. That's how we built the chip dip business. This association was conveyed in our promotion and in our shelf placement with salty snacks."

EXHIBIT 6

Frito-Lay's® Dips Trade Promotions

4 COLUMN INCHES

6 COLUMN INCHES

EXHIBIT 7

Frito-Lay's® Dips Television Commercial

TRACY-LOCKE
CLIENT: Frito-Lay, Inc.
PRODUCT: Frito Lay's® Dips

TITLE: "Magnetism"
LENGTH: 15 Seconds
COMM'L. NO.: PECD 6193
FIRST AIR DATE: 2/21/86

SFX: LABORATORY SOUNDS
SCIENCE EDITOR: Do you forget Frito-Lay's®
Dip?

Use the theory of magnetism,

so when you pick up the chips you automatically
. . .

SFX: METALLIC CLINK
SCIENCE EDITOR: pick up the Dip.

ANNCR (VO) AND SCIENCE EDITOR EATING:
The best way to remember Frito-Lay's® Dip is to
taste [CRUNCH! Mmmmm!] what it does to our
chips.

SCIENCE EDITOR: What an attractive concept!

■ FUTURE GROWTH OPPORTUNITIES

Two opportunities for the Frito-Lay's® Dips product line were raised at the planning review meeting. Frito-Lay could continue to develop the chip dip market, where it already had a strong foothold, or it could pursue the vegetable dip market as well, using the new sour cream–based dip as a spearhead. The decision would have significant resource allocation consequences, since it was unlikely that funds for dip advertising and merchandising would be increased in 1987 beyond the $4.73 million budgeted for 1986.

Chip Dip Opportunity

One view expressed at the planning meeting was that Frito-Lay should capitalize on its foothold in the chip dip market and attempt to expand the market and build market share. Several arguments were made for this strategy. First, research indicated that only 20 percent of chips were currently eaten with dips; furthermore, only 45 percent of all U.S. households used dips in 1985, whereas 97 percent used salty snacks. "This indicated a major opportunity to build penetration through more aggressive advertising," according to a Frito-Lay executive. Second, research indicated that in 1985 the average number of times shelf-stable dips were purchased by households was four. It was felt that this frequency could be increased through frequency-building promotions such as on-pack coupon offers to encourage repeat sales. In 1985, the purchase frequency of all Frito-Lay's® Dips was 3.6 times per year. A third argument in favor of focusing attention on the chip dip market was the increased competitive activity: 40 new Mexican-style cheese dips had been introduced since 1983. Although many were regional products, each vied for shelf space in or near the salty snack section of supermarkets. At the same time, it was believed that Kraft would be introducing additional products that would compete in the chip dip market. A fourth argument was that historically Frito-Lay had not promoted dips aggressively. It was believed that the typical ratio of advertising and merchandising spending to sales (A/S ratio) for prepared dips was 10 percent.[1] Refrigerated salad dressings had an A/S ratio of 3 percent, and salad dressing dry mixes had an A/S ratio of 13.6 percent. In 1985, Frito-Lay's A/S ratio for its dip product line was 2.7 percent. Therefore, the 1986 advertising and merchandising budget had been more than double 1985 expenditures. (A breakdown of these expenses is shown in Exhibit 8.) A fifth argument was that Frito-Lay could spin off other products from its sour cream–based dip.

EXHIBIT 8

Planned Frito-Lay's® Dips Advertising and Merchandising Expenditures by Product Line, 1986

Product Line	Consumer Advertising	Consumer Promotion	Trade Promotion	Total
Mexican and cheese dips[a]	$1,170,000	$2,740,320	$ 56,790	$3,967,110
Sour cream dip	0	648,900	112,500	761,400
Total	$1,170,000	$3,389,220	$169,290	$4,728,510

[a] Total advertising and merchandising expenditures for Mexican and cheese dips were roughly proportional to 1985 sales of the two product lines.

---

[1] The A/S ratio is calculated by dividing total expenditures for consumer advertising and promotion and trade promotion by total sales for a given year.

Other executives argued that the opportunity in the chip dip category was less promising. They based their argument on three points. First, competitive activity was such that Frito-Lay could only hope to hold, not improve, its position in the chip dip category. The effort and expense necessary to increase penetration and/or increase purchase frequency in the congested chip dip category could be better spent on attacking vegetable dips, where the competition (such as Marie's) was less formidable and more fragmented. Second, Frito-Lay's recent sales growth in dips was due to new products (for example, cheese-based dips), and it was not clear that further product line extensions could produce continued growth. There was also significant potential for cannibalization of existing cheese dips if the line was expanded further. Third, the new sour cream dip represented a break with Mexican-style dips and cheese dips and was probably more suitable for vegetable dipping. To promote and distribute this new dip solely as a chip dip rather than as a vegetable dip could mean a missed opportunity.

Vegetable Dip Opportunity

Executives who voiced concern about focusing on the chip dip category also raised several points in favor of the vegetable dip opportunity. First, they noted that 33 percent of dip sales were linked to vegetables. Moreover, industry research indicated that only one-fourth of the dollar volume associated with vegetable dipping was accounted for by refrigerated salad dressings, such as Marie's. The remainder was accounted for by dip mixes and refrigerated dips, and no major competitors had a strong competitive position in the market. Second, research indicated that sour cream-based dips were more popular than cheese dips for vegetable dipping. Third, trend data indicated that consumers were becoming concerned about the nutritional value and salt content of prepared foods.[2] It was felt that this trend could affect preferences for vegetables and salty snacks and, as a result, dips. Fourth, the Frito-Lay's® Dips line now had a sour cream–based dip that had not yet been promoted and merchandised for vegetable dipping. Fifth, no major competitor had introduced a shelf-stable dip for vegetables. Frito-Lay had pioneered the shelf-stable business for chip dips, and some executives felt that a similar opportunity existed for vegetable dips. Finally, a cost analysis indicated that the gross margins would be largely unaffected. The gross margin on Frito-Lay's sour cream dip was 45 percent.

Other executives expressed the view that pursuing the vegetable dip segment would not be easy, however. These executives cited research indicating that supermarket executives preferred that dips suitable for vegetable dipping be handled by their produce warehouse. This meant that Frito-Lay's front-door delivery system would not be favored. Distribution through the produce warehouse would also involve dealing with supermarket produce buyers and managers. Frito-Lay had never dealt with these individuals in the past, and some company executives believed that a totally new sales approach would be necessary. Even though a complete cost analysis had not been conducted, it was estimated that selling expenses could increase to 25 percent of sales. Current sales expense was 22.7 percent. Freight expense would not be affected. As of 1986, the sour cream dip was not allocated any general and administrative overhead. Furthermore, Frito-Lay driver/salespeople were unfamiliar with merchandising practices in the produce section of supermarkets. This same research indicated that any new vegetable dip should be shelved next to refrigerated salad dressing or near produce.

---

[2]Bob Messenger, "Consumers See the Light. . . and the Lean, with a Touch of Pizzazz," *Prepared Foods* (November 1985): 46–49.

A second concern was that Frito-Lay's® Dips would lose some economies in advertising and merchandising. Frito-Lay's® Dips had been promoted jointly with the company's chips in the past and thus traded on the "halo effect" of Frito-Lay salty snacks. Mirabito acknowledged that vegetable dips would have to "go it alone" because Frito-Lay's halo effect might not translate to vegetable dips.

A third concern expressed at the meeting was that any foray into vegetable dips would require more than a single item. In addition to the French onion flavor, other flavors (such as ranch style) would be necessary. Such line extensions would require added research and development expenses and promotional support, as had been the case with the successful introduction of cheese dips.

The planning meeting adjourned without resolution of the issue. Ben Ball asked Ann Mirabito to give the "chip dip versus vegetable dip" question further consideration. She was to prepare a recommendation for another meeting to be scheduled within 30 days.

South Delaware Coors, Inc.

Larry Brownlow was just beginning to realize the problem was more complex than he had thought. The problem, of course, was giving direction to Manson and Associates regarding what research should be completed by February 20, 1990, to determine market potential of a Coors beer distributorship for a two-county area in southern Delaware. With data from this research, Larry would be able to estimate the feasibility of such an operation before the March 5 application deadline. Larry knew his decision on whether to apply for the distributorship was the most important career choice he had ever faced.

■ LARRY BROWNLOW

Larry was just completing his MBA and, from his standpoint, the Coors announcement of expansion into Delaware could hardly have been better timed. He had long ago decided the best opportunities and rewards were in smaller, self-owned businesses and not in the jungles of corporate giants. Because of a family tragedy some three years earlier, Larry found himself in a position to consider small business opportunities such as the Coors distributorship. Approximately $500,000 was held in trust for Larry, to be dispersed when he reached age 30. Until then, Larry and his family were living on an annual trust income of about $40,000. It was on the basis of this income that Larry had decided to leave his sales engineering job and return to graduate school for his MBA.

The decision to complete a graduate program and operate his own business had been easy to make. Although he could have retired and lived off investment income, Larry knew such a life would not be to his liking. Working with people and the challenge of making it on his own, Larry thought, were far preferable to enduring an early retirement.

Larry would be 30 in July, about the time money would actually be needed to start the business. In the meantime, he had access to about $15,000 for feasibility research. Although there certainly were other places to spend the money, Larry and his wife agreed the opportunity to acquire the distributorship could not be overlooked.

■ COORS, INC.

Coors' history dated back to 1873, when Adolph Coors built a small brewery in Golden, Colorado. Since then, the brewery had prospered and become the fourth-largest seller of beer in the country. Coors' operating philosophy could be summed

This case was prepared by Professor James E. Nelson and doctoral student Eric J. Karson, of the University of Colorado, as a basis for class discussion and is not designed to illustrate effective or ineffective handling of an administrative situation. Certain data have been disguised. Copyright 1990 by the Business Research Division, College of Business and Administration and the Graduate School of Business Administration, University of Colorado, Boulder, Colorado 80309-0419.

up as "hard work, saving money, devotion to the quality of the product, caring about the environment, and giving people something to believe in." Company operation is consistent with this philosophy. Headquarters and most production facilities are still located in Golden, Colorado, with a new Shenandoah, Virginia, facility aiding in nation-wide distribution. Coors is still family operated and controlled. The company had issued its first public stock, $127 million worth of nonvoting shares, in 1975. The issue was enthusiastically received by the financial community despite its being offered during a recession.

Coors' unwillingness to compromise on the high quality of its product is well known both to its suppliers and to its consuming public. Coors beer requires constant refrigeration to maintain this quality, and wholesalers' facilities are closely controlled to ensure that proper temperatures are maintained. Wholesalers are also required to install and use aluminum can recycling equipment. Coors was one of the first breweries in the industry to recycle its cans.

Larry was aware of Coors' popularity with many consumers in adjacent states. However, Coors' corporate management was seen by some consumers to hold anti-union beliefs (because of a labor disagreement at the brewery some ten years ago and the brewery's current use of a nonunion labor force). Some other consumers perceived the brewery to be somewhat insensitive to minority issues, primarily in employment and distribution. These attitudes—plus many other aspects of consumer behavior—meant that Coors' sales in Delaware would depend greatly on the efforts of the two wholesalers planned for the state.

■ MANSON RESEARCH PROPOSAL

Because of the press of his studies, Larry had contacted Manson and Associates in January for their assistance. The firm was a Wilmington-based general research supplier that had conducted other feasibility studies in the South Atlantic region. Manson was well known for the quality of its work, particularly with respect to computer modeling. The firm had developed special expertise in modeling such things as population and employment levels for cities, counties, and other units of area for periods of up to 10 years into the future.

Larry had met John Rome, senior research analyst for Manson, in January and discussed the Coors opportunity and appropriate research extensively. Rome promised a formal research proposal (Exhibit 1) for the project, which Larry now held in his hand. It certainly was extensive, Larry thought, and reflected the professionalism he expected. Now came the hard part—choosing the more relevant research from the proposal—because he certainly couldn't afford to pay for it all. Rome had suggested a meeting for Friday, which gave Larry only three more days to decide.

Larry was at first overwhelmed. All the research would certainly be useful. He was sure he needed estimates of sales and costs in a form allowing managerial analysis, but what data in what form? Knowledge of competing operations' experience, retailer support, and consumer acceptance also seemed important for feasibility analysis. For example, what if consumers were excited about Coors and retailers indifferent, or the other way around? Finally, several of the studies would provide information that could be useful in later months of operation, in the areas of promotion and pricing, for example. The problem now appeared more difficult than before!

It would have been nice, Larry thought, to have had some time to perform part of the suggested research himself. However, there just was too much in the way of class assignments and other matters to allow him that luxury. Besides, using Manson and Associates would give him research results from an unbiased source. There would be plenty for him to do once he received the results anyway.

E X H I B I T 1

Research Proposal by Manson and Associates

January 16, 1990

Mr. Larry Brownlow
1198 West Lamar
Chester, PA 19345

Dear Larry:

It was a pleasure meeting you last week and discussing your business and research interests in Coors wholesaling. After further thought and discussion with my colleagues, the Coors opportunity appears even more attractive than when we met.

Appearances can be deceiving, as you know, and I fully agree some formal research is needed before you make application. Research that we recommend would proceed in two distinct stages and is described below.

Stage One Research, Based on Secondary Data and Manson Computer Models:

Study A: National and Delaware Per-Capita Beer Consumption for 1988–1992.
Description: Per-capita annual consumption of beer for the total population and for population age 21 and over in gallons is provided.
Source: Various publications, Manson computer model
Cost: $1,000

Study B: Population Estimates for 1986–1996 for Two Delaware Counties in Market Area.
Description: Annual estimates of total population and population age 21 and over are provided for the period 1986–1996.
Source: U.S. Bureau of Census, *Sales Management Annual Survey of Buying Power,* Manson computer model
Cost: $1,500

Study C: Estimates of Coors' Market Share for 1990–1995.
Description: Coors' market share for the two-county market area based on total gallons consumed is estimated for each year in the period 1990–1995. These data will be projected from Coors' nationwide experience.
Source: Various publications, Manson computer model
Cost: $2,000

Study D: Estimates of Number of Liquor and Beer Licenses for the Market area, 1990–1995.
Description: Projections of the number of on-premise sale operations and off-premise sale operations are provided.
Source: Delaware Department of Revenue, Manson computer model
Cost: $1,000

Study E: Beer Taxes Paid by Delaware Wholesalers for 1988 and 1989 in the Market Area.
Description: Beer taxes paid by each of the six presently operating competing beer wholesalers are provided. These figures can be converted to gallons sold by applying the state gallonage tax rate ($.06 per gallon).
Source: Delaware Department of Revenue
Cost: $200

Study F: Financial Statement Summary of Wine, Liquor, and Beer Wholesalers for Fiscal Year 1988.
Description: Composite balance sheets, income statements, and relevant measures of performance for 510 similar wholesaling operations in the United States are provided.
Source: Robert Morris Associates Annual Statement Studies, 1989 ed.
Cost: $49.50

Stage Two Research, Based on Primary Data:

Study G: Consumer Study.
Description: Study G involves focus-group interviews and a mail questionnaire to determine consumers' past experience, acceptance, and intention to buy

(continued on next page)

EXHIBIT 1 *(continued)*

Coors beer.[a] Three focus-group interviews would be conducted in the two counties in the market area. From these data, a questionnaire would be developed and sent to 300 adult residents in the market area, utilizing direct questions and a semantic differential scale to measure attitudes toward Coors beer, competing beers, and an ideal beer.
Source: Manson and Associates
Cost: $6,000

Study H: Retailer Study.
Description: Group interviews would be conducted with six potential retailers of Coors beer in one county in the market area to determine their past beer sales and experience and their intention to stock and sell Coors. From these data, a personal-interview questionnaire would be developed and executed at all appropriate retailers in the market area to determine similar data.
Source: Manson and Associates
Cost: $4,800

Study I: Survey of Retail and Wholesale Beer Prices.
Description: In-store interviews would be conducted with a sample of 50 retailers in the market area to estimate retail and wholesale prices for Budweiser, Miller Lite, Miller, Busch, Bud Light, Old Milwaukee, and Michelob.
Source: Manson and Associates
Cost: $2,000

Examples of the final report tables are attached [Exhibit 2, pages 147–151]. This should give you a better idea of the data you will receive.

As you can see, the research is extensive and, I might add, not cheap. However, the research as outlined will supply you with sufficient information to make an estimate of the feasibility of a Coors distributorship, the investment for which is substantial.

I have scheduled 9:00 A.M. next Friday as a time to meet with you to discuss the proposal in more detail. Time is short, but we firmly feel the study can be completed by February 20, 1990. If you need more information in the meantime, please feel free to call.

Sincerely,

John Rome
Senior Research Analyst

---

[a] A focus-group interview consists of a moderator's questioning and listening to a group of 8 to 12 consumers.

EXHIBIT 2

Examples of Final Research Report Tables

Table A
National and Delaware Residents' Annual Beer Consumption per Capita, 1988–1992 (Gallons)

	U.S. Consumption		Delaware Consumption	
Year	Based on Entire Population	Based on Population Age 21 and Over	Based on Entire Population	Based on Population Age 21 and Over
1988				
1989				
1990				
1991				
1992				

Source: Study A.

Table B
Population Estimates for 1986–1996 for Two Delaware Counties in Market Area

County	Entire Population					
	1986	1988	1990	1992	1994	1996
Kent						
Sussex						

County	Population Age 21 and Over					
	1986	1988	1990	1992	1994	1996
Kent						
Sussex						

Source: Study B.

Table C
Estimates of Coors' Market Share for 1990–1995

Year	Market Share (%)
1990	
1991	
1992	
1993	
1994	
1995	

Source: Study C.

(continued on next page)

EXHIBIT 2 (continued)

Table D
Estimates of Number of Liquor and Beer Licenses for the Market Area, 1990–1995

Type of License	1990	1991	1992	1993	1994	1995
All beverages						
Retail beer and wine						
Off-premise beer only						
Veterans beer and liquor						
Fraternal						
Resort beer and liquor						

Source: Study D.

Table E
Beer Taxes Paid by Beer Wholesalers in the Market Area, 1988 and 1989

Wholesaler	1988 Tax Paid ($)	1989 Tax Paid ($)
A		
B		
C		
D		
E		
F		

Source: Study E.

Note: Delaware beer tax is $0.06 gallon.

Table F
Financial Statement Summary for 510 Wholesalers of Wine, Liquor, and Beer in Fiscal Year 1988

Assets	Percentage
Cash and equivalents	
Accounts and notes receivable, net	
Inventory	
All other current	
Total current	
Fixed assets, net	
Intangibles, net	
All other noncurrent	
Total	100.0

EXHIBIT 2 *(continued)*

Table F *(continued)*

Liabilities	Percentage
Notes payable, short term	
Current maturity long-term debt	
Accounts and notes payable, trade	
Accrued expenses	
All other current	
Total current	
Long-term debt	
All other noncurrent	
Net worth	
Total liabilities and net worth	100.0
Income Data	
Net sales	100.0
Cost of sales	
Gross profit	
Operating expenses	
Operating profit	
All other expenses, net	
Profit before taxes	
Ratios	
Quick	
Current	
Debt/worth	
Sales/receivables	
Cost of sales/inventory	
Percentage profit before taxes, based on total assets	

Interpretation of Statement Studies Figures:
RMA recommends that Statement Studies data be regarded only as general guidelines and not as absolute industry norms. There are several reasons why the data may not be fully representative of a given industry:
1. The financial statements used in the Statement Studies are not selected by any random or statistically reliable method. RMA member banks voluntarily submit the raw data they have available each year, with these being the only constraints: (a) The fiscal year-ends of the companies reported may not be from April 1 through June 29, and (b) their total assets must be less than $100 million.
2. Many companies have varied product lines; however, the Statement Studies categorize them by their primary product Standard Industrial Classification (SIC) number only.
3. Some of the industry samples are rather small in relation to the total number of firms in a given industry. A relatively small sample can increase the chances that some of our composites do not fully represent an industry.
4. There is the chance that an extreme statement can be present in a sample, causing a disproportionate influence on the industry composite. This is particularly true in a relatively small sample.
5. Companies within the same industry may differ in their method of operations, which in turn can directly influence their financial statements. Since they are included in our sample, too, these statements can significantly affect our composite calculations.
6. Other considerations that can result in variations among different companies engaged in the same general line of business are different labor markets, geographical location, different accounting methods, quality of products handled, sources and methods of financing, and terms of sale.

For these reasons, RMA does not recommend that Statement Studies figures be considered as absolute norms for a given industry. Rather, the figures should be used only as general guidelines and in addition to the other methods of financial analysis. RMA makes no claim as to the representativeness of the figures printed in this book.

Source: Study F (Robert Morris Associates, © 1989).

EXHIBIT 2 *(continued)*

Table G
Consumer Questionnaire Results

	Percentage			Percentage
Consumed Coors in the past:				
Attitudes toward Coors:	%	Usually buy beer at:		
Strongly like		Liquor stores		
Like		Taverns and bars		
Indifferent/no opinion		Supermarkets		
Dislike		Corner grocery		
Strongly dislike				
Total	100.0	Total		100.0
Weekly beer consumption:		Features considered		
Less than 1 can		important when buying beer:		
1–2 cans		Taste		
3–4 cans		Brand name		
5–6 cans		Price		
7–8 cans		Store location		
9 cans and over		Advertising		
Total	100.0	Carbonation		
Intention to buy Coors:		Other		
Certainly will		Total		100.0
Maybe will				
Not sure				
Maybe will not				
Certainly will not				
Total	100.0			

Semantic Differential Scale, Consumers[a]

	Extremely	Very	Somewhat	Somewhat	Very	Extremely	
Masculine	—	—	—	—	—	—	Feminine
Healthful	—	—	—	—	—	—	Unhealthful
Cheap	—	—	—	—	—	—	Expensive
Strong	—	—	—	—	—	—	Weak
Old-fashioned	—	—	—	—	—	—	New
Upper-class	—	—	—	—	—	—	Lower-class
Good taste	—	—	—	—	—	—	Bad taste

[a] Profiles would be provided for Coors, three competing beers, and an ideal beer.

Source: Study G.

EXHIBIT 2 *(continued)*

Table H
Retailer Questionnaire Results

	Percentage		Percentage
Brands of beer carried:		Beer sales:	
Budweiser		Budweiser	
Miller Lite		Miller Lite	
Miller		Miller	
Busch		Busch	
Bud Light		Bud Light	
Old Milwaukee		Old Milwaukee	
Michelob		Michelob	
Intention to sell Coors:		Others	
Certainly will		Total	100.0
Maybe will			
Not sure			
Maybe will not			
Certainly will not			
Total	100.0		

Semantic Differential Scale, Retailers[a]

	Extremely	Very	Somewhat	Somewhat	Very	Extremely	
Masculine	—	—	—	—	—	—	Feminine
Healthful	—	—	—	—	—	—	Unhealthful
Cheap	—	—	—	—	—	—	Expensive
Strong	—	—	—	—	—	—	Weak
Old-fashioned	—	—	—	—	—	—	New
Upper-class	—	—	—	—	—	—	Lower-class
Good taste	—	—	—	—	—	—	Bad taste

[a] Profiles would be provided for Coors, three competing beers, and an ideal beer.

Source: Study H.

Table I
Retail and Wholesale Prices for Selected Beers in the Market Area

Beer	Wholesale Six-Pack Price[a] (dollars)	Retail Six-Pack Price[b] (dollars)
Budweiser		
Miller Lite		
Miller		
Busch		
Bud Light		
Old Milwaukee		
Michelob		

[a] Price at which the wholesaler sold to retailers.

[b] Price at which the retailer sold to consumers.

Source: Study I.

■ INVESTMENT AND OPERATING DATA

Larry was not completely in the dark regarding investment and operating data for the distributorship. In the past two weeks he had visited two beer wholesalers in his home town of Chester, Pennsylvania, who handled Anheuser-Busch and Miller beer, to get a feel for their operation and marketing experience. It would have been nice to interview a Coors wholesaler, but Coors management had instructed all of their distributors to provide no information to prospective applicants.

Although no specific financial data had been discussed, general information had been provided in a cordial fashion because of the noncompetitive nature of Larry's plans. Based on his conversations, Larry had made the following estimates:

Inventory		$240,000
Equipment:		
Delivery trucks	$150,000	
Forklift	20,000	
Recycling and miscellaneous equipment	20,000	
Office equipment	10,000	
Total equipment		200,000
Warehouse		320,000
Land		40,000
Total investment		$800,000

A local banker had reviewed Larry's financial capabilities and saw no problem in extending a line of credit on the order of $400,000. Other family sources also might loan as much as $400,000 to the business.

To get a rough estimate of fixed expenses, Larry decided to plan on having four route salespeople, a secretary, and a warehouse manager. Salaries for these people and himself would run about $160,000 annually, plus some form of incentive compensation he had yet to determine. Other fixed or semifixed expenses were estimated as follows:

Equipment depreciation	$35,000
Warehouse depreciation	15,000
Utilities and telephone	12,000
Insurance	10,000
Personal property taxes	10,000
Maintenance and janitorial services	5,600
Miscellaneous	2,400
	$90,000

According to the two wholesalers, beer in bottles and cans outsold keg beer by a three-to-one margin. Keg beer prices at the wholesale level were about 45 percent of prices for beer in bottles and cans.

■ MEETING

The entire matter deserved much thought. Maybe it was a golden opportunity, maybe not. The only thing certain was that research was needed, Manson and Associates was ready, and Larry needed time to think. Today is Tuesday, Larry thought—only three days until he and John Rome would get together for direction.

CHAPTER 5

Product and Service Strategy and Brand Management

 The fundamental decision in formulating a marketing mix concerns the offering of an organization. Without something to satisfy target market wants and needs, there would be nothing to price, distribute, or communicate. In essence, the ultimate profitability of an organization depends on its product or service offering(s) and the strength of its brand(s). Accordingly, issues in the development of a product, service, and brand strategy are of special interest to all levels of management in an organization.

The three basic kinds of offering-related decisions facing the marketing manager concern (1) modifying the offering mix, (2) positioning offerings, and (3) branding offerings. Aspects of each decision are described in this chapter.

In certain ways, offering decisions are extensions of product-market matching strategies described in Chapter 1. Like other marketing-mix decisions, offering decisions must be based on consideration of organization and marketing objectives, organization resources and capabilities, customer needs and wants, and competitive forces in the marketplace.

■ THE OFFERING PORTFOLIO

The Offering Concept

Before proceeding to a discussion of offering-related decisions, we should define the term *offering*. In an abstract sense, an *offering* consists of the benefits or satisfaction provided to target markets by an organization. More concretely, an offering consists of a tangible product or service (a physical entity) plus related services (such as delivery and setup), brand name(s)' warranties or guarantees, packaging, and the like.

Use of the term *offering* rather than *product* or *service* has numerous benefits for strategic marketing planning. By focusing on benefits and satisfaction offered, it establishes a conceptual framework. This framework is potentially useful in analyzing competing offerings, identifying the unmet needs and wants of target markets, and developing or designing new products or services. It forces a marketer to go beyond the single tangible entity being marketed and to consider the entire offering, or extended product or service.

In a broader view, an organization's offerings are an extension of its business definition. Offerings illustrate not only the buyer needs served, but also the types of customer groups sought and the means (technology) for satisfying their needs.

The Offering Mix

Seldom do organizations market a solitary offering; rather, they tend to market many product or service offerings. The typical supermarket contains over 40,000 different products; General Electric offers over a quarter million. Banks provide hundreds of services to customers, including computer billing, automatic payroll deposits, checking accounts, and loans of numerous kinds. Similarly, hospitals maintain a complete "inventory" of services ranging from pathology to obstetrics to food services. The totality of an organization's offerings is known as its product or service *offering mix* or *portfolio*. This mix usually consists of distinct offering lines—groups of offerings similar in terms of usage, buyers marketed to, or technical characteristics. Each offering line is composed of individual offers or items.

Offering decisions concern primarily the width, depth, and consistency of the offering portfolio. Marketing managers must continually assess the number of offering lines (the width decision) and the number of individual items in each line (the depth decision). Although these decisions depend, in part, on the existing competitive or industry situation, as well as organizational resources, they are most often determined by overall marketing strategy. The options are many. At one extreme, an organization can concentrate on one offering; at the other, it can offer complete lines to its customers. In between, it can specialize in high-profit and/or high-volume offerings. Furthermore, managers must consider the extent to which offerings satisfy similar needs, appeal to similar buyer groups, or utilize similar technologies (the consistency decision).

Increasingly, organizations have turned to "bundling" as a means to enhance their offering mix. *Bundling* involves the marketing of two or more product or service items in a single "package" that creates a new offering. For example, McDonald's offers "value meals" that include a sandwich, soft drink, and french fries. Travelocity offers complete vacations, including travel, lodging, and leisure activities. IBM sells computer hardware, software, and maintenance contracts together. Bundling is based on the idea that consumers value the package more than the individual items. This is due to benefits received from not having to make separate purchases and enhanced satisfaction from one item given the presence of another. Moreover, bundling often provides a lower total cost to buyers and lower marketing costs to sellers. For instance, SBC Communications, Inc. offers a telephone service "bundle" that includes Internet, entertainment, and local telephone service with numerous add-on features such as caller ID and voice mail for one price of $137.00 per month. Priced separately, items in the bundle cost a buyer up to $185.00 per month.[1]

■ MODIFYING THE OFFERING MIX

The first offering-related decision confronting the manager is whether to modify the offering mix. Rarely, if ever, will an organization's offering mix stand the test of changing competitive actions and buyer preferences, or satisfy an organization's desire for growth. Accordingly, the marketing manager must continually monitor target markets and offerings to determine when new offerings should be introduced and existing offerings modified or eliminated.

Additions to the Offering Mix

Additions to the offering mix may take the form of a single offering or of entire lines of offerings. ConAgra Foods is an example. The company successfully launched an eight-item line of complete dinner kits with meat under the Homestyle Bakes brand and notched sales of $100 million in less than a year.[2]

Whatever the reason for considering new offerings, three questions should direct the evaluation of this action:

- How consistent is the new offering with existing offerings?
- Does the organization have the resources to adequately introduce and sustain the offering?
- Is there a viable market niche for the offering?

First, in evaluating the consistency of the new offering with existing offerings, offering interrelationships—whether substitute, complementary, or whatever—must be carefully taken into account. This is necessary to avoid situations in which sales of the new offering may excessively cannibalize those of other offerings. Eastman Kodak did not originally introduce 35mm cameras and camcorders because of the potential for cannibalizing its core products—cameras. Today, a similar situation exists with electronic imaging cameras, which could cannibalize sales of existing cameras.[3] Determining a new offering's consistency also involves considering the degree to which the new offering fits the organization's existing selling and distribution strategies. For example, will the new offering require a different type of sales effort, such as new sales personnel or selling methods? The Metropolitan Life Insurance Company faced such a situation when it added automobile insurance to its line of life and health insurance, since the sales task for auto insurance differs from that for life insurance. Or will the new offering require a different marketing channel to reach the target market sought? Both the cannibalization question and the question of fit with sales and distribution strategies raise a fundamental third question relating to the buyers sought for the new offering. Will the new offering satisfy the target markets currently being served by the existing offering mix? If it will, then the sales and distribution issue may be settled, but the cannibalization question remains. If it will not, then the situation is just the opposite.

The second issue arising from the addition of new offerings is the adequacy of an organization's resources. In particular, the financial strength of the organization must be objectively appraised. New offerings often require large initial cash outlays for research, development, and introductory marketing programs. Gillette, for example, spent $750 million for research and development and another $300 million in advertising and marketing support to launch its Mach 3 razor.[4] Other costs of sustaining the new offering before it returns a profit to the organization must also be measured. These costs will be determined, in part, by the speed and magnitude of competitive response to new offerings in the market and by market growth itself. The experience of Royal Crown Company, the maker of RC Cola, is a case in point. The company pioneered the first can in 1954, the first diet cola in 1962, and the first caffeine-free cola in 1980. All three offerings achieved a respectable market presence only to lose it when larger competitors such as Coca-Cola and Pepsi-Cola introduced competitive products.[5]

Finally, one must determine whether a market niche exists for the new offering. Important questions here are whether the new offering has a relative advantage over existing competitive offerings and whether a distinct buyer group exists for which no offering is satisfactory. Careful market analysis is necessary to answer these questions.

New-Offering Development Process

Marketing managers are often faced with new-offering decisions. In dealing with the often chaotic process of developing and marketing new offerings, most managers attempt to follow some sort of structured procedure.[6] This procedure typically includes four multifaceted steps: (1) idea generation/idea screening, (2) business analysis, (3) market testing, and (4) commercialization.

Briefly, the process is as follows. New-offering ideas are obtained from many sources—employees, buyers, and competitors—through formal (marketing research) and informal means. These ideas are screened, both in terms of organizational definition and capability and from the viewpoint of prospective buyers. Ideas deemed incompatible with organizational definition and capability are quickly eliminated. The match between prospective buyers and offering characteristics is assessed through questions such as the following. First, does the offering have a *relative advantage* over existing offerings? Second, is the offering *compatible* with buyers' use or consumption behavior? Third, is the offering *simple* enough for buyers to understand and use? Fourth, can the offering be *tested* on a limited basis prior to actual purchase? Fifth, are there *immediate benefits* from the offering, once it is used or consumed? If the answers to these questions are yes and the offering satisfies a *felt need*, then the new-offering idea passes on to the next stage. At that point, the idea is subjected to a business analysis to assess its financial viability in terms of estimated sales, costs, and profitability. Those ideas that pass the business analysis are then developed into prototypes, and various testing procedures are implemented. Marketing-related tests may include product concept or buyer preference tests in a laboratory situation, or even field market tests. Offering ideas that pass through these stages are commercially introduced into the marketplace in the hope that they will become profitable to the organization. Research on the new-offering development process indicates that upwards of 3,000 raw ideas are needed to produce a single commercially successful, innovative new product. This research also emphasizes that two major factors contribute to the success of new offerings: (1) a fit with market needs and (2) a fit with the internal strengths of the organizations.[7]

Although the stages just outlined are relatively straightforward from a managerial perspective, two require further elaboration: the business analysis and testing stages. Sales analysis and profit analysis are two fundamental aspects of the business analysis stage. Forecasting sales volume for a new offering is an enormously difficult task; nevertheless, preliminary forecasts must be made before further investigation of the offering is warranted. For the most part, profitability analyses are related to investment requirements, break-even procedures, and payback periods. Break-even procedures can be used to determine estimates of the number of units that must be sold to cover fixed and variable costs. An extension of this procedure—and one that is frequently used in evaluating new offerings—is to compute the payback period of the new offering. *Payback period* refers to the number of years required for an organization to recapture its initial offering investment. The shorter the payback period, the sooner an offering will prove profitable. Usually the payback period is computed by dividing the fixed costs of the offering by the estimated incoming cash flows from it. Though widely used, the method is limited in that it does not distinguish among offering investments according to their absolute sizes. A final method often used is to calculate the common return on investment (ROI). ROI equals the ratio of average annual net earnings (return) divided by average annual investment, discounted to the present time. Like the payback method, the ROI method does not always distinguish among offering alternatives according to their riskiness. Risk must still be subjectively assessed.

Test marketing is a major consideration in the development and testing stage. A test market is a scaled-down implementation of one or more alternative marketing strategies for introducing the new offering. Test markets provide several benefits to managers. First, they generate benchmark data for assessing sales volume when the product is introduced over a wider area. Second, if alternative marketing strategies are tested, the relative impacts of the two programs can be examined under actual market conditions. In a similar vein, test markets allow the manager to assess the incidence of offering trial by potential buyers, repeat-purchasing behavior, and quantities purchased. A manager should remember, however, that test markets of new offerings inform competitors of the organization's activities and, thus, may increase the speed and effectiveness of competitive response. This recently happened to Procter & Gamble.[8] Its Olay cosmetics line featuring a skin health benefit was test-marketed for three years, only to be discontinued. Revlon's Almay and Johnson & Johnson's Neutrogena had beat it to the marketplace with the same benefit supported by heavy marketing spending.

Life-Cycle Concept

An important managerial tool related to the development and management of offerings is the concept of the life cycle. A *life cycle* plots sales of an offering (such as a brand of coffee) or a product class (such as all coffee brands) over a period of time. Life cycles are typically divided into four stages: (1) introduction, (2) growth, (3) maturity-saturation, and (4) decline. Exhibit 5.1 shows the general form of a product life cycle and the corresponding stages.

The sales curve can be viewed as being the result of offering trial and repeat-purchasing behavior. In other words,

$$\text{Sales volume} = (\text{number of triers} \times \text{average purchase amount} \times \text{price})$$
$$+ (\text{number of repeaters} \times \text{average purchase amount} \times \text{price})$$

Early in the life cycle, management efforts focus on stimulating trial of the offering by advertising, giving out free samples, and obtaining adequate distribution. The vast majority of sales volume is due to trial purchases. As the offering moves through its life cycle, an increasing share of volume is attributable to repeat purchases, and management efforts focus on retaining existing buyers of the offering through offering modifications, enhanced brand image, and competitive pricing.

Anticipating and recognizing movement into advanced stages of the life cycle are crucial to managing the various stages. Movement into the maturity-saturation stage is often indicated by (1) an increase in the proportion of buyers who are repeat purchasers (that is, few new buyers or triers exist), (2) an increase in the standardization of production operations and product-service offerings, and (3) an increase in the

EXHIBIT 5.1

General Form of a Product Life Cycle

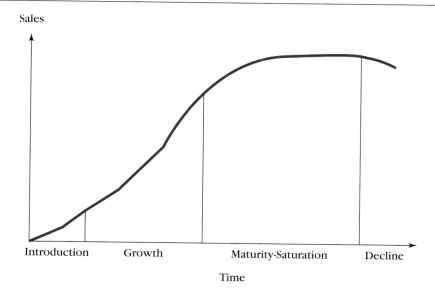

incidence of aggressive pricing activities of competitors. As the offering enters into and moves through this stage, management efforts typically focus on finding new buyers for the offering, significantly improving the offering, and/or increasing the frequency of usage among current buyers. Ultimately, the decline stage must be addressed. The decision criteria at this stage are outlined in the following discussion on modifying, harvesting, and eliminating offerings.

Services often follow a life cycle similar to the product life cycle described previously. As a service firm approaches maturity, it typically modifies its operations to attract new buyers or purchase frequency. Examples include Starbucks with its expanded breakfast menu and barbershops that become hair-stylist operations featuring hair-cutting services for men and women. Often service firms expand their geographical scope by reproducing facilities through franchising and licensing agreements to become multisite operators.

Modifying, Harvesting, and Eliminating Offerings

Modifying offerings is a common practice. Firms must always be on the lookout for new ways to improve the value their offerings provide customers in terms of quality, functions, features, and/or price.

Modification decisions typically focus on trading up or trading down the offering. *Trading up* involves a conscious decision to improve an offering—by adding new features and higher-quality materials or augmenting the offering with attendant services—and raising the price. Examples of augmenting products with services are found in the computer industry. Manufacturers of computers enhanced the image and suitability of their products through programming services, information-system assistance, and user training. *Trading down* is the process of reducing the number of features or quality of an offering and lowering the price.

The elimination of offerings as a specific decision is given less attention than new-offering or modification decisions. However, the elimination decision has grown in importance in recent years because of the realization that some offerings may be an unnecessary burden in light of potential opportunities. As an alternative to total elimination, management might consider harvesting the offering when it enters the late-maturity or decline stage of the life cycle. *Harvesting* is the strategic management decision to reduce the investment in a business entity in the hope of cutting costs and/or improving cash flow. In other words, the decision is not to abandon the offering outright but, rather, to minimize human and financial resources allocated to it. Harvesting should be considered when (1) the market for the offering is stable, (2) the offering is not producing good profits, (3) the offering has a small or respectable market share that is becoming increasingly difficult or costly to defend from competitive inroads, and (4) the offering provides benefits to the organization in terms of image or "full-line" capabilities, despite poor future potential.

Outright abandonment, or elimination, means that the offering is dropped from the mix of organizational offerings. Generally speaking, if the answer to each of the following questions is "very little" or "none," then an offering is a candidate for elimination.

1. What is the future sales potential of the offering?
2. How much is the offering contributing to the overall profitability of the offering mix?
3. How much is the offering contributing to the sale of other offerings in the mix?
4. How much could be gained by modifying the offering?
5. What would be the effect on channel members and buyers?

Each of these questions was considered by General Motors when it made the decision to discontinue its Oldsmobile line of automobiles.[9]

■ POSITIONING OFFERINGS

A second major offering-related decision confronting the manager concerns the positioning of offerings. *Positioning* is the act of designing an organization's offering and image so that it occupies a distinct and valued place in the target customer's mind relative to competitive offerings. There are a variety of positioning strategies available, including positioning by (1) attribute or benefit, (2) use or application, (3) product or service user, (4) product or service class, (5) competitors, and (6) price and quality.[10]

Positioning Strategies

Positioning an offering by attributes or benefits is the strategy most frequently used. Positioning an offering by attributes requires determining which attributes are important to target markets, which attributes are being emphasized by competitors, and how the offering can be fitted into this offering-target market environment. This kind of positioning may be accomplished by designing an offering that contains appropriate attributes or by stressing the appropriate attributes if they already exist in the offering. This latter tactic has been employed by a number of cereal manufacturers, who have emphasized the "naturalness" of their products in response to the growing interest in nutrition among a sizable number of cereal buyers.

In practice, operationalizing the positioning concept requires the development of a matrix relating attributes of the offering to market segments. Using toothpaste as an example, Exhibit 5.2 shows how particular attributes may vary in importance for different market segments.[11] Several benefits accrue from viewing the market for toothpaste in this manner. First, the marketing manager can spot potential opportunities for new offerings and determine if a market niche exists. Second, looking at offering attributes and their importance to market segments permits subjective estimation of the extent to which a new offering might cannibalize existing offerings. If two offerings emphasize the same attributes, then they can be expected to compete with each other for the same market segment. Alternatively, if the offerings have different mixes of attributes, they probably will appeal to different segments. For this reason, Procter & Gamble's introduction of Crest tartar-control-formula toothpaste for adults did not have a major adverse effect on its sales of the existing Crest toothpaste for children. Third, the competitive response to a new offering can be judged more

EXHIBIT 5.2

Attributes and Marketing Segment Positioning

Toothpaste Attributes	Market Segments			
	Children	Teens, Young Adults	Family	Adults
Flavor	*			
Color	*			
Whiteness of teeth		*		
Fresh breath		*		
Decay prevention			*	
Price			*	
Plaque prevention				*
Stain prevention				*
Principal brands for each segment	Aim, Stripe	Ultra Brite, McCleans	Colgate, Crest	Topol, Rembrandt

Note: An asterisk (*) indicates principal benefits sought by each market segment.

effectively using this framework. By determining which brands serve specific markets, one can evaluate offerings in terms of financial strength and market acceptance.

Organizations can also position their offerings by use or application. Arm & Hammer used this approach to position its baking powder as an odor-destroying agent in refrigerators and a water softener in swimming pools. Public television was originally positioned as a source of educational and cultural programming.

Positioning by user is a third strategy. This strategy typically associates a product or service with a user group. Federal Express positions its delivery service for the busy executive. Certain deodorant brands position themselves for females (Jean Naté by Charles of the Ritz), whereas others focus on males (Brut by Fabergé).

Products and services can be positioned by product or service class as well. For example, margarine brands position themselves against butter. Savings associations position themselves as "banks."

An organization can position itself or its offerings directly against competitors. Avis positions itself against Hertz in the rental car business. Sabroso, a coffee liqueur, positions itself against Kahlua. For many years, the National Pork Producers Council positioned its product as being like poultry: "Pork: The Other White Meat." Often a political candidate will position himself or herself against the opponent.

Finally, positioning along a price-quality continuum is also possible. Hewlett-Packard consciously prices its line of office personal computers below Compaq and IBM in an attempt to convey a "value" position among corporate buyers. Ford Motor Company, on the other hand, has pursued a quality positioning stance evidenced by its "Quality Is Job One" advertising program.

Repositioning

Repositioning is necessary when the initial positioning of a product, service, brand, or organization is no longer competitively sustainable or profitable or when better positioning opportunities arise. However, given the time and cost to establish a new position, repositioning is not advisable without careful study.

Examples of successful repositionings include the efforts behind Johnson & Johnson's St. Joseph Aspirin and Carnival Cruise Lines.[12] Johnson & Johnson repositioned the aspirin from one for babies to an adult "Low Strength Aspirin" to reduce the risk of heart problems or strokes. This repositioning produced a significant boost in sales. Carnival Cruise Lines repositioned itself from a vacation alternative for older people to a "Fun Ship" for younger adults and families. After expanding its service offering to include Las Vegas–style shows, Camp Carnival, and Nautica Spa programs, Carnival became the largest and most successful company in the cruise industry.

Making the Positioning Strategy Decision

The challenge facing a manager is deciding which positioning strategy is most appropriate in a given situation. The choice of a strategy is made easier when the following three questions are considered. First, who are the likely competitors, what positions have they staked out in the marketplace, and how strong are they? Second, what are the preferences of the target consumers sought and how do these consumers perceive the offerings of competitors? Finally, what position, if any, do we already have in the target consumer's mind? Once answered, attention can then be focused on a series of implementation questions:

1. What position do we want to own?
2. What competitors must be outperformed if we are to establish the position?
3. Do we have the marketing resources to occupy and hold the position?

The success of a positioning strategy depends on a number of factors. First, the position selected must be clearly communicated to targeted customers. Second, as the development of a position is a lengthy and often expensive process, frequent positioning changes should be avoided. Finally, and perhaps most important, the position taken in the marketplace should be sustainable and profitable.

■ BRAND EQUITY AND BRAND MANAGEMENT

Branding offerings is a third responsibility of marketing managers. A brand name is any word, "device" (design, sound, shape, or color), or combination of these that are used to identify an offering and set it apart from competing offerings. The major managerial implication of branding offerings is that consumer goodwill, derived from buyer satisfaction and favorable associations with a brand, can lead to *brand equity*— the added value a brand name bestows on a product or service beyond the functional benefits provided. This value has two distinct marketing advantages for the brand owner. First, brand equity provides a competitive advantage, such as the Sunkist label that signifies quality citrus fruit and the Gatorade name that defines sports drinks. A second advantage is that consumers are often willing to pay a higher price for a product or service with brand equity. Brand equity, in this instance, is represented by the premium a consumer will pay for one brand over another when the functional benefits provided are identical. Duracell batteries, Coca-Cola, Kleenex facial tissues, Louis Vuitton luggage, Bose audio systems, and Microsoft software all enjoy a price premium arising from brand equity.

Creating and Valuing Brand Equity

Brand equity doesn't just happen. It is carefully crafted and nurtured by marketing programs that forge strong, favorable, and unique consumer associations and experiences with a brand. Brand equity resides in the minds of consumers and results from what they have learned, felt, seen, and heard about a brand over time. Marketers recognize that brand equity is not easily or quickly achieved. It arises from a sequential building process consisting of four steps (see Exhibit 5.3 on page 162).[13] The first step is to develop positive brand awareness and an association of the brand in consumers' minds with a product class or need to give the brand an identity. Gatorade and Kleenex have done this in the sports drink and facial tissue product classes, respectively. Next, a marketer must establish a brand's meaning in the minds of consumers. Meaning arises from what a brand stands for and has two dimensions—a functional, performance-related dimension and an abstract, imagery-related dimension. Nike has done this through continuous product development and improvement and its links to peak athletic performance in its integrated marketing communications program. The third step is to elicit the proper consumer responses to a brand's identity and meaning. Here attention is placed on how consumers think and feel about a brand. Thinking focuses on a brand's perceived quality, credibility, and superiority relative to other brands. Feeling relates to the consumer's emotional reaction to a brand. Michelin elicits both responses for its tires. Not only is Michelin thought of as a credible and superior-quality brand, but consumers also acknowledge a warm and secure feeling of safety, comfort, and self-assurance without worry or concern about the brand. The final, and most difficult, step is to create a consumer-brand resonance evident in an intense, active loyalty relationship between consumers and the brand. A deep psychological bond characterizes consumer-brand resonance and the personal identification consumers have with the brand. Examples of brands that have achieved this status include Harley-Davidson, Apple, and eBay.

Brand equity also provides a financial advantage for the brand owner.[14] Successful, established brand names, such as Gillette, Nike, IBM, and Campbell's, have an economic value because they represent intangible assets. These assets enable their owner to enjoy a competitive advantage, to create earnings and cash flows in excess of the

EXHIBIT 5.3

Customer-Based Brand Equity Pyramid

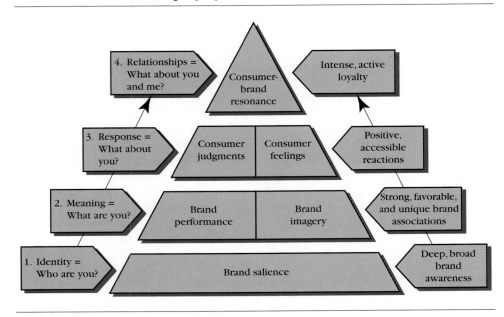

return on its tangible (plant and equipment) assets, and to achieve a high rate of return relative to competitors. The recognition that brands are assets and have an economic value is apparent in the strategic marketing decision to buy and sell brands. For example, Procter & Gamble bought the Hawaiian Punch brand from Del Monte in 1990 for $150 million and sold it to Cadbury Schweppes in 1999 for $203 million. This example illustrates that brands, unlike tangible assets that depreciate with time and use, appreciate in value when effectively managed. However, brands can lose value when they are not managed properly. The purchase and sale of Snapple brand noncarbonated fruit-flavored drinks and iced tea by Quaker Oats is a case in point. Quaker bought Snapple for $1.7 billion in 1994, only to sell it to Triarc Companies in 1997 for $300 million. The challenge of brand valuation is illustrated in the case study, Frito-Lay Company: Cracker Jack, at the end of this chapter.

Branding Decisions

Two branding decisions commonly confront marketing managers. The first relates to the strategy used to assign brands to multiple offerings or multiple lines of offerings. A manufacturer must decide whether to assign one brand name to *all* of the organization's offerings (such as General Electric), to assign one brand name to *each line* of offerings (Sears' appliances are Kenmore, and Sears' tools are Craftsman), or to assign individual names to *each offering* (Tide, Cheer, and Downy are all laundry detergents sold by Procter & Gamble). The branding strategy selected will depend on the consistency of the offering mix. If the offerings are related in terms of needs satisfied, then a common (family) brand strategy is favored. A common brand name for offerings is often selected if the organization wishes to establish dominance in a class of product or service offerings, as in the case of Campbell soups. The decision to use a single brand name has advantages and disadvantages. Among the advantages is the fact that it is usually easier to introduce new offerings when the brand name is familiar to buyers—

an outgrowth of brand equity. However, a single brand name strategy can have a negative effect on existing offerings if a new offering fails.

Some companies employ *sub-branding*, which combines a family brand with a new brand, when introducing new product or service offerings. The intent is to build on the favorable associations consumers have toward the family brand while differentiating the new offering. For example, ThinkPad is a sub-brand to the IBM name. Gatorade used sub-branding with the introduction of Gatorade Frost, Gatorade Fierce, and Gatorade Ice, with unique flavors developed for each.

The second branding decision relates to supplying an intermediary with its own brand name. From the intermediary's perspective, the decision is whether or not to carry its own brands. Distributors favor carrying their own brands for a number of reasons.[15] By carrying a private brand, a distributor avoids price competition to some extent, since no other distributor carries an identical brand that consumers can use for comparison purposes. Also, any buyer goodwill attributed to an offering accrues to the distributor, and buyer loyalty to the offering is tied to the distributor, not the producer. If a distributor desires a private brand, it must locate a producer willing to manufacture the brand. A marketing manager is then placed in the position of having to decide whether to be the producer. A potential producer of private brands, or distributor brands, should consider a number of factors when making this decision. If a producer has excess manufacturing capacity and the variable costs of producing a distributor's brand do not exceed the sale price, the possibility exists for making a contribution to overhead and utilizing production facilities. Even though a distributor's brand will often compete directly with a producer's brand, the combined sales of the brands and the profit contribution to the producer may be greater than if a competitor obtained the rights to produce the distributor brand. For these reasons and others, firms such as H. J. Heinz, Ralston Purina, and Dial produce private brands of pet foods, cereals, and bar soap for their distributors. However, a danger in producing private brands is the possibility of becoming too reliant on private-brand revenue, only to have it curtailed when a distributor switches suppliers or builds its own production plant. Overreliance on distributor brands will also affect trade relationships between a producer and distributor. As a generalization, the influence of a producer, in terms of price and channel leadership, is inversely related to the proportion of its output or revenue obtained from a distributor's brand.

Brand Growth Strategies

An organization has four strategic options for growing its brands (see Exhibit 5.4).[16] The options are dictated by whether a marketing manager wishes to extend existing brands or develop new brands and whether the manager chooses to deploy these brands in product classes presently served or not served by the organization.

Line Extension Strategy The most frequently employed growth strategy is a *line extension strategy*. Line extensions occur when an organization introduces additional offerings with the same brand in a product class that it currently serves. New flavors, forms, colors, different ingredients or features, and package sizes are examples of line extensions. As an example, Campbell Soup Company offers regular Campbell soup, homecooking style, chunky, and "healthy request" varieties, more than 100 soup flavors, and several different package sizes of prepared soups. Line extensions respond to customers' desire for variety. They also can eliminate gaps in a product line that might be filled by competitive offerings or to neutralize competitive inroads. This strategy also lowers advertising and promotion costs because the same brand is used on all items, thus raising the level of brand awareness. Line extensions do involve risk. There is a likelihood of product cannibalism occurring rather than incremental volume gains as buyers substitute one item for another in the extended

EXHIBIT 5.4

Brand Growth Strategies

		Product/Service Class Served by the Organization	
		New Product Class	*Existing Product Class*
Brand Name	*New Brand*	New Brand Strategy	Fighting/Flanker Brand Strategy
	Existing Brand	Brand Extension Strategy	Line Extension Strategy

product line. Also, proliferation of offerings within a product line can create production and distribution problems and added costs without incremental sales. For example, 8 percent of personal-care and household products sold in the United States account for 84.5 percent of total sales. Such statistics led companies that market these products to prune their product lines in the late 1990s.[17]

Brand Extension Strategy　Strong brand equity makes possible a *brand extension strategy*, the practice of using a current brand name to enter a completely different product class. This strategy can reduce the risk associated with introducing an offering in a new market by providing consumers the familiarity of and knowledge about an established brand. For instance, the equity in the Tylenol name as a trusted pain reliever allowed Johnson & Johnson to successfully extend this name to Tylenol Cold & Flu and Tylenol PM, a sleep aid. Fisher-Price, an established name in children's toys, was able to extend its brand to children's shampoo and conditioners and baby bath and lotion products. Transferring an existing brand name to a new product class requires care. Research indicates that the perceptual fit of the brand with and the transfer of the core product benefit to the new product class must exist for a brand extension to be successful. This happened with Tylenol and Fisher-Price, and both ventures produced sizable sales volume gains for the brands. However, it did not with Levi business attire and Dunkin Donuts cereal. Both efforts failed. Even successful brand extensions involve a risk. Too many uses for a brand name can dilute the meaning of a brand for consumers. Some marketing analysts claim this has happened to the Arm & Hammer brand given its extension to toothpaste, laundry detergent, cat litter, air freshener, carpet deodorizer, antiperspirant, and chewing gum.[18]

A variation on brand extensions is *co-branding*, the pairing of two brand names of two manufacturers on a single product. For example, Hershey Foods has teamed with General Mills to offer a co-branded breakfast cereal called Reese's Peanut Butter Puffs and with Nabisco to provide Chips Ahoy cookies using Hershey's chocolate morsels. Citibank co-brands MasterCard and Visa with American Airlines. Co-branding benefits firms by allowing them to enter new product classes and capitalize on an already established brand name in those product classes.

New Brand Strategy　In situations in which an organization concludes that its existing brand name(s) cannot be extended to a new product class, a new brand strategy is appropriate. A *new brand strategy* involves the development of a new brand and often a new offering for a product class that has not been previously served by the organization. Examples of successful new brand strategies include the introduction of Prego spaghetti sauce by Campbell Soup, and Aleve, a nonprescription pain reliever, by Roche Holding, Ltd. In both examples, existing company brand names were not deemed extendable to the new product classes for which they were targeted.

A new brand strategy may be the most challenging to successfully implement and the most costly. The cost to introduce a new brand in some consumer markets ranges from $50 million to $100 million. In many ways, this strategy is akin to diversification, with all the attendant challenges associated with this product-market strategy. The marketing of Eagle brand snacks by Anheuser-Busch described in Chapter 1 is an example of a new brand strategy failure. Launching a new brand (Eagle) in a product class new to the company (salty snacks) meant competing with Frito-Lay, the market leader, and its well-entrenched brands. Without a cost/price or quality advantage, focused distribution, effective advertising, promotion, or sales effort, the Eagle brand never achieved more than a modest market share and operated at a loss for 17 years before its demise in 1996.[19]

Flanker/Fighting Brand Strategy   Sometimes new brands are created for a product class already served by the organization when a line extension strategy is deemed inappropriate. These brands expand the product line to tap specific consumer segments not attracted to an organization's existing products/brands or represent defensive moves to counteract competition. As the name suggests, a *flanker brand strategy* involves adding new brands on the high or low end of a product line based on a price–quality continuum. The Marriott Hotel group has done this to attract different traveler segments. In addition to its medium-priced Marriott hotels, it has added Marriott Marquis hotels to attract the upper end of the traveler market. It has added Courtyard hotels for the economy-minded traveler and the Fairfield Inn for those with a very low travel budget. Each brand offers a different amenities assortment and a corresponding room rate. A *fighting brand strategy* involves adding a new brand whose sole purpose is to confront competitive brands in a product class being served by an organization. A fighting brand is typically introduced when (1) an organization has a high relative share of the sales in a product class, (2) its dominant brand(s) is susceptible to having this high share sliced away by aggressive pricing or promotion by competitors, or (3) the organization wishes to preserve its profit margins on its existing brand(s). Frito-Lay successfully used its Santitas brand tortilla chip as a fighting brand to confront lower-price and lower-quality regional tortilla chip brands. This was done without changing the premium price and quality of its flagship Doritos and Tostitos brand tortilla chips. Similarly, Kodak introduced its Funtime brand of film priced 20 percent below its dominant Kodak brand to compete against lower-priced film sold by Fuji and Konica.

Like line extensions, fighting and flanker brand strategies incur the risk of cannibalizing the other brand(s) in a product line. This is particularly likely with lower-priced brands. However, advocates of these brand strategies argue that it is better to engage in *preemptive cannibalism*—the conscious practice of stealing sales from an organization's existing products or brands to keep customers from switching to competitors' offerings—than lose sales volume.[20]

NOTES

1. "SBC Launches Phone-Service 'Bundles' in Two Markets to Compete with AT&T," *Wall Street Journal* (January 6, 2000): B3.

2. "Shopping List: Quick, Classic, Cool for Kids," *BRANDWEEK* (June 17, 2002): S52–S53.

3. "Film vs. Digital: Can Kodak Build a Bridge?" *Business Week* (August 2, 1999): 66–69.

4. Glenn Rifkin, "Mach 3: Anatomy of Gillette's Latest Global Launch," *Strategy & Business* (2nd quarter 1999): 34–41.

5. This and other examples appear in Gerard J. Tellis and Peter N. Golder, *Will and Vision: How Latecomers Grow to Dominate Markets* (New York: McGraw-Hill, 2002).

6. For an extended treatment of the new product development process, see C. Merle Crawford and Anthony DiBenedetto, *New Products Management*, 7th ed. (Burr Ridge, IL: McGraw-Hill/Irwin, 2003).

7. "A Survey of Innovation in Industry," *The Economist* (February 20, 1999).

8. "Is Testing the Answer?" *Advertising Age* (July 9, 2001): 13.

9. Bill Sharfman, "One Last Look at Oldsmobile," *BRANDWEEK* (January 8, 2001): 28–32.

10. Portions of the following discussion are based on Rajeev Batra, John G. Myers, and David A. Aaker, *Advertising Management*, 5th ed. (Upper Saddle River, NJ: Prentice Hall, 1996): 190–201.

11. This example is adapted and updated from Russell Haley, "Benefit Segmentation: A Decision-Oriented Research Tool," in Ben Enis and Keith Cox (eds.), *Marketing Classics*, 7th ed. (Boston: Allyn and Bacon, 1991): 208–215.

12. "St. Joseph: From Babies to Baby Boomers," *Advertising Age* (July 9, 2001): 1, 38; "Few Icebergs on the Horizon," *Business Week* (June 14, 1999): 80–81.

13. This discussion is based on Kevin Lane Keller, *Strategic Brand Management: Building, Measuring, and Managing Brand Equity*, 2nd ed. (Upper Saddle River, NJ: Prentice Hall, 2003).

14. This discussion is based on Roger A. Kerin and Raj Sethuraman, "Exploring the Brand Value–Shareholder Value Nexus for Consumer Goods Companies," *Journal of the Academy of Marketing Science* (Winter 1998); 260–273; "P&G Sells to Cadbury Hawaiian Punch Label in $203 Million Accord," *Wall Street Journal* (April 16, 1999): B2; and "Will Triarc Make Snapple Crackle" *Business Week* (April 28, 1997): 64.

15. This discussion is based on Stephanie Thompson, "The New Private Enterprise," *BRANDWEEK* (May 3, 1999): 36–48; and David Dunne and Chakravarthi Narasimhan, "The New Appeal of Private Labels," *Harvard Business Review* (May–June 1999): 41–52.

16. For different views on brand growth strategies, see David C. Court, Mark G. Leitter, and Mark A. Loch, "Brand Leverage," *The McKinsey Quarterly* (number 2, 1999): 100–110; and John A. Quelch and David Kenny, "Extend Profits, Not Product Lines," *Harvard Business Review* (September–October 1994): 153–160.

17. "Make it Simple," *Business Week* (September 9, 1996): 96–105.

18. "When Brand Extension Becomes Brand Abuse," *BRANDWEEK* (October 26, 1998): 20–22.

19. "How Eagle Became Extinct," *Business Week* (March 4, 1996): 68–69.

20. For an extended discussion on product cannibalism and preemptive cannibalism, see Roger A. Kerin and Dwight Riskey, "Product Cannibalism," in Sidney Levy, ed., *Marketing Manager's Handbook* (Chicago: Dartnell Company, 1994): 880–895.

Dr Pepper/Seven Up, Inc.
Squirt® Brand

In mid-summer 2001, Kate Cox, the brand manager at Dr Pepper/Seven Up, Inc. responsible for Squirt, began to draft the brand's annual advertising and promotion plan. Squirt is a caffeine-free, low-sodium carbonated soft drink brand with a distinctive blend of grapefruit juices that gives it a tangy, fresh citrus taste. Squirt is the best-selling carbonated grapefruit soft drink brand in the United States.

Cox believed that market targeting and product positioning might require attention early in Squirt's advertising and promotion plan development. Both topics were highlighted in a June 2001 presentation by the brand's advertising agency, Foote, Cone & Belding, shortly after she assumed responsibility for Squirt. Actions by competitors, notably Coca-Cola and Pepsi-Cola; a recent dip in Squirt case sales volume; and implications of the growing Hispanic community in markets where Squirt was popular were foremost in her mind.

■ DR PEPPER/SEVEN UP, INC.

Dr Pepper/Seven Up, Inc. is the largest division of Cadbury Schweppes PLC. Cadbury Schweppes PLC is the world's third largest soft drink company and the fourth largest confectionary company, with product sales in almost 200 countries. Headquartered in London, England, Cadbury Schweppes PLC has the distinction of being the world's first soft drink maker and the world's largest non-cola soft drink producer and marketer.

Dr Pepper/Seven Up, Inc. (DPSU) is the largest non-cola soft drink enterprise in North America. The company markets such national brands as Dr Pepper, Seven Up, RC Cola, A&W Root Beer, Canada Dry, Squirt, Hawaiian Punch, and Schweppes, among others. DPSU also owns regional brands including Sundrop and Vernors, among others.

DPSU is the third largest soft drink company in the United States. Its flagship brands—Dr Pepper and Seven Up—are consistently ranked among the top-ten soft drink brands in the United States as measured by market share. Its other brands were often the market leader in their specific categories. For example, Canada Dry is the top-selling ginger ale in the United States, Schweppes is the leading tonic water, and Canada Dry seltzers lead the club soda/seltzer category. Squirt is the best-selling grapefruit soft drink, and A&W Root Beer is the leading root beer sold in bottles and cans.

The cooperation of Dr Pepper/Seven Up, Inc. in the preparation of this case is gratefully acknowledged. This case was prepared by Professor Roger A. Kerin, of the Edwin L. Cox School of Business, Southern Methodist University, as a basis for class discussion and is not designed to illustrate effective or ineffective handling of an administrative situation. Certain company information has been disguised and is not useful for research purposes. Squirt® is a registered trademark used under license (© 2002 Dr Pepper/Seven Up, Inc.) and used in this case with permission from Dr Pepper/Seven Up, Inc. Copyright © 2002 by Roger A. Kerin. This case may not be reproduced without the written permission of the copyright holder.

■ CARBONATED SOFT DRINK INDUSTRY IN THE UNITED STATES

U.S. consumers drink more carbonated soft drinks than tap water. In 2000, Americans consumed 53 gallons of soft drinks per person, compared with about 47 gallons in 1990. Population growth compounded by rising per capita consumption produced an estimated $60.3 billion in carbonated soft drink retail sales in 2000. However, soft drink consumption growth has slowed in recent years.

Industry Structure

There are three major participants in the production and distribution of carbonated soft drinks in the United States.[1] They are concentrate producers, bottlers, and retail outlets. For regular soft drinks, concentrate producers manufacture the basic flavors (for example, lemon-lime and cola) for sale to bottlers, which add a sweetener to carbonated water and package the beverage in bottles and cans, which are then sold to retailers. For diet soft drinks, concentrate producers include an artificial sweetener, such as aspartame, with their flavors. Concentrate producer prices to bottlers differ slightly between regular and diet soft drinks. For example, a concentrate producer's price for regular flavored (non-cola) concentrate is about $1.02 per unit. The diet flavored (non-cola) concentrate price is about $1.18 per unit. A concentrate unit produces the equivalent of one 192-ounce soft drink case (a standard case consists of twenty-four 8-ounce bottles). The Coca-Cola Company, The Pepsi-Cola Company, and Dr Pepper/Seven Up, Inc. are the three major concentrate producers in the United States.

Approximately 500 bottlers in the United States convert flavor concentrate into carbonated soft drinks. Concentrate producers either (1) own or have an equity interest in bottlers or (2) franchise their brands to independent bottlers to produce their products. For example, Coca-Cola Enterprises, Inc. (CCE), with multiple bottler operations, is the largest U.S. bottler of Coca-Cola brand beverage products. CCE accounts for 80 percent of The Coca-Cola Company's soft drink bottle and can volume in North America. Similarly, the Pepsi Bottling Group, Inc., with multiple operations, accounts for 55 percent of Pepsi-Cola brand beverage volume in North America. Independent franchised bottlers are typically granted a right to package and distribute a concentrate producer's branded line of soft drinks in a defined territory and not allowed to market a directly competitive major brand. However, franchised bottlers can represent noncompetitive brands and decline to bottle a concentrate producer's secondary lines. These arrangements mean that a franchised bottler of Coca-Cola cannot sell Pepsi-Cola but can bottle and market Squirt rather than Coca-Cola's Fresca.

The principal retail channels for carbonated soft drinks are supermarkets, convenience stores, vending machines, fountain service, mass merchandisers, and thousands of small retail outlets. Soft drinks are typically sold in bottles and cans, except for fountain service. In fountain service, syrup is sold to a retail outlet (such as McDonald's), which mixes the syrup with carbonated water for immediate consumption by customers. Supermarkets and grocery stores account for about 31 percent of carbonated soft drink industry retail sales.

Competition in the Soft Drink Industry

Three companies command over 90 percent of carbonated soft drink sales in the United States. The Coca-Cola Company leads the industry with a 44.1 percent market share, followed by The Pepsi-Cola Company (31.4 percent), and Dr Pepper/Seven Up, Inc. (14.7 percent). These three companies also market the top ten brands, measured

---

[1]A portion of this discussion is based on "Industry Surveys: Foods & Nonalcoholic Beverages," *Standard & Poor's* (New York: Standard & Poor's, December 6, 2001).

in market share. Coca-Cola owns five of the top-ten brands; Pepsi-Cola owns three; and Dr Pepper/Seven Up owns two. These ten brands account for almost 73 percent of soft drink sales in the United States. Exhibit 1 shows the top-ten carbonated soft drink companies and brands in 2000.

Soft Drink Marketing

Soft drink marketing is characterized by heavy investment in consumer advertising and promotion, selling and trade promotion to and through bottlers to retail outlets, and consumer price discounting. Concentrate producers usually assume responsibility for developing national consumer advertising and promotion programs, product development and planning, and marketing research. Bottlers usually take the lead in developing local trade promotions to retail outlets and local consumer promotions.

EXHIBIT 1

Top-Ten Carbonated Soft Drink Companies and Brands in 2000

		Top-Ten Soft Drink Companies		
Rank	**Companies**	**Market Share %**	**Share Change**[a]	**Volume % Change**[b]
1	Coca-Cola Co.	44.1	flat	+0.1
2	Pepsi-Cola Co.	31.4	flat	+0.1
3	Dr Pepper/7 Up (Cadbury Schweppes)	14.7	+0.1	+1.1
4	Cott Corp.	3.3	+0.2	+5.8
5	National Beverage	2.1	flat	+4.2
6	Royal Crown[b]	1.1	−0.1	−1.9
7	Big Red	0.4	flat	+13.4
8	Seagram	0.3	flat	+7.2
9	Monarch Co.	0.1	flat	−35.8
10	Private label/other	2.5	−0.2	−12.2
	Total Industry	100.0		+0.2

		Top-Ten Soft Drink Brands			
Rank	**Companies**	**Brand Owner**	**Market Share %**	**Share Change**[a]	**Volume % Change**[b]
1	Coke Classic	Coca-Cola	20.4	+0.1	+0.5
2	Pepsi-Cola	Pepsi-Cola	13.6	−0.2	−1.0
3	Diet Coke	Coca-Cola	8.7	+0.2	+2.5
4	Mountain Dew	Pepsi-Cola	7.2	+0.1	+1.5
5	Sprite	Coca-Cola	6.6	−0.2	−2.0
6	Dr Pepper	Dr Pepper/7 Up	6.3	flat	+0.1
7	Diet Pepsi	Pepsi-Cola	5.3	+0.2	+4.0
8	7Up	Dr Pepper/7 Up	2.0	−0.1	−0.6
9	CF Diet Coke	Coca-Cola	1.7	−0.1	−1.0
10	Barq's Root Beer	Coca-Cola	1.1	flat	+3.0
	Total Top-Ten		72.9		

Notes: [a] Share change and volume change data are based on the difference from 1999.

[b] Royal Crown was purchased by Dr Pepper/Seven Up in the 4th quarter 2000, but treated as a separate company for 2000 data.

Source: "Top-10 U.S. Soft Drink Companies and Brands for 2000," *Beverage Digest* (February 15, 2001). Special Issue. Used with permission.

Bottlers are also responsible for selling and servicing retail accounts, including the placement and maintenance of in-store displays and the restocking of retailer shelves and vending machines with their brands. The different marketing roles assumed by concentrate producers and bottlers are apparent in their comparative income statements. As shown in Exhibit 2, concentrate producers spend about 39 cents of every sales dollar on advertising and promotion. Bottlers spend about 28 cents of every sales dollar on selling and delivery expenses.

Soft Drink Advertising and Promotion.   Local advertising and promotion programs are jointly implemented and financed by concentrate producers and bottlers. Concentrate producers and bottlers often split local advertising costs 50–50. For example, if $1 million were spent for local television brand advertising in a bottler's territory, $500,000 would be paid by the brand's local bottler and $500,000 would be paid by the concentrate producer. Bottlers and concentrate producers split the cost of local retail-oriented merchandise promotions and consumer promotions 50–50. However, advertising and promotion programs are negotiated, sometimes at the individual bottler level. A bottler may choose, or not choose, to participate in a concentrate producer's advertising or promotion program or negotiate its own financial arrangement.

A variety of merchandising and consumer promotions are used in the soft drink industry. Merchandising promotions include end-of-aisle displays, other types of special freestanding displays, and shelf banners. Concentrate producers will often provide up to 20 cents per case sold to bottlers who implement these merchandising promotions. Consumer promotions include sponsorship of local sports, cultural and entertainment events, plastic cups and napkins with the brand logo, and stylish baseball caps, T-shirts, or sunglasses featuring the brand name. Assorted other promotions are also used, including coupons, on-package promotions, and sweepstakes. Concentrate producers will offer anywhere from 5 cents (for cups, caps, or glasses) to 25 cents (for local event marketing including cups, caps, or glasses) per case sold to bottlers who use these promotions.

Concentrate producers occasionally offer bottlers price promotions in the form of merchandising incentives. These incentives are typically based on case sales and are

EXHIBIT 2

Comparative Income Statements for the Typical Flavored Concentrate Producer and Soft Drink Bottler in the United States (per standard twenty-four 8-ounce bottle case)

	Concentrate Producer	*Soft Drink Bottler*
Net sales	100%	100%
Cost of goods sold	-17	-57*
Gross profit	83%	43%
Selling and delivery	2	28
Advertising and promotion**	39	2
General and administrative expense	13	4
Pretax profit	29%	9%

* Packaging represents the major element of a bottler's cost of goods sold.

** Advertising and promotion includes production costs, fees, and media placement expenses.

Source: Industry analysts and case writer estimates.

frequently used to stimulate bottler sales and participation in merchandising activities. These incentives are often in the range of 15 to 25 cents per case depending on the amount of effort requested.

Brand and Flavor Competition   There are more than 900 registered brand names for carbonated soft drinks in the United States. Most of these brands are sold regionally and reflect taste and flavor preferences of consumers in different parts of the United States.

Colas are the dominant flavor in the U.S. carbonated soft drink industry, accounting for about 60 percent of total retail sales in 2000. The dominance of colas has eroded in the past decade from roughly two-thirds of total retail sales in 1990. By comparison, flavored soft drinks have grown in popularity. Flavors such as orange, lemon-lime, cherry, grape, and root beer now represent about one-quarter of carbonated soft drink sales following a 30 percent increase in sales from 1990 to 2000. The changing composition of the U.S. population has been an important factor in the growing popularity of flavored carbonated soft drinks.

Demographics of Soft Drink Consumption   Industry research indicates that the average American consumes 849 eight-ounce servings of carbonated soft drinks annually, or roughly 2.3 servings per day. Nearly all Americans consume at least one soft drink serving in a given year. Most carbonated soft drink volume in the United States is consumed by individuals aged 20 to 49. The prominence of this age group is due mainly to the fact that it is the largest segment of the U.S. population. Consumption of diet soft drinks is more pronounced among consumers over 25 years of age. Teens and young adults generally are heavier consumers of regular soft drinks. Conventional wisdom in the soft drink industry holds that teens and young adults are the primary audience for soft drink marketing, since taste and brand preferences are formed between 12 and 24 years of age.

Per capita consumption of soft drinks is higher among Hispanics and African Americans than other racial and ethnic groups and among teens than adults. Furthermore, the trend favoring flavored carbonated soft drinks has been attributed in part to the changing demographic mix in the United States. Today, about 25 percent of Americans are younger than 18 and one-quarter of the U.S. population is Hispanic and African American. These population groups tend to consume flavored carbonated soft drinks. "The bottom line is that young consumers in recent years have been galvanized by flavor (citrus) brands," notes the editor and publisher of *Beverage Digest*, an industry trade publication.[2] By 2005, Hispanic youth will overtake African Americans to become the largest ethnic youth population, according to U.S. Census 2000 figures. They will account for 17 percent of all youth under age 18, and 45 percent of all minority minors in the United States. By 2010, one minor in five will be Hispanic, amounting to a 22 percent increase in nine years, while during the same period, the number of white youth will experience a decrease of 5 percent.[3]

Major soft drink companies have responded to the growing prominence of Hispanic and African American consumers and teens in different ways. The Coca-Cola Company has elevated Hispanics from its sixth priority to second after teens, according to the senior brand manager for multicutural marketing at Coca-Cola North America.[4] Following this change in priorities, Coca-Cola North America and Coca-

---

[2]"Flat Colas Anxiously Watch Gen Yers Switch," *Advertising Age* (September 25, 2000), p. 510.

[3]"Targeting Teens," *Hispanic Business* (September 2001), pp. 15–17.

[4]This discussion is based on Hillary Chura, "Identifying a Demographic Sweet Spot," *Advertising Age* (November 12, 2001), p. 16; "New Apple-flavored Manzana Mia and Popular Fanta Soft Drinks Roll Out in Southern California," The Coca-Cola Company News Release, April 20, 2001; and "Coke Relaunches Fanta, New Drink, Targets Southern California Hispanics," Reuters News Service, April 11, 2001.

Cola Bottling Company of Southern California recently introduced two flavored soft drinks to the Southern California market. In March 2001, Coca-Cola launched Manzana Mía, an apple-flavored soft drink similar to Manzana Lift, a Coca-Cola Company brand sold in Mexico. In addition, Fanta, The Coca-Cola Company's second largest brand that is distributed primarily outside the United States, was introduced to Southern California featuring orange, grape, strawberry, and pineapple flavors. According to a spokesperson at The Coca-Cola Bottling Company of Southern California, "Many Southern Californians know about Manzana Lift and have expressed enthusiasm for having it available here in the United States. They have also told us that they want more fruit-flavored carbonated beverages." Company research specifically indicated that fruit flavored soft drinks held a special appeal for Hispanics in Southern California. A senior executive at Coca-Cola North America added, "In this case, we evaluated our international beverage portfolio and decided to introduce the Manzana Lift and Fanta beverage concepts in Southern California, adapting their positioning and packaging to meet local consumer preferences."

Marketers of Pepsi-Cola's Mountain Dew also have attended to the growing prominence of Hispanic consumers. Mountain Dew—the fourth largest U.S. soft drink brand and the best-selling flavored (citrus) carbonated beverage—now features advertising that specifically caters to the Hispanic market. According to Mountain Dew's director of marketing, "Ethnic markets are a huge growth opportunity for us and we are investing more in that area." The brand's primary target audience is teens and its base positioning and advertising feature a fun, exhilarating, daring, and adventurous "Dew-x-perience." Twenty- to 39-year-olds make up the brand's secondary market.[5]

Both Coca-Cola and Pepsi-Cola now rank among the top 25 advertisers to the Hispanic community in the United States. It was estimated that Coca-Cola would spend $18.7 million and Pepsi-Cola $16 million in media advertising to the Hispanic market in 2001, or about 2 percent of each company's advertising expenditure.[6]

■ SQUIRT BRAND HERITAGE AND MARKETING

Squirt has been marketed by Dr Pepper/Seven Up, Inc. since 1995 and by Cadbury Schweppes PLC since 1993. However, the brand's origins are found in the Great Depression of the 1930s.

History of Squirt

The origin of Squirt is traced to Herb Bishop of Phoenix, Arizona, who in 1938, began experimenting with Citrus Club, a then-popular, regional non-carbonated beverage. Bishop created a new carbonated soft drink that required less fruit and less sugar to produce. The new drink "seemed to squirt onto the tongue just like squeezing a grapefruit," so Bishop named the drink Squirt. For advertising, Bishop and his partner, Ed Mehren, created a likeable character named "Little Squirt" (see Exhibit 3). The appeal of "Little Squirt" was immediate and subsequently broadened Squirt's attraction. Squirt sales grew during World War II because its low sugar content helped bottlers restricted by sugar rationing rules. Squirt established itself as a mixer in the 1950s. By the mid-1970s, Squirt was introduced internationally in Central and South America.

In 1977, Brooks Products, a bottler in Holland, Michigan, purchased Squirt from Bishop. The company reformulated Squirt, updated Squirt's logo, and positioned the brand as a mainstream soft drink. In 1983, taking advantage of new low-calorie soft drink technology, Diet Squirt became the first soft drink in the United States to be

---

[5]"Being True to Dew," *Brandweek* (April 24, 2000), p. 24.

[6]"Top 60 Advertisers in the Hispanic Market, 2001," *Hispanic Business* (December 2001), p. 18.

EXHIBIT 3

Little Squirt Character

sweetened with Nutra Sweet (Aspertame). Squirt joined A&W Brands in 1986, which was subsequently purchased by Cadbury Schweppes PLC in 1993. After the March 1995 acquisition of Dr Pepper/Seven Up Companies, Inc. by Cadbury Schweppes PLC, responsibility for manufacturing, marketing, and distribution of Squirt was assigned to Dr Pepper/Seven Up, Inc. in the United States.

Squirt Marketing

Squirt sales since 1995 have exceeded preacquisition levels due to a broadened bottling and distribution network supported by increased marketing attention and investment. Exhibit 4 shows Squirt case sales volume for the period 1990 through 2000.

Squirt Bottler and Sales Distribution   Squirt is bottled and sold by some 250 bottlers in the United States. One-third of these bottlers were independent franchised
bottlers or part of the Dr Pepper/Seven Up, Inc. Bottling Group. Two-thirds of Squirt
bottlers were affiliated with Coca-Cola Enterprises, Inc. and the Pepsi Bottling Group,
Inc. The geographical distribution of these bottlers meant that Squirt was available in
about 83 percent of U.S. bottler markets that represented about 85 percent of total
soft drink volume in the United States. The New York City metropolitan area was the
largest market without a Squirt bottler.

   Five bottler markets accounted for 50 percent of Squirt case sales volume. These
were Los Angeles (30 percent), Chicago (7 percent), Detroit (6 percent), San Diego (4
percent), and Portland, Oregon (3 percent). Another ten bottler markets represented
20 percent of Squirt case volume. Ten additional bottler markets accounted for 10 percent of Squirt case volume. The remaining 20 percent of Squirt case volume was
divided among other Squirt bottlers. Some 100 bottlers in the western United States
accounted for about one-half of Squirt case volume. California alone represented 38
percent of Squirt's case volume in 2000. Squirt bottlers in Southern California were
affiliated with Coca-Cola Enterprises, Inc. and in Northern California with the Pepsi
Bottling Group, Inc.

Squirt Product Line and Competitive Brands   The Squirt product line consists of regular and diet Squirt and regular and diet Ruby Red Squirt—a berry flavor extension
introduced in 1993. The diet version of Squirt and Ruby Red Squirt account for about
20 percent of sales. Exhibit 5 displays the Squirt product line.

   As a carbonated grapefruit soft drink, Squirt competes directly with Coca-Cola's
two carbonated grapefruit soft drink brands—Fresca and Citra. Introduced in the
1960s, Fresca is a caffeine-free, diet soft drink targeted principally at adults (30 years
of age and older) and, more recently, used as a mixer.[7] As recently as 1992, Fresca was

EXHIBIT 4

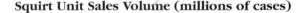

Squirt Unit Sales Volume (millions of cases)

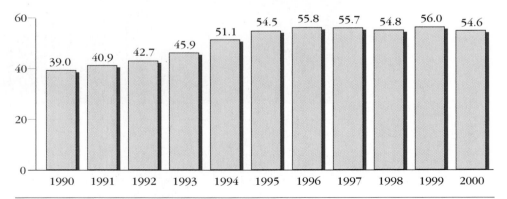

Source: *Beverage Digest.* Used with permission.

---

[7]"Fresca Enjoys New Bubble of Popularity," *Wall Street Journal* (September 11, 2001), p. A11.

EXHIBIT 5

Squirt Product Line

one of the fastest-growing soft drinks in the United States. Citra was introduced by Coca-Cola in early 1997 as a "sugared" counterpart to Fresca and does not have a diet version. The brand is targeted at teens and young adults and is caffeine free.[8]

In the broader citrus-flavored soft drink category, Squirt also competes with two Coca-Cola brands, Mello Yellow and Surge, Pepsi-Cola's Mountain Dew, and Sundrop, marketed by Dr Pepper/Seven Up. All four brands contain caffeine. Except for Surge, all brands are sold in regular and diet versions. Mountain Dew is the largest selling citrus-flavored carbonated soft drink brand in the United States. Industry analysts attribute the brand's popularity to its association with everyday youth culture and connecting with it across alternative sports, hip-hop, and college basketball. Mountain Dew Code Red, a cherry-flavored extension introduced in mid-2001, has leveraged these associations with its tag line: "New Code Red. A cherry rush that'll bring you right back to the streets."[9]

Coca-Cola's Surge brand was introduced in 1997 to attract consumers before they became Mountain Dew drinkers. However, industry analysts speculated in early 2001 that some Coca-Cola's Surge bottlers were discontinuing the brand.[10] Mello Yellow, a nationally distributed citrus-flavored brand marketed by Coca-Cola, is most prominent in the southeastern United States. Sun Drop, marketed by Dr Pepper/Seven Up, is a popular regional brand in the southeastern United States. The brand's slogan—"Tastes Good. Nothing Else Matters"—emphasizes the refreshing taste of this beverage. Exhibit 6 shows case volume sales data for Squirt and competitive brands for the period 1996–2000.

EXHIBIT 6

Case Volume Trend for Major Carbonated Grapefruit and Citrus-Flavored Brands in the United States: 1996–2000

Company/Brand(s)	Case Volume (millions) by Year				
	1996	1997	1998	1999	2000*
Coca-Cola					
Fresca	28.0	26.2	25.9	25.5	24.1
Citra	NA	NA	21.0	26.2	15.6
Mello Yellow	59.0	46.6	42.4	41.6	45.7
Surge	NA	69.0	51.8	26.7	11.8
Pepsi-Cola					
Mountain Dew	605.9	683.2	748.1	793.0	809.8
Regular	535.6	605.2	665.1	705.0	715.6
Diet	70.3	78.0	83.0	88.0	94.2
Dr Pepper/Seven Up					
Sundrop	19.7	20.1	20.4	20.1	20.2
Squirt/Ruby Red	55.8	55.7	54.8	56.0	54.6
Total Case Volume	768.4	900.8	964.4	989.1	981.8

*Note: 2000 competitor case volume data represent estimated figures.

Source: Beverage Digest. Used with permission.

---

[8]"Citra: Coke Debuts Yet Another Soft Drink in U.S.," Beverage Digest (January 22, 1997), p. 38; "Coke Takes Citra National," Beverage Digest (February 5, 1999), p. 22.

[9]"Code Red Soft Drink Sales Explode," AdAge.com, downloaded August 27, 2001.

[10]"Coke Shifts Strategy as Surge Fizzles," AdAge.com, downloaded February 12, 2001.

Squirt Advertising and Promotion Expenditures and Competitor Spending A variety of media have been used to advertise Squirt. These media include freestanding inserts in newspapers, spot television, cable television, and spot radio. Squirt also uses retail, consumer, and trade promotions and has a number of cooperative advertising arrangements with individual bottlers. Media advertising expenditures for Squirt are typically less than competitors. However, due to consistent advertising over an extended time period, Squirt enjoys the highest consumer brand awareness among carbonated grapefruit soft drinks in the United States. Squirt expenditures for retail, trade, and consumer promotions and cooperative advertising arrangements often exceed media advertising expenditures. Combined, these expenditures amount to 20 to 25 percent of dollar sales.[11]

Coca-Cola and Pepsi-Cola typically spend more on media advertising and promotion than does Dr Pepper/Seven Up, Inc. for its major carbonated grapefruit and citrus-flavored brands. Mountain Dew is the most heavily advertised brand in this category. As a rule, media advertising expenditures are typically higher, both in dollar terms and as a percent of sales, for new brands. Also, expenditures for retail, trade, and consumer programs often exceed the amount spent for media advertising. Exhibit 7 shows the estimated media advertising spending for major carbonated grapefruit and citrus-flavored brands by concentrate producers in the United States for the period 1996–2000. Planned media expenditures for Squirt in 2001 were the same as 2000.

Squirt Positioning Squirt positioning was addressed soon after Cadbury Schweppes PLC acquired the brand. In 1994, Foote, Cone & Belding recommended, and brand management agreed, that Squirt's unique thirst-quenching attribute should be the

EXHIBIT 7

Estimated Media Advertising Spending for Major Carbonated Grapefruit and Citrus-Flavored Brands in the United States:1996–2000

Company/Brand(s)	Estimated Media Advertising Expenditures ($000) by Year				
	1996	1997	1998	1999	2000
Coca-Cola					
Fresca	2,471.5	730.2	672.6	N.S.	N.S.
Citra	NA	1,119.1	6,711.6	10,100.4	98.4
Mellow Yellow	1,407.8	1,524.2	1,199.7	1,010.6	773.1
Surge	NA	13,611.0	17,846.7	18,967.4	243.8
Pepsi-Cola					
Mountain Dew (Regular & Diet)	28,991.3	33,951.1	40,104.3	37,074.3	50,384.6
Dr Pepper/Seven Up					
Sundrop	10.9	429.6	3.0	391.8	314.1
Squirt Regular/Diet	3,485.1	1,657.6	955.8	601.5	390.0
Squirt Ruby Red	1,807.6	537.2	N.S.	N.S.	N.S.

Key: NA = Not Available; N.S. = No Significant Expenditures

Source: CMR/TNS Media Intelligence U.S. Used with permission.

---

[11]*Case writer note*: Dr Pepper/Seven Up, Inc. does not disclose promotion expenditure data for its brands. The percent-of-sales figure is provided for case analysis and discussion purposes only.

dominant positioning dimension upon which to build the brand. Squirt was targeted at adults, 18–44 years old. Ruby Red Squirt was positioned as a "fruity bold way to refresh your thirst," and targeted at teens and young adults, 12–24 years old. Advertising for Squirt emphasized the "hip, cool, experiential nature" of the brand with the message: "Beyond the ordinary refreshment—the great citrus taste is incredibly thirst quenching." Ruby Red Squirt advertising emphasized its *bold* taste and extraordinary refreshment with the message: "It's fruity berry and citrus taste is incredibly *exciting*." Advertising featured two television commercials labeled "Mountain Bike" and "Rollerblade" and portrayed Squirt and Ruby Red Squirt in action-oriented biking and skating settings.

In mid-1995, following the acquisition of Dr Pepper/Seven Up by Cadbury Schweppes PLC, Foote, Cone & Belding was asked to revise its creative strategy. The reasoning was that the creative execution was "a bit too intense to fit with the brand." Instead of sport situations that may have suggested Squirt might be an isotonic beverage (a believability issue), Squirt's creative strategy migrated to "everyday, on-the-go experiences." The emphasis on Squirt's thirst-quenching benefit remained but was now portrayed in "spunky, lively, sociable, colorful, and music-driven" advertising vignettes that depicted fun-loving, individualistic young adults. The target market was also narrowed to adults, 18–34 years old. Advertising copy described Squirt as "Fun relief when you're dry" with the tag line "Squirt Your Thirst." Exhibits 8 and 9 show television commercials for Squirt and Ruby Red Squirt with this creative execution.

Squirt's positioning and creative execution were revisited in 1999 and again in 2000, following the introduction of Citra by Coca-Cola, but no changes were made. Citra debuted in March 1997 in the southeastern and southwestern United States with English and Spanish language television and radio advertising.[12] Citra was positioned as a light-hearted, youthful, and thirst-quenching soft drink. The brand's advertising emphasized the slogan "No Thirst Is Safe" and featured the adventures and misadventures of teenagers roaming the country in a recreational vehicle.[13] By 1998, Citra was available in 50 percent of U.S. bottler markets. In February 1999, Coca-Cola announced that Citra would be available in 95 percent of U.S. bottler markets by 2000.[14]

DPSU consumer research indicated that few Squirt users considered Citra's positioning or advertising appealing to them. Additional DPSU consumer research and taste testing of Squirt and Citra indicated that Squirt scored higher on the thirst-quenching attribute. "Brand name, packaging, and Citra's newness supported by advertising appeared to drive [Citra's] initial sales," said an advertising agency executive. Subsequent consumer research uncovered potential opportunities for Squirt positioning and the creative execution in the brand's advertising. This research indicated that Squirt advertising effectively communicated the intended fun and thirst-quenching message, portrayed Squirt users in an interesting, unique, and involving manner, and engaged the target audience with music. However, a portion of both younger and older Squirt users considered aspects of the imagery in the commercials "juvenile." Furthermore, focus group interviews indicated that Citra users (mostly 18- to 74-year-olds) did not consider Squirt's positioning and creative execution in its advertising as speaking to their current lifestyle. Squirt's brand management requested a formal positioning review for Squirt in early 2001 by Foote, Cone & Belding and scheduled a presentation for June.

---

[12]"Coca-Cola Rolling Out Citra in Two New Test Markets," *The Atlanta Journal and Constitution* (April 12, 1997), p. 2H.

[13]"Coca-Cola to Promote Citra on MTV's 'Road Rules' Show; Grapefruit Drink's Territory Expands," *The Atlanta Journal and Constitution* (March 4, 1999), p. 2G.

[14]"Coke Takes Citra National," *Beverage Digest* (February 5, 1999), p. 22.

EXHIBIT 8

Squirt Television Commercial

(MUSIC BEGINS)

MALE VOCALIST: Everybody's a little wild, everybody's a little child.

Everybody's a little squirt. Be a squirt and squirt your thirst.

Everybody's a little cool, everybody breaks a little rule.

Everybody's a little squirt. Be a squirt and squirt your thirst.

Everybody's a little juvenile, everybody's a little infantile.

Everybody's a little squirt. Be a squirt and squirt your thirst.

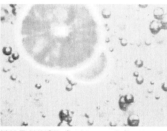

MALE ANNCR: Squirt, a cool citrus blend.

MALE VOCALIST: Everybody's a little squirt.

Be a squirt

and squirt your thirst.

Everybody's a little squirt. Be a squirt and squirt your thirst. (MUSIC ENDS)

EXHIBIT 9

Ruby Red Squirt Television Commercial

(MUSIC IN) MALE VOCALIST SINGS: Everybody's a little wild.

Everybody's a little shy.

Everybody's a little squirt. Here, squirt, squirt your thirst.

Everybody's a little cool. Everybody breaks the little rules.

Everybody's a little squirt.

Here, squirt, squirt your thirst. Everybody a little juvenile.

Everybody's a little infantile. Everybody's a little squirt. Here,

Squirt, squirt your thirst.

MALE ANNCR: Ruby Red Squirt,

a citrus berry blast.

Everybody's a little Squirt. Here, squirt, squirt your thirst.

Everybody's a little squirt. Here, squirt, squirt-- (MUSIC OUT)

■ SQUIRT POSITIONING REVIEW: JUNE 2001

The Squirt positioning review was presented to brand management on June 25, 2001. The review consisted of two parts: (1) a positioning analysis and (2) a recommendation.

Positioning Analysis

The Foot, Cone & Belding (FCB) presentation began by stating the purpose of the positioning review: "To develop a strategic platform to help grow volume and maintain Squirt's leadership as the number one grapefruit carbonated soft drink." After providing an historical review of Squirt advertising copy and creative strategy since 1994, attention turned to brand positioning.

Exhibit 10 shows FCB's analysis of the relative positioning of the seven major grapefruit and citrus brands in mid-June 2001. According to the FCB analysis, these seven brands were positioned along two prominent dimensions. Squirt was the most

EXHIBIT 10

Perceptual Map of Grapefruit and Citrus Brands: Mid-2001

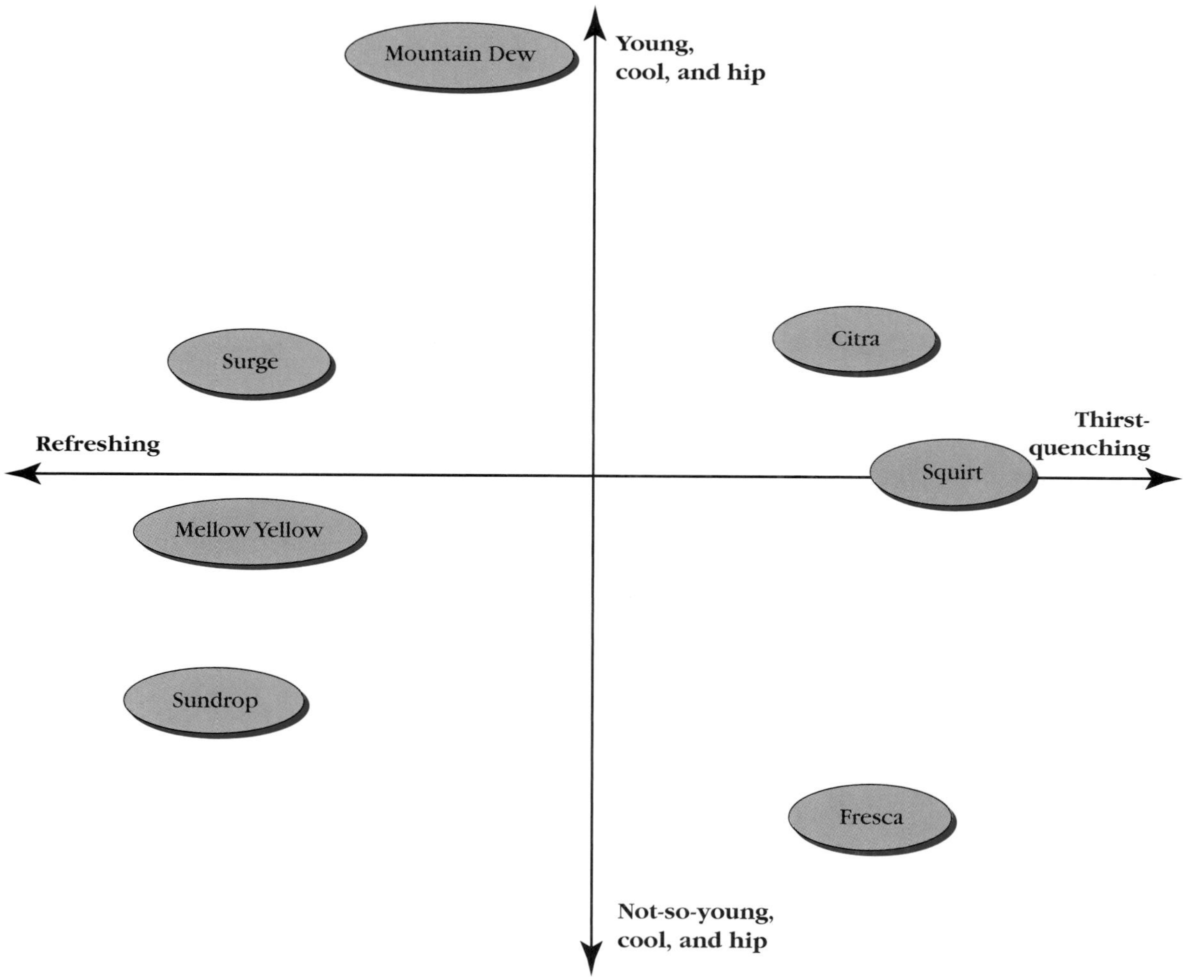

Source: Squirt Positioning Review, June 25, 2001.

"thirst-quenching" beverage. Mountain Dew was the most "young, cool, and hip" beverage. Coca-Cola's Citra brand was the most closely positioned brand next to Squirt based on FCB's analysis. FCB personnel concluded, "A creative strategy needed to be developed to increase relevancy with a younger target [market] and focus on Squirt's thirst-quenching property."

Target Market and Positioning Recommendation

Following a review of U.S. Census 2000 statistics, Squirt consumption data, and its own and Dr Pepper/Seven Up research, FCB proposed a refinement in Squirt's target market and positioning. Citing research that featured Squirt's consumption by racial/ethnic group and age relative to carbonated soft drink users (Exhibit 11), FCB recommended that Squirt be targeted at multicultural, 18- to 24-year-olds to tap into this heavy carbonated soft drink user segment.

Squirt positioning would continue to emphasize its "thirst-quenching" benefit. To increase the brand's relevancy to this segment, Squirt's positioning and advertising would speak to the unique 21- to 24-year-old life stage marked by the straddling of adult responsibilities and more carefree times. This recommendation was based on focus group interviews and other research suggesting that 21- to 24-year-old consumers experience a transition stage into adulthood bringing new challenges. These consumers also want to make the most out of life, work hard, and play even harder. The formal positioning statement for Squirt, upon which a creative advertising execution could be built, was stated as follows:

> For young multicultural adults who thrive on the excitement and spontaneity of living up to the max, Squirt citrus soda fuels your thirst for living life loud, with an exhilarating taste that's powerfully thirst-quenching!

This new positioning had five benefits, according to FCB personnel. First, it is appropriate for the carbonated soft drink category. Second, like carbonated soft drinks, it emphasizes instant gratification. Third, the positioning emphasizes the freedom that this demographic segment strives to maintain. Fourth, with proper creative execution, this positioning has the potential to break through the clutter of soft drink advertising. Finally, the new positioning is consistent with Squirt's product look and feel.

■ THE HISPANIC MARKET OPPORTUNITY

Kate Cox met briefly and informally with the Squirt brand management team the day following the FCB presentation. During the meeting, the popularity of fruit-flavored carbonated beverages among African American and Hispanic teens and young adults was discussed. Also, the reference to making Squirt relevant to multicultural, 18- to 24-year-olds initiated a discussion about simultaneously reaching current and potentially new Hispanic as well as African American Squirt customers. The meeting concluded with an assignment given to Jaxie Stollenwerck, the associate brand manager for Squirt, to prepare a profile of Hispanic and African American consumers in the United States from recently released U.S. Census 2000 data and any other relevant sources.

Hispanic Consumers in the United States

Kate Cox received an e-mail from Jaxie Stollenwerck the following week while on a visit with a Squirt bottler concerning a local promotion. A paraphrased summary of the report is reproduced here:

1. According to the U.S. Census 2000, the Hispanic population in the United States increased by 57.9 percent from 22.4 million in 1990 to 35.3 million in 2000, compared with an increase of 13.2 percent for the total U.S. population.

EXHIBIT 11

Demographics of Squirt Consumption

(A) Squirt Volume Breakdown by Racial/Ethnic Group: Total U.S. Market

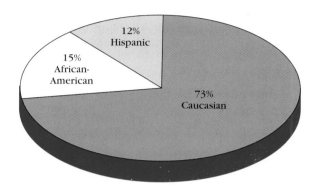

(B) Consumption Volume and Age Relationship Among Carbonated Soft Drink Users and Squirt Users: Total U.S. Market

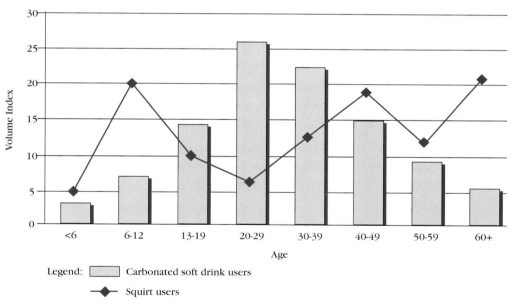

Source: Squirt Positioning Review, June 25, 2001.

In 2000, 58.5 percent of Hispanics in the United States were Mexican, 9.6 percent were Puerto Rican, 3.5 percent were Cuban, 8.6% were of Central or South American ancestry, and 19.7 percent were of other Hispanic ancestry or origins not classified. Hispanics accounted for 12.5 percent of the U.S. population in 2000. African Americans accounted for 12.3 percent of the U.S. population, or 34.7 million people.

2. More than 75 percent of Hispanics live in the western and southern United States (43.5 percent live in the West; 32.8 percent live in the South).

Mexicans, Puerto Ricans, and Cubans are concentrated in different regions. Among Mexicans, 55.3 percent live in the West; 31.7 percent live in the South. Among Puerto Ricans, 60.4 percent live in the Northeast; 22.3 percent live in the South. Among Cubans, 74.2 percent live in the South; 13.6 percent live in the Northeast. For comparison, 54.8 percent of African Americans live in the South; just 8.4 percent live in the West.

3. More than half of all Hispanics live in just two states: California and Texas. There are 11 million Hispanics in California (77 percent of which are of Mexican ancestry) and 6.7 million Hispanics in Texas (76 percent of which are of Mexican ancestry).

4. The 10 largest "places" (defined by the U.S. Census Bureau) where Hispanics reside are shown here:

Rank	Place and State	Hispanic Population	Percent Hispanic of Total Population
1	New York, NY	2,160,554	27.0
2	Los Angeles, CA	1,719,073	46.5
3	Chicago, IL	753,644	26.0
4	Houston, TX	730,865	37.4
5	San Antonio, TX	671,394	58.7
6	Phoenix, AZ	449,972	34.1
7	El Paso, TX	431,875	76.6
8	Dallas, TX	422,587	35.6
9	San Diego, CA	310,752	25.4
10	San Jose, CA	269,989	30.2

Among the 10 places with the largest Hispanic populations, Puerto Ricans represented the largest share (36.5 percent) of all Hispanics in New York, while Mexicans represented the largest share (varying from 63.5 percent in Los Angeles to 83.4 percent in San Diego) of all Hispanics in the nine other places. In Chicago, Mexicans represented 70.4 percent of all Hispanics. Of the 10 largest places where African Americans reside, just four overlap with Hispanic places: New York (first), Chicago (second), Houston (fifth), and Los Angeles (seventh), Detroit, one of our largest markets, ranks third in places where African Americans reside.

5. The relative youthfulness of the Hispanic population is reflected in its population under age 18 and its median age. While 25.7 percent of the U.S. population was under 18 in 2000, 35 percent of Hispanics were under 18. The median age for Hispanics was 25 years in 2000, while the median age for the entire U.S. population was 35.3 years. Mexicans had a median age of 24.2 years, Puerto Ricans 27.2 years, and Cubans 40.7 years. In high density Hispanic markets like Los Angeles, Hispanics under 20 represent 58 percent of all Los Angeles youth in that age group. This group will grow to capture 80 percent by 2003. The median age of African Americans was 30.2; 32.4 percent of African Americans were under 18, and 42.6 percent were under 25.

6. The diversity of nationalities that make up the U.S. Hispanic population is apparent in language and cultural differences. For example, research shows that, even though all nationalities speak Spanish, dialects differ. Also, since about 50 percent of Hispanics in the United States are immigrants, many prefer to converse in their native language. This seems relevant for advertising. According to Strategy Research Corp., 55.4 percent of Hispanics prefer to see and hear ads in Spanish, while 30.3 percent would choose English and 13.2

percent don't have a preference between the two languages. Young Hispanics aged 18–24 are about evenly split on language, with 44 percent preferring ads in English and 46 percent in Spanish. As an aside, I also ran across other interesting tidbits worth noting. It seems there is a strong brand link with heritage among Hispanics; authenticity is important as is an emotional connection with brands; Hispanics don't like "hard sell" approaches and prefer messages that are real and relevant to them.

7. Hispanics prefer shopping close to home and tend to patronize mom-and-pop grocery outlets, convenience stores, and bodegas (a small shop that sells food and other items, mostly to Spanish-speaking customers).

8. Finally, I came across some interesting statistics about the Mexican CSD (carbonated soft drink) market. Mexico is the second largest CSD market in the world and Squirt is the eighth largest CSD brand in Mexico. Squirt is the second most popular brand in the grapefruit category, which happens to be the second largest category (after cola) in Mexico, with a 41 percent share. Squirt is owned and marketed by Refremex AG in Mexico.

The information provided confirmed Kate Cox's suspicion about the size of the Hispanic community in major Squirt bottler markets. She also thought that the mention made to authenticity and the importance of an emotional link to brands coupled with being real and relevant in advertising paralleled the FCB analysis. Cox was particularly interested in the reference made to Squirt's prominence in Mexico. She knew Squirt was sold in Mexico, but not by Dr Pepper/Seven Up, and had heard the brand was popular there. However, this information, later confirmed, was particularly intriguing. She thought, "Could Squirt's popularity in Mexico be leveraged in the United States or had Squirt already benefited from its Mexican linkages?" She scheduled a meeting of the Squirt brand management team upon her return to discuss market targeting and positioning topics related to the annual advertising and promotion plan.

Squirt Advertising and Promotion Plan Development

Kate Cox assembled the Squirt brand management team in mid-summer 2001 to begin drafting the annual advertising and promotion plan for Squirt in the United States. Once drafted, the plan would be formally presented to senior management for review and approval prior to its implementation.

Kate Cox began the meeting by echoing FCB's purpose behind the recent Squirt positioning review. She emphasized that her strategic intent was to lay a solid foundation for Squirt's future growth with this year's advertising and promotion plan—her first as Squirt's brand manager. Market targeting and positioning for Squirt was the first agenda item. Three general options existed. First, the present market targeting and positioning strategy could be continued. Second, the market targeting and positioning recommendation made by FCB could be adopted. Third, another market targeting and positioning strategy could be developed, which may or may not include elements of the current and recommended strategy. She added that any examination of options should consider what role the multicultural market for carbonated soft drinks, the grapefruit/citrus category, and Squirt played in formulating a market targeting and positioning strategy and implementing the advertising and promotion plan.

More broadly, Cox asked the team members to consider how a "multicultural marketing mind-set" might guide the overall planning process itself. She said, "If we choose to focus on multicultural 18- to 24-year-olds, what might we need to do differently than if we simply focus on 18- to 24-year-olds or for that matter, 18- to 34-year-olds as we've done in the past?"

"Ultimately, our market targeting and positioning decision and recommendation will determine where and how we deploy our advertising and promotion dollars," Kate Cox continued. She reminded the brand management team that Squirt was roughly the ninth largest brand in the company brand portfolio and the objectives, strategy, and budget for advertising and promotion should consider this reality. "That certainly has implications for where and how we choose to spend the budget," injected an M.B.A. student summer intern who recently joined the brand management team. He continued, "Suppose we choose to run a bilingual media advertising and bottler promotion campaign, or a Spanish-only program for selected markets that corresponds to FCB's estimate of Hispanic Squirt consumption. Don't we incur the risk of spreading the budget too thinly across the country, other things being equal?" Cox replied, "That's a possibility. But we may be getting ahead of ourselves by discussing spending. This may be a good time to discuss the topic of market targeting and positioning and see where it takes us."

Zoëcon Corporation
Insect Growth Regulators

In January 1986, Zoëcon Corporation executives met to assess future growth and profit opportunities for its Strike® brand insect growth regulator (IGR) called Strike ROACH ENDER®. The meeting was prompted by a recent change in top management and corporate objectives, which now emphasized a focus on high financial-return businesses and products.

The first item on the agenda was the marketing program for Strike ROACH ENDER. This product had been in a consumer test market for six months in four cities: Charleston, South Carolina; Beaumont, Texas; Charlotte, North Carolina; and New Orleans, Louisiana. The results of the test market and future directions for the product were to be discussed. Ideas had already surfaced in informal meetings, however. Some executives believed Zoëcon (pronounced Zoy-con) should expand distribution of Strike ROACH ENDER to 19 cities in April 1986, with the intent of distributing the product nationally in April 1987. Other executives felt that Zoëcon should concentrate its effort on opportunities in the professional pest control market. Still other executives held the view that Zoëcon should reconsider any plans to market the product itself. Rather, these executives said Zoëcon should sell its IGR compound to firms actively engaged in reaching the consumer insecticide market. These firms included d-Con Company, S. C. Johnson and Son (Raid), and Boyle-Midway Division of American Home Products (Black Flag).

Further discussions indicated that some alternatives were mutually exclusive and others were not. For example, Zoëcon could sell to the consumer market under the Strike name or through other firms and also distribute its IGR to professional pest control operators. However, if Zoëcon was able to sell its IGR compound to, say, d-Con, then selling Strike ROACH ENDER would be infeasible. According to one Zoëcon executive, "The decision is basically how can we best allocate our technical, financial, and marketing resources for our IGR compounds."

■ ZOËCON CORPORATION

Zoëcon Corporation was founded in 1968 in Palo Alto, California, by Dr. Carl Djerassi to research endocrinological methods of insect population control. Djerassi was a pioneer in the development of chemical methods for human birth control, which subsequently led to the introduction of the birth control pill. The name Zoëcon is a combination of the Greek words *zoe* for life and *con* for control.

Zoëcon Corporation was acquired in 1983 by Sandoz, Ltd., a Swiss-based producer of pharmaceuticals, agrichemicals, and colors and dyes. Zoëcon's mission was to be the marketing arm of Sandoz, Ltd., in the animal health and insect control areas.

This case was prepared by Dr. Larry Smith, graduate student, under the supervision of Professor Roger A. Kerin, of the Edwin L. Cox School of Business, Southern Methodist University, as a basis for classroom discussion and is not designed to illustrate effective or ineffective handling of an administrative situation. Certain names and data have been disguised. The cooperation of Zoëcon Corporation in the preparation of this case is gratefully acknowledged. Copyright © 1986 by Roger A. Kerin. No part of this case may be reproduced without written permission of the copyright holder.

EXHIBIT 1

Selected Zoëcon Products and Applications

Brand/Product	Target Insects and Rodents
Consumer	
Strike ROACH ENDER®	Cockroaches, fleas, ticks, mosquitoes, spiders, crickets
Strike FLEA ENDER®	
VAPORETTE® flea collars	
Methoprene	
Roach traps	
Insect strips	
Animal Health	
VET-KEM®—flea collars, dips, flea aerosols and foggers, flea powders, flea shampoos ZODIAC®—flea collars, dips, flea aerosols and foggers, flea powders, flea and regular shampoos	Fleas, ticks, sarcoptic mange
STARBAR®—flybait; cattle dusts, sprays, and dips; swine dusts, sprays, and dips; insect strips; rodenticides; pet products; Altosid® feed-through	Houseflies, cattle hornflies, grubs, lice, mosquitoes, rats and mice, fleas, ticks, and sarcoptic mange
Pest Control	
SAFROTIN®	Cockroaches, fleas, houseflies, pharaoh ants, stored-product pests, tobacco moths, cigarette beetles, mosquitoes, and blackflies
PRECOR®	
GENCOR®	
FLYTEK®	
PHARORID®	
DIANEX®	
KABAT®	
ALTOSID®	
TEKNAR®	

Source: Company records. STRIKE, ROACH ENDER, FLEA ENDER, VAPORETTE, VET-KEM, ZODIAC, STAR-BAR, SAFROTIN, PRECOR, GENCOR, FLYTEK, PHARORID, DIANEX, KABAT, ALTOSID, and TEKNAR are trademarks of Sandoz, Ltd.

Zoëcon sells (1) animal health products to small-animal veterinarians and clinics, (2) pest control chemicals for farm animals, (3) insecticides for household pets and pest control to supermarkets, pet stores, veterinarians, and pest control companies, and (4) products and chemical compounds to firms engaged in marketing pest control products to the consumer market. For example, Zoëcon produces the chemicals for the Black Flag Roach Motel sold by Boyle-Midway. The company recorded $100 million in sales from these products and a 25 percent pretax profit on sales. A partial list of company products and applications is shown in Exhibit 1.

■ INSECT CONTROL

The use of chemical toxins to control insect pests is commonplace. Although these toxins are potentially harmful to people as well as insects, recent advances in chemistry have reduced the threat to people. Surviving insects, however, may produce successive generations that are resistant to toxins.

Public concern over the toxic effect of agricultural and household insecticides has remained widespread despite the advances in chemistry. In particular, consumers have evidenced increasing concern that safer household insecticides be used where children and pets might come in contact with the residual chemicals. The demand for safer compounds caused a change in the focus of research and development from new insect adulticides, which kill adult insects, to chemical compounds that disrupt insect reproduction.

Insect Life Cycles

Insects reproduce by laying eggs. The life patterns after hatching from the egg vary among different insect species. The flea has a complete metamorphic cycle, passing in sequence through the egg, larval, and pupal stages to the adult stage in 23 days. Cockroach metamorphosis is incomplete. Wingless nymphs hatch from eggs and grow by shedding their exoskeletons, molting six times through six nymphal stages, called instars. Molting of the sixth instar produces winged, sexually mature adult roaches in 74 days.

Metamorphosis is controlled by the insect's endocrine system. In fleas, hormones regulate development and transition from larval to pupal to adult stages. Analogously, in roaches, molting is initiated when the brain produces a neurohormone that activates prothoracic gland production of a molting hormone. Additionally, a juvenile hormone is produced by the brain in decreasing amounts, until at the sixth and final molt no juvenile hormone is produced. This molting produces sexually mature adult cockroaches up to two inches long.

The life cycle of the cockroach is shown in Exhibit 2. It begins with formation of about 40 eggs in a capsule called an ootheca. The adult female produces one ootheca

EXHIBIT 2

Normal Life Cycle of the Cockroach

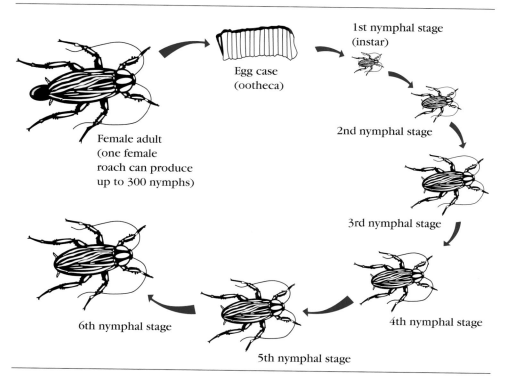

Female adult (one female roach can produce up to 300 nymphs)

Egg case (ootheca)

1st nymphal stage (instar)

2nd nymphal stage

3rd nymphal stage

4th nymphal stage

5th nymphal stage

6th nymphal stage

every 23 days over an average life span of 150 days, for a total of about 260 roaches. Research on cockroaches indicates that a roach population will increase geometrically if ample food, water, and shelter are available. Research also indicates that roaches are omnivorous and have a particular liking for beer.

Insect Growth Regulators

Insect growth regulators are effective against insects that are problems as adults, such as cockroaches. Roaches have been shown to carry bacteria, viruses, fungi, and protozoa, which cause diseases such as food poisoning, diarrhea, dysentery, hepatitis B, polio, and encephalitis. They are also capable of carrying organisms causing cholera, plague, typhus, leprosy, and tuberculosis. Furthermore, in susceptible individuals, cockroach contaminations may produce allergic reactions similar to hay fever, asthma, food allergies, and dermatitis.

Insect growth regulators are synthetic analogs of the natural insect juvenile hormones produced in the normal sequence of metamorphosis. The concentration of juvenile hormone produced decreases with each molting, to permit emergence of an adult insect after the pupal stage (for fleas) or after the last nymph stage (for roaches). If the larva or nymph is exposed to an IGR during the stage prior to molting, however, subsequent development into an adult is prevented or altered. Fleas exposed to an IGR during the larval stage pupate but fail to emerge to continue the reproductive cycle. Similarly, cockroaches exposed to an IGR in the sixth instar molt will become deformed, sexually immature adults incapable of reproducing.

As chemicals, IGRs are much less toxic than compounds typically used in household insecticides. Because they are synthetic chemical analogs of juvenile hormones specific to insects, they are not physiologically active in human or animal endocrine systems.

IGRs are extremely effective in eliminating insect populations. Only a few tenths of a milligram per square foot is required for effective control of insect reproduction. When an IGR is combined with an adulticide, many insects are killed and those that survive are prohibited from reproducing. In time, an insect infestation is controlled and, ideally, eliminated.

A unique feature of IGRs is that the immediate effects of an application are not observable. That is, since an IGR affects the reproductive cycle of an insect, it does not kill insects that come in contact with the compound. Controlled tests of a cockroach IGR indicate that a significant reduction in roach population occurs after 120 days and continues with applications spaced at 120-day intervals. When the IGR is combined with an adulticide, adult roaches and nymphs are killed upon contact with the adulticide. Short-term residual effects of the adulticide can repel roaches from treated areas, however. Therefore, the adulticide can hamper the effect of an IGR, since insects avoid treated areas.

■ PREMISE INSECTICIDE MARKET

The premise insecticide market is divided into two segments: the consumer market and the professional pest control market. The distinction is based on distribution systems and product forms. Insecticides for the consumer market are packaged in easy-to-use, do-it-yourself containers sold mostly through supermarkets. The professional pest control market consists of sales of insecticides, often in diluted form, to professional applicators. Orkin and Terminix are examples of professional applicators.

Consumer Market

Estimated annual sales for all consumer-disbursed insecticides in 1985 were $400 million at manufacturers' prices. Sales were forecasted to grow at an average rate of 10 percent per year through 1990. S. C. Johnson and Son, Inc. captured 45 percent of this market with its Raid brand. The Boyle-Midway Division of American Home Products accounted for 12 percent of the market with Black Flag, and d-Con Company captured 10 percent. No other company had a market share greater than 8 percent.

Supermarkets accounted for 70 percent of insecticide sales, followed by drugstores (9 percent) and a host of other retailers such as home improvement centers and house and garden outlets (21 percent). Aerosol sprays, including foggers, were the preferred method for applying insecticides and accounted for 74 percent of retail sales. Liquid sprays followed with 14 percent. Solids, strips, pastes, traps, and baits generated 12 percent of retail sales. Differences in packaging were based on consumers' preferences for quick-kill, residual control, or a margin of safety. Quick-kill dominated the consumer mindset, hence the popularity of aerosols and liquids that allowed for a "chase and squirt" routine when a roach was seen.

The consumer market was further subdivided into insect-specific insecticides. Ant and roach killers captured 40 percent of the market, flying insect killers 20 percent, flea killers 11 percent, and other insect-specific products 29 percent.

As expected, household insecticide sales were seasonal and varied by geography. The six-month period from May through October was the prime sales time for insecticides; 75 percent of annual sales were made during this period. The southern tier of 14 states (from the East Coast to the West Coast) accounted for 50 percent of annual sales.

Insecticides sold to the consumer market are heavily promoted. In 1983, the most recent year for which advertising expenditures were available, manufacturers spent $28.6 million for magazine, newspaper, television, radio, and outdoor advertising. For example, it was estimated that S. C. Johnson and Son spent $1.4 million to advertise Raid Ant & Roach Killer, Roach and Flea Killer, and Roach Traps. Boyle-Midway spent almost $3 million to advertise its Black Flag Roach & Ant Killer and Roach Motel. Past history of product introductions indicated that a minimum $10 million promotion investment was required to successfully launch a new product when consumers were familiar with the brand name.

Professional Pest Control Market

The professional pest control market produced revenues of $2.5 billion in 1985. Revenues were forecasted to be $3.7 billion in 1990, representing an annual average growth rate of 8 percent. About 6 percent of the revenues produced by pest control operators (PCOs) were accounted for by chemical compound cost.

The majority (52 percent) of professional pest control revenues resulted from general insect control (for example, of cockroaches, fleas, or ants). Termite control accounted for 21 percent of professional pest control revenues. The remaining 27 percent were from specialty pest control applications, especially rodent control.

This market was dominated by many small PCOs. There were an estimated 14,000 PCOs, of which only two (Orkin and Terminix) had annual sales greater than $100 million. About 28 PCOs had annual sales greater than $3 million, whereas over 6,000 had revenues under $50,000 annually.

Insecticides were sold to PCOs through distributors. These distributors purchased insecticides in bulk quantities (cases and pallets) from producers and then sold them to PCOs in smaller quantities. These distributors typically received an average gross margin of 27 percent on the selling price to PCOs. Although percentages varied, industry sources estimated that the producer's average gross profit on chemicals sold to the professional pest control market was 51 percent. By comparison, the average gross profit on insecticides sold to the consumer market was 55 percent.

Producer marketing expenses associated with selling to the professional pest control market were small in comparison to the costs of selling to the consumer market.

As a general rule, about 27 percent of sales were spent for marketing to PCOs. Most of these expenses were for trade advertising and sales efforts.

■ ZOËCON PRODUCT DEVELOPMENT AND MARKETING

From its beginning, Zoëcon made a large commitment to ongoing research on IGRs. By the mid-1970s, Zoëcon research scientists, who comprised more than 25 percent of the company's employees, had synthesized more than 1,250 IGRs, and 175 patents had been issued for these inventions.

Development and Marketing of Flea Compound

The first commercialized IGR, methoprene, was introduced in 1974 for mosquito control. This IGR was made available in a variety of product forms over the years for multiple control uses. In 1980, Zoëcon obtained EPA approval for the use of methoprene under the trade name PRECOR® as a flea control compound. Given the company's already established trade relations with PCOs, veterinary clinics, and pet stores, Zoëcon began selling its flea control compound to these outlets. By 1985, Zoëcon executives estimated that the company had captured 80 percent of all flea product sales made through these outlets. Some company executives attributed the success of PRECOR to the fact that PCOs, veterinarians, and pet store sales personnel could explain the unique benefits and application of methoprene.

The early success of PRECOR led Zoëcon to look for opportunities outside of PCOs, animal clinics, and pet stores. Market analysis revealed that supermarkets accounted for a rapidly growing percentage of flea product sales volume. Since Zoëcon had no significant experience dealing with supermarkets, it approached the makers of d-Con, Black Flag, and Raid products about including PRECOR in their products. Only d-Con expressed interest. In 1981, d-Con introduced Flea Stop, a fogger for fleas containing only PRECOR—no adulticide was included among the ingredients. Flea Stop sold well in supermarkets, given the sales and marketing support provided by d-Con.

PRECOR's success prompted Zoëcon to again approach the makers of Black Flag and Raid in 1982. No agreement could be reached, however. This setback resulted in the decision by Zoëcon to develop its own brand for sales through supermarkets. In early 1983, Zoëcon introduced Strike FLEA ENDER®, which includes PRECOR and an adulticide, in 19 cities that accounted for the majority of flea product sales. By late 1983, Strike FLEA ENDER had captured 11 percent of flea product sales in those cities. This success led to an agreement with S. C. Johnson and Son, in December 1983, to include PRECOR in its Raid Flea Killer Plus. This agreement allowed Zoëcon to continue marketing PRECOR under the STRIKE brand name. Strike FLEA ENDER had an 18 percent market share in 1985; however, the product had not yet achieved its profit objective.

Development and Marketing of Roach Compound

Continuing research efforts resulted in the development of hydroprene, an IGR that was particularly useful for preventing normal cockroach maturation. This discovery was viewed as a major breakthrough in the creation of synthetic chemical analogs of naturally occurring insect juvenile hormones. In early 1984, Zoëcon obtained Environmental Protection Agency (EPA) registrations for hydroprene. By late 1984, the company was marketing hydroprene under the GENCOR® trade name only to PCOs, since pet stores and veterinary clinics had little or no use for this compound.

In late 1984, Zoëcon executives responsible for Strike FLEA ENDER proposed that a hydroprene-based product with the name Strike ROACH ENDER® be introduced to supermarkets. This proposal requested that Strike ROACH ENDER, which would contain hydroprene and an adulticide, be introduced in the same 19 cities where Strike FLEA ENDER was being sold. Top management believed that an opportunity existed but that Strike ROACH ENDER should be test marketed before an investment in all 19 markets was made. Accordingly, a test market plan was drafted in early 1985.

Test Marketing Strike Roach Ender

Two objectives were set for the test market: to determine consumer acceptance of the product and to qualify the trade and consumer marketing program. The four cities chosen for the test were Charlotte, North Carolina; Charleston, South Carolina; Beaumont, Texas; and New Orleans, Louisiana. These cities were considered representative of the 19-city market where 80 percent of roach insecticides were sold. The cities contained 1.17 million households, or 5.3 percent of the 22 million households in that market area. The test market ran from May through October 1985. Product shipments to supermarkets in the four cities began in April.

Segmentation and Positioning   Research on roach insecticide users indicated that three segments existed, based on the primary benefit sought. The primary target market for Strike ROACH ENDER was the "end problem permanently" segment. A secondary market was the "product that lasts" segment. The "convenience/low cost" segment was not considered a primary or secondary target.

Strike ROACH ENDER was positioned as a scientific breakthrough with unique qualities desired by the targeted segments. A print advertisement for the product is shown in Exhibit 3 on page 194.

Product Packaging and Price   Strike ROACH ENDER was packaged in a 10-ounce aerosol spray and a 6-ounce fogger. The retail price for the aerosol was $4.49 and for the fogger was $3.99. These prices were 50 to 75 percent higher than those of existing roach insecticides. The premium price was justified on the basis of the product's unique compound and long-lasting effect. The higher price also provided supermarkets with a higher margin than they received from competitive products. Price and cost data are shown in Exhibit 4 on page 195.

Consumer and Trade Promotion   Television and newspaper advertising was used to build consumer awareness, and cents-off coupons were employed to stimulate product trial. The consumer promotion and media strategy focused on 25- to 54-year-old women living in households of three or more. A "blitz" strategy was used, with the heaviest promotion scheduled for the first three months of the test. A public relations effort was also launched, featuring press kit mailings to newspapers, guest appearances on local radio and television talk shows, and an 800-number consumer hotline to answer consumers' questions.

The trade promotion included discounts for first-time supermarket buyers, a calendar to assist buyers in coordinating store promotion with consumer advertising, freestanding in-store displays, and sales aids. Exhibit 5 on page 195 shows a Strike ROACH ENDER trade promotion.

Test-Market Expenditures and Results   The cost of the test market was $1,478,000. An itemized summary is shown in Exhibit 6 on page 196.

Results of the test market were tracked by an independent marketing research firm. At the end of the test in November 1985,57 percent of the households in the

EXHIBIT 3

Strike ROACH ENDER Print Advertisement

test cities were aware of the product, 6 percent of the households in the test cities had tried the product, and 30 percent of those households that had tried the product had repurchased during the test period. The average number of units purchased by all trier households was 1.3 units. Households that repurchased bought an average of 3.5 units in addition to their initial purchase. Sixty-six percent of Strike ROACH ENDER sales were of the aerosol spray; 34 percent were of foggers. This breakdown was identical for first purchases and subsequent purchases. Product shipments data indicated that 44,700 cases (at 12 units per case) of 10-ounce aerosol units and 24,300

EXHIBIT 4

Strike ROACH ENDER Package Economics

	10-oz. Aerosol	6-oz. Fogger
Price to trade[a]	$3.14	$2.79
Cost of goods sold[b]	1.41	1.26
Zoëcon's gross profit	$1.73	$1.53

[a]Price to trade is the price at which Zoëcon sells directly to the retailer.

[b]Cost of goods sold includes the cost of the can, solvent, propellant, active ingredients, and freight. Note that the cost of goods sold represents virtually all of the variable costs associated with the product forms.

EXHIBIT 5

Strike ROACH ENDER Trade Promotion

EXHIBIT 6

Summary of Marketing Expenses for the Strike ROACH ENDER Test Market

Activity	Expense
Promotion and advertising[a]	$1,016,000
Setup/auditing[b]	377,000
Marketing research[c]	65,000
Miscellaneous[d]	20,000
	$1,478,000

[a]Includes consumer advertising and promotion to supermarket buyers.

[b]Includes point-of-purchase materials, monitoring of shelf placement, sales aids, and free goods.

[c]Includes consumer tracking studies (for example, product awareness and purchase behavior).

[d]Includes public relations campaign.

cases (at 12 units per case) of 6-ounce fogger units were shipped to supermarket warehouses in the four cities prior to the test period.

■ JANUARY MEETING

When Zoëcon executives met in January 1986, the first item on the agenda was to review the test-market results and prepare marketing plans for 1986. Different points of view had already been expressed in informal discussions among Zoëcon executives. One position advanced was that Strike ROACH ENDER distribution should be expanded to the 19 cities where Strike FLEA ENDER was being sold. Marketing research indicated that these 19 cities accounted for 80 percent of roach insecticide volume. These executives reasoned that the up-front investment in marketing research, public relations, and set-up/auditing costs would not have to be repeated in the expanded distribution. Rather, the primary direct costs associated with the rollout to all 19 cities would be for promotion and advertising.

A second view was that Zoëcon should direct its resources to PCOs. These executives noted that GENCOR® (hydroprene) had been well received by PCOs in late 1984 and many PCOs were promoting its benefits to their customers. These executives felt that an ongoing investment of $500,000 per year above the 27 percent of sales typically budgeted for trade advertising and sales efforts would accelerate its use.

A third opinion was that Zoëcon should pursue opportunities for selling hydroprene to the makers of d-Con, Black Flag, and Raid for use in their products. This strategy had worked in the past for PRECOR (methoprene). A product cost analysis performed on Strike ROACH ENDER indicated that the cost of goods sold for the 10-ounce aerosol package without hydroprene would be $0.80. For the 6-ounce fogger package without hydroprene, the cost of goods sold would also be $0.80. Furthermore, Zoëcon could realize a 50 percent gross margin on hydroprene sold to another insecticide marketer with no investment in marketing or sales. These costs would be absorbed by the marketer of the product—d-Con, Black Flag, or Raid. Executives favoring this option believed the test-market experience could be used to interest insecticide marketers in the product. Specific aspects of the proposal, including the price for hydroprene, would have to be developed if this option was adopted. Executives favoring the continued marketing of Strike ROACH ENDER cautioned that this action could spell the end for Zoëcon's presence in the consumer market.

Zoëcon executives present at the January 1986 meeting were acutely aware of the importance of the decision they faced. Moreover, the peak season for roach insecticides was approaching, and a decision needed to be made quickly.

Soft and Silky Shaving Gel

On Friday, January 5, 2001, Phoebe Masters, the newly appointed Product Manager for hand and body lotions at Ms-Tique Corporation, was faced with her first decision one day after her promotion. She had to decide whether to introduce a new package design for the company's Soft and Silky Shaving Gel. The major questions were whether a $5^{1}/_{2}$-ounce or a 10-ounce aerosol container should be introduced and whether she should approve additional funds for a market test. Timing was critical because the incidence of women's shaving would increase during the spring months and reach its peak during the summer months.

■ THE COMPANY AND THE PRODUCT

Soft and Silky Shaving Gel is marketed by Ms-Tique Corporation, a manufacturer of women's personal-care products with sales of $225 million in 2000. The company's line of products includes facial creams, hand and body lotions, and a full line of women's toiletries. Products are sold by drug and food-and-drug stores through rack jobbers. Rack jobbers are actually wholesalers that set up retail displays and keep them stocked with merchandise. They receive a margin of 20 percent off the sales price to retailers.

Soft and Silky Shaving Gel was introduced in the spring of 1986. The product was viewed as a logical extension of the company's line of hand and body lotions and required few changes in packaging and manufacturing. The unique dimension of the introduction was that Soft and Silky Shaving Gel was positioned as a high-quality women's shaving gel. The positioning strategy was successful in differentiating Soft and Silky Shaving Gel from existing men's and women's shaving creams and gels at the time. Moreover, rack jobbers were able to obtain product placement in the women's personal-care section of drug and food-and-drug stores, thus emphasizing the product's positioning statement. Furthermore, placement apart from men's shaving products minimized direct price comparisons with men's shaving creams, since Soft and Silky Shaving Gel was premium-priced—with a suggested retail price of $3.95 per $5^{1}/_{2}$-ounce tube. Retailers received a 40 percent margin on the suggested retail selling price.

Soft and Silky Shaving Gel has been sold in a tube since its introduction. This packaging was adopted because the company did not have the technology to produce aerosol containers in 1986. Furthermore, the company's manufacturing policy was and continues to be to utilize existing production capacity whenever possible. As of early 2001, all products sold by Ms-Tique Corporation were packaged in tubes, bottles, or jars.

EXHIBIT 1

Soft and Silky Shaving Gel Income Statement for the Year Ending December 31, 2000

Sales		$3,724,000
Cost of goods sold (incl. freight)[a]		784,000
Gross profit		$2,940,000
Assignable costs:		
Advertising and promotion costs	$1,154,540	
Overhead and administrative costs	421,560	$1,576,100
Brand contribution		$1,363,900

[a] For analysis purposes, treat the cost of goods sold and freight cost as the only variable cost.

Soft and Silky Shaving Gel had been profitable from the time of its introduction. Although the market for women's shaving cream and gels was small, compared to men's shaving cream and gels, Soft and Silky's unique positioning had created a "customer franchise," in the words of Heather Courtwright, the Soft and Silky brand assistant. "We have a unique product for the feminine woman who considers herself special." Soft and Silky Shaving Gel sales were $3,724,000 in 2000 with a 1,960,000 unit volume (see Exhibit 1).

■ WOMEN'S SHAVING

Research on women's shaving commissioned by Masters' predecessors over the past decade had produced a number of findings useful in preparing annual marketing plans for Soft and Silky Shaving Gel. The major findings and selected marketing actions prompted by these findings are described below.

Methods of Hair Removal and Shaving Frequency

Women use a variety of methods for hair removal. The most popular method is simply shaving with razors and soap and water. Shaving with razors and shaving cream and gels is the next most used method, followed by shaving with electric razors. Women typically have their own razors and purchase their own supplies of blades. Approximately 45 million women shave with a razor; 15 million women use electric shavers.

Over 80 percent of women shave at least once per week, and women who work outside the home shave more frequently than those who do not. On average, women shave eleven times per month and shave nine times more skin than men per shaving occasion (men shave 24 times per month on average). Shaving frequency varies by season, with the summer months producing the greatest shaving activity (see Exhibit 2). Accordingly, in-store promotions and multipack deals were scheduled during the summer.

Attitudes Toward Shaving

Women view shaving as a necessary evil. When queried about their ideal shaving cream or gel, women typically respond that they want a product that contains a moisturizer, reduces irritation, and makes shaving easier. It appears that four out of five women use a moisturizer after shaving.

EXHIBIT 2

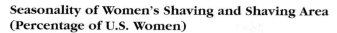

**Seasonality of Women's Shaving and Shaving Area
(Percentage of U.S. Women)**

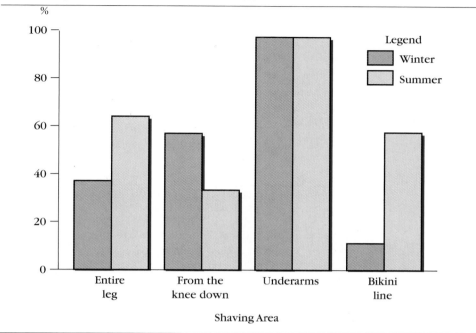

These specific findings resulted in a change in the Soft and Silky Shaving Gel ingredient formulation in 1991. Prior to 1991, the product contained only aloe. In 1991, three additional moisturizers were added to the product, including vitamin E. These ingredients were emphasized on the package and in-store promotions and media advertising.

Market Size and Competitive Products

Industry sources estimate the U.S. dollar value of women's "wet shaving" products to be over $400 million in 2000, at manufacturer's prices. Sales growth has been in the range of 3 to 5 percent per year since 1995. Razors and blades account for the bulk of sales growth and annual sales.

Historically, women who used shaving cream or gels had few "women's-only" products to choose from. However, since 1995, a vibrant women's shaving cream and gel category has emerged due to new-product activity, increased advertising and promotion, and improved shaving technology. Some industry analysts pointed toward the introduction of Gillette's Sensor Razor for Women and the recently launched Gillette Venus Razor for Women as important growth stimulants. Other analysts cited improvements in the quality of shaving creams and gels for women and increased advertising. Until late 1993, only two competitive products were normally available in the drug and food-and-drug stores served by Ms-Tique Corporation rack jobbers. These products were S. C. Johnson's Skintimate (formerly called Soft Sense) and Soft Shave, a lotion sold by White Laboratories. By late 2000, several competing brands existed in the women's shaving cream or gel category, even though all were not stocked by stores that carried Soft and Silky Shaving Gel. Exhibit 3 on page 200 shows representative brands, sizes, forms (cream, gel, lotion), and typical retail prices. Ms-Tique Corporation advertising and promotion for Soft and Silky Shaving Gel had responded to the

EXHIBIT 3

Representative Women's Shaving Products

Brand (Manufacturer)	Size[a]	Form	Price/Price per Oz.
Skintimate (S. C. Johnson)	7 oz.	Gel	$2.79/$.40
Skintimate (S. C. Johnson)	10 oz.	Cream	$2.79/$.28
Satin Care (Gillette)	7 oz.	Gel	$2.99/$.43
Soft Shave (White Labs)	9 oz.	Lotion	$1.82/$.20
Aveeno Therapeutic Shaving Gel (S. C. Johnson)	7 oz.	Gel	$3.99/$.57
Inverness Ultra-Lubricating Shaving Gel (Inverness Corp.)	6 oz.	Gel	$6.95/$1.16
Soft and Silky Shaving Gel (Ms-Tique Corp.)	5.5 oz.	Gel	$3.95/$.72

[a] Several manufacturers also sold smaller 2-, $2\frac{1}{2}$-, and $2\frac{3}{4}$-ounce sizes designed for travel purposes

increase in competition. Expenditures had increased each year since 1995, reaching 31 percent of sales in 2000.

By 2000, the dominant packaging for women's shaving cream or gels had become the aerosol container. Only a few shaving gels and brands were sold in tubes or plastic bottles, including Soft and Silky Shaving Gel, Soft Shave lotion, and Inverness Ultra-Lubricating Shaving Gel.

■ NEW PACKAGE DESIGN

The idea for a new package design was provided by Masters' brand assistant, Heather Courtwright. She originally proposed the new package to Masters' predecessor in July 2000. Her recommendation was based on four developments. First, unit sales volume for Soft and Silky Shaving Gel had slowed and then plateaued in recent years (see Exhibit 4). Second, the growth of Soft and Silky Shaving Gel had strained manufacturing capacity. In the past, production of Soft and Silky Shaving Gel had been easily integrated into the firm's production schedules. However, growth in the entire line of hand and body lotions, coupled with Soft and Silky Shaving Gel sales, had overburdened production capacity and scheduling. Moreover, inspection of shipping records indicated that the product's fill rate (that is, Ms-Tique Corporation's ability to supply quantities requested by retailers) had dropped, leading to out-of-stock situations and lost sales. Third, the company had no manufacturing capacity expansion plans for the next three years. And finally, the aerosol packaging had become the dominant design for women's shaving creams and gels.

Courtwright's observations prompted a preliminary study of outsourcing opportunities for a new package design. Her study included visits to several firms specializing in "contract filling" and requests for production proposals. A contract filler purchases cans, propellants, caps, and valves from a variety of sources and then assembles these components, including the product fill (that is, shaving gel), into the final container. The production method is called pressure filling. In this method, the cap and valve are inserted in the can and then sealed. At the same time, a vacuum is created in the container. The product fill and propellant are then injected under high pressure through the valve into the can.

Her review of supplier proposals led her to choose one that was capable of meeting production requirements and providing certain "value-added" features. For example,

EXHIBIT 4

Soft and Silky Shaving Gel Unit Sales Volume, 1987–2000

Unit Volume

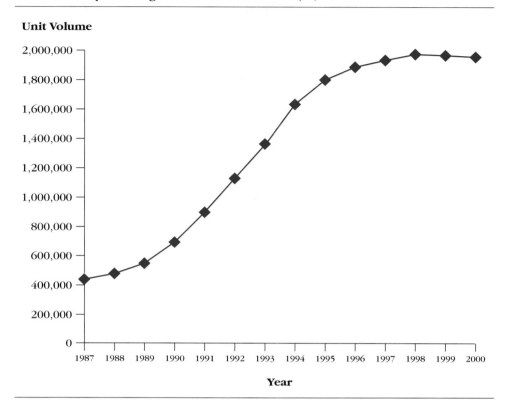

Year

the chosen supplier could deliver a propellant with no chlorofluorocarbons (CFCs), which are harmful to the earth's ozone layer. Also, the container's bottom would be rust-proof and leave no rust ring when wet. This feature was desired because most women shave in the bathtub or shower and tend to leave a wet can on the tub's porcelain, which can leave a rust stain. In addition, the supplier could produce and ship product directly from its manufacturing facility at a lower per unit cost than the tube container and was prepared to maintain an adequate safety stock of inventory. The only drawback in the supplier's proposal was that only $5^1/_2$- and 10-ounce containers could be produced without making significant and expensive changes in its equipment. The typical sizes for women's shaving creams and gels ranged from 6-ounce to 10-ounce containers.

The estimated total cost of producing and delivering to retailers a 10-ounce aerosol can of shaving gel was $0.29. A minimum order of 100,000 10-ounce cans would be required. Courtwright believed the suggested retail price would be set at $4.25 per 10-ounce can, reflecting Soft and Silky's premium-price strategy. The estimated total cost of producing and delivering to retailers a $5^1/_2$-ounce aerosol can of shaving gel was $0.24, and the suggested retail price would be $3.50. A 100,000-unit minimum order would be required. Courtwright recognized that the price per ounce for the aerosol containers was lower than the equivalent price per ounce for the tube package. She said the lower price reflected competitive realities in the category: "The dominant players (S. C. Johnson and Gillette) are very price competitive. We can retain our relative premium image even at the lower prices. I fully expect some cannibalization of the tube will take place just as I am confident the incremental volume will more than offset it." A one-time set-up charge for the Soft and Silky Shaving Gel production line and package graphics was $10,000, due and payable by Ms-Tique Corporation upon the signing of the supply agreement. This charge would be the same whether one or both sizes were produced.

■ PRELIMINARY TESTS

In November 2000, Courtwright received authorization from Masters' predecessor to spend $35,000 to assess consumer response to the proposed container. Her proposal was approved on the basis of the cost data provided and the recognition that use of a contract filler would require no incremental investment in company manufacturing capacity.

Courtwright commissioned a large marketing research firm to conduct four focus-group studies. Two focus groups would involve current users of Soft and Silky Shaving Gel, and two focus groups would involve users of shaving creams and gels other than Soft and Silky Shaving Gel and soap and water users. The principal information sought from these focus group studies was as follows:

1. Are present customers and noncustomers receptive to the new package?

2. At what rate would present customers convert to the aerosol can, and would noncustomers switch over to Soft and Silky Shaving Gel?

3. Where, in drug and food-and-drug stores, would customers and noncustomers expect to find the aerosol can?

4. Is the suggested retail price acceptable?

In addition, the marketing research firm was asked to examine analogous situations of package changes and report its findings.

In late December 2000, the marketing research firm presented its findings to Courtwright, two days after Masters' predecessor resigned to take a position with another company. There were six principal findings from the focus groups:

1. Customers and noncustomers were unanimously in favor of the aerosol can. The 10-ounce can was the favorite, since it would require fewer purchases.

2. Twenty percent of Soft and Silky Shaving Gel customers said they would convert to the 10-ounce can; 25 percent said they would convert to the $5^{1}/_{2}$-ounce can.

3. One-fourth of the noncustomers said they would switch over to the aerosol can irrespective of can size. These consumers' preference for the aerosol over the tube package was their principal reason (in addition to price) for not buying Soft and Silky Shaving Gel previously.

4. Customers expected to find the aerosol can next to the tube container. Noncustomers expected to find the aerosol container stocked with women's toiletries.

5. The pricing was acceptable and actually favored by current customers. Noncustomers thought the suggested retail price was somewhat high, but liked the value-added features and would try the product.

6. Current Soft and Silky Shaving Gel customers are extremely loyal to the brand. None of the brand's current customers had used a competing brand in the past two years. These was no evidence of such loyalty among noncustomers.

In addition to these findings, the marketing research firm presented ten case histories in which marketers of men's shaving cream had introduced a new package. (There was no distinction made with respect to size of package, whether the package

EXHIBIT 5

Soft and Silky Shaving Gel Sales Forecasts by Size and Type of Container

Forecast A: Low estimate for 5 ^{1}/$_2$-ounce aerosol package addition

5^1/$_2$-ounce tube package volume		8,600,000 ounces
5^1/$_2$-ounce aerosol package volume:		
Cannibalized volume	2,145,174	
Net new volume	300,000	2,445,174
		11,044,174 ounces

Forecast B: High estimate for 5 ^{1}/$_2$-ounce aerosol package addition

5^1/$_2$-ounce tube package volume		8,400,000 ounces
5^1/$_2$-ounce aerosol package volume:		
Cannibalized volume	2,345,174	
Net new volume	500,000	2,845,174
		11,245,174 ounces

Forecast C: Low estimate for 10-ounce aerosol package addition

5^1/$_2$-ounce tube package volume		9,000,000 ounces
10-ounce aerosol package volume:		
Cannibalized volume	1,745,174	
Net new volume	800,000	2,545,174
		11,545,174 ounces

Forecast D: High estimate for 10-ounce aerosol package addition

5^1/$_2$-ounce tube package volume		9,600,000 ounces
10-ounce aerosol package volume:		
Cannibalized volume	1,145,174	
Net new volume	1,500,000	2,645,174
		12,245,174 ounces

change was from aerosol to nonaerosol, or vice versa, or previous sales performance.) Two statistics were highlighted: first-year sales with the combined packages and the cannibalization rate for the existing package. According to the report,

> It is difficult to draw one-to-one comparisons between the experience of other shaving creams and gels and that of Soft and Silky Shaving Gel, given its unique market position. We have tried to do so after examining ten product-design changes. Our estimates [Exhibit 5] are broken down into a "high" and a "low" forecast for each package size. Seven out of the ten products studied experienced the "high" situation presented; three experienced the "low" situation. We see the 10-ounce package as producing the largest increase in ounces sold. Even with the cannibalism effect operating, we believe that an additional package will produce higher sales, in ounces, than the Soft and Silky Shaving Gel forecasted volume of 10,745,174 ounces (1,953,668 5^1/$_2$-ounce tubes) for 2001. Only a market test can indicate what will actually occur.

■ THE PACKAGING AND TEST MARKET DECISION

Courtwright presented the research firm's findings to Phoebe Masters on January 5, 2001, one day after Masters became Product Manager for hand and body lotions. Masters listened attentively as Courtwright summarized the research findings and recommended that a market test be conducted to determine the best package size.

Courtwright's test-market recommendation included a proposal to introduce the new package design in a limited cross-section of drug and food-and-drug stores, including heavy-volume and low-volume stores, that presently carried Soft and Silky Shaving Gel. Test stores would be isolated geographically from nontest stores. The new package would be placed among women's toiletries, and the test would run for three months, beginning April 1, 2001. The April 1 start date was necessary to assure that adequate supply of the new package was available. One-half of the stores would carry the $5\frac{1}{2}$-ounce container, and the other half would carry the 10-ounce container. The test would include a full complement of promotional aids, including newspaper ads and point-of-purchase displays, and would approximate a full-scale introduction.

Courtwright's estimated cost for the test market was $30,000, which included the cost of gathering marketing research data on the cannibalization rate and incremental sales growth. In addition, the $10,000 supplier set-up charge would have to be paid. However, Courtwright negotiated a 20,000 unit minimum order for each package size for the test market. No other incremental costs would be charged against the products. Sales and marketing efforts for the existing tube package would remain unchanged during the course of the test.

Late in the evening of Friday, January 5, 2001, Masters found herself considering whether the $5\frac{1}{2}$-ounce or the 10-ounce container should be introduced. She believed it unwise to introduce both sizes, given the uncertainty of market acceptance and packaging practices of most competitors. She also wondered whether Courtwright's test-market proposal should be adopted. Masters was confident that, given the product's sales history, the existing Soft and Silky Shaving Gel tube package would produce sales of 1,953,668 units (a .32 percent decrease from 2000) in 2001 if no new package was introduced. She was also confident that a new package would simultaneously cannibalize the existing package and generate incremental unit volume. Therefore, she knew that her decision on the package sizes and test market would have to focus on what was best for the Soft and Silky Shaving Gel product line, assuming an aerosol container would be marketed alongside the original tube container.

Masters also sensed that the new package had become a pet project for Courtwright. Courtwright had championed the idea for six months in addition to working on a variety of other assignments. Furthermore, she had heard that Courtwright felt that she, not Masters, should have been promoted to Product Manager for hand and body lotions given her association with the line for five years. Given the situation, Masters believed that her handling of this decision would affect her working relationship with Courtwright.

Perpetual Care Hospital

Downtown Health Clinic

In mid-April 2000, Sherri Worth, Assistant Administrator at Perpetual Care Hospital (PCH) in charge of PCH's Downtown Health Clinic (DHC), uncovered an unsettling parcel of news. During a call on the employee benefits director at a downtown department store, she was told that a firm was conducting a study to determine whether sufficient demand existed to establish a clinic five blocks north of PCH's Downtown Health Clinic. The description of the clinic's services sounded similar to those offered by the DHC, and the planned opening date was May 2001.

As Worth walked back to her office, she could not help but think about the possible competition. Upon arriving at her office, Worth called Dr. Roger Mahon, PCH's administrator, to tell him what she had learned. He asked her to contact other employee benefits directors and query patients to see whether they had been surveyed. He expressed concern for two reasons. First, a competitive clinic would attract existing and potential patients of the Downtown Health Clinic. Second, a clinic that provided similar services could hamper the DHC's progress toward achieving its service and profitability objectives. Mahon requested that Worth summarize the DHC's performance to date so that he could speak to members of the board of trustees' executive committee on what action, if any, the DHC should take to compete for patients.

■ THE HOSPITAL INDUSTRY AND AMBULATORY HEALTH CARE SERVICES

Health care, and specifically the hospital industry, has undergone a dramatic transformation in the past four decades. Until the 1960s, hospitals were largely charitable institutions that prided themselves on their not-for-profit orientation. Hospitals functioned primarily as workshops for physicians and were guided by civic-minded boards of trustees.

Federal legislation introduced in the 1960s created boom times for the hospital industry. The Hill-Burton Act provided billions of dollars for hospital construction, to be repaid by fulfilling quotas for charity care. Additional funds were poured into expansion and construction of medical schools. Medicare and Medicaid subsidized health care for the indigent, disabled, and elderly. These programs reimbursed hospitals for their incurred costs plus an additional return on investment. This period also saw dramatic increases in commercial insurance coverage, offered as employee fringe benefits and purchased in additional quantities by a more affluent public. Accordingly, health care became accessible to an overwhelming majority of U.S. citizens, regardless of where they lived or their ability to pay. Federal intervention had changed the concept of health care services from privilege to entitlement.

This case was prepared by Professor Roger A. Kerin, of the Edwin L. Cox School of Business, Southern Methodist University, as a basis for class discussion and is not designed to illustrate effective or ineffective handling of an administrative situation. Certain names and data have been disguised. Copyright © 2000 by Roger A. Kerin. No part of this case may be reproduced without written consent of the copyright holder.

By the 1980s, however, skyrocketing health care costs had forced the federal government to reassess its role in health care. Stringent controls were placed on hospital construction and expansion, and utilization and physician-review programs were implemented to ensure against too-lengthy inpatient stays. By the end of the decade, hospitals were initiating voluntary cost-cutting programs to stave off additional government intervention. Despite all efforts, however, health care expenditures continued to outpace the Consumer Price Index into the 1990s.

The late 1980s and early 1990s ushered in a very different health care environment, and hospitals particularly were hard hit by the changes. On the one hand, the federal government sought to reduce health care costs through cutbacks in subsidy programs and cost-control regulations, such as the Balanced Budget Act of 1997. On the other hand, innovations in health care delivery severely reduced the number of patients serviced by hospitals.

One innovation was preventive health care programs. These fall into two categories: health maintenance organizations (HMOs) and preferred provider organizations (PPOs). An HMO encourages preventive health care by providing medical services as needed for a fixed monthly fee. HMOs typically enter into contractual relationships with designated physicians and hospitals and have been successful in reducing hospital inpatient days and health care expenditures. PPOs establish contractual arrangements between health care providers (physicians and/or hospitals) and large employer groups. Unlike HMOs, PPOs generally offer incentives for using preferred providers rather than restricting individuals to specific hospitals or physicians. PPOs have the same effect on inpatient days and health care expenditures that HMOs have, and Mahon planned to expand the PPO for Perpetual Care Hospital using the Downtown Health Clinic as a link to large employers in the downtown area.

A second innovation has been ambulatory health care services and facilities. Ambulatory health care services consist of treatments and practices that consumers use on an episodic or emergency basis. Examples include physical examinations, treatment of minor emergencies (such as cuts, bruises, and minor surgery), and treatment of common illnesses (such as colds and flu).

Ambulatory health care facilities are split into two categories: (1) minor emergency centers, known by acronyms such as FEC (Free-Standing Emergency Clinic) and MEC (Medical Emergency Clinic) and (2) clinics that focus on primary or episodic care.[1] Although regulation is nominal, if a clinic positions itself as an emergency care center, expressing this focus in its name, it generally is required (or pressured by area physicians) to be staffed 24 hours a day by a licensed physician and to have certain basic life support equipment.

Three factors account for the growth of ambulatory health care services. First, advances in medical technology, miniaturization, and portable medical equipment have made more diagnostic and surgical procedures possible outside the traditional hospital setting. Second, consumers have adopted a more proactive stance on where they will receive their health and medical care. Consumers often choose the hospital at which they wish to be treated, and the incidence of "doctor shopping" is common. Third, the mystique of medical and health care has been altered with the growth of paramedical professionals and standardized treatment practices.

Most of the early centers emphasized quick, convenient, minor emergency care. Many new centers have positioned themselves as convenient, personalized alternatives to primary care physicians' practices. These operations typically employ aggressive, sophisticated marketing techniques, including branding, consistent logos and

---

[1]*Primary care* is the point of entry into the health care system. It consists of a continuous relationship with a personal physician who takes care of a broad range of medical needs. Primary care physicians include general practitioners, internal medicine and family practice specialists, gynecologists, and pediatricians.

atmospherics, promotional incentives, and mass-media advertising (giving rise to vernacular designations such as "Doc-in-the-Box" and "McMedical"). Although ambulatory care facilities vary considerably among communities and owners, the following characteristics appear to be universal: (1) branding, (2) extended hours, (3) lower fees than emergency rooms, (4) no appointments necessary, (5) minor emergencies treated, (6) easy access and parking, (7) short waiting times, and (8) credit cards accepted.

■ PERPETUAL CARE HOSPITAL

Perpetual Care Hospital is a 600-bed, independent, not-for-profit, general hospital located on the southern periphery of a major western city. It is one of six general hospitals in the city and twenty in the county. It is financially stronger than most of the metropolitan-based hospitals in the United States. It is debt-free and has the highest overall occupancy rate among the city's six general hospitals. Nevertheless, the hospital's administration and board of trustees have serious concerns about its patient mix, which reflects unfavorable demographic shifts. Most of the population growth in recent years occurred in the suburban areas to the north, east, and west. These suburban areas attracted young, upwardly mobile families from the city. They also attracted thousands of families from other states—families drawn to the area's dynamic, robust business climate.

As hospitals sprang up to serve the high-growth suburban areas, PCH found itself becoming increasingly dependent on inner-city residents, who have a higher median age and higher incidence of Medicare coverage. Without a stronger stable inflow of short-stay, privately insured patients, the financial health of the hospital would be jeopardized. Accordingly, in the summer of 1998, the board of trustees authorized a study to determine whether to open an ambulatory facility in the downtown area about ten blocks north of the hospital.

■ DOWNTOWN HEALTH CLINIC

The charter for the Downtown Health Clinic contained four objectives:

1. To expand the hospital's referral base
2. To increase referrals of privately insured patients
3. To establish a liaison with the business community by addressing employers' specific health needs
4. To become self-supporting three years after opening

The specific services to be offered by the DHC would include (1) preventive health care (for example, physical examinations and immunizations), (2) minor-emergency care, (3) referral for acute and chronic health care problems, (4) specialized employer services (for example, preemployment examinations and treatment of worker's compensation injuries), (5) primary health care services (for example, treatment of common illnesses), and (6) basic x-ray and laboratory tests. The DHC would be open 260 days a year (Monday-Friday) from 8:00 A.M. to 5:00 P.M.

The location for the DHC would be in the Greater West Office and Shopping Complex, situated on the corner of Main and West Streets (see Exhibit 1 on page 208). This location was chosen because a member of the board of trustees owned the Greater West Complex and was willing to share construction, design, and equipment expenses with the hospital.

EXHIBIT 1

Present and Planned Locations of Downtown Health Clinics and Service Areas

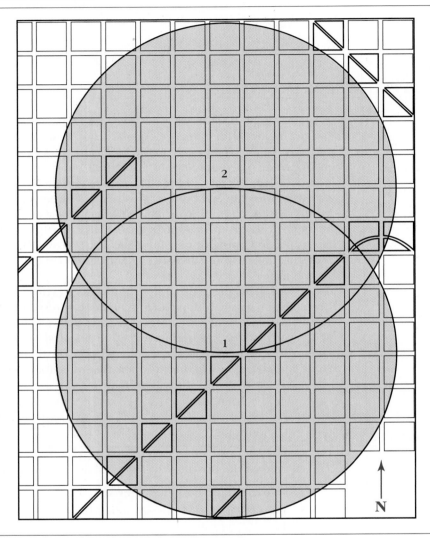

Key:

1. Original DHC and five-block service radius.

2. Planned location of competitor and five-block service radius.

During the fall of 1998, construction plans for erecting the DHC were well under way, and the expense budget was developed (see Exhibit 2). During the winter months, PCH commissioned a study to determine the service radius of the DHC, estimate the number of potential users of the DHC, assess responsiveness to the services to be offered by the DHC, and review the operations of suburban ambulatory care clinics. The results indicated that the service area would have a five-block radius, since this was the longest distance office workers would walk. Discussions with city planners indicated the service area contained 11,663 office workers during the 9:00–5:00 Monday–Friday work week. The population in the area was expected to grow 6 per-

EXHIBIT 2

Downtown Health Clinic: Preliminary 12-Month Expense Budget

Item	Expenditure
Physician coverage: 260 days times 8 hr/day at $66/hr	$137,280
Professional fees	43,720
Lease	76,500
Supplies	46,894
Utilities	6,630
Personnel, including fringe benefits (director, nurse, laboratory assistant, x-ray technician, receptionist)	168,376
Amortization	30,648
Annual expenditure	$510,048

Note: Expenditures were based on the assumption that the DHC would have 4 visits per hour, or 32 visits per day, when operating at full capacity.

cent per year, given new building and renovation activity. Personal interviews with 400 office workers, selected randomly, indicated that 50 percent would use or try the DHC if necessary and that 40 percent of these prospective users would visit the DHC at least once per year (see Exhibit 3 on page 210 for additional findings). Finally, the study of suburban ambulatory care facilities revealed the data shown in Exhibit 4 on page 211. Given their locations in suburban areas, these facilities were not considered direct competition, but their existence indicated that "the city's populace was attuned to ambulatory health care facilities," remarked Worth.

These results were viewed favorably by the board of trustees and "confirmed our belief that an ambulatory facility was needed downtown," noted Worth. The DHC was formally opened May 1, 1999. Except for the publicity surrounding the opening, however, no advertising or other types of promotion were planned. "Several members of the hospital staff shied away from advertising or solicitation, since it hinted at crass commercialism," said Worth.

Performance: May 1999–March 2000

A financial summary of DHC performance through March 2000 is shown in Exhibit 5 on page 212. According to Mahon:

> We are pleased with the performance to date and hope the DHC will be self-supporting by April 2001. We are getting favorable word of mouth from satisfied patients that will generate both new and repeat patients. We expect 410 patient visits in April [2000]. In addition, we have taken steps to improve our financial standing. For example, our bad debts have been costing us 4 percent of gross revenue. With a better credit and collection procedure established just last month, we will reduce this figure to 2 percent. We plan to initiate an 8 percent across-the-board increase in charges on May 1 and will experience only a 5 percent increase in personnel and professional services expenses next year.

Records kept by PCH revealed that the DHC was realizing its objectives. For example, the referral objective was being met, since the DHC had made 105 referrals to PCH and produced slightly over $378,000 in revenue and an estimated $30,000 in net profit. Almost all of these patients were privately insured. The service mix, though dominated by treatment of common illnesses and examinations, did indicate

EXHIBIT 3

Profile of DHC Service Area, Based on City and Survey Data

1999 Population Estimate (Source: City Planning Department)

Total office worker population in five-block radius	11,663
Expected annual growth, 1998–2003	6.0% yr
Sex breakdown in five-block radius:	
Male	40%
Female	60%

Results from Personal Interviews (January 1998)

Would use/try DHC if necessary for personal illness/exams	50%
Expected frequency of DHC use for personal illness/exams among those saying would use/try if necessary:[a]	
Once every other year	60%
Once per year	25%
Twice per year	10%
Three or more times per year	5%

Selected Cross-Tabulations

	Sex		
	Male	**Female**	**Total**
Would you use or try DHC if necessary?			
Yes	88[b]	168	256
No	72	72	144
Total	160	240	400

	Have Regular Physician (Excluding Gynecologist)		
	Yes	**No**	**Total**
Would you use or try DHC if necessary?			
Yes	58	198	256
No	130	14	144
Total	188	212	400

[a] No difference between males and females on frequency of use.

[b] Of the 160 males interviewed, 88 (55 percent) said they would use the DHC; 88 of the 256 interviewees (34 percent) who said they would use the DHC were male.

that the DHC was being used for a variety of purposes. A breakdown of the reasons for patient visits for the first 11 months of operations is as follows:

Personal illness exams	53%
Worker's compensation exam/treatment	25
Employment/insurance physical exams	19
Emergency	3
Total	100%

Patient records indicated that 97 percent of all visits were by first-time users of the DHC and 113 visits were by repeat patients. Approximately 5 percent of the visits in each month from October 1999 through March 2000 were repeat visits. "We are pleased that we are already getting repeat business because it shows we are doing

EXHIBIT 4

Suburban Ambulatory Care Clinics: Operations Profile

Operations	EmerCenter #1	EmerCenter #2	Adams Industrial Clinic	Health First	Medcenter
Opening	March 1990	November 1992	June 1992	May 1991	June 1997
Patients/year	9,030	6,000	8,400	5,700	8,661
Hours of operation	10:00 A.M.–10:00 P.M. Monday–Friday	10:00 A.M.–10:00 P.M. Monday–Sunday	8:00 A.M.–5:00 P.M. Monday–Friday	5:00 P.M.–11:00 P.M. Monday–Friday 10:00 A.M.–10:00 P.M. Saturday–Sunday	8:00 A.M.–8:00 P.M. Monday–Sunday
Physicians/8-hr shift	2	2	2	2	2
Estimated patient visits/hour	3.8/hr	3.4/hr	5.0/hr	3.0/hr	3.0/hr
Estimated average charge per visit	$60.00	$62.00	$76.00	$62.00	$64.00
Services provided:					
Preventive health care			✓	✓	✓
Minor emergencies	✓	✓	✓	✓	✓
Employer services			✓	✓	✓
X-ray/lab tests	✓	✓	✓	✓	✓
Miscellaneous	✓	✓	✓	✓	✓
Use direct-mail advertising	✓	✓		✓	✓

EXHIBIT 5

Downtown Health Clinic Financial Summary

	1999								2000			Total Year to Date
	May	June	July	Aug.	Sept.	Oct.	Nov.	Dec.	Jan.	Feb.	Mar.	
Gross revenue	$ 8,150	$ 16,774	$ 17,688	$ 19,394	$ 22,412	$ 22,812	$ 23,344	$ 23,516	$ 25,692	$ 27,758	$ 29,430	$ 236,970
Variable expenses:												
Bad debt	326	710	708	776	896	912	934	940	1,026	1,110	1,176	9,514
Medical/surgical supplies	13,182	1,596	1,870	1,286	2,126	2,426	3,322	1,224	1,052	3,106	2,156	33,346
Drugs	318	108	130	104	610	186	0	112	372	506	152	2,598
Office supplies	1,294	444	1,192	1,436	630	(380)	48	562	934	0	128	6,288
Total variable expense	$ 15,120	$ 2,858	$ 3,900	$ 3,602	$ 4,262	$ 3,144	$ 4,304	$ 2,838	$ 3,384	$ 4,722	$ 3,612	$ 51,746
Contribution	$ (6,970)	$ 13,916	$ 13,788	$ 15,792	$ 18,150	$ 19,668	$ 19,040	$ 20,678	$ 22,308	$ 23,036	$ 25,818	$ 185,224
Fixed expenses:												
Personnel	15,632	14,918	13,340	11,800	13,632	22,980	14,640	12,498	13,410	17,990	15,288	166,128
Professional services[a]	20,018	13,890	15,564	14,316	14,770	13,600	14,400	14,900	14,484	14,156	14,374	164,472
Facility[b]	6,444	5,074	5,780	5,810	5,244	5,310	5,240	5,226	5,672	5,244	5,438	60,482
Miscellaneous	1,410	214	266	280	476	90	222	152	212	246	114	3,682
Amortization	2,554	2,554	2,554	2,554	2,554	2,554	2,554	2,554	2,554	2,544	2,544	28,074
Total fixed expense	$ 46,058	$ 36,650	$ 37,504	$ 34,760	$ 36,676	$ 44,534	$ 37,056	$ 35,330	$ 36,332	$ 40,180	$ 37,758	$ 422,838
Net gain (loss)	$(53,028)	$(22,734)	$(23,716)	$(18,968)	$(18,526)	$(24,866)	$(18,016)	$(14,652)	$(14,024)	$(17,144)	$(11,940)	$(237,614)
Number of patient visits	109	231	275	277	322	320	321	366	383	463	423	3,490
Number of working days	22	21	21	22	20	23	22	20	22	21	23	237

[a] Includes professional fees paid (see Exhibit 2).
[b] Includes lease payments, utilities, and maintenance.

our job," Worth commented. The average revenue per patient visit during the first 11 months was $67.90.[2] A breakdown of the average charge by type of visit follows. The average charge was to increase 8 percent on May 1, 2000.

Personal illness/exam	$50 per visit
Worker's compensation exam/treatment	$78 per visit
Employment/insurance physical examination	$94 per visit
Emergency	$134 per visit

In an effort to monitor the performance of the DHC, patients were asked to provide selected health care information as well as demographic information. This information was summarized monthly, and Exhibit 6 shows the profile of patients visiting the DHC for the first 11 months of operation. In addition to this information, patients were asked for suggestions on how the DHC could serve the downtown area. Suggestions typically fell into three categories: service hours, services offered, and waiting time. Thirty percent of the patients suggested expanded service hours, with an opening time of 7:00 A.M. and a closing time of 7:00 P.M. One-half of the female patients requested that gynecological services be added.[3] A majority of the patients expressed concern about the waiting time, particularly during the lunch hours (11:00 A.M.–2:00 P.M.). A check of DHC records indicated that 70 percent of patient visits occurred during the 11:00 A.M.–2:00 P.M. period and that one-half of the visits were for personal illnesses.

Worth believed all three suggestions had merit, and she had already explored ways to expand the DHC's hours and reduce waiting time. For example, the reason for her call on the employee benefits director at a local department store was to schedule employee physical examinations in the morning or late afternoon hours to minimize crowding during the lunch hour. Nevertheless, she believed a second licensed physician might be necessary, with one physician working the hours from 7:00 A.M. to 3:00 P.M. and the other working between 11:00 A.M. and 7:00 P.M. The overlap during the lunch period would alleviate waiting times, she thought. Expanding from 9- to 12-hour days would entail a 33 percent increase in personnel costs, however, as well as the cost of another physician.[4]

Worth believed that scheduling was more of a problem than she or the PCH staff had expected. "You just can't schedule the walk-ins," she said, "and pardon me for saying it, but the people coming in with personal care needs have really caused the congestion." She added that the problem would get worse because the mix of patient needs was moving toward personal illnesses and examinations. "If the trend continues, we should have 20 percent more personal illness visits next year than last year."

Worth believed that gynecological services would be a plus, since 70 percent of the visits were made by women and almost all were under 35 years of age. She said:

> Women should see a gynecologist regularly at least once a year and often twice a year. We could add an additional 2,000 visits per year by having a hospital gynecologist work at the DHC two eight-hour days a week by appointment. An average charge per visit would be about $104 including lab work, and the physician cost would be $70 per hour.

Worth had also given some thought to how the DHC could improve its relations with the business community. Currently, business-initiated visits (worker's compensation examinations and treatments and employment/insurance physical examinations) accounted for 44 percent of the visits to the DHC. Construction in the downtown area had stimulated worker's compensation activity, and growth in employment in the

---

[2]The average charge per patient visit excluded the charge for basic x-ray and laboratory tests.

[3]*Gynecology* is that branch of medicine dealing with the female reproductive tract.

[4]Expanded hours would be staffed by part-time personnel, who would receive the same wages as full-time personnel.

EXHIBIT 6

Profile of Downtown Health Clinic Patients: Personal Illness/Exam Visits Only

Occupation

Clerical	48%
Professional/technical/managerial	23
Operator	19
Other	10
	100%

Sex

Male	30%
Female	70
	100%

Referral Source

Friend/colleague	35%
Employer	60
Other	5
	100%

Patient Origin

Distance:

One block	25%
Two blocks	28
Three blocks	22
Four blocks	15
Five blocks	8
More than five blocks	2
	100%

Direction:

North of DHC	10%
South of DHC	25
Northeast of DHC	5
Southwest of DHC	15
East of DHC	20
West of DHC	10
Southeast of DHC	10
Northwest of DHC	5
	100%

Have Regular Physician

Yes	18%
No	82
	100%

five-block service radius had contributed to employment physicals. Worth believed worker's compensation visits would stabilize at about 81 per month and then decline with slowed building activity. Employment physicals accounted for 50 visits per month and were expected to remain at this level with the current operating hours.

Insurance physicals were not expected to increase beyond current levels, nor were emergency visits.

Commenting on her calls on businesses, Worth remarked:

I have actively called on businesses under the guise of community relations because the PCH staff has not sanctioned solicitation. My guess, after talking with business people, is that we could get virtually every new employment physical if we didn't interfere with employment hours and scheduled them before 8:00 A.M. or after 5:00 P.M. Given net new employment in the area and new employees due to turnover, I'd guess we could schedule an additional 65 employment physicals every month—that is, a total of 115 a month.

Worth added that she had also received approval to run an "informational advertisement" in the downtown weekly newspaper each week next year provided that the advertisement did not feature prices or appear to be commercial in its presentation. The weekly advertisement would cost $10,400 per year.

The Possibility of Competition

Worth's calls on local businesses and patient interviews indicated that someone was conducting a survey. She believed that Medcenter, a privately owned suburban ambulatory facility, was the sponsor. Medcenter appeared to be successful in its suburban location (see Exhibit 4) and had a reputation for being an aggressive, marketing-oriented operation. Even though Medcenter did not provide employer services at its suburban location, Worth thought the fact that an employee benefits director had been interviewed suggested that such services might be offered.

The proposed location for the new clinic was five blocks directly north of the DHC. Based on the research for the DHC, Worth estimated that the number of office workers within a five-block radius of the competitive clinic would be 11,652 in 2001 and 13,590 in 2002, and would grow at an annual rate of 7 percent through 2005 because of new construction and building renovation. Worth believed the competitor's service area had the same socioeconomic profile and the same usage and employment characteristics as the DHC's service area.

The overlap in service areas was due to the layout of the downtown area and the availability of high-quality street-level space. According to Worth, "It is possible that a third of our current personal illness/exam patients from the northern portion of our service area will switch to the new clinic and about 40 percent of potential personal illness/exam patients in this area will go to the new location." Worth went on to say that the overlap in service areas would cover 3,424 office workers in 2000.

The effect of the competing clinic on the volume of emergency, worker's compensation, and employment/insurance exam work was more difficult to assess. Worth felt that worker's compensation visits would not be materially affected because most construction was being undertaken in areas south, east, and west of the DHC. Emergency visits were so random that it was not possible to assess what effect the competing clinic would have. The projected volume of employment and insurance physicals could change with the addition of a competing clinic, however. Worth guessed, "At worst, we would see no increase in these types of visits over last year since we have not gotten many visits from this area."

A week after she first heard about the possibility of competition, Worth and Mahon met to review the information on the DHC. Just before Worth finished giving her overview, Mahon's administrative assistant interrupted to tell him he had to leave to catch a plane for a three-day hospital administration conference. As he left the room, Mahon asked Worth to draft a concise analysis of the DHC's position. He also asked her to specify and evaluate the alternatives for the DHC, assuming Medcenter either did or did not open a facility. "Remember," Mahon said, "we have a lot riding on the DHC. Making it work involves not only dollars and cents, but our image in the community as well."

Procter & Gamble, Inc.

Scope

As Gwen Hearst looked at the year-end report, she was pleased to see that Scope held a 32 percent share of the Canadian mouthwash market for 1990. She had been concerned about the inroads that Plax, a prebrushing rinse, had made in the market. Since its introduction in 1988, Plax had gained a 10 percent share of the product category and posed a threat to Scope. As Brand Manager, Hearst planned, developed, and directed the total marketing effort for Scope, Procter & Gamble's (P&G) brand in the mouthwash market. She was responsible for maximizing the market share, volume, and profitability of the brand.

Until the entry of Plax, brands in the mouthwash market were positioned around two major benefits: fresh breath and killing germs. Plax was positioned around a new benefit—as a "plaque fighter"—and indications were that other brands, such as Listerine, were going to promote this benefit. The challenge for Hearst was to develop a strategy that would ensure the continued profitability of Scope in the face of these competitive threats. Her specific task was to prepare a marketing plan for P&G's mouthwash business for the next three years. It was early February 1991, and she would be presenting the plan to senior management in March.

■ COMPANY BACKGROUND

Based on a philosophy of providing products of superior quality and value that best fill the needs of consumers, Procter & Gamble is one of the most successful consumer goods companies in the world. The company markets its brands in more than 140 countries and had net earnings of $1.6 billion in 1990. The Canadian subsidiary contributed $1.4 billion in sales and $100 million in net earnings in 1990. It was recognized as a leader in the Canadian packaged-goods industry, and its consumer brands led in most of the categories in which the company competed.

Between 1987 and 1990, worldwide sales of P&G had increased by $8 billion and net earnings by $1.3 billion. P&G executives attributed the company's success to a variety of factors, including the ability to develop truly innovative products to meet consumers' needs. Exhibit 1 contains the statement of purpose and strategy of the Canadian subsidiary.

P&G Canada has five operating divisions, organized by product category. The divisions, and some of the major brands, are:

1. *Paper products*: Royale, Pampers, Luvs, Attends, Always
2. *Food and beverage*: Duncan Hines, Crisco, Pringles, Sunny Delight
3. *Beauty care*: Head & Shoulders, Pantene, Pert, Vidal Sassoon, Clearasil, Clarion, Cover Girl, Max Factor, Oil of Olay, Noxzema, Secret

This case was prepared by Professors Gordon H. G. McDougall and Franklin Ramsoomair, of the Wilfrid Laurier University, as a basis for class discussion and is not designed to illustrate effective or ineffective handling of an administrative situation. Used with permission.

EXHIBIT 1

A Statement of Purpose and Strategy: Procter & Gamble, Canada

We will provide products of superior quality and value that best fill the needs of consumers.

We will achieve that purpose through an organization and a working environment which attracts the finest people, fully develops and challenges our individual talents; encourages our free and spirited collaboration to drive the business ahead; and maintains the Company's historic principles of integrity, and doing the right thing.

We will build a profitable business in Canada. We will apply P&G worldwide learning and resources to maximize our success rate. We will concentrate our resources on the most profitable categories and on unique, important Canadian market opportunities. We will also contribute to the development of outstanding people and innovative business ideas for worldwide company use.

We will reach our business goals and achieve optimum cost efficiencies through continuing innovation, strategic planning, and the continuous pursuit of excellence in everything we do.

We will continuously stay ahead of competition while aggressively defending our established profitable businesses against major competitive challenges despite short-term profit consequences.

Through the successful pursuit of our commitment, we expect our brands to achieve leadership share and profit positions and that, as a result, our business, our people, our shareholders, and the communities in which we live and work, will prosper.

Source: Company records.

4. *Health care*: Crest, Scope, Vicks, Pepto-Bismol, Metamucil
5. *Laundry and cleaning*: Tide, Cheer, Bounce, Bold, Oxydol, Joy, Cascade, Comet, Mr. Clean

Each division had its own Brand Management, Sales, Finance, Product Development and Operations line management groups and was evaluated as a profit center. Typically, within each division a Brand Manager was assigned to each brand (for example, Scope). Hearst was in the Health Care division and reported to the Associate Advertising Manager for oral care, who, in turn, reported to the General Manager of the division. After completing her business degree (B.B.A.) at a well-known Ontario business school in 1986, Hearst had joined P&G as a Brand Assistant. In 1987 she became the Assistant Brand Manager for Scope, and in 1988 she was promoted to Brand Manager. Hearst's rapid advancement at P&G reflected the confidence that her managers had in her abilities.

■ THE CANADIAN MOUTHWASH MARKET

Until 1987, on a unit basis the mouthwash market had grown at an average of 3 percent per year for the previous 12 years. In 1987, it experienced a 26 percent increase with the introduction of new flavors such as peppermint. Since then, the growth rate had declined to a level of 5 percent in 1990 (Exhibit 2 on page 218).

The mouthwash market was initially developed by Warner-Lambert with its pioneer brand Listerine. Positioned as a therapeutic germ-killing mouthwash that eliminated bad breath, it dominated the market until the entry of Scope in 1967. Scope, a green, mint-tasting mouthwash, was positioned as a great-tasting, mouth-refreshing brand that provided bad-breath protection. It was the first brand that offered both effective protection against bad breath and a better taste than other mouthwashes. Its advertising focused, in part, on a perceived weakness of Listerine—a medicine breath (for example, "Scope fights bad breath. Don't let the good taste fool you")—and in 1976, Scope became the market leader in Canada.

EXHIBIT 2

Canadian Mouthwash Market

	1986	1987	1988	1989	1990
Total retail sales (millions)	$43.4	$54.6	$60.2	$65.4	$68.6
Total factory sales (millions)	$34.8	$43.5	$48.1	$52.2	$54.4
Total unit sales (thousands)[a]	863	1,088	1,197	1,294	1,358
(% change)	3	26	10	8	5
(% change—"breath only")[b]	3	26	0	3	5
Penetration (%)[c]	65	70	75	73	75
Usage (number of times per week)[d]	2.0	2.2	2.3	2.4	3.0

[a] One unit or statistical case equals 10 liters or 352 fluid ounces of mouthwash.

[b] Excludes Plax and other prebrushing rinses.

[c] Percentage of households having at least one brand in home.

[d] For each adult household member.

Source: Company records.

In 1977, Warner-Lambert launched Listermint mouthwash as a direct competitor to Scope. Like Scope, it was a green, mint-tasting mouthwash and positioned as a "good tasting mouthwash that fights bad breath." Within a year it had achieved a 12 percent market share, primarily at the expense of Listerine and smaller brands in the market.

In the 1970s, Merrell Dow, a large pharmaceutical firm, launched Cepacol, which was positioned very close to Listerine. It achieved and held approximately 14 percent of the market in the early 1980s.

During the 1980s, the major competitive changes in the Canadian mouthwash market were:

- Listerine, which had been marketed primarily on a "bad breath" strategy, began shifting its position and in 1988 introduced the claim "Fights plaque and helps prevent inflamed gums caused by plaque." In the United States, Listerine gained the American Dental Association seal for plaque but, as yet, did not have the seal in Canada.

- Listermint added fluoride during the early 1980s and added the Canadian Dental Association seal for preventing cavities in 1983. More recently, Listermint had downplayed fluoride and removed the seal.

- In early 1987, flavors were introduced by a number of brands including Scope, Listermint, and various store brands. This greatly expanded the market in 1987 but did not significantly change the market shares held by the major brands.

- Colgate Fluoride Rinse was launched in 1988. With the seal from the Canadian Dental Association for cavities, it claimed that "Colgate's new fluoride rinse fights cavities. And, it has a mild taste that encourages children to rinse longer and more often." Colgate's share peaked at 2 percent and then declined. There were rumors that Colgate was planning to discontinue the brand.

- In 1988, Merrell Dow entered a licensing agreement with Strategic Brands to market Cepacol in Canada. Strategic Brands, a Canadian firm that markets a variety of consumer household products, had focused its efforts on gaining greater distribution for Cepacol and promoting it on the basis of price.

- In 1988, Plax was launched on a new and different platform. Its launch and immediate success caught many in the industry by surprise.

■ THE INTRODUCTION OF PLAX

Plax was launched in Canada in late 1988 on a platform quite different from the traditional mouthwashes. First, instead of the usual use occasion of "after brushing," it called itself a "prebrushing" rinse. The user rinses before brushing, and Plax's detergents are supposed to help loosen plaque to make brushing especially effective. Second, the product benefits were not breath-focused. Instead, it claimed that "Rinsing with Plax, then brushing normally, removes up to three times more plaque than just brushing alone."

Pfizer Inc., a pharmaceutical firm, launched Plax in Canada with a promotion campaign that was estimated to be close to $4 million. The campaign, which covered the last three months of 1988 and all of 1989, consisted of advertising estimated at $3 million and extensive sales promotions, including (1) trial-size display in three drugstore chains ($60,000), (2) co-op mail couponing to 2.5 million households ($160,000), (3) an instantly redeemable coupon offer ($110,000), (4) a professional mailer to drug and supermarket chains ($30,000), and (5) a number of price reductions ($640,000). Plax continued to support the brand with advertising expenditures of approximately $1.2 million in 1990. In 1990, Plax held a 10 percent share of the total market.

When Plax was launched in the United States, it claimed that using Plax "removed up to 300% more plaque than just brushing." This claim was challenged by mouthwash competitors and led to an investigation by the Better Business Bureau. The investigation found that the study on which Plax based its claim had panelists limit their toothbrushing to just 15 seconds—and didn't let them use toothpaste. A further study, where people were allowed to brush in their "usual manner" and with toothpaste, showed no overall difference in the level of plaque buildup between those using Plax and a control group that did not use Plax. Plax then revised its claim to "three times more plaque than just brushing alone." Information on plaque is contained in the Appendix.

■ THE CURRENT SITUATION

In preparing for the strategic plan, Gwen Hearst reviewed the available information for the mouthwash market and Scope. As shown in Exhibit 2, in 1990, 75 percent of Canadian households used one or more mouthwash brands, and, on average, usage was three times per week for each adult household member. Company market research revealed that users could be segmented on frequency of use; "heavy" users (once per day or more) comprised 40 percent of all users, "medium" users (two to six times a week) comprised 45 percent, and "light" users (less than once a week) comprised 15 percent. No information was available on the usage habits of prebrushing rinse users. Nonusers currently don't buy mouthwash because they either (1) don't believe they get bad breath, (2) believe that brushing their teeth is adequate, and/or (3) find alternatives like gums and mints more convenient. The most important reasons why consumers use mouthwash are:

Most Important Reason for Using a Mouthwash	%
It is part of my basic oral hygiene	40[*]
It gets rid of bad breath	40
It kills germs	30
It makes me feel more confident	20
To avoid offending others	25

[*]Multiple reasons allowed.

During 1990, a survey was conducted of mouthwash users' images of the major brands in the market. Respondents were asked to rate the brands on a number of attributes, and the results show that Plax had achieved a strong image on the "removes plaque/healthier teeth and gums" attributes (Exhibit 3).

Market share data revealed there was a substantial difference in the share held by Scope in food stores, 42 percent (for example, supermarkets) versus drugstores, 27 percent (Exhibit 4). Approximately 65 percent of all mouthwash sales went through drugstores, while 35 percent went through food stores. Recently, wholesale clubs, such as Price Club and Costco, were accounting for a greater share of mouthwash sales.[1] Typically, these clubs carried Cepacol, Scope, Listerine, and Plax.

Competitive data were also collected for advertising expenditures and retail prices. As shown in Exhibit 5 (on page 222), total media spending of all brands in 1990 was $5 million, with Scope, Listerine, and Plax accounting for 90 percent of all advertising. Retail prices were calculated based on a 750-ml bottle, both Listerine and Plax were priced at a higher level in food stores, and Plax was priced at a premium in drugstores.

EXHIBIT 3

Consumer Perceptions of Brand Images

	All Users[a]					
Attributes	Cepacol	Colgate	Listerine	Listermint	Plax	Scope
Reduces bad breath	. . .	. . .	. . .	. . .	—	. . .
Kills germs	+	. . .	+	. . .	. . .	—
Removes plaque	. . .	. . .	. . .	. . .	+	—
Healthier teeth and gums	. . .	. . .	. . .	. . .	+	—
Good for preventing colds	. . .	. . .	+	. . .	. . .	. . .
Recommended by doctors/dentists	. . .	—	. . .	. . .	+	. . .
Cleans your mouth well	. . .	. . .	. . .	. . .	. . .	. . .

	Brand Users[b]					
Attributes	Cepacol	Colgate	Listerine	Listermint	Plax	Scope
Reduces bad breath	+	—	+	+	—	+
Kills germs	+	. . .	+	—	—	. . .
Removes plaque	—	+	+	—	+	—
Healthier teeth and gums	. . .	+	+	—	+	—
Good for preventing colds	+	—	+	—	—	—
Recommended by doctors/dentists	+	+	+	—	+	—

[a]Includes anyone who uses mouthwash. Respondents asked to rate all brands (even those they haven't used) on the attributes. A "+" means this brand scores *higher than average*. A ". . ." means this brand scored *about average*. A "—" means this brand scored *below average*. For example, Cepacol is perceived by those who use mouthwash as a brand that is good/better than most at "preventing germs."

[b]Includes only the users of that brand. For example, Cepacol is perceived by those whose "usual brand" is Cepacol as a brand that is good/better than most at "reducing bad breath."

Source: Company records.

---

[1]Wholesale clubs were included in food store sales.

EXHIBIT 4

Canadian Mouthwash Market Shares

	Units			1990 Average	
	1988	*1989*	*1990*	*Food*	*Drug*
Scope	33.0%	33.0%	32.3%	42.0%	27.0%
Listerine	15.2	16.1	16.6	12.0	19.0
Listermint	15.2	9.8	10.6	8.0	12.0
Cepacol	13.6	10.6	10.3	9.0	11.0
Colgate oral rinse	1.4	1.2	0.5	0.4	0.5
Plax	1.0	10.0	10.0	8.0	11.0
Store brands	16.0	15.4	16.0	18.0	15.0
Miscellaneous other	4.6	3.9	3.7	2.6	4.5
Total	100.0%	100.0%	100.0%	100.0%	100.0%
Retail sales (000,000)	$60.2	$65.4	$68.6	$24.0	$44.6

Source: Company records.

Information on the U.S. market for 1989 was also available (see Exhibit 6 on page 223). In contrast to Canada, Listerine held the dominant share in the U.S. market. Since early 1989, Listerine had been advertised heavily in the United States as "the only nonprescription mouthwash accepted by the American Dental Association for its significant help in preventing and reducing plaque and gingivitis." In clinical tests in the United States, Listerine significantly reduced plaque scores by roughly 20 to 35 percent, with a similar reduction in gingivitis. In Canada, the 1990 advertising campaign included the claim that Listerine has been clinically proven to "help prevent inflamed and irritated gums caused by plaque build-up." Listerine's formula relied on four essential oils—menthol, eucalyptol, thymol, and methyl salicylate—all derivatives of phenol, a powerful antiseptic.

Listerine had not received the consumer product seal given by the Canadian Dental Association (CDA) because the association was not convinced a mouthrinse could be of therapeutic value. The CDA was currently reviewing American tests for several products sold in Canada. In fact, any proposed changes to the formulation of mouthwashes or advertising claims could require approval from various regulatory agencies.

■ THE REGULATORY ENVIRONMENT

1. **Health Protection Branch:** This government body classifies products into "drug status" or "cosmetic status" based on both the product's action on bodily functions and its advertising claims. Drug products are those that affect a bodily function (for example, prevent cavities or prevent plaque buildup). For "drug status" products, all product formulations, packaging, copy, and advertising must be pre-cleared by the Health Protection Branch (HPB), with guidelines that are very stringent. Mouthwashes like Scope that claim to only prevent bad breath are considered as "cosmetic status." However, if any claims regarding inhibition of plaque formation are made the product reverts to "drug status," and all advertising is scrutinized.

EXHIBIT 5

Competitive Market Data, 1990

Advertising Expenditures (000)

Scope	$1,700
Listerine	1,600
Plax	1,200
Listermint	330
Cepacol	170

Media Plans

	Number of Weeks on Air	GRPs[a]
Scope	35	325
Listerine	25	450
Plax	20	325

Retail Price Indices

	Food Stores	Drugstores
Scope	98	84
Listerine	129	97
Listermint	103	84
Colgate	123	119
Plax	170	141
Store brand	58	58
Cepacol	84	81
Total Market[b]	100	100

[a]GRP (Gross Rating Points) is a measurement of advertising impact derived by multiplying the number of persons exposed to an advertisement by the average number of exposures per person. The GRPs reported are monthly.

[b]An average weighted index of the retail prices of all mouthwash brands is calculated and indexed at 100 for both food stores and drugstores. Scope is priced slightly below this index in food stores and about 16 percent below in drugstores.

Source: Company records.

2. **The Canadian Dental Association:** Will, upon request of the manufacturer, place its seal of recognition on products that have demonstrated efficacy against cavities or against plaque/gingivitis. However, those products with the seal of recognition must submit their packaging and advertising to the CDA for approval. The CDA and the American Dental Association (ADA) are two separate bodies and are independent of each other and don't always agree on issues. The CDA, for example, would not provide a "plaque/gingivitis" seal unless clinical studies demonstrating actual gum health improvements were done.

3. **Saccharin/Cyclamate sweeteners:** All mouthwashes contain an artificial sweetener. In Canada, cyclamate is used as the sweetener, as saccharin is considered a banned substance. In contrast, the United States uses saccharin because cyclamate is prohibited. Thus, despite the fact that many of the same brands compete in both Canada and the United States, the formula in each country is different.

EXHIBIT 6

Canada–U.S. Market Share Comparison, 1989 (% units)

Brands	Canada	United States
Scope	33.0	21.6
Listerine	16.1	28.7
Listermint	9.8	4.5
Cepacol	10.6	3.6
Plax	10.0	9.6

Source: Company records.

■ THE THREE-YEAR PLAN

In preparing the three-year plan for Scope, a team had been formed within P&G to examine various options. The team included individuals from Product Development (PDD), Manufacturing, Sales, Market Research, Finance, Advertising, and Operations. Over the past year, the team had completed a variety of activities relating to Scope.

The key issue, in Hearst's mind, was how P&G should capitalize on the emerging market segment within the rinse category that focused more on "health-related benefits" than the traditional breath strategy of Scope. Specifically with the launch of Plax, the mouthwash market had segmented itself along the "breath-only" brands (like Scope) and those promising other benefits. Plax, in positioning itself as a prebrushing rinse, was not seen as, nor did it taste like, a "breath refreshment" mouthwash like Scope.

Gwen Hearst believed that a line extension positioned against Plax, a recent entry into the market, made the most sense. If the mouthwash market became more segmented, and if these other brands grew, her fear was that P&G would be left with a large share of a segment that focused only on "breath" and hence might decline. However, she also knew that there were questions regarding both the strategic and financial implications of such a proposal. In recent meetings, other ideas had been proposed, including "doing nothing" and looking at claims other than "breath" that might be used by Scope instead of adding a new product. Several team members questioned whether there was any real threat, as Plax was positioned very differently from Scope. As she considered the alternatives, Hearst reviewed the activities of the team and the issues that had been raised by various team members.

Product Development

In product tests on Scope, PDD had demonstrated that Scope reduced plaque better than brushing alone because of antibacterial ingredients contained in Scope. However, as yet P&G did not have a clinical database to convince the HPB to allow Scope to extend these claims into the prevention of inflamed gums (as Listerine does).

PDD had recently developed a new prebrushing rinse product that performed as well as Plax but did not work any better than Plax against plaque reduction. In fact, in its testing of Plax itself, PDD was actually unable to replicate the plaque reduction claim made by Pfizer that "rinsing with Plax, then brushing normally removes up to three times more plaque than brushing alone." The key benefit of P&G's prebrushing rinse was that it did taste better than Plax. Other than that, it had similar aesthetic qualities to Plax—qualities that made its "in-mouth" experience quite different from that of Scope.

The Product Development people in particular were concerned about Hearst's idea of launching a line extension because it was a product that was only equal in efficacy to Plax and to placebo rinses for plaque reduction. Traditionally, P&G had only launched products that focused on unmet consumer needs—typically superior performing products. However, Gwen had pointed out, because the new product offered similar efficacy at a better taste, this was similar to the situation when Scope was originally launched. Some PDD members were also concerned that if they couldn't replicate Plax's clinical results with P&G's stringent test methodology, and if the product possibly didn't provide any greater benefit than rinsing with any liquid, then P&G's image and credibility with dental professionals might be impacted. There was debate on this issue, as others felt that as long as the product did encourage better oral hygiene, it did provide a benefit. As further support they noted that many professionals did recommend Plax. Over all, PDD's preference was to not launch a new product but, instead, to add plaque-reduction claims to Scope. The basic argument was that it was better to protect the business that P&G was already in than to launch a completely new entity. If a line extension was pursued, a product test costing $20,000 would be required.

Sales

The sales people had seen the inroads Plax had been making in the marketplace and believed that Scope should respond quickly. They had one key concern. As stock-keeping units (SKUs) had begun to proliferate in many categories, the retail industry had become much more stringent regarding what it would accept. Now, to be listed on store shelves, a brand must be seen as different enough (or unique) from the competition to build incremental purchases—otherwise retailers argued that category sales volume would simply be spread over more units. When this happened, a retail outlet's profitability was reduced because inventory costs were higher, but no additional sales revenue was generated. When a new brand was viewed as not generating more sales, retailers might still list the brand by replacing units within the existing line (for example, drop shelf facings of Scope), or the manufacturer could pay approximately $50,000 per stock-keeping unit in listing fees to add the new brand.

Market Research

Market Research (MR) had worked extensively with Hearst to test the options with consumers. Its work to date had shown:

1. A plaque reassurance on current Scope (that is, "Now Scope fights plaque") did not seem to increase competitive users' desire to purchase Scope. This meant that it was unlikely to generate additional volume, but it could prevent current users from switching.

   MR also cautioned that adding "reassurances" to a product often takes time before the consumer accepts the idea and then acts on it. The issue in Hearst's mind was whether the reassurance would ever be enough. At best it might stabilize the business, she thought, but would it grow behind such a claim?

2. A "Better-Tasting Prebrushing Dental Rinse" product did research well among Plax users, but did not increase purchase intent among people not currently using a dental rinse. MR's estimate was that a brand launched on this positioning would likely result in approximately a 6.5 percent share of the total mouthwash and "rinse" market on an ongoing basis. Historically, it has taken approximately two years to get to the ongoing level. However, there was no way for them to accurately assess potential Scope cannibalization. "Use your judgment," they had said. However, they cautioned that although it was a product for a different usage occasion, it was unlikely to be 100 percent incremental business. Hearst's best rough guess was that this product might cannibalize

somewhere between 2 and 9 percent of Scope's sales. An unresolved issue was the product's name—if it were launched, should it be under the Scope name or not? One fear was that if the Scope name was used it would either "turn off" loyal users who saw Scope as a breath refreshment product or confuse them.

MR had questioned Hearst as to whether she had really looked at all angles to meet her objective. Because much of this work had been done quickly, they wondered whether there weren't some other benefits Scope could talk about that would interest consumers and hence achieve the same objective. They suggested that Hearst look at other alternatives beyond just "a plaque reassurance on Scope" or a "line extension positioned as a 'Better-Tasting Prebrushing Rinse.'"

Finance

The point of view from Finance was mixed. On the one hand, Plax commanded a higher dollar price/liter and so it made sense that a new rinse might be a profitable option. On the other hand, they were concerned about the capital costs and the marketing costs that might be involved to launch a line extension. One option would be to source the product from a U.S. plant where the necessary equipment already existed. If the product was obtained from the U.S., delivery costs would increase by $1 per unit. Scope's current marketing and financial picture is shown in Exhibits 7 and 8 and an estimate of Plax's financial picture is provided in Exhibit 9 on page 226.

EXHIBIT 7

Scope Historical Financials

Year	1988		1989		1990	
Total market size (Units) (000)	1,197		1,294		1,358	
Scope market share	33.0%		33.0%		32.4%	
Scope volume (Units) (000)	395		427		440	
	$(000)	**$/Unit**	**$(000)**	**$/Unit**	**$(000)**	**$/Unit**
Sales	16,767	42.45	17,847	41.80	18,150	41.25
COGS	10,738	27.18	11,316	26.50	11,409	25.93
Gross margin	6,029	15.27	7,299	15.30	6,741	15.32

Scope Marketing Plan Inputs
Scope "Going" Marketing Spending

Year	1990	1989	1988
Advertising (000)	$1,700	—	—
Promotion (000)	1,460	—	—
Total (000)	$3,160	$3,733	$2,697

Marketing Input Costs

Advertising:		(See Exhibit 5)
Promotion:	Samples	(Including Distribution): $0.45/piece
	Mailed couponing	$10.00 per 1,000 for printing distribution
		$0.17 handling per redeemed coupon (beyond face value) redemption rates: 10% to 15%
	In-store promotion	$200/store (fixed)
		$0.17 handling per redeemed coupon (beyond face value) redemption rates: 85% +

Source: Company records.

EXHIBIT 8

Scope 1990 Financials

	$(000)	$/Unit
Net sales[a]	18,150	41.25
Ingredients	3,590	8.16
Packaging	2,244	5.10
Manufacturing[b]	3,080	7.00
Delivery	1,373	3.12
Miscellaneous[c]	1,122	2.55
Cost of goods sold	11,409	25.93
Gross margin	6,741	15.32

[a] Net sales = P&G revenues.

[b] Manufacturing: 50 percent of manufacturing cost is fixed of which $200,000 is depreciation; 20 percent of manufacturing cost is labor.

[c] Miscellaneous: 75 percent of miscellaneous cost is fixed. General office overhead is $1,366,000. Taxes are 40 percent. Currently the plant operates on a five-day one-shift operation. P&G's weighted average cost of capital is 12 percent. Total units sold in 1990 were 440,000.

Source: Company records.

Purchasing

The Purchasing Manager had reviewed the formula for the line extension and had estimated that the ingredients cost would increase by $2.55 per unit due to the addition of new ingredients. But, because one of the ingredients was very new, Finance felt that the actual ingredient change might vary by ± 50%. Packaging costs would be $0.30 per unit higher owing to the fact that the setup charges would be spread over a smaller base.

Advertising Agency

The Advertising Agency felt that making any new claims for Scope was a huge strategic shift for the brand. They favored a line extension. Scope's strategy had always been "breath refreshment and good tasting" focused, and they saw the plaque claims as

EXHIBIT 9

Plax Financial Estimates ($/Unit)

Net Sales	65.09
COGS	
Ingredients	6.50
Packaging	8.30
Manufacturing	6.50
Delivery	3.00
Miscellaneous	1.06
Total	25.36

Notes: General overhead costs estimated at $5.88/unit.

Source: P&G estimates.

very different, with potentially significant strategic implications. The one time they had focused advertising only on taste and didn't reinforce breath efficacy, share fell. They were concerned that the current Scope consumer could be confused if plaque or any "nonbreath" claims were added and that Scope could actually lose market share if this occurred. They also pointed out that trying to communicate two different ideas in one commercial was very difficult. They believed the line extension was a completely different product from Scope with a different benefit and use occasion. In their minds, a line extension would need to be supported on a going basis separately from Scope.

■ WHAT TO RECOMMEND?

Hearst knew the business team had thought long and hard about the issue. She knew that management was depending on the Scope business team to come up with the right long-term plan for P&G—even if that meant not introducing the new product. However, she felt there was too much risk associated with P&G's long-term position in oral rinses if nothing was done. There was no easy answer—and compounding the exigencies of the situation was the fact that the business team had differing points of view. She was faced with the dilemma of providing recommendations about Scope, but also needed to ensure that there was alignment and commitment from the business team, or Senior Management would be unlikely to agree to the proposal.

■ APPENDIX

Plaque

Plaque is a soft, sticky film that coats teeth within hours of brushing and may eventually harden into tartar. To curb gum disease—which over 90 percent of Canadians suffer at some time—plaque must be curbed. Research has shown that, without brushing, within 24 hours a film (plaque) starts to spread over teeth and gums and, over days, becomes a sticky, gelatinous mat, which the plaque bacteria spin from sugars and starches. As the plaque grows it becomes home to yet more bacteria—dozens of strains. A mature plaque is about 75 percent bacteria; the remainder consists of organic solids from saliva, water, and other cells shed from soft oral tissues.

As plaque bacteria digest food, they also manufacture irritating malodorous byproducts, all of which can harm a tooth's supporting tissues as they seep into the crevice below the gum line. Within 10 to 21 days, depending on the person, signs of gingivitis—the mildest gum disease—first appear, gums deepen in color, swell, and lose their normally tight, arching contour around teeth. Such gingivitis is entirely reversible. It can disappear within a week after regular brushing and flossing are resumed. But when plaque isn't kept under control, gingivitis can be the first step down toward periodontitis, the more advanced gum disease in which bone and other structures that support the teeth become damaged. Teeth can loosen and fall out— or require extraction.

The traditional and still best approach to plaque control is careful and thorough brushing and flossing to scrub teeth clean of plaque. Indeed, the antiplaque claims that toothpastes carry are usually based on the product's ability to clean teeth mechanically, with brushing. Toothpastes contain abrasives, detergent, and foaming agents, all of which help the brush do its work.

Frito-Lay Company
Cracker Jack

In mid-July 1997, Lynne Peissig, Vice President and General Manager for New Ventures at the Frito-Lay Company, a division of PepsiCo, Inc., assembled the business team responsible for studying the possible acquisition of Cracker Jack from Borden Foods Corporation. Cracker Jack had been owned by Borden since 1964 and was one of the oldest and best-known trademarks in the United States. Borden's intention to sell the Cracker Jack brand and related assets had become public in June 1997. Peissig and the New Ventures Division initiated a study of the Cracker Jack business potential within days of the announcement.

The purpose of the all-day meeting was to (1) consolidate the findings of the business team, (2) outline a plan for how Cracker Jack might be marketed as a Frito-Lay brand, and (3) estimate the "fair market value" of the Cracker Jack business. The valuation would assist senior PepsiCo executives in determining an acquisition price should they decide to submit a bid on the Cracker Jack brand and related assets.

The effort of the business team benefited from the involvement of Frito-Lay brand marketing, sales, distribution, manufacturing, finance, legal, and research and development personnel and PepsiCo merger and acquisition staff working with the New Ventures Division. Peissig was scheduled to deliver a formal presentation and recommendation to senior PepsiCo executives within two weeks. She knew that the marketing issues identified, the plan outline, and the financial valuation by the business team would carry considerable weight in her recommendation to pursue or pass on the business opportunity made possible by the acquisition of the Cracker Jack brand and related assets.

■ FRITO-LAY COMPANY

Frito-Lay Company is a division of PepsiCo, Inc. Frito-Lay recorded an operating profit of $1.63 billion on net sales of $9.68 billion in 1996, which represented 31 percent of PepsiCo's net sales and 60 percent of PepsiCo's operating profit. The sales and operating profit compounded annual growth rate for Frito-Lay was 13 percent for the five-year period, 1991 to 1996. Frito-Lay Company is composed of Frito-Lay North America and Frito-Lay International. Frito-Lay North America, consisting of operations in the United States and Canada, recorded 68 percent of company sales and 79 percent of company operating profit in 1996.

The cooperation of the Frito-Lay Company in the preparation of this case is gratefully acknowledged. BAKED LAY'S, BAKED TOSTITOS, CHEE·TOS, DORITOS, FRITOS, FUNYUNS, LAY'S, ROLD GOLD, RUFFLES, SANTITAS, SUN CHIPS, TOSTITOS, SMARTFOODS, and GRANDMA'S are trademarks used by the Frito-Lay Company. After the acquisition, CRACKER JACK, SAILOR JACK, and BINGO would be trademarks used by the Frito-Lay Company. This case was prepared by Professor Roger A. Kerin, of the Edwin L. Cox School of Business, Southern Methodist University, with the assistance of Daniel Goe and Rebecca Kaufman, graduate students, as a basis for class discussion and is not designed to illustrate effective or ineffective handling of an administrative situation. Certain company information, including names of Frito-Lay executives, are disguised and not useful for research purposes. Copyright © 1999 by Roger A. Kerin. No part of this case may be reproduced without written permission of the copyright holder.

Company Background

Frito-Lay is a worldwide leader in the manufacturing and marketing of snacks. Well-known company brands include Lay's and Ruffles potato chips, Fritos corn chips, Doritos, Tostitos, and Santitas tortilla chips, Chee-tos cheese-flavored snacks, and Rold Gold pretzels. Other well-known Frito-Lay brands include Sun Chips multigrain snacks and Funyuns onion-flavored snacks. In addition, the company markets a line of dips, salsas, nuts, peanut butter and cheese-filled sandwich crackers, processed beef sticks, Smartfood brand ready-to-eat popcorn, and Grandma's brand cookies.

The company is the leading manufacturer of snack chips in the United States, capturing 54 percent of the retail sales in this category in 1996. Nine of Frito-Lay's snack chips are among the top 10 best-selling snack brands in U.S. supermarkets (see Exhibit 1). Doritos tortilla chips and Lays and Ruffles potato chips each have the distinction of being the only snack chips with over $1 billion in retail sales in the world.

A major source of volume growth for Frito-Lay in the 1990s was due to the introduction of "better-for-you" low-fat and no-fat snacks. These snacks, including Baked Lay's potato crisps, Baked Tostitos tortilla chips, and Rold Gold pretzels, accounted for 47 percent of Frito-Lay's total pound volume growth in 1995 and 1996, and 40 percent of pound volume growth in 1994. Better-for-you products represented 15 percent of Frito-Lay's total snack volume in 1996, up from 5 percent in 1993.

Frito-Lay's U.S. snack food business spans every aspect of snack food production and distribution, from agriculture to stocking retailer shelves. During 1996 in the United States alone, Frito-Lay used 2.7 billion pounds of potatoes, one billion pounds of corn, and over 15 million pounds of cheese to produce its products. The company has 45 manufacturing plants in 26 states, including the world's largest snack food plant

EXHIBIT 1

Top-Selling Snack Chip Items in U.S. Supermarkets (Retail Sales in $ millions)

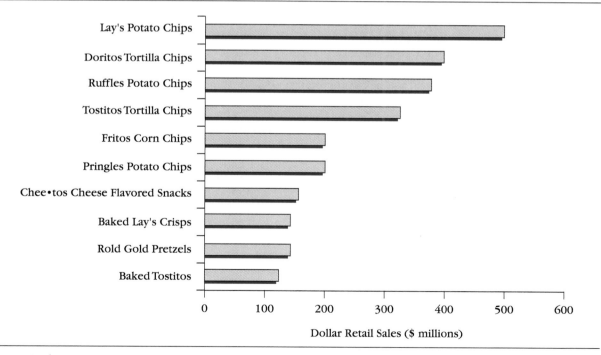

Source: 1996 PepsiCo, Inc., annual report.

in Frankfort, Indiana, and operates more than 1,800 warehouses and distribution facilities. Frito-Lay employs 17,500 salespeople—the largest store-door-delivery sales force in the world—who make 750,000 sales and delivery calls on approximately 350,000 retail store customers each week. Frito-Lay's products receive constant attention from the company's sales force, which ensures constant replenishment of fresh product and proper facings of products on store shelves. Supermarkets and grocery stores accounted for more than 50 percent of Frito-Lay's total U.S. retail sales in 1996, followed by convenience stores (15 percent), mass merchandise/warehouse/club stores (11 percent), vending and food service operators (8 percent), and other retailers and institutions (10 percent).

Frito-Lay consistently ranks among the leading national advertisers in the United States, both in terms of dollars spent and creative execution. The company also uses trade and consumer promotions and sponsors special events, such as the Tostitos Fiesta Bowl postseason collegiate football game.

New Ventures Division

The New Ventures Division at Frito-Lay originated in December 1996 with a well-defined mission:

> To drive significant Frito-Lay growth by seeking and creating new business platforms and products which combine the best of Frito-Lay advantages with high-impact consumer food solutions.

According to Casey Joseph, Frito-Lay's Senior Vice President–Worldwide Marketing, the primary purpose of the New Ventures Division was to create meaningful growth outside of Frito-Lay's already successful existing snack businesses, and secondarily augment ongoing internal product development activities.

During the winter of 1997, the New Ventures mission manifested itself as a deliberate approach for identifying and developing sales and profit growth opportunities for Frito-Lay. After considerable discussion, three broad opportunity avenues emerged as possible routes for achieving meaningful future growth. One growth avenue consisted of opportunities for building Frito-Lay's existing snack business by expanding into new eating occasions for current or new products. Ongoing internal research and development efforts to identify "better-for-you" products for morning and all-day consumption fell into this category. A second growth avenue was the opportunity to successfully enter new product categories by capitalizing on Frito-Lay's store-door-delivery sales force strengths, broad distribution coverage, and brand marketing skills. This opportunity could be realized through internal research and development or through targeted distribution alliances and acquisitions. Possible new product categories for Frito-Lay included confectioneries (e.g., candies) and baked sweet pastries, single-serve cakes, or snack bars. A third growth avenue was labeled "opportunistic acquisitions" made possible by related food companies offering products or entire businesses for sale as a result of corporate restructuring. These acquisitions would be screened by the New Ventures Division on the basis of their strategic and operating fit with Frito-Lay's sales, distribution, manufacturing, and brand marketing capabilities and meaningful sales and profit growth potential.

The announcement by Borden of its intention to divest the Cracker Jack brand and related assets represented a potential fit with all three growth avenues. According to Lynne Peissig:

> Early in our discussions, the New Ventures Division came to believe that sweet snacks represented a potential incremental growth opportunity for Frito-Lay. Cracker Jack appeared to be a logical "step out" versus a "leap" into sweet snacks from a strategic perspective. It could provide the foundation for a sweet snack platform to build a successful business on and complement Frito-Lay's salty snack business. Cracker Jack,

with its strong brand equities, was certainly worth the time and effort to explore as an acquisition.

■ THE READY-TO-EAT CARAMEL POPCORN PRODUCT CATEGORY

The ready-to-eat (RTE) caramel popcorn product category recorded U.S. retail sales of $192 million in 1996 and $205 million in 1995. Manufacturer sales of RTE caramel popcorn were $167.3 million in 1996, down 6.2 percent from 1995. The decline in 1996 category dollar sales followed a steady annual sales increase since 1993. Pound volume in the RTE caramel popcorn category declined from 59.3 million pounds in 1995 to 57 million pounds in 1996, following a steady annual volume growth since 1993. Category sales and volume growth in the 1990s was due primarily to the introduction of new flavors (i.e., butter toffee) and low-fat and no-fat varieties of established brands.

Competitors

Several different types of competitors serve the RTE caramel popcorn category: (1) national brand firms, (2) seasonal/specialty firms, (3) regional firms, and (4) private label firms. National brand firms, which distribute products throughout the United States, include Borden Foods (Cracker Jack brand), International Home Foods, Inc. (Crunch 'n Munch brand), Lincoln Foods (Fiddle Faddle brand), and SIM-GT Licensing Corporation, which markets the Richard Simmons brand. A second category of competitors consists of seasonal/specialty firms that produce and market their caramel popcorn on a seasonal basis (often around December and the Christmas holiday season) or as a specialty item frequently sold in collectible tins. Seasonal/specialty firms include Houstons Foods and Harry and David. A large number of small, regional firms produce and distribute RTE caramel popcorn in only certain parts of the United States. Private brands are produced by regional or local manufacturers on a contractual basis for major U.S. supermarket chains. Estimated 1996 sales and pound volume market shares for individual national brands, seasonal/specialty/regional brands, and private labels are shown in Exhibit 2 on page 232.

International Home Foods, Inc. (Crunch 'n Munch) and Borden Foods (Cracker Jack) are the RTE caramel popcorn category dollar and volume market share leaders in the United States. Prior to 1996, International Home Foods was the consumer foods unit of American Home Products Corporation (AHP). AHP is a multinational human and animal health care and agricultural products company with net sales exceeding $14 billion in 1996. In November 1996, AHP sold a majority interest (80%) in the food unit for approximately $1.2 billion to a limited partnership, of which the investment firm of Hicks, Muse, Tate & Furst is the general partner. International Home Foods produces and markets name-brand preserved foods. Its nationally known products include Chef Boyardee pastas (which represents nearly 30% of sales), Bumble Bee tuna, Polaner fruit spread, and PAM cooking spray. The company also sells southwestern cuisine foods (Ro*Tel canned tomatoes, Dennison's canned chili, and Ranch Style beans) and snack foods (Crunch 'n Munch caramel popcorn and Jiffy Pop popcorn). International Home Foods recorded net sales of $942.8 million in 1996.

Borden, Inc. is owned by the investment firm of Kohlberg Kravis Roberts & Co., which purchased the company for $1.9 billion in 1994. Although widely known for its dairy products, Borden divested its dairy business in 1997. Today, the company makes pasta, soup mixes, and bouillon (Borden Foods), snack foods (Wise Foods and Cracker Jack), consumer adhesives (Elmer's products), and industrial adhesives, coatings, and resins (Borden Chemical). Borden, Inc. recorded net sales of about $5.8 billion in 1996.

EXHIBIT 2

Caramel Corn Category Dollar and Volume Share at Retail: 1996

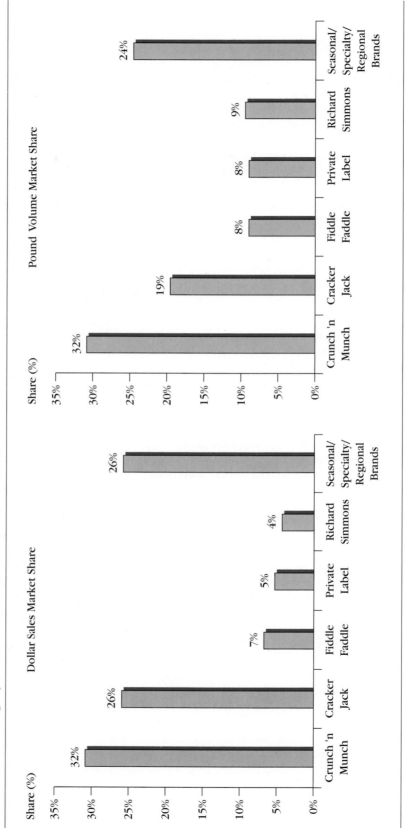

Source: Company records.

The decision by Borden to divest itself of Cracker Jack and related assets was prompted by a strategic assessment of the company's focus and resources. The company chose to focus on its pasta business and expand into grain-based meals that would require a significant resource investment. As a consequence of this assessment and growth plan, Borden Foods announced that Cracker Jack, along with Borden Brands North America and Borden Brands International, would be sold in 1997.

Marketing Practice

RTE caramel popcorn is generally viewed among snack food industry analysts as an "undermarketed" category, when compared with microwave popcorn and most other snack categories. Most brands in the category offer both caramel and butter toffee flavors and feature both regular and low-fat/fat-free varieties in different package sizes. An exception is the Richard Simmons brand, which is sold only as a fat-free product.

Only Crunch 'n Munch and Cracker Jack have been recently advertised in consumer media. Crunch 'n Munch leads the category in advertising expenditures, outspending Cracker Jack by a wide margin since 1993 (see Exhibit 3). The last time Cracker Jack spent significant funds for consumer advertising occurred in 1992, when $2.1 million was spent to launch the brand's butter toffee flavor. Consumer and trade

EXHIBIT 3

Competitive Spending for Consumer Media Advertising: 1993–1997

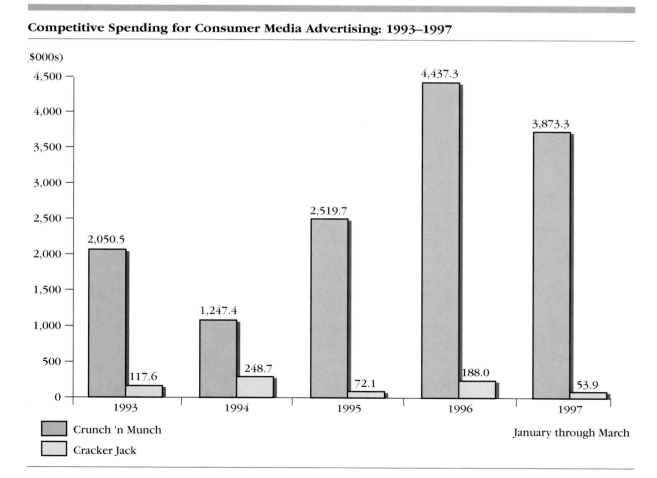

($000s)

January through March

Crunch 'n Munch
Cracker Jack

promotions are often used by national and regional brands. Consumer promotions include in-store and newspaper couponing and product sampling; trade promotions include sales aids and off-invoice allowances for retailers.

Supermarkets and grocery stores and mass merchandise/warehouse/club stores are the principal retail outlets for RTE caramel popcorn. Supermarkets and grocery stores account for an estimated 44.7 percent of category dollar sales. About 42 percent of sales occur in mass merchandise/warehouse/club stores (Target, Kmart, Wal-Mart). Drugstores account for 13 percent of sales. Remaining sales arise from a variety of other retail and food service outlets. In 1996, Crunch 'n Munch had an estimated 31 percent volume share in supermarkets and grocery stores, an 18 percent share in mass merchandise/warehouse/club stores, and a 13 percent share in drugstores. Cracker Jack's market share in these channels was 23 percent, 8 percent, and 11 percent, respectively, according to industry sources.

Retail outlets for RTE caramel popcorn are typically serviced via warehouse delivery systems. With a warehouse system, product is delivered from a manufacturer's plant or distribution center to a retailer's warehouse. The retailer assumes responsibility for distributing the product to its stores and stocking shelves.

Cracker Jack is the premium-priced brand in the RTE caramel popcorn category. Its total brand average price premium relative to Crunch 'n Munch has averaged about 28 percent over the past three years. Private (store) labels are typically the lowest-priced brands. Regional brands are often priced between national brands and private labels. In some areas, regional "gourmet" brands and seasonal/specialty brands are priced at or near national brands.

Caramel Popcorn Consumer

Industry research shows that RTE caramel popcorn is a snack primarily eaten at home in the afternoon and evening as a treat or reward. Four of five users eat RTE caramel popcorn at home, and 80 percent of eating occasions are in the afternoon or evening hours. Only about 12 percent of U.S. households consume RTE caramel popcorn. Average consumption frequency is also low relative to other snack categories at less than two purchases per year. Whereas 2 percent of U.S. households consume RTE caramel popcorn at least once in a typical two-week period, 70 percent consume a salty snack (e.g., potato chips) and 31 percent consume candy (excluding gum and mints).

Industry research also shows that U.S. households with a female household head between the ages of 25 and 44, with children ages 4 to 17, is the heavy user of RTE caramel popcorn and Cracker Jack. This research further documents that:

1. Adult females consume 44 percent of caramel popcorn sold, adult males consume 29 percent, and children under age 18 consume 27 percent.

2. Fifty-four percent of heavy caramel popcorn users and 60 percent of heavy Cracker Jack purchasers reside in households with more than two members.

3. Fifty percent of heavy Cracker Jack purchasers and 42 percent of heavy caramel popcorn users are in households with children under age 18.

■ CRACKER JACK BRAND

Cracker Jack is one of the most recognized consumer food brands in the United States. The brand name enjoys a 97 percent awareness among persons between the ages of 15 and 60. Cracker Jack has a 95 percent brand name awareness among heavy users of caramel popcorn.

Brand Heritage

Cracker Jack is the original caramel popcorn. Invented by F. W. Ruekheim, the confection of popcorn, peanuts, and molasses was first made and sold in 1893 at the World's Fair Columbian Exhibition in Chicago, Illinois. The Cracker Jack name was coined in 1896 when a visiting salesman tasted the product and exclaimed, "That's a cracker jack!"—a nineteenth-century slang phrase meaning, "That's great." In 1899, Cracker Jack was packaged in moisture-proof boxes making possible broadened distribution of the product.

Three developments in the early 1900s had lasting effects on the image of Cracker Jack. In 1908, the brand was immortalized in the song, "Take Me Out to the Ball Game," with its lyric "Buy me some peanuts and Cracker Jack." In 1912, F.W. Ruekheim introduced the prize-in-every-box novelty, featuring magnifying glasses, little books, beads, metal trains and whistles, and baseball cards, among other items. More than 17 billion Cracker Jack toys have been distributed since 1912. A patriotic flair was added to the Cracker Jack box during World War I (1914–1918) with the inclusion of red, white, and blue stripes. A saluting Sailor Jack and his dog, Bingo, were also added to the box and soon became the national Cracker Jack logo. Sailor Jack and Bingo have appeared on Cracker Jack packages with only slight variations since 1918.

Cracker Jack Product Line and Positioning

For 100 years, the Cracker Jack product line consisted only of caramel-coated popcorn and peanuts, using the original recipe developed by F. W. Ruekheim. In 1992, a Butter Toffee flavor was introduced, followed by Nutty Deluxe in 1994, and Cracker Jack Fat Free (in Original and Butter Toffee flavors) in 1995. Approximately 23 percent of Cracker Jack dollar and pound volume sales growth between 1993 and 1995 could be attributed to these product introductions. The breakdown of Cracker Jack 1996 net dollar sales by formulation is shown below:

Product Formulation	Net Dollar Sales (%)
Original/Butter Toffee	63.0%
Original/Butter Toffee Fat Free	26.0
Nutty Deluxe	6.7
Other*	4.3
Total	100.0%

*The other category consists primarily of inventory with limited shelf-life sold to a number of prequalified off-price retailers.

Cracker Jack is sold in a variety of packages. The product is packaged in 1.05-ounce and 1.25-ounce single-serve boxes and bags (introduced in December 1996) and 7-ounce and 8-ounce family-size bags and bags-in-boxes (introduced in 1992). The combinations of flavors, package sizes, and package forms (boxes, bags, and bags-in-boxes) resulted in a product line with 32 separate items or stock-keeping units (SKUs) in 1996. Family-size bags-in-boxes accounted for 75 percent of net dollar sales; single-serve boxes accounted for 25 percent of net dollar sales in 1996. Single-serve and family-size bags represented an insignificant percentage of net dollar sales in 1996. Representative items in the Cracker Jack product line are shown in Exhibit 4 on page 236.

Cracker Jack positioning over the past 30 years focused on its brand heritage as a traditional fun treat. This positioning manifested itself in the primary message for Cracker Jack advertising as illustrated below:

1. "What do you want when you've gotta have something . . . candy coated popcorn, peanuts and a prize" (1960s)

EXHIBIT 4

Cracker Jack Product Line

2. "When you're really good they call you Cracker Jack," featuring contemporary children excelling in athletics (1970s and early 1980s)

3. "Delicious then, delicious now," featuring a dual child/adult appeal reminding mothers how much they enjoyed Cracker Jack when growing up (mid-1980s)

4. "Only one snack says Cracker Jack," featuring its unique brand heritage (early 1990s). In 1992, the Butter Toffee flavor was introduced and positioned as a unique, all-family, all-occasion snack that provided a delicious-tasting, fun experience.

Cracker Jack's positioning was broadened in mid-1997 to emphasize the "better-for-you" qualities of Cracker Jack Fat Free in both Original and Butter Toffee flavors: "Cracker Jack, the sweet and crunchy fun snack you remember, has surprisingly less fat than you thought." The new positioning was being applied to all forms of brand communication, including packaging, consumer promotion, public relations, and consumer advertising.

Advertising and Promotion

Annual advertising and promotion spending for the Cracker Jack brand, as a percentage of sales, has ranged between 28 and 40 percent since 1993. Trade promotion, including incentives given retailers to reduce their cost or gain merchandising performance (off-invoice allowances, slotting fees, and market-development funds), represented the principal expense since 1993. Consumer promotion, including in-store and Sunday newspaper coupon insertions and redemption cost, and "other" promotions such as sales aids and samples accounted for the second largest expense item. Consumer advertising represented the smallest expense category. Cracker Jack has not been advertised nationally since 1993. However, as recently as 1980, Cracker Jack was the most advertised sweet snack in the United States, with a $6 million spending level.

The Cracker Jack toy surprise is another element of the advertising and promotion program. The choice of prizes is based on research among mothers and children to determine appeal. All toys must also pass rigorous safety testing to be considered as Cracker Jack prizes. In addition to long-time favorites, such as miniature baseball cards, Cracker Jack has licensed high-profile children's properties (e.g., Animaniacs, Looney Tunes, Wishbone, Scooby Doo) since 1995 to add value to the toy surprise. This effort has focused on promoting impulse purchases, particularly for Cracker Jack's highest gross margin items—the 1.05-ounce and 1.25-ounce single-serve box and bag.

Sales and Distribution

Cracker Jack sales volume is concentrated in the United States, where 98.9 percent of sales occur. Sales in Canada and a small export business represent the remaining 1.1 percent of volume. In 1996, 52 percent of Cracker Jack sales arose from supermarkets and grocery stores, 31 percent from mass merchandisers, 7 percent from drugstores, 4 percent from warehouse and club stores, and 6 percent from other outlets.

Cracker Jack is sold through a shared Borden sales force that also sells cheese and other Borden grocery brands such as Eagle Brand, Cremora, and ReaLemon. The retail grocery sales force includes 47 people who sell product to supermarkets and grocery stores through 65 independent food brokers. An independent broker organization of 20 people sells product directly to mass merchandise, military, drugstore, and club store customers.

Cracker Jack is shipped from 13 company distribution centers to retail store distribution centers or warehouses and subsequently delivered to retail outlets for stocking on store shelves by retail store personnel. Accordingly, Cracker Jack is typically placed in what is called the "warehouse-delivered snack aisles" of supermarkets and grocery stores versus the "direct-store delivery aisles," which are stocked and merchandised by a manufacturer's sales force and not retail store personnel.

Pricing

Borden Foods has employed a premium pricing strategy for Cracker Jack relative to competing national brands (e.g., Crunch 'n Munch). Cracker Jack prices have risen by an average of 5 to 6 percent per year since 1993. As a consequence, Cracker Jack's average retail price premium relative to Crunch 'n Munch was about 28 percent on a per-ounce basis since 1993. The price premium was expanded in January 1997, when the price for Cracker Jack was increased by 6 percent. However, this price premium margin quickly eroded when the 10- and 5-ounce Crunch 'n Munch packages were downsized to 8- and 4-ounce packages, respectively, without a change in price. The effect of this move was to reduce the Cracker Jack price premium for the 7-ounce and 8-ounce family-size packages to 14 percent.

Manufacturing

Borden Foods manufactures Cracker Jack at its Northbrook, Illinois, facility along with selected Borden Foods soup products. Cracker Jack equipment occupies about 32 percent of the facility's manufacturing space. This space houses 15 production lines,

11 box lines, and 4 bag lines. The production lines operate at approximately 33 percent capacity, and the box and bag lines operate at 85 percent capacity based on a five-day week and two eight-hour shifts per day. Approximately 450,000 to 500,000 packages are produced per day, warehoused at the site, and subsequently shipped to company distribution centers.

A unique feature of the production and packaging process is the Cracker Jack prize insertion activity. Prizes are collated on custom-made equipment designed by the company, and electric eyes are placed within the production lines to ensure that these prizes are inserted in boxes. In 1994, about 85 percent of the company's total capital expenditures was spent to automate the family-size bag-in-box packaging line and change the filling operation from a volumetric cup filler to a more accurate scale system.

Cracker Jack Strategy and Financial Performance: 1993–1996

Exhibit 5 contains Cracker Jack Direct Product Contribution Income Statements for the period 1993 to 1996.[1] Cracker Jack recorded a negative Direct Product Contribution in each of the three previous years (1994 to 1996). Borden's current management attributed this performance to a variety of sources. Beginning in 1992, prior management pursued a volume-based strategy that focused on introducing family-size packages (7- and 8-ounce bags and bags-in-boxes) while reducing emphasis on the smaller box packages (e.g., 1.25-ounce box). This strategy achieved its intended effect. Cracker Jack pound volume in supermarkets and grocery stores, mass merchandisers, warehouse clubs, and drugstores combined increased to 12.4 million pounds in 1993, 13.5 million pounds in 1994, and 16.3 million pounds in 1995. However, the Cracker Jack gross margin percentage suffered due to a smaller margin contribution on large packages, which cannibalized higher margin small packages. In addition, rising material prices in 1994 and 1995 reduced margins since the added costs were not passed on with comparable price increases. Also, the introduction of Nutty Deluxe and Fat Free varieties in 1994 and 1995 was supported by a heavy financial investment in trade promotions. Even though these varieties accounted for almost one-fourth of Cracker Jack dollar and volume sales growth between 1993 and 1995, this growth was not large enough to offset the incremental trade promotion costs.

Direct Product Contribution improved in 1996 due to a number of changes made by current Borden management. For example, trade promotion spending was reduced. The number of Cracker Jack SKUs was reduced from 47 in 1995 to 32 in 1996, which reduced inventory levels and improved the sales mix gross margin. However, Cracker Jack dollar sales declined by 9 percent and unit volume fell to 11.2 million pounds in 1996.

Exhibit 6 on page 240 shows the Cracker Jack balance sheet for the year ended December 31, 1996. In addition to the physical assets shown, other Cracker Jack assets include the trademarks Cracker Jack, the Sailor Jack and Bingo representation, Nutty Deluxe, and "When you're really good they call you Cracker Jack," and certain patents related to the manufacturing of Cracker Jack.

---

[1]Direct Product Contribution Income Statements exclude certain direct and indirect expenses which customarily are allocated to products in accordance with Borden Foods' internal policies. These allocated expense categories, which change from time to time, represent the costs associated with the functional infrastructure of Borden Foods and include certain fixed sales and administrative expenses. In addition, costs related to certain systems, legal expenses, finance/accounting, and human resource/benefit services provided by Borden Foods Corporate headquarters have also been excluded in determining Direct Product Contribution. All financial information contained in these exhibits has been disguised and is not useful for external research purposes.

EXHIBIT 5

Cracker Jack Direct Product Contribution Income Statement: 1993–1996 ($ in Millions)

	1993	1994	1995	1996
Net trade sales	$51.4	$ 51.7	$ 53.2	$48.4
Cost of goods sold	26.0	33.8	32.2	27.1
Gross margin	$25.4	$ 17.9	$ 21.0	$21.3
Distribution expense	$ 4.6	$ 6.1	$ 5.5	$ 4.4
Trade promotion	11.4	16.0	15.6	8.6
Advertising, consumer, & other promotion	5.9	4.8	5.2	5.0
Variable sales	1.1	1.4	1.3	1.2
A & P management	0.3	0.4	0.8	0.8
Market research	0.3	1.0	2.3	2.5
Technical research	0.1	0.2	0.4	0.6
Direct product contribution[a]	$ 1.7	($ 12.0)	($ 10.1)	($ 1.8)
Other financial information:				
Depreciation expense	$ 1.5	$ 1.6	$ 1.4	$ 1.4
Capital expenditures	$ 1.4	$ 5.3	$ 0.8	$ 0.3
Working capital[b]	$ 16.4	$ 12.8	$ 6.3	$ 2.3

[a] Excludes effects of allocated selling costs, overhead, and other income and expense.

[b] Current assets (other than cash) minus current liabilities.

Explanatory Notes for Revenue and Expense Items:

Revenue recognition. Net trade sales are generally recognized when products are shipped. Liabilities are established for estimated returns, allowances, and consumer and trade discounts when revenues are recognized.

Cost of goods sold. Includes all variable costs associated with producing the product, including raw materials, packaging supplies, direct and indirect labor, and plant fixed overhead expenses including a BFC allocation for quality assurance and engineering.

Distribution expense. Expenses associated with moving finished good from distribution centers to customers and all handling and storage charges of moving goods into, within, and out of third-party warehouses.

Variable sales. Commission or other payments to brokers associated with volume.

A & P management. Costs associated with business unit marketing personnel.

Market research. Syndicated consumer information, taste tests, package tests, focus groups, and other market research.

Advertising costs. Production costs of future media advertising are expensed on the first airdate or print-release date of the advertising. All other advertising is expensed as incurred.

Trade promotion. All incentives to the trade related to tactics to reduce price or gain merchandising performance. Included are off-invoice allowances, slotting, and market development funds.

Consumer promotion. Promotion expenses targeted at consumers including coupon insertion and redemption and consumer refunds/premiums in return for certain purchase level requirements.

Other promotion. Includes sales aids, samples, packaging development, and racks.

Technical research. Costs associated with product or process research and development.

Note: All financial information in this exhibit has been disguised and is not useful for external research purposes.

Cracker Jack Strategy and Financial Projections: 1997–2001

The financial performance of Cracker Jack through 1995 prompted a change in strategy in 1996. The new Cracker Jack strategy arose from a general strategic review of the entire Borden Foods Corporation begun in 1995. The strategy, adopted in 1996, had three objectives: (1) revitalize the base business, (2) improve operating efficiencies,

EXHIBIT 6

Cracker Jack Balance Sheet: December 31, 1996 ($ in Millions)

Assets

Cash and marketable securities	—
Net trade receivables[*]	$ 2.0
Inventories	4.2
Other current assets	0.2
Other long-term assets and intangibles	12.2
Net property, plant, and equipment	15.4
Total assets	**$34.0**

Liabilities and equity

Trade and drafts payable[*]	$ 3.1
Other current liabilities	1.1
General insurance	2.2
Pension liability	0.3
Nonpension postemployment benefits	2.5
Total liabilities	**$ 9.2**
Owner's investment	**$24.8**

[*]Net trade receivables, trade and drafts payable, and certain other current liabilities are not being sold and are presented for informational purposes only.

Note: All financial information in this exhibit has been disguised and is not useful for external research purposes.

and (3) extend the Cracker Jack trademark. These objectives would be realized by (1) expanded distribution within retail snack and food service marketing channels, (2) developing new packaging and flavors, (3) impactful product positioning, (4) enhanced gross margins via sustained price leadership, and (5) additional resources being allotted to consumer advertising.

Initial efforts in 1996 were designed to arrest the losses incurred in 1994 and 1995. The elimination of unprofitable trade promotions, the pruning of Cracker Jack SKUs from 47 to 32, and a higher gross margin resulted in a sizable improvement in the 1996 Direct Product Contribution. In late 1996 and early 1997, other actions were taken consistent with the new Cracker Jack strategy:

1. In December 1996, a single-serve (1.05- and 1.25-ounce) bag was introduced, primarily for distribution through vending machines and to Sam's Warehouse Clubs.

2. A 6 percent price increase was implemented in January 1997.

3. A new positioning that emphasized the low-fat content of Cracker Jack was initiated in mid-1997. This positioning—"Cracker Jack, the sweet and crunchy fun snack you remember, has surprisingly less fat than you thought"—highlighted the low-fat content of Original Cracker Jack (2.5 grams of fat per 1.25-ounce serving) and Cracker Jack Fat Free (0 grams of fat per serving).

Cracker Jack management believed that broadened distribution was the most important element of the new strategy. In December 1996, efforts were made to develop the vending machine business with the new single-serve bag using specialty distributors. Vending sales were projected to be almost $2 million in 1997. However, Cracker Jack management was of the view that the brand needed a totally new sales and delivery infrastructure to grow sales and product profitability. Specifically, the shared Borden sales force and broker/distributor network currently in use should be replaced by a direct-store-delivery (DSD) sales force. It was believed that a DSD sales force could provide product placement in grocery DSD snack aisles, which is the highest-velocity snack aisle in supermarkets. Limited, controlled store tests commissioned by Cracker Jack management indicated that placement in DSD snack aisles could initially boost dollar retail sales by as much as 38 percent. However, a DSD sales force is more resource intensive than Borden's present sales and distribution network. Borden Foods management was neither prepared to make the investments required nor equipped to handle a DSD sales force for Cracker Jack given the resource demands of other business opportunities.

Exhibit 7 details projected Direct Product Contribution Income Statements prepared by Cracker Jack management for the period 1997 to 2001. The projections reflect the new strategy initiatives adopted by Borden's management and the integration of Cracker Jack into a national manufacturing, distribution, and sales infrastructure of a potential acquirer with an existing snack-related business.

The projection assumes significant revenue increases resulting from distribution expansion, primarily into grocery DSD, vending, and food service sales. It is also assumed that the acquirer would be willing and able to (1) fund trade promotions and consumer advertising to bolster sales of existing products and extend the product line and (2) raise prices. The projections also include capital expenditures, notably in 1999, that will be required to support the volume projections.

The Direct Product Contribution Income Statement projected for 1997 reflects Cracker Jack management's estimate of year-end results without a DSD sales force. Projected 1998 revenues demonstrate the estimated impact of a fully operational DSD sales force. These estimates focus exclusively on domestic opportunities for Cracker Jack and do not include potential export sales growth.

EXHIBIT 7

Cracker Jack Projected Direct Product Contribution Income Statements: 1997–2001 ($ in Millions)

	1997	1998	1999	2000	2001
Net trade sales	$50.5	$78.5	$191.4	$209.1	$258.9
Cost of goods sold	27.3	37.4	97.5	108.3	127.8
Gross margin	$23.2	$41.1	$ 93.9	$100.8	$131.1
Distribution expense	$ 4.4	$ 4.6	$ 9.7	$ 11.0	$ 13.0
Trade promotion	6.2	10.2	23.8	22.3	23.9
Advertising, consumer, & other promotion	5.3	11.3	19.9	20.1	24.8
Variable sales	1.4	2.4	3.6	3.9	4.6
A & P management	0.9	0.4	0.4	0.4	0.6
Market research	1.0	1.6	2.6	3.0	3.4
Technical research	0.7	0.8	1.8	2.1	2.6
Direct product contribution[a]	$ 3.3	$ 9.8	$ 32.1	$ 38.0	$ 58.2
Other financial information:					
Depreciation expense	$ 1.4	$ 1.9	$ 3.7	$ 4.2	$ 4.7
Capital expenditures	$ 0.4	$ 4.0	$ 19.3	$ 4.3	$ 6.4
Working capital[b]	$ 3.0	$ 5.0	$ 13.2	$ 14.4	$ 18.0

[a] Excludes effects of allocated selling costs, overhead, and other income and expense.

[b] Current assets (other than cash) minus current liabilities.

Note: All financial information in this exhibit has been disguised and is not useful for external research purposes.

■ PROJECT BINGO

The New Ventures team met in June 1997 to decide whether or not to explore the Cracker Jack acquisition. Following a review of financial and operating data supplied by Borden in its Offering Memorandum, the decision was made to examine Cracker Jack as an acquisition. The effort was code-named "Project Bingo."

Project Bingo consisted of commissioned studies, internal company reviews, and cross-functional team analyses and evaluations orchestrated by Lynne Peissig. The target completion date was July 15, 1997, with a presentation and recommendation to Frito-Lay senior management scheduled for August 1, 1997. A nonbinding open bid for Cracker Jack and its related assets from prospective buyers was due August 6, 1997. The top bidders would be invited to Northbrook, Illinois, for a plant visit and a Borden management presentation. A binding letter of intent and bid would be submitted by interested parties toward the end of September 1997. Peissig believed that bids for Cracker Jack would be submitted by a number of investment firms and consumer foods companies, including General Mills, Nabisco, and Procter & Gamble.

The data-gathering effort was substantially complete by mid-July 1997. Preliminary analyses had been conducted in four areas: (1) brand management, (2) sales and distribution, (3) manufacturing and product assurance, and (4) finance and administration.

Brand Management

The consensus opinion among the New Ventures team was that brand management considerations would drive Project Bingo. Two studies were commissioned, including (1) a brand awareness, image, equity, and usage study; and (2) a simulated test market.

Brand Awareness, Image, Equity, and Usage Study An independent research firm that specialized in ongoing brand-tracking studies for consumer goods companies submitted its report to Project Bingo's brand marketing team in late June 1997. The principal findings are summarized below:

1. The Cracker Jack name registers virtually universal awareness. However, Cracker Jack Fat Free, Butter Toffee, and Nutty Deluxe exhibit consumer awareness levels below 50 percent.

2. The Cracker Jack name evokes distinct imagery and icons in consumers' minds. These include the product form itself (caramel, popcorn, peanuts), the prize/toy in the box, the boy/sailor and dog on the box, and taste/flavor. Overall, Cracker Jack was perceived to be:

   - Traditional and old-fashioned in a way that evokes fond memories of growing up (but not very contemporary, and less contemporary than Crunch 'n Munch).
   - Popular with kids more than teens, adults, or the family.
   - More of a personal snack than a snack for sharing.
   - A good treat, but not necessarily extendible across eating occasions.
   - Fairly unique, particularly compared to other RTE caramel popcorn.
   - Not at all "better for you" compared to many other snacks.
   - Not as available for purchase, nor as easy to find in the stores as other RTE caramel popcorn.
   - Lacking a good variety of flavors/types.

3. Cracker Jack has a respectable brand equity due largely to its heritage and generally favorable image foundation. It is a recognized brand with a positive reputation that appears to have lost momentum (popularity) in recent years.

4. Only 7.1 percent of U.S. households consume Cracker Jack. These households consume less than one pound of Cracker Jack annually. Exhibit 8 on page 244 shows the major reasons why consumers do not buy Cracker Jack more often.

The study results were viewed favorably by the brand marketing team. According to one team member, "Cracker Jack is a trademark living off residual heritage with untapped opportunity."

Simulated Test Market Preliminary results from the simulated test market (STM) also proved "encouraging," according to a brand marketing team member. Unlike the brand awareness, image, equity, and usage study, the STM was commissioned to obtain an initial assessment of Cracker Jack's commercial potential.

The STM, conducted by another marketing research firm, consisted of four steps. First, consumers between the ages of 12 and 64, who had purchased a sweet or salty snack during the past three months, were recruited at shopping malls in 16 U.S. cities and escorted to a nearby research facility. These consumers were then exposed to an advertisement for Cracker Jack (see Exhibit 9 on page 245). Following this exposure, consumers proceeded to a mock store setup where Cracker Jack was available for sale along with competing RTE caramel popcorn brands. Consumers were given money and could purchase whatever brands they wished, keeping any money left over. Finally, consumers who bought Cracker Jack were given two complimentary packages of Cracker Jack to take home. These consumers were called after a 2- to 3-week time period, asked a series of questions about the product, and offered a chance to repeat purchase the brand.

Diagnostic information was also gathered as part of the Cracker Jack STM. Consumer attitudes toward the brand (likes and dislikes) and usage intentions were obtained. These data were incorporated into computer simulation models that also included elements of the brand's intended marketing plan. The STM output included estimates of household brand trial and repeat rates, purchase amounts and frequency, product cannibalism, and first-year sales volume estimates.[2]

Fifteen different marketing plan options were tested in the Cracker Jack STM. Planned distribution coverage was set at levels comparable for Frito-Lay potato, corn, and tortilla chips. Two different store locations were tested: placement in the salty snack aisle versus the alternative snack aisle of stores. The present retail price of $1.69 for an 8-ounce box was tested, but the package type was varied to compare the 8-ounce box with a 7-ounce flex bag. Also, a $1.99 retail price was tested with an 8-ounce flex bag. Finally, three advertising and promotion expenditure levels ($15 million, $22 million, and $32 million) were simulated.

Diagnostic information gathered during the STM indicated that consumers had more "likes" than "dislikes" about Cracker Jack. Consumers gave favorable ratings to Cracker Jack's taste/flavor and texture/consistency. However, most consumers said there were not enough peanuts. Cracker Jack scored highly as an afternoon, early evening, and late evening snack, but low as a morning treat. Almost one-half (46%) of consumers said that the nuts, popcorn, and snack mix aisle was the preferred store location for buying Cracker Jack. The next most preferred store aisle was with salty snacks (24%), followed by the candy and cookie aisles and the checkout counter.

Exhibit 10 (on page 246) shows preliminary first-year pound and net sales dollar volume estimates for each of the marketing plan options. First-year net sales estimates ranged from $46.6 million to $124.4 million at manufacturer prices. Estimates of product cannibalism indicated that 22 percent of Cracker Jack pound volume would come

---

[2] For an extended description of STMs, see K. Clancy, R. Shulman, and M. Wolf, *Simulated Test Marketing: Technology for Launching Successful New Products* (New York: Lexington Books, 1994).

EXHIBIT 8

Most Important Reasons for Not Buying Cracker Jack More Often

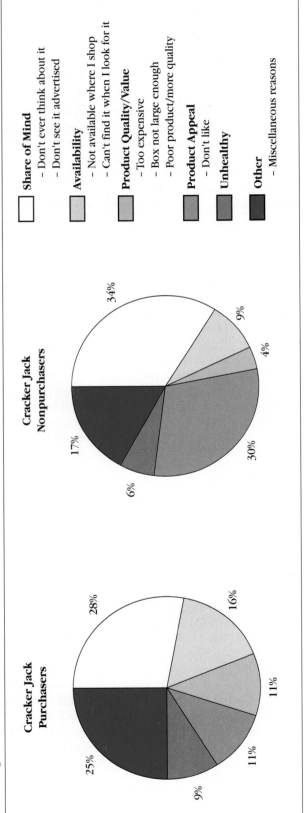

Share of Mind
- Don't ever think about it
- Don't see it advertised

Availability
- Not available where I shop
- Can't find it when I look for it

Product Quality/Value
- Too expensive
- Box not large enough
- Poor product/more quality

Product Appeal
- Don't like

Unhealthy

Other
- Miscellaneous reasons

Cracker Jack
Nonpurchasers

34%
9%
4%
30%
6%
17%

Cracker Jack
Purchasers

28%
16%
11%
11%
9%
25%

Source: Company records.

EXHIBIT 9

Cracker Jack Simulated Test Market Advertisement

EXHIBIT 10

Cracker Jack Simulated Test Market First-Year Volume Projections

Marketing Plan Elements	Preliminary Marketing Plan Options														
Distribution/Product Placement	**Salty Snack Aisle**									**Alternative Snack Aisle**					
	8-oz. Bag-in-Box @ $1.69			7-oz. Flex Bag @ $1.69			8-oz. Flex Bag @ $1.99			8-oz Bag-in-Box @ $1.69			7-oz. Flex Bag @ $1.69		
Package form and retail (consumer) price															
Advertising and promotion ($ million)[a]	$15	$22	$32	$15	$22	$32	$15	$22	$32	$15	$22	$32	$15	$22	$32
First-Year Volume Projections[b]															
Pound volume (millions)	24.3	34.0	40.7	22.6	31.6	37.8	26.0	36.4	43.8	20.5	32.2	38.9	19.0	29.9	36.2
Dollar sales volume (millions) @ manufacturer price to retailer (mfr. net sales)	$59.6	$83.4	$99.0	$55.1	$77.1	$92.5	$73.9	$103.7	$124.4	$50.4	$79.1	$95.7	$46.6	$72.6	$88.6

[a]Advertising and Promotion Breakdown:

	At $15 million	At $22 million	At $32 million
Consumer Advertising	$0	$10	$15
Consumer Promotion	8	5	10
Trade Promotion	7	7	7

[b]Volume forecasts are subject to a ± 15% accuracy range.

Note: All financial information in this exhibit has been disguised and is not useful for external research purposes.

246

from other Frito-Lay snack chip brands when the advertising and promotion expenditure was $32 million.[3](*Case writer note*: Footnote 3 contains important information for case analysis purposes.) This percentage was 7 percent at the $15 million expenditure level. No estimates were made for the $22 million expenditure level. The incidence of product cannibalism did not vary by store location (salty snack versus alternative snack aisle). According to a New Ventures team member, "These preliminary results indicate that Cracker Jack has considerable upside potential given broadened availability through our extensive sales and distribution network and advertising and promotion support."

Cracker Jack Extensions   In subsequent meetings with the brand marketing team, discussions focused on Cracker Jack extension possibilities beyond the first year. Brand marketing personnel believed that attention in the first year should focus on establishing the Cracker Jack base business given a new sales and distribution infrastructure. However, brand and flavor extensions should be pursued in the second and third year of Cracker Jack marketing as a Frito-Lay brand.

Several brand marketing team members advocated a brand extension in the second year. Specifically, they proposed that a Cracker Jack snack bar be introduced. Cereal marketers had experienced considerable success with these bars following the trend toward "grab-and-go" eating. For example, Kellogg's Rice Krispies Treats snack bar recorded over $100 million in supermarket retail sales over the past two years. Quaker Oats recently extended its oatmeal cereal with the launch of Fruit & Oatmeal Cereal bars supported by $20 million in trade promotion and consumer advertising. Brand marketing team members speculated that a Cracker Jack snack bar could generate $50 to $100 million in incremental manufacturer net sales in the second year if supported by a $10 million trade and consumer advertising and promotion program. It was believed that incremental snack bar sales would be somewhat dependent on first-year sales; that is, higher first-year sales would result in higher incremental snack bar sales.

A flavor extension, added to the current caramel and butter toffee flavors, might be introduced in the third year, according to brand marketing team members. A specific flavor had not been proposed, but likely candidates were chocolate and peanut butter. The snack bar and flavor extension might produce an incremental dollar sales boost of 5 to 10 percent over the second-year sales volume if supported by a $5 to $10 million trade and consumer advertising and promotion program.

Sales and Distribution

Frito-Lay sales and distribution personnel were consulted soon after the Cracker Jack acquisition opportunity became public. Their initial reaction was positive, noting that Cracker Jack would fit the existing Frito-Lay sales and distribution infrastructure.

Sales and distribution personnel raised two issues related to the acquisition. First, the number of Cracker Jack SKUs (32) seemed large. The typical Frito-Lay brand had five to ten SKUs and the number of Cracker Jack SKUs could present a challenge in getting retailer shelf and display space. Second, the estimated cost of a direct-store-delivery (DSD) like that employed by Frito-Lay appeared to be understated. According to industry analysts, the selling and distribution cost of a DSD sales force selling comparable products was understated by a factor of one-half when stated as a percent of net sales.

---

[3]Frito-Lay does not divulge profitability data on individual products and product lines. However, for case analysis and class discussion purposes, Frito-Lay snack chip brands can be assumed to have a gross profit of $1.05 per pound.

Manufacturing and Product Assurance

Frito-Lay manufacturing and product assurance personnel were also favorably disposed toward the Cracker Jack acquisition. Like sales and distribution personnel, they expressed concerns about the number of Cracker Jack SKUs and the added complexity caused by this large number from a production perspective.

Without actually inspecting the Cracker Jack plant, manufacturing and product assurance personnel could not assess the condition of the facility and Cracker Jack production, box, and bag lines. However, they believed that it was highly unlikely that Frito-Lay would buy the Northbrook, Illinois, facility. The production, box, and bag lines might be purchased depending on their condition and relocated to an existing Frito-Lay manufacturing plant along with peanut and prize-insertion equipment. The ongoing capital expenditures projected by Borden management seemed appropriate if this were done.

Manufacturing personnel also said it was unlikely that Frito-Lay would need to make the substantial new plant and equipment capital expenditures indicated in Borden management's projection for 1999 (see Exhibit 7). Rather, Frito-Lay had a long-standing and successful relationship with an independent supplier that produced caramel popcorn, among other savory and salty snack products, and also had the manufacturing capacity to produce the equivalent of $100 million in sales. Space was available at existing Frito-Lay manufacturing facilities to install additional production, box, and bag lines if Cracker Jack sales exceeded $100 million. These lines could be added incrementally for a minimal capital investment. Each $10 million capital investment for production and lines was estimated to provide capacity to manufacture the equivalent of $50 million in sales. The equipment itself would be most likely depreciated over 15 years using the straight-line method.

A senior Frito-Lay manufacturing executive also believed that the Cracker Jack cost of goods sold could be 10 percent less than Borden management's projections. This cost reduction could be realized by simplifying the Cracker Jack product line and building the flex bag volume relative to Cracker Jack sold in boxes and bags-in-boxes.

Finance and Administration

Lynne Peissig engaged Frito-Lay planning personnel and PepsiCo merger and acquisition specialists to begin a valuation analysis of the Cracker Jack business in June 1997. By mid-July, a variety of data had been gathered pertaining to recent acquisitions in the consumer foods industry. According to Diane Tousley, the New Ventures division finance director, the transaction prices for these types of acquisitions represented one to three times net revenues and 10 to 12 times after-tax earnings of the acquired companies. The higher multiples were associated with businesses that had strong brand names or trademarks, established distribution channels and trade relations, and a positive earnings history.

Tousley acknowledged that these data needed to be supplemented with a more rigorous financial appraisal, including a discounted cash flow valuation for Cracker Jack (see Appendix: Note on Valuing a Business at the end of this case). She noted that Frito-Lay commonly applied a risk-adjusted discount rate to calculate the present value of after-tax future cash flows when performing a discounted cash flow analysis for new investments. (*Note*: According to the PepsiCo, Inc. annual report, 1997, p. 29, the effective 1997 PepsiCo, Inc. corporate income tax rate for continuing operations was 35.4 percent.) Depending on the level of the risk, the discount rate ranged from 12 to 18 percent with an average risk-adjusted discount rate of 15 percent. New Ventures team members agreed that an investment in Cracker Jack represented an "average risk" for Frito-Lay.

Revenue forecasts associated with marketing Cracker Jack as a Frito-Lay brand had not been finalized as of July 15, 1997. However, Peissig believed that the preliminary first-year sales projections provided by the STM and incremental dollar sales estimates resulting from brand and flavor extensions in the second and third year offered a starting point for making revenue forecasts. She also thought Cracker Jack dollar sales growth would likely stabilize at a rate of 2 or 3 percent in the fourth and fifth year following modest price and pound volume increases. Peissig added: "I suspect that considerable discussion will focus on Cracker Jack revenue projections when the business team is assembled."

Peissig also expected an animated discussion related to the Cracker Jack trade promotion and consumer advertising budget. She believed three years of focused brand development efforts supported by promotion and advertising spending would be necessary to rebuild and grow the business. After that, the Cracker Jack business might be sustained with an annual promotion and advertising budget representing about 4 to 8 percent of manufacturer net sales. Other costs would also be incurred by Cracker Jack. For example, Tousley estimated that initial and ongoing general and administrative costs associated with the marketing of Cracker Jack as a Frito-Lay brand would range from 4 to 7 percent of manufacturer net sales. These costs included product and process research and development, marketing research, and brand management and administrative salaries and fringe benefits.

Finally, Peissig believed that her presentation to senior PepsiCo executives should include consideration of the Cracker Jack acquisition relative to the internal development and commercialization of a new consumer food brand. According to industry sources, the financial investment to internally develop and launch a new brand (trademark) in a consumer food category was $75 to $100 million, including the cost of product research and development, test marketing, and a national introduction. The time interval from concept development to full-scale commercialization ranged from two to three years. The likelihood of a new product success was roughly one in ten.

■ APPENDIX: NOTE ON VALUING A BUSINESS

Estimating a company's fair market value is a necessary first step in determining the purchase price for an acquisition. Fair market value is the cash, or cash-equivalent, price at which an asset would trade between a willing buyer and seller, with each in command of all information necessary to value the asset and neither under any pressure to trade.

Valuation experts have developed a variety of valuation techniques to assist in establishing a company's fair market value, although this value often may not represent the final transaction price. In practice, a transaction price involves consideration of a variety of factors that may vary depending on the characteristics of the company to be acquired and the objectives of the buyer and seller. For example, obtaining valuable trade names, taking control of another entity, or acquiring an increased market share for a particular product may affect the final purchase price. Still, determination of a transaction or purchase price or a reasonable price range generally involves quantitative techniques. This appendix briefly describes the discounted cash flow (DCF) technique that is used by investment bankers, research analysts, and valuation experts to estimate a company's fair market value. It is assumed that the reader is familiar with the vocabulary and mechanics of present value and discounted cash flow analysis.[4]

---

[4]For background reading on the time value of money, present value analysis, and discounted cash flow, see the most recent edition of S. Ross, R. Westerfield, and B. Jordan, *Fundamentals of Corporate Finance* (Burr Ridge, IL: Irwin McGraw-Hill) or R. Higgins, *Analysis for Financial Management* (Burr Ridge, IL: Irwin McGraw-Hill).

The Discounted Cash Flow Technique

The DCF valuation approach is the most frequently used fair market valuation technique. It provides a "going concern" value, which is the value indicated by the future commercial possibilities of a business. Using this technique, fair market value is calculated by the summation of the present value of projected cash flows for a determined period plus the present value of the residual or terminal value at the end of the projection period for a business. Typically, a 5- to 10-year projection period of after-tax operating cash flows, with various terminal or residual value estimates, will be discounted back to the present by the risk-adjusted, weighted-average cost of capital for the acquiring company. The cash flows are derived from the projected income statements and working and fixed capital expenditure plans. This calculation produces a result that represents the fair market value to both debt and equity holders. To arrive at the (owner's) equity value, the outstanding debt at the time of the acquisition is subtracted from the total capital value.

Four key areas must be assessed for accuracy and appropriateness when using the DCF technique. These include the (1) assumptions underlying the projection of cash flows, (2) length of the projection period, (3) residual or terminal value at the end of the projection period, and (4) appropriate discount rate.

Financial Projection Assumptions and Projection Period   Five factors form the basis for basic financial projections: (1) historical sales growth; (2) business plans of the company to be acquired; (3) prevailing relevant business conditions including growth expectations and trends in light of competitive positioning, general market growth, and price pressure; (4) anticipated needs for working capital and fixed asset expenditures; and (5) historical and expected levels and trends of operating profitability. Each factor affects the estimation of projected cash flows for the business to be acquired.

Determining the length of the projection period is a matter of judgment. As a general rule, it is expected that at the end of the projection period, the operations of a business should be at a normal and sustainable operating level in order to more easily estimate a terminal or residual value (discussed next). Unusual circumstances, such as an excessive sales growth factor, an increase or decrease in operating profit margins, or an improvement in the accounts receivable or inventory levels, should no longer exist by the end of the projection period. For companies projecting normal sales growth rates and profitability margins, a 5- to 10-year projection period is usually employed.

Estimating the Terminal or Residual Value   The value of a business at the end of the projection period is often the least analyzed element of a valuation. However, it can represent a significant portion of the company's entire fair market value. The proper method for estimating the terminal or residual value depends on the financial projection factors described earlier and the length of the projection period in addition to the specifics of the business. A trade-off exists between the degree of reliability inherent within the two factors (DCFs during the projection period and the terminal value) used to calculate an ultimate fair market value. A shorter projection period places greater importance on the ability to develop a meaningful terminal or residual value estimate. A longer projection period places less reliance on the estimated terminal value but makes the annual cash flow assumptions more important.

The two most frequently used approaches for estimating a terminal value are the income capitalization and the multiple techniques. Both techniques estimate the future value of the business at the end of the projection period. This future value is then discounted back to determine the present value.

The income capitalization technique method adjusts either after-tax earnings or cash flow from the final year of the projection period by the discount rate. This technique assumes that after-tax earnings will either be constant or increasing at a constant rate from the last year of the projection period and that the proper risk-adjusted weighted-average cost of capital is the discount rate. The multiple approach applies some multiplier to either after-tax earnings or cash flow from the last year of the projection period. The resulting terminal value is then discounted to its present value using the discount rate from the final year of the projection period. The multiples are developed from publicly traded comparable companies or recent merger and acquisition transactions. A point to remember about the income capitalization and multiple approaches is that the calculated terminal value is dependent on the assumptions underlying the projection period. For example, aggressive sales growth rates will overstate after-tax earnings or cash flow for the last year of the projection period, which will in turn overstate the terminal value. Similarly, multiples may be distorted because of extrinsic influences on recent merger and acquisitions transactions and the fact that two companies are rarely alike.

Discount Rate   The proper discount rate is one of the most significant elements in a DCF. Because the present value changes inversely with changes in the discount rate, it is critical to the valuation to properly assess the inherent risk and thus the required yield of the business to be acquired.

The Capital Asset Pricing Model (CAPM) is generally accepted by the financial community as a means for estimating an investor's yield requirement and hence a company's cost of equity capital. Essentially, the CAPM states that the required cost of equity is equal to the cost of risk-free debt plus some additional risk premium relating to the company. A detailed discussion of CAPM can be found in most finance textbooks. The required rates of return on equity and debt are then weighted in order to arrive at the weighted-average cost of capital. The weighted-average cost of capital for *Fortune* 500 consumer goods companies averages around 10 to 12 percent.

■ DISCOUNTED CASH FLOW TECHNIQUE ILLUSTRATION

Exhibit A-1 provides a simple illustration of the DCF computation for valuing a business. The upper portion of the illustration contains a five-year *pro forma* income statement, including projected business revenues, cost of goods sold, operating expenses, and earnings (net income) before interest and taxes. Also indicated is the provision for corporate income tax and after-tax earnings.

Cash Flow Calculation   The bottom portion of Exhibit A-1 details the cash flow calculation. The projected cash flows are obtained by adjusting the pro forma income statement for noncash items and changes in balance sheet items affecting cash.[5] This is shown by first adding depreciation expense (a noncash cost) for each year to after-tax earnings. After-tax earnings plus depreciation represents the annual cash flow from operations for a business.

The cash flow from operations then needs to be adjusted to reflect cash outflows. This is done by subtracting the estimated year-to-year *increase* in working capital (current assets minus current liabilities) and planned capital expenditures for each year from the estimated cash flow from operations. Increases to working capital in this illustration suggest that current assets, such as inventories and accounts receivables, net of current liabilities (e.g., accounts payable), increase each year at a constant amount of $100,000 given the constant (10%) annual revenue growth rate over the projection period shown in Exhibit A-1. The dollar amount for capital expenditures reflect annual cash investments in plant and equipment. In summary, after-tax

---

[5]For simplicity, deferred taxes and amortization of goodwill are omitted from this example.

EXHIBIT A-1

Business Valuation Discounted Cash Flow Illustration ($000s)

	Year 1	Year 2	Year 3	Year 4	Year 5	Residual Value	Fair Market Value
Revenues (10% growth)	$10,000	$11,000	$12,100	$13,310	$14,641		
Cost of goods sold (40% of revenues)	4,000	4,400	4,840	5,324	5,856		
Gross profit (60% of revenues)	6,000	6,600	7,260	7,986	8,785		
Operating expenses (20% of revenues)	2,000	2,200	2,420	2,662	2,928		
Earnings before interest and taxes (EBIT) (40% of revenues)	4,000	4,400	4,840	5,324	5,856		
Income tax provision on EBIT (40% of EBIT)	1,600	1,760	1,936	2,130	2,343		
After-tax earnings before interest and taxes on interest (24% of revenues)	$ 2,400	$ 2,640	$ 2,904	$ 3,194	$ 3,514		
Add noncash items, including depreciation expense	700	850	1,050	1,300	1,600		
Funds provided	$ 3,100	$ 3,490	$ 3,954	$ 4,494	$ 5,114		
Subtract:							
Increases to working capital	(100)	(100)	(100)	(100)	(100)		
Capital expenditures	(500)	(750)	(1,000)	(1,250)	(1,500)		
Total cash flows exclusive of interest (net of tax)	$ 2,500	$ 2,640	$ 2,854	$ 3,144	$ 3,514	$45,682[a]	
Present value factor at 15%	0.87	0.756	0.658	0.572	0.497	0.497	
Present value	$ 2,174	$ 1,996	$ 1,877	$ 1,798	$ 1,747	$22,704	
Total present value of cash flows							$ 9,592
Present value of residual							22,704
Fair market capital value for the firm							$32,296

[a]Residual value using an after-tax earnings (cash flow) multiple. After-tax earnings (cash flow) from Year 5 times the multiple selected of twelve ($3,514 × 12).

earnings plus noncash expenses (e.g., depreciation) minus projected increases to working capital and annual capital expenditures result in a projected total annual cash flow for a business.

Present Value of Projected Cash Flows and Residual or Terminal Value   As described earlier, the fair market value of a business is calculated by the summation of the present value of projected cash flows for a determined period plus the present value of the residual or terminal value at the end of the projection period. Exhibit A-1 shows the present value calculation using a 15 percent discount rate (other discount rates are shown in Exhibit A-2). The discount rate reflects the acquiring company's weighted-average cost of capital, plus any amount to be added for special risks entailed in the acquisition; hence, the frequently used term *risk-adjusted discount rate*. The summed, or cumulative, present value of projected cash flows over the 5- year projection period is $9,592,000, shown in Exhibit A-1.

EXHIBIT A-2

Present Value of $1.00 Discounted at Discount Rate K, for N Years

Period (N)	Discount Rate (K)						
	12%	13%	14%	15%	16%	17%	18%
1	0.893	0.885	0.877	0.870	0.862	0.855	0.847
2	0.797	0.783	0.769	0.756	0.743	0.731	0.718
3	0.712	0.693	0.675	0.658	0.641	0.624	0.609
4	0.636	0.613	0.592	0.572	0.552	0.534	0.515
5	0.567	0.543	0.519	0.497	0.476	0.456	0.437

As mentioned earlier, the residual or terminal value at the end of a projection period often represents a significant portion of the fair market value of a business. This is apparent in Exhibit A-1, which illustrates the multiple approach for estimating the residual or terminal value. In this illustration, an after-tax earnings (cash flow) multiple (12) is used, which is then discounted to its present value using the discount rate from the final year of the projection period. This results in a residual value of $22,704,000. The sum of the cumulative present value of projected cash flows ($9,592,000) and the present value of the residual or terminal value is the estimated fair market value shown as $32,296,000 in Exhibit A-1.

Alternatively, the income capitalization approach can be used. This approach adjusts either after-tax earnings or cash flow from the final year of the projection period by the discount rate. It can be assumed that after-tax earnings or cash flow will be either constant or increasing at a constant rate from the last year of the projection period.

The income capitalization approach for estimating a residual or terminal value can be applied given information contained in Exhibit A-1. Assuming that after-tax earnings (or cash flow) in Year 5 remain constant at $3,514,000 and a 15 percent discount rate applies, then the present worth of the residual value is $11,643,053 ([$3,514,000/.15] × 0.497). When added to the present value of projected cash flows, the estimated fair market value is $21,235,053 ($9,592,000 + $11,643,053). Alternatively, if a 10 percent annual growth in after-tax earnings (or cash flow) is expected in the future as was apparent in Exhibit A-1 projections, then the present value of a perpetually growing after-tax earnings (cash flow) stream can be estimated. This is done using the formula, $E/K - g$, where E represents after-tax earnings (cash flow) in the last year of the projection period, K is the discount rate, and g is the growth rate in perpetuity. Applying this formula, the estimated residual value is $70,280,000 ($3,514,000/[.15 − .10]). The present value of this amount is $34,929,160 (0.497 × $70,280,000). By adding the present value of the terminal value to the present value of projected cash flows, the estimated fair market value is $44,521,160.

Summary

The estimation of fair market value requires both a qualitative and quantitative appraisal of the future commercial possibilities of a business as a going concern. As demonstrated in this note, the determination of fair market value is by no means a simple matter and will often yield different dollar figures given different assumptions. The DCF valuation approach featured in this note, while conceptually correct, often requires a heavy dose of judgment in its application. Fair market value of a business lies in the eyes of the beholder, whether he or she is the buyer or the seller.

Swisher Mower and Machine Company
Evaluating a Private Brand Opportunity

In early 1996, Wayne Swisher, President and Chief Executive Officer (CEO) of Swisher Mower and Machine Company (SMC), received a certified letter from a major national retail merchandise chain inquiring about a private branding arrangement for SMC's line of riding mowers. Wayne Swisher had only recently assumed his position as President and CEO from Max Swisher, his father and company founder. Wayne Swisher was previously Vice President of Sales, a position he held for six years following completion of the MBA Program at Southern Methodist University in Dallas, Texas. Prior to graduate school, he had worked in a sales and marketing position for three years at a large *Fortune* 500 corporation.

The private branding proposal represented the first major decision he faced as President and CEO. He thought the inquiry presented an opportunity worth consideration, since unit volume sales of the SMC riding mower had plateaued in recent years. However, details concerning the proposal would have to be studied more closely.

■ COMPANY BACKGROUND

The origins of Swisher Mower and Machine Company can be traced to the mechanical aptitude of its founder, Max Swisher. He received his first patent for a gearbox drive assembly when he was 18 years old. Shortly thereafter, he developed a self-propelled push mower utilizing this drive assembly. He began selling these mowers to neighbors after converting his parents' garage into a small manufacturing operation and formed Swisher Mower and Machine Company in 1945. In the early 1950s, Swisher decided to integrate his drive mechanism into a riding mower and, after service in the Korean War, began selling these mowers under the Ride King name in 1956.

In 1966, unit volume for SMC riding mowers peaked at 10,000 units with sales of $2 million. In the early 1970s, sales volume began a downward trend as a result of poor economic conditions in the geographic markets served by SMC. From 1975 to 1989, unit volume remained relatively constant. Sales improved in the 1990s, with an average unit volume of 4,250 riding mowers. In 1995, the company sold 4,200 riding mowers and recorded total company sales of $4.3 million. Exhibit 1 shows SMC's riding mower unit sales history since 1956.

The company manufactures mowers at its plant in Warrensburg, Missouri, but utilizes outside suppliers for some machine tool work and subassembly. Its facilities have

The cooperation of Swisher Mower and Machine Company in the preparation of this case is gratefully acknowledged. This case was prepared by Professor Roger A. Kerin, of the Edwin L. Cox School of Business, Southern Methodist University, and Wayne Swisher, Swisher Mower and Machine Company, as a basis for class discussion and is not designed to illustrate effective or ineffective handling of an administrative situation. Company financial and operating data are disguised and not useful for research purposes. © 1999 by Roger A. Kerin. No part of this case may be reproduced without written permission of the copyright holder.

EXHIBIT 1

Unit Sales History for SMC Riding Mowers

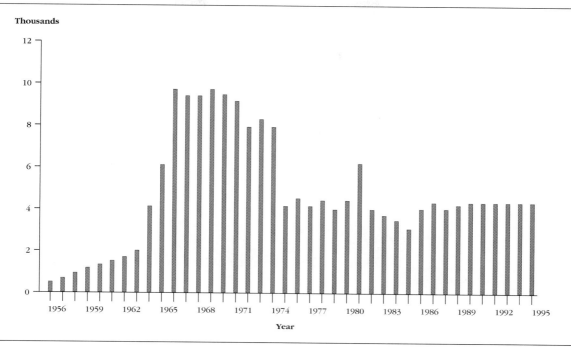

an annual production capacity of 10,000 riding mower units on a single 40-hour-per-week shift. The company's production facility and office space are rented from a related firm.

Max Swisher has always insisted that his company be customer-oriented in recognizing and providing for both dealer and end-user needs. Maintaining a "small company" image had also been an important aspect of Max Swisher's business philosophy, which in turn has resulted in personal relationships with dealers and customers alike. A special loyalty has been demonstrated to the original SMC dealers and distributors that helped build the sales foundation of the company. SMC continues to guarantee protection of these and other dealers' trade territories whenever possible.

Product Line

SMC produced three types of lawn mower units in early 1996. Its flagship product, the Ride King, is a three-wheel riding mower that has a zero turning radius. Developed by Max Swisher in the 1950s, this design is distinct from competitors' in that the single steerable front wheel is also the drive unit. This feature allows the mower to be put in reverse without changing gears and by simply turning the steering wheel 180 degrees. The company is credited with producing the first zero-turning-radius riding mower.

The manufacturer's list price for the standard Ride King is $650. Manufacturer gross profit margin on this unit is approximately 15 percent. The cost of goods sold for this product is approximately $100 for labor and $453 for parts.

SMC has a reputation for producing high-quality riding mowers that have a simple design allowing for ease of customer use and maintenance. These features and benefits are prominently displayed in the product literature for Ride King (see Exhibit 2 on page 256). The reliability and ruggedness of the riding mower are demonstrated by the

EXHIBIT 2

Ride King Product Literature

SWISHER ZERO TURNING RADIUS MOWER
For a quick, clear cut around trees, shrubs, and lawn ornaments.

Swisher, the originator of the ZERO TURNING RADIUS MOWER, has continually refined the mower with updated operating features since its exclusive patent. Swisher's riding mowers are guided by a single, steerable front wheel, pivoting 360 degrees for sharp turns or reversing without stopping or changing gears. Its 32" cutting deck is powered by an 8HP Briggs & Stratton engine. Swisher's ZERO TURNING RADIUS MOWER is another innovation in a long line of Swisher lawn and garden equipment – developed over the past 50 plus years.

Deluxe ergonomic seat with spring suspension

Simple, reliable design

Quick and easy height adjustment handle and wide wheels

Optional quick change chute for mulch or side discharge

1

Anti-scalp rollers

360 degree pivoting front wheel, zero turning radius

ZERO TURNING RADIUS MOWER ZERO TURNING RADIUS MOWER ZERO TURNING RADIUS MOWER

product's longevity. SMC mowers often run for more than 25 years before having to be replaced. The company provides a one-year warranty on all parts and labor. Riding mowers accounted for 63.6 percent of SMC's total sales and 57.8 percent of total gross profit in 1995.

Most current mowers' parts are interchangeable with the parts of older models that date back to 1956. Even though the patent for the zero-turning-radius drive unit has expired, no competitors have copied this exact design.

SMC also produced a "trailmower" called T-44. This unit consists of a trailer-type mower that has a cutting width of 44 inches. When hitched to any riding lawn mower, this unit effectively increases the cutting width by 44 inches. The "trailmower" can also be pulled behind all-terrain vehicles. The T-44 accounted for 8.2 percent of SMC's total sales and 13.2 percent of total gross profit in 1995. Exhibit 3 on page 258 shows the product literature for the T-44.

SMC deemphasized the sale of its self-propelled push mower in the early 1960s due to lagging sales and increased demand for the riding mower. When it phased out these units, the company began offering push lawn mower "kits." There are three different push mower kits available, and each consists of all the component parts necessary to assemble push mowers. Kits do not provide a material contribution to the company's gross profit. Kits accounted for 8.2 percent of SMC's total sales in 1995.

The replacement parts business for mowers accounts for the remainder (20 percent) of SMC sales. Since little standardization exists among mower parts in the industry, SMC must provide customers with replacement parts for its mowers. Replacement parts accounted for 29 percent of the company's total gross profit.

Plans were under way to broaden the SMC product line in 1996 with the introduction of a high-wheel string trimmer product. The "Trim-Max" is a high-wheel, walk-behind product that combines a trimmer, mower, and edger in one unit. Exhibit 4 on page 259 shows the product literature for the "Trim-Max."

Distribution and Promotion

SMC distributes its lawn mowers through farm supply stores, lawn and garden stores, home centers, and hardware stores located primarily in nonmetropolitan areas. About 75 percent of company sales are made in nonmetropolitan areas.

SMC sells the Ride King mower through wholesale distributors that supply independent dealers and directly to dealers. Wholesalers that represent SMC are located throughout the country, but they mainly supply farm dealers situated in the south central and southeastern United States. Wholesalers account for 30 percent of riding mower sales; direct-to-dealer sales account for 25 percent of sales.

Private-label riding mower sales account for 40 percent of SMC sales. Its private-label Big Mow mowers are produced for two buying networks: Midstates (Minneapolis, Minnesota) and Wheat Belt (Kansas City, Missouri). These two organizations represent independent farm supply stores and home centers in the upper and central midwestern United States and provide a central purchasing service. Even though these buying groups operate in roughly the same territory, their stores are not generally located in the same towns. Exhibit 5 on page 260 shows the geographic scope of SMC's distribution in the United States by brand name.

In recent years the company has developed distributor arrangements in parts of Europe and in the South Pacific. These arrangements produce 5 percent of total company sales.

Prior to 1985, SMC advertising focused on trade-oriented promotion to wholesalers and dealers. Since 1985, SMC has used consumer advertising to promote Ride King through a co-op advertising program with its dealers utilizing radio, television, and newspapers. Ride King has been featured in publications such as *National Gardening, Country Journal*, and *Popular Mechanics*, among others.

EXHIBIT 3

T-40 Product Literature

SWISHER T-44 TRAILMOWER
For quick, versatile mowing.

1. The ultimate way to save time on large areas, Swisher's T-44 TRAILMOWER quickly attaches to almost any lawn tractor or ATV for a faster, wider cut. The T-44 can be offset left or right; it features non-incremented, easy changing adjustment handles for variable ground clearance heights. For convenience, the optional remote ignition is located near the operators' position and features an optional 12 volt electric starter. Swisher's T-44 TRAILMOWER is another innovative product in a long line of Swisher lawn and garden equipment – developed over the past 50 plus years.

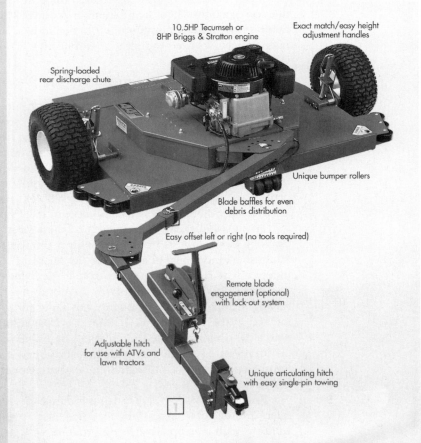

10.5HP Tecumseh or
8HP Briggs & Stratton engine

Exact match/easy height
adjustment handles

Spring-loaded
rear discharge chute

Unique bumper rollers

Blade baffles for even
debris distribution

Easy offset left or right (no tools required)

Remote blade
engagement (optional)
with lock-out system

Adjustable hitch
for use with ATVs and
lawn tractors

Unique articulating hitch
with easy single-pin towing

T-44 TRAILMOWER T-44 TRAILMOWER T-44 TRAILMOWER T-44 TRAILMOWER

EXHIBIT 4

Trim-Max Product Literature

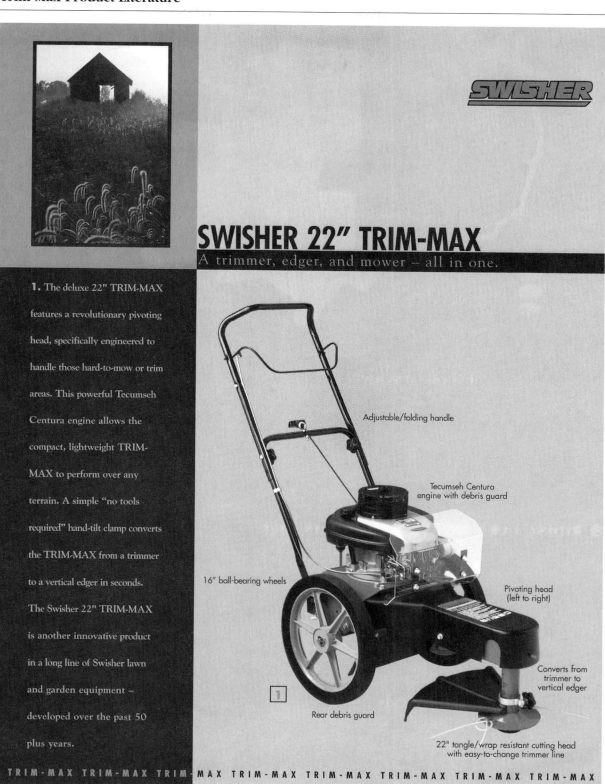

1. The deluxe 22" TRIM-MAX features a revolutionary pivoting head, specifically engineered to handle those hard-to-mow or trim areas. This powerful Tecumseh Centura engine allows the compact, lightweight TRIM-MAX to perform over any terrain. A simple "no tools required" hand-tilt clamp converts the TRIM-MAX from a trimmer to a vertical edger in seconds. The Swisher 22" TRIM-MAX is another innovative product in a long line of Swisher lawn and garden equipment – developed over the past 50 plus years.

SWISHER 22" TRIM-MAX
A trimmer, edger, and mower – all in one.

Adjustable/folding handle

Tecumseh Centura engine with debris guard

16" ball-bearing wheels

Pivoting head (left to right)

Converts from trimmer to vertical edger

Rear debris guard

22" tangle/wrap resistant cutting head with easy-to-change trimmer line

TRIM-MAX TRIM-MAX TRIM-MAX TRIM-MAX TRIM-MAX TRIM-MAX TRIM-MAX TRIM-MAX

EXHIBIT 5

Geographic Scope of SMC Distribution

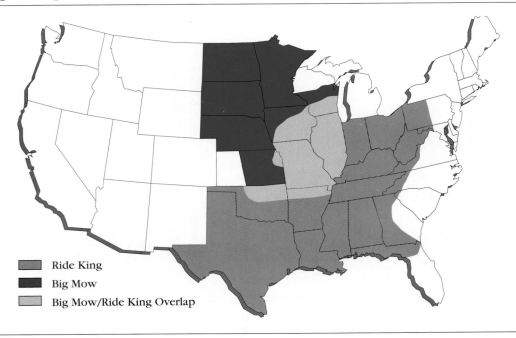

Ride King

Big Mow

Big Mow/Ride King Overlap

Financial Position

SMC has remained a profitable company since its founding. The company has consistently generated a net profit return on sales of 10 percent or more annually. Moreover, SMC has been able to produce cash flow at levels large enough to minimize the need for any major short-term or long-term financing. During 1995, Ride King riding mower accounts receivable and inventory had turns of 8.1 and 5.8, respectively. Exhibit 6 shows SMC financial statements for 1995.

■ RIDING LAWN MOWER INDUSTRY IN 1995

Riding lawn mowers are classified as lawn and garden equipment. This category is composed of numerous products, including walk-behind rotary mowers, riding mowers and tractors, garden tillers, snow throwers, and other outdoor power equipment designed primarily for the consumer market.

Industry sources estimated that the lawn and garden equipment industry produced sales of $5.5 billion in 1995, at manufacturers' prices. Of this amount, 74 percent was for finished goods and 25 percent was for engines. Components, including parts, accounted for the remainder of industry sales.

Sales Trends

Industry statistics show that riding mower unit volume is cyclical. Unit sales had grown in the early 1970s, but dropped dramatically in 1975 following a decline in the U.S. economy. By 1979, unit shipments had gradually risen, but with slowed economic conditions in the early 1980s, unit volume again declined. This same pattern was repeated during the 1983 to 1992 period. In 1993 and 1994, the industry posted

EXHIBIT 6

Swisher Mower and Machine Company Financial Statements: 1995[a]

Income Statement
(Year ended September 30, 1995)

Sales		$4,292,000
Cost of goods sold		3,587,150
Gross profit		$ 704,850
Sales and administrative expenses	$264,700	
Depreciation	2,300	
Total expenses		267,000
Income from continuing operations		$ 437,850
Other income (expenses)		(7,650)
Net income[b]		$430,200

Balance Sheet
(September 30, 1995)

Assets	
Current assets	$1,133,000
Net property and equipment	53,000
Total assets	$1,186,000
Liabilities and owner's equity	
Current liabilities	212,800
Owner's equity	973,200
Total liabilities and owner's equity	$1,186,000

[a] All figures disguised and not useful for research purposes.

[b] SMC is an "S" Corporation and, therefore, pays no corporate federal or state income taxes.

record unit sales. Projections for 1995 and 1996 point toward further increases in unit volume. Exhibit 7 on page 262 shows industry riding mower and lawn tractor unit sales for the period 1974 to 1994.

The riding lawn mower industry is highly seasonal. About one-third of riding lawn mower retail sales occur in March, April, and May. Over half of manufacturer shipments of these products occur in the four-month period from January to April.

Product Configuration

Riding lawn mowers are usually designed in two basic configurations: (1) front-engine lawn tractors and (2) rear-engine riding mowers. However, there are some mid-engine riding mowers on the market, such as those produced by SMC. Lawn tractors with larger engines (20 horsepower or more) are classified as garden tractors.

Riding lawn mowers are targeted at consumers who have large mowing areas, usually an acre or more. Front-engine lawn tractors are the most popular design followed by rear-engine and mid-engine models. According to industry surveys, the front-engine configuration (lawn and garden tractors) is perceived to be more powerful than the rear-engine configuration and capable of handling bigger jobs. Because the physical dimensions of the front-engine configuration tend to be larger than the rear-engine configuration, consumers tend to perceive lawn tractors and garden tractors as stronger and more durable.

EXHIBIT 7

Unit Sales of Riding Lawn Mowers and Lawn Tractors: 1974–1994

(in thousands)

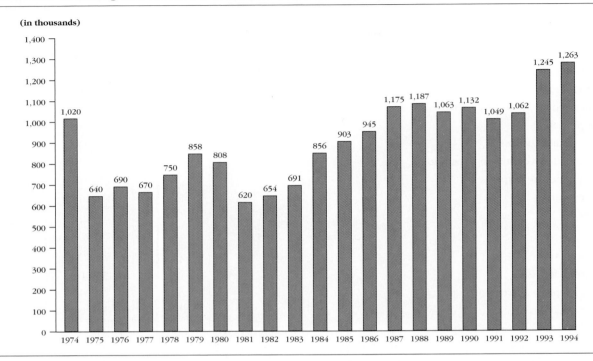

Competition and Retail Distribution

Ten manufacturers comprised the major competitors in the riding lawn mower market in 1995: American Yard Products, Ariens, Honda, John Deere, Kubota, MTD, Inc., Murray of Ohio, Snapper, Toro, and Garden Way/Troy-Bilt.

Ariens, Honda, John Deere, Kubota, American Yard Products, Murray, MTD, Snapper, Toro, and Garden Way/Troy-Bilt sell their products through lawn and garden stores and specialty retailers. MTD, Murray, and American Yard Products also sell to national mass-merchandise stores. All of these companies manufacture riding mowers under a nationally branded name and engage in private-label production. Several companies produce a combination of nationally branded riding mowers and private labels for mass merchandisers (e.g., Sears, Wal-Mart, Kmart), home centers (e.g., Lowe's, Home Depot), and hardware chains (e.g., True Value Hardware).

Private-label riding mowers have captured a growing percentage of unit sales in the industry. It is estimated that private-label mowers currently account for 65 to 75 percent of total industry sales.

Each of the major competitors produces several riding mowers at different price points. Although retail prices vary by type of retail outlet, representative retail prices for national and private-label riding mowers typically range from $800 to $5,000.

Outdoor power equipment (OPE), including riding mowers, is distributed through a variety of retail outlets. National retail merchandise chains such as Wal-Mart, Home Depot, and Sears account for the largest percentage of sales. These chains, plus outdoor power equipment/farm equipment and supply stores, lawn and garden stores, discount department stores, home centers, and hardware stores, account for 90 percent of total industry sales (see Exhibit 8).

EXHIBIT 8

Retail Distribution of Outdoor Power Equipment (Percentage of Sales)

National retail merchandise chains	24%
OPE/Farm equipment & supply stores	22%
Lawn/Garden stores	19%
Discount department stores	13%
Home centers	10%
Hardware stores	2%
Others	10%

■ THE PRIVATE-BRAND PROPOSAL

The inquiry received by SMC concerning a private-brand arrangement requested a sample order of 700 standard riding mower units to be delivered in January 1997. The national retail merchandise chain expected to make an annual order of approximately 8,200 units. The proposed arrangement had features that made it quite different from SMC's typical manner of doing business with its other private-label organizations. The chain wanted to purchase the mowers at a price 5 percent lower than SMC's manufacturer's list price for its standard model. The chain also wished to be a house account without manufacturers' representatives or company sales representatives calling on it. It did not want any seasonal or promotional discounts but only a single guaranteed low price. Reorders would be at the same price. The mowers would be shipped free on board (FOB) factory (that is, the chain would pay for all freight charges).

The chain wanted to carry inventories in its regional warehouses, but did not want title to transfer to itself until the mowers were shipped to a specific company store. From that point, payment would be made in 45 days. However, the chain agreed to take title to mowers that had been in one of its warehouses for two months. A 45-day payment period would follow the title transfer.

There would be small changes in the appearance of the mower to help differentiate it from SMC's Ride King. The chain requested a different seat and a particular color and type of paint and specified that all parts be American-made or that the mower at least display an "American name" as its producer. The chain would supply all decals displaying its brand name.

The chain did not propose any mechanical specifications for the mower. The letter expressed satisfaction with the design and performance of the machine and noted that only minor cosmetic changes were necessary. SMC's standard warranty would be required for all mower parts. The chain expected SMC to reimburse it for any labor costs resulting from warranty work at $22.00 per hour. Replacement parts would be purchased at present price points and shipped FOB factory.

A two-year contract was offered, which could be automatically extended on a year-to-year basis. Either party could terminate the contract with a six-month notice. A new price would be negotiated at the end of the original two-year period. The contract would be negotiated annually thereafter. The chain also required SMC to assume liability for personal injury that might result from the use and maintenance of the mowers. The chain would supply all advertising related to the product and would not allow SMC to mention its relationship with the chain in any of its advertising or promotion.

■ EVALUATING THE PROPOSAL

The private-brand proposal required careful consideration, according to Wayne Swisher. The opportunity to expand production, given excess capacity, coupled with the added benefit of broadened distribution in metropolitan areas, seemed inviting. Moreover, increased sales of parts were likely, and the potential for selling the "trailmower" was possible. At the same time, other factors would have to be considered. For example, SMC was self-insured and had not experienced any significant product-liability claims with some 175,000 units having been sold or used since 1956. However, if the private-brand proposal was pursued, greater exposure to liability claims was possible.

Furthermore, although increased production could be handled by paying overtime to SMC production workers, the cost of overtime, reflected in the direct labor cost, would represent an additional 4 percent of the current manufacturer's sales price for riding mowers. Additional direct material costs could represent another 1 percent of the current manufacturer's price. Additional overhead costs were estimated to be another 1 percent; other related costs, including additional inventory insurance, pilferage and breakage, additional wear and maintenance on machines, and a county property tax based on inventory, would account for an additional 1.5 percent.

A production agreement would create some one-time added costs for SMC. These costs would include arranging sources for specific materials that differed from those used in standard production and a rearrangement of production facilities to accommodate the new output levels. These one-time costs would be in the range of $10,000 to $12,000.

The added financing costs were of particular importance. Normally, SMC obtained short-term funds from local banks at 2.5 percentage points above the prime rate (currently 7 percent). These funds were used to finance accounts receivable and riding mower inventories, both of which would increase with the new arrangement. For example, the additional average inventory carried with this proposal would be 2,100 units.

Sales of SMC mowers by the national merchandiser could cannibalize some existing sales. Although the chain's outlets were located in metropolitan areas, there would be some overlap in trade areas with SMC's current dealers. Swisher felt that, as a result, SMC could initially lose approximately 300 units a year of Ride King sales volume. In addition, dealers directly affected would not welcome the added competition. Wayne Swisher believed that a small percentage of independent dealers would be likely to drop the SMC line.

Some aspects of the proposal might be negotiable, such as the title transfer and payment dates. From his experience, he knew that the unit price in the proposal was probably fixed and that the cosmetic changes were not negotiable. He knew that his bargaining position was limited because the chain would be approaching other manufacturers with the same opportunity. However, he also knew that SMC offered a highly differentiated and proven riding mower. This would be an advantage, because many other manufacturers' mowers were indistinguishable.

Wayne Swisher had been concerned for several years about SMC's future prospects. The private-brand arrangement might offer numerous benefits to SMC, but he wondered if other actions might be even more attractive. For example, a more aggressive advertising and sales effort to recruit new dealers and assist current dealers was being considered. Also, the new Trim-Max product was soon to be introduced under the Swisher name and an expanded line of "trailmowers" was a possibility. Still, he thought, the proposal is a "bird in the hand" while the other initiatives still had to prove themselves.

CHAPTER 6

Integrated Marketing Communication Strategy and Management

 Marketing communication is the process by which information about an organization and its offerings is disseminated to selected markets. Given the role communication plays in facilitating mutually beneficial exchange relationships between an organization and prospective buyers, its importance cannot be overstated. The goal of communication is not just to induce initial purchases; it is also to achieve postpurchase satisfaction, thus increasing the probability of repeat sales. Even if prospective buyers possessed a pressing need and an organization possessed an offering that precisely met that need, no exchange would occur without communication. Communication is necessary to inform buyers of the following:

- The availability of an offering
- The unique benefits of the offering
- The where and how of obtaining and using the offering

Exactly how potential buyers are to be informed—the actual message communicated—is one of the most subjective communication decisions. Although message development can be somewhat aided by research, there are no guaranteed message strategies available for all offerings, markets, or organizations. Each individual situation must determine whether the message is to be hard-sell, humorous, or informational. Whatever message format is chosen, the message communicated should be desirable to those to whom it is directed, exclusive or unique to the offering being described, and believable in terms of the benefit claims made for the offering.

It is the task of the marketing manager to manage the communication process most effectively. Marketing managers have at their disposal specific communication activities, often called *elements, functions, tools*, or *tasks*. These include advertising, personal selling, and sales promotion. Collectively, the activities are termed the *marketing communication mix*.[1] Elements of the communication mix range from very flexible (for example, personal selling) to very inflexible (for example, mass advertising), and each has a unique set of characteristics and capabilities. To a certain extent, however, they are interchangeable and substitutable. It is the responsibility of the marketing manager to find the most effective communication mix at the least possible cost.

Marketing managers should not limit their thinking to which communication activity to use when designing communication strategies. Rare is the organization that employs only one form of communication. Rather, managers should broaden their perspective to think of *integrated marketing communications*—the practice of blending different elements of the communication mix in mutually reinforcing ways. In this context, attention is directed to which activity should be emphasized, how intensely it should be applied, and how communication activities can be most effectively combined and coordinated. For instance, advertising activities might be employed to develop offering awareness and comprehension; sales promotion might be used to increase purchase intention; and personal selling might be utilized to obtain final conviction and purchase.

Increasingly, marketers are looking to the Internet as a potential platform for integrated marketing communications. This technology has the capability to take consumers and industrial users through the entire purchase process, from creating awareness to providing information in an interactive manner, to placing an order, to customer service after the sale. The role of the Internet in marketing communications is addressed in this chapter. The Internet's role as a distribution channel is featured in Chapter 7.

■ INTEGRATED MARKETING COMMUNICATION STRATEGY FRAMEWORK

From a managerial perspective, the formulation of an integrated marketing communication strategy requires six major decisions. Once the offering and target markets have been defined, the manager must consider the following decisions:

1. What are the information requirements of target markets as they proceed through the purchase process?

2. What objectives must the communication strategy achieve?

3. How might the mix of communication activities be combined to convey information to target markets?

4. How much should be budgeted for communicating with target markets, and in what manner should resources be allocated among various communication activities?

5. How should the communication be timed and scheduled?

6. How should the communication process be evaluated as to its effectiveness, and how should it be controlled?

Theoretically, these questions are distinct and, thus, can be approached in a sequential manner. In practice, however, they are likely to be approached simultaneously, because they are closely interrelated.

■ INFORMATION REQUIREMENTS IN PURCHASE DECISIONS

The first step in designing an integrated marketing communication strategy is to determine how buyers purchase a particular offering and to define the role of information in the purchase process. This often requires use of a purchase-process (or adoption-process) model. Usually, such a model treats buyers as though they were moved through a series of sequential stages in their purchase processes, such as

Unawareness → Knowledge → Preference → Purchase

At any point in time, different buyers are in different stages of the model, and each stage requires a different communication strategy.

Most models allow the marketing manager to distinguish between solitary and joint decision making. In any purchase decision, the person or persons involved can play several possible roles—purchaser, influencer, decision maker, and/or consumer. In certain purchase situations, one individual may play more than one role. In other purchase situations, such as a joint purchase decision, the roles may be played by different individuals. Whereas a mother may be the family member who purchases breakfast cereal, her children may influence the brand purchase, and the father may consume the product. A similar situation could exist in an industrial setting. A purchasing agent may be the buyer, an engineer the influencer and decision maker, and a technician the user. Understanding who is playing the roles is a prerequisite for successfully determining what the communication message should be, as well as to whom it should be directed and how it should be communicated.

Similarly, the process used by buyers to purchase an offering influences the role of information, and hence the most effective communication strategy. For example, in industrial settings purchasing procedures are often prescribed. Therefore, understanding when, where, how, and what information is employed in the purchase decision will enable an organization to direct the proper communication to the proper individual at the proper time. These remarks also apply to communication directed toward consumers. Consider the case of consumers making a decision to buy a house. To communicate effectively, an organization must know *what* information these consumers think is necessary (price, location, size), *where* they will seek it (newspapers, the Internet, brokers, friends), *when* they will seek it (how far in advance, on what days), and *how* they will apply the information once obtained.

Finally, the way in which buyers perceive an organization and its offering is closely related to their information needs. The perceived importance of the offering and the perceived risk in making an incorrect purchase decision influence the extent to which buyers receive information, as well as their choice of information source(s). The more important or risky an offering is perceived to be (because of large dollar outlays, ego involvement, or health and safety reasons), the more likely it is that buyers will seek information from sources other than the organization providing the offering.

■ SETTING REASONABLE COMMUNICATION OBJECTIVES

The objectives set for communication programs will depend on the overall offering-market strategies of the organization and the stage of a product or service life cycle. Communication objectives will differ according to whether the strategy being employed is market penetration, market development, or product development. For instance, a market penetration strategy will suggest communication objectives that emphasize more frequent offering usage or that build preference for or loyalty to the offering. On the other hand, a market development strategy will encourage communication that will stimulate awareness and trial of the offering.

Life-cycle stage plays a role in determining whether communication objectives should stimulate primary demand or selective demand. Early in the life cycle, communication efforts focus on stimulating *primary demand*—demand for the product or service class, such as dairy products, personal computers, or financial planning. Typically, the message conveyed focuses on introducing the benefits of a product or service or overcoming objections to the product or service. Later in the life cycle, when substitute products or services exist, communication efforts focus on stimulating *selective demand*—demand for a particular brand, product, or service such as Borden milk, Apple personal computers, or Merrill Lynch financial planning. Typically, the message conveyed extols the benefits of a particular competitive offering and seeks to differentiate that offering from others.

Objectives must also be delineated for individual communication tools. Both general and specific communication objectives need to relate directly to the tasks that the tools are to accomplish. Communication objectives and the tasks must be reasonable—*consistent* both among themselves and with other marketing elements, *quantifiable* for measurement and control purposes, and *attainable* with an appropriate amount of effort and expenditure and within a specific time frame.

■ DEVELOPING AN INTEGRATED MARKETING COMMUNICATION MIX

Development of an integrated marketing communication mix requires the assignment of relative weights to particular communication activities, based on communication objectives. Although no established guidelines exist for designing an optimal communication mix, several factors that influence the mix need to be considered. These factors are:

- The information requirements of potential buyers
- The nature of the offering
- The nature of the target markets
- The capacity of the organization

Information Requirements of Buyers

As a starting point in crafting an integrated communication mix, an analysis of the relative value of the communication tools used at various stages in the purchase-decision process ought to be undertaken. Consider the purchase-decision process for a new automobile. Through advertising and Web sites, such as *GMBuyPower.com*, manufacturers seek to stimulate awareness of the new models and to indicate where they can be purchased. Sales personnel provide information on specific options available, financing, and delivery. Sales promotion, brochures, and catalogs provide descriptions of performance characteristics and other salient features. Which communication tool has the greatest impact on prospective buyers? The answer to this question, while difficult to arrive at, will lead to a weighing of the importance of the communication tools. The manager will achieve an effective communication mix only by understanding the information requirements of potential buyers and by meeting those requirements with the appropriate communication-mix elements.

Nature of the Offering

A major consideration in developing the communication mix is the organization's offering. A highly technical offering, one with benefits not readily apparent (such as performance or quality), or one that is relatively expensive is likely to require personal selling. On the one hand, advertising is a potent communication tool when the offering is not complex, is frequently purchased, is relatively inexpensive, or has benefits that readily differentiate it from competing offerings. Sales promotion lends itself to nearly every offering type because of the wide variety of forms it can assume. Its main use is to induce immediate action on frequently purchased products.

Target-Market Characteristics

The nature of the target market is another consideration. A target market consisting of a small number of potential buyers, existing in close proximity to one another and each purchasing in large quantities, might suggest a personal selling strategy. In contrast, a mass market that is geographically scattered generally calls for an emphasis on advertising. However, firms are finding that direct marketing also can be used to reach a geographically dispersed target market. This realization has led many firms to substitute mail and telephone solicitations for mass media (radio, print, and television) advertising and use the Internet as a communication medium to complement advertising for consumer products and services and a supplement to personal selling for industrial goods and services.

Organizational Capacity

A fourth consideration is the ability or willingness of the organization to undertake certain communication activities. The organization is continually faced with *make-or-buy decisions*. If an organization decides to employ a particular communication activity, should it perform the activity internally (that is, make it) or contract it out (in other words, buy it)?

One such make-or-buy decision is the choice between a company sales force and independent sales representatives.[2] The decision has both economic and behavioral dimensions. The economic dimension relates to the issue of fixed versus variable costs. The cost of independent representatives is variable; they are paid on sales commission only. A company sales force, on the other hand, typically includes a variable-cost component *and* a fixed-cost component. If independent representatives fail to sell, no costs are incurred; however, if a company sales force fails to sell, the fixed costs still have to be paid. These concepts are useful in determining whether independent representatives or company sales representatives are more cost-effective at different sales levels.

Suppose independent representatives received a 5 percent commission on sales and company sales personnel received a 3 percent commission in addition to incurring a salary and administration cost of $500,000. At what sales level would company representatives become more or less costly than independent representatives? This question can be resolved by setting the cost equations for both types of representatives equal to each other and solving for the sales level amount, as follows:

$$\frac{\text{Cost of company reps}}{0.03(x) + \$500,000} = \frac{\text{Cost of independent reps}}{0.05(x)}$$

where x = sales volume. Solving for x, we get $25 million as the sales volume at which the costs of company and independent representatives are equal. This relationship is shown in Exhibit 6.1 on page 272.

The calculation indicates that if the sales volume were below $25 million, the independent representative would be cheaper; above that amount, the company sales force would be cheaper. Of course, a fundamental issue is the likelihood of achieving a $25 million sales level.

Behavioral dimensions of this decision focus on issues of control, flexibility, effort, and availability of independent and company sales representatives. There is considerable difference of opinion as to the relative advantages and disadvantages of company and independent representatives with respect to each factor. Proponents of a company sales force argue that this strategy offers greater control, since the company selects, trains, and supervises sales personnel. The sales effort is enhanced because sales personnel are representing only one company's product line. Flexibility exists because the firm can change sales-call patterns and customers and can transfer personnel. Finally, availability of sales personnel is superior, because an independent representative might not exist in a geographical area, whereas a company representative can be relocated. Proponents of independent sales representatives argue that selection, training, and supervision of sales personnel can be done equally well by sales agencies and at no cost to the firm. Flexibility is improved, since fixed investment in a sales force is minimal. Effort is increased, since independent representatives live on their commissions. Finally, availability is no problem, because the entrepreneurial

EXHIBIT 6.1

**Break-Even Chart for Comparing Independent Agents
and a Company Sales Force**

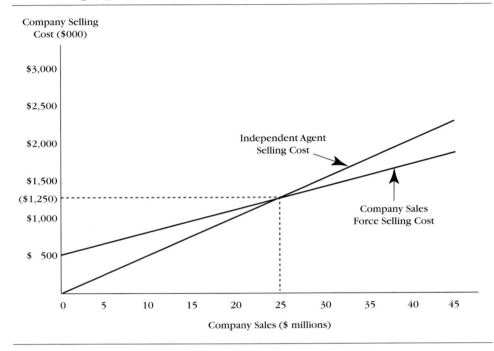

spirit of these individuals will take them wherever effective demand exists. Today, 50 percent of all companies operating in North America use independent sales representatives in some capacity, whether for a piece of their product line or a certain geographic region.[3]

Another make-or-buy decision relates to advertising. Often, it is advantageous to have intermediaries (such as wholesalers, retailers, and dealers) assume advertising costs and placement responsibilities. Cooperative advertising, in which a manufacturer and intermediaries share the costs of advertising or sales promotion, is an example of this type of strategy.

Push Versus Pull Communication Strategies

Two approaches that incorporate the topics just discussed are termed *push* and *pull communication strategies*. A *push communication strategy* is one in which the offering is pushed through a distribution channel in a sequential fashion, with each channel level representing a distinct target market. A push strategy concentrates on channel intermediaries, building relationships that can have long-term benefits. With such a strategy, advertisements are likely to appear in trade journals and magazines, and sales aids and contests are likely to be used as incentives to gain shelf space and distribution. A principal emphasis, however, is on personal selling to wholesalers and retailers. This strategy is typically used when (1) an organization has easily identifiable buyers, (2) the offering is complex, (3) buyers view the purchase as being risky, (4) a product or service is early in its life cycle, and/or (5) the organization has limited funds for direct-to-consumer advertising.

A *pull communication strategy* seeks to create initial interest among potential buyers, who in turn demand the product from intermediaries, ultimately pulling the offering through a channel. A pull strategy normally employs heavy end-user (consumer) advertising, free samples, and coupons to stimulate end-user awareness and interest. Consumers might be encouraged to ask their favorite retailer for the offering to pressure retailers into carrying the product. Pennzoil Motor Oil's "Ask for Pennzoil" and Claritin's "Talk to your doctor . . ." advertising campaigns are prime examples of a pull communication strategy in practice.

The conditions favoring a pull strategy are virtually opposite to those favoring a push strategy. A central issue in choosing a push strategy is the ability and willingness of wholesalers and retailers to implement selling and sales promotion programs advocated by manufacturers. An important consideration in using a pull strategy is whether an *advertising opportunity* exists for a product or service. Such an opportunity exists when (1) there is a favorable primary demand for a product or service category, (2) the product or service to be advertised can be significantly differentiated from its competitors, (3) the product or service has hidden qualities or benefits that can be portrayed effectively through advertising, and (4) there are strong emotional buying motives involved, such as buyers' concern for health, beauty, or safety. The value of an advertising opportunity decreases if one or more of these conditions is not met. Nonprescription drugs and cosmetics often satisfy most of these conditions and are frequently advertised. Commodities such as unprocessed foods (for example, corn, oats, and wheat) are rarely advertised; however, when they are processed and dietary supplements and flavors are added to produce cereals, they are advertised effectively.

Nevertheless, push and pull communication strategies are often used together. Investment in end-user advertising stimulates consumer demand and hence product or service sales volume. Investment in efforts to gain display space for products, promote specific services, and educate retail salespeople builds channel relationships that have long-term benefits.

■ MARKETING WEB SITES AND INTEGRATED MARKETING COMMUNICATIONS

A continuing challenge for companies is the development and execution of an integrated marketing communication strategy that capitalizes on the evolving capabilities of Internet/Web-enabled technology and marketing Web sites. Simply stated, a *Web site* is a place where information is made available to users of the Internet by the provider. Marketing Web sites engage buyers and potential buyers in interactive communication for the purpose of selling an organization's products or services or moving potential buyers closer to a purchase. They come in two general forms: (1) transactional sites and (2) promotional sites.

Purpose of Marketing Web Sites

Transactional Web sites are essentially electronic storefronts such as those operated by L. L. Bean, the catalog marketer, FAO Schwartz, a toy retailer, and Ethan Allen, a furniture manufacturer. They focus principally on converting an online browser into an online buyer. Successful transactional Web sites feature well-known, branded products and services and a technological infrastructure designed to create a favorable shopping and buying experience. Gap clothes, for example, have sold well via its Web site (*gap.com*) because most consumers know the brand and the merchandise and its site is easy to navigate. Gap generates more sales volume from its Web site than any of its stores save one.[4] Transactional Web sites, which represent a form of direct distribution, are discussed further in Chapter 7 in the context of electronic marketing channels and multichannel marketing.

Promotional Web sites have a very different purpose than transactional sites. They promote a company's products and services and provide information on how items can be used and where they can be purchased. These sites often engage the visitor in an interactive experience involving games, contests, and quizzes with electronic coupons and other gifts as prizes. Procter & Gamble maintains separate promotional Web sites for 24 of its leading brands, including Pringles potato chips, Vidal Sassoon hair products, Scope mouthwash, Folgers coffee, and Pampers diapers. Promotional sites can be effective in generating awareness of, interest in, and trial of a company's products and services. By doing so, promotional sites can support a company's advertising program and traditional marketing channel.[5] For example, General Motors reports that 80 percent of the people visiting a Saturn store first visited the brand's Web site (*Saturn.com*). The Metropolitan Life Insurance Web site (*metlife.com*) is a proven vehicle for qualifying prospective buyers of its insurance and financial services for its agents. These sites also can be used for customer research and feedback. Cathay Pacific Airlines is a case in point. Its Web site (*cathay-usa.com*) is used to interview frequent fliers to determine their travel preferences and buying habits in addition to offering travel promotions.

Promotional Web sites also can be used to create *buzz*, a popular term for word-of-mouth behavior made possible by Internet/Web-enabled technology. Marketers have long known that word of mouth is the most powerful information source for consumers because it involves brand, product, and service recommendations from friends. Some marketers have capitalized on this phenomenon by creating buzz through viral marketing.[6] *Viral marketing* is an Internet/Web-enabled promotional strategy that encourages individuals to forward marketer-initiated messages to others via e-mail. A popular application of viral marketing is to offer consumers incentives (discounts, sweepstakes, or free merchandise) for referrals. Procter & Gamble did this when it introduced Physique shampoo. People who referred 10 friends to the shampoo's promotional Web site (*physique.com*) received a free, travel-sized styling spray and were entered in a sweepstakes to win a year's supply of the shampoo. This promotion generated 2 million referrals and made Physique the most successful new shampoo ever launched in the United States.

Leveraging Advertising and Personal Selling with Promotional Web Sites

Promotional Web sites can assume a unique role in leveraging different elements of the communication mix. Most companies employ a mix of communication tools to achieve various objectives in the marketing communication process, judiciously combining personal selling, advertising, and sales promotion in mutually reinforcing ways. Promotional Web sites and the Internet/Web-enabled technology that supports them can leverage personal selling and advertising efforts, as described here:

> Personal selling is usually the largest single item in the industrial marketing communications mix. On the other hand, broadcast advertising is typically the dominant way used to reach consumers by marketers. Where do Web sites fit? The Web site is something of a mix between direct selling (it can engage the visitor in a dialogue) and advertising (it can be designed to generate awareness, explain/demonstrate the product, and provide information—without interactive involvement). It can play a cost-effective role in the communication mix, in the early stages of the process-need recognition, development of product specifications, and supplier search, but can also be useful as the buying process progresses toward evaluation and selection. Finally, the site is also cost-effective in providing feedback on product/service performance. Web sites might typically be viewed as complementary to the direct selling activity by industrial marketers, and as supplementary to advertising by consumer marketers.[7]

■ COMMUNICATION MIX BUDGETING

As one might expect, the question of how much to spend on communication is difficult to answer. Many factors, including those previously mentioned, must be considered in communication budget determination. In general, the greater the geographic dispersion of a target market, the greater the communication expenditure required; the earlier an offering is in its life cycle, the greater the necessary expenditure; and so forth.

The primary rule in determining a communication budget is to *make the budget commensurate with the tasks required of the communication activities*. The more important communication is in a marketing strategy, the larger the amount of funds that should be allocated to it. Conceptually, budget determination is straight forward—set the budget so that the marginal costs of communication equal the marginal revenues resulting from it. This, however, requires an assessment of the effectiveness of communication.

Because it is difficult to evaluate communication effectiveness, attempts to establish a relationship between budget size and communication effectiveness have generally proven unproductive. For this reason, there is no widely agreed-on criterion for establishing the size of a communication budget. Instead, numerous guidelines have been suggested. These guidelines can be roughly grouped as *formula based* or *qualitatively based*.

The most widely used formula-based approach is the *percentage-of-sales approach*. Most frequently, past sales are employed, but anticipated sales are also occasionally used. Hence, when sales increase, communication activity increases. Although it creates certain conceptual problems (for example, which should come first—sales or communication?), this approach is commonly used as a starting point because of its simplicity. A second formula-based method is to allocate for communication a fixed dollar amount per offering unit, and then to calculate the communication budget by multiplying this per-unit allocation by the number of units expected to be sold. This method is most often used by durable-goods manufacturers such as appliance and automobile companies.

In practice, the formula-based approaches tend to be rather inflexible and not marketing oriented, so they are often supplemented by qualitatively based approaches. Management may use the *competitive-parity approach*, whereby an organization attempts to maintain a balance between its communication expenditures and those of its competitors. Another approach is to use *all available funds* for communication. This strategy might be employed in introducing a new offering for which maximum exposure is desired; it is also sometimes used by nonprofit organizations.

A final approach is termed the *objective-task* approach. Here an organization budgets communication as a function of the objectives set for a communication program and the costs of the tasks to be performed to accomplish the objectives. The approach involves three steps: (1) define the communication objectives, (2) identify the tasks needed to attain the objectives, and (3) estimate the costs associated with the performance of these tasks.

Although all of these approaches are useful, each has limitations. Most managers would say that the objective-task approach is the best approach but the most difficult to apply in practice.[8] More often than not, managers use these approaches in conjunction with one another.

Communication Budget Allocation

Once a communication budget has been settled on, it must be allocated across the communication activities. This can be accomplished by using guidelines similar to those discussed previously for general communication budget determinations. Advertising and personal selling will be used to illustrate necessary budgetary allocation decisions. As a general rule, marketers of consumer products and services spend more for advertising as a percentage of their communication budget; marketers of industrial products and services spend more for personal selling as a percentage of their communication budget.[9]

Advertising Budget Allocation   Decisions about advertising budget allocation revolve around media selection and scheduling considerations. Basically, there are six mass media—television, radio, magazine, newspaper, outdoor (billboard) and the Internet— that an organization can use in transmitting its advertising messages to target markets. Each of these media, or *channels*, consists of *vehicles*—specific entities in which advertisements can appear. In magazines, the vehicles include *Newsweek* and *Mechanics Illustrated*. *Newsweek* can be thought of as a mass-appeal vehicle, whereas *Mechanics Illustrated* might be considered a selective-appeal vehicle. Moreover, media can be *vertical* (reaching more than one level of a distribution channel) or *horizontal* (reaching only one level of a channel).

Media selection is based on numerous factors, the most important of which are cost, reach, frequency, and audience characteristics. Cost frequently acts as a constraint— for example, a one-minute national television commercial (spot) during the Super Bowl costs over $3 million, not including associated production costs. *Cost* is usually expressed as cost per thousand (CPM) readers or viewers to facilitate cross-vehicle comparisons. *Reach* is the number of buyers potentially exposed to an advertisement in a particular vehicle. *Frequency* is the number of times buyers are exposed to an advertisement in a given time period; total exposure equals reach multiplied by frequency. The more closely the characteristics of the target market match those of a vehicle's audience, the more appropriate the vehicle.

Other considerations include the purpose of the advertisement (image building, price, and so on), product needs, and the editorial climate of the vehicle. Whereas price advertisements (those emphasizing an immediate purchase) are more likely to be found in newspapers than in magazines, the opposite is true for advertisements of products requiring color illustration and detailed explanation. Finally, audience characteristics determine which advertisements are acceptable, as well as which are appropriate. For example, 89 percent of wives either influence or make outright purchases of men's clothing. Knowing this, Haggar Clothing, a menswear marketer, advertises in women's magazines such as *Vanity Fair* and *Red-book*.[10]

The timing, or scheduling, of advertisements is critical to their success. Purchases of many offerings (such as skis, snowblowers, and swimsuits) are seasonal or are limited to certain geographic areas. Thus, the advertising budgeting must take into account purchasing patterns. For example, advertising snowblowers in Ohio during the month of July is probably not a worthwhile endeavor.

There are numerous timing strategies that a marketing manager can employ when undertaking an advertising campaign. One alternative is to concentrate advertising dollars in a relatively short time period—a *blitz strategy*. This strategy is often used when new products or services are introduced. For example, movie studios spend 75 percent of an average new film's advertising budget of $22 million in the four to five days preceding the film's opening weekend.[11] Another alternative is to spend advertising dollars over the long term to maintain continuity. A *pulse strategy* might be employed, whereby an organization periodically concentrates its advertising but also attempts to maintain some semblance of continuity.

Sales-Force Budget Allocation   The sales-force budgeting problem is two-faceted: How many salespeople are needed, and how should they be allocated? A commonly used formula is

$$NS = \frac{NC \times FC \times LC}{TA}$$

where

NS = number of salespeople
NC = number of customers (actual or potential)
FC = necessary frequency of customer calls
LC = length of average customer call, including travel time
TA = average available selling time per salesperson (less time spent on administrative duties)

In most instances, the time period is one business year. Although this formula can be used for nearly all types of salespeople, from retail clerks to highly creative salespeople, it is more likely used with the latter.

Assume that the number of potential customers is 2,500 and four calls should be made per customer per year. If the length of the average call and travel time is two hours and there are 1,340 working hours per year available for selling (50 weeks × 40 hours × 67 percent available selling time per week), then

$$NS = \frac{2,500 \times 4 \times 2}{1,340} = 15 \text{ salespeople needed}$$

The formula is flexible. It is possible to create several different strategies simply by varying (1) how the various elements in this formula are defined and (2) the elements themselves; such as the frequency of calls with actual customers and potential customers.

A related decision concerns the allocation of salespeople. Every salesperson must have a territory, whether defined as square feet of selling space, a geographical area, or a delivery route. In determining how large the sales territory should be, decision makers should attempt to equate selling opportunities with the workload associated with each sales territory.

The question of how the sales force should be organized is perhaps more difficult to answer, as it directly relates to organization and marketing objectives, offering characteristics, competitor and industry practices, and the like. The alternatives include having salespeople specialize in certain offerings or in customer types or in a combination of offerings and customer types.[12] For instance, Procter & Gamble and Black & Decker organize their sales forces by customer size, with large customers (Wal-Mart and Home Depot) having "customer specialists" who focus on delivering superior customer service. Firestone Tire and Rubber has a sales force that calls on its own dealers and another that calls on independent dealers, such as gasoline stations. Lone Star Steel has a sales force that sells drilling pipe to oil companies and another that sells specialty steel products to manufacturers.

■ EVALUATION AND CONTROL OF THE COMMUNICATION PROCESS

As part of every communication strategy, there must be mechanisms for evaluation and control. Without them, a marketing manager would be hard-pressed to manage the communication process effectively. There would be no way to determine whether a strategy had achieved its objectives, nor would there be a way to make changes in a strategy in response to competitive activities or environmental occurrences, whether fortuitous or not.

Implicit in both mechanisms is the concept of *continuousness*. The marketing manager must continuously monitor the execution of any communication plan or strategy to ensure that the communication objectives are being attained.

Ideally, evaluation and control should incorporate some measure of sales or profits. Although this is possible for certain communication tools (the sales effectiveness of a direct-mail program can be judged in a relatively straightforward way), for others, it is not. It is nearly impossible to isolate the contribution of institutional advertising to any individual sales transaction.

Budgeting is the ultimate form of control because slashing or adding to the budget of a communication activity effectively eliminates or accentuates the activity itself. The budgeting element is illustrated by the decision to add an additional sales representative with a yearly salary and fringe benefits of $75,000 or to allocate the same amount to a direct-mail sales promotion program, when the product mix contribution margin is 25 percent. A simple break-even calculation ($75,000 ÷ 0.25) reveals that $300,000 in additional sales must be generated to cover the incremental cost. The issue is therefore whether the new sales representative or the sales promotion is more likely to achieve this break-even sales volume. Incremental analysis of this type is increasingly being viewed as the appropriate approach for evaluating and controlling expenditures for sales promotion, advertising, and personal selling.

NOTES

1. Publicity is a fourth element often included in the communication mix, but it is not considered here for two reasons. First, publicity is often uncontrollable except through the broader public relations function of an organization; hence, it is not typically the responsibility of the marketing manager. Second, even if publicity is the responsibility of the marketing manager, it is often managed as a mixture of advertising and personal selling and, thus, does not require separate treatment.

2. Independent representatives are individuals or firms paid commissions for selling a manufacturer's product. These individuals or companies represent several noncompeting products that are sold to one or several categories of customers. They do not carry product inventories or take legal title to goods. Their functions vary from selling only a firm's products to broader activities including applications engineering, in-store merchandising support (point-of-purchase displays, stocking), and product maintenance. Independent representatives go by a variety of names, including broker, manufacturer's representative, and sales agent.

3. "Making the Case for Outside Sales Reps," *Knowledge@Wharton* (February 1, 2002).

4. "Click Till You Drop," *Time* (July 20, 1998): 34–39.

5. Tom Duncan, *IMC: Using Advertising and Promotion to Build Brands* (New York: McGraw-Hill, 2002); and Larry Chiagouris and Brandt Wansley, "Branding on the Internet," *Marketing Management* (Summer 2000): 35–38.

6. "Pass It On," *Wall Street Journal* (January 14, 2002): R6, R7; and "Why Are These CEOs Smiling?" *Time* (November 5, 2001): 41–44.

7. Richard T. Watson, Pierre Berthon, Leyland F. Pitt, and George Zinkhan, *Electronic Commerce: The Strategic Perspective* (Ft. Worth, TX: The Dryden Press, 2000): 79.

8. George E. Belch and Michael A. Belch, *Introduction to Advertising and Promotion: An Integrated Marketing Communications Perspective*, 6th ed. (Chicago: McGraw-Hill/Irwin, 2004).

9. "Business-to-Business Captures 37.4% of All Marketing Spending," *Advertising Age* (June 3, 1997): 46.

10. "Wearing the Pants," *BRANDWEEK* (October 20, 1998): 20–22.

11. "AdAge Special Report: Leading National Advertisers," *Advertising Age* (June 24, 2002): S-26; and "The Won and Lost Weekend," *The Economist* (November 29, 1997): 87–88.

12. Douglas J. Dalrymple, William L. Cron, and Thomas E. DeCarlo, *Sales Management*, 7th ed. (New York: John Wiley & Sons, 2001).

Carrington Furniture, Inc. (A)

Late in the evening of January 6, 2003, Charlton Bates, President of Carrington Furniture, Inc., called Dr. Thomas Berry, a marketing professor at a private university in the Northeast and a consultant to the company. The conversation went as follows:

BATES: Hello, Tom. This is Chuck Bates. I'm sorry to call you this late, but I wanted to get your thoughts on the tentative 2003 advertising program proposed by Mike Hervey of Hervey and Bernham, our ad agency.

BERRY: No problem, Chuck. What did they propose?

BATES: The crux of their proposal is that we should increase our advertising expenditures by $225,000. They suggested that we put the entire amount into our consumer advertising program for ads in several shelter magazines.[1] Hervey noted that the National Home Furnishings Foundation has recommended that furniture manufacturers spend 1 percent of their sales exclusively on consumer advertising.

BERRY: That increase appears to be slightly out of line with your policy of budgeting 5 percent of expected sales for total promotion expenditures, doesn't it? Hasn't John Bott [Vice President of Sales] emphasized the need for more sales representatives?

BATES: Yes, John has requested additional funds. You're right about the 5 percent figure too, and I'm not sure if our sales forecast isn't too optimistic. Your research has shown that our sales historically follow industry sales almost perfectly, and trade economists are predicting about a 6 percent increase for 2003. Yet, I'm not too sure.

BERRY: Well, Chuck, you can't expect forecasts to be always on the button. The money is one thing, but what else can you tell me about Hervey's rationale for putting more dollars into consumer advertising?

BATES: He contends that we can increase our exposure and tell our quality and styling story to the buying public—increase brand awareness, enhance our image, that sort of thing. He also cited industry research data that showed that as baby boomers [consumers born between 1946 and 1964] age they are becoming more home oriented and are replacing older, cheaper furniture with more expensive, longer-lasting pieces. Baby boomers make up 44 percent of all U.S. households based on the U.S. Census 2000. All I know is that my contribution margin will fall to 25 percent next year.

BERRY: I appreciate your concern. Give me a few days to think about the proposal. I'll get back to you soon.

---

[1]Shelter magazines feature home improvement ideas, new ideas in home decorating, and so on. *Better Homes and Gardens* is an example of a shelter magazine.

This case was prepared by Professor Roger A. Kerin, of the Edwin L. Cox School of Business, Southern Methodist University, as a basis for class discussion and is not designed to illustrate effective or ineffective handling of an administrative situation. All names and data have been disguised. Copyright © 2003 by Roger A. Kerin. No part of this case may be reproduced without written permission of the copyright holder.

After hanging up, Berry began to think about Bates's summary of the proposal, Carrington's present position, and the furniture industry in general. He knew that Bates expected a well-thought-out recommendation on such issues and a step-by-step description of the logic used to arrive at that recommendation.

■ THE COMPANY

Carrington Furniture is a manufacturer of medium- to high-priced wood bedroom, living room, and dining room furniture. The company was formed at the turn of the century by Charlton Bates's grandfather. Bates assumed the presidency of the company upon his father's retirement. Year-end net sales in 2002 were $75 million with a before-tax profit of $3.7 million.

Carrington sells its furniture through 1,000 high-quality department stores and independent furniture specialty stores nationwide, but all stores do not carry the company's entire line. The company is very selective in choosing retail outlets. According to Bates, "Our distribution policy, hence our retailers, should mirror the high quality of our products." As a matter of policy, Carrington does not sell to furniture chain stores or discount outlets.

The company employs 10 full-time salespeople and two regional sales managers. Sales personnel receive a base salary and a small commission on sales. A company sales force is atypical in the furniture industry; most furniture manufacturers use sales agents or representatives who carry a wide assortment of noncompeting furniture lines and receive a commission on sales. "Having our own sales group is a policy my father established years ago," noted Bates, "and we've been quite successful in having people who are committed to our company. Our people don't just take furniture orders. They are expected to motivate retail salespeople to sell our line, assist in setting up displays in stores, and give advice on a variety of matters to our retailers and their salespeople." He added, "It seems that my father was ahead of his time. I was just reading in the *Standard & Poor's Industry Surveys* for household furniture that the competition for retail floor space will require even more support, including store personnel sales training, innovative merchandising, inventory management, and advertising."

In early 2002, Carrington allocated $3,675,000 for total promotional expenditures for the 2002 operating year, excluding the salary of the Vice President of Sales. Promotion expenditures were categorized into four groups: (1) sales expense and administration, (2) cooperative advertising programs with retailers, (3) trade promotion, and (4) consumer advertising. Sales costs included salaries for sales personnel and sales managers, selling-expense reimbursements, fringe benefits, and clerical/office assistance, but did not include salespersons' commissions. Commissions were deducted from sales in the calculation of gross profit. The cooperative advertising budget is usually spent on newspaper advertising in a retailer's city. Cooperative advertising allowances are matched by funds provided by retailers on a dollar-for-dollar basis. Trade promotion is directed toward retailers and takes the form of catalogs, trade magazine advertisements, booklets for consumers, and point-of-purchase materials, such as displays, for use in retail stores. Also included in this category is the expense of participating in trade shows. Carrington is represented at two shows per year. Consumer advertising is directed at potential consumers through shelter magazines. The typical format used in consumer advertising is to highlight new furniture and different bedroom, living room, and dining room arrangements. The dollar allocation for each of these programs in 2002 is shown in Exhibit 1.

EXHIBIT 1

Allocation of Carrington's Promotion Dollars, 2002

Sales expense and administration	$ 995,500
Cooperative advertising allowance	1,650,000
Trade advertising	467,000
Consumer advertising	562,500
	$3,675,000

Source: Company records.

■ THE HOUSEHOLD FURNITURE INDUSTRY

The household furniture industry is divided into three general categories: wood, upholstered, and other (ready-to-assemble furniture and casual furniture). Total furniture industry sales in 2002 were estimated to be $23.9 billion at manufacturers' prices.

Household wood furniture sales represent 48 percent of total household furniture sales, followed by upholstered furniture (42 percent) and other forms (10 percent), according to the American Furniture Manufacturers Association (AFMA). The principal types of wood furniture are dressers, tables, and dining room suites. Bedroom and dining room furniture accounts for the majority of wood furniture sales.

In recent years, wood furniture manufacturers have increased their emphasis on quality by monitoring the entire production process from the raw materials used, to construction, finishes, and packaging. In addition to improving quality controls, companies also stress price points and basic styling features, and are trying to improve shipping schedules. Wood furniture manufacturers' sales rose 5 percent in 2002 but are expected to rise by 6 percent in 2003, according to the AFMA.

More than 1,000 furniture manufacturers operate in the United States. Two manufacturers have annual sales of more than $2 billion and represent about 20 percent of industry sales. These are Furniture Brands International, Inc. (owner of the Drexel Heritage, Maitland-Smith, Henredon, Broyhill, Lane, and Thomasville brands) and La-Z-Boy, Inc. Other well-known manufacturers include Ethan Allen, Bassett, and Sherrill. The top 25 manufacturers account for about 50 percent of U.S. furniture sales. Exports are not a major factor in the U.S. household wood furniture industry.

Consumer Expenditures for Furniture

Consumer spending for wood furniture is highly cyclical and closely linked to the incidence of new housing starts, consumer confidence, and disposable personal income. Because wood furniture is expensive and often sold in sets, such as a dining room table and chairs, consumers consider these purchases deferrable.

Expenditures for furniture of all kinds have fluctuated as a percentage of consumer disposable personal income since 1979. It has been estimated that about 1 percent of a U.S. household's disposable income is spent for household furniture and home furnishings. Forecasted retail sales for 2003 are about $70 billion. Exhibit 2 shows annual furniture sales at retail prices from 1992 through 2002.

Furniture Buying Behavior

Even though industry research indicates many consumers consider the furniture shopping process to be enjoyable, consumers acknowledge that they lack the confidence

EXHIBIT 2

Total Retail Furniture Sales in the United States, 1992–2002 (In Billions of Dollars at Retail Prices)

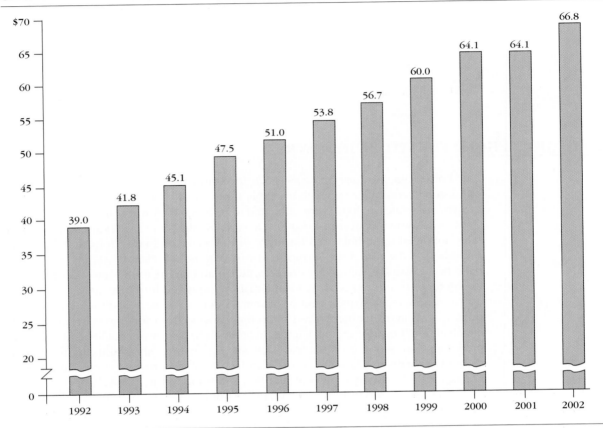

Source: U.S. Department of Commerce, Bureau of Economic Analysis.

to assess furniture construction, make judgments about quality, and accurately evaluate the price of furniture. Consumers also find it difficult to choose among the many styles available, fearing they will not like their choice several years later or that their selection will not be appropriate for their home and they will be unable to return it. According to a recent summary of furniture-buying behavior published in *Standard & Poor's Industry Surveys*:

> Consumers are quite finicky when it comes to buying furniture—a procedure fraught with concerns that are often not associated with buying other consumer durables, such as appliances and cars. With appliances and cars, consumers may have a more limited selection, they can do their own research, and they know what they are buying and what to expect. On the other hand, most consumers know little about evaluating the price or quality of furniture. It is also difficult for consumers to imagine how furniture will look in their homes, or whether they will still like their purchase in several years. Furthermore, there are questions about delivery—as in whether the item will arrive on time and in good condition and whether it can be returned for a full refund.

The furniture industry's efforts to educate consumers over the past years have failed for the most part. These efforts have included in-depth market studies to learn what consumers look for when they buy furniture, improved distribution, and new programs for training sales personnel. Despite these efforts, consumers still find the quality of furniture difficult to discern, and tend to base their furniture choice on price.

Results of a consumer panel sponsored by *Better Homes and Gardens* and composed of its subscribers provide the most comprehensive information available on furniture-buying behavior. Selected findings from the *Better Homes and Gardens* survey are reproduced in the appendix following this case. Other findings arising from this research are as follows:

- 94 percent of the subscribers enjoy buying furniture somewhat or very much.
- 84 percent of the subscribers believe "the higher the price, the higher the quality" when buying home furnishings.
- 72 percent of the subscribers browse or window-shop furniture stores even if they don't need furniture.
- 85 percent read furniture ads before they actually need furniture.
- 99 percent of the subscribers agree with the statement "When shopping for furniture and home furnishings, I like the salesperson to show me what alternatives are available, answer my questions, and let me alone so I can think about it and maybe browse around."
- 95 percent of the subscribers say they get redecorating ideas or guidance from magazines.
- 41 percent of the subscribers have requested a manufacturer's booklet.
- 63 percent of the subscribers say they need decorating advice to "put it all together."

Consumer research data have prompted both furniture retailers and manufacturers to stress the need for well-informed retail sales personnel to work with customers. For example, many manufacturers have established education centers where they train retail salespersons in the qualitative and construction details of the furniture they sell. Some manufacturers also distribute product literature to customers via retailers. Drexel Heritage, for instance, provides a series of books, entitled *Living with Drexel Heritage*, to its authorized retailers, who then give them to customers.

Distribution

Furniture is sold through over 100,000 specialty furniture and home furnishing stores, department stores, and mass-merchandise stores in the United States. Industry trends indicate that the number of independently owned furniture stores has declined while furniture store chains have grown. The top 10 furniture retailers in the United States captured approximately 19 percent of total U.S. furniture retail sales. Ethan Allen is the largest furniture retailer in terms of retail sales.

Furniture manufacturers have eschewed the Internet as a sales channel for the most part. Smaller manufacturers consider the up-front cost of $1.5 million to build a Web site coupled with the ongoing cost of $250,000 to maintain a furniture Web site to be prohibitive. Also the costs of delivering and returning heavy items are a concern. These costs, plus the limited success of Internet furniture retailers, has led some larger manufacturers to instead build and operate promotional Web sites at roughly half the cost. These Web sites feature new styles and list retailer locations that sell their products. Examples of these Web sites are *drexelheritage.com* and *thomasville.com*. Ethan Allen is an exception. As a vertically integrated furniture manufacturer that sells exclusively through company-owned and franchised stores, Ethan Allen sells selected furniture and accessories at its *ethanallen.com* Web site.

A significant trend among furniture retailers is the movement toward the "gallery concept"—the practice of dedicating an amount of space and sometimes an entire freestanding retail outlet to one furniture manufacturer. There are currently 11,000 galleries, and it is estimated this number will reach 12,500 by 2004. Commenting on the gallery concept, Charlton Bates said:

> The gallery concept has great appeal for a furniture manufacturer, since product is displayed in a unique and comfortable setting without the lure of competitive brands. We have galleries in a small number of our furniture stores. The fact that we are not getting our full line in all of our retailers galls me because the opportunity to even discuss the gallery concept with many of our retailers doesn't exist.

Bates added: "Galleries and upscale furniture and department stores attract and serve our target customer, the 38- to 56-year-old home owner with an annual household income over $100,000. That's where our customers get ideas and buy the quality furniture we sell" (see Exhibit 3).

The selling of furniture to retail outlets centers on manufacturers' expositions held at selected times and places around the country. The major expositions occur in High Point, North Carolina, in October and April. Regional expositions are also scheduled during the June–August period in locations such as Los Angeles, New York, and Boston. At these *marts*, as they are called in the furniture industry, retail buyers view manufacturers' lines and often make buying commitments for their stores. However, Carrington's experience has shown that sales efforts in the retail store by company representatives account for as much as one-half of the company's sales in any given year.

Advertising Practices

Manufacturers of household furniture spend approximately 3.5 percent of annual net sales for advertising of all types (consumer, trade, and cooperative advertising). This percentage has remained constant for many years. The typical vehicles used for consumer advertising are shelter magazines such as *Better Homes and Gardens, House Beautiful*, and *Southern Living*. Trade advertising directed primarily toward retailers includes brochures, point-of-purchase materials to be displayed on a retailer's sales floor, and technical booklets describing methods of construction and materials. Cooperative advertising, shared with retailers, usually appears in newspapers, but there are also some television and radio spots featuring the brands carried by retailers.

EXHIBIT 3

Furniture Retailers That Upscale Shoppers (Household Income $100,000 and Up) Have Used for Ideas and Where They Buy

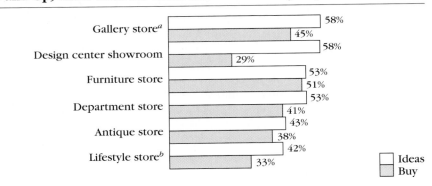

	Ideas	Buy
Gallery store[a]	58%	45%
Design center showroom	58%	29%
Furniture store	53%	51%
Department store	53%	41%
Antique store	43%	38%
Lifestyle store[b]	42%	33%

[a] *Furniture from single company*

[b] *Crate & Barrel, Pottery Barn, Ikea, etc.*

EXHIBIT 4

Home Furnishings Council Print Advertisement

Home Furnishings Tips From Kathie Lee Gifford.

Second In A Series:
"How Do I Start?!" My Answer: Don't Panic, Breathe Easy, And Read This.

Nobody ever said that decorating a room, or a whole house, was a piece of cake. But it's definitely *not* hard, and can actually be fun—especially if you start off right.

You can do that by following the terrific "Getting Started" tips found in Haven. It's the incredibly easy to use, complete decorating guide that's *free* at home furnishings stores everywhere that display the "heart and home" sign of the Home Furnishings Council.

Here are a few of Haven's time-saving, money-saving, sanity-saving ideas on starting off right.

1. For Step One, you don't even have to step out of your home, just go through all the decorating magazines you've been saving to find the rooms, the home furnishings, the colors and styles you like. Then take a grand tour of your own home, to see what you like, and what you'd like to never see again. Put all your thoughts on paper.

2. Next comes my favorite part, visiting home furnishings stores and galleries.

3. Take advantage of all the help and advice that these stores' sales experts have to offer you. Tell them your budget (don't be timid about it!) so they can help you get the best value for your dollar. Show them the pictures you tore out of magazines, bring along your room dimensions, your likes and dislikes—the more they know, the more they can help.

For the store nearest you offering free copies of Haven, please call 1-800-521-HOME, ext. 345

4. And, most important, work with them to realistically plan your decorating in phases—no one expects you to buy *everything* you want at once.

See, making a beautiful home for the most wonderful family in the world *is* a whole lot easier than you thought.

HOME FURNISHINGS COUNCIL

Home Is Where The Heart Is.

Source: Courtesy of the Home Furnishings Council.

Occasionally, industry groups sponsor advertising designed to stimulate consumer demand for home furnishings in general. For example, Exhibit 4 (on page 285) shows one of the print advertisements sponsored by the Home Furnishings Council. (The Home Furnishings Council merged with the Home Furnishings International Association in August 2002.)

■ THE BUDGET MEETING

At the January 6 meeting attended by Hervey and Bernham executives and Carrington executives, Michael Hervey proposed that the expenditure for consumer advertising be increased by $225,000 in 2003. Cooperative advertising and trade advertising allowances would remain at 2002 levels. Hervey further recommended that shelter magazines account for the bulk of the incremental expenditure for consumer advertising.

John Bott, Carrington's Vice President of Sales, disagreed with the budget allocation and noted that sales expenses and administration costs were expected to rise by $65,000 in 2003. Moreover, Bott believed that an additional sales representative was needed to service Carrington's accounts because 50 new accounts were being added. He estimated that the cost of the additional representative, including salary and expenses, would be at least $70,000 in 2003. "That's about $135,000 in additional sales expenses that have to be added into our promotional budget for 2003," Bott noted. He continued:

> We recorded sales of $75 million in 2002. If we assume a 6 percent increase in sales in 2003, that means our total budget will be $3,975,000, if my figures are right—a $300,000 increase over our previous budget. And I need $135,000 of that. In other words, $165,000 is available for other kinds of promotion, some of which should go to trade promotion to assist our salespeople servicing new accounts.

Hervey's reply to Bott noted that the company planned to introduce several new styles of living room and dining room furniture in 2003 and that these new items would require consumer advertising in shelter magazines to be launched successfully. He agreed with Bott that increased funding of the sales effort might be necessary and thought that Carrington might draw funds from cooperative advertising allowances and trade promotion.

Bates interrupted the dialogue between Bott and Hervey to mention that the $225,000 increase in promotion was about $75,000 less than the 5 percent percentage-of-sales policy limit. He pointed out, however, that higher material costs plus a recent wage increase were forecasted to squeeze Carrington's gross profit margin and threaten the company objective of achieving a 5 percent net profit margin before taxes. "Perhaps some juggling of the figures is necessary," he concluded. "Both of you have good points. Let me think about what's been said and then let's schedule a meeting for a week from today."

As Bates reviewed his notes from the meeting, he realized that the funds allocated to promotion were only part of the question. How the funds would be allocated within the budget was also crucial. A call to Tom Berry might be helpful in this regard, too.

■ APPENDIX: SELECTED FINDINGS FROM THE *BETTER HOMES AND GARDENS*® CONSUMER PANEL REPORT—HOME FURNISHINGS[2]

Question: If you were going to buy furniture in the near future, how important would the following factors be in selecting the store to buy furniture? (Respondents: 449)

---

[2]Reprinted courtesy of the *Better Homes and Gardens*® Consumer Panel.

Factor	Very Important	Somewhat Important	Not Too Important	Not at All Important	No Answer
Sells high-quality furnishings	62.6%	31.0%	3.8%	1.1%	1.5%
Has a wide range of different furniture styles	58.8	29.2	8.2	2.9	0.9
Gives you personal service	60.1	29.9	7.8	0.9	1.3
Is a highly dependable store	85.1	12.7	1.1	—	1.1
Offers decorating help from experienced home planners	26.5	35.9	25.4	10.9	1.3
Lets you "browse" all you want	77.1	17.8	3.3	0.7	1.1
Sells merchandise that's a good value for the money	82.0	15.6	0.9	0.2	1.3
Displays furniture in individual room settings	36.3	41.2	18.7	2.4	1.3
Has a relaxed, no-pressure atmosphere	80.0	17.1	1.6	—	1.3
Has well-informed salespeople	77.5	19.8	1.6	—	1.1
Has a very friendly atmosphere	68.2	28.1	2.4	—	1.3
Carries the style of furniture you like	88.0	10.0	0.9	—	1.1

Question: Please rate the following factors as to their importance to you when you purchase or shop for case-goods furniture, such as a dining room or living room suite, *1* being the most important factor, *2* being second most important, and so on, until all factors have been rated. (Respondents: 449)

Factor	1	2	3	4	5	6	7	8	9	10	No Answer
Construction of item	24.1%	16.0%	18.5%	13.1%	10.5%	6.9%	4.9%	1.6%	0.2%	1.1%	3.1%
Comfort	13.6	14.7	12.9	12.3	12.7	10.9	8.2	4.5	4.0	2.4	3.8
Styling and design	33.6	19.8	11.1	9.6	4.7	7.3	4.5	1.6	2.9	1.6	3.3
Durability of fabric	2.2	7.6	9.8	14.5	15.1	14.7	12.9	5.6	5.8	7.8	4.0
Type and quality of wood	10.9	17.8	16.3	15.8	14.7	5.8	5.3	3.1	4.9	2.0	3.4
Guarantee or warranty	1.6	3.8	1.6	5.3	8.7	10.0	13.8	25.2	14.5	11.1	4.4
Price	9.4	6.2	8.7	8.5	10.0	12.5	14.2	11.8	6.9	8.0	3.8
Reputation of manufac-turer or brand name	6.2	3.6	4.7	5.6	6.2	6.2	12.7	17.1	22.7	11.6	3.4
Reputation of retailer	1.6	1.8	1.6	2.4	4.0	7.3	7.4	13.6	22.0	34.5	3.8
Finish, color of wood	4.7	7.6	10.2	8.0	8.9	13.4	10.7	10.0	10.2	12.7	3.6

Question: Below is a list of 15 criteria that may influence what furniture you buy. Please rate them from *1* as most important to *5* as least important. (Respondents: 449)

Criterion	*1*	*2*	*3*	*4*	*5*	*No Answer*
Guarantee or warranty	11.4%	11.1%	26.3%	16.9%	5.3%	29.0%
Brand name	9.1	6.5	14.3	25.6	11.6	32.9
Comfort	34.7	27.8	14.5	8.5	4.7	9.8
Decorator suggestion	4.0	2.4	2.7	8.2	44.8	37.9
Material used	14.9	24.1	14.9	13.4	6.2	26.5
Delivery time	0.7	0.5	1.3	2.9	55.2	39.4
Size	7.6	10.7	13.6	30.9	4.0	33.2
Styling and design	33.4	17.8	21.8	13.6	2.2	11.2
Construction	34.3	23.6	13.1	11.4	2.9	14.7
Fabric	4.0	25.6	24.9	14.0	4.5	27.0
Durability	37.0	19.4	13.6	6.9	4.9	18.2
Finish on wooden parts	5.8	14.7	16.7	10.7	16.7	35.4
Price	19.4	21.8	16.0	10.9	15.4	16.5
Manufacturer's reputation	4.2	9.1	15.4	22.9	14.3	34.1
Retailer's reputation	2.2	4.7	10.5	21.2	26.5	34.9

Question: Listed below are some statements others have made about shopping for furniture. Please indicate how much you agree or disagree with each one. (Respondents: 449)

Statement	*Agree Completely*	*Agree Somewhat*	*Neither Agree nor Disagree*	*Disagree Somewhat*	*Disagree Completely*	*No Answer*
I wish there were some way to be really sure of getting good quality in furniture	61.9%	24.7%	4.7%	4.2%	3.6%	0.9%
I really enjoy shopping for furniture	49.2	28.3	7.6	9.8	4.2	0.9
I would never buy any furniture without my husband's/wife's approval	47.0	23.0	10.9	9.8	7.1	2.2
I like all pieces in the master bedroom to be exactly the same style	35.9	30.7	12.7	11.1	7.6	2.0
Once I find something I like in furniture, I wish it would last forever so I'd never have to buy again	36.8	24.3	10.0	18.9	9.1	0.9
I wish I had more confidence in my ability to decorate my home attractively	23.1	32.3	12.5	11.6	18.7	1.8
I wish I knew more about furniture styles and what looks good	20.0	31.0	17.1	13.4	16.7	1.8

Statement	Agree Completely	Agree Somewhat	Neither Agree nor Disagree	Disagree Somewhat	Disagree Completely	No Answer
My husband/wife doesn't take much interest in the furniture we buy	6.5	18.0	12.3	17.8	41.4	4.0
I like to collect a number of different styles in the dining room	3.3	10.5	15.2	29.8	38.3	2.9
Shopping for furniture is very distressing to me	2.4	11.6	14.3	18.0	51.9	1.8

Question: Listed below are some factors that may influence your choice of furnishings. Please rate them with *1* being most important, *2* being second most important, and so on, until all factors have been rated. (Respondents: 449)

Factor	1	2	3	4	5	No Answer
Friends and/or neighbors	1.3%	16.9%	15.8%	22.1%	41.7%	2.2%
Family or spouse	62.8	9.4	14.3	9.8	2.0	1.7
Magazine advertising	16.3	30.3	29.6	17.6	4.2	2.0
Television advertising	1.1	6.7	14.7	32.5	42.3	2.7
Store displays	18.9	37.2	22.1	14.0	5.6	2.2

Question: When you go shopping for a *major piece* of furniture or smaller pieces of furniture, who, if anyone, do you usually go with? (Respondents: 449—multiple responses)

Person	Major Pieces	Other Pieces
Husband	82.4%	59.5%
Mother or mother-in-law	6.2	9.1
Friend	12.0	18.9
Decorator	4.2	1.6
Other relative	15.6	15.4
Other person	2.9	3.3
No one else	5.1	22.3
No answer	0.9	3.1

Question: When the time comes to purchase a *major* item of furniture or other smaller pieces of furniture, who, if anyone, helps you make the final decision about which piece to buy? (Respondents: 449—multiple responses)

Person	Major Pieces	Other Pieces
Husband	86.0%	63.5%
Mother or mother-in-law	2.4	4.5
Friend	3.6	8.0
Decorator	3.1	2.7
Other relative	10.0	12.9
Other person	1.6	1.8
No one else	7.1	24.3
No answer	0.9	2.2[2]

Carrington Furniture, Inc. (B)

In April 2003, Carrington Furniture, Inc. merged with Lea-Meadows, Inc., a manufacturer of upholstered furniture for living and family rooms. The merger was not planned in a conventional sense. Charlton Bates's father-in-law died suddenly in early February 2003, leaving his daughter with controlling interest in Lea-Meadows. The merger proceeded smoothly, since the two firms were located on adjacent properties and the general consensus was that the two firms would maintain as much autonomy as was economically justified. Moreover, the upholstery line filled a gap in the Carrington product mix, even though it would retain its own identity and brand names.

The only real issue that continued to plague Bates was merging the selling effort. Carrington had its own sales force, but Lea-Meadows relied on sales agents to represent it. The question was straightforward, in his opinion: "Do we give the upholstery line of chairs and sofas to our sales force, or do we continue using the sales agents?" John Bott, Carrington's Vice President of Sales, said the line should be given to his sales group; Martin Moorman, National Sales Manager at Lea-Meadows, said the upholstery line should remain with sales agents.

■ LEA-MEADOWS, INC.

Lea-Meadows, Inc. is a small, privately owned manufacturer of upholstered furniture for use in living and family rooms. The firm is more than 75 years old. The company uses some of the finest fabrics and frame construction in the industry, according to trade sources. Net sales in 2002 were $5 million. Total industry sales of upholstered furniture manufacturers in 2002 were $10 billion. Forecasted 2003 industry sales for upholstered furniture were $10.4 billion. Company sales had increased 7 percent annually over the past five years, and company executives believed this growth rate would continue for the foreseeable future.

Lea-Meadows employed 15 sales agents to represent its products. These sales agents also represented several manufacturers of noncompeting furniture and home furnishings. Often, a sales agent found it necessary to deal with several buyers in a store in order to represent all the lines carried. On a typical sales call, a sales agent first visited buyers to discuss new lines, in addition to any promotions being offered by manufacturers. New orders were sought where and when it was appropriate. The sales agent then visited the selling floor to check displays, inspect furniture, and inform salespeople about furniture styles and construction. Lea-Meadows paid an agent commission of 5 percent of net company sales for these services. Moorman thought sales agents spent 10 to 15 percent of their in-store time on Lea-Meadows products.

The company did not attempt to influence the type of retailers that agents contacted, although it was implicit in the agency agreement that agents would not sell to

This case was prepared by Professor Roger A. Kerin, of the Edwin L. Cox School of Business, Southern Methodist University, as a basis for class discussion and is not designed to illustrate appropriate or inappropriate handling of administrative situations. All names and data are disguised. Copyright © 2003 by Roger A. Kerin. No part of this case may be reproduced without permission from the copyright holder.

discount houses. Sales records indicated that agents were calling on specialty furniture and department stores. An estimated 1,000 retail accounts were called on in 2001 and 2002. All agents had established relationships with their retail accounts and worked closely with them.

■ CARRINGTON FURNITURE, INC.

Carrington Furniture, Inc. is a manufacturer of medium- to high-priced wood bedroom, living room, and dining room furniture.[1] Net sales in 2002 were $75 million; before-tax profit was $3.7 million. Industry sales of wood furniture in 2002 were $11.5 billion at manufacturers' prices. Projected industry sales for 2002 were $12.2 billion.

The company employed 10 full-time sales representatives, who called on 1,000 retail accounts. These individuals performed the same function as sales agents but were paid a salary plus a small commission. In 2002, the average sales representative received an annual salary of $70,000 (plus expenses) and a commission of 0.5 percent on net company sales. Total sales administration costs were $130,000.

Carrington's salespeople were highly regarded in the industry. They were known particularly for their knowledge of wood furniture and willingness to work with buyers and retail sales personnel. Despite these advantages, Bates knew that all retail accounts did not carry the complete Carrington furniture line. He had therefore instructed Bott to "push the group a little harder." At present, sales representatives were making 10 sales calls per week, with the average sales call running three hours. Salespersons' remaining time was accounted for by administrative activities and travel. Bates recommended that the call frequency be increased to seven calls per account per year, which was consistent with what he thought was the industry norm.

■ MERGING THE SALES EFFORTS

Through separate meetings with Bott and Moorman, Bates was able to piece together a variety of data and perspectives on the question of merging the sales efforts. These meetings also made it clear that Bott and Moorman differed dramatically in their views.

John Bott had no doubts about assigning the line to the Carrington sales force. Among the reasons he gave for this view were the following. First, Carrington had developed one of the most well respected, professional sales forces in the industry. The representatives could easily learn the fabric jargon, and they already knew personally many of the buyers who were responsible for upholstered furniture. Second, selling the Lea-Meadows line would require only about 15 percent of present sales call time. Thus, he thought that the new line would not be a major burden. Third, more control over sales efforts was possible. Bott noted that Charlton Bates's father had created the sales group 30 years earlier because of the commitment it engendered and the service "only our own people are able and willing to give." Moreover, the company salespeople have the Carrington "look" and presentation style, which is instilled in every one of them. Fourth, Bott said that it wouldn't look right if both representatives and agents called on the same stores and buyers. He noted that Carrington and Lea-Meadows overlapped on all their accounts. He said, "We'd be paying a commission on sales to these accounts when we would have gotten them anyway. The difference in commission percentages would not be good for morale."

---

[1]Additional background information on the company and industry can be found in the case titled "Carrington Furniture, Inc. (A)."

Martin Moorman advocated keeping sales agents for the Lea-Meadows line. His arguments were as follows. First, all sales agents had established contacts and were highly regarded by store buyers, and most had represented the line in a professional manner for many years. He, too, had a good working relationship with all 15 agents. Second, sales agents represented little, if any, cost beyond commissions. Moorman noted, "Agents get paid when we get paid." Third, sales agents were committed to the Lea-Meadows line: "The agents earn a part of their living representing us. They have to service retail accounts to get the repeat business." Fourth, sales agents were calling on buyers not contacted by the Carrington sales force. Moorman noted, "If we let Carrington people handle the line, we might lose these accounts, have to hire more sales personnel, or take away 25 percent of the present time given to Carrington product lines." Finally, Moorman took issue with Bott's view that Carrington salespeople could easily learn about upholstered furniture. He said, "Lea-Meadows has some 1,000 different frames for sofas and upholstered chairs. If all combinations of fabric, skirts, pillow, springs, and fringes are considered, a sales rep would need to be conversant in no fewer than 1 billion possibilities."

As Bates reflected on the meetings, he felt that a broader perspective was necessary beyond the views expressed by Bott and Moorman. One factor was profitability. Existing Carrington furniture lines typically had gross margins that were 5 percent higher than those for Lea-Meadows upholstered lines. Another factor was the "us and them" references apparent in the meetings with Bott and Moorman. Would merging the sales effort overcome this, or would it cause more problems? The idea of increasing the sales force to incorporate the Lea-Meadows line did not sit well with him. Adding new salespeople would require restructuring of sales territories, involve potential loss of commissions by existing salespeople, and be "a big headache." Still, it had been Carrington's policy for many years to have its own sales force and not use sales agents. In addition, there was the subtle issue of Moorman's future. Moorman, who was 55 years old, had worked for Lea-Meadows for 25 years and was a family friend and godfather to Bates's youngest child. If the Lea-Meadows line was represented by the Carrington sales force, Moorman's position would be eliminated. Given these circumstances, Bates also thought his wife's views had to be considered. He could bring up the topic on their way to the High Point, North Carolina, furniture exposition early next week.

Cadbury Beverages, Inc.
Crush® Brand

In January 1990, marketing executives at Cadbury Beverages, Inc. began the challenging task of relaunching the Crush, Hires, and Sun-Drop soft drink brands. These brands had been acquired from Procter & Gamble in October 1989.

After considerable discussion, senior marketing executives at Cadbury Beverages, Inc. decided to focus initial attention on the Crush brand of fruit-flavored carbonated beverages. Three issues were prominent. First, immediate efforts were needed to rejuvenate the bottling network for the Crush soft drink brand. Second, according to one executive, "[we had] to sort through and figure out what the Crush brand equity is, how the brand was built . . . and develop a base positioning."[1] Third, a new advertising and promotion program for Crush had to be developed, including setting objectives, developing strategies, and preparing preliminary budgets.

Kim Feil was assigned responsibility for managing the relaunch of the Crush soft drink brand. She had joined Cadbury Beverages, Inc. on December 12, 1989, as a Senior Product Manager, after working in various product management positions at a large consumer goods company for five years. Recounting her first day on the job, Feil said, "I arrived early Wednesday morning to find 70 boxes of research reports, print ads, sales and trade promotions and videotapes stacked neatly from the floor to the ceiling." Undaunted, she began to sift through the mountains of material systematically, knowing that her assessment and recommendations would soon be sought.

■ CADBURY BEVERAGES, INC.

Cadbury Beverages, Inc. is the beverage division of Cadbury Schweppes PLC, a major global soft drink and confectionery marketer. In 1989, Cadbury Schweppes PLC had worldwide sales of $4.6 billion, which were produced by product sales in more than 110 countries. Cadbury Schweppes PLC headquarters are located in London, England; Cadbury Beverages, Inc., worldwide headquarters are in Stamford, Connecticut. Exhibit 1 shows the product list sold worldwide by Cadbury Beverages, Inc. Exhibit 2 on page 295 details the product list for the United States.

History

Cadbury Schweppes PLC has the distinction of being the world's first soft drink maker. The company can trace its beginnings to 1783 in London, where Swiss national

---

[1]Patricia Winters, "Fresh Start for Crush," *Advertising Age* (January 6, 1990):47.

The cooperation of Cadbury Beverages, Inc. in the preparation of this case is gratefully acknowledged. This case was prepared by Professor Roger A. Kerin, of the Edwin L. Cox School of Business, Southern Methodist University, as a basis for class discussion and is not designed to illustrate effective or ineffective handling of an administrative situation. Certain information has been disguised and is not useful for research purposes. Crush is a registered trademark used by permission from Cadbury Beverages, Inc. Copyright © 1995 by Roger A. Kerin. No part of this case may be reproduced without written permission of the copyright holder.

EXHIBIT 1

Worldwide Product List for Cadbury Beverages, Inc.

Carbonates	Waters	Still Drinks/Juices
Canada Dry	Schweppes	Oasis
Schweppes	Canada Dry	Atoll
Pure Spring	Pure Spring	Bali
Sunkist	Malvern	TriNaranjus
Crush		Vida
'C' Plus		Trina
Hires		Trina Colada
Sussex		Red Cheek
Old Colony		Allen's
Sun-Drop		Mitchell's
Gini		Mott's
		Clamato
		E. D. Smith
		Rose's
		Mr & Mrs "T"
		Holland House

Jacob Schweppe first sold his artificial mineral water. Schweppe returned to Switzerland in 1789, but the company continued its British operations, introducing a lemonade in 1835 and tonic water and ginger ale in the 1870s. Beginning in the 1880s, Schweppes expanded worldwide, particularly in countries that would later form the British Commonwealth. In the 1960s, the company diversified into food products.

In 1969, Schweppes merged with Cadbury. Cadbury was a major British candy maker that traced its origins to John Cadbury, who began his business making cocoa in Birmingham, England, in the 1830s. By the middle of this century, Cadbury had achieved market presence throughout the British Commonwealth, as well as other countries.

In 1989, Cadbury Schweppes PLC was one of the world's largest multinational firms and was ranked 457th in *Business Week*'s Global 1000. Beverages accounted for 60 percent of company worldwide sales and 53 percent of operating income in 1989. Confectionery items accounted for 40 percent of worldwide sales and produced 47 percent of operating income.

Soft Drinks

Cadbury Schweppes PLC is the world's third largest soft drink marketer behind Coca-Cola and PepsiCo. The company has achieved this status through consistent marketing investment in the Schweppes brand name and extensions to different beverage products such as tonic, ginger ale, club soda, and seltzer in various flavors. In addition, the company has acquired numerous other brands throughout the world, each with an established customer franchise. For example, Cadbury Schweppes PLC acquired the Canada Dry soft drink brands and certain rights to Sunkist soft drinks in 1986. In 1989, the company acquired certain soft drink brands and associated assets (for TriNaranjus, Vida, Trina, and Trina Colada) in Spain and Portugal and purchased the Gini brand, which is the leading bitter lemon brand in France and Belgium. Also, in

EXHIBIT 2

U.S. Product List for Cadbury Beverages, Inc.

Schweppes	Canada Dry	Sunkist	Crush, Hires, Sun-Drop	Mott's, Red Cheek, Holland House, Mr & Mrs "T," Rose's
Tonic Water	Tonic Water	Sunkist Pineapple Soda	Crush Orange	Mott's 100% Pure Apple Juices
Diet Tonic Water	Sugar-Free Tonic Water	Sunkist Grape Soda	Crush Diet Orange	Mott's 100% Pure Juice Blends
Club Soda	Club Soda	Sunkist Fruit Punch	Hires Root Beer	Mott's Juice Drinks
Seltzer Water	Seltzer Waters	Sunkist Strawberry Soda	Hires Diet Root Beer	Mott's Apple Sauce
Sparkling Waters	Sparkling Mineral Waters	Sunkist Orange Soda	Hires Cream Soda	Mott's Apple Sauce Fruit Snacks
Grapefruit Soda	Barrelhead Root Beer	Sunkist Diet Orange Soda	Hires Diet Cream Soda	Mott's Prune Juice
Collins Mix	Barrelhead Sugar-Free	Sunkist Sparkling	Crush Strawberry	Clamato
Grape Soda	Root Beer	Lemonade	Crush Grape	Beefamato
Ginger Ale	Wink	Sunkist Diet Sparkling	Crush Cherry	Grandma's Molasses
Diet Ginger Ale	Ginger Ale	Lemonade	Crush Pineapple	Rose's Lime Juice
Raspberry Ginger Ale	Diet Ginger Ale		Crush Cream Soda	Rose's Grenadine
Diet Raspberry Ginger Ale	Cherry Ginger Ale		Sun-Drop Cherry Citrus	Red Cheek Apple Juice
Bitter Lemon	Diet Cherry Ginger Ale		Sun-Drop Diet Citrus	Red Cheek Juice Blends
Lemon Sour	Bitter Lemon			Mr & Mrs "T" Margarita Salt
Lemon Lime	No-Cal Brand Soft Drinks			Mr & Mrs "T" Bloody Mary Mix
	Cott Brand Soft Drinks			Mr & Mrs "T" Liquid Cocktail Mixers
	Lemon Ginger Ale			Mr & Mrs "T" Rich & Spicy
	Diet Lemon Ginger Ale			Holland House Cooking Wines
				Holland House Dry Mixers
				Holland House Wine Marinades
				Holland House Smooth & Spicy
				Holland House Coca Casa Cream of Coconut
				Holland House Liquid Mixers

October 1989, the company acquired all the Crush brand worldwide trademarks from Procter & Gamble for $220 million.

Cadbury Schweppes PLC (Cadbury Beverages, Inc.) was the fourth largest soft drink marketer in the United States in 1989, with a carbonated soft drink market share of 3.4 percent. (The three leading U.S. soft drink companies, in order, were Coca-Cola, PepsiCo, and Dr. Pepper/7Up.) Nonetheless, the company's brands were often the market leader in their specific categories. For example, Canada Dry is the top-selling ginger ale in the United States, Schweppes is the leading tonic water, and Canada Dry seltzers top the club soda/seltzer category. The combined sales of Sunkist and Crush brand orange drinks lead the orange-flavored carbonated soft drink category.

According to industry analysts, the 1989 acquisition of Crush meant that Canada Dry would account for 39 percent of Cadbury Beverages soft drink sales in the United States. Sunkist, Crush, and Schweppes would account for 22 percent, 20 percent, and 17 percent of U.S. sales, respectively. The remaining 2 percent of U.S. sales would come from other soft drink brands.[2]

■ CARBONATED SOFT DRINK INDUSTRY

American consumers drink more soft drinks than tap water. In 1989, the average American consumed 46.7 gallons of carbonated soft drinks, or twice the 23 gallons consumed in 1969. Population growth compounded by rising per capita consumption produced an estimated $43 billion in retail sales in 1989.

Industry Structure

There are three major participants in the production and distribution of carbonated soft drinks in the United States. They are concentrate producers, bottlers, and retail outlets. For regular soft drinks, concentrate producers manufacture the basic flavors (for example, lemon-lime and cola) for sale to bottlers, which add a sweetener to carbonated water and package the beverage in bottles and cans. For diet soft drinks, concentrate producers include an artificial sweetener, such as aspartame, with their flavors.

There are over 40 concentrate producers in the United States. However, about 82 percent of industry sales are accounted for by three producers: Coca-Cola, PepsiCo, and Dr. Pepper/7Up.

Approximately 1,000 bottling plants in the United States convert flavor concentrate into carbonated soft drinks. Bottlers are either owned by concentrate producers or franchised to sell the brands of concentrate producers. For example, roughly one-half of Pepsi-Cola's sales are through company-owned bottlers; the remaining volume is sold through franchised bottlers. Franchised bottlers are typically granted a right to package and distribute a concentrate producer's branded line of soft drinks in a defined territory and not allowed to market a directly competitive major brand. However, franchised bottlers can represent noncompetitive brands and decline to bottle a concentrate producer's secondary lines. These arrangements mean that a franchised bottler of Pepsi-Cola cannot sell Royal Crown (RC) Cola but can bottle and market Orange Crush rather than PepsiCo's Mandarin Orange Slice.

Concentrate producer pricing to bottlers was similar across competitors within flavor categories. Exhibit 3 shows the approximate price and cost structure for orange concentrate producers and bottlers.

The principal retail channels for carbonated soft drinks are supermarkets, convenience stores, vending machines, fountain service, and thousands of small retail outlets.

---

[2]Patricia Winters, "Cadbury Schweppes' Plan: Skirt Cola Giants," *Advertising Age* (August 13, 1990): 22–23.

EXHIBIT 3

Approximate Price and Cost Structure for Orange Concentrate Producers and Bottlers

| | Concentrate Producers | | | |
| | Regular (Sugar) | | Diet (Aspartame) | |
	$/Case	Percentage	$/Case	Percentage
Net selling price	$0.76	100%	$0.92	100%
Cost of goods sold	0.11	14	0.12	13
Gross profit	$0.65	86%	$0.80	87%
Selling and delivery	0.02	3	0.02	2
Advertising and promotion	0.38	50	0.38	41
General and administrative expense	0.13	17	0.13	14
Pretax cash profit/case	$0.12	16%	$0.27	30%

| | Bottlers | | | |
| | Regular (Sugar) | | Diet (Aspartame) | |
	$/Case	Percentage	$/Case	Percentage
Net selling price	$5.85	100%	$5.85	100%
Cost of goods sold	3.16	54	3.35	57
Gross profit	$2.69	46%	$2.50	43%
Selling and delivery	1.35	23	1.35	23
Advertising and promotion	0.40	7	0.40	7
General and administrative expense	0.05	1	0.05	1
Pretax cash profit/case	$0.89	15%	$0.71	12%

Soft drinks are typically sold in bottles and cans, except for fountain service. In fountain service, syrup is sold to a retail outlet (such as McDonald's), which mixes the syrup with carbonated water for immediate consumption by customers. Supermarkets account for about 40 percent of carbonated soft drink industry sales. Industry analysts consider supermarket sales the key to a successful soft drink marketing effort.

Soft Drink Marketing

Soft drink marketing is characterized by heavy investment in advertising, selling and promotion to and through bottlers to retail outlets, and consumer price discounting. Concentrate producers usually assume responsibility for developing national consumer advertising and promotion programs, product development and planning, and marketing research. Bottlers usually take the lead in developing trade promotions to retail outlets and local consumer promotions. Bottlers are also responsible for selling and servicing retail accounts, including the placement and maintenance of in-store displays and the restocking of supermarket and convenience store shelves with their brands.

Flavor and Brand Competition Colas account for slightly less than two-thirds of total carbonated soft drink sales. Other flavors, such as orange, lemon-lime, cherry, grape, and root beer account for the remaining sales. Estimates of market shares for flavors in 1989 were as follows:

Flavor	Market Share
Cola	65.7%
Lemon-lime	12.9
Orange	3.9
Root beer	3.6
Ginger ale	2.8
Grape	1.1
Others	10.0
	100.0%

Diet soft drinks represented 31 percent of industry sales in 1989. Industry trend data indicate that sales of diet drinks accounted for a large portion of the overall growth of carbonated soft drink sales in the 1980s.

There are more than 900 registered brand names for soft drinks in the United States. Most of these brands are sold only regionally. Exhibit 4 shows the top 10 soft drink brands in 1989. Six of these brands were colas, and all 10 brands were marketed by Coca-Cola, PepsiCo, or Dr. Pepper/7Up.

Soft Drink Purchase and Consumption Behavior   Industry research suggests that the purchase of soft drinks in supermarkets is often unplanned. Accordingly, soft drink purchasers respond favorably to price (coupon) promotions, in-store (particularly end-of-aisle) displays, and other forms of point-of-sale promotions (such as shelf tags). The importance of display is evidenced in the view held by an industry analyst who estimated that a brand is "locked out of 60 percent of the [supermarket soft drink] volume if it can't get end-aisle displays."[3] The typical supermarket purchaser of soft drinks is a married woman with children under 18 years of age living at home.

Soft drink buying is somewhat seasonal, with consumption slightly higher during summer months than winter months. Consumption also varies by region of the country. Per capita consumption in the East South Central states of Kentucky, Tennessee,

EXHIBIT 4

Market Share of Top 10 Soft Drink Brands in the United States, 1989

Brand	Market Share
1. Coca-Cola Classic	19.8%
2. Pepsi-Cola	17.9
3. Diet Coke	8.9
4. Diet Pepsi	5.7
5. Dr. Pepper	4.5
6. Sprite	3.7
7. Mountain Dew	3.6
8. 7Up	3.2
9. Caffeine-free Diet Coke	2.5
10. Caffeine-free Diet Pepsi	1.6
Top 10 brands	71.4
Other brands	28.6
Total industry	100.0%

[3]Patricia Winters, "Crush Fails to Fit on P&G Shelf," *Advertising Age* (July 10, 1989): 1, 42–43.

Alabama, and Mississippi was highest in the United States in 1989, with 54.9 gallons compared with the national per capita average of 46.7 gallons. In the Mountain states of Montana, Idaho, Wyoming, Colorado, New Mexico, Arizona, Utah, and Nevada, per capita consumption was 37.1 gallons—the lowest in the nation.

Consumption of diet beverages was more pronounced among consumers over 25 years of age. Teenagers, and younger consumers generally, were heavier consumers of regular soft drinks.

■ ORANGE CATEGORY

Orange-flavored carbonated soft drinks recorded sales of 126 million cases in 1989, or 3.9 percent of total industry sales sold through supermarkets.[4] Prior to 1986, annual case volume had hovered in the range of 100 to 102 million cases. In the mid-1980s, PepsiCo introduced Mandarin Orange Slice, and Coca-Cola introduced Minute Maid Orange. Entry of these two brands, supported by widespread distribution and heavy advertising and promotion, revitalized the category and increased supermarket sales to 126 million cases. Annual supermarket case volume for the period 1984–1989 was as follows:

Year	Annual Supermarket Case Volume of Orange-Flavored Soft Drinks
1984	102,000,000
1985	100,000,000
1986	126,000,000
1987	131,000,000
1988	131,000,000
1989	126,000,000

Major Competitors

Four brands captured the majority of orange-flavored soft drink sales in 1989. Mandarin Orange Slice marketed by PepsiCo was the category leader with a market share of 20.8 percent. Sunkist, sold by Cadbury Beverages, Inc., and Coca-Cola's Minute Maid Orange had market shares of 14.4 percent and 14 percent, respectively. Orange Crush had a market share of 7.5 percent. Other brands accounted for the remaining 43.3 percent of sales of orange-flavored soft drinks. Exhibit 5 shows the market shares for the major competitors for the period 1985–1989.

The major competitors sold both regular and diet varieties of orange-flavored drink. As shown in Exhibit 6, slightly over 70 percent of sales in this category were regular soft drinks. Orange Crush sales mirrored this pattern. Sunkist, however, exceeded the category average, with 82 percent of its case volume sales being the regular form. For Mandarin Orange Slice and Minute Maid Orange, case volume was almost evenly split between regular and diet drinks.

Major competitors also differed in terms of market coverage in 1989. Sunkist was available in markets that represented 91 percent of total orange category sales. By comparison, Orange Crush was available in markets that represented only 62 percent of orange category sales. Mandarin Orange Slice and Minute Maid Orange were available

---

[4]*Case author's note:* The soft drink industry uses supermarket sales and market shares as a gauge to assess the competitive position of different brands and flavors, since supermarket volumes affect sales through other retail outlets and fountain service. As an approximation and for analysis purposes, *total case* volume for a brand or flavor can be estimated as 2.5 times supermarket case volume. Therefore, total sales of orange-flavored soft drinks are 2.5 × 126,000,000 = 315 million cases.

EXHIBIT 5

Orange Carbonated Soft Drink Brand Market Shares, 1985–1989 (Rounded)

	Year				
Brand	*1985*	*1986*	*1987*	*1988*	*1989*
Sunkist	32%	20%	13%	13%	14%
Mandarin Orange Slice	NA	16	22	21	21
Minute Maid Orange	NA	8	14	13	14
Crush	22	18	14	11	8
Total top four brands	54	62	63	58	57
Others	46	38	37	42	43

in markets that represented 88 percent of orange category sales. Exhibit 7 shows the market coverage by the four major competitors for the period 1985–1989.

Competitor Positioning and Advertising

Each of the four major competitors attempted to stake out a unique position within the orange category. For example, Minute Maid Orange appeared to emphasize its orange flavor, while Sunkist focused on the teen lifestyle. Mandarin Orange Slice and Minute Maid Orange appeared to be targeted at young adults and households without children. These brands also appeared to be emphasizing the "better for you" idea. Crush and Sunkist targeted teens and households with children at home. Exhibit 8 summarizes the apparent brand positionings of the major competitors and selected performance data compiled by the Crush marketing research staff.

Slightly over $26 million was spent on advertising by the four major brands in 1989. Mandarin Orange Slice and Minute Maid Orange accounted for 84 percent of all advertising expenditures in the orange category. Although both brands were advertised on network and cable television and both used spot television commercials in local markets, their advertising differed in other respects. Minute Maid Orange used outdoor billboards and network radio for advertising, but Mandarin Orange Slice did not. In comparison, Mandarin Orange Slice was advertised in magazines and newspapers, but Minute Maid Orange was not.

Crush and Sunkist spent less on advertising and used fewer advertising vehicles than did Minute Maid Orange and Mandarin Orange Slice. Crush was promoted most frequently on spot television, in newspapers, and on outdoor signage. Sunkist used newspapers, spot television, outdoor billboards, and some syndicated television.

EXHIBIT 6

Case Volume in 1989 by Type of Drink: Regular Versus Diet

Type	*Total Soft Drinks*	*Total Orange*	*Crush*	*Sunkist*	*Mandarin Orange Slice*	*Minute Maid Orange*
Regular	68.9%	73.2%	71.3%	82.1%	49.0%	53.1%
Diet	31.1	26.8	28.7	17.9	51.0	46.9
	100.0%	100.0%	100.0%	100.0%	100.0%	100.0%

EXHIBIT 7

Market Coverage of Orange Category by Major Competitors, 1985–1989

Brand	Year				
	1985	1986	1987	1988	1989
Crush	81%	81%	78%	78%	62%
Sunkist	95	83	79	86	91
Mandarin Orange Slice	10	68	87	88	88
Minute Maid Orange	10	60	87	88	88

Two advertising trends were evident in the orange category since 1986. First, total expenditures for measured print and broadcast media declined each year since 1986, when $52.2 million was spent for advertising. In that year, Mandarin Orange Slice and Minute Maid Orange were introduced nationally. Second, competitors increased the variety of media used for advertising. In 1986, spot television and outdoor billboards were used almost exclusively. By 1989, a broader spectrum of vehicles was used, including broadcast media (network, spot, syndicated, and cable television and network radio) and print media (outdoor, magazines, and newspapers). Exhibit 9 shows advertising expenditures for the four major brands for the period 1985–1989.

Competitor Pricing and Promotion

Concentrate pricing among the four major competitors differed very little. Typically, no more than a one-cent difference existed. The price differential between regular (with sugar) and diet (with aspartame) concentrate was virtually the same across competitors. The similarity in pricing as well as in raw material costs resulted in similar gross profit margins across competitors in the orange category. However, as noted in Exhibit 3, the gross profit margin differs between regular and diet soft drink concentrate.

Advertising and promotion programs were jointly implemented and financed by concentrate producers and bottlers. Concentrate producers and bottlers split adver-

EXHIBIT 8

Competitive Positioning and Performance, 1989

	Sunkist	Mandarin Orange Slice	Minute Maid Orange	Crush
Positioning	"Teens on the Beach"; "Drink in the Sun"	"Who's Got the Juice?" Contemporary youth culture	"The orange, orange" orange flavor, taste of real orange	"Don't just quench it, CRUSH it"; bold user imagery with thirst-quenching benefit
Target	Teens, 12–24	Young adults, 18–24	Young adults, 18–34	Teens, 13–29
Household size of purchaser	3–4 (children at home)	1–2 (no children)	1–2 (no children)	3–5 (children at home)
Package sales mix	Two-liter 51% Cans 42% Other 7%	Two-liter 54% Cans 42% Other 4%	Two-liter 54% Cans 41% Other 5%	Two-liter 64% Cans 31% Other 5%
Loyalty (percentage of brand buyer's orange volume)	36%	55%	48%	46%

Source: Crush Marketing Research Staff Report. Based on trade publications and industry sources.

EXHIBIT 9

Concentrate Producers' Advertising Expenditures for Broadcast and Print Media for Major Orange Soft Drink Brands, 1985–1989 (In Thousands of Dollars)

Brand	1985	1986	1987	1988	1989
Mandarin Orange Slice (total)	$17,809.4	$32,079.9	$29,555.8	$15,001.3	$11,388.1
Regular	12,739.4	27,704.2	20,123.2	10,247.9	11,199.5
Diet	5,070.0	4,375.7	2,676.4	1,881.9	
Regular and Diet			6,756.2	2,872.5	188.6
Sunkist (total)	$ 7,176.2	$ 4,013.0	$ 910.7	$ 1,719.3	$ 2,301.9
Regular	4,816.5	1,340.6	887.2	309.4	281.5
Diet	2,316.0	1,269.5	1.3		
Regular and Diet	43.7	1,402.9	22.2	1,409.9	2,020.4
Crush (total)	$ 4,371.2	$ 7,154.9	$ 4,296.7	$ 6,841.1	$ 1,853.6
Regular	3,282.7	4,712.9	2,729.8	2,561.6	1,382.2
Diet	1,004.6	2,413.1	959.4	1.2	127.7
Regular and Diet	83.9	28.9	607.5	4,278.3	343.7
Minute Maid Orange (total)	$ 174.4	$ 7,952.3	$ 9,027.2	$12,811.3	$10,463.1
Regular	174.4	7,508.2	7,211.6	9,252.5	10,191.9
Diet			1,745.1	3,450.2	
Regular and Diet		444.1	70.5	108.6	271.2

tising costs 50–50. For example, if $1 million were spent for television brand advertising, $500,000 would be paid by the brand's bottlers and $500,000 would be paid by the concentrate producer. Bottlers and concentrate producers split the cost of retail-oriented merchandise promotions and consumer promotions 50–50.

A variety of merchandising promotions are used in the soft drink industry. One kind of promotion, called a "dealer loader," is a premium given to retailers. A common form is a "display loader" such as ice chests, insulated can coolers, T-shirts, or sweatshirts, which are part of an in-store or point-of-purchase display. After the display is taken down, the premium is given to the retailer. End-of-aisle displays and other types of special free-standing displays are also provided, as are shelf banners. Concentrate producers will often allocate 10 cents (for shirts) to 20 cents (for displays) per case sold to bottlers who implement these merchandising promotions. Consumer promotions include sponsorship of local sports and entertainment events, plastic cups and napkins with the brand logo, and stylish baseball caps, T-shirts, or sunglasses featuring the brand name. Assorted other promotions are also used, including coupons, on-package promotions, and sweepstakes. Concentrate producers will offer anywhere from 5 cents (for cups, caps, or glasses) to 25 cents (for local event marketing including cups, caps, or glasses) per case sold to bottlers who use these promotions. Examples of trade and consumer promotions are shown in Exhibit 10 and Exhibit 11.

Concentrate producers occasionally offer bottlers price promotions in the form of distribution incentives. These incentives are typically based on case sales and are frequently used to stimulate bottler sales and merchandising activity. These incentives are often in the range of 15 to 25 cents per case depending on the amount of effort desired or needed.

EXHIBIT 10

Example of Crush Trade Promotion

HAVE A CRUSH ON US!
DEALER LOADERS

Item

A Crush Adventure Back Pack
B Beach Bag/Blanket
C Neon Cap
D Sony® Walkman
E Dirty Dunk®

EXHIBIT 11

Example of Crush Consumer Promotion

■ CRUSH MARKETING PROGRAM

In January 1990, several strategic marketing decisions were made concerning the Crush brand. Most notably, a decision was made to focus initial attention on the orange flavor. Even though the Crush line featured several flavors, orange (regular and diet) accounted for almost two-thirds of total Crush case volume. (Exhibit 12 shows the Crush product line.) Second, marketing executives at Cadbury Beverages, Inc. decided to focus immediate attention and effort on reestablishing the bottling network for the Crush line, particularly Orange Crush. Third, it was decided that careful consideration of Crush positioning was necessary to build on the existing customer franchise and provide opportunities for further development of the Crush brand and its assorted flavors. Finally, the executives agreed to the development of an advertising and promotion program, including the determination of objectives, strategies, and expenditures.

Bottler Network Development

Recognizing the traditional and central role that bottlers play in the soft drink industry, company marketing and sales executives immediately embarked on an aggressive effort to recruit bottlers for the Crush line. The Crush bottling network had gradually eroded in the 1980s due in part to Procter & Gamble's decision to test a distribution system for selling Crush through warehouses rather than through bottlers. This action, which centralized bottling in the hands of a limited number of bottlers that shipped product to warehouses for subsequent delivery to supermarkets and other

EXHIBIT 12

Crush Product Line

retail outlets, had led many in the Crush bottler network to question their future role with Crush. An outgrowth of this action was that Crush had the lowest market coverage of orange category sales potential among major competitors.

Recruitment efforts in early 1990 broadened the bottler network. By mid-1990, new bottling agreements had been arranged, and trade relations with 136 bottlers were established. The revitalized bottler network meant that Crush would be available in markets that represented 75 percent of total orange category sales in time for the Crush relaunch. The broadened bottler network would also require promotional support. According to Kim Feil, "We knew that reestablishing trade relations was an important first step. However, we also knew that new and existing bottlers would be gauging the kind and amount of advertising and promotional support we would provide when we relaunched Crush."

Positioning Issues

Numerous issues related to positioning were being addressed while the bottler recruitment effort was under way. First, since the company already marketed Sunkist, questions arose concerning the likely cannibalization of Sunkist sales if a clearly differentiated position for Orange Crush in the marketplace was not developed and successfully executed. A second issue concerned the relative emphasis on regular and diet Crush with respect to Mandarin Orange Slice and Minute Maid Orange. These two competitors had outpaced Crush and Sunkist in attracting the diet segment of orange drinkers. Third, viable positions had to be considered that did not run contrary to previous positionings and would build on the customer franchise currently held by Orange Crush. In this regard, a historical review of Crush positioning was conducted. The results of this effort are reproduced in Exhibit 13.

Company executives recognized that issues relating to positioning needed to be addressed in a timely manner. Without a clear positioning statement, the creative process underlying the advertising program could not be initiated.

Advertising and Promotion

Crush marketing executives were pleasantly surprised to learn that the Crush brand had high name awareness in the markets served by existing and new bottlers. According to the company's consumer awareness tracking research, of the four major brands, Crush had the highest orange-brand awareness in Seattle, San Francisco, New York, Miami, Los Angeles, Chicago, and Boston. Nevertheless, numerous issues had to be addressed concerning the Crush advertising and promotion program.

In particular, objectives for the advertising and promotion had to be established and communicated to the advertising agency that would represent Crush. Next, the relative emphasis on consumer advertising and on types of trade and consumer promotion had to be determined. Specifically, this meant setting the budget for advertising expenditures and the amounts to be spent on a per case basis for promotions. Ultimately, a *pro forma* statement of projected revenues and expenses would be necessary for presentation to senior management at Cadbury Beverages, Inc. Implicitly, this required a case volume forecast for Orange Crush that realistically portrayed market and competitive conditions and "the quality of my marketing program," said Feil.

EXHIBIT 13

Positioning of Crush, 1954–1989

Year	Positioning	Target	Campaign
1954	Natural flavor from Valencia oranges	All-family	"Naturally—it tastes better, Orange Crush"
1957–Late 1960s (est.)	Good for you; fresh juice from specially selected oranges	All-family	"Tastes so good . . . so good for you!"
1963–1964 (est.)	Introduced full line of flavors: grape, strawberry, grapefruit, root beer, cherry	All-family	No clear introduction effort: • "Thirsty? Crush that thirst with Orange Crush" • "Delicious, refreshing, satisfying—Grape Crush" • "Clean fruit taste—Grapefruit Crush" • "Mellow Crush Root Beer"
Early 1970s (est.)	Unique taste, the "change of pace" drink	All-family directed toward purchaser who is female 18–35, promotions targeted children/young adults	"Ask for Crush, the taste that's all its own."
1979–1980	Competitive taste superiority	Maintained early 1970s TV but focused on young males with sports	Added "There is no orange like Orange Crush . . ." to "Ask for Crush, the taste that's all its own."
1980	Competitive taste superiority in fruit flavors	Added new radio for 10–19 target	Same as above
1981	100% natural flavors, contemporary wholesome brand	13–39 Teens and young adults	"Orange lovers have a Crush on us"
1980–1985	Great, irresistible taste	13–39	"Orange lovers have a Crush on us"
1981–1982	Great taste	13–39	Test: "First Crush"
1983	More orangery taste	13–39	"Orange lovers"
1984	Sugar-free Crush, great taste of Nutrasweet	13–49	"Celebrate"
1986–1987	Taste with 10% real juice	Teens, 12–17	"Peel Me a Crush"
1987	The drink that breaks monotony	Teens, 12–17	Test: "Color Me Crush"
1987–1989	Bold user imagery with thirst-quenching benefit	Teens, 13–29	"Don't just quench it, Crush it"

Drypers Corporation
National Television Advertising Campaign

In late 1997, senior executives at Drypers Corporation were discussing the merits of spending upwards of $10 million on national television advertising in 1998 for its Drypers brand of disposable diapers. The matter was significant for two reasons. First, the company had not used television advertising in its 10-year history. Second, a $10 million expenditure represented a 33 percent increase in the company's combined advertising and promotion budget, which was budgeted at about $30 million in 1997.

The reasoning behind the national television advertising campaign was explained as follows:

> In the United States, diapers are highly promoted since many retailers rely on their diaper products to attract customers to their stores. In addition, Procter & Gamble and Kimberly-Clark spend a significant amount on mass media advertising to create demand for their products. In contrast, Drypers has relied more heavily on promotional spending and cooperative merchandising arrangements with retailers. Promotional activity, such as couponing, is geared toward initiating consumer trial and has been especially effective at targeting spending when less than full distribution has yet to be achieved.
>
> [Television] advertising will build consumer awareness for Drypers as a national brand that stands for quality and innovation. Awareness will boost demand, and increased demand will yield three important results. One, we will increase our penetration of grocery outlets. Two, increased grocery penetration will help mass merchants see us in a new light and help us break into this all-important retail channel. And three, we will move away from higher-cost, promotion-driven sales to brand-driven sales.

The marketing rationale for television advertising was clear. However, discussions related to the national advertising campaign, including its short- and long-term sales and brand-building effect and profit impact, continued as part of the business planning process for 1998.

■ U.S. DISPOSABLE DIAPER AND TRAINING PANTS MARKET

The market for disposable diapers and training pants is often described as infants and children, primarily below age four, who use diapers and training pants, and their mothers, primarily between the ages of 18 and 49, who decide on the brand of diapers and

---

[1]Laurie Freeman, "Flanking Maneuver," *Marketing News* (October 27, 1997): 1, 16.

[2]Drypers Corporation, *U.S. Securities and Exchange Commission Form 10-K*, for the fiscal year ended December 31, 1997, at p. 9.

[3]Drypers Corporation, *1997 Annual Report*, p. 11.

This case was prepared by Professor Roger A. Kerin, of the Edwin L. Cox School of Business, Southern Methodist University, as a basis for class discussion and is not designed to illustrate effective or ineffective handling of an administrative situation. This case is based on published sources, including the Drypers Corporation annual reports, U.S. Securities and Exchange Commission Form 10-K and 10-Q reports, company news releases, published articles, and information provided by individuals knowledgeable about the industry. The information presented in the case does not necessarily depict the explicit situation faced by Drypers Corporation, but is introduced only for class discussion purposes. Where appropriate, quotes, statistics, and published information are footnoted for reference purposes. Copyright © 1999 Roger A. Kerin. No part of this case may be reproduced without written permission of the copyright holder.

EXHIBIT 1

Trends in the U.S. Disposable Diaper and Training Pants Market

	1994	1995	1996	1997
Infants (millions): birth to 30 months	10.0	9.8	9.7	9.7
Diapers sold (billions of units)	17.2	17.2	17.3	17.5
Diaper retail dollar sales (millions)	$3,880.0	$3,825.0	$3,855.0	$3,930.0
Children (millions): 18 months to 8 years	26.1	26.3	26.3	26.2
Training and youth pants sold (millions of units)	970.0	1,070.0	1,250.0	1,410.0
Training and youth pants retail dollar sales (millions)	$485.0	$510.0	$540.0	$595.0

training pants and usually make the purchase. A baby, on average, uses five diapers per day for 30 months, for a total of 5,475 diapers. At an average retail price in the range of 18 to 27 cents per diaper, each baby represents about $1,125.00 in retail sales.

The retail dollar value of unit volume of the U.S. disposable diaper market has recorded modest growth in recent years due to the trend in fewer infants under 30 months of age and diaper improvements in absorbency and leakage control. The retail dollar value of the U.S. disposable diaper market was estimated to be $3.93 billion in 1997. The retail dollar value of the training and youth pants market was estimated to be $595 million in 1997. Trends in U.S. retail sales, diaper and training pants unit volume, and population are shown in Exhibit 1.

Distribution Channels

Disposable diapers and training pants are distributed principally through grocery stores, drugstores, and mass merchants. Grocery stores accounted for approximately $2 billion in diaper and training pants retail sales in 1997. Grocery store distribution of diapers and training pants has been decreasing as a percentage of total retail sales since 1994. Grocery stores accounted for 51.2 percent of retail sales in 1997, compared with 60 percent in 1994.

Mass merchants and drugstores recorded diaper and training pants retail sales of about $1.9 billion in 1997. Mass merchants have increased their share of total diaper and training pants retail sales from 30 percent in 1994 to 39.4 percent in 1997. The drugstore share of diaper and training pants retail sales has declined from 10 percent in 1994 to 9.2 percent in 1997.

Competitors

Manufacturers of disposable diapers and training pants are typically grouped into three general categories: (1) premium-priced branded manufacturers, (2) value-priced branded manufacturers, and (3) private-label manufacturers. Procter & Gamble and Kimberly-Clark are the leading premium-priced branded manufacturers with their well-known Pampers and Huggies premium brands, respectively. They compete on the basis of product quality, product features and benefits, and price. Both manufacturers invest heavily in research and development. For example, Kimberly-Clark pioneered the first premium training pants for children and presently captures 77 percent of this market on a unit volume basis. Procter & Gamble and Kimberly-Clark also invest heavily in consumer advertising and marketing support for their brands. In 1997, Procter & Gamble spent an estimated $69.6 million in measured media advertising for its Pampers brand; Kimberly-Clark spent $75.6 million in measured media advertising for its Huggies brand. The following is a breakdown of their media expenditures:

Manufacturer	Brand	1997 Media Advertising ($ Millions)		
		Television	Print	Total
Kimberly-Clark	Huggies	$57.2	$18.5	$75.6
Procter & Gamble	Pampers	$52.8	$16.8	$69.6

Kimberly-Clark and Procter & Gamble brands commanded an estimated 78.9 percent of total U.S. retail dollar sales of disposable diapers and training pants in 1997. The combined share of these two companies has increased since 1994 (see Exhibit 2), due in part to their extensive distribution coverage in grocery, mass-merchant, and drugstore markets. For example, both companies sell their products in stores that account for over 90 percent of U.S. diaper and training pants sales. However, Kimberly-Clark and Procter & Gamble market shares differ by distribution channel. For example, Kimberly-Clark's 1997 market share in U.S. grocery stores is an estimated 40.6 percent whereas Procter & Gamble's market share is 34.1 percent. Kimberly-Clark has an estimated 41.8 percent share of the mass merchant and drugstore channel; Procter & Gamble's share is 39.4 percent.

Value-priced branded manufacturers, such as Drypers Corporation, typically market their products through grocery stores due to their general lack of national brand-name recognition and less extensive national production and distribution capabilities necessary to supply large mass-merchant and drugstore chains. Value-priced branded manufacturers' strategies vary widely, ranging from an emphasis on quality and "good value for the money" to simply low prices. Products vary from premium-quality to low-quality diapers. Few of these manufacturers engage in extensive research and development or invest in national advertising. Instead, they rely on instore promotions and couponing, often using local or regional print advertising, and cooperative advertising and promotion programs with retailers.

Private-label manufacturers, such as Paragon Trade Brands, Inc. and Arquest, Inc. (the two largest U.S. private-label manufacturers), market their diapers and training pants under retailer-affiliated labels. These manufacturers typically emphasize lower

EXHIBIT 2

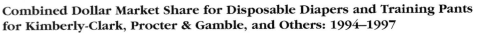

**Combined Dollar Market Share for Disposable Diapers and Training Pants
for Kimberly-Clark, Procter & Gamble, and Others: 1994–1997**

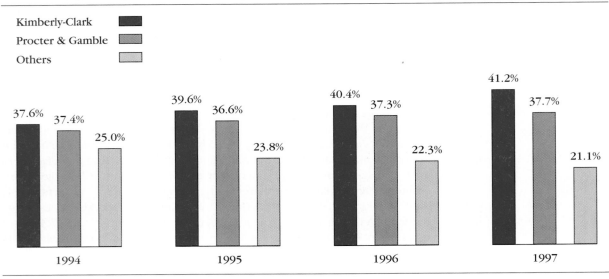

EXHIBIT 3

Dollar and Unit Market Share of Private-Label Diapers and Training Pants by Distribution Channel

| | Private Label | |
Distribution Channel	*Unit Share*	*Dollar Share*
Grocery stores	23.0%	15.9%
Drugstores	31.3	21.7
Mass merchandisers	21.5	15.3
U.S. market share for private-label diapers and training pants	23.2%	16.1%

price over quality and product features. Private-label manufacturers spend little on consumer advertising and marketing; however, retailers often promote their individual private-label brands. Private labels account for approximately 16 percent of 1997 retail dollar sales and 23 percent of unit sales for diapers and training pants. Private labels are the most prominent in the drugstore channel. The breakdown of private-label sales by channel is shown in Exhibit 3.

■ DRYPERS CORPORATION

Drypers Corporation (*www.drypers.com*) is a producer and marketer of premium-quality, value-priced disposable baby diapers and training pants sold under the Drypers brand name in the United States and under the Drypers name and other brand names internationally. The company also manufactures and sells lower-priced disposable diapers under other brand names (Comfees) in the United States and internationally, in addition to private-label diapers, training pants, and premoistened baby wipes. In 1997, branded products represent 88.9 percent of company net sales in the United States; sales of private-label and other products account for remaining sales. The company's Drypers premium-brand diapers and training pants account for 52.3 percent of total company net sales in 1997, down from 62.3 percent in 1996 and 61.3 percent in 1995. The company leases manufacturing, distribution, and administrative space in nine locations in the United States, Brazil, Puerto Rico, Argentina, and Mexico. Corporate headquarters are in Houston, Texas.

The company is the world's sixth largest producer of disposable baby diapers and the third largest marketer of brand-name disposable diapers in the United States. In 1997, the company's Drypers brand was the fourth largest selling diaper brand in the United States and the second largest selling training pants brand in U.S. grocery stores.

Company Sales and Profit History

Drypers Corporation has recorded double-digit sales growth since 1995. A tenfold increase in international sales accounted for much of the sales increase, as shown below:

	1995		*1996*		*1997*	
	(Dollars in Millions)					
Domestic[a]	$154.5	94.3%	$179.2	86.6%	$191.3	66.7%
International	9.4	5.7	27.8	13.4	95.7	33.3
Total net sales	$163.9	100.0%	$207.0	100.0%	$287.0	100.0%

[a]Domestic sales include the United States, Puerto Rico, and exports from these manufacturing operations.

The company's foreign-produced and exported products are sold in over 28 countries, but international marketing efforts have focused principally in Latin America. For example, in February 1997 the company acquired the Brazilian Puppet brand name and formed a joint venture to market this brand in Brazil. In addition, Drypers Corporation is the exclusive private-label supplier to Wal-Mart stores in Latin America and also supplies Drypers premium-branded products to Wal-Mart stores in Latin America.

The company has recorded a significant improvement in sales and profitability since 1995. In 1995, the company's financial performance was adversely affected by events outside its control.[4] Devaluation of the Mexican peso in December 1994, followed by economic uncertainty in Brazil, had a severe impact on sales and profitability. In addition, aggressive diaper promotional spending and pricing by Kimberly-Clark and Procter & Gamble in the United States and a rise in raw-material costs dampened the company's gross profit margin. These events occurred just as the company was converting its four regional U.S. brands (Drypers in the South, Baby's Choice in the West, Wee-Fits in the Midwest, and Cozies in the Northeast) into one common package design and brand name, Drypers. The lack of Drypers brand awareness in the markets previously served by regional brands materially affected sales.

Exhibit 4 shows abbreviated income statements for Drypers Corporation for the years ended December 31, 1995, 1996, and 1997. The company generated earnings before interest, taxes, depreciation, and amortization (EBITDA) of $28.8 million for 1997. This strong cash flow, along with sales growth, enabled the company to raise $115 million in capital through a bond offering. Proceeds from the issuance of bonds were used to refinance debt and finance additional production capacity in the United States and Latin America. The company's working capital stood at $48.7 million at the end of 1997.

EXHIBIT 4

Drypers Corporation Abbreviated Income Statements: 1995–1997 (Expressed as a Percentage of Net Sales)

	Year Ended December 31		
	1995	*1996*	*1997*
Net sales	100.0%	100.0%	100.0%
Cost of goods sold	69.6	60.9	61.2
Gross profit	30.4	39.1	38.8
Selling, general, and administrative expenses	32.8	34.0	31.3
Unusual expenses	1.9	—	—
Restructuring charge	2.6	—	—
Operating income (loss)	(6.9)	5.1	7.5
Interest expense, net	4.9	4.3	3.5
Other income	—	—	0.1
Income (loss) before income tax provision (benefit) and extraordinary item	(11.8)	0.8	4.1
Income tax provision (benefit)	(2.4)	0.2	0.8
Extraordinary item	—	—	(2.7)
Net income (loss)	(9.4)%	0.6%	0.6%

Source: Drypers Corporation, U.S. Securities and Exchange Commission, Form 10-K, 1997, at p. 17.

[4]Alexandra M. Biesada, "The Poop on Drypers," *Texas Monthly* (July 1996): 50ff.

Market Position

Drypers Corporation distributes its products principally through grocery stores in the United States. In 1997, the company estimated that its products were sold through 635 grocery retailers with an estimated 20,000 retail outlets. The sales of these retailers represented 66 percent of the total U.S. grocery store market for disposable diapers and training pants. In 1995, the company's distribution coverage in the grocery store channel represented 54 percent of the total U.S. grocery store market for these products. The company estimates that its brands captured 6.4 percent of the total dollar volume and 6.6 percent of the total unit volume for disposable diapers and training pants in the U.S. grocery store channel in 1997. However, in some grocery store markets, including Minneapolis, Minnesota, where Drypers are sold in grocery stores such as Super Valu and Cub Foods, the company estimates that its market share is as high as 20 percent, a figure comparable to Procter & Gamble's Pampers brand.

The company had less widespread distribution in mass-merchant and drugstore chain channels. As a consequence, Drypers' dollar market share in the total U.S. disposable diaper and training pants market is about 3.1 percent.[5] However, the company has recently obtained distribution through selected mass-merchant and drugstore chains, including Super Kmart stores of Kmart, Meijer, and Caldor. "We're trying to break into mass [merchants], to get on the shelf in Wal-Mart and Target," said Dave Olsen, Vice President of Marketing. "We're doing that by showing retailers that we really do have product differentiation in Drypers while maintaining our value position."[6] Terry Tognietti, co-CEO and President of Drypers North America, added, "What mass merchandisers want to see is that your product will move off the shelf on its own merit with little promotion, versus having them move it off the shelf for you."[7]

Marketing at Drypers Corporation

As the third largest marketer of brand-name disposable diapers in the United States, Drypers Corporation has found it necessary to compete against Kimberly-Clark and Procter & Gamble in novel ways. According to Terry Tognietti:

> We've always tried to compete with Kimberly-Clark and P&G in areas where they can't beat us by throwing money at us. When it comes to money, they beat us every time. So we need, and we try, to put ourselves in competitive situations where we are competing on ideas and quickness, not just who has the deeper pockets.[8]

Product Innovation and Pricing Drypers Corporation has demonstrated an ability to shift the ground rules in diaper marketing through product innovation. For example, in 1996 and 1997, the company was the first to introduce diapers that focused on skin care, in addition to diaper fit, absorbency, and leakage control. "We felt it was time for Drypers as a brand to begin to differentiate itself from the other brands," said Terry Tognietti. He added:

> We do not want to be just a high-quality, low-price, me-too diaper. We want consumers to buy Drypers because they're Drypers, and to do that, we've made significant strides in rolling out diapers that have different features—like the baking soda to address odor control, and the aloe vera as a skin-smoothing treatment.[9]

---

[5]Laurie Freeman, "Flanking Maneuver," *Marketing News* (October, 27, 1997): 16.

[6]*Ibid.*

[7]*Ibid.*

[8]*Ibid.*

[9]*Ibid.*

Drypers with Natural Baking Soda and Drypers with Aloe Vera, introduced in 1996 and 1997, respectively, were believed to be responsible for the increased penetration of the U.S. grocery store channel between 1995 and 1997. In addition, Drypers Corporation was presented the American Marketing Association's prestigious "Gold Edison" award in 1997 for the most innovative children's product on the basis of its Drypers with Aloe Vera product. The company also has provided value-added features to training pants, including a one-piece design and fit to make them look more like real underwear. These innovations, coupled with the addition of baking soda and aloe vera, have contributed to the company's market share in training pants. Drypers Corporation is second only to Kimberly-Clark in training pants sales, with a U.S. market share of 7.8 percent on a unit volume basis.

In 1997, Drypers Corporation entered into a licensing agreement to use the Sesame Street trademark and characters on the company's products, packaging, and advertising materials. This agreement was viewed as a validation of the company's product innovation efforts for children's products. "Children's Television Workshop is very careful who they license the Sesame Street characters to," according to Dave Olsen. "Sesame Street characters are seen as high end. That's the sizzle part."[10]

Drypers Corporation delivers on its value proposition with retail prices that are often 40 percent lower than premium-priced brands for comparable items. "Once consumers understand that our diapers are equal to the other national brands—and offered at a better price—we feel confident that we'll get our share of the diaper business," Terry Tognietti said.

Advertising, Promotion, and Sales   Drypers Corporation has historically relied on print advertising in parent-oriented magazines and regularly places coupons in daily newspapers' food sections and Sunday newspaper free-standing inserts (FSIs). The company also does large volumes of direct mail, in-store promotions, and sampling in pediatricians' offices. For example, the company ships 8,000 to 10,000 diaper samples to pediatricians annually, along with several million coupons and/or diapers to day-care centers. Drypers Corporation's combined advertising and promotion budget was about $30 million in 1997. Of this amount, $3,219,000 was spent for advertising. Advertising expense in 1996 was $1,854,000.

The company does not have a dedicated sales force in the United States. Rather, the company uses in-house managers to coordinate brokerage companies that facilitate the distribution of products through grocery stores on a nonexclusive basis. This approach has expedited the company's entry into grocery store chains and independent grocers because of the favorable long-term relationships that many of these brokers have with these retailers. The use of brokers also minimized corporate overhead expense.

■ BUSINESS PLANNING FOR 1998

Senior executives at Drypers Corporation outlined an ambitious business plan for 1998. The company was registering its strongest year ever in 1997 in terms of sales and profitability, which was reflected in the upward trend in its common stock price (Exhibit 5). The time seemed right to continue existing efforts that had yielded favorable results and pursue new initiatives. The business plan focused on six key elements:

---

[10]*Ibid.*

EXHIBIT 5

Drypers Corporation High and Low Quarterly Common Stock Price: 1996–1997

	1996		1997	
	High	Low	High	Low
Quarter:				
First	$4.13	$2.75	$4.75	$3.63
Second	4.00	2.75	7.75	3.88
Third	4.25	2.63	7.94	6.13
Fourth	5.63	3.50	9.00	5.13

The Company's common stock, $.001 par value, was listed on the NASDAQ National Market under the symbol "DYPR" from March 11, 1994, through January 28, 1996. Effective January 29, 1996, the Company's stock began trading on the NASDAQ SmallCap Market. The table sets forth, for the periods indicated, the high and low sales prices of the common stock as reported by the NASDAQ National Market and the NASDAQ SmallCap Market.

Source: Drypers Corporation, U.S. Securities and Exchange Commission, Form 10-K, 1997, at p. 12.

1. Continue product innovation to differentiate the Drypers brand.
2. Offer "Everyday Value" branded products to consumers.
3. Continue to pursue international expansion opportunities.
4. Expand product lines to include additional consumer products.
5. Provide higher-margin products for retailers.
6. Increase brand awareness and retail penetration.

Each element is described below.

Continue product innovation to differentiate the Drypers brand. Drypers Corporation has built its business on meaningful product differentiation that creates value for its customers. The 1998 business plan continued this focus with the scheduled introduction of Drypers Supreme with Germ Guard Liner in September 1998. The product would position Drypers as the only diaper in the industry to include an antibacterial treatment.

Offer "Everyday Value" branded products to consumers. Drypers Corporation's value position emphasizes premium-quality, value-priced diapers and training pants that offer consumers the recognition and reliability of a national brand coupled with product quality and features comparable to premium-priced diapers at generally lower prices. The 1998 business plan reaffirmed this value position and ongoing efforts for continuous improvement.

Continue to pursue international expansion opportunities. The international disposable diaper market is estimated to be $12 billion in annual manufacturers' sales. Growth opportunities exist in regions of the world with low consumer penetration of disposable diapers, including Latin America, the Pacific Rim, and Eastern Europe. Drypers Corporation will continue to expand its operations in Argentina, Mexico, and Brazil and seek further expansion opportunities through acquisition, joint venture, or other arrangements in the Pacific Rim and Latin America.

Expand product lines to include additional consumer products. Drypers Corporation will seek to produce and market additional high-quality consumer products that occupy specialty niches in large and fragmented consumer product categories and can be sold primarily through grocery stores, drugstores, and mass merchants. In October 1997, Drypers Corporation acquired an option to purchase NewLund Laboratories, Inc., a start-up company with a breakthrough laundry detergent technology. The technology provides a detergent, fabric softener, and static-control product in a single-sheet form. The 1998 business plan included a scheduled roll-out of this product by year-end 1998.

Provide higher-margin products for retailers. Drypers Corporation will continue to sell its products to retailers at a generally lower price than leading premium-priced national brands, which allows retailers to offer a lower price to consumers while achieving substantially higher margins. The ability to maintain attractive profit margins for retailers and a favorable price–value relationship for consumers will continue as a result of the company's ongoing emphasis in four areas: (1) delivering innovative product features that differentiate its products, (2) producing high-quality products at substantially the same cost as leading national brand manufacturers, (3) significantly lower advertising, promotion, and research and development expenditures, and (4) maintaining a low corporate overhead structure.

Increase brand awareness and retail penetration. Drypers Corporation has been building its brand equity in a deliberate manner since 1992 with consolidation of the three largest U.S.-branded regional disposable diaper producers. By 1995, the different operations, technology, and the brands themselves had been converted to Drypers. Through distinctive product innovations in 1996 and 1997, the Drypers brand had differentiated itself in the marketplace. All of these efforts have been aimed at achieving a single, clear corporate objective: full U.S. distribution of Drypers diapers and training pants. The decision to invest in a national television media campaign in 1998 by senior Drypers Corporation executives was considered a logical step toward realizing this objective: "We strongly believe that this investment in a national television campaign to build brand awareness is key to achieving full product distribution and higher overall sales."[11]

The 1998 business plan included an expenditure budget for upwards of $10 million for a national television advertising campaign in the United States. The campaign would run during the first two quarters or six months of 1998, in combination with the company's existing promotional programs. In the second half of 1998, total advertising and promotion costs, as a percentage of sales, would be reduced to preadvertising levels. It was believed that building brand recognition through advertising should allow the company to gradually reduce its dependence on direct promotional spending and should increase the distribution of Drypers brand diapers and, in turn, increase sales in the second half of 1998.

Although it was clear why an investment in a national television advertising campaign should be made and what this investment should do, discussions continued as to what a national television advertising campaign would do. Discussions related to this initiative, including its short- and long-term sales and brand-building effect and profit impact, continued as the 1998 business plan took shape.

---

[11]Drypers Corporation, *1997 Annual Report*, p. 3.

Craft Marine Corporation

In October 2001, Brayden Frank marked his first six months as vice-president of Marketing for the Craft Marine Corporation. Frank, who had joined Craft Marine after five years with a management consulting firm, had spent the first six months familiarizing himself with all aspects of the company and meeting with Craft Marine dealers. At present, he was in the process of drafting Craft Marine's 2002 advertising plan. The uncertain economic and consumer climate following the terrorist attacks on the World Trade Center in New York City on September 11, 2001, loomed large in his thinking.

Craft Marine's advertising plan for the coming year was to (1) showcase product development activities undertaken in 2001, (2) increase top-of-mind awareness among boat owners and those likely to become involved in boating, and (3) maintain the sales growth momentum of the previous year. The company had spent $2.8 million in 2001 for product development that produced three breakthroughs. First, a new hull design for 17- and 18-foot family outboard boats had been perfected and would be introduced in 2002. Second, the company had developed three 20-foot offshore boats (boats designed for saltwater usage) that were to be introduced in 2002. These boats were the first offshore models ever produced by the company. Third, the company had developed a new lightweight fishing boat. The emphasis on top-of-mind awareness had been prompted by a recent study conducted by Craft Marine, which showed that among new boat owners, the Craft Marine brand name had the lowest awareness level of the ten major brand names studied. Finally, company dollar sales had risen 15 percent in 2000 and 2001, and top management wanted to repeat this growth rate in 2002.

Although the details of the 2002 advertising program and its execution would be left to the company's advertising agency, it was Frank's responsibility to make the budgeting decision. Specifically, he would have to recommend the total advertising budget to top management and recommend how the budget was to be allocated.

■ THE COMPANY

Craft Marine Corporation was among the first companies to produce fiberglass pleasure boats. By 2001, with the company's product development efforts, Craft Marine's product line would include 32 different models in five product groups, varying from small fishing boats to cruisers. A breakdown of product groups follows:

Product Group	Number of Models
Family (pleasure)	18
Offshore	3
Cruiser	7
Fishing/water skiing	4

Craft Marine's boats are competitively priced. "The company competes on quality and performance rather than price," said Frank.

For the year ending December 31, 2001, Craft Marine Corporation would post sales of $120.5 million. After-tax earnings were expected to be $5 million.

Distribution

Approximately 95 percent of Craft Marine's sales occur in the continental United States. Canada accounts for the remaining 5 percent of sales. The company maintains trade relationships with 241 dealers. These dealers represent several competing brands of boats and marine products. The largest U.S. dealer accounted for 17 percent of total company sales. This dealer was situated in the West North Central region, which included Iowa, Kansas, Minnesota, Nebraska, and North and South Dakota. The next two largest dealers, with each accounting for 16 percent of total company sales, were located in the East North Central region (Wisconsin, Indiana, Michigan, Illinois, and Ohio). All three dealers had been selling Craft Marine boats for more than 20 years.

Historically, Craft Marine distribution had been weakest in areas where offshore boat sales were highest (for example, Florida and California). Company executives believed the introduction of the three 20-foot offshore boats in 2002 would bolster sales in these areas.

Sales and Promotion

Craft Marine's sales organization consists of a national sales manager, two regional sales managers, and a sales staff. The two regional sales managers operate east and west of the Mississippi River, respectively. Their function is to coordinate the firm's sales effort with the sales efforts of dealers.

In the past, sales promotion activities had been limited to the development and distribution of traditional accoutrements such as jackets, banners, and cups and glasses.[1] Recently, however, Craft Marine had been increasingly active in boat trade and consumer shows. Trade shows are typically scheduled in the late fall and blend into consumer shows in the winter months. Both types of shows take place at multiple locations across the country, and it is during these shows that new boat models are introduced. Craft Marine had introduced its new hull designs and offshore boats in the fall trade shows and planned to exhibit these innovations during the winter of 2002 at consumer boat shows.

As part of his more aggressive marketing strategy for 2002, Frank had expanded the sales promotion program. The expanded program included a promotion kit for company dealers, which consisted of five packages of sales promotion materials, each organized around a seasonal theme. Included in the materials were T-shirt transfers, display posters, balloons, and flags. These kits were to be made available to dealers in February 2002.

Advertising

During 2001, Craft Marine spent $600,000 for advertising, compared with $500,000 in 2000 and $415,000 in 1999. As was typical in the industry, advertising focused exclusively on print media. The percentage and dollar breakdowns for the 2001 advertising budget are shown in Exhibit 1.

Frank was sensitive to achieving parity with other national boat manufacturers in terms of advertising in vertical boating magazines, which reach dealers, boat owners, and boating enthusiasts. Although it was difficult to determine how much Craft

---

[1]Sales promotion expenditures and the cost of trade shows and consumer boat shows were paid for out of a separate budget account, according to company accounting procedures.

EXHIBIT 1

Advertising Budget for 2001

Budget Item	Expenditure	
National, vertical boating magazines[a]	$312,000	(52%)
Dealer catalogs/consumer brochures[b]	66,000	(11%)
Cooperative newspaper advertising with dealers[c]	132,000	(22%)
Production costs[d]	90,000	(15%)
	$600,000	(100%)

[a]Vertical magazines reach distribution channel members (dealers) and consumers. Examples of vertical boating magazines appear in Exhibit 5.

[b]Dealer catalogs/consumer brochures show Craft Marine's product line, including product performance specifications. These are used by dealers for point-of-sale information for prospective buyers.

[c]Cooperative advertising involves splitting newspaper advertising costs with dealers on a 50-50 basis. A typical cooperative advertisement would show Craft Marine products with a dealer tag line.

[d]Production costs include the costs of preparing advertisements and agency fees.

Marine's competition was budgeting for advertising in these magazines, the company's advertising agency provided some estimates. The agency estimated that two major competitors spent, respectively, 0.53 percent and 0.4 percent of sales in vertical boating magazines in 2001. These percentages were obtained from public announcements made by two large competitors in feature articles about the industry. Craft Marine spent 0.26 percent of sales on advertising in these publications in 2001. A color Craft Marine advertisement appeared six times in each magazine during peak sales periods.

Frank was also sensitive to the level of advertising spending in the industry as a whole. The industry average was 0.7 percent of sales.[2] Large, national manufacturers of pleasure boats spent an estimated 0.9 percent of sales on advertising, according to Craft Marine's advertising agency.

Finally, Frank was informed by his advertising agency that the major concentration of industry media dollars was spent during peak selling months. Moreover, his own observation of competitive print advertising suggested to him that advertising in the industry tended toward sameness. Most advertising featured a single model or product line. Advertisements for smaller models had a factual emphasis, whereas those for larger, more expensive, and more sophisticated models emphasized the boat's "sizzle," along with the facts. This was particularly true for cruisers. "People buy boats to escape stress and get away from on-land cares," said Frank.

■ THE U.S. PLEASURE BOAT INDUSTRY

Pleasure boat industry sales are heavily dependent on general economic conditions. Industry sales tend to reflect personal discretionary income patterns in the United States. Projected 2001 year-end sales of $25.6 billion were attributed primarily to a 13 percent increase in the price of an average new boat. Unit sales in the industry actually dropped 6 percent in 2001. Industry dollar sales were $25.5 billion in 2000 and $22.2 billion in 1999.

[2]"2001 Advertising-to-Sales Ratios for the 200 Largest Ad Spending Industries," *Advertising Age* (September 17, 2001), p. 20.

There are over 100 full-line boat manufacturers in the United States. Between 20 and 30 of these manufacturers distribute their products nationally and compete directly with Craft Marine in the continental United States. No one manufacturer holds more than a 10 percent industry market share. For example, Genmar Holdings, Inc., a leading U.S. boat manufacturer that markets the well-known Glastron, Ranger, and Wellcraft brands with more than 400 different models, had sales estimated to be $1.2 billion. (*Note*: Sales of U.S. boat manufacturers are difficult to estimate because most manufacturers are privately owned or are part of larger companies that sell a variety of products. For example, the well-known Sea Ray and Bayliner boat brands are manufactured by the Brunswick Corporation, a leader in the broad leisure products industry.)

Market Distribution and Seasonality

Geographically, boat sales are segmented by state and region. Exhibit 2 shows the distribution of boat registrations by state. Ten states account for the majority of sales. Michigan and California are the largest markets. Florida and Minnesota also represent major markets. Three regions account for over half of all sales. The East North Central Region (Illinois, Indiana, Michigan, Ohio, and Wisconsin) and the South Atlantic Region (Delaware, District of Columbia, Florida, Georgia, Maryland, North and South Carolina, Virginia, and West Virginia) each account for 20 percent of annual U.S. boat registrations. The West North Central Region (Iowa, Kansas, Minnesota, Missouri, Nebraska, and North and South Dakota) accounts for 12.5 percent of annual U.S. boat registrations

Three-quarters of retail boat sales take place between March and August, with April, May, and June being the primary purchase months. For example, boat sales typically vary from a low of 2 percent in December to a high of 15 percent in May. Accordingly, factory shipments are heaviest in February, March, April, and May, with earlier purchase agreements with dealers representing normal operating procedure for national manufacturers. Craft Marine, for instance, typically builds up boat inventories from September through February and offers an off-season price discount program to encourage prepeak purchasing by dealers. "All of our sales growth in 2001 occurred

EXHIBIT 2

Top Ten States in Boat Registrations: 2001

State	*Percentage*
Michigan	7.75
California	7.74
Florida	6.98
Minnesota	6.40
Texas	4.81
Wisconsin	4.47
New York	4.08
Ohio	3.22
South Carolina	2.96
Illinois	2.87
	51.28

Total U.S. Boat Registrations: 12.9 million

Source: Company records (based on U.S. Coast Guard data).

prior to September 11, 2001," said Frank. "November and December sales at our dealers have been virtually nonexistent and they are carrying excess inventory into the winter."

Behavior of Boat Buyers

Research on boat-buying behavior commissioned by Craft Marine in early 2001 produced a profile of boat owners and their reasons for purchasing boats. The study employed a nationwide random sample of boat owners.

According to the study, the typical boat owner was a married male in his mid- to late forties with two teenage children. The median annual household income of a boat owner was $40,450. Fishing was the most popular boating activity, followed by cruising and water skiing.

Findings dealing with boat attributes and information sources yielded a few surprises. Frank was not too surprised to see that quality of construction was easily the most important boat characteristic influencing a boat purchase (see Exhibit 3). However, he wondered how a boat buyer could presumably determine construction quality without the assistance of a dealer or a salesperson. He knew that it had taken him a few months to learn to distinguish between good and average construction quality—and he had been taught what to look for by Craft Marine's vice-president of manufacturing. He was also surprised at the relative unimportance of low price and thought this finding might be an artifact of the study. The rankings of the information sources for selecting a brand of boat were consistent with what he expected (see Exhibit 4 on page 322). Finally, Frank was particularly intrigued with three study findings:

- Of those present boat owners planning to purchase a boat in the next six months (March through August of 2001), 34 percent stated that this boat would be an 18-foot or smaller family pleasure boat, whereas 47 percent said it would be a family cruiser type.

- In all decisions except those concerning color, the husband dominated.

- Before making a purchase decision, the typical boat buyer visited a minimum of two marine dealers.

EXHIBIT 3

Product Attributes Affecting Boat Purchases

Attribute	Relative Importance
Quality of construction	100%
Performance	81
Design purpose	78
Value	68
Smooth ride	46
Service after purchase	42
Economy of operation	29
Resale value	25
Brand	19
Amount of horsepower available	9
Low price	4
Accessories included	2

Source: Company records.

EXHIBIT 4

Source of Information on Brand of Boat Purchased

Source	Relative Importance[a]
Friends and relatives	100%
Marine dealer	98
Catalog/brochure	97
Magazine advertising	93
Salesperson	86
Magazine/newspaper story	85
Newspaper advertising	69
Radio/TV advertising	67

[a]"Friends and relatives" were arbitrarily assigned a 100-percent rating.

Source: Company records.

■ THE ADVERTISING BUDGET DECISION

The 2002 advertising plan represented Frank's first major presentation to Craft Marine's president and executive committee. Therefore, the presentation meant more than merely making a request for funds. He felt that the thoroughness of the advertising plan and the logic behind it would be as important as the final budget itself. He knew that the final budget would likely be a compromise between what ideally should be done and what was realistic from a funding perspective. It also had to reflect economic realities. "It is impossible to get a fix on 2002 sales given the stagnant U.S. economy and the tragedies of September 11," Frank said. However, he felt that if he could clearly articulate the role advertising played in the marketing of boats, then his proposal might be given more careful consideration and his specific recommendations on how the budget should be allocated would carry greater weight.

The budget itself would be an itemized statement like that shown in Exhibit 1. Supplementary exhibits would document the figures reported.

At Frank's request, the advertising agency prepared for his consideration a summary of advertising in different media. Principal vertical boating magazines and general-interest magazines are described in Exhibit 5. Craft Marine had not advertised in general-interest magazines in the past due to their cost. In addition, agency personnel prepared estimates of the cost of producing dealer catalogs and consumer brochures that would feature the new hull designs, the three offshore boats, and the new fishing boat. A summary of the costs for catalogs and brochures is shown in Exhibit 6. Finally, the agency projected a 5-percent increase in cooperative advertising, given the higher costs forecasted for newspaper advertising in Craft Marine's dealer markets.

EXHIBIT 5

Comparison of Selected Media

	Major Boating Magazines		
	Boating Magazine	Yachting	Motor Boating
Frequency of Publication	Monthly	Monthly	Monthly
1 page b/w	$19,005	$14,235	$11,700
1 page color	$22,630	$15,910	$13,400
Circulation	202,265	133,899	153,282
Editorial description	The most general boating magazine.	Covers both sail and power boats, lists major events, and describes new products.	For the boat owner/yacht interested in entertainment.

	General-Interest Magazines*			
	Business Week	Time	National Geographic	Sports Illustrated
Frequency of Publication	Weekly	Weekly	Monthly	Weekly
1 page b/w	$57,400	$128,100	$135,130	$133,000
1 page color	$85,000	$183,000	$156,755	$190,000
Circulation	923,786	4,122,699	10,000,000	3,251,117
Editorial description	For management news as it affects business.	Gives national affairs news briefs.	International in scope; cultural environment, scientific information.	Reports on sports, recreation, and leisure.

*Note: All cost and circulation estimates are based on national distribution.
Regional issues are also available, which cost from 15 to 25 percent of national coverage costs.

Source: Company records.

EXHIBIT 6

Catalog and Brochure Cost Estimates

Catalog		Brochure	
Units Produced	Cost	Units Produced	Cost
500	$10,000	5,000	$ 25,000
1,000	18,000	10,000	45,000
1,500	24,000	15,000	63,700
2,000	28,000	20,000	80,000
2,500	30,000	25,000	93,750
		30,000	105,000

Orders over 2,500 would be priced at $12.00 per hundred.

Orders over 30,000 would be priced at $3.00 per thousand.

Note: Catalogs and brochures for 2002 would be in color and feature new hull designs, offshore models, and the new fishing boat. Catalogs would include all new products, including photos and boat specifications. Catalogs would be three-hole punched for inclusion in dealer binders and also be available to boat buyers. Brochures would be individually produced for the new hull designs, offshore models, and the new fishing boat, respectively (e.g., 5,000 brochures for offshore models, 5,000 brochures for the new hull designs, and 5,000 brochures for the new fishing boat). Brochures would typically contain 2 or 4 pages.

Godiva Europe

In July 1991, Charles van der Veken, President of Godiva Europe, examined with satisfaction the financial results of Godiva Belgium for the last period, which showed an operating profit of 13 million Belgian francs. "We've come a long way," he thought to himself, remembering the financial situation he inherited just one year ago, which showed a loss of 10 million francs.[1] Over the course of the past year van der Veken had completely restructured the company. He started by firing the marketing and sales staff and then changed the retail distribution network by removing Godiva's representation from numerous stores. He then completely rethought the decoration and design of the remaining stores, and established precise rules of organization and functioning applicable to those stores. These changes made the Godiva–Belgium network of franchises comparable to those in the United States and Japan. For, while in all other countries Godiva stores conveyed an image of luxury and of high scale products, in Belgium, where the Godiva concept was originally conceived, this image was scarcely maintained. Fearing what he called the "boomerang effect," van der Veken had first focused on restructuring the Godiva retail network, an objective that was today on the road to realization. "It is time," thought van der Veken, "to communicate the desired image of Godiva more widely, now that we have a retail network capable of maintaining that image on the level of the Triad Countries."[2]

■ THE GODIVA EUROPE COMPANY

Godiva has its roots in Belgium, where the handcrafting of chocolates stems from a long tradition. Joseph Draps, founder of Godiva in the 1920s, took control of the family business upon the death of his father and created an assortment of prestigious chocolates for which he lacked a name. He finally chose the name "Godiva" because it had an international sound and a history, that of Lady Godiva:

> Lady Godiva is the heroine of an English legend. She was the wife of Leofric, Count of Chester in the 11th century, whom she married around 1050. Roger de Wendower (13th century) tells that Godiva implored Leofric to lower the taxes that were crushing Coventry. The Count would not consent unless his wife would walk through the town completely naked, which she did, covered only by her long hair. John Brompton (16th century) added that nobody saw her. According to a ballad from the 17th century, Godiva ordered all the inhabitants to remain at home. The only one to see her was an indiscreet Peeping Tom. Since 1678, every three years in Coventry, a Godiva Procession is held (Grand Larousse, Vol. 5, p. 522).

Godiva was purchased in 1974 by the multinational Campbell Soup Company. Godiva International is made up of three decision centers: Godiva Europe, Godiva USA,

---

[1] In 1991, 34 Belgian francs (bf) = $1.00 U.S.

[2] The Triad Countries include the United States, Japan, and countries in Western Europe.

This case study was prepared by Professeur Jean-Jacques Lambin, of Louvain University, Louvain-la-Neuve, Belgium, with the cooperation of Jean-Francois Buslain and Sophie Lambin. Certain names and data have been disguised, and the case cannot be used as a source of information for market research. Used with permission.

EXHIBIT 1

Campbell Soup Organizational Structure

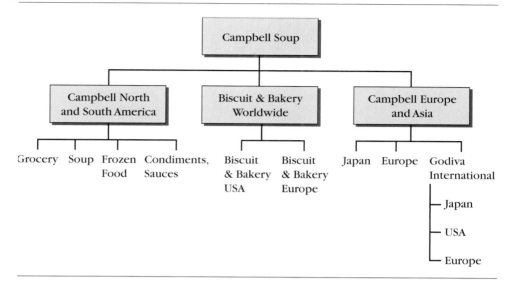

and Godiva Japan, as shown in Exhibit 1. An essentially Belgian company in the beginning, Godiva has become an almost entirely triadic enterprise with a presence in the United States, Japan, and Western Europe.

Godiva Europe is headquartered in Brussels, Belgium. The company's factory, which has 3,000 tons of annual production capacity, is also situated in Brussels, from where products are exported to more than 20 countries throughout the world, including Japan. There is another production unit in the United States, which can provide about 90 percent of the needs of the U.S. market, with the remainder being imported from Belgium.

In 1990, Godiva Europe had annual sales of 926 million Belgian francs. The company is well placed to serve Belgium, its largest market. After Belgium, the principal European markets are France, Great Britain, Germany, Spain, and Portugal. Godiva USA and Godiva Japan distribute Godiva products to their respective markets and constitute the two other most important markets.

The largest part of European production volume (55 percent) is sold under the Godiva brand name, about 10 percent is sold through private labels arrangements, and another 10 percent is sold under the brand Corné Toison d'Or; 25 percent of Godiva Europe's production is sold directly to Godiva Japan and Godiva USA at a company transfer price. Thus, only 65 percent of the total sales are made in Europe under the brand name Godiva. A significant share of Godiva Europe's sales is made through more than 20 airport duty-free shops throughout the world. Those sales, free of a value-added tax (VAT), are made at the expense of local country sales, but they help to establish the international image of Godiva.[3]

Godiva Europe also owns the Corné Toison d'Or brand, which is distributed through 40 stores in Belgium, which are mostly located in the Brussels area. This brand has an image very similar to Godiva: a refined, handmade, luxury product. The acquisition of Corné Toison d'Or was made in 1989 to fully exploit the production capacity of the Brussels plant modernized two years earlier. The original objective

---

[3]A value-added tax is a government tax levied upon the value that is added to products as they progress from raw material to consumer goods.

was to differentiate the positioning of the brand Corné Toison d'Or from Godiva, but this objective was never pursued by management. A further complication stemmed from the fact that another Corné brand, Corné Port Royal, also exists in the Belgian market with a retail network of 18 stores.

Godiva USA has a factory in Pennsylvania that serves the U.S. market. Godiva Japan, which is solely concerned with marketing, distribution, and sales of Godiva chocolates, imports the product from Belgium. The Japanese market is very important for Godiva International because of the price level, 4,000 bf per kilogram compared to 2,000 bf in the United States, and 1,000 bf in Belgium.[4]

The reference market of Godiva International consists of the Triad Nations. As a branch of Campbell Soup Company, Godiva benefits from a privileged position. Godiva International is directly attached to the Campbell Soup Company Vice President Europe-Asia without an intermediary.

■ THE WORLD CHOCOLATE MARKET

Unlike coffee or tea, chocolate lends itself to multiple preparations. It can be eaten or drunk, munched or savored. The official journal of the European Community divides chocolate into four categories: bars of chocolate that are filled or not filled, chocolate candies or chocolates (called "pralines" in Belgium) such as Godiva's chocolates, and other chocolate preparations.

Chocolate consumption stabilized in the mid-1980s as a result of increasing raw material costs and an ensuing price rise of finished products. As depicted in Exhibit 2, the past three years have shown very good performances with worldwide consumption of confectionery chocolate (all categories included) of just over 3 million tons in 1989, or an increase of 30.7 percent compared with 1980 consumption. Overproportional consumption was observed in Japan (+54.2 percent), Italy (+102.1 percent), Australia (+45.1 percent), and the United States since 1980.

A distinction is made between industrial and chocolate pralines within the chocolate candies category. Industrial chocolates are sold in prewrapped boxes with or without brand names. The generic boxes are mostly sold through large retail chains at Christmas or Easter; brand boxes are luxurious, offer a high-quality assortment of chocolates, and emphasize the brand name on the package and through mass-media advertising. Typical of this subcategory is the brand Mon Chéri from Ferrero. The sales of generic boxes are stable in Europe, while sales of brand boxes are increasing. This suggests that consumers pay attention to brand names and to the quality image communicated by chocolate packaging and advertising.

Chocolate pralines, on the other hand, designate chocolate products that are handmade or decorated by hand. The distinctive characteristics of pralines are their delicate flavor and luxurious packaging. They are also highly perishable and fragile

EXHIBIT 2

Chocolate Confectionery World Consumption (In Thousands of Tons)

Year	1980	1985	1986	1987	1988	1989
Tons	2,359.6	2,778.1	2,780.2	2,862.0	2,990.8	3.083.6
Index	100	118	118	121	127	131

Source: IOCCC, December 1990, p. 45.

[4]1 kilogram = 2.205 pounds.

with regard to conservation and transport. Typically, Godiva chocolates belong to this last product category.

Chocolate Consumption per Country

The per capita consumption of chocolate varies among countries as shown in Exhibit 3. Chocolate consumption is higher in the northern part of Europe and lower in the Mediterranean region. In 1990, Switzerland had the highest per capita consumption, with 9.4 kilograms per person. The lowest per capita consumption rate is observed in Spain, with 1.2 kilograms per person.

Exhibit 3 also shows that the share of chocolate candies (namely, pralines) with respect to total chocolate confectionery consumption, is strongest in Belgium, with 44 percent against 41 percent in Great Britain, 37 percent in France, 35 percent in Italy, and 34 percent in Switzerland. Switzerland is the largest consumer of chocolate candies, followed closely by the United Kingdom and Belgium, while the other countries are found far behind these three leaders.

In examining the level of consumption reached in countries such as Switzerland, the United Kingdom, and Belgium, it is possible to get an idea of the enormous potential that the world chocolates market holds. In fact, countries like Spain, Italy, and Japan are susceptible to one day reaching such a level of consumption roughly comparable to Switzerland, the United Kingdom, and Belgium provided effective marketing programs are implemented. Available industry statistics do not allow more precise estimates of the share of "chocolate pralines" in the category of chocolate candies.

Evolution of Consumption

Growth rates of chocolate confectionery are also very different among countries as shown in Exhibit 4. Countries experiencing the highest growth rates are Italy, Japan, the United Kingdom, and the United States. With the exception of the United Kingdom, these are the countries where the per capita consumption is the lowest. The largest consumer countries like Belgium, Germany, and Switzerland have probably reached a plateau in terms of per capita consumption.

EXHIBIT 3

Chocolate Confectionery Consumption per Country

Country	Per Capita Consumption in Kilograms in 1989		Share of Chocolates in Confectionery Chocolate
	Chocolate Candies	Chocolate Confectionery	
Belgium	2.65	6.09	43.5%
Denmark	1.17	5.61	20.9%
France	1.69	4.59	36.8%
Spain	0.14	1.21	11.6%
Italy	0.65	1.84	35.3%
Japan	0.44	1.59	27.8%
German Federal Republic	1.64	6.81	24.1%
Switzerland	3.17	9.41	33.9%
United Kingdom	2.96	7.15	41.4%
United States	1.14	4.77	23.9%

Source: IOCCC, Statistical Bulletin, Brussels, December 1990. Chocolate candies: candy bars, pralines, and other chocolate products. Solid and filled bars and chocolate products.

EXHIBIT 4

Evolution of Chocolate Confectionery Consumption: Average Yearly Growth Rates, 1980–1989

Country	Consumption (Kilograms per Person)		Average Growth	
	1980	1989	1980 = 100	Average Growth Rate
Belgium	6.04	6.09	100.8	1.76%
Denmark	4.80	5.61	116.9	1.79%
France	3.96	4.59	115.9	1.65%
Spain	nd	1.21	nd	—
Italy	0.92	1.84	200.0	8.00%
Japan	1.09	1.59	145.9	4.28%
German Federal Republic	6.56	6.81	103.8	0.42%
Switzerland	8.44	9.41	111.5	1.22%
United Kingdom	5.48	7.15	130.5	3.00%
United States	3.69	4.77	129.3	2.89%

nd = no data.

Source: IOCCC, December 1990, p. 49.

Purchase Behavior of the Chocolate Consumer

Chocolate was imported to Europe by the Spanish at the time of the exploration of the New World. At that time, only the wealthy ate chocolate.

Today, chocolate is a mass-consumption product, accessible to everyone. Consumers are demanding and desire variety. In making chocolate a luxury product, chocolatiers have given chocolates a certain nobleness. The hand-worked character of production and refined decoration give chocolates their status. Chocolates are offered at holidays and other special occasions, and are eaten among friends in an atmosphere of warmth. They are not purchased like bars of chocolate; the behavior of the consumer of chocolate pralines is much more deliberate and involved. The higher prices of chocolate pralines with respect to the other categories of chocolate do not inhibit the consumer but limit more impulsive purchases.

The consumption of chocolate of all categories is associated with pleasure. A qualitative study of the Belgian market shows that this pleasure is associated with the ideas of refinement, taste pleasure, and gift:". . . chocolate pralines are offered as a gift while chocolate bars are purchased for self-consumption. A praline would be mainly feminine, . . . women seem to appreciate them more and pralines are described by them as refined and fine." In addition, the strong and powerful taste, a particular form, the consistency of chocolate that melts in the mouth, and the feel of the chocolate to the touch are also factors to which the consumer is sensitive. Finally, the idea of health, of a pure product devoid of chemicals, is also in the consumer's mind.

■ GODIVA CHOCOLATES IN THE WORLD

The ancestry of chocolates can be traced to the chef of the Duke of Choiseul de Plessis-Praslin, an ambassador of Louis XIII of France, when he prepared almonds browned in caramelized sugar. However, chocolates as we know them today, a filling surrounded by chocolate, were born in Belgium. It was at the end of the nineteenth century that Jean Neuhaus, son of a confectioner from Neuchatel living in Brussels, created the first chocolates that he named "pralines."

The current concern of Godiva International is to convey a similar image of Godiva chocolates across the world: the image of a luxury chocolate that is typically Belgian. In what follows, the main characteristics of consumers in each country where Godiva is distributed will be briefly presented.

Belgium

Belgium is the birthplace of chocolates and where their consumption is strongest. While there are no significant differences in the consumption rate among the different Belgian regions, differences do exist among the four main socioprofessional categories, as shown in Exhibit 5.

In 60 percent of purchases, chocolates are offered as gifts, and consumers make a clear distinction between a purchase for self-consumption and for a gift. The customer prefers a package where he or she may select the assortment. However, the image of chocolate pralines has aged; chocolates have become a product more comparable to flowers than to a luxury product. The results of a brand image study conducted in the Brussels area (see Appendix A) shows that, while Godiva is strongly associated with the items "most expensive," "nicest packaging," and "most beautiful stores," it is not clearly perceived as very different from its main competitors, Neuhaus mainly, on items associated with superior quality or a significant quality differential. Neuhaus and Corné, two directly competing brands, are perceived in a very similar way, as shown in the perceptual map presented in Exhibit 6.

In Belgium, Godiva holds a 10 percent market share and Léonidas 43 percent. Léonidas also has a large international coverage with more than 1,500 outlets throughout the world and a production capacity of 10,000 tons, or three times that of Godiva Europe. In 1991, the size of the total Belgian market for chocolate pralines was estimated to be 3.6 billion Belgian francs (VAT included) or about 8,800 tons. This estimate is based on the data presented in Exhibit 5.

France

French chocolate is darker, drier, and more bitter than Belgian chocolates. Belgian chocolates are, however, well known and appreciated due to Léonidas, which introduced chocolates in France and today holds the largest market share and sells through 250 boutiques. Belgian chocolates are represented as well by Jeff de Bruges, which belongs to Neuhaus. Godiva has a share in a small niche, which is also occupied by several French chocolatiers, none of whom have national market coverage. In France, chocolates are above all regarded as a gift that is offered on certain special occasions, and their purchase is very seasonal (60 percent of all purchases are made at Christmas), which poses problems of profitability during periods of lower sales. Estimates of market size are presented in Exhibit 7.

EXHIBIT 5

The Demand for Pralines in Belgium: Average Expenditures per Household in 1988 (bf)

Regions	Belgium	Brussels	Wallonie	Flanders
	814	884	812	793
Households	Independent	White Collar	Blue Collar	Inactive
	1,239	800	567	755

Source: INS, Enquête sur less budgets des ménages (1988). The total population includes 3,876,549 households.

EXHIBIT 6

Brand Image Study: Chocolate Pralines in Belgium (Bubble Area = Awareness)

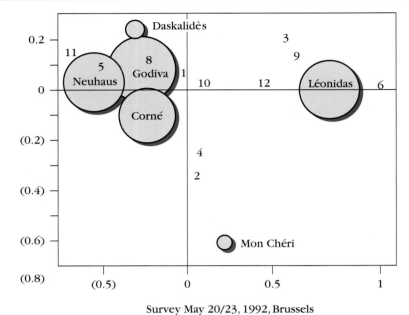

1. Queen of chocolate
2. Ideal for gift
3. For self-indulgence
4. Special occasions
5. Beautiful boutique
6. Attractive price
7. Nice packaging
8. Refined chocolate
9. Belgian chocolate
10. Taste I like best
11. Expensive chocolate
12. Worldly known brand

Survey May 20/23, 1992, Brussels
Sample Size = 128

United Kingdom

An assortment of confectionery products, in which different types of chocolate are mixed, is most appreciated in the United Kingdom. Godiva is currently being introduced to the British market and seeks to create the concept of high-quality and more refined Belgian chocolates. The change in mentality is progressing, but the British are viewed as rather conservative and the economic climate is not very favorable for a luxury product. Marks and Spencer, an upscale British retailer, is selling Belgian chocolates under the private brand name Saint Michael. The Belgian origin of the chocolates is clearly indicated in the packaging, however.

EXHIBIT 7

Estimated Consumption of Chocolates in France, 1988–1990 (In Tons)

Year	1988	1989	1990
Production	44,302	47,660	50,720
Imports (+)	9,677	10,478	11,546
Exports (−)	3,788	5,739	7,970
Total consumption	50,191	52,399	54,365
Per capita consumption	0.900 kg	0.935 kg	0.965 kg

Source: "Production des IAA," SCEES (Décembre 1991): 61 (bonbons de chocolat); Eurostat "Foreign Trade"—Categories; 1806.90.11 and 1806.90.19. The category "bonbons de chocolat" includes other products than chocolate pralines. Thus, total consumption is overestimated.

Spain and Portugal

In Spain and Portugal, chocolate pralines are a completely new concept. Godiva was the first to introduce chocolates a few years ago, and the reception was excellent. Godiva chocolates immediately acquired the image of a refined, luxury product. In Spain, Godiva is sold through the upscale department store Corte Inglese and by several franchises. Consumers' attitudes toward chocolate is very positive. Chocolates are principally offered as gifts and most often in luxurious boxes.

Germany

In Germany, a "chocolates culture" does not really exist. Germans appear to be satisfied with a classic chocolate bar and do not yet place much importance on the distinctive qualities of fine chocolates. Godiva pralines are distributed through five franchised dealers.

Other European Countries

In Holland, chocolate pralines are perceived as too expensive. In Italy and in the Nordic countries, chocolate praline consumption is still a very marginal phenomenon.

United States

Chocolates are very popular in the United States. Chocolates are given as presents on special occasions such as birthdays, Valentine's Day, and Christmas. Chocolates are typically offered in prewrapped packages, with an interior form to house them. The output of the Godiva facility in Pennsylvania almost suffices to cover the needs of present domestic consumption. A small proportion of the Brussels plant output is exported to the United States. The Belgian factory delivers only new products or some products that cannot be produced by the Pennsylvania plant, such as the Godiva golf balls and the chocolate cartridges. In addition to 95 company-owned stores, 800 outlets carry Godiva chocolates in the United States. These outlets are generally located in upscale department stores situated in suburban shopping malls, like Lord & Taylor, Neiman Marcus, Saks Fifth Avenue, Filenes, and I Magnin.

Japan

In Japan, the Godiva chocolate is perceived foremost as European (60 percent as Belgian and 40 percent as Swiss or French). Chocolates are a prestigious and luxury gift. A large problem of seasonality exists in Japan as 75 percent of purchases take place near Valentine's Day. A unique feature of this market is that Japanese women give Japanese men chocolates on Valentine's Day. The Japanese market is a very attractive market for Godiva International and is still expanding.

The Duty-Free Market

In addition to these countries, one must also include the duty-free market, which represents a very significant market segment in terms of output. The number of duty-free stores is still increasing, and sales are closely linked to the development of passenger traffic. Godiva holds a very strong position in this market where Léonidas is not present.

Generally speaking, the annual growth potential in Europe is very different and varies from country to country. In the United States, growth varies between 5 and 10 percent annually, while in Japan growth is very strong, varying between 20 and 25 percent annually.

■ GODIVA'S MARKETING STRATEGY

Godiva pralines are produced by four means of fabrication: those that are formed in a mold, those that are hollowed then filled, those where a solid filling is coated with chocolate, and finally those that are produced entirely by hand: handmade chocolates. Seventy percent of Godiva pralines are machine-made, and 30 percent are handmade. However, 60 percent of the 70 percent machine-made chocolates must be decorated by hand. Hand decoration is necessary to assure the quality level and the look of the praline.

Godiva strives to find an optimal compromise between automation and handwork, hoping both to ensure the profitability and to perpetuate the name of Godiva as a producer of handmade luxury chocolates. However, the difference in production costs between machine-made and handmade chocolates is considerable (handmade chocolates can cost up to seven times more than machine-made). Charles van der Veken often had second thoughts about the wisdom of maintaining this product policy. He thought:

> Isn't the investment in making hand-made chocolates disproportional to the expectations of our customers? Do they really perceive the added value of these handmade chocolates? Aren't these chocolates just a bit too sophisticated?

Whatever the case, the objective pursued by Godiva is to convert the European market to the quality level of the Godiva praline. The Belgian consumer is the reference point: "Shouldn't a product that has passed the test of the Belgian consumer, a fine connoisseur of chocolate and a demanding customer, be assured of success throughout the world?"

The Godiva facility in Belgium produces chocolates for the entire world, with the exception of the United States. Products exported from Belgian are identical for all countries, but sales by item are different. For example, in France the demand for drier and more bitter chocolates is stronger, while in the United Kingdom cream and white chocolates are more popular. The production capacity of the Belgian factory is not fully utilized, and there is a significant available capacity. Today, the U.S. factory still produces a slightly different and more limited assortment of chocolate pralines. These differences will progressively vanish, and the trend is toward similar production. The planning of production is particularly complex, however, because of the high seasonality of consumption combined with the emphasis on chocolate freshness.

Packaging Policy

Only packaging will distinguish one country from another in order to better meet national and local chocolate consumption habits. In the United States, the tradition is to purchase chocolates prewrapped, while in Europe and Japan the custom-made assortment dominates. What's more, in Japan, chocolates are purchased in very small quantities (given the price); thus, the beauty of the packaging becomes predominant, whereas in Europe and more precisely in Belgium, the value of the gift is more often related to the judicious assortment of chocolates that was chosen. As stated by a Godiva dealer, "Customers have very precise ideas on the type of assortment they want, even for gifts, and they don't like to buy prewrapped standard assortments."

Currently, the trend in packaging at Godiva is packaging by themes called "collections." With these "collections," Godiva leaves the food industry for the luxury products sector. These handmade creations constitute a research and development activity that ensures continuous innovation and provides renewed promotional displays in the Godiva boutiques. In these "collections," beautiful fabric boxes, handcrafted according to the principles of "haute couture," will illustrate through the calendar Valentine's Day, Spring, Easter, Mother's Day, Christmas, and so on. In Belgium, the price of such a box (1,000 bf) is exorbitant with respect to the price of the chocolates; thus, these boxes serve more often for in-store decoration than for sales.

EXHIBIT 8

Price of One Kilo of Godiva Pralines (bf)

Country	Price to Franchisees	Retail Price (VAT Included)	VAT (%)
Belgium	640	1,080	6.0
France	763	1,920	18.6
Spain	640	2,145	6.0
United Kingdom	757	1,782	17.5
Italy	640	2,009	9.0
Holland	640	1,261	6.0
Germany	640	1,641	7.0
Portugal	640	2,408	16.0
United States	na	2,040	—
Japan	na	4,000	—

Source: Trade publications.

For several years, Godiva has also tried to develop tea rooms attached to Godiva boutiques where customers can eat fine pastries or ice cream. The people who stop here see these rooms as havens of peace where they can rest between purchases while shopping and buy a few chocolates or even a box of chocolates.

Pricing Policy

Making a Godiva chocolate requires an enormous amount of manual labor and the gross margins are modest (35 to 40 percent on average). Top management of Campbell Soup requires a 15 percent rate of return on capital invested for Godiva, a normal rate of return for a luxury product.

From one country to another, the price differences are great, as shown in Exhibit 8. One of the main preoccupations of Godiva Europe is to standardize retail prices at the European level, in view of the unified European Union in 1993.

Previously, Godiva franchisees were held to a contract with the Godiva organization and had to be supplied within that country. From 1993 on, it will no longer be possible to keep French franchisees from getting their supplies directly from the Belgian factory, which sells its chocolates at a much lower price. This is why prices must be modified. This adaptation has been started in Belgium, with a 10 percent increase in prices effective August 1, 1991. The price of one kilo of Godiva chocolates is 1,080 bf, whereas the average market price for chocolates in Belgium is 450 bf per kilo.

This price policy, however, has not been easily accepted by the market, particularly in Belgium, where the price gap between the high and the low end of the market is already very large (see Exhibit 9). Charles van der Veken observed that, in Belgium, a 10 percent price increase has generated a loss in volume of about 7 percent. He is also aware that this lost volume goes to Léonidas for the most part.

Distribution Policy

The ultimate goal that Godiva is pursuing in its distribution policy is to obtain across the world something akin to the Benetton model: boutiques with a uniform look. This "look" includes a logo with golden letters on a black background, a facade incorporating these same colors, interior fixtures in pink marble, glass counters, and so forth.

The current retail distribution problem lies in the great disparity between the Godiva boutiques in different countries, mainly in Europe and even more particularly

EXHIBIT 9

Retail Price Comparison Among Brands

Belgium		France		United Kingdom	
Brands (bf/kg)	Price	Brands (ff/kg)	Price	Brands (£/lb)	Price
Godiva	1,080	Godiva	320	Godiva	13.50
Neuhaus	980	Hédiard	640	Gérard Ronay	20.00
Corné PR	880	Fauchon	430	Valrhona	16.80
Corné TO	870	Maison ch.	390	Charbonel	14.00
Daskalidès	680	Le Notre	345	Neuhaus	12.00
Jeff de Bruges	595	Fontaine ch.	327	Léonidas	6.75
Léonidas	360	Léonidas	120	Thorton's	5.80

in Belgium (Exhibit 10 shows the Godiva distribution network). Through the years the boutiques in Belgium have become less and less attractive. As a consequence, the Godiva brand image has aged. Abroad, however, Godiva benefits from an extremely prestigious image, and the boutiques merit their name. Nevertheless, Charles van der Veken fears the worst:

> If we don't react quickly, we could compromise the world brand image of Godiva. What would a Spanish tourist think in comparing the boutique of a local distributor in Brussels to the refined boutiques that he finds in Spain, although Belgium is the birthplace of chocolates?

Godiva's retail distribution action plan for Belgium covers a period of 18 months. A contract has been made with the franchisees in which Godiva imposes both exclusivity and design; all the boutiques must have completed renovation. Once the movement is well established in Belgium, Godiva hopes this will create a spillover effect to

EXHIBIT 10

The Godiva Distribution Network

Country	Company-Owned Stores	Franchised Dealers	Department Stores and Others	Total Outlets
Belgium	3	54	—	57
France	1	19	—	20
Spain	—	6	18	24
United Kingdom	2	—	15	17
Italy	—	2	—	2
Holland	—	2	—	2
Germany	—	4	1	5
Portugal	—	3	7	10
Total Europe	6	90	41	137
United States	95	—	800	895
Japan	—	22	67	89

Source: Trade publications and yellow pages.

all of Europe, because the new boutiques will constitute a reference for the recruitment of new franchisees or for spontaneous requests for renovations.

This renovation movement has already begun and every two weeks a "new" boutique is inaugurated. The renovated boutiques have been transformed so that everything is in black and gold, and the entire interior decoration is redone according to the same single standard of luxury.

Generally, consumer reactions in Belgium seem favorable, although in certain respects consumers find the stores almost too beautiful. As for the franchisees, they feel as though they have a new business, and appear to be changing some of their former bad habits. If the effects remain favorable in the medium term, van der Veken said he will increase the margin provided to franchisees, which is still different from one country to the other (see Exhibit 8).

The Chairman of Godiva International, Mr. Partridge, has frequently questioned the wisdom of this costly exclusive distribution system because he believes chocolate is not really a destination purchase. In Europe, the adoption of a broader distribution system is difficult, however, because of the reluctance of consumers vis-à-vis prewrapped assortments of chocolates. Van der Veken is convinced, however, that the Godiva boutique is a key component of the Godiva image of a luxury good.

The Competitive Environment

The handmade luxury chocolate segment is occupied by many other brands. Exhibit 11 presents a ranking of the specialty brands for Belgium, France, and the United Kingdom, in descending order of market share. The strength of the Léonidas competitive position in Europe is clearly shown by this comparison. Léonidas was created in 1910. It did for chocolate pralines what Henry Ford did for the car: a mass-consumption product sold at a low price. Their recipe is simple: a price of 360 bf per kilogram, 8,600 square meters of industrial space, a production capacity of 10,000 tons. Léonidas is a very important competitor for Godiva. With total sales of over 2.6 billion Belgian francs, and a 32 percent operating profit margin, Léonidas has 1,500 stores worldwide, and is now expanding rapidly in the international market. The next major competitor is Neuhaus, which recently merged with Mondose and Corné Port Royal and which is also pursuing an international development strategy. The "others" include the many small confectionery chocolatiers who nibble at the market share of the larger companies in offering fresh, original products made from pure cocoa.

However, given its broad market coverage, Charles van der Veken believes that Godiva has a significant competitive advantage due to its integration into Campbell Soup 13 years ago, which provided Godiva with an opportunity for global expansion

EXHIBIT 11

Main European Competitors

Belgium		France		United Kingdom	
Brands	*Share*	*Brands*	*Share*	*Brands*	*Tons*
Léonidas	42.8%	Léonidas	62.0%	Thornton's	1,200
Godiva	10.3	Thornton's	18.0	Léonidas	300
Neuhaus	7.1	Jeff de Bruges	14.0	Godiva	40
Mondose	5.4	Godiva	3.0		
Corné TO	2.7	Le Notre	1.0		
Others	31.7	Others	2.0		

Source: Industry trade publications (market shares are calculated on sales revenues).

much more quickly than its competitors. Thus, Godiva is present everywhere, and even if it often skirts a competitor in a particular market, it is rarely the same one across the world. Godiva can thus currently be considered the global leader in the luxury chocolate segment.

Only in Belgium is Godiva having difficulties making use of its competitive advantage. The volume growth has proven important everywhere, except in Belgium. According to Charles van der Veken, the market is already too saturated, and it is up to the best to make the difference.

Advertising Strategy

Today, Godiva does not need to make itself known on the international level: Its brand name is already globally recognized. Its current concern, in line with the policy that has been pursued for the past several months, is to create a common advertising message for the entire world. However, this will not be an easy task, as evidenced by a comparison of the situation in Belgium, the United States, and Japan. In the United States and Japan, the product is relatively new and has a strong image inasmuch as there is no direct competitor. In Belgium, the consumer has followed the evolution of Godiva chocolates and the progressive commoditization of the brand. It is therefore more difficult to impress Belgians with a product that is already well known. What's more, Belgians are in daily contact with other brands of chocolates, with which they can easily compare Godiva.

Thus, as van der Veken pointed out, Godiva finds itself faced with very different worlds. Until now, in the United States advertising was focused on prestige, luxury, and refinement, with a communication style similar to the one adopted by Cartier, Gucci, or Ferrari. These advertisements were presented in magazines well adapted to the desired positioning: gourmet, fashion, or business magazines that cater to higher-income echelons (see Exhibit 12).

In Belgium, however, this type of advertising tended only to reinforce the aged, grandmotherish image of Godiva chocolates. What's more, the gap between the "perceived image" (a food item interchangeable with others of the same type) and the "desired image" (an exceptional luxury product) was so large that spectacular results could not be expected.

A study performed by Godiva seems to show that nobody could remember these advertisements, nor the promises that were made. In Belgium, Godiva had also made use of event marketing: being represented at events at which the target population had a large chance of being present. Thus, two years ago, Godiva was the sponsor of a golf competition in Belgium that held its name (Godiva European Masters). Such actions are, however, extremely costly, and their effectiveness is difficult to measure. The total advertising budget of Godiva Europe is 31 million Belgian francs per year.

■ THE ADVERTISING DECISION

Aware of this problem, Godiva Europe is in the process of evaluating its advertising strategy. The following situation had to be solved: creating a common advertising message targeted at the three main markets while taking into consideration the inevitable cultural differences among countries.

Godiva USA had just sent Charles van der Veken the briefing of an international advertising campaign, which is summarized in Exhibit 13. He said that adopting this advertising style on the European market worried him to a certain degree:

> The least one can say is that differences of mentality exist between our two continents. We certainly need to wake up our old-fashioned Godiva, but we should also be careful of overly radical changes.

EXHIBIT 12

Typical Godiva Print Advertisement in the United States

SPEND YOUR BIRTHDAY WITH THE ONES YOU LOVE.

Whether it's luscious hazelnut praliné, butterscotch caramel or mocha buttercream enveloped in milk chocolate, a gift of Godiva is a true surprise party for your taste buds. To send Godiva, call 1-800-643-1579.

GODIVA
Chocolatier

EXHIBIT 13

The Briefing from Godiva International

1. Current Positioning
- To adults who want a quality product for special moments, Godiva is an accessible luxury branded by Godiva Chocolatier and distinguished by superior craftsmanship.

2. Consumer Benefit
- Whether you give Godiva or consume it yourself, you will relish its uniquely sensual pleasures: taste and presentation.

3. Promise
- Using the finest ingredients and Belgian recipes for a remarkable taste experience.
- Godiva heritage of fine chocolate making.
- Beautifully crafted packaging.
- Handcrafted in fine European heritage/style.
- Created by an expert chocolatier.

4. Psychographic Characteristics
- Godiva purchasers are discerning and driven by quality expectations. While they are value-oriented, they will pay a higher price if a significant quality differential exists, since they aspire to have or share the best.
- Godiva men and women are sensual individuals, enjoying the pleasures that things of exceptional look, feel, taste, sound, and smell can offer them.

5. Competitive Frame
- Gift: flowers, perfume, wine, other fine chocolates, giftables of the same price range.
- Self-consumption: any item meant to provide a range of self-indulgences at Godiva's basic price-points.

6. Target Audience
- The Godiva target covers a range of demographic characteristics:
  - Broad age range (25–54 primarily)
  - Women and men
  - Across breadth of income levels, but with reasonable to high disposable incomes.

7. Advertising Objectives
- To revitalize Godiva's worldwide premium position most specifically as it pertains to the superior quality of the chocolate product.
- To motivate our current Godiva franchise to purchase on more frequent occasions (gifting and self-consumption).
- To motivate current purchasers of competitive chocolates and nonchocolate giftables to convert to the Godiva franchise.

8. Message
- Godiva chocolates are expertly crafted to provide an unparalleled sensory experience.

9. Tone and Manner
- Luxurious—Energetic—Modern—Upscale—Emotionally involving.

Reflecting with his marketing staff, van der Veken tended to define the advertising objective in the following manner.

> The objective of Godiva USA is to increase the frequency of the purchase of chocolates for gifts as well as for self consumption, whereas Belgium wants to make its brand image more youthful. Thus, the United States should adjust its advertising slightly "downward," in making the product more accessible through convivial advertising and less "plastic beauty." Belgium should strive, jointly with other marketing efforts (redesign of boutiques, increased quality of service, creation of "collections"), to adjust its advertising slightly "upward," in affirming itself as a prestigious luxury product, only younger.

The upward adjustment for Belgium was a daring challenge. Charles van der Veken wondered if it would not be preferable to pass through a transitory period before beginning a global marketing campaign, which would take into consideration the historical and cultural context of Belgium.

Just then, Mrs. Bogaert, van der Veken's assistant, entered his office holding a fax from Godiva International:

> The campaign cannot be launched in time for Christmas; prepare as quickly as possible your advertising campaign for Belgium and contact your agencies. Meeting in five weeks in New York for the confirmation of our projects.

Charles van der Veken immediately called his Director of Marketing, informed her of the freshly arrived news, and asked her to submit for the Belgian market a campaign project based on the American model, targeted in a first step to the Belgian market, but which could be extended to the other European markets, if not to the entire world. Together they agreed on objectives in three main categories:

1. Qualitative objectives:
   - Rapidly reinforce the luxury image of Godiva
   - Make visibility a priority
2. Quantitative objectives:
   - Increase the frequency of purchase
3. Other objectives:
   - Concentrate all efforts on Belgium during several months (months of peak sales)
   - Synergy of all other methods of promotion and advertising

An additional 13 million bf advertising budget would be allocated to the campaign. After some thought, it seemed possible to Mr. van der Veken that a triad campaign would, on a long-term basis, be feasible in spite of cultural differences. He did not believe, however, that business generated in the other European countries would be high enough today to justify the same advertising budget as for Belgium. This became even more obvious when one considered that, in terms of media costs and for a same impact, 1 bf in Belgium is equivalent to 1.6 bf in France and 1.9 bf in the United Kingdom.

Charles van der Veken was also convinced that a European advertising campaign was useless without having first improved and reinforced Godiva European distribution.

■ APPENDIX: RESULTS OF THE BRAND IMAGE STUDY IN THE BRUSSELS MARKET AREA

Aided Brand Awareness (%)

Brand Name	Not at All	Only by Name	By Experience	Total
Corné	24.2%	28.9%	46.9%	100%
Corné Toison d'Or	31.3	25.8	43.0	100
Corné Port Royal	69.3	16.5	14.2	100
Daskalidès	54.3	26.0	19.7	100
Godiva	2.3	19.5	78.1	100
Léonidas	2.3	10.9	86.7	100
Mon Chéri	4.7	23.6	71.7	100
Neuhaus	13.3	25.0	61.7	100

Don't know any of brands Corné, Corné Toison d'Or, Corné Port Royal: 22.7%. Known "by name" or "by experience" at least one of the following brands: Corné, Corné Toison d'Or, Corné Port Royal: 77.3%.

Brand Image Analysis

	Brand Associated Most with Each Attribute (%)									
Attribute	Corné (1)	Corné Toison d'Or (2)	Corné Port Royal (3)	Corné Total (1 + 2 + 3)	Daska-lidès	Godiva	Léoni-das	Mon Chéri	Neu-baus	Total
The queen of chocolates	7.1%	5.5%	0.8%	(13.4%)		37.8%	27.6%	1.6%	19.7%	100%
Ideal for gift	11.0	3.1		(14.1)		29.1	26.8	10.2	19.7	100
For self-indulgence	4.8	3.2	0.8	(8.8)	0.8%	26.4	48.0	1.6	14.4	100
For special occasions	6.5	8.9	0.8	(16.2)	0.8	26.8	28.5	8.1	19.5	100
The most beautiful boutique	6.0	9.4		(15.4)		40.2	12.0	0.9	31.6	100
The most attractive price	3.3	2.5		(5.8)	0.8	5.7	81.1	4.9	1.6	100
The nicest packaging	7.2	7.2	0.8	(15.2)	0.8	49.6	6.4	3.2	24.8	100
The most refined chocolate	8.8	7.2	1.6	(17.6)	0.8	35.2	18.4	0.8	27.2	100
Typically Belgian chocolate	6.5	2.4		(8.9)		30.1	48.1	2.4	10.6	100
Taste I like best	5.6	4.0	1.6	(11.2)		32.3	37.9	3.2	15.3	100
The most expensive chocolate	6.7	8.4		(15.1)	2.5	40.3	5.9	0.8	35.3	100
Worldly known brand	4.0	0.8		(4.8)	0.8	42.7	39.5	4.8	7.3	100

Brand Preferences by Situation

For Self-Consumption		For Gift	
Corné:	2.4%	Corné:	3.9%
Corné Toison d'Or:	4.1	Corné Toison d'Or:	3.9
Corné Port Royal:	0.8	Corné Port Royal:	0.8
Daskalidès:	—	Daskalidès:	0.8
Godiva:	24.4	Godiva:	29.1
Léonidas:	48.0	Léonidas:	27.6
Mon Chéri:	2.4	Mon Chéri:	5.5
Neuhaus:	12.2	Neuhaus:	25.2
Other:	5.7	Other:	3.2
	100%		100%

Make-Up Art Cosmetics (M.A.C) Ltd.

In July 1999, Gabe Monnetti was appointed director, M.A.C Online, for Make-Up Art Cosmetics Ltd. (M.A.C), a Canadian-based cosmetics company. This was a new position created in the company as a result of M.A.C's growing desire to be active on the Internet. Monnetti's mandate was to design and manage the development of the company's new Web site.

It was only recently that M.A.C had decided to investigate the possibilities of the Internet. Senior management was not yet convinced that it needed the Internet to communicate and interact with its customers. Support for an online strategy, however, was growing. In the first few months of 1999, customers were complaining to the company's customer service department that they expected M.A.C to have a Web site. Many customers were also requesting the ability to purchase M.A.C products online.

Monnetti was asked to consider the possibility of developing a new retail channel for the company through the Internet. Should M.A.C take advantage of the Web to create a new relationship with the customer? Monnetti had to decide which of several potential Internet strategies to select and make a recommendation to senior management.

■ THE COMPANY

M.A.C was founded in 1985 in Toronto, with the original goal of developing products specifically for use by professional make-up artists. These cosmetics first found their way onto the faces of fashion models, actors and stage performers. Soon the public wanted the same products that were being used by the professionals.

M.A.C created a whole new face for the cosmetics industry. Contrary to industry norms, M.A.C did not advertise or do gift-with-purchase promotions, and it did not pay commissions to its retail staff. M.A.C also focused on developing professional quality products and staffed its counters with make-up artists to support those products rather than simply salespeople. It also enlisted Rupaul—a six-foot tall man who dressed as a woman—to help raise money for AIDS awareness and to support activities. This fresh, new image caught on quickly and M.A.C was soon very popular.

Vic Casale prepared this case under the supervision of John S. Hulland solely to provide material for class discussion. The authors do not intend to illustrate either effective or ineffective handling of a managerial situation. The authors may have disguised certain names and other identifying information to protect confidentiality.

The company experienced phenomenal growth following its inception, primarily through word of mouth and repeated, favorable media attention. By 1999, the company's annual retail sales had grown to over Cdn$500 million worldwide. M.A.C products were available in over 200 locations in 15 countries, and the company had 2,500 employees.[1]

M.A.C sold its products through three retail channels:

Partnered Stores—These were primarily upscale department stores such as Bloomingdale's, Nordstrom and The Bay. The company would set up a counter in the department store's cosmetics area and sell its products using department store employees.

Company Owned and Operated Stores—A significant volume of sales was generated through these M.A.C-owned cosmetics stores.

1–800—A small portion of sales was managed through a 1–800 customer service call center, which shipped product directly to the consumer.[2]

M.A.C customers generally fell into two categories. The professionals were those who used the products for work. These were primarily make-up artists, but they also included models and actors. These professionals represented about 50 percent of the overall sales by dollar volume. The remaining customer group was referred to as the retail consumer, comprised mostly of younger women. The typical M.A.C consumer was a young, fashion-conscious individual who was seeking a unique look.

■ THE M.A.C STRATEGY

Initially, the company's market was primarily professional make-up artists in Canada. M.A.C serviced these make-up artists by appointment only from a store on Carlton Street in Toronto. Distribution was mainly through the store and several professional distributors across Canada. Within a few years, the distribution network spread into the U.S., with key distributors in New York and Los Angeles. As demand grew with make-up artists, a new customer segment began to appear. This segment was referred to as the professional market, and included celebrities, actors, models, photographers and hairstylists. These newer customers were served through M.A.C's own stores, which were opened in Toronto, Montreal, Vancouver, New York, Chicago and Los Angeles.

As media attention increased and demand continued to grow, nonprofessional but fashion-conscious women started wanting to purchase M.A.C cosmetics for themselves. To meet this demand, M.A.C expanded its distribution to include major department stores across North America. By 1992, this strategy was well established, and in 1995 the company opened its first counter outside of North America at Harvey Nichols in London. From the U.K., M.A.C expanded into central Europe and Asia and was selling products in 15 countries by 1999, including France, Italy, Germany, Spain, Switzerland, Hong Kong, Japan and Singapore.

In 1998, the company opened several Proshops—new warehouse-type stores that catered solely to professional make-up artists—to ensure that this segment was

---

[1]In February 1998, the original M.A.C owners sold the company to Estée Lauder Companies Inc. (ELC) of New York. The company purchased M.A.C as part of a new strategy to take small, primarily North American brands, like Bobbi Brown Cosmetics, Aveda and Jane Cosmetics, and develop them into international players.

[2]This service was not openly promoted, as management wanted customers to shop the M.A.C counters. Instead, it was offered as an improved customer service to existing customers. Special order representatives were not encouraged to push sales; rather, they would take an order only if the customers knew what they wanted.

being properly serviced. By 1999, 27 percent of revenues came from sales to the professional make-up artists segment, approximately 23 percent came from the professional industry, with the remaining balance coming from retail customers. Although this represented a major shift in the company's distribution emphasis from its early days, M.A.C's vision statement remained the same:"To be the most preferred brand of professional cosmetics in the world." M.A.C's distribution system as it existed in mid-1999 is summarized in Exhibit 1.

Products

M.A.C products were developed for the professional artist. They were available in a large selection of colors and textures and were formulated to stand up to bright lights and to be worn for longer periods than normal. The packaging was minimalist—black and inexpensive in appearance. Each make-up color was individually packaged, and there were no cheap brushes put into the individual eye shadow containers. M.A.C stressed the use of professional-quality brushes with its make-up and carried a complete line of professional cosmetics and accessories, including lipsticks, eye shadows, blush, foundations, brushes, make-up bags, cases and skin treatment products.

In the fall of 1998, the company had launched a new product line called M.A.C-PRO, made available solely through the company's Proshops and Special Order Department. It was an exclusively professional line of products that included cream colors, primary colors, mixable lip-cream, and numerous professional tools such as brushes, sponges, and make-up cases.

The In-Store Experience

Trained make-up artists, many of whom were working freelance, staffed all M.A.C locations. They wore black clothing and whatever accessories they desired. It was

EXHIBIT 1

M.A.C Distribution Channels

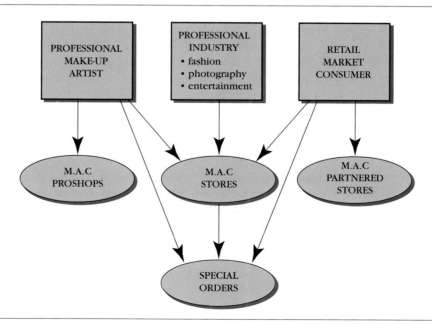

Source: Company records.

not uncommon to see a M.A.C artist with orange hair, or a pierced lip, or dressed in drag. The retail artists were not paid commission on sales but rather were paid above-average salaries.

All products were displayed and open on the counter to encourage a touch-and-play atmosphere for the customer. The store fixtures were all uniquely designed and included black granite, brushed metal and stained wood finishes. Customers frequently commented on the unique experience of shopping at a M.A.C counter.

Not all customers enjoyed this experience. Some complained that the artists were unapproachable, or that they looked too perfect, too weird, too confident. This put the customer into an insecure position. However, it was these same well-trained retail artists that added to the M.A.C brand's credibility and differentiation. Many younger, fashion-trendy customers also found it off-putting to have to shop for M.A.C products in a department store. They associated department stores as places for older, more mainstream consumers.

Price

All M.A.C products were priced at the lower end of the prestige market. For example, a M.A.C lipstick retailed for $12, whereas a competitor's product would range in price from $14 to $20 in a department store. A premium, mass-market lipstick retailed for considerably less, in the $4 to $8 range.

An important early entry strategy used by the company to encourage professional sales was a discount policy called the Preferred Professional Industry Discount (PPID). M.A.C issued PPID cards to certified professionals. Make-up artists received a 40 percent discount, while models, actors and make-up students received a 20 percent discount. To receive a PPID card, the professional was required to submit a request form each year. This allowed M.A.C to track many professionals in the industry and monitor their sales.

Promotion

M.A.C's promotion strategy was a first for the cosmetics industry. It did no advertising and offered no in-store gift-with-purchase promotions. Its products were never put on sale or discounted to the retail customer. Instead, M.A.C developed several socially conscious programs to help raise awareness for the environment and AIDS. For example, it established a program called "Back-to-M.A.C" that rewarded customers with one free lipstick for returning six empty plastic containers. These containers were then sorted and sent off to recycling facilities. M.A.C also had a program called Viva Glam that raised money, through the sale of a particular shade of lipstick, for people living with AIDS and HIV. M.A.C also employed a special group of celebrity make-up artists who traveled around the world to provide make-up services at fashion shows and special events.

The M.A.C Phenomenon

Over the years, M.A.C had developed strong brand awareness. Thanks to its unique strategy and wide media support, many consumers around the world knew M.A.C. The market success of the company was due to a combination of its creativity, products, people, services and company culture. This formula was believed to be the key to the company's success. The M.A.C brand was seen to represent professional quality make-up. It was perceived as being socially responsible and unconventional. Customers were very brand loyal. Many would drive great distances to shop at a M.A.C counter. Dedicated customers even asked traveling friends to pick up their favorite products when they traveled to a city selling M.A.C. The company was seen to be "edgy," part of the "in" crowd, and very "hip."

■ THE COMPETITION

By the early 1990s, the cosmetics industry had started to recognize that M.A.C had created an entirely new approach to selling make-up. There were no other companies at the time selling professional-quality products through mainstream retail channels. Most competitors at that time were found in the department stores; companies such as Lancome, Estée Lauder, Clinique, Elizabeth Arden and Shiseido were the larger, more recognized brands. Their price points were generally higher than M.A.C's, and their product selection was limited in the make-up category. Most competitors concentrated on selling expensive fragrances and skin care products—none were known for their color products. The customers of these brands were usually older, more conservative women.

As the M.A.C model grew in popularity, others attempted to copy it. New professional make-up brands were launched; by 1996, approximately 10 new make-up brands were on the market. The more successful of these new companies included Bobbi Brown Essentials, Trish MacEvoy, Nars, Stila and Make-up Forever. All of these companies claimed to sell professional cosmetics and to employ professional make-up artists. These new brands sold their products at much the same price as M.A.C, and most copied the packaging, the black dress code, and the product line. This new "Professional Artist" category was gaining momentum and establishing a presence in department stores. Department store managers supported the growth in this category both because it generated new revenue and because it attracted a new, younger customer segment into the stores. Despite the increased competition, in mid-1999 M.A.C continued to be the market leader in the department store channel.

Another group of competitors for M.A.C was the purely professional brands that did not sell their products in mainstream channels. These brands focused only on the professionals and the professional industry, and the major players were Visiora, Bill Tuddle, Kryolan, RCMA and Joe Bolasco. They were considered strictly professional and sold their products directly to film production studios through industry distributors. It was very important for M.A.C to maintain a presence in this market because of the credibility it gave M.A.C.

To compete in this environment, companies would support make-up artists with their special needs. For example, sometimes a special product or color was made for a show. It was also common for companies to offer free products and training to make-up artists. It was very difficult to compete in this segment; make-up artists wanted special products that were not available to the mainstream, and they had to have the products first. Around this time, make-up artists began to see M.A.C as a retail, mass-market line, a potential threat to the credibility of the company. Although M.A.C still maintained a market leadership position with this customer segment in mid-1999, it was beginning to lose some of its original artist customers.

There were several competitors retailing online, although with varying degrees of success. Clinique, another brand owned by ELC, had launched its online shopping a year earlier. According to one of Clinique's online managers, "The channel has had limited impact on new revenue." Customers were using the site for information gathering rather than online purchases.

New, unauthorized online retailers sold the majority of Internet-based cosmetics sales. They acted as discount houses for most of the popular brands, offering a limited selection and only listing what was currently available to them. Major retailers such as Nordstrom, Macy's and Bloomingdale's were also attempting to sell cosmetics online. For most of these department stores, the Internet had forced them to attempt to retail their traditional in-store brands online. Their initial sites were very basic in design and offered only a limited range of products. They also needed the permission of their suppliers to list products on their Web sites.

■ ONLINE RETAILING

By the end of 1998, online retailing reached approximately US$15 billion in transaction revenues, far exceeding industry projections. It was expected that this new retail channel would grow at rates well above 200 percent per year for the next few years. Major categories, such as computer goods, consumer electronics, books, music, and videos, accounted for about 42 percent of sales. Discount brokerages, including travel, auctions, and financial services, accounted for 32 percent of online sales. All other consumer goods accounted for just 2.5 percent. The top 10 sites were responsible for over 50 percent of total online sales. Importantly, the Internet also supported a much larger volume of offline sales from referrals. This number was difficult to track, but, for example, automotive referral sites facilitated US$12 billion in offline sales while recording only US$28 million in online sales.

Through the Internet, retailers could disassociate information from the physical environment, whereas the traditional retail channel blended information with a physical environment. The online model deconstructed the traditional value chain, as retailers restructured physical activities and information to create a unique retailing experience. This new channel was breaking the trade-off between richness and reach. Traditionally, if a retailer wanted a rich communication with the customer, it would have to be done face-to-face. And, conversely, a retailer who wanted to reach many customers would sacrifice richness because only a very simple message could be communicated. The Internet broke down this fundamental trade-off, allowing a retailer to reach many customers with a very rich shopping experience.

Retailers currently selling their products online had identified six key barriers to success:

Increasing consumers' comfort levels. Online retailers needed to improve convenience and value for customers and assist them in overcoming their concerns about security and trust.

Resolving technological limitations. The ability for online retailers to deliver unique experiences is linked to technology improvements. The Internet is still constrained by lack of bandwidth and problems with reliability.

Rapidly scaling internal operations. Online retailers face the challenges of managing significant growth, internal organizational change and developing and scaling their customer service and fulfillment infrastructure—all while the technology is still evolving.

Engineering comprehensive convenience. Customers identify many convenience problems with today's online environment. Among them are the need for customers to reenter personal data on different sites, the wide variation in customer service across sites, and the lack of coordination between online and offline retail environments on the part of retailers using both channels.

Resolving channel conflict. Many offline retailers believe that there is a risk of cannibalizing sales through existing channels by going online. Many manufacturers fear alienating their existing distribution partners by providing an alternative channel for customers to purchase. These perceived channel conflicts are keeping some traditional retailers and manufacturers from joining the Internet.

Developing low-cost distribution. Distribution systems can be expensive. Online fulfillment systems are still developing and there is a disconnect between what is required and what is currently offered by existing offline systems.

Finally, multi-channel retailers—those who sold through traditional channels while moving online—accounted for 59 percent of online revenues. Multi-channel retailers usually outperformed purely online retailers on conversion rates and customer loyalty.

■ M.A.C'S ONLINE OPTIONS

There were many issues facing Monnetti as he thought about taking M.A.C online. He had to consider every aspect of the M.A.C business model, the competition, and the current issues surrounding online retailing.

M.A.C had developed a unique brand image through an unconventional approach. The company had managed to create a whole new segment of customers in a fairly traditional retail environment. How could this be translated into a new, online channel? Part of the success of the company was through the unique retail shopping experience that it offered. Customers were serviced by make-up artists in a well-designed space, with products open on the counter and available for trial. Would traditional cosmetic shoppers feel comfortable buying make-up, a very personal purchase, online? Choosing the right colors, textures and products could prove to be very complex.

Also, there was the concern about the existing retail channels. M.A.C had developed an extensive network of stores across North America. These retailers wanted M.A.C products to be sold on their own Web sites along with their other cosmetic brands. At the same time, some of M.A.C's competitors were starting to offer direct online retailing—new Web sites were coming online every day, and there were even a few unofficial M.A.C Web sites selling products in Canada. The low Canadian dollar provided a significant margin when selling to customers in the United States.

Monnetti had identified three distinct Internet options that he believed might be suitable for building M.A.C's online presence. The first option would involve creating an information-oriented Web site without offering any of M.A.C's products for sale directly through the Web. Option two was based on expanding M.A.C's interactions with its existing retail partners to sell the company's products on their own Web sites. Finally, Monnetti believed that M.A.C could establish a site that would allow consumers to make online purchases directly from the company. He saw strengths and weaknesses associated with each of the three options.

Information-Oriented Web Site

Launching an information-based Web site initially, without offering any products for sale, was an option that had a number of advantages going for it. First, the site would serve as the company's online flagship store, allowing customers to move an online camera around the page and to zoom in on specific products or news. The Web site would be designed with a "fashion at the forefront" image in mind by having clips of fashion shows where M.A.C products were used. Monnetti felt that such a site would be very attractive to consumers, allowing them to visit the M.A.C site and browse without fears about security.

Second, the widespread availability of the Internet would increase market awareness of M.A.C and its products worldwide, allowing M.A.C to expand into new markets around the world. This would involve building its conventional retail operations through additional retail partners and corporate stores in new markets. The ability to maintain this traditional shopping experience would ensure that M.A.C maintained its prestige status. Under this option, M.A.C's Web site would include the addresses of nearby retailers, thereby driving sales to those stores.

M.A.C could also use its site to promote awareness of AIDS and other causes that the company had long supported. As part of M.A.C's Web site, for example, an online support line and information service for AIDS victims could be created, providing a chat room and information about services and community support groups.

Third, the Web site would provide the company with an effective medium to introduce new and upcoming products by offering advance information to both existing and new customers. M.A.C could accomplish ongoing communications with its online visitors through the use of an e-mail announcement system, and it could allow online users to become members of a "M.A.C Internet club." This would create customer excitement about the products, helping to maintain M.A.C's vibrant image as an innovative fashion cosmetic company while simultaneously creating greater and advance demand for the new products.

Online Selling Through Retail Partners' Web Sites

Monnetti believed that encouraging existing retail partners to sell M.A.C products on their own Web sites could also be a successful strategy. These retailers would offer cheaper distribution, the strength of their own brand names, and existing customer bases. Most of M.A.C's key retailers were well known in their own markets, providing an assurance to online customers that if they had a problem they could always travel to the retailer's closest store to resolve it. Furthermore, these retailers had substantial distribution networks that included regional distribution warehouses and local stores spread throughout local communities, leading to faster shipments and lower costs.

This option would also create fewer logistics problems for M.A.C. For example, this option would not put unnecessary strains on the company's working relationships with its retail partners, who might otherwise be concerned about the potential of lost sales to a M.A.C Web site. Similarly, the existing sales division within M.A.C would not need to worry about sales erosion to a newly created online division. Furthermore, M.A.C would not have to make major investments in internal logistics improvements.

On the other hand, Monnetti believed that M.A.C's retail partners were unlikely to make major investments in building the M.A.C brand. They carried thousands of products that they wanted to feature online. Thus, M.A.C products were likely to receive only limited online representation under this option. Furthermore, M.A.C would have limited input into how its products were presented on the retailers' sites. Monnetti feared that this might lead to the presentation of a dated image of the brand. This was particularly an issue in the case of retailers that were themselves still inexperienced at Web site design and maintenance.

Finally, there would be limited potential for new customers, since the retailers' Web sites were likely to appeal primarily to their existing customers. Even if the customer base was expanded, M.A.C would learn little about these new consumers, thus limiting the company's ability to develop an extensive customer database that could be used for direct electronic marketing, marketing research and improving customer service.

Online Direct Selling Through a M.A.C Web Site

The online strategy for M.A.C could range from basic to innovative. A basic approach would allow consumers to purchase products, choosing from itemized lists with brief descriptions and product photographs, along with information about how the selected products should be applied. This was essentially the approach taken by two of M.A.C's sister companies—Clinique and Bobbi Brown Essentials.

A more innovative approach would involve replenishment buying: customers initially buy in a store, but then reorder through the Internet once familiar with the product. Following such a strategy had proven highly effective for 1-800-Flowers. M.A.C could include product showrooms on its site that allowed consumers to examine goods more extensively before placing orders.

Another possibility for M.A.C would be to integrate store-based and Internet shopping. For example, it might place a scanner and an imager in kiosks in its stores. A customer's photograph would be taken and entered into the system. After answering questions about preferences and physical requirements, she could securely access this photo and see the effects of choosing and applying various M.A.C products.[3] Such a system had been used successfully by Eye-Web in New York. Given the sen-

---

[3]Customers having limited or no access to a M.A.C store could instead send a photograph directly to the company for system entry.

sory nature of M.A.C's products, this approach had significant potential. On the other hand, it would require substantial programming and capital investment.

Monnetti believed that the advantages of pursuing an online sales strategy in the near term were considerable. First, it was likely to attract new customers to M.A.C stores. Research by New York–based Cyber Dialogue Inc. had found that for every dollar spent online, consumers were likely to purchase another $5 of goods offline (in the retailer's store). Second, M.A.C could more quickly and easily introduce and test new products. Third, the company could broaden its product line beyond what could effectively be displayed in stores. Lines that were discontinued in stores, for example, could be available for an extended period through the Web. Finally, an online sales site might remove excess repeat traffic from M.A.C store counters, easing lineups and crowding.

The biggest concern that Monnetti had about this option was that it could pose a threat to the company's credibility with the professional segment of the market. If M.A.C was perceived by these customers to be too accessible and mass-market, it risked losing its prestige status. The company had already begun to lose some of its original artist customers, and the move to online could, if not handled properly, accelerate the defections. In addition, this option would involve a relatively large initial investment without any guarantee of success or payback in the near to mid-term.

Customer Research and Competitor Analysis

Using measures taken from a recent M.A.C customer survey that had asked customers to rank the factors influencing their satisfaction and, therefore, their buying behaviors, the company had developed more detailed profiles of the professional artists, professional industry and retail consumer segments of the market (see Exhibit 2). It also

EXHIBIT 2

M.A.C Customer Segment Analysis—North America

	Professional Artists	*Professional Industry*	*Retail Consumer*
Demographics			
Age	32% between 36–45	40% between 26–35	47% between 26–35
Gender	56% female	83% female	98% female
Education	High school	20% college	37% college
Size	50,000	375,000	2,000,000
Average Visit Purchase	$120	$78	$38
Average Yearly Purchase	$2,700	$305	$125
Purchase Use	For work	Both work and personal	Personal
Purchase Where	Proshops/M.A.C stores	78% M.A.C stores	84% Partnered stores
Average length of time as customer	58% between 4–7 years	35% between 4–7 years	46% between 1–3 years
	Professional Artists	*Professional Industry*	*Retail Consumer*
Psychographics			
	Wants the latest	Looks to the artists	Looks to the industry
	Willing to try new products	Will try what is recommended	Willing to try new looks
	Needs to be exclusive	Spends more time shopping	Fashion conscious
	Little time to shop	Has several different brands	Uses many brands
	Is the leader		
	Commits to a few brands		

Source: Company records.

created a "Shopping Experience Analysis" chart (see Exhibit 3) that assessed how well both M.A.C's existing, offline approach and the three potential online strategies affected customer satisfaction levels within each segment.

In order to get a sense of what its competitors were currently offering online, the company looked at 10 competitive Web sites. Various aspects of these sites are described in Exhibit 4, including a qualitative assessment of the overall site quality. Monnetti was not necessarily looking to duplicate these offerings but felt that understanding the competitive landscape was an important precursor to choosing an online strategy for M.A.C.

EXHIBIT 3

M.A.C Shopping Experience Analysis

Segment	Benefits (ranked for importance)			
	Current Strategy	Information Web site	Retailer Selling Online	M.A.C Selling Online
Professional				
Product range available	3	1	1	3
Ease of making purchase	2	2	3	3
Product availability	2	1	2	3
Try products on	3	1	1	1
Expertise of artists	3	2	1	2
Products demonstrated	3	1	1	2
Consistency of service	1	3	2	3
Totals	17	11	11	17
Professional Industry				
Expertise of artists	3	2	1	2
Try products on	3	1	1	1
Product availability	2	1	2	3
Consistency of service	1	3	2	3
Ease of making purchase	2	2	3	3
Location convenience	2	2	3	3
Product range available	3	1	1	3
Totals	16	12	13	18
Retail Industry				
Expertise of artists	3	2	1	2
Product availability	2	1	2	3
Products demonstrated	3	1	1	2
Try products on	3	1	1	1
Consistency of service	1	3	2	3
Ease of making purchase	2	2	3	3
Convenience of location	2	2	3	3
Totals	16	12	13	17
M.A.C Totals	49	35	37	52

LEGEND: 1 = Low Satisfaction; 2 = Medium Satisfaction,; 3 = High Satisfaction

Source: Company records.

EXHIBIT 4

Web Functionality for M.A.C's Principal Competitors

Brand	Web Site	Information Available on Site (Company only; Brands only; Major products/lines, New product lines, All products/lines)	Depth of Information (Shallow, Moderate, Useful, Extensive)	E-Commerce Capability (Not yet, Est'd products, Product launches, Full range, Distinct e-commerce line)	Special Features (Beauty tips, Coupons for use in stores, Customer Survey; E-mail sign up, Gifts, Links to other sites, Register, Store location, Video clips)	Quality Assessment (Poor, Good, Excellent)	Innovation (Basic, Safe, Tries too hard, Fun, Innovative)
Bobbi Brown Essentials	bobbibrowncosmetics.com	A	U	F(USA)	G, R	G	S
Chanel Inc.	chanel.com	N	U		B, CS, E, R, S	G	T
Clinique	clinique.com	A	U	F(USA)	B,CS,E, G, L, R, S	E	F
Elizabeth Arden	elizabetharden.com	Under construction					
Estée Lauder Cosmetics Ltd.	esteelauder.com	Under construction		N			
Lancome	lancome.com	A	U	N	CS, E	G	S
L'Oréal	lorealcosmetics.com	A	U	N	B, C, E, R	G	S
Prescriptives	prescriptives.com	No site					
Revlon	revlon.com	A	M	N	B, C, CS, R	G	S
Shiseido	shiseido.com	A	S	N	B, E	P	B

Source: Company records.

351

Financial Implications

The company had prepared pro forma income statements for each of the three online options under consideration (see Exhibit 5). In all three cases, M.A.C anticipated a 2 percent increase in offline retail sales as a result of going online. This was consistent with Clinique's experience.

For option one, it was believed that incremental advertising and promotion expenses would increase by about $75,000. An additional $75,000 for e-messaging would also be required. Finally, $100,000 was allocated for future site enhancement/updating. All sales made under this option were made through traditional retail outlets, so retailer discounts and traditional cost of goods sold calculations applied.

As already described, option two allowed for online sales through associated retailers. It was felt that this would generate incremental online sales totaling $1.5 million. The operating costs of employing this option were similar to option one, but a larger sum of money was set aside for site enhancement/updating.

EXHIBIT 5

M.A.C Online Sales—Pro Forma Income Statements (In Thousands)

	Information Web Site Only	Retailer Site	M.A.C E-Commerce Site
Existing Retail Sales (North America only)	$350,000	$350,000	$350,000
Incremental Retail Sales (@ 2% of Retail)[1]	7,000	7,000	7,000
Less: Retailers Discount (@ 40%)	−2,800	−2,800	−2,800
Net Incremental Revenue from Retail	4,200	4,200	4,200
Online Revenues[2]		1,500	1,500
Less: Retailer's Discount (@ 40%)		−600	
Net Online Revenue		900	1,500
Total Incremental Revenue	**4,200**	**5,100**	**5,700**
Cost of Goods Sold—on Incremental Retail Sales	−1,050	−1,050	−1,050
Cost of Goods Sold—Online Sales		−225	−225
Total Cost of Goods Sold	**−1,050**	**−21,275**	**−1,275**
Gross Profit	**3,150**	**3,825**	**4,425**
Operating Expenses			
Selling Expenses (incl. Customer-service staff)			230
Warehousing and Shipping			25
Advertising and Promotion	75	75	250
E-Messaging	75	75	125
Site Enhancement/Updating[3]	100	160	200
Total Operating Expenses	**250**	**310**	**830**
Operating Income	**2,900**	**3,515**	**3,595**
Operating Income Margin	69%	69%	63%

Notes:

1. Consistent with Clinique's experience, which has been that retail sales increased by an estimated 2 percent as a result of its site.

2. Selling, warehousing/shipping, advertising/promotion and e-messaging are all assumed to be at roughly half of the increase in orders.

3. Site enhancement is an ongoing experience as the site must be regularly refreshed to stay competitive and interesting to customers.

Source: Company records.

The third option led to the most extreme changes in revenues and costs. Because online sales would be made directly to the customer, M.A.C would not have to offer retailer discounts on any products sold through this channel. On the other hand, the projected operating costs for this option were significantly higher, reflecting the need for improved logistics and more aggressive marketing communications.

■ CONCLUSION

It was late November 1999, just six months before M.A.C planned to launch its Web site. Monnetti needed to present senior management with a recommendation on how M.A.C should proceed to take its brand online. As part of his recommendation, he would need to choose one of the three proposed online strategies for M.A.C. He knew that the company's decision would attract considerable media coverage and that his recommendation would, therefore, need to be clearly communicated. He also knew that once the site was operating, customers would question whichever strategy M.A.C pursued. Monnetti had one week to finalize his recommendation.

CHAPTER **7**

Marketing Channel
Strategy and Management

 Marketing channels play an integral role in an organization's marketing strategy. A *marketing channel* consists of individuals and firms involved in the process of making a product or service available for consumption or use by consumers and industrial users. Channels not only link a producer of goods to the goods' buyers but also provide the means through which an organization implements its marketing strategy. Marketing channels determine whether the target markets sought by an organization are reached. The effectiveness of a communications strategy is determined, in part, by the ability and willingness of channel intermediaries to perform sales, advertising, and promotion activities. An organization's price strategy is influenced by the markup and discount policies of intermediaries. Finally, product strategy is affected by intermediaries' branding policies, willingness to stock and customize offerings, and ability to augment offerings through installation or maintenance services, the extension of credit, and so forth.

Marketing channel strategy and management has assumed greater significance with the onset of electronic commerce. Growth in the sophistication and usage of Internet/Web-based technology has revolutionized the way products and services are made available for consumption or use by consumers and industrial users. The Internet has challenged marketers to innovatively employ this technology in channel strategy and management in a manner that creates customer value at a profit. This topic is addressed in this chapter from the perspective of multi-channel marketing.

■ THE CHANNEL-SELECTION DECISION

Making the channel-selection decision is not so much a single act as it is a process of making various component decisions. The process of channel selection involves specifying the type, location, density, and functions of intermediaries, if any, in a marketing channel. However, before addressing these decisions, the marketing manager must conduct a thorough market analysis in order to identify the target markets that will be served by a prospective marketing channel. The target markets sought and their buying requirements form the basis for all channel decisions. In other words, the marketing manager needs answers to fundamental questions such as these: Who are potential customers? Where do they buy? When do they buy? How do they buy? What do they buy? By working backward from the ultimate buyer or user of an offering, the manager can develop a framework for specific channel decisions and can identify alternative channel designs.[1]

Consider Avon Products, Inc., the world's leading direct seller of beauty and related items to women in 139 countries.[2] For more than 115 years, the company successfully marketed its products through an extensive network of independent representatives, which number 3.4 million worldwide. However, Avon's marketing research indicated that 59 percent of women who don't buy Avon products would if they were more accessible. The message to Avon's senior management was clear: Give busy women a choice in how, where, and when they do their buying—through an Avon representative, in a retail store, or online. According to Avon's chief executive officer, "While direct selling will always be our principal sales channel, expanding access to new customers will help accelerate top-line [sales] growth." Today, Avon products are sold by independent representatives, on its Web site (avon.com), and in a shop-within-a-store format in selected department stores.

The Design of Marketing Channels

Exhibit 7.1 illustrates traditional channel designs for consumer and industrial offerings. Also indicated is the number of levels in a marketing channel, which is determined by the number of intermediaries between the producer and the ultimate buyers or users. As the number of intermediaries between the producer and the ultimate buyer increases, the channel increases in length.

Direct Versus Indirect Distribution   The first decision facing a manager is whether the organization should (1) use intermediaries to reach target markets or (2) contact ultimate buyers directly using its own sales forces or distribution outlets, or the Internet through a marketing Web site or electronic storefront. If the manager elects to use intermediaries, then the type, location, density, and number of channel levels must be determined.

EXHIBIT 7.1

Traditional Marketing Channel Designs

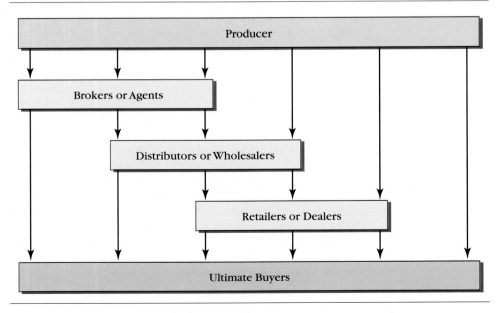

Organizations usually elect to contact ultimate buyers directly rather than through intermediaries when the following conditions exist. Direct distribution is usually employed when target markets are composed of buyers who are easily identifiable, when personal selling is a major component of the organization's communication program, when the organization has a wide variety of offerings for the target market, and when sufficient resources are available to satisfy target market requirements that would normally be handled by intermediaries (such as credit, technical assistance, delivery, and postsale service). Direct distribution must be considered when intermediaries are not available for reaching target markets, or when intermediaries do not possess the capacity to service the requirements of target markets. For example, Procter & Gamble sells its soap and laundry detergents direct, door to door in the Philippines because there are no other alternatives in many parts of the country. Also, when Ingersoll-Rand first introduced pneumatic tools, a direct channel was used because considerable buyer education and service were necessary. As buyers became more familiar with these products, the company switched to using industrial distributors. Certain characteristics of offerings also favor direct distribution. Typically, sophisticated technical offerings such as mainframe computers, unstandardized offerings such as custom-built machinery, and offerings of high unit value are distributed directly to buyers. Finally, the overall marketing strategy might favor direct distribution. An organization might seek a certain aura of exclusivity not generated by using intermediaries, or an organization might want to emphasize the appeal of "buying direct," presumably important to certain market segments. Direct distribution may also be appropriate if the organization seeks to differentiate its offering from others distributed through intermediaries. A part of the successful differentiation strategy used by Dell, Inc. is its emphasis on Internet purchases of personal computers.

Even though a variety of conditions favor direct distribution, an important caveat must be noted. The decision to market directly to ultimate buyers involves the absorption of all functions (contacting buyers, storage, delivery, and credit) typically performed by intermediaries. The marketing principle "You can eliminate intermediaries but not their functions" is particularly relevant to the manager considering direct distribution. This point is occasionally overlooked by marketing managers when they elect to distribute directly. The costs of performing these functions can be prohibitive, depending on the organization's financial resources and the opportunity cost of diverting financial resources from other endeavors. Therefore, even though all signs favor direct distribution, the capacity of the organization to perform tasks normally assigned to intermediaries may eliminate this alternative from final consideration. A similar caveat must be noted with respect to intermediaries who consider acquiring functions typically performed by channel members above or below them in the channel (for example, a retailer who wishes to perform wholesaling functions).

Electronic Marketing Channels The availability of the Internet and the World Wide Web adds a technological twist to the analysis of direct versus indirect distribution.[3] *Electronic marketing channels* employ some form of electronic communication, including the Internet, to make products and services available for consumption or use by consumers and industrial users.

Exhibit 7.2 on page 358 shows the electronic marketing channels for books (*Amazon.com*), automobiles (*Auto-By-Tel.com*), reservations services (*Travelocity.com*), and personal computers (*Dell.com*). A feature of these channels is that they often combine electronic and traditional intermediaries. The inclusion of traditional intermediaries for product marketing (distributors for books and dealers for cars) is due to the logistics function they perform—namely, handling, storage, shipping, and so forth. This function remains with traditional intermediaries or with the producer, as evident with Dell, Inc. and its Dell.com direct channel. It is also noteworthy that two-thirds of the sales through Dell.com involve human sales representatives—a common practice with direct distribution as described earlier.

EXHIBIT 7.2

Representative Electronic Marketing Channels

Amazon.com	Autobytel.com	Travelocity.com	Dell.com
Book Publisher	Auto Manufacturer	Commercial Airline	Dell Computer
↓	↓		
Book Distributor	Auto Dealer		
↓	↓	↓	
Amazon.com (Virtual Retailer)	Auto-By-Tel (Virtual Broker)	Travelocity (Virtual Agent)	

Ultimate Buyers

Many services can be distributed through electronic marketing channels, such as travel reservations marketed by Travelocity.com, financial securities by Schwab.com, and insurance by *MetLife.com*. Software also can be marketed this way. However, many other services such as health care and auto repair still involve traditional intermediaries. Electronic marketing channels represent yet another, albeit important, channel design option available for marketers. Like all options, it too must be assessed on its revenue-producing capability relative to the costs of achieving market coverage and satisfying buyer requirements.

Channel Selection at the Retail Level

In the event that traditional intermediaries are chosen as the means for reaching target markets, the channel-selection decision then focuses on the type and location of intermediaries at each level of the marketing channel, beginning with the retail level.

Consider the case of a manufacturer of sporting goods. If retail outlets are chosen, the question becomes, What type of retail outlet? Should hardware stores, department stores, sporting goods stores, or some combination be selected to carry the line of sporting goods? Also, where should these retail outlets be located? Should they be in urban, suburban, or rural areas, and in what parts of the country?

Recognizing that numerous routes to buyers exist, three questions need to be addressed when choosing a marketing channel and intermediaries:

1. Which channel and intermediaries will provide the best coverage of the target market?

2. Which channel and intermediaries will best satisfy the buying requirements of the target market?

3. Which channel and intermediaries will be the most profitable?

Target Market Coverage   Achieving the best coverage of the target market requires attention to the density and type of intermediaries to be used at the retail level of distribution. Three degrees of distribution density exist: intensive, exclusive, and selective.

1. *Intensive distribution* at the retail level means that a manager attempts to distribute the organization's offerings through as many retail outlets as possible. More specifically, a manager may seek to gain distribution through as many outlets of a specific type (such as drugstores) as possible. In its extreme form, intensive distribution refers to gaining distribution through almost all types of retail outlets, as soft drink and candy manufacturers do. For example, Coca-Cola's retail distribution objective is to place its products "within an arm's reach of desire."

2. *Exclusive distribution* is the opposite of intensive distribution in that typically *one* retail outlet in a geographic area or *one* retail chain carries the manufacturer's line. Usually, the geographic area constitutes the defined trade area of the retailer. Mark Cross wallets and Regal shoes are distributed under an exclusive distribution arrangement. Sometimes retailers sign exclusive distribution agreements with manufacturers. For instance, Radio Shack now sells only Compaq's Presario home computers and Thomson SA's RCA brand of audio and video products in its 7,000 stores.[4]

   Occasionally, the exclusive-distribution strategy involves a contractual arrangement between a retailer and a manufacturer or service provider that gives the retailer exclusive rights to sell a line of products or services in a defined area in return for performing specific marketing functions. A common form of an exclusive agreement is a franchise agreement. Franchise agreements now exist in more than 70 industry categories ranging from tax preparation services (H & R Block) to donuts (Dunkin' Donuts). There are nearly 3,000 franchise retail chains in the United States with 600,000 units, which account for 41 percent of all retail sales.[5]

3. *Selective distribution* is between these two extremes. This strategy calls for a manufacturer to select a few retail outlets in a specific area to carry its offering. This approach is often used for marketing furniture, some brands of men's clothing, and quality women's apparel. Selective distribution weds some of the market coverage benefits of intensive distribution to the control over resale evident with the exclusive distribution strategy. For this reason, selective distribution has become increasingly popular in recent years among marketers.

The popularity of selective distribution has come about also because of a phenomenon called effective distribution. *Effective distribution* means that a limited number of outlets at the retail level account for a significant fraction of the market potential. An example of effective distribution is a situation in which a marketer of expensive men's wristwatches distributes through only 40 percent of available outlets, but these outlets account for 80 percent of the volume of the wristwatch market. Increasing the density of retail outlets to perhaps 50 percent would probably increase the percentage of potential volume to 85 percent; however, the attendant costs of this action might lead to only a marginal profit contribution at best.

The decision as to which of the three degrees of density to select rests on how buyers purchase the manufacturer's offering, the amount of control over resale desired by the manufacturer, the degree of exclusivity sought by intermediaries, and the contribution of intermediaries to the manufacturer's marketing effort. Intensive distribution is often chosen when the offering is purchased frequently and when buyers wish to expend minimum effort in its acquisition. Almost by definition, convenience goods such as confectionery products, personal care products, and gasoline fall into this category. Limited-distribution strategies (exclusive and selective) are chosen when the offering requires personal selling at the point of purchase. Major appliances and industrial goods are typically distributed exclusively or selectively.

The density of retail distribution varies inversely with the amount of control over resale and aura of exclusivity desired by manufacturers and retailers. That is, retail density decreases as control over resale practices and desired exclusivity increases. Gucci, one of the world's leading luxury goods producers with its Yves Saint Laurent, Sergio Rossi, Boucheron, Opium, and Gucci brands, has systematically dropped retail outlets for its brands that have not met its stringent sales, service, and display standards. Large toy retailers routinely obtain proprietary rights to market specific toys sold by Mattel, Hasbro, and other producers. Such exclusivity gives these retailers a competitive advantage and higher profit margins.[6]

Satisfying Buyer Requirements   A second consideration in channel selection is the identification of channels and intermediaries that satisfy at least some of the interests buyers want fulfilled when purchasing a firm's products or services. These interests fall into four broad categories: (1) information, (2) convenience, (3) variety, and (4) attendant services.

Information is an important requirement when buyers have limited knowledge or desire specific data about a product or service. Properly chosen intermediaries communicate with buyers through in-store displays, demonstrations, and personal selling. Personal computer manufacturers such as Gateway and Apple Computer have opened their own retail outlets staffed with highly trained personnel to inform buyers how their products can better meet each customer's needs.

Convenience has multiple meanings for buyers, such as proximity or driving time to a retail outlet. For example, 7-Eleven stores with more than 5,300 outlets nationwide satisfy this interest for buyers, and candy and snack food firms benefit by gaining display space in these stores. For other consumers, convenience means a minimum of time and hassle. Jiffy Lube and Q-Lube, which promise to change engine oil and filters quickly, appeal to this aspect of convenience. For those who shop on the Internet, convenience means that Web sites must be easy to locate and navigate, and image downloads must be fast. A commonly held view among Web site developers is the "8-second rule": Consumers will abandon their efforts to enter or navigate a Web site if download time exceeds 8 seconds.[7]

Variety reflects buyers' interest in having numerous competing and complementary items from which to choose. Variety is evident in both the breadth and depth of products and brands carried by intermediaries, which enhances their attraction to buyers. Thus, manufacturers of pet food and supplies seek distribution through pet superstores such as Petco and PetsMart, which offer a wide array of pet products.

Attendant services provided by intermediaries are an important buying requirement for products such as large household appliances that require delivery, installation, and credit. Therefore, Whirlpool seeks dealers that provide such services.

Profitability   The third consideration is channel profitability, which is determined by the margins earned (revenues minus cost) for each channel member and for the channel as a whole. Channel cost is the critical dimension of profitability. These costs include distribution, advertising, and selling expenses associated with different types of marketing channels. The extent to which channel members share these costs determines the margins received by each member and by the channel as a whole.

Channel Selection at Other Levels of Distribution

After having determined the nature of retail distribution, the marketing manager must then specify the type, location, and density (if any) of intermediaries that will be used to reach retail outlets. These specific selection decisions closely parallel the retail network decisions made earlier.

If a second-level intermediary (wholesaler, broker, or industrial distributor) is decided on, the question becomes, What type of wholesaler? Should the manager select a specialty wholesaler, which carries a limited line of items within a product line; a general-merchandise wholesaler, which carries a wide assortment of products; a general-line wholesaler, which carries a complete assortment of items in a single retailing field; or a combination of wholesalers? Obviously, an important consideration is what types of wholesalers sell to the retail outlets desired. When Mr. Coffee decided to use supermarkets to sell its replacement coffee filters, it had to recruit food brokers to call on these retailers. Often the decision is based on what is available. If the available wholesalers do not meet the requirements of the manufacturer in terms of satisfying retailers' requirements for delivery, inventory assortment and volume, credit, and so forth, then direct distribution to retailers becomes the only viable alternative. However, careful study of a wholesaler's role in distribution should precede any decision to bypass it, particularly in countries outside the United States. The Gillette Company's experience in Japan is a case in point.[8] Gillette attempted to sell its razors and blades through company salespeople in Japan as it does in the United States, thus eliminating wholesalers traditionally involved in marketing toiletries. Warner-Lambert Company sold its Schick razors and blades through the traditional Japanese channel involving wholesalers. The result? Gillette captured 10 percent of the Japanese razor and blade market and Schick captured 62 percent.

The location of wholesalers is determined by the location of retail outlets to the extent that geographical proximity affects logistical considerations such as transportation costs and fast delivery service. The density of wholesalers is influenced by the density of the retail network and wholesaler service capabilities. Generally, as the density of retail outlets increases, the density of wholesalers necessary to service them also increases. Retail bookseller Barnes & Noble, Inc. faced this issue. It attempted to acquire the Ingram Book Group, the largest U.S. book wholesaler with 11 strategically placed distribution locations. The addition of these wholesalers could have cut transportation costs to its more than 1,000 stores and reduced delivery time for its growing number of online customers reached through barnesandnoble.com. The acquisition did not materialize, and Barnes & Noble found it necessary to expand its own wholesale distribution network.[9]

Similar kinds of decisions are required for each level of distribution in a particular marketing channel; their determination will depend on the extent of market coverage sought and the availability of intermediaries. Suffice it to say that the number of levels in a marketing channel generally varies directly with the breadth of the market sought.

■ DUAL DISTRIBUTION AND MULTI-CHANNEL MARKETING

The discussion thus far has focused on the selection of a single marketing channel. However, many organizations use multiple channels simultaneously. Two common approaches are dual distribution and multi-channel marketing.

Dual Distribution

Dual distribution occurs when an organization distributes its offering through two or more different marketing channels that may or may not compete for similar buyers. For example, General Electric sells its appliances directly to house and apartment builders but uses retailers to reach consumers.

Dual distribution is adopted for a variety of reasons. If a manufacturer produces its own brand as well as a private store brand, the store brand might be distributed directly to that particular retailer, whereas the manufacturer's brand might be handled by wholesalers. Or a manufacturer may distribute directly to major large-volume retailers, whose service and volume requirements set them apart from other retailers, and may use wholesalers to reach smaller retailer outlets. Finally, geography itself may affect whether direct or indirect methods of distribution are used. The organization might use its own sales group in high-volume and geographically concentrated markets but use intermediaries elsewhere. In some instances, companies use multiple channels when a multibrand strategy is used (see Chapter 5). Hallmark sells its Hallmark brand greeting cards through its franchised Hallmark stores and select department stores, and its Ambassador brand of cards through discount and drugstore chains.

The viability of the dual-distribution approach is highly situational and will depend on the relative strengths of the manufacturer and retailers. If a manufacturer decides to distribute directly to ultimate buyers in a retailer's territory, the retailer may drop the manufacturer's line. The likelihood of this depends on the importance of the manufacturer's line to the retailer and the availability of competitive offerings. If a retailer accounts for a sufficiently large portion of the manufacturer's volume, elimination of the line could have a negative effect on the manufacturer's sales volume. This happened to Shaw Industries, the world's largest carpet and rug manufacturer. When Shaw Industries announced it would begin operating its own retail stores and commercial dealer network, Home Depot dropped Shaw Industries as a carpet and rug supplier and switched to Mohawk Industries' products.[10]

Multi-Channel Marketing

Like dual distribution, multi-channel marketing involves the use of two or more marketing channels that may or may not compete for similar buyers. *Multi-channel marketing* involves the blending of an electronic marketing channel (electronic storefront or Web site) and a traditional channel in ways that are mutually reinforcing in attracting, retaining, and building relationships with customers.

Multi-channel marketing is pursued for a number of reasons.[11] First, the addition of an electronic marketing channel can provide incremental revenue. Consider Victoria's Secret, the well-known specialty retailer of intimate apparel for women age 18 to 45. It reports that almost 60 percent of the buyers at its Web site are men, most of whom generate new sales for the company. Second, an electronic marketing channel can leverage the presence of a traditional channel. Ethan Allen, the furniture manufacturer, markets its products through ethanallen.com and also through some 300 retail stores in the United States. Customers can browse and buy at its electronic storefront or in its retail furniture store. Ethan Allen's Web site prominently lists retail store locations, and customers who buy online can have their furniture shipped from a nearby store, reducing delivery charges. Finally, multi-channel marketing can satisfy buyer requirements. The Clinique Division of Estée Lauder Companies, which markets cosmetics through department stores and through clinique.com, provides information about its products, skin care, and cosmetic applications through its Web site. Clinique reports that 80 percent of current customers who visit its Web site later purchase a Clinique product at a department store; 37 percent of browsers make a Clinique purchase after visiting the company's Web site.

The viability of multi-channel marketing depends on a variety of considerations.[12] A major consideration is the extent to which an electronic marketing channel generates incremental revenue or simply cannibalizes sales from traditional channel intermediaries. In general, incremental revenue is more likely if (1) an electronic channel reaches a different segment of customers than the traditional channel or (2) traditional and electronic channels are mutually reinforcing in attracting, retaining, and building customer relationships. Relatedly, companies are increasingly focused on the incremental cost to launch and sustain an electronic storefront relative to forecasted incremental revenues. Although estimates vary, the up-front cost to build a Web site with static content, simple search tools, and merchandising that is not personalized is about $350,000 with ongoing costs of $140,000. The up-front cost to build a Web site with interactive content, sophisticated search tools, and highly personalized merchandising can run as high as $4 million with an ongoing cost of $2 million. Not surprisingly, high-margin and high-volume products are best suited for electronic marketing channels. Relationships between a manufacturer or service provider and traditional channel intermediaries also must be considered. Intermediaries, and particularly retailers, are concerned with *disintermediation*—the practice whereby a traditional intermediary member is dropped from a marketing channel and replaced by an electronic storefront. Disintermediation is considered more serious than cannibalization by intermediaries. Whereas cannibalism affects only a portion of an intermediary's sales, disintermediation affects their survival. Companies have avoided multi-channel marketing because of complaints by intermediaries and threats to discontinue carrying their products and delivering their service. For example, Levi Strauss and Norwegian Cruise Line discontinued their electronic storefronts for jeans and online booking reservations, respectively, following retailer and travel agent complaints.

■ SATISFYING INTERMEDIARY REQUIREMENTS AND TRADE RELATIONS

The role of intermediaries in channel selection has been cited several times; however, a number of specific points require elaboration. The impression given so far may be that intermediaries are relatively docile elements in a marketing channel. Nothing could be further from the truth!

Even though reference has been made to "selecting" intermediaries, selection in actual practice is a two-way street. Intermediaries often choose those suppliers with whom they wish to deal. The previously described decisions by Radio Shack to sell only Compaq Computers and RCA audio and video products and Home Depot to replace carpeting from Shaw Industries with Mohawk Industries' products vividly illustrate this point.

Intermediary Requirements

Experienced marketing managers know that they must be sensitive to possible requirements of intermediaries that must be met in order to establish profitable exchange relationships. Intermediaries are concerned with the adequacy of the manufacturer's offering in improving its product assortment for its own target markets. If the product line or individual offering is inadequate, then the intermediary must look elsewhere. Intermediaries also seek marketing support from manufacturers. For wholesalers, support often involves promotional assistance; for industrial distributors, it includes technical assistance. As noted previously, intermediaries concerned with competition usually seek a degree of exclusivity in handling the manufacturer's offering. The ability of the intermediary to provide adequate market coverage, given an exclusive agreement, will determine whether this interest can be satisfied by the manufacturer. Finally, intermediaries expect a profit margin on sales consistent with the functions they are expected to perform. In short, trade discounts, fill-rate standards (that is, the ability of the manufacturer to supply quantities requested by intermediaries), cooperative advertising and other promotional support, lead-time requirements (that is, the length of time from order placement to receipt), and product-service exclusivity agreements each contribute to the likelihood of long-term exchange relationships. A manager who fails to recognize these facts of life often finds that the functions necessary to satisfy buyer requirements, such as sales contacts, display, adequate inventory, service, and delivery, are not being performed.

Trade Relations

Trade relations also are an important consideration in marketing channel management and strategy. Marketing managers recognize that conflicts often arise in trade relations.

Channel Conflict   *Channel conflict* arises when one channel member (such as a manufacturer or an intermediary) believes another channel member is engaged in behavior that is preventing it from achieving its goals. Four sources of conflict are most common.[13] First, conflict arises when a channel member bypasses another member and sells or buys direct. When Wal-Mart elected to purchase products directly from manufacturers rather than through manufacturers' agents, these agents picketed Wal-Mart stores and placed ads in the *Wall Street Journal* critical of the company. Second, there can be conflict over how profit margins are distributed among channel members. For example, when General Motors and Fiat demanded lower prices for original equipment tires supplied by Michelin, the tire maker refused and canceled the supply contract when its term ended. The lower prices prohibited Michelin from achieving its targeted profit margin goals. A third source of conflict arises when manufacturers believe wholesalers or retailers are not giving their products adequate attention. For example, H. J. Heinz Company became embroiled in a conflict with supermarkets in Great Britain because the supermarkets were promoting and displaying private brands at the expense of Heinz brands. The fourth source of conflict occurs when a manufacturer engages in dual distribution and particularly when different retailers or dealers carry the same brands. For instance, the launch of Elizabeth Taylor's Black Pearls fragrance by Elizabeth Arden was put on hold when department store chains such as May and Dillard refused to stock the item once they learned that mass merchants Sears and J.C. Penney would also carry the brand. Elizabeth Arden subsequently introduced the brand only through department stores.

Channel Power   Conflict can have destructive effects on the workings of a marketing channel. To reduce the likelihood of conflict, one member of the channel sometimes seeks to coordinate, direct, and support other channel members. This channel member assumes the role of a *channel captain* because of its power to influence the behavior of other channel members.

This type of power can take four forms. First, economic power arises from the ability of a firm to reward or coerce other members, given its strong financial position or customer franchise. Microsoft Corporation and Wal-Mart have economic power. Expertness is a second source of power. For example, American Hospital Supply helps its customers—hospitals—manage order processing for hundreds of medical supplies. Identification with a particular channel member may also bestow power on a firm. For instance retailers may compete to carry Ralph Lauren, or clothing manufacturers may compete to be carried by Neiman-Marcus or Nordstrom. Finally, power can arise from the legitimate right of one channel member to dictate the behavior of other members. This would occur under contractual arrangements (such as franchising) that allow one channel member to legally direct how another behaves.

■ CHANNEL-MODIFICATION DECISIONS

An organization's marketing channels are subject to modification but less so than product, price, and promotion. Shifts in the geographical concentration of buyers, the inability of existing intermediaries to meet the needs of buyers, and the costs of distribution represent common reasons for modifying existing marketing channels. An organization might initiate a channel-modification program if the product-market strategy changed with the adoption of a market development or diversification strategy. Honda (Acura), Toyota (Lexus), and Nissan (Infiniti) created separate dealer networks to sell their new luxury models designed for upscale consumer markets. Whatever the reason for modifying an organization's marketing channels, at the base of the channel-modification decision should lie the marketing manager's intent to (1) provide the best coverage of the target market sought, (2) satisfy the buying requirements of the target market, and (3) maximize revenue and minimize cost. Channel modification decisions involve an assessment of both the benefits and costs of making a change.

Qualitative Factors in Modification Decisions

The qualitative assessment of a modification decision rests on a series of questions. These questions imply that the modification decision involves a comparative analysis of the existing and new channels.

1. Will the change improve the effective coverage of the target markets sought? How?
2. Will the change improve the satisfaction of buyer needs? How?
3. Which marketing functions, if any, must be absorbed in order to make the change?
4. Does the organization have the resources to perform the new functions?
5. What effect will the change have on other channel participants?
6. What will be the effect of the change on the achievement of long-range organizational objectives?

Quantitative Assessment of Modification Decisions

A quantitative assessment of the modification decision considers the financial impact of the change in terms of revenues and expenses. Suppose an organization is considering replacing its wholesalers with its own distribution centers. Wholesalers receive $5 million annually from the margin on sales of the organization's offering. The organization's cost of servicing the wholesalers is $500,000 annually. Therefore, the cost of using wholesalers in this instance is the margin received by wholesalers plus the $500,000 devoted to servicing them, for a total of $5.5 million. Stated differently, the organization would save this amount if the wholesalers were eliminated.

If it eliminated the wholesalers, however, the organization would have to assume their functions, including the costs of sales to retail accounts formerly assumed by the wholesalers. Sales administration costs would be incurred also. In addition, since the wholesalers carry inventories to service retail accounts, the cost of carrying the inventory would have to be assumed, as well as the expenses of delivery and storage. Finally, since wholesalers extend credit to retailers, the cost of carrying the accounts receivable must be included.

Once the costs incurred by eliminating the wholesaler have been estimated, an evaluation of the modification decision from a financial perspective is possible. Such an evaluation follows with illustrative dollar values.

Cost of Wholesalers		Cost of Distribution Centers	
Margin to wholesalers	$5,000,000	Sales to retailers	$1,500,000
Service expense	500,000	Sales administration	250,000
Total cost	$5,500,000	Inventory cost	935,000
		Delivery and storage	1,877,000
		Accounts receivable	438,000
		Total cost	$5,000,000

Since using wholesalers costs $5.5 million and the cost of distribution centers would be $5 million, a cost perspective suggests selection of the latter option. However, the effect on revenues must be considered. This effect can be determined by first addressing the questions noted earlier and then translating market coverage, the satisfaction of buyer needs, and channel-participant response into dollar values.

NOTES

1. Anne T. Couglan, Erin Anderson, Louis W. Stern, and Adel I. El-Ansary, *Marketing Channels*, 6th ed. (Upper Saddle River, NJ: Prentice Hall, 2001): Chapter 2.

2. Avoncompany.com; Rochelle Kass, "Experimental Beauty," *The Journal News* (July 21, 2001): 1D, 2D; and Nanette Byrnes, "Avon: The New Calling," *Fortune* (September 18, 2000): 136–148.

3. Portions of this discussion are based on Bert Rosenbloom, *Marketing Channels*, 7th ed. (Cincinnati, OH: Southwestern Publishing, 2003): Chapter 15.

4. "Radio Shack Campaign Touts Its RCA Alliance," *Advertising Age* (June 5, 2000): 61; "Radio Shack, Compaq Pact Is Extended," *Dallas Morning News* (April 20, 2000): 2D.

5. International Franchise Association, January 10, 2003.

6. Joshua Levine and Matthew Swibel, "Dr. No," *Forbes* (May 28, 2001): 72–76; "Retailers Won't Share Their Toys," *Wall Street Journal* (December 4, 2001): B1, B4.

7. Jonathan Mandell, "Speed It Up Webmaster, We're Losing Billions Every Second," *New York Times* (September 22, 1999): 58D.

8. "Gillette Tries to Nick Schick in Japan," *Wall Street Journal* (February 4, 1991): B3, B4.

9. "Barnes & Noble Likely to Build Centers for Distribution If Ingram Deal Fails," *Wall Street Journal* (June 2, 1999): B8.

10. "Carpet Firm's Dynamic Chief Must Weave Succession," *Wall Street Journal* (August 19, 1998): B4.

11. This discussion is based on *Multi-Channel Integration: The New Retail Battleground* (Columbus, OH: PricewaterhouseCoopers, March 2001): "Battle-Tested Rules of Online Retail," *eCompany* (April 2001); "No Sale," *Wall Street Journal* (December 10, 2002): R10.

12. This discussion is based on "The Dell Myth," *Wall Street Journal* (September 16, 2002): R12; *The Next Chapter in Business-to-Consumer E-Commerce* (Boston: The Boston Consulting Group, March 2001).

13. This discussion is based, in part, on Christine B. Bucklin, et al., "Channel Conflict: When Is It Dangerous?" *The McKinsey Quarterly* (Number 3, 1997): 36–43; and "Michelin Cancels Supply Contract with GM Europe," *Wall Street Journal* (May 30, 2002): D6.

Gateway, Inc.

Early on a sunny mid-March 2001 morning, Ted Waitt entered the cafeteria in the North Sioux City, South Dakota, manufacturing plant of Gateway, Inc. Upon entering, a plant supervisor shouts, "Ted is in the house!" The music shifts to Smash Mouth's "All Star" as Waitt steps onto a small makeshift stage at the center of the room surrounded by hundreds of Gateway employees. As the room becomes suddenly quiet, Waitt says softly, in a low, throaty voice, "It's good to be home."[1]

In January 2001, Gateway, Inc. founder and Chairman of the Board, Ted Waitt was named chief executive officer. His predecessor had suddenly retired after serving as the company's chief executive officer since January 1, 2000. Waitt's appointment came at a challenging time. With the U.S. economy in a slowdown in 2000, Gateway recorded a 14 percent decline in year-end annual operating income and posted a $25 million operating loss in the fourth quarter of 2000. The company's common stock, which traded as high as $73.00 per share in the first quarter of 2000, would trade as low as $16.82 in the fourth quarter of 2000.

In early 2001, Waitt and a newly formed senior executive team undertook a strategic review of Gateway's business and established the following objectives for the year: (1) simplify Gateway's business, (2) reduce the company's cost structure, and (3) return to a path to long-term sustainable profitability. "As we exit 2001, our goal is to have this business normalized and operating at a level that will drive healthy shareholder returns through a sustainable long-term business model," said Waitt.[2] The need for decisive action was apparent as the operating results for the first quarter of 2001 were unfolding. Gateway would soon announce a first quarter 2001 operating loss of $576 million compared with a $186 million operating income in the first quarter of 2000.

■ GATEWAY, INC.

Gateway, Inc. is a major U.S. marketer of personal computers (PCs) and related products and services to consumers and businesses. The company is one of the leading suppliers of PCs to the U.S. consumer market, with a market share greater than 20 percent in 2000 based on revenue. With 65 percent of its U.S. sales going to consumers in 2000 (versus 61 percent in 1999), Gateway is one of the top two manufacturers of consumer PCs in the United States. The company recorded an operating income of $511 million on net sales of $9.6 billion in 2000. Exhibit 1 on page 368 shows Gateway's annual operating results for the period 1994 through 2000 and quarterly operating results for 1999 and 2000.

---

[1] Katrina Brooker, "I Built This Company, I Can Save It," *Fortune* (April 30, 2001), pp. 94ff.

[2] Ted Waitt, "Fellow Shareholders," *Gateway Annual Report 2000*.

This case was prepared by Professor Roger A. Kerin, of the Edwin L. Cox School of Business, Southern Methodist University, as a basis for class discussion and is not designed to illustrate effective or ineffective handling of an administrative situation. This case is based on published sources including Gateway, Inc. annual reports, U.S. Securities and Exchange Commission Form 10-K reports, company news releases, published articles, and information provided by individuals knowledgeable about the industry. Consequently, the interpretation and perspectives presented in the case are not necessarily those of Gateway, Inc. or any of its employees. Where appropriate, quotes, statistics, and published information are footnoted for reference purposes. Copyright © 2002 Roger A. Kerin. No part of this case may be reproduced without the written permission of the copyright holder.

EXHIBIT 1

Gateway, Inc. Annual and Quarterly Operating Results

Annual Operating Results: 1994–2000

	1994	1995	1996	1997	1998	1999	2000
Net sales ($ in millions)	$2,701	$3,676	$5,035	$6,294	$7,468	$8,965	$9,601
Operating expense and income as a percent of net sales							
Net sales	100.0%	100.0%	100.0%	100.0%	100.0%	100.0%	100.0%
Cost of goods sold	86.8	83.5	81.4	82.9	79.3	79.5	78.6
Gross profit	13.2	16.5	18.6	17.1	20.7	20.5	21.4
Selling, general, and administrative expense (S,G&A)	8.0	9.7	11.5	12.5	14.1	13.8	16.1
Operating income	5.2	6.8	7.1	2.8	6.6	6.6	5.3

Quarterly Operating Results: 1999–2000

1999	1st Quarter	2nd Quarter	3rd Quarter	4th Quarter
Net sales ($ in thousands)	$2,181,901	$1,969,376	$2,263,900	$2,549,723
Operating expense and income as a percent of net sales				
Net sales	100.0%	100.0%	100.0%	100.0%
Gross profit	19.7	20.1	20.9	21.1
S,G&A	13.2	13.9	13.9	14.3
Operating income	6.5	6.2	7.0	6.8
2000	1st Quarter	2nd Quarter	3rd Quarter	4th Quarter
Net sales ($ in thousands)	$2,398,950	$2,207,017	$2,548,290	$2,446,343
Operating expense and income as a percent of net sales				
Net sales	100.0%	100.0%	100.0%	100.0%
Gross profit	21.6	22.6	22.7	18.9
S,G&A	13.9	15.2	15.4	19.9
Operating income (loss)	7.8	7.4	7.3	(1.0)

Source: Gateway, Inc. Annual Reports, 1994-2000.

Company Background

With a $10,000 loan secured by his grandmother, Ted Waitt and a partner founded Gateway as a computer-parts distributor in 1985. What began in a small barn on Waitt's father's cattle farm in Iowa evolved into the second largest custom manufacturer and direct marketer of PCs behind Dell Computer Corporation in 2000. In February 2001, Gateway was ranked as the most admired American company in the computers and office equipment industry in a *Fortune* magazine survey of business executives, corporate directors, and securities analysts.[3] Today, the company is headquartered in Poway, California.

Gateway's strategy is to deliver the best value to its customers by offering quality, high-performance PCs and other products and services employing the latest technology at competitive prices and by providing outstanding service and support. The company has shipped over 21.6 million PCs through 2000, including approximately 5.1 million units in 2000 and 4.7 million units in 1999.

Gateway expanded into Europe in 1993 when it opened a sales, service, and production facility in Ireland. In 2000, "Gateway Europe" had operations and facilities in most Western European countries. Gateway began doing business in the Asia Pacific region in 1995. By 2000, "Gateway Asia Pacific" had a manufacturing operation in Malaysia, as well as sales and service facilities in Singapore, Malaysia, Australia, New Zealand, and Japan. In 1999, Gateway entered the Canadian computer market supported by product, service, and support offerings. International sales were 14 percent of total Gateway sales in 1999 and 2000.

Gateway Customer Base and Product Line

Gateway develops, manufactures, markets, and supports a broad line of desktop and portable PCs, servers, and workstations used by consumers, small and medium-sized businesses, government agencies, educational institutions, and large businesses. Gateway provides PC products that are custom-configured to conform to customer specifications. Each PC is generally shipped from Gateway's manufacturing facilities ready for use, with an operating system and certain applications software already installed. PC replacement parts are also generally shipped directly from Gateway to its customers.

In addition, the company markets a broad range of "beyond-the-box" offerings including peripheral products (monitors, printers, fax/modems, CD-ROM drives, external storage devices, and third-party software titles), Internet access services, financing programs, training programs, and services and support. Beyond-the-box offerings accounted for about 20 percent of 2000 sales, compared with about 9 percent of company sales in 1999. The surge in beyond-the-box revenue was driven in part by an expansion in Internet access and portal income through an alliance with America Online, Inc. (AOL) established in late 1999 and the delivery of Gateway training programs.

The growing attention to beyond-the-box products and particularly services by Gateway reflected the company's view of its future business. As explained by Ted Waitt in 1998:

> We're about customer relations a lot more than we are about PCs. If we get a 5 percent margin on a $1,500 PC, we make $75. But if we can make $3 a month on Internet access, that's another $100 over three years. Three years from now, I don't think just selling PC hardware will allow anyone to have a great business.[4]

Gateway Direct Marketing and Distribution

Gateway sells its products and services to PC customers primarily through three complementary distribution channels—telephone sales, an Internet Web site (*www. gateway.com*), and Gateway Country Stores. The company estimates that over half of its consumer customers take advantage of at least two of these channels before making their purchases.

---

[3]Ahmad Diba and Lisa Muñoz, "America's Most Admired Companies," *Fortune* (February 19, 2001), pp. 64ff.
[4]David Kirkpatrick, "Old PC Dogs Try New Tricks," *Fortune* (July 6, 1998), p. 187.

EXHIBIT 2

Unit Growth of Gateway Country Stores

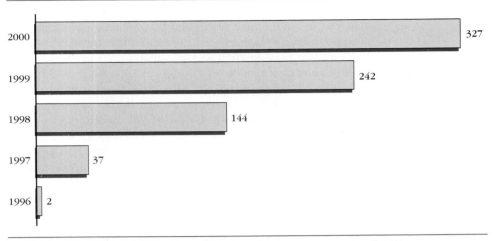

Source: Gateway, Inc., U.S. Securities and Exchange Commission Form 10K, 1996–2000.

Gateway originally sold its PCs directly to customers over the telephone. The company has had an Internet Web site since 1995. In April 1996, Gateway became the first major PC manufacturer to provide its customers the ability to custom configure, order, and pay for a personal computer via the World Wide Web. In November 1996, Gateway opened two Gateway Country Store locations in the United States, following the debut of this concept in France and Germany in 1994 and later in Japan, the United Kingdom, Sweden, and Australia. Ten stores were opened in Canada in late 2000. By the end of 2000, Gateway was operating 327 Gateway Country Stores in the United States and some 360 stores worldwide. According to company estimates, 75 percent of the U.S. population had a Gateway Country Store located within a 30-minute drive in 1999. In 2000, 85 percent of the U.S. population were within this driving distance of a Gateway Country Store.[5] Exhibit 2 shows the growth of Gateway Country Stores in the United States.

Gateway Country Stores   A novel feature of Gateway Country Stores is that Gateway does not stock PCs ready for sale at the stores. Rather, the stores function principally as showrooms and allow customers to see, test, and handle Gateway's products and have their questions answered by trained customer service representatives. Customers can order a PC while at a store, can visit the Gateway Web site later to place an order, or can call to ask further questions and order their PC over the telephone. PCs, built to the customer's specifications, are then shipped to the customer's home or business within five days. Another feature of the stores is the emphasis placed on information dissemination, product demonstration and servicing, customer relationship building, and training by Gateway personnel in a comfortable setting. In 1999, Gateway formally introduced its Gateway Business Solution centers in its stores to meet the needs of small business and home office customers. The company subsequently added approximately 300 dedicated business sales representatives working out of its stores to address the technology needs of small and medium-sized business clients in 2000.

---

[5]Brad Graves, "Gateway Aims to Cut 'Tech Overload'," *San Diego Business Journal* (August 14, 2000), pp. 1ff.; Susan Chandler, "Gateway Wants to Market to Shoppers Out of Internet's Reach," *Knight-Ridder Business News* (October 26, 1999).

According to industry research, 60 percent of small businesses purchase PCs through retail stores and Gateway "could attract a big segment with this effort," noted an industry analyst.[6]

The stores reflect Gateway's midwestern roots and the décor includes tractor seats, mock silos, and grain bins. Gateway Country Stores typically occupy 4,000 to 8,000 square feet and are staffed by as many as 15 training personnel, technical specialists, and customer service representatives. In 2000, the 327 U.S. Gateway Country Stores housed about 6,000 classroom seats, offering training on general PC usage, popular third-party software, Internet usage, and networking services. Gateway has annual sales of about $8 million emanating from each of its U.S. Gateway Country Stores according to industry analysts.[7] (Gateway does not formally report store sales separately.)

Multi-Channel Distribution   Gateway's practice of using three complementary distribution channels to sell its products and services is believed to be a competitive advantage. According to company sources:

> Gateway believes that this direct distribution and multi-channel approach provides several competitive advantages. First, Gateway believes it can offer competitive pricing by avoiding the additional markups, inventory and occupancy costs associated with distributors, dealers and traditional retail stores. Second, by alleviating the need for the high levels of finished goods inventory required by traditional retail channels, Gateway believes it can respond more quickly to changing customer demands—offering new products on a timely basis and reducing its exposure to the risk of product obsolescence. Third, Gateway believes that working directly with customers promotes brand awareness and customer loyalty as evidenced by the high number of repeat customers.[8]

Gateway's complementary distribution channels also have been recognized by an industry observer as having "the potential to shake up the business of selling PCs as much as Dell's direct model first did in the early 1990s."[9] According to this observer:

> Gateway is forcing the industry to recognize that it's no longer in the same category as archrival Dell. While Michael Dell has resolutely championed a direct strategy—denouncing storefront sales—Gateway's "hybrid direct" approach has let consumers choose the buying experience that fits them best, at the same time giving the company the cost advantages and efficiency of direct-from-the-factory production.

Competitors as well have monitored the growth of Gateway Country Stores and multi-channel sales and distribution effort. Apple Computer, for example, was believed to be planning to open its own chain of retail stores in 2001.[10]

In February 2000, Gateway looked to further expand its retail presence with the announcement of an alliance with OfficeMax, a major office products retailer in the United States.[11] Under the terms of the alliance, a Gateway store-within-a-store would occupy about 400 square feet near the entrance of OfficeMax stores and be staffed by Gateway customer service representatives. In turn, OfficeMax would phase out its own computer department. Gateway would invest $50 million in OfficeMax convertible

[6]Gary McWilliams, "PCs: Gateway to Use Its Stores to Lure Small Businesses," *Wall Street Journal* (April 8, 1999), p. B1.

[7]Cliff Edwards, "Sorry Steve, Here's Why It Won't Work," *Business Week* (May 21, 2001), p. 44.

[8]Gateway, Inc., U.S. Securities and Exchange Commission, Form 10-K, 2000, pp. 3-4.

[9]Deborah Claymon, "Strip Malls Are Gateway Country," *The Industry Standard* (November 27, 2000), at p. 56.

[10]"Apple Is Mulling Own Store Chain to Expand Sales," *Wall Street Journal* (September 29, 2000), pp. B1, B2.

[11]"OfficeMax and Gateway Announce Major Long-Term, Multi-Channel Strategic Alliance," Gateway Inc. Press Release, February, 23, 2000.

preferred stock and pay OfficeMax for store refixturing costs and rent. Gateway expected to be present in 1,000 OfficeMax stores by the end of the first quarter of 2001. Gateway had 463 stores in OfficeMax locations by year-end 2000.

Expansion of Gateway's retail presence shifted revenue obtained from telephone and online sources to retail stores. According to one industry analyst, Gateway's revenue from telephone and Internet sales dropped from 76 percent of total company revenue in the first quarter of 2000 to 65 percent in the fourth quarter of 2000. By contrast, retail-derived sales increased from 24 percent to 35 percent of total revenue during the same period.[12]

■ THE PERSONAL COMPUTER INDUSTRY MARKETING ENVIRONMENT

Personal computers represent the largest sector of the computer hardware industry in terms of both units sold and revenue. Desktop computers represent approximately 61 percent of PC hardware revenues; notebooks and portable PCs account for 28 percent of revenues, and PC servers register 11 percent of revenues. The United States is the largest single geographical market for PCs, accounting for 35 percent to 40 percent of worldwide PC unit volume. Business customers, including small, medium, and large companies, educational institutions, and government entities, buy more PCs than consumers (households and individuals) both in the United States and internationally. Exhibit 3 shows the percentage breakdown of PC unit shipments by business and consumer customer segments in and outside the United States for the 1998–2001 period (estimated).

The Market for Personal Computers

The heyday of the personal computer arrived in the early 1990s. Growth in worldwide PC shipments averaged more than 20 percent annually between 1991 and 1995, driven largely by increasing PC affordability and performance. However, after a 26

EXHIBIT 3

Distribution of PC Unit Shipments by Geographic Market and Customer Segment for the Period 1998–2001 (estimated)

Geographic Market	Customer Segment	Percentage of PC Shipments by Year			
		1998	*1999*	*2000*	*2001 est.*
United States	Consumer	34%	39%	40%	36%
	Business	66	61	60	64
		100%	100%	100%	100%
Non-U.S.	Consumer	27%	32%	37%	35%
	Business	73	68	63	65
		100%	100%	100%	100%
Worldwide (U.S. + Non-U.S.)	Consumer	30%	35%	38%	36%
	Business	70	65	62	64
		100%	100%	100%	100%

Source: Based on "Computers: Hardware," *Standard & Poor's Industry Surveys*, May 2001 and Company 10-K Reports.

---

[12]"Gateway Shuts 10 Percent of U.S. Stores," CNET News.com (March 28, 2001).

percent sales increase in 1995, annual growth trended downward to about 13 percent in 1998. In 1999, worldwide PC shipments increased 23 percent due in part to Internet-driven demand and customer interest in upgrades.

The U.S. personal computer industry posted moderate unit volume gains for the year 2000. Personal computer unit sales in the United States grew 10 percent in 2000 compared with a worldwide sales growth of 14.5 percent. "The PC industry was hurt by a sluggish 2000 fourth quarter when worldwide PC shipments increased just 10 percent and U.S. shipments increased 6.4 percent," according to an analyst from Gartner Dataquest, a major supplier of industry information.[13]

PC sales in the first quarter of 2001 continued the slide from the fourth quarter of 2000. Industry analysts were predicting 2001 PC unit shipments in the United States over all to be 11 percent below 2000 levels. The last time the PC industry experienced such a significant yearly downturn was 1985, when U.S. personal computer shipments dropped 21.8 percent.[14]

The average system price for PCs has evidenced a downward trend in recent years. The average PC price fell from $1,877 in 1998 to $1,709 in 1999 (down 9 percent) to an estimated $1,609 in 2000 (down 5.9 percent). The average system price was projected to be $1,456 in 2001 (down 9.5 percent). The largest price decline has been in desktops, where the average price fell 12 percent in 1999, 7 percent in 2000, and an expected 9.6 percent in 2001.[15] PC manufacturers have sought to offset the declining gross profit margins due to lowered system prices by broadening their revenue stream beyond PCs, commonly called "beyond-the-box" revenues. These offerings include warranty service, product integration and installation services, Internet access, customer financing, PC peripherals, technology consulting and training, and other products and services. In general, beyond-the-box products and services typically have gross margins two to three times higher than PC gross margins.

PC Manufacturers and Marketing Practices

Five large U.S.-based manufacturers compete globally and domestically in the marketplace for PCs in 2000. They are Compaq Computer Corporation, Dell Computer Corporation, Gateway, Inc., Hewlett-Packard, and IBM. These five companies commanded over 46 percent of worldwide PC shipments and 60 percent of PC shipments in the United States in 2000. Compaq Computer was the worldwide market share leader and Dell Computer the U.S. market share leader in 2000. Industry analysts speculated that Dell Computer could become the world's largest PC manufacturer in 2001. Exhibit 4 on page 374 shows PC manufacturer unit shipment and market share data for 1999 and 2000.

Market Positions PC manufacturers differed in terms of their respective market positions. For example, 55 percent of Compaq's revenue was derived from sales outside the United States and PC sales to consumers accounted for about 18 percent of the company's revenue in 2000. By comparison, 14 percent of Gateway's revenue was derived from international sales and PC consumer sales represented 56 percent of total company 2000 sales. Approximately 65 percent of Dell's PC sales were to businesses and about 33 percent of its sales were outside the United States.

Market positioning affected the pricing and profitability of PC manufacturers. In general, PCs sold to businesses tend to be on the higher end of the price continuum and have higher gross margins. PCs sold to consumers tend to be on the lower end of the price continuum and have lower gross margins.

[13]"PC Market Hits Pothole in Q4," CyberAtlas.internet.com, January 2001.

[14]"PC Market Has Nowhere to Go but Up," CyberAtlas.internet.com, March 2001.

[15]"Computers: Hardware," *Standard & Poors Industry Surveys*, May, 2001.

EXHIBIT 4

PC Manufacturer Shipment and Market Share Data: 1999 and 2000[*]

PC Manufacturer Unit Shipments Worldwide: 1999 and 2000
(Thousands of Units)

Manufacturer	1999 Shipments	1999 Market Share (%)	2000 Shipments	2000 Market Share (%)	Year-to-Year Growth (%)
Compaq	15,870	13.5%	17,203	12.8%	8.4%
Dell	11,459	9.7	14,536	10.8	26.9
Hewlett-Packard	7,600	6.5	10,237	7.6	34.7
IBM	9,331	7.9	9,162	6.8	− 1.8
Gateway	4,745	4.0	5,110	3.8	7.7
Others	68,621	58.4	78,490	58.1	16.1
Total Market	117,626	100.0%	134,738	100.0%	14.5%

PC Manufacturer Unit Shipments in U.S.: 1999 and 2000
(Thousands of Units)

Manufacturer	1999 Shipments	1999 Market Share (%)	2000 Shipments	2000 Market Share (%)	Year-to-Year Growth (%)
Dell	7,493	16.7%	9,433	19.1%	25.9%
Compaq	7,222	16.1	7,599	15.4	5.2
Gateway	4,002	8.9	4,271	8.7	6.7
Hewlett-Packard	3,955	8.8	5,642	11.4	42.7
IBM	3,274	7.3	2,677	5.4	− 18.2
Others	18,937	42.2	19,723	40.0	4.2
Total Market	44,882	100.0%	49,344	100.0%	10.0%

[*] Data include desk-based PCs, mobile PCs, and PC servers.

Source: Company 10-K Reports. International Data Corporation and Gartner Dataquest total market estimates.

Differentiation　PC manufacturers compete on the basis of price, technology availability, performance, quality, reliability, service, and support. However, as PCs have migrated to the status of a commodity product in the minds of many consumer and business buyers, PC manufacturers have found it necessary to find innovative ways to differentiate their products and their total offering. According to a Gateway executive, "In a mature industry, the smart players begin to think about how to differentiate around a commodity."[16] Apple Computer's "Think Different" advertising campaign coupled with the introduction of iMac—the most innovative PC ever created according to many PC and business analysts—is one example of differentiation.[17] The growing

---

[16]Deborah Claymon, "Strip Malls Are Gateway Country," *The Industry Standard* (November 27, 2000), p. 55.

[17]Jim Carlton, "Apple to Post Profit Again on Sales Gains," *Wall Street Journal* (January 6, 1999), pp. A3, A8.

emphasis on beyond-the-box offerings is another example of differentiation as well as an additional revenue and gross profit stream.

Production and Distribution Business Models By the late 1990s, PC manufacturers came to recognize that their fundamental production-distribution business model represented a potential source of differentiation and competitive advantage. Each of the five large U.S.-based PC manufacturers tend to emphasize one of two production and distribution business models. Compaq Computer, Hewlett-Packard, and IBM employ the "build-to-stock/reseller" business model for the most part. Dell Computer and Gateway use the "build-to-order/sell direct" business model for the most part. The two business models are shown in Exhibit 5.

Build-to-Stock/Reseller Model The "build-to-stock/reseller" model involves the mass production of PCs for sale to and through a network of resellers to businesses and consumers. Resellers include value-added resellers, distributors, and retailers. value-added resellers (VARs) specialize in selling to a particular market segment (such as educational institutions) and offer specialized services, such as complete PC hardware and software systems or special expertise in an application area. PC distributors provide warehousing functions and logistics support and sell to retailers. Retailers

EXHIBIT 5

Production and Distribution Business Models for Personal Computers

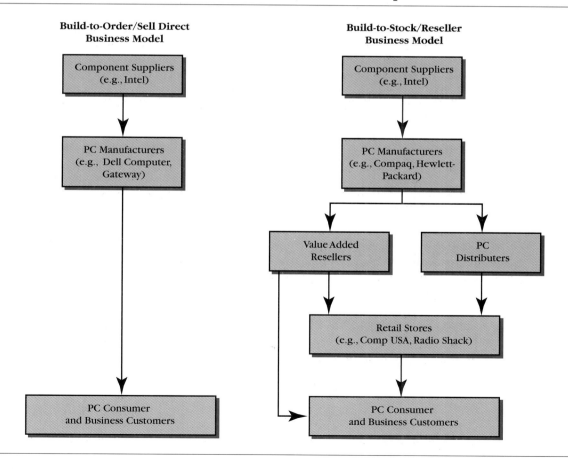

include consumer electronics specialty stores and mass merchandisers that typically serve the household consumer and small office/home office business customer.

Build-to-Order/Sell Direct Model   The "build-to-order/sell direct" model involves the customized production of PCs to customer specifications and direct shipment to the buyer. With this model, a PC is not produced until it has been ordered by a customer. This model avoids (1) having to keep many differently equipped PCs in a manufacturer's distribution center or on distributor and retailer shelves to fill buyer requests for one or another configuration of options and components, and (2) having to clear out slow-selling machines at a discount before introducing a new generation of PCs. In addition, selling direct eliminated reseller selling, general and administrative (S,G&A) expenses, and resulting retailer margins (typically in the 4 to 10 percent range) that increased PC prices or decreased manufacturer gross margins. Industry observers were of the view that the "build-to-order/sell direct" model was particularly appealing to customers well versed in PC technology who knew what options and features they wanted and who were knowledgeable of price differences among brands.

By 2000, industry analysts and PC manufacturers alike were of the view that the "build-to-order/sell direct" model was the more economically efficient production and distribution business model for PCs. Accordingly, this model is now applied to some degree by most U.S.-based PC manufacturers and several PC retailers. Compaq Computer, for example, has invested in its own build-to-order manufacturing capability and sells PCs directly through its toll-free telephone number and Internet site (*www.compaq.com*). Nevertheless, by the end of 2000, the overwhelming majority of Compaq's PC unit sales came from its extensive reseller network in more than 100 countries. At the same time, computer retailers such as CompUSA and Wal-Mart Stores have begun to offer their own "build-to-order/sell direct" option on their Web sites.

Gateway, Inc. Versus Dell Computer Corporation   Gateway and Dell Computer Corporation pioneered the "build-to-order/sell direct" business model for PCs in the 1980s. Both companies were founded by young entrepreneurs—Ted Waitt at Gateway and Michael Dell at Dell Computer—who dropped out of college to build their businesses. Both companies embraced the philosophy that PCs could be built to order and sold directly to customers at a profit. And both companies recognized the potential of offering customers the ability to custom configure, order, and pay for a PC via the World Wide Web as an integral part of their business model in 1995. As recently as 1996, the two companies were virtually identical in terms of their sales and operating income. (Compare Exhibit 6 for a summary of Dell Computer's annual operating results for the period 1994 through 2000 with Gateway results shown in Exhibit 1.) It was during this time that Gateway and Dell Computer were frequently called "archrivals."

About this time, Gateway and Dell Computer began to differentiate the sales and distribution element of their business models. From 1997 through 2000 Gateway broadened its sell-direct initiative by adding company-owned and operated Gateway Country Stores to its telephone and Internet sales practice—becoming the only PC manufacturer to do so. According to a Gateway executive, "Over the years, Gateway has learned that many customers simply aren't willing to place an order for a computer sight unseen."[18] Some industry observers also applauded this effort noting:

> The stores are useful. There are people who like to go in and kick the tires. In the stores, the customer can get better sales support. You can go in and actually talk to a human being and some people like to do that. There's a kind of customer interaction that you're going to get at Gateway that you're not going to get at Best Buy or Circuit City.

---

[18]"Direct Seller Gateway Gets Closer to Buyer with Stores," *Dallas Morning News* (December 9, 1998), pp. 1D, 11D.

EXHIBIT 6

Dell Computer Corporation Operating Results: Fiscal Years 1994–2000*

	1994	1995	1996	1997	1998	1999	2000
Net sales ($ in millions)	$2,873	$3,475	$5,296	$7,759	$12,327	$18,243	$25,265
Operating expense and income as a percent of net sales							
Net sales	100.0%	100.0%	100.0%	100.0%	100.0%	100.0%	100.0%
Cost of sales	84.9	78.8	79.8	78.5	77.9	78.5	79.3
Gross profit	15.1	21.2	20.2	21.5	22.1	22.5	20.7
Operating expenses:							
Selling, general, and administrative expense	14.7	12.2	11.3	10.6	9.8	9.8	9.4
Research, development, and engineering	1.7	1.9	1.8	1.6	1.6	1.5	2.2
Operating income (loss)	(1.3)	7.1	7.1	9.3	10.7	11.2	9.1

*Fiscal years generally run from February through January.

Source: Dell Computer Corporation Annual Reports, 1994–2000.

> The stores give customers real human beings to talk to, and in the end, Gateway doesn't care whether those customers buy the computer right there in the stores, or go home and make the transaction via the Web or by telephone. Either way they get the sale. . . . It's certainly driving their revenue.[19]

However, all industry observers were not favorably disposed toward Gateway's retail emphasis and expansion.[20] One observer called the stores "an albatross." Another believed the stores' expenses have forced it to raise its PC prices above those of rival Dell Computer and Compaq Computer by as much as 25 percent by year-end 2000 for comparable machines. Although estimates varied, industry analysts thought the average selling, general and administrative (S,G&A) expenses to operate a store ranged from $1.5 million to $2 million annually (including the rental costs of multi-year leases; personnel staffing costs, utilities, etc.).

Dell Computer, on the other hand, put greater emphasis on its direct-sales, build-to-order business model during the past three years. This emphasis was prompted, in part, by the company's ill-fated decision in the early 1990s to sell its PCs through retailers as well by direct sales. Believing its direct-sales business would not grow fast enough, Dell Computer began distributing its PCs through Soft Warehouse Superstores (now CompUSA), Staples (a leading office products chain), Wal-Mart Stores, Sam's Club, Price Club (now Costco), and Best Buy stores in 16 states in 1990 through 1993. However, when the company saw how thin its gross margins were in selling through retailers and other intermediaries in 1994, it abandoned this effort to refocus on direct sales.[21] According to Michael Dell in 1994, "The strength we see in our own direct

---

[19]Robert Scally, "The Crown Prince of Clicks-and-Mortar," *DSN Retailing Today* (May 8, 2000), pp. 24–26.

[20]Gary McWilliams, "PCs: Gateway to Use Its Stores to Lure Small Businesses," *Wall Street Journal* (April 8, 1999), p. B1.

[21]"Dell Forsakes Retail for Direct Approach," *Computer World* (July 18, 1994), pp. 32ff.

business to consumers has convinced us that focusing on this business will be far more valuable to our organization than traditional retail expansion."[22] Since 1995, Dell Computer has emphasized the importance of keeping its operating costs down and wringing efficiency out of its build-to-order/sell direct business model. In 2000, over 40 percent of Dell Computer's sales were Web-enabled and almost 45 percent of the company's technical support activities were conducted via the Internet. Dell Computer sales in 2000 were almost five times higher than sales in 1996 and operating income increased sixfold during the period.

■ GATEWAY SITUATION IN MARCH 2001

By the end of March 2001, Ted Waitt and a newly formed senior management team had identified three objectives that Gateway had to meet to revitalize the company's fortunes. These were to (1) simplify Gateway's business, (2) reduce the company's cost structure, and (3) return to a path to long-term sustainable profitability. Since January 2001, Waitt and Gateway senior executives have promptly made several decisions consistent with 2001 objectives.[23]

To simplify Gateway's business, the company began cutting the number of components used to build Gateway PCs, thus reducing product variations from 2 million to 1,000. In addition, while the company would continue to offer beyond-the-box products and services, Gateway's focus would be on selling "one computer, one customer at a time," said Waitt. The renewed attention to PC sales was evident in a revised sales commission plan. During 2000, Gateway sales people earned higher commissions for beyond-the-box offerings than PCs. Waitt reversed this policy, paying salespeople higher commissions for PC sales.

To reduce the company's cost structure, Gateway executives decided to discontinue company-owned manufacturing, sales, and service operations outside North America in the third quarter of 2001. These operations employed 3,500 people representing almost 18 percent of Gateway's total workforce in 2000. Technical and service support to customers outside North America would be contracted to third-party service providers. In addition, Gateway would terminate its store-within-a-store retail relationship with OfficeMax in July 2001. Despite substantial costs to launch this initiative, anticipated sales did not materialize. The company also closed 10 percent of its Gateway Country Stores in the United States and its recently opened stores in Canada, which affected about 700 employees. Planned openings of an additional 60 Gateway Country Stores were put on hold. Finally, Gateway decided to drop its advertising agency and develop corporate advertising in-house, which was expected to save the company "millions" of dollars in advertising fees in 2001.

Looking forward, Waitt recognized that revenue growth was important to Gateway's future. He said:

> In addition to getting our cost structure back in line, we simply have to get growing again. There's growth to be had even in a downturn, and we plan to grab more than our fair share of the market with great products and beyond-the-box services that are competitively priced to offer the best value in the industry.[24]

---

[22]"Dell to Discontinue Retail Sales," *PR Newswire* (July 11, 1994).

[23]This summary is based on "Gateway to Drastically Slim Down Its Product Line," CNET News.com (February 28, 2001); "Gateway Provides Guidance and Revises 2000 Financial Results," Gateway Press Release (February 28, 2001); "Gateway Ads Set to Return to House Unit," *Advertising Age* (February 26, 2001), p. 1C; Katrina Brooker, "I Built This Company, I Can Save It," *Fortune* (April 30, 2001), pp. 94ff; and "Gateway Closes Canadian Retail Outlets," *DSN Retailing Today* (May 1, 2001), p. 31.

[24]Ted Waitt, "Fellow Shareholders," *Gateway Annual Report 2000*.

Gateway Operating and Financial Performance in the First Quarter of 2001

During the first quarter of 2001, Gateway sold 1.1 million PC units worldwide.[25] This unit volume was 12 percent below the first quarter of 2000 and 14 percent less than the fourth quarter of 2000. U.S. consumer revenues declined 19 percent year over year in the quarter and U.S. business customer sales posted a 6 percent increase in revenues. Sales to small and medium-sized businesses increased 13 percent compared with the first quarter of 2000. Gateway's European operations recorded a 38 percent decrease in revenues for the quarter over the same period last year. Gateway's Asia-Pacific operations reported a 32 percent decline. Company sales over all in the first quarter of 2001 were $2.03 billion compared with sales of $2.4 billion in first quarter of 2000.

Gateway recorded an operating loss of $576 million in the first quarter of 2001, compared with an operating income of $186 million for same quarter of 2000. Included in this loss was $533 million of special charges incurred by Gateway due to restructuring decisions made in the first quarter of which $430 million were noncash charges. In addition, while Gateway would continue to offer consumer financing, it sold its outstanding loan portfolio. When the financial effects of this action were accounted for along with restructuring charges, Gateway recorded a net loss before income taxes of about $6 million for the first quarter of 2001.

Excluding the effects of Gateway's special charges and consumer loan portfolio, the company's gross profit margin would have been about 18.5 percent for the first quarter of 2001, compared with 21.6 percent for the first quarter of 2000. The gross profit for the fourth quarter of 2000 was 18.9 percent. Omitting extraordinary charges, Gateway's S,G&A expenses in the fourth quarter represented about 18.9 percent of revenue, compared with 19.9 percent of revenue in the fourth quarter of 2000. S,G&A expenses were 13.8 percent of revenue in the first quarter of 2000. Commenting on the company's 2001 first-quarter performance, Gateway's chief financial officer said:

> We have essentially broken even from an operating perspective in the first quarter, as per our earlier guidance, excluding the effects of the special charges and losses on the now discontinued lower quality consumer financing business.[26]

Looking Toward Year-End 2001 and Beyond

The decisive executive actions in the first quarter of 2001 were focused on achieving Waitt's announced goal for the year: "to have this business normalized and operating at a level that will drive healthy shareholder returns through a sustainable long-term business model." However, challenges remained. The U.S. personal computer market continued its sluggish pace and Dell Computer had just dropped its PC prices by as much as 20 percent. On April 5, Dell's stock price jumped 13 percent on reports that it was taking market share away from Gateway and other PC manufacturers.[27]

An immediate decision facing Gateway executives was how to respond to Dell Computer's recent PC price cut. A price cut could further depress the company's gross profit margin. On the other hand, Gateway's unit volume was already down and additional lost sales loomed as a possibility.

Resource allocation issues also required attention. For example, what emphasis should be placed on building U.S. consumer sales versus U.S. business customer sales given that Gateway planned to discontinue company-owned operations outside North

---

[25]This discussion is based on "Gateway Reports First Quarter Results," Gateway Press Release (April 19, 2001); Gateway, Inc. Securities and Exchange Commission Form 10Q, 2001 First Quarter Report.

[26]"Gateway Reports First Quarter Results," Gateway Press Release (April 19, 2001).

[27]Katrina Brooker, "I Built This Company, I Can Save It," *Fortune* (April 30, 2001), pp. 94ff.

America in the third quarter of 2001? Relatedly, how might Gateway's sales and advertising effort be directed? That is, how much sales and advertising emphasis should be placed on driving PC and PC-related unit sales versus beyond-the-box products and services? Similarly, should advertising dollars be spent directing prospective buyers to Gateway Country Stores or Gateway's Web site or toll-free telephone number? Gateway's advertising expenditure would be $239.6 million in 2001, compared with $328 million in 2000 and $256.8 million in 1999.

Operating issues related to selling, general and administrative (S,G&A) expenses also required further attention. The planned closure of manufacturing, sales, and service operations outside North America, a reduction in the number of Gateway Country Stores along with advertising fees and expenditures, and the termination of the store-within-a-store agreement with OfficeMax would reduce company-wide S,G&A expenses. Nevertheless, ongoing S,G&A costs associated with continuing operations still needed attention if Gateway was to post an operating profit in 2001. Might the role of the Gateway Country Store concept itself require further thought in the company's business model?

Looking ahead, Gateway's senior executive team recognized that the company's future depended a lot on its customer sales mix, its product sales mix, and its sales mix across three distribution channels. Attention to Gateway's gross margin and operating expenses was also of paramount concern if the company was to return to profitability.

GolfLogix

Measuring the Game of Golf

It was a sunny May afternoon in 2002 as the employees of GolfLogix—all six of them—assembled around the company's conference table in Scottsdale, Arizona. It was 106°F outside, but it was comfortable inside—partly due to the air conditioning, and partly due to the company's finally gaining traction in the market. After three years and nearly $2 million in investments, things were looking up.

GolfLogix was founded in May 1999 on a simple concept—using the satellite-based global positioning system (GPS) to aid golfers in playing the sport they loved. In its simplest form, the GolfLogix product consisted of a customized, handheld GPS receiver, called an "xCaddie," that indicated the distance to the green to which a golfer was hitting (see Exhibit 1 on page 382). Rather than having to "guesstimate" how far he was, the golfer could simply look at his xCaddie, see that he was, say, 157 yards from the green, and pick the club appropriate for that distance. GolfLogix was offering 60 of these "Distance Only" units to golf courses for approximately $1,500 per month on a three-year lease. In turn, courses could provide the units to golfers free of charge, rent them for a nominal fee (say $1 per round), or bundle their cost with the greens fee.

But GolfLogix's system could do much more. Rather than simply indicate distance, the system also could be used to record a golfer's progress around the course. Using an enhanced version of the xCaddie, a golfer could record the exact location of his ball at the beginning and end of every shot as well as the club used to make that shot. At the end of the round, he could download these data to a kiosk in the course's pro shop. In return, he would receive a three-page color printout mapping his progress around the course, along with statistics on how often he used certain clubs, how far he hit the ball using those clubs, and how accurate his shots were (see Exhibit 2 on pages 383–385). This information also was forwarded to a dedicated Web site (*www.golflogix.com*), where it could be combined with data from previous rounds to let the golfer track his progress over time. This "Complete System," which consisted of 60 GPS devices, a GolfLogix kiosk, and a color printer, was being leased to golf courses for approximately $2,000 per month for three years.

Getting courses to adopt these systems had proven elusive, however. But this was beginning to change. In the first four months of 2002, GolfLogix had leased 15 systems (see Exhibit 3 on page 386), with many additional courses requesting a 30-day trial.

The purpose of that day's meeting was to discuss the merits of a recent proposal from one of the members of the GolfLogix team to make and market a direct-to-consumer version of the Distance Only xCaddie. The thinking was that GolfLogix could outsource production of such a device to an original equipment manufacturer

EXHIBIT 1

The GolfLogix Distance Only xCaddie

Source: GolfLogix Web site (*www.golflogix.com*).

and then market it directly to golfers under the GolfLogix name. The device could be marketed through TV infomercials, the Internet, mass merchandisers (such as Wal-Mart), consumer electronics firms (such as Best Buy), and golf outlet stores. It would likely retail for about $300.

While this concept was intriguing, there was debate within GolfLogix as to its merits. Diane DiCioccio, the chief marketing officer of GolfLogix, summed up the situation:

> Six months ago, I would have jumped at this proposal. All along, we've known that we have a great product; we were just having trouble getting buy-in from the courses because of the bad economic conditions. Now that's beginning to change, and we're headed in the right direction. Why screw that up now? If we go with a direct-to-consumer product, even if we get an initial surge, there is no telling if it will last. The last thing I want is for the xCaddie to be this year's golfing fad.

But Jeff Saltz, the CEO of GolfLogix, offered a different opinion:

> Why shouldn't we take the chance? Going through golf courses is one channel, but going directly to consumers gives us a second, complementary channel. The more success we have with consumers, the more the courses will see the value of our product. Our job is to build the GolfLogix brand name by making our product an indispensable tool. Direct-to-consumer offers a very visible, very rapid way of doing that. And if we don't do it, one of our competitors will.

EXHIBIT 2

A Typical Three-Page Printout Following the Use of the Complete System

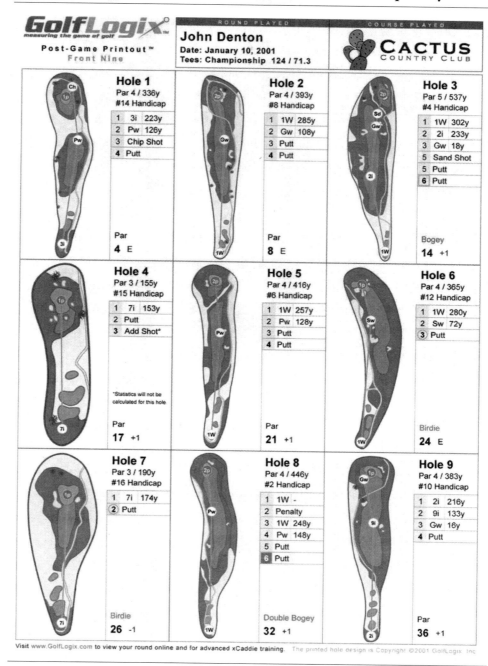

EXHIBIT 2 *(continued)*

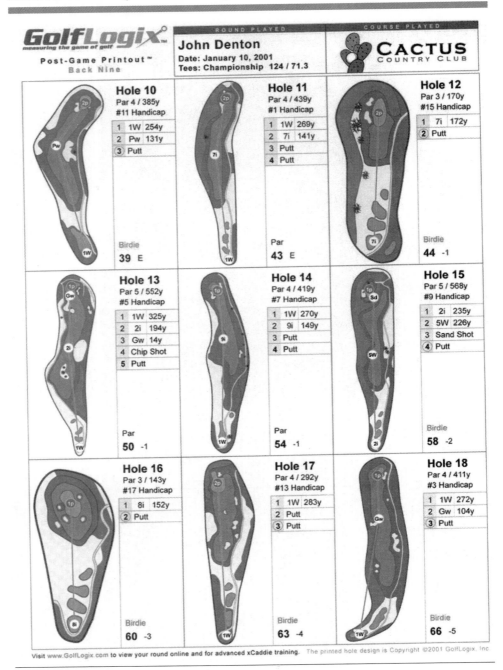

EXHIBIT 2 *(continued)*

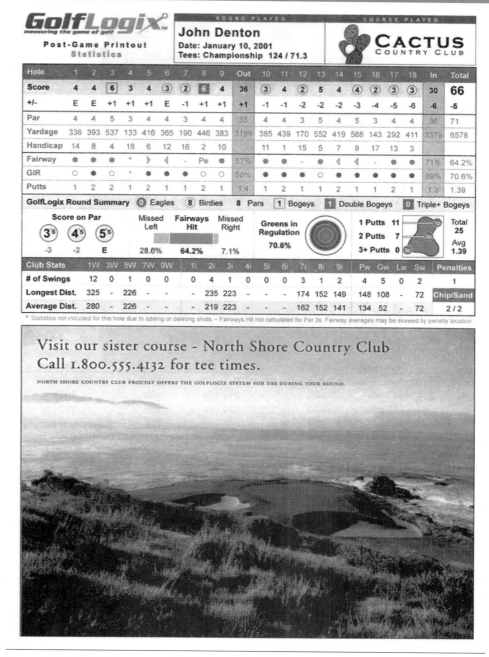

GolfLogix — *measuring the game of golf*

Post-Game Printout Statistics

ROUND PLAYED
John Denton
Date: January 10, 2001
Tees: Championship 124 / 71.3

COURSE PLAYED
CACTUS COUNTRY CLUB

Hole	1	2	3	4	5	6	7	8	9	Out	10	11	12	13	14	15	16	17	18	In	Total
Score	4	4	6	3	4	3	2	6	4	36	3	4	2	5	4	4	2	3	3	30	66
+/-	E	E	+1	+1	+1	E	-1	+1	+1	+1	-1	-1	-2	-2	-2	-3	-4	-5	-6	-6	-5
Par	4	4	5	3	4	4	3	4	4	35	4	4	3	5	4	5	3	4	4	36	71
Yardage	336	393	537	133	416	365	190	446	383	3199	385	439	170	552	419	568	143	292	411	3379	6578
Handicap	14	8	4	18	6	12	16	2	10		11	1	15	5	7	9	17	13	3		
Fairway	●	●	●	*	◗	◖	-	Pe	●	57%	●	●	-	●	◖	◖	-	●	●	71%	64.2%
GIR	○	●	○	*	●	●	●	○	○	50%	●	●	●	○	●	●	●	●	●	89%	70.6%
Putts	1	2	2	1	2	1	1	2	1	14	1	2	1	1	2	1	1	2	1	13	1.39

GolfLogix Round Summary   **0** Eagles   **8** Birdies   **8** Pars   **1** Bogeys   **1** Double Bogeys   **0** Triple+ Bogeys

Score on Par			Missed Left	Fairways Hit	Missed Right	Greens in Regulation		1 Putts	11	Total 25
3's	**4's**	**5's**				70.6%		2 Putts	7	
-3	-2	E	28.6%	64.2%	7.1%			3+ Putts	0	Avg 1.39

Club Stats	1W	3W	5W	7W	9W	1i	2i	3i	4i	5i	6i	7i	8i	9i	Pw	Gw	Lw	Sw	Penalties
# of Swings	12	0	1	0	0	0	4	1	0	0	0	3	1	2	4	5	0	2	1
Longest Dist.	325	-	226	-	-	-	235	223	-	-	-	174	152	149	148	108	-	72	Chip/Sand
Average Dist.	280	-	226	-	-	-	219	223	-	-	-	162	152	141	134	52	-	72	2 / 2

* Statistics not included for this hole due to adding or deleting shots. - Fairways Hit not calculated for Par 3s. Fairway averages may be skewed by penalty location

Source: GolfLogix Web site *www.golflogix.com*.

EXHIBIT 3

Product Rollout for GolfLogix xCaddie Systems

Golf Course	Location	System	Date of Adoption
Sun Ridge Canyon	Scottsdale, AZ	Complete	May 2001
Ocotillo Golf Course	Scottsdale, AZ	Complete	June 2001
The Country Club at DC Ranch	Scottsdale, AZ	Distance Only	February 2002
Arizona Traditions	Surprise, AZ	Distance Only	February 2002
Whistler Country Club	British Columbia, CAN	Complete	March 2002
Sandy Burr Country Club	Wayland, MA	Distance Only	April 2002
Wedgewood Pines Country Club	Stow, MA	Distance Only	April 2002
Stowe Acres North Country Club	Stow, MA	Distance Only	April 2002
Fresh Meadows	Flushing, NY	Distance Only	May 2002
Cyprian Keyes	Boylston, MA	Distance Only	May 2002
Wachusett Country Club	W. Boylston, MA	Distance Only	May 2002
Stowe Acres South Country Club	Stow, MA	Distance Only	May 2002
Fresh Pond Golf Course	Cambridge, MA	Distance Only	July 2002

Source: GolfLogix company documents.

■ THE GAME OF GOLF

The game of golf was invented in Scotland in the 15th century and brought to the United States in the late 19th century. In its current form, it involved the use of wooden or metal clubs to hit a small, hard ball into a cup on each of 18 different holes on a golf course. These holes could range in length from slightly over 100 yards to 500 yards or more. Each swing a golfer took was called a stroke and counted toward his or her total score. The number of strokes a player took through an entire round was the player's score, with the lowest score winning.

Players began each hole from the tee box. They tried to drive the ball onto the fairway, hit an approach shot onto the green, and putt the ball into the cup. Along the way, different hazards (ponds, sand traps, high grass) hindered progress and increased the difficulty of a hole. Each hole was designated either as a par 3, a par 4, or a par 5, where the number indicated the benchmark number of strokes allowed for that hole. For the entire 18 holes, "par" was typically 72. If a player took fewer than 72 strokes, he shot "under par." If he took more than 72 strokes, he shot "over par."

The typical golfer used as many as 14 different clubs during a single round, including several woods (for example, driver, 5-wood), a series of irons (3-iron through 9-iron), several wedges (pitching wedge, sand wedge), and a putter. Each club was used to hit the ball a particular distance. For example, a driver typically was used to hit the ball from 200 to 300 yards, a 7-iron was used to hit the ball from 120 to 150 yards, and a pitching wedge was used to hit the ball 120 yards or less. Using the same clubs, an expert golfer would tend to hit the ball farther, more accurately, and more consistently than a novice. (Exhibit 4 shows how far and how consistently golfers of different skills might hit the ball using various clubs.)

There were several critical elements to achieving a low score. The first was to hit the ball straight so as to avoid the various hazards around the course. The second was to advance the ball the desired distance. This required that a golfer know two things—the distance to a particular target and how far he could hit the ball with each golf club that he carried. The third critical element was the ability to putt the ball well. Many

EXHIBIT 4

Average Distance and Accuracy Achieved by Golfers of Different Skill Levels[a]

Golf Club	Expert Golfer[b]		Average Golfer[b]		Novice Golfer[b]	
	Average Distance	Accuracy[c]	Average Distance	Accuracy	Average Distance	Accuracy
Driver (1 Wood)	275 yds	±25	240 yds	±40	200 yds	±50
3 Wood	240 yds	±20	210 yds	±30	190 yds	±40
5 Wood	220 yds	±20	200 yds	±25	180 yds	±40
3 Iron	215 yds	±20	200 yds	±30	180 yds	±40
4 Iron	200 yds	±15	185 yds	±25	170 yds	±40
5 Iron	190 yds	±15	175 yds	±20	160 yds	±30
6 Iron	175 yds	±10	165 yds	±15	150 yds	±20
7 Iron	160 yds	±10	150 yds	±15	135 yds	±20
8 Iron	145 yds	±10	135 yds	±15	125 yds	±20
9 Iron	135 yds	±10	125 yds	±15	110 yds	±20
Pitching Wedge	125 yds	±10	115 yds	±15	100 yds	±20
Sand Wedge	90 yds	±5	75 yds	±10	50 yds	±20

[a] These distances are for the prototypical expert, average, and novice golfers. However, many experts do not hit the ball as far as shown here, while many novices hit the ball farther than shown.

[b] Experts typically have handicaps below 10, average golfers have handicaps of about 20, and novices have handicaps of 30 or more.

[c] "Accuracy" is the variance in distance achieved by a single golfer. For instance, when a particular expert hits his driver, he can reliably predict that his ball will travel between 250 yards (if he hits it poorly) to 300 yards (if he hits it perfectly).

Source: Casewriter discussions with golfers of various skill levels.

golfers could hit the ball straight and long but had no skill at putting the ball into the cup when on the green.

■ THE GOLFLOGIX SOLUTION

The concept for GolfLogix came about in 1998 during a round of golf between two friends—Todd Kuta and Scott Lambrecht. Lambrecht had only recently taken up the game and often asked Kuta, a more seasoned golfer, to estimate the distance to the green and advise him on what club to hit for that distance. Kuta welcomed these questions at first but soon become frustrated with the constant inquiries.

Over drinks at the clubhouse after the round, Kuta and Lambrecht realized that these problems—judging the distance to the green and choosing the right club for that distance—were common challenges for many golfers, from beginners to experienced players. Kuta had read that 60 percent of golfers' shots ended up short of the green, while only 10 percent went past the green—and he attributed this to two factors. First, golfers often underestimated their distance to the green. Second, golfers often thought, "It's 150 yards to the center of the green . . . I can hit my 8-iron 150 yards . . . so I'll hit my 8-iron." Unfortunately, they failed to consider that they hit their 8-iron 150 yards only when they hit it perfectly. Instead, Kuta pointed out, they should have been thinking, "Which club do I hit an average of 150 yards?"

Kuta noted that there ought to be a way to automatically measure a golfer's distance to the green. Lambrecht, who had used GPS technology in the past, suggested that it might do the trick. He reasoned that a small, handheld GPS receiver could pinpoint a golfer's location on the course. And if the receiver "knew" the location of the center of the green to which that golfer was hitting, it could calculate and display the distance to the green.

As Kuta and Lambrecht thought about this solution, they realized that such a system could do much more. Rather than just report distances, it could also actively record a golfer's progress around the course, capturing the location of the ball at the start and end of every shot as well as the club used to make that shot. This would provide the golfer with a detailed record of his round. He would know how far and how accurately he had hit the ball with every club, how many times he had putted, and how many shots he had taken. Instead of knowing that he had shot an 85, he would have a record of *why* he had shot an 85. Thus began GolfLogix.

The Company

As Lambrecht and Kuta set out to develop their concept, one of the first questions they asked was, "Under the rules of golf, is such a system legal?" The answer turned out to be both "no" and "yes." The United States Golf Association (USGA), the governing body for golf in the United States, indicated that a GPS yardage device *could not be used* during tournament play but could be used for all other types of play.[1] The reason for allowing its use during regular play was that it provided distance to the center of the green and was no different from existing means of marking distances to the center of the green, such as the 150-yard marker found on almost every fairway.

With their concept in place, Lambrecht and Kuta formally incorporated GolfLogix in May 1999. By May 2002 the company consisted of six full-time employees and a handful of commissioned sales reps. In its short existence, GolfLogix had raised about $2 million and taken on moderate debt. Spending had gone toward executive salaries, facilities rental, and the development of the xCaddie software and the GolfLogix Web site. Moving forward, the company expected to incur operating expenses of about $50,000 to $75,000 per month for at least the next three years, which it hoped to support out of operating revenues.

To date, the task of selling the xCaddie systems had largely fallen to Pete Charleston, GolfLogix's executive vice president of sales, and CEO Saltz. Over time, however, the company planned to take on an increasing number of distributors. One of the first of these was Steve Goodwin (*www.goodwingolf.com*), a New England–based golf technology provider largely responsible for the recent flurry of GolfLogix's leases in Massachusetts.

With a distributor, GolfLogix would lease its systems at full price—$1,500 per month for the Distance Only System and $2,000 per month for the Complete System. In turn, the distributor would lease the systems to a golf course at whatever price it believed it could charge. Recent leases suggested that the typical distributor markup was 20 percent to 30 percent.

The Underlying Technology

The core technology for the GolfLogix solution was GPS, originally developed by the U.S. Department of Defense to help determine the position of military troops, ships, vehicles, and missiles. Consisting of 24 satellites, the system could pinpoint a GPS receiver anywhere on the globe with an accuracy of several feet to several yards. The system determined this location by "triangulation," which involved simultaneously measuring the distance and direction of the GPS receiver from four or more of the satellites.

---

[1]Unlike the use of illegal clubs or balls, the use of a GPS device did not invalidate a round of golf. In fact, for handicapping purposes, the USGA *required* that a golfer record a round of golf played with a GPS device no differently than he or she would record a round of golf played without such a device.

Originally limited to military use, GPS was gradually made available for civilian use, free of charge, beginning in the 1980s. By 2000 roughly 1 million GPS receivers per year were being manufactured for commercial use in devices ranging from on-board map systems for cars (such as the OnStar System) to marine navigation systems to handheld devices for hikers and campers.

The GPS receiver employed by GolfLogix was manufactured by Garmin International, a leading maker of GPS receivers for consumer and commercial use in the United States with over $350 million in sales. The xCaddie GPS receiver developed for GolfLogix was designed to be accurate to within two yards and was being sold by Garmin to GolfLogix for about $200 per unit. This cost was expected to come down over time.

Making the Solution Operational

But having a GPS receiver pinpoint a person's location was only half the battle. To make that information useful to a golfer, the system also had to "know" the location of various landmarks around the golf course. For the Distance Only units, these landmarks were the centers of every green. For the Complete System, they were the tee boxes, fairways, greens, and various hazards. To collect these course-specific data, GolfLogix had to map each course that adopted its system.

The Distance Only System
The easier of the two systems to get up and running was the Distance Only System. The data required for distance only were GPS readings for the center of every green on the golf course. A GolfLogix employee could collect these data by walking the course, standing in the center of every green, and recording each location with a GPS receiver.

Lambrecht estimated that it took one GolfLogix employee about four hours to fully outfit a golf course with 60 Distance Only xCaddie units—two hours to record the center of every green plus two hours to download that information to the 60 xCaddie units. He estimated the labor cost to outfit a course with a Distance Only system to be $500, with one installer able to outfit up to 10 courses per week.

The Complete System
Making a Complete System operational was more time consuming. In addition to knowing the GPS location of the center of every green, the system also needed to know the locations and dimensions of the tee boxes, the fairways, the greens, and any hazards on the course. In most cases, the starting point for such a mapping was a detailed aerial photograph of the course (usually available commercially). Using this photograph, a team of three people could then take 20 to 30 GPS location readings for each of the 18 holes. This took about four hours. Finally, by overlaying the readings on the aerial photograph, a technician could "fill in the details" and produce a digital map with precise GPS coordinates for the entire course. This took about eight hours and could be conducted in GolfLogix's office. Altogether, Lambrecht estimated that it took about 20 man hours and $2,000 to map a Complete System.

In addition, a Complete System required a touch-screen kiosk (connected to the Internet) and a high-quality color printer. Most often, these devices were placed in the course's pro shop. The kiosk and printer had a combined cost of about $5,000 and an expected life of about three years.

The last required element of the Complete System was the GolfLogix Web site, where performance data from each round for a particular golfer could be collected and analyzed. Lambrecht estimated that the cost to maintain this Web site was about $100,000 per year.

Playing Golf with the GolfLogix Systems

Once the GolfLogix systems were ready for use, a golfer merely needed to request an xCaddie at the course's pro shop and follow a simple set of directions.

The Distance Only System   The Distance Only xCaddie employed a scrolling feature no more complex than that on a cellular telephone. A golfer scrolled to the hole that he was playing, stood over or near his ball, and read the yardage to the green on the xCaddie's digital readout. Regardless of whether he was in the center of the fairway, buried in a sand trap, or off in the woods, he would know that he was exactly, say, 212 yards from the center of the green. When not being used, the xCaddie could be clipped to the golfer's belt or bag or could be cradled in a special bracket attached to the golfer's cart. For a first-time user, a pro shop employee could adequately explain the workings of the Distance Only device in about two minutes.

The Complete System   The Complete System took a bit more explaining on the part of the pro shop employees—perhaps five minutes. First, upon receiving the xCaddie, a golfer needed to register his name and e-mail address using the touch-screen GolfLogix kiosk. Then the golfer was provided a small, laminated card with directions on the use of the xCaddie (see Exhibit 5).

Prior to taking his first shot on the first hole, the golfer could look at his xCaddie to determine his distance to the green. Once he selected the club he wished to hit, he used the xCaddie's scrolling feature until that club appeared on the digital screen. The golfer then stood over his ball and hit the "Enter" key. This did two things—it recorded the club being used and took a location reading for the golf ball. The golfer

EXHIBIT 5

Instruction Card for the Complete System xCaddie

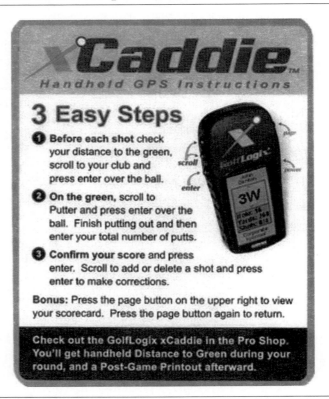

Source: GolfLogix product literature.

then slipped the xCaddie into his pocket or clipped it to his belt and proceeded to hit the ball as he normally would.

After walking to his ball and prior to hitting his second shot, the golfer repeated the process—that is, he checked his distance, chose his club, scrolled to that club on the xCaddie, stood over the ball, and pressed "Enter." This provided a second location reading, which coincided with the landing point of the first shot and the starting point of the second shot.[2]

Upon reaching the green, the golfer scrolled to "Putter," stood over his ball, and again pressed "Enter." He then proceeded to take as many putts as he needed to get the ball in the cup. When finished, he entered that number and pressed "Enter." The xCaddie then confirmed the total number of shots taken on the hole. If this number was correct, the golfer pressed "Enter," and the xCaddie screen advanced to the next hole. If the number was incorrect (for example, because the golfer forgot to record one of his shots), he could add or remove a shot to get the correct score.

Finally, upon finishing his round, the golfer connected his xCaddie via a cable to the GolfLogix kiosk and received a three-page, full-color printout of his round (refer back to Exhibit 2). At the same time, an e-mail message was sent to the golfer inviting him to view the same postgame data on a personalized Web page on GolfLogix.com—where he could also view data from all previous rounds during which he used the xCaddie.

■ THE U.S. GOLF MARKET

In 2000, 26.7 million Americans played 586 million rounds of golf on just over 17,000 public and private courses around the United States (see Exhibit 6 for trends over time). Each year about 2 million new golfers began playing the sport, with a slightly smaller number giving it up, resulting in a net growth of 200,000 to 400,000 golfers per year. Once considered a sport for older, affluent men, the game had attracted more women and younger golfers through much of the 1980s and 1990s. Nevertheless, the prototypical golfer was still male, over 40 years old, and with a household income over $70,000 (see Exhibit 7 on page 392 for a demographic profile of golfers).

EXHIBIT 6

Growth of Golf in the United States (1970 to 2000)

Year	Golfers (in millions)	Rounds Played (in millions)	Golf Courses
1970	11.2	266	10,848
1975	13.0	309	12,306
1980	15.1	358	12,849
1985	17.5	415	13,254
1990	24.2	469	13,738
1995	25.0	490	15,390
2000	26.7	586	17,108

Source: Adapted from The National Golf Foundation's "Frequently Asked Questions—The Growth of U.S. Golf."

---

[2]Recognizing the many ways a golfer can "screw up" a particular hole, the xCaddie had several features embedded in it. First, the golfer could record penalty shots. Second, the golfer could record recovery shots, so that if he used his 7-iron to hit out from under a tree, the distance for that shot would not be tallied as a 7-iron but as a recovery shot.

EXHIBIT 7

A Demographic Profile of U.S. Golfers in 2000

Population	Participation Rate Among Population	Percentage of All Golfers
Gender:		
Male[a]	20%	86%
Female	4%	14%
Age:		
18–29 years	10%	17%
30–39 years	14%	24%
40–49 years	14%	22%
50–59 years	16%	16%
60 and over	15%	21%
Household Income:		
Under $29,999	12%	11%
$30,000–49,999	21%	20%
$50,000–74,999	16%	25%
$75,000–99,999	21%	25%
$100,000 and over	24%	19%
Education:		
Non-HS Grad	7%	3%
High School Grad	8%	15%
Some College	12%	35%
College Grad	20%	47%
Occupation:		
Professional/Management	16%	45%
Clerical/Sales	14%	17%
Blue Collar	10%	20%
Retired	14%	18%

[a]To be read: 20 percent of adult males play golf, and they represent 86 percent of all golfers.

Source: Adapted from the National Golf Foundation's "Golf Participation in the United States."

The Golfer

Golfers could be segmented in many different ways. One basis was frequency of play—approximately 25 percent of all golfers were considered "avid" golfers and played 25 rounds or more per year, another 50 percent were considered "core" golfers and played from 8 to 24 rounds per year, and the remainder were considered "occasional" golfers.

A second basis for segmentation was expertise, typically measured by a golfer's handicap. A handicap was a historical average of how many strokes a golfer took, relative to par, for an entire round. For instance, a golfer with a "5" handicap averaged 5 strokes over par, while a golfer with a "20" handicap averaged 20 strokes over par. About 20 percent of American golfers maintained an official handicap, with the average handicap being "20" (Table A provides a breakdown.) The 80 percent of golfers who did not maintain an official handicap tended to be less avid and less accomplished than those who did. By one estimate, the average unofficial handicap for these golfers exceeded "25."

TABLE A

Range of Handicaps for Golfers Who Maintained an Official Handicap

Men's Handicaps		Women's Handicaps	
Handicap	*Percent*	*Handicap*	*Percent*
0 to 5	7	0 to 5	1
6 to 10	18	6 to 10	2
11 to 15	27	11 to 15	6
16 to 20	23	16 to 20	12
21 to 25	14	21 to 25	18
26 to 30	6	26 to 30	20
30+	5	30+	41

Source: Adapted from the USGAWeb site. (*www.usga.org/handicap.*)

A third way to segment golfers was based on the courses they played—public versus private. About 80 percent of golfers played on public courses, which required a daily greens fee. The remaining 20 percent belonged to private courses, which typically required a one-time initiation fee and a yearly membership fee. Golfers who played on public courses tended to play multiple courses over the course of a year (three or four different courses), while golfers who belonged to a private course tended to play it almost exclusively.

In 1999, golfers spent over $22 billion on their sport. Over 70 percent of this was in the form of private ($8.5 billion) or public ($7.5 billion) course fees, followed by the purchase of golf clubs ($2.5 billion), golf-related clothing such as hats, shoes, and shirts ($1 billion), golf balls ($0.8 billion), and miscellaneous items ($1.2 billion). Avid golfers accounted for 50 percent of this spending.

Aside from course fees, the purchase of golf clubs was the single largest expense a golfer encountered. A high-quality set of clubs could easily cost $1,000, with some top-of-the-line sets costing $2,000 or more. Depending on how frequently a golfer played, a good set of clubs might last anywhere from 5 to 20 years. It was also common for golfers to add to an existing set of clubs through the purchase of a new driver, fairway wood, wedge, or putter. (Exhibit 8 on page 394 lists some of the best-selling items in the golf industry in recent years, while Exhibit 9 on page 394 provides an overview of where golfers were doing their buying.)

Golf courses

As of 2000, there were slightly over 17,000 golf courses in the United States, most of which fell into one of four categories:

- ***Municipal and lower-end public courses (7,000)***—Municipal and lower-end public courses represented the backbone of golf in the United States. Charging $20 to $50 per round, these courses tended to attract all levels of golfers, but especially beginners and those with high handicaps. They also attracted golfers in large numbers, averaging over 40,000 rounds per course per year and having to turn away golfers during periods of peak demand. As a rule, these courses tended to be less well maintained and less challenging than other types of courses.

- ***High-end public courses (4,000)***—Higher-end public courses charged between $50 and $100 per round, offered more of a challenge than municipal courses, and attracted more avid and accomplished golfers. They also experienced heavy use during peak playing periods, with each supporting more than 30,000 rounds per year. Many avid golfers played a small set of high-end public courses regularly or semiregularly.

EXHIBIT 8

Examples of Best-Selling Golf Items in 2002

Item	Typical Retail Price
Titleist Pro V1 Golf Balls	$45 per dozen
Cleveland Tour Action Wedges	$120 per club
Callaway Odyssey White Hot Putters	$120 per putter
Sun Mountain Golf Bags	$120
FootJoy DryJoy Golf Shoes	$125
Callaway Steelhead III Woods	$199 per club
TaylorMade 200 Series Woods	$199 per club
Callaway Hawkeye VFT Woods	$279 per club
TaylorMade R500 Series Driver	$399 per club
Hogan Apex Edge Irons	$599 per set
Cleveland Tour Action Irons	$700 per set
Ping i3 Irons	$729 per set

Source: Based on casewriters' interviews with Boston-based golf retailers.

- *Resort courses (2,000)*—Resort courses, while open to the public, often gave preference to those staying at the resort. They tended to be of high quality, with daily greens fees in the $100 to $200 range. Many of the golfers who played these courses did so only while on vacation or at a conference at the resort.

- *Private courses (4,000)*—Finally, private courses represented the aspiration of many golfers. The quality of these courses tended to be very high, and members were charged accordingly. The typical initiation fee might be $20,000 to $100,000, and the typical annual membership fee might be $5,000 to $10,000 per year. Such a course could have 300 to 500 members and support anywhere from 20,000 to 25,000 rounds per year by members and their guests.

EXHIBIT 9

A Breakdown of Where Golfers Obtain Their Merchandise

	Type of Golfer		
	Avid Golfer (25+ rounds/yr)	Core Golfer (8–24 rounds/yr)	Occasional Golfer (1–7 rounds/yr)
Course-Based Pro Shops	30%	15%	5%
Golf Specialty Stores	25%	20%	10%
Golf Discount Stores (e.g., Nevada Bobs)	20%	25%	30%
Mass Merchants (e.g., Wal-Mart)	10%	15%	25%
Sporting Goods Stores (e.g., Sports Authority)	10%	15%	25%
Internet (e.g., *mygolf.com*)	5%	10%	5%

Source: Casewriters' estimates.

EXHIBIT 10

Typical Golf Course Development Costs (in thousands)

Component	Municipal Course	Public Course	High-End Resort Course	Private Course
Land (200 acres)	$1,500	$2,000	$2,500	$2,500
Course Construction	2,000	3,000	4,000	4,000
Clubhouse Construction	500	800	1,000	3,500
Maintenance Facilities	200	350	350	400
Maintenance Equipment	300	350	350	400
Other[a]	500	800	1,100	1,400
Total	$5,000	$8,300	$9,300	$12,200

[a] Other includes design expenses, financing expenses, and overhead.

Source: Adapted from "How to Pencil Out Your Golf Development," Economics Research Associates, August 1996.

New courses were being built in the United States at a rate of about 300 to 400 per year. The vast majority were higher-end public, resort, and private courses. By one estimate, the cost to build a typical course ranged from $8 million to over $15 million, depending on the type of course (see Exhibit 10). Such courses could generate revenues of about $2.5 million per year and incur expenses of $1.5 million to $2 million per year, for a net operating income of $500,000 to $1 million. (Exhibit 11 provides the economics for a typical high-end golf course.)

EXHIBIT 11

Revenues and Expenses for a Typical High-End Public Golf Course (in thousands)

Operating Revenues:

Greens fees	$1,500
Golf cart rentals	300
Driving range fees	200
Pro shop merchandise (net of cost of goods sold)	200
Food and beverage (net of cost of goods sold)	300
Total	$2,500

Operating Expenses:

Course operations/Maintenance	$700
Golf operations[a]	400
Food and beverage	300
General and administrative	400
Total	$1,800

Net Operating Income	**$ 700**

[a] Golf operations includes pros, assistant pros, and all other pro shop personnel.

Source: Adapted from "How to Pencil Out Your Golf Development," Economics Research Associates, August 1996.

The Golf Professional

The person responsible for running the golf-related activities at a course was the head professional.[3] At smaller courses, he might be assisted by several part-time employees, while at larger courses he would likely be assisted by one or two assistant pros and several full-time employees. Collectively, they handled the scheduling of tee times, the payment of greens fees, the rental of clubs and carts, and the selling of merchandise (balls, caps, and so on). The intensity of these activities peaked from early morning through mid-afternoon, especially on Friday, Saturday, and Sunday. And they were magnified when the course was hosting a golf outing, such as a charity fundraiser, which tended to attract golfers unfamiliar with the course.

The pros were also responsible for selling large-ticket items such as clubs, bags, clothing, and shoes. Golf clubs, in particular, demanded the attention of the head pro or assistant pro to ensure that they matched the buyer's skill level. Pros generally received a 5 percent to 10 percent commission on the items they sold.

A third responsibility of golf professionals was giving lessons, which might range from a single half-hour lesson for $30 to a series of hour-long lessons for several hundred dollars. For beginning golfers, a lesson might consist of the basics, such as how to properly grip and swing a club. For more advanced golfers, lessons might focus on correcting or perfecting particular parts of the golfer's game. This required the golfer to have a good sense of what parts of his or her game needed work. Sometimes, the pro might play several holes with the golfer to get a clearer sense of what to work on. On a typical summer day, a pro or assistant pro might spend several hours giving lessons. Generally, whichever pro gave a lesson got to keep the payment for that lesson.

A final responsibility and constant headache for pro shop personnel was managing the pace of play on the course. Golf was played in foursomes, with a new group of four players beginning play every 10 to 12 minutes. Without delays, a foursome *should* be able to play an entire round of golf in about four hours. However, rounds of five to six hours were increasingly common on many public and resort courses, especially on weekends. The reasons for this were many. The difficulty of the course, the inexperience of the golfers, an unfamiliarity with the course, and a congestion of tee times all contributed to delays. Efforts to speed play included the use of a ranger to monitor slower golfers and the threat of removal from the course for continued slow play. In the end, however, the pro shop staff faced the constant dilemma of getting as many paying customers onto the course as possible while not slowing play to the point of frustration. In one survey, 70 percent of public-course golfers reported slow play as their number-one complaint.

■ SELLING THE GOLFLOGIX SOLUTION

The job of selling the GolfLogix solutions to golf courses fell to Charleston, GolfLogix's executive vice president of sales. A co-founder of the company, Charleston was instrumental in developing the selling message for both the Distance Only System and the Complete System. Both versions, he pointed out, possessed features and benefits for both golfers and courses. For the Distance Only System, he noted the following benefits:

- ***Better golf*** By knowing the exact distance to the green, golfers were more likely to choose the appropriate club, leading to more accurate shots and lower scores.

[3]Head pros and assistant pros were different from the tournament pros who appeared on television each weekend. The primary responsibilities of a head pro or assistant pro were to oversee the golf activities at a course and to give lessons.

- *Improved pace of play* The xCaddie eliminated the need to search for yardage markers or sprinkler heads.
- *Affordability* The GolfLogix system was affordable for all types of courses.
- *Portability* The size of the xCaddie unit made it convenient and unobtrusive.
- *Ease of use* Operating the Distance Only xCaddie was virtually self-explanatory.
- *Ease of installation* Making the system operational required no effort on the part of course personnel and did not interfere with normal course operations.

In addition to those benefits, Charleston highlighted other benefits achieved by an upgrade to the Complete System:

- *Performance statistics* Use of the Complete System allowed the golfer to capture data on shot distances, shot accuracy, fairways hit, greens hit, number of putts, and so on.
- *Game history* After each round, the golfer received a full-color, postgame printout.
- *Personalized Web site* After each round, a golfer's performance data were uploaded to a personal Web site maintained by GolfLogix, allowing for further analysis.
- *An aid to teaching* Teaching pros could evaluate a golfer's ability and progress over time by analyzing his performance statistics and postgame printouts, helping to focus lessons on the areas most in need of improvement.

According to Charleston and the entire GolfLogix team, these benefits offered a compelling value proposition to golfers and courses. Some early feedback suggested that this was the case. In one survey of 50 golfers who had just used the Distance Only System on a trial basis, over 90 percent reported that it was easy to use, and over 80 percent reported that they would regularly use the system if it were available on the courses they played.

In a second survey of 120 golfers who tried the Complete System, 88 percent reported that it was either easy to use (38 percent) or somewhat easy to use (50 percent). In addition, 100 percent reported that they would either always use (75 percent) or occasionally use (25 percent) the system if it were available at the courses they played. When asked to identify the feature that they most liked, 50 percent identified distance to the green, 45 percent the postgame printout, and 5 percent the automatic scoring. Finally, when asked how much they would be willing to pay to use this system, 20 percent claimed that they would pay $3 or more per round, 70 percent claimed that they would pay $1 to $3, and only 10 percent reported that they would be unwilling to pay.

Enthusiasm was no less evident among courses that had adopted these systems. An employee at one course reported:

> Since installing the GolfLogix Distance Only System this past May, we have had many great comments about our golfing experience. The owner of our course used the system when he was in Arizona and thought it was the best in its class. Now we know he was right. We have increased our golf cart fees by $1 and include the GPS device with each cart rental. By doing this, the pace of play has improved by 20 to 30 minutes per round.

At the same time, the GolfLogix team knew that golfers and courses tended to be a conservative crowd. When presented with the idea of a GPS-based distance device, one golfer noted, "What's next? Do they also provide a robot to hit the ball for you?" Similarly, courses were understandably slow to adopt any innovation that might be perceived as deviating from the traditions of the game. They also expressed concern that using the GolfLogix systems might prove problematic and confusing for golfers, resulting in slower play and less satisfaction on the golf course.

All of this led to a rather slow adoption curve for the GolfLogix systems. As Charleston noted:

> Golf is a very traditional sport, and there is great sensitivity to adding anything new to the ritual of the game. In addition, when it comes to anything high-tech, course owners and managers tend to be slow adopters. This makes for a long sales cycle. But if we can find the courses that are forward thinking, we can create competitive demand. As more courses adopt the system, our sales cycle will shorten and our sales task will become easier. We're already starting to see this in Massachusetts.

■ COMPETITION

The need to assess yardage and track performance was nothing new in the game of golf. Over the years, many solutions had been developed to address these needs.

Distance: Low-Tech Solutions

Yardage Markers   Perhaps the most widely used tools to assess distance to the green were yardage markers—colored plastic or concrete plates embedded down the center of the fairway at distances of 100, 150, and 200 yards from the center of the green. Many golfers had grown accustomed to pacing off distances between their ball and these yardage markers to determine their distance to a green. But this grew more difficult and more unreliable the farther a golfer was from the center of the fairway. Nearly all courses used some form of yardage marker.

Sprinkler Heads   A second tool that many courses employed involved marking distances on sprinkler heads. With as many as 10 or 12 sprinklers per hole, this provided the golfer with more points of reference for estimating his distance to the green. However, golfers still needed to pace off distances between their ball and the nearest sprinkler head and, as with yardage markers, sprinkler heads tended to be located only in the fairway. About half of all courses marked yardage using sprinkler heads.

Yardage Booklets   A third tool used by some courses to indicate distance was a yardage booklet. These booklets diagrammed each of the 18 holes on the course indicating the distances to and from various landmarks (see Exhibit 12). For instance, a diagram might show that the distance from the tee box to the nearest sand trap was 267 yards, or that the distance from the edge of a pond to the center of the green was 143 yards. The availability of these booklets tended to be limited to resort courses and high-end public courses, which charged golfers $3 to $5 per booklet.

Rangefinders   Finally, some golfers used optical or laser rangefinders to estimate distances. Priced from $25 to $300, these devices allowed a golfer to view any target and see the approximate distance on a digital readout. However, many golfers viewed these devices as illegal under the rules of the USGA, resulting in their lack of use among serious golfers.[4] Nevertheless, they could be found in various sporting goods and discount stores.

---

[4]Rangefinders, like GPS systems, were prohibited from use during tournament play but were allowed for handicapping purposes, meaning that golfers could submit their score from a round of golf played with a rangefinder.

EXHIBIT 12

An Example of the Information Contained in a Yardage Booklet

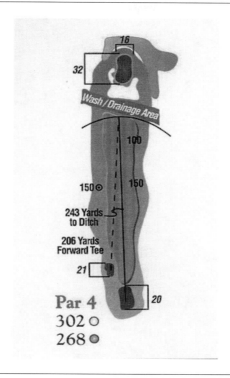

Source: GolfLogix company documents.

Distance: High-Tech Solutions

More recently, several high-tech, GPS-based solutions had appeared in the marketplace, including cart-mounted systems and personal digital assistant (PDA) based solutions.

Cart-mounted systems   Perhaps the most visible high-tech distance devices were cart-mounted GPS systems, including products by ProShot, ProLink, and UpLink (see Exhibit 13 on page 400 for an example). These GPS-based video units were permanently suspended from the roof of a golf cart and provided golfers with (1) a graphical display of the hole to be played, (2) distances from the cart to the green, (3) two-way communication with the pro shop, and (4) the ability to order food and drinks while on the course.

An added benefit of these systems was that they allowed the pro shop to monitor the pace of play by showing the exact location of every cart on the course. If a particular foursome was holding up play, the pro shop could relay a warning to that foursome to speed play or run the risk of being thrown off the course. The sellers of these systems claimed that their use sped play by as much as 30 minutes per round, reducing a 5-hour round to $4^{1}/_{2}$ hours.

The primary drawback to these systems was cost. According to one maker of cart-mounted systems, the price to outfit 80 golf carts could exceed $250,000. To recoup such costs, some courses charged a rental fee (about $5 per round). Through early 2002, about 500 high-end public, resort, and private courses had adopted these cart-mounted systems.

EXHIBIT 13

An Example of a Cart-Mounted GPS System

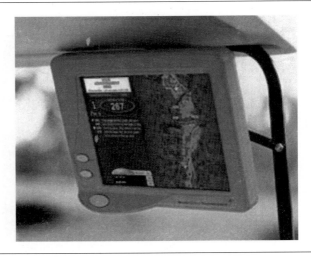

Source: GolfLogix company documents.

PDA-Based Systems   Taking a different approach were companies such as SkyGolf GPS and GolfPS that sold GPS adapters that attached to a golfer's PDA (see Exhibit 14 for an example). These companies sold directly to consumers through the Internet, mass merchandisers, consumer electronic stores, and golf shops. For a golfer who already owned a PDA, the cost of one of these GPS adapters ranged from $150 to $500. The purchase of a PDA would add $200 to $300 to this price.

    The capabilities of these devices varied, but almost all had the ability to indicate distance to the green, with more expensive devices allowing the golfer to collect data on the length and accuracy of shots and overall scoring. But to make these PDA-based systems operational, one first needed to map a course. This could be done in two ways. First, a golfer recorded the center of every green in one round of golf and used his PDA to measure distances in subsequent rounds. Second, each manufacturer allowed golfers to download mappings made previously and uploaded by other golfers (one manufacturer boasted over 2,000 such mappings in its database). To date, there was little information on how well these products were selling.

Performance Tracking

In contrast to solutions for tracking yardage, few solutions existed to help a golfer develop a detailed record of his game. Some booklets did exist that allowed a golfer to manually record whether his tee shots landed in the fairway, whether his approach shots landed on the green, and how many putts he took per round, but most golfers found the use of these booklets to be tedious, time consuming, and distracting. Alternatively, software packages had been developed for PDAs to help golfers collect these statistics electronically, but the same drawbacks existed. In short, the dominant method for keeping track of one's progress was the USGA handicap system, which allowed a golfer to track scores but little else.

    For details on what parts of their game were good and what parts needed work, most golfers simply relied on memory and gut feel. But as GolfLogix CEO Saltz pointed out:

EXHIBIT 14

An Example of a PDA-Based GPS System

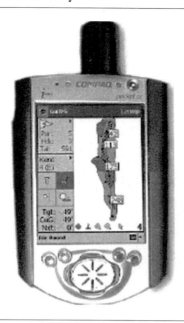

Source: GolfLogix company documents.

Most golfers have a very lousy sense of how often and how well they hit the ball with each club. They remember the really good shots and the really bad shots, but they have no sense of all the shots in between. Something as simple as the number of putts per round is a mystery to most golfers. As a result, they work on the wrong things. Just look at how the average golfer practices. They go to the driving range and hit driver after driver after driver. But only 10 percent of their shots are made with a driver. In contrast, they rarely practice their putting and chipping, even though they account for 40 percent to 50 percent of all the shots in a round. If golfers ever want to get better, they need to work on those parts of their game where they waste the most strokes.

■ GOING STRAIGHT TO CONSUMERS

By almost any measure, the pace of adoption of the GolfLogix systems had picked up dramatically in recent months. After very limited sales in 2001, 2002 was showing lots of promise. Already, over a dozen new courses had adopted either the Distance Only or Complete System, and almost every week another course or two seemed to agree to a 30-day free trial. Moreover, most courses that had agreed to a trial had subsequently signed lease agreements.

In the midst of this long-awaited sales growth, the concept of introducing a consumer-based offering presented an intriguing wrinkle in the firm's business planning. Lambrecht quickly sketched some preliminary numbers on the white board. The units would retail for approximately $300 (perhaps $250, when on sale), with a 50 percent to 65 percent gross margin, depending on volume. But what would the target market be? Lambrecht speculated that a direct-to-consumer xCaddie would appeal to serious, veteran golfers intent on improving their game. He argued that such a device could capture 1 percent to 2 percent of the "avid" and "core" segments of the market in the first year. How the market would evolve after that, however, he was not sure. Others argued that such a device would have far greater appeal among novice golfers still struggling to understand the nuances of the game. For these golfers, accurately judging distances was a constant struggle.

At a more strategic level, company executives were divided as to whether a direct-to-consumer product represented a smart move for GolfLogix. Targeting consumers directly might jeopardize relationships with golf courses that the firm had worked hard to establish. On the other hand, it might open up a new revenue stream that could give the company a shot in the arm while it continued to pursue the golf course market.

In either case, the GolfLogix team knew it was time to make a decision.

Goodyear Tire and Rubber Company

In early 1992, Goodyear Tire and Rubber Company executives were reconsidering a proposal made by Sears, Roebuck and Company. Sears management had approached Goodyear about selling the company's popular Eagle brand tire in 1989. The proposal was declined. At the time, Goodyear's top management believed that such an action would undermine the tire sales of company-owned Goodyear Auto Service Centers and franchised Goodyear Tire Dealers, which were the principal retail sources for Goodyear brand tires. However, following a $38 million loss in 1990 and a change in Goodyear top management in 1991, the Sears proposal resurfaced for consideration.

Two factors contributed to the renewed interest in the Sears proposal.[1] First, between 1987 and 1991, Goodyear brand tires recorded a 3.2 percent decline in market share for passenger car replacement tires in the United States. This share decline represented a loss of about 4.9 million tire units. It was believed that the growth of warehouse membership club stores and discount tire retail claims coupled with multibranding among mass merchandisers contributed to the market share erosion (see Exhibit 1 on page 404). Second, it was believed that nearly 2 million worn-out Goodyear brand tires were being replaced annually at some 850 Sears Auto Centers in the United States. According to a Goodyear executive, the failure to repurchase Goodyear brand tires happened by default "because the remarkable loyalty of Sears customers led them to buy the best tire available from those offered by Sears," which did not include Goodyear brand tires.

The Sears proposal raised several strategic considerations for Goodyear. First, as a matter of distribution policy, Goodyear had not sold the Goodyear tire brand through a mass merchandiser since the 1920s, when it sold tires through Sears. A decision to sell Goodyear brand passenger car tires again through Sears would represent a significant change in distribution policy and could create conflict with its franchised dealers. Second, if the Sears proposal was accepted, several product policy questions loomed. Specifically, should the arrangement with Sears include (1) only the Goodyear Eagle brand or (2) all of its Goodyear brands? Relatedly, should Goodyear allow Sears to carry one or more brands exclusively and have it, own dealers carry certain brands on an exclusive basis? Goodyear presently has 12 brands of passenger and light-truck tires sold under the Goodyear name, ranging from lower-priced tire brands to a very expensive special high-speed tire for a Corvette that bears the Goodyear name.

---

[1] "Newsfocus," *Modern Tire Dealer* (March 1992), p. 13.

This case was prepared by Professor Roger A. Kerin, of the Edwin L. Cox School of Business, Southern Methodist, University, as a basis for class discussion and is not designed to illustrate effective or ineffective handling of an administrative situation. The case is based on published sources. The author wishes to thank Professor Arthur A. Thompson, Jr., of the University of Alabama, for kindly granting permission to extract information from his industry note, "Competition in the World Tire Industry, 1992," for use in this case, the Goodyear Tire and Rubber Company for comments on a previous draft of the case and permission to reproduce its advertising copy, and Michelin Tire Corporation for permission to reproduce its advertising copy. Copyright © 1995 by Roger A. Kerin. No part of this case may be reproduced without written permission of the copyright holder.

EXHIBIT 1

U.S. Market Share of Replacement Tire Sales by Type of Retail Outlet, 1982 and 1992

Type of Retail Outlet	1982	1992*
Traditional multibrand independent dealers	44%	44%
Discount multibrand independent dealers	7	15
Chain stores, department stores	20	14
Tire company stores	10	9
Service stations	11	8
Warehouse clubs	—	6
Other	8	4
	100%	100%

*Estimate.

Source: Goodyear Tire and Rubber Company.

■ THE TIRE INDUSTRY

The tire industry is global in scope, and competitors originate, produce, and market their products worldwide.[2] World tire production in 1991 was approximately 850 million tires, of which 29 percent were produced in North America, 28 percent in Asia, and 23 percent in Western Europe. Ten tire manufacturers account for 75 percent of worldwide production. Groupe Michelin, with headquarters in France, is the world's largest producer and markets the Michelin, Uniroyal, and BF Goodrich brands. Goodyear is the second-largest producer, with Goodyear, Kelly-Springfield, Lee, and Douglas being its most well-known brands. Bridgestone Corporation, a Japanese firm, is the third-largest tire producer. Its major brands are Bridgestone and Firestone. These three firms account for almost 60 percent of all tires sold worldwide.

The Original Equipment Tire Market

The tire industry divides into two end-use markets: (1) the original equipment tire market and (2) the replacement tire market. Original equipment tires are sold by tire manufacturers directly to automobile and truck manufacturers. Original equipment tires represent 25 to 30 percent of tire unit production volume each year. Goodyear is the perennial market share leader for original equipment tires capturing 38 percent of this segment in 1991. Exhibit 2 shows the original equipment tire market shares for major tire suppliers.

Demand for original equipment tires is derived; that is, tire volume is directly related to automobile and truck production. Overall original equipment tire demand is highly price inelastic given the derived demand situation. However, the price elasticity of demand for individual tire manufacturers (brands) was considered highly price elastic, since car and truck manufacturers could easily switch to a competitor's brands. Accordingly, price competition among tire manufacturers was fierce and motor vehicle manufacturers commonly relied upon two sources of tires. For example, General Motors split its tire purchases among Goodyear, Uniroyal/Goodrich, General Tire, Michelin, and Firestone brands in the early 1990s. Even though the original equipment

[2]Portions of the tire industry overview are based on "Competition in the World Tire Industry, 1992," in Arthur A. Thompson, Jr., and A. J. Strickland III, *Strategic Management: Concepts & Cases*, 7th ed. (Homewood, IL, 1993), pp. 581–614.

EXHIBIT 2

Manufacturer Brand U.S. Market Share for Original Equipment Passenger Car Tires

Original Equipment (OE) Buyer	Tire Manufacturer (Brand)						
	Goodyear	Firestone	Michelin	Uniroyal Goodrich	General Tire	Dunlop	Bridgestone
General Motors	33.5%	1.5%	14.5%	32.5%	18.0%	0.0%	0.0%
Ford	26.0	39.0	23.5	0.0	11.5	0.0	0.0
Chrysler	83.0	0.0	0.0	0.0	17.0	0.0	0.0
Mazda	15.0	50.0	0.0	0.0	0.0	0.0	35.0
Honda of U.S.	30.0	0.0	47.0	0.0	0.0	16.0	7.0
Toyota	15.0	40.0	0.0	0.0	3.0	42.0	0.0
Diamond Star	100.0	0.0	0.0	0.0	0.0	0.0	0.0
Nissan	0.0	35.0	22.0	0.0	35.0	8.0	0.0
Nummi (GM-Toyota)	50.0	50.0	0.0	0.0	0.0	0.0	0.0
Volvo	0.0	0.0	100.0	0.0	0.0	0.0	0.0
Saturn	0.0	100.0	0.0	0.0	0.0	0.0	0.0
Isuzu	15.0	35.0	0.0	50.0	0.0	0.0	0.0
Subaru	0.0	0.0	100.0	0.0	0.0	0.0	0.0
Hyundai	35.0	0.0	65.0	0.0	0.0	0.0	0.0
Overall OE market share	38.0%	16.0%	16.0%	14.0%	11.5%	2.75%	1.25%

Source: Modern Tire Dealer, January 1991, p. 27.

market was less profitable than the replacement tire market, tire manufacturers considered this market strategically important. Tire manufacturers benefited from volume-related scale economics in manufacturing for this market. Furthermore, it was believed that car and truck owners who were satisfied with their original equipment tires would buy the same brand when they replaced them.

The Replacement Tire Market

The replacement tire market accounts for 70 to 75 percent of tires sold annually. Passenger car tires account for 75 percent of annual sales. Primary demand in this market is affected by the average mileage driven per vehicle. Every 100-mile change in the average number of miles traveled per vehicle produces a 1 million unit change in the unit sales of the replacement market, assuming an average treadwear life of 25,000 to 30,000 miles per tire.[3] Worldwide unit shipments in this segment have been "flat" due in part to the longer treadlife of new tires. Exhibit 3 on page 406 shows original equipment and replacement unit sales in the United States for the period 1987 to 1991.

Tire manufacturers produce a large variety of grades and lines of tires for the replacement tire market under both manufacturers' brand names and private labels. Branded replacement tires are made to the tiremaker's own specifications. Some private-label tires supplied to wholesale distributors and large chain retailers are made to the buyer's specifications rather than to the manufacturer's standards.

The major tire producers often used network TV campaigns to promote their brands, introduce new types of tires, and pull customers to their retail dealer outlets. Their network TV ad budgets commonly ran from $10 million to $30 million, and their budgets for

---

[3]"Competition in the World Tire Industry, 1992," p. 587.

EXHIBIT 3

Unit Tire Sales in the United States, 1987–1991

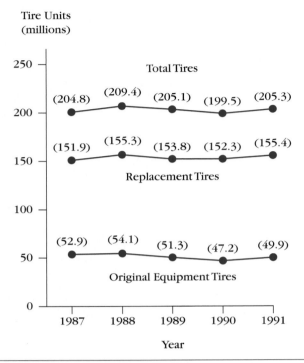

Source: *Modern Tire Dealer*, 1993 Facts/Directory.

cooperative ads with dealers were from $20 million to $100 million. Print media were also used extensively. As an illustration, a Michelin print ad featuring the slogan "Michelin. Because So Much Is Riding on Your Tires" is shown in Exhibit 4. Several tire companies also sponsored auto racing events to promote the performance capabilities of their tires.

Goodyear is the perennial market-share leader in the U.S. replacement tire market. The company holds a leadership position in the passenger car, light-truck, and highway truck product categories (see Exhibit 5 on page 408).

Retail Distribution   Major brand-name tire manufacturers capitalized on their reputation and experience as producers of original equipment tires by building strong wholesale and retail dealer relationships and networks through which to sell their brand-name replacement tires to vehicle owners. The tire industry uses "retail points of sale" to gauge the retail coverage of tire manufacturers and their brands. Goodyear brand tires have the broadest retail coverage with almost 8,000 "retail points of sale," most of which are company-owned Goodyear Auto Service Centers or franchised Goodyear Tire Store dealers with multiple locations. Groupe Michelin is estimated to have almost 14,000 "points of sale" for its three major brands—Michelin, Goodrich, and Uniroyal. The number of "retail points of sale" for major tire brands is shown in Exhibit 6 on page 408.

Retail Marketing[4]   Independent tire dealers usually carried the brands of several different major manufacturers and a discount-priced private-label brand so as to give

---

[4]This material is extracted from "Competition in the World Tire Industry, 1992," pp. 588–591.

EXHIBIT 4

Michelin Print Advertisement

replacement buyers a full assortment of qualities, brands, and price ranges to choose from. Service stations affiliated with Exxon, Chevron, and Amoco marketed Atlas brand tires produced by Firestone (Bridgestone). Other service stations, especially those that emphasized tire sales, stocked one or two manufacturers' brand tires and a private-label brand. Retail tire outlets that were owned or franchised by the manufacturers (that is, Goodyear Tire Stores and Firestone Auto Master Care Centers) carried only the manufacturer's name brands and perhaps a private-label or lesser-known, discount-priced line made by the manufacturer. Department stores and the major retail chains such as Montgomery Ward and Sears Roebuck and Company occasionally carried manufacturers' label tires but usually marketed only their own private-label brands.

Manufacturers found it advantageous to have a broad product line to appeal to most buyer segments to provide tires suitable for many different types of vehicles driven under a variety of road and weather conditions. When vehicle owners went to a tire dealer to shop for replacement tires, they had a variety of tread designs, tread widths, tread durabilities, performance characteristics, and price categories to choose from. Car and light-truck owners were often confused by the number of choices they

EXHIBIT 5

Estimated U.S. Market Shares of the Top Ten Brands in the Replacement Tire Market, 1991

Passenger Car Tires		*Light-Truck Tires*		*Highway-Truck Tires*	
Brand	*Share*	*Brand*	*Share*	*Brand*	*Share*
Goodyear	15.0%	Goodyear	11.0%	Goodyear	23.0%
Michelin	8.5	BF Goodrich	10.0	Michelin	15.0
Firestone	7.5	Firestone	5.0	Bridgestone	11.0
Sears	5.5	Michelin	6.0	General Tire	7.0
General	4.5	Cooper/Falls	5.0	Firestone	6.0
BF Goodrich	3.5	Kelly-Springfield	5.0	Kelly-Springfield	6.0
Bridgestone	3.5	Armstrong	4.0	Dunlop	6.0
Cooper	3.5	General Tire	4.0	Yokohama	5.0
Kelly-Springfield	3.0	Bridgestone	3.0	Cooper	4.0
Multi-Mile	3.0	Dunlop	2.0	Toyo	3.0
Others	42.5%	Others	44.0	Others	14.0
	100.0%		100.0%		100.0%

Source: Modern Tire Dealer, January 1991, p. 27; *Market Data Book*, 1991; *Tire Business*, January 1992, p. 13.

had; few buyers were really knowledgeable about tires. Many buyers ended up choosing a tire on the basis of price, while others followed the recommendation of the local dealer whom they regularly patronized. The retail prices of replacement tires ranged from retreaded (or recapped) tires selling for under $20 to $35 each to top-of-the-line tires going for $125 to $175 each. Tire dealers ran frequent price promotion ads in the local newspapers, making it easy for price-sensitive buyers to watch for sales and buy at off-list prices. In recent years, consumers had become more price conscious and less brand loyal (thus eroding the importance of securing replacement sales through origi-

EXHIBIT 6

Estimated Number of Retail Points of Sale for Major Tire Brands in the United States, 1991

Tire Brand (Parent Company)	*Number of Retail Points of Sale*
Armstrong (Pirelli)	978
Bridgestone (Bridgestone Corp.)	5,960
Cooper (Cooper Tire and Rubber)	1,518
Dunlop (Sumitomo)	2,046
Firestone (Bridgestone Corp.)	4,208
General (Continental A.G.)	2,107
Goodrich (Groupe Michelin)	4,215
Goodyear (Goodyear Tire and Rubber)	7,964
Kelly-Springfield (Goodyear Tire and Rubber)	2,421
Michelin (Groupe Michelin)	7,159
Pirelli (Pirelli Group)	2,133
Uniroyal (Groupe Michelin)	2,321

Source: *Market Data Book*, 1991; *Tire Business*, January 1992, p. 14.

nal equipment sales to vehicle manufacturers). However, it was often difficult for car owners to comparison shop on the basis of tire quality and tread durability because of the proliferation of brands, lines, grades, and performance features. Manufacturers had resisted the development of standardized specifications for replacement tires, and there was a general lack of common terminology in describing tire grades and construction features.

In most communities, the retail tire market was intensely competitive. Retailers advertised extensively in newspapers, on outdoor billboards, and occasionally on local TV to establish and maintain their market shares. Price was the dominant competitive appeal. Many dealers featured and pushed their private-label "off-brand" tires because they could obtain higher margins on them than they could selling the name-brand tires of major manufacturers. Dealer-sponsored private-label tires accounted for 15 to 20 percent of total replacement tire sales in the United States in 1991. Surveys showed dealers were able to influence a car owner's choice of replacement tires, both as to brand and type of tire. Most replacement car tire buyers did not have strong tire brand preferences, making it fairly easy for tire salespeople to switch customers to tire brands and grades with the highest dealer margins. Normal dealer margins on replacement tires were in the 35 to 40 percent range, but many dealers shaved margins to win incremental sales.

Retailer Profitability   Since the mid-1970s, tire retailers' profit margins had been under competitive pressure, partly because of stagnant growth in tire sales and partly because of declining retail prices since 1980. To bolster profitability, tire dealers had expanded into auto repair services (engine tune-ups, shock-absorber and muffler replacement, and brake repair), retreading, and automobile accessories. Some tire retailers were experimenting with becoming "total car care centers." Auto service work was very attractive because gross profit margins were bigger than the margins earned on replacement tire sales. A recent survey of independent tire dealers indicated that 38.2 percent of their sales and 45.8 percent of their earnings came from automobile service.[5]

■ GOODYEAR TIRE AND RUBBER COMPANY

Goodyear Tire and Rubber Company, headquartered in Akron, Ohio, was founded in 1898 by Frank and Charles Seiberling. The company began as a supplier of bicycle and carriage tires, but soon targeted the fledgling automotive industry. The introduction of the Quick Detachable tire and the Universal Rim (1903) helped make Goodyear the world's largest tire manufacturer by 1916, the same year the company introduced the pneumatic truck tire. Goodyear held the distinction as the world leader in tire production until November 1990, when Groupe Michelin acquired the Uniroyal Goodrich Tire Company (then the second largest U.S. tire manufacturer) for a purchase price of $1.5 billion.

Goodyear's principal business is the development, manufacture, distribution, and sale of tires throughout the world. Tires and tire tubes represented 83 percent of Goodyear's corporate sales of $10.9 billion in 1991. Corporate-wide earnings in 1991 were $96.6 million. In addition to Goodyear brand tires, the company owns the Kelly-Springfield Tire Company, Lee Tire and Rubber Company, and Delta Tire. The company also manufactures private-label tires.

Goodyear controls 20 to 25 percent of the world's tire manufacturing capacity and about 37 percent of U.S. tire-making capacity. Sales outside of the United States accounted for about 42 percent of company revenues.

---

[5]"Dealer Attitude Survey Concerning Automotive Service," *Modern Tire Dealer* (Spring 1992), p. 1.

Market Presence

Approximately 60 percent of Goodyear worldwide sales were in the tire replacement market and 40 percent were to the original equipment market. The Goodyear brand is the market share leader in North America and in Latin America and number two throughout Asia outside of Japan (behind Bridgestone). The Goodyear brand is third in market share in Europe behind Michelin and Pirelli. Goodyear is second to Groupe Michelin (Michelin, Uniroyal-Goodrich) in terms of worldwide market share for auto, truck, and farm tires (see Exhibit 7). The company operates 44 tire products plants in 28 countries and seven rubber plantations.

Tire Product Line and Pricing

Goodyear produces tires for virtually every type of vehicle. It has the broadest line of tire products of any tire manufacturer. The broad market brand names sold under the Goodyear umbrella include the Arriva, Corsa, Eagle, Invicta, Tiempo, Decathlon, Regatta, S4S, T-Metric, Wrangler (light-truck tire), and Aquatred. The Aquatred brand was the most recent introduction and featured a new tread design that prevented hydroplaning (see Exhibit 8). Sales of this brand were expected to reach 1 million units in 1992 based on initial sales figures.

The Goodyear name is one of the best known brand names in the world. Goodyear brand tires have been traditionally positioned and priced as premium quality brands. Nevertheless, the company has recently introduced mid-priced tire brands. These include the Decathlon and T-Metric brands with lower treadwear and traction performance characteristics than its other brands (see Exhibit 9 on page 412).

Kelly-Springfield Tire Company and Lee Tire and Rubber Company, two Goodyear subsidiaries, also sell some 16 tire brands and engage in private-label manufacturing. For example, Wal-Mart sells the Douglas brand made by the Kelly-Springfield unit.

Goodyear Advertising and Distribution

Goodyear is one of the leading national advertisers in the United States. The company also has maintained a high profile in auto racing to emphasize the high-performance capabilities of its tires and the company's commitment to product innovation. The Goodyear name is prominently featured on the company's well-known blimps frequently seen at special events in communities throughout the United States. The company's advertising slogan, "The best tires in the world have Goodyear written all over them," communicates the Goodyear positioning as a high-quality, worldwide tire manufacturer and marketer.

EXHIBIT 7

Worldwide Market Shares of Tire Makers, 1990

Tire Manufacturer (Brands)	Market Share
Michelin/Uniroyal-Goodrich	21.5%
Goodyear	20.0
Bridgestone/Firestone	17.0
Continental/General	7.5
Pirelli/Armstong	7.0
Sumitomo/Dunlop	7.0
Others	20.0
	100.0%

Source: Goodyear Tire and Rubber Company, 1991 annual report, p.5.

EXHIBIT 8

Aquatred Print Adverisement

ONE GALLON PER SECOND.

POURING BUCKETS? GOODYEAR AQUATRED® PUMPS UP TO A GALLON OF WATER AWAY AS YOU DRIVE.

The award-winning* Aquatred, with its deep-groove AquaChannel™ moves up to one gallon of water away per second at highway speeds. This keeps more of the tire's tread area in contact with the road for superb wet traction. **ONLY FROM GOODYEAR.** For your nearest Goodyear retailer call 1-800-GOODYEAR.

*Which awards? *Popular Science,* 1991 Best of What's New. *Popular Mechanics,* 1992 Design & Engineering Award. *Fortune,* a 1992 "Product of the Year." Industrial Designers Society of America, Gold Industrial Design Excellence IDEA Award. *Discover,* Discover Award for Technological Innovation.

Aquatred features a 60,000-mile treadlife limited warranty. Ask your retailer for details.

THE BEST TIRES IN THE WORLD HAVE GOODYEAR WRITTEN ALL OVER THEM.

Experience Goodyear traction for your high-performance, passenger and multi-purpose vehicles.

EAGLE GS-C.®
Dual tread zone for high-performance traction.

AQUATRED.®
Deep-groove design for outstanding wet traction.

WRANGLER GS-A.®
"Triple Traction" tread for all-surface traction.

GOODYEAR
#1 in Tires

Source: Courtesy of the Goodyear Tire and Rubber Company.

EXHIBIT 9

Goodyear Brand Passenger-Car Tires (Including Minimum Assigned Grades for Treadwear, Traction, and Temperature)

Brand	Treadwear[a] Rim Diameter 13"	All Others	Traction[b]	Temperature[c]
Aquatred	320	340	A	B
Arriva	260	310	A	B
Corsa GT	280	280	A	B
Decathlon	220	240	B	C
Eagle GA	280	300	A	B
Eagle GA (HNIZ)	280	300	A	A
Eagle GS-C	—	220	A	A
Eagle GS-D	—	180	A	A
Eagle GT (H)	—	200	A	A
Eagle GT II	—	320	A	B
Eagle GT + 4	—	240	A	B
Eagle GT + 4 (HNIZ)	—	240	A	A
Eagle ST IV	280	300	A	B
Eagle VL	—	220	A	A
Eagle VR	—	220	A	A
Eagle ZR	—	220	A	A
Invicta	—	280	A	B
Invicta GA	—	280	A	B
Invicta GA (HN)	—	280	A	A
Invicta GA (L)	—	300	A	B
Invicta GA (L) (HN)	—	220	A	A
Invicta GFE	280	300	A	B
Invicta GL	260	280	A	B
Invicta GL (H)	—	280	A	A
Invicta GLR	260	280	A	B
Invicta GS	320	340	A	B
Regatta	300	320	A	B
S4S	240	280	A	B
Tiempo	240	280	A	B
T-Metric	240	240	B	C

Note: The U.S. Department of Transportation (DOT) requires tire manufacturers to state the size, load and pressure, treadwear, traction, and temperature on their tires. This information is provided by manufacturers based on their own tests and not provided by the DOT. Treadwear, traction, and temperature are all useful quality indicators and appear on the tire sidewall.

[a] Treadwear. This is an index based on how quickly the tire tread wears under conditions specified by the U.S. Government, relative to a "standard tire." The index does not specify how long a tire tread will last on a car because driving conditions vary. However, a tire with a treadwear index of 200 should wear about twice as long as a tire with an index of 100 under similar conditions.

[b] Traction. This is a measure of a tire's ability to stop on wet pavement under specific conditions. Grades range from A (highest) to C (lowest).

[c] Temperature. This is a measure of a tire's resistance to heat buildup under simulated high-speed driving. Grades range from A (highest) to C (lowest).

Source: "How to 'Read' a Tire," *Consumer Reports* (February 1992): 78.

Goodyear distributes its tire products through almost 8,000 retail points of sale in the United States and some 25,000 retail outlets worldwide. The company operates about 1,000 company-owned Goodyear Auto Service Centers and sells through 2,500 franchised Goodyear Tire Dealers in the United States, many of which are multisite operators. These retail outlets account for a major portion of Goodyear brand annual tire sales. In addition, the company sells its tires through some multibrand dealers. As of early 1992, the company did not typically sell Goodyear brand tires through discount multibrand dealers, mass-merchandise chain stores, or warehouse clubs.[6]

■ STRATEGIC CONSIDERATIONS IN BROADENING DISTRIBUTION

Interest in reconsidering Sears Auto Centers for selling Goodyear brand tires meant that Goodyear executives would have to revisit the company's long-standing distribution policy. Furthermore, a product policy question relating to which brands might be sold through Sears had to be considered. Decisions on these policy issues were further complicated by Goodyear Tire dealer franchisee reaction to broadened distribution and estimates of incremental sales possible through expanded distribution.

An immediate reaction was forthcoming from franchised Goodyear tire dealers who heard about the Sears proposal. According to comments appearing in the *Wall Street Journal*, one dealer said, "We went with them through thick and thin, and now they're going to drown us."[7] Other dealers indicated they would add private-label brands to their product line. One dealer said: "We [will] sell what we think will give the customer the best value, and that's not necessarily Goodyear." While it was clear that some franchise dealers were critical of broadened distribution of any kind, the pervasiveness of this view was unknown. Furthermore, it was not readily apparent how many dealers would actually carry competitive brands.

Tire industry analysts expected Sears to benefit from carrying Goodyear brand tires. According to market share estimates made by *Modern Tire Dealer*, an industry trade publication, Sears' share of the U.S. replacement passenger car tire market had declined from 6.5 percent in 1989 to 5.5 percent in 1991.[8] Goodyear brand tires would certainly enhance the company's product mix and draw tire buyers who were already Sears customers. The extent of the draw, however, would depend on how many or which Goodyear brands were sold through Sears Auto Centers.

Cannibalization of company-owned Goodyear Auto Service Center and franchised Goodyear Tire Dealers tire sales also meant that Goodyear executives had to consider the incremental replacement passenger car tire sales from broadened distribution. In other words, even though distribution through Sears could increase sales of Goodyear brand tires from the manufacturer's perspective, the danger would be that company-owned and franchised Goodyear Tire Dealers might incur a loss in unit sales. This could be particularly evident in communities where Sears had a strong market presence.

---

[6]Goodyear brand tires could sometimes be purchased at discount multibrand dealers because of "diverting." Diverting is the practice whereby a manufacturer's authorized distributors/dealers sell the manufacturer's products to unauthorized distributors/dealers who, in turn, distribute the manufacturer's products to customers. This practice is common for many consumer products. See W. Bishop, Jr., "Trade Buying Squeezes Marketers," *Marketing Communications* (May 1988): pp 52-53.

[7]"Independent Goodyear Dealers Rebel," *Wall Street Journal* (July 8, 1992): p B2.

[8]Statistics reported in *Modern Tire Dealer* (January 1991): 27; "Tire Makers Are Traveling Bumpy Road as Car Sales Fall, Foreign Firms Expand," *Wall Street Journal* (October 19, 1990): B1.

Steel Door Technologies, Inc.

In November 2002, the corporate planning process for Steel Door Technologies, Inc. had just concluded, and Richard Hawly, Director of Sales and Marketing, was reviewing the corporate sales goal for 2003. The plan established a sales goal of $12.5 million for 2003, which represented a 36 percent increase in sales over projected 2002 year-end sales.

During the planning process, a number of fellow executives had voiced concern over whether the distribution approach used by Steel Door was appropriate for the expanded sales goal. Hawly felt that their concerns had merit and should be given careful consideration. Though he had considerable latitude in devising the distribution strategy, the final choice would have to be consistent with achieving the 2003 sales goal. His approach and action plan had to be prepared in a relatively short time to permit implementation in January 2003.

■ THE COMPANY

Steel Door Technologies, Inc. is a privately owned regional manufacturer of residential and commercial garage doors. Projected year-end company sales were $9.2 million in 2002 with a net income of $460,000 (see Exhibit 1). The company manufactures both insulated and noninsulated steel residential and commercial garage doors and supplies springs, cables, rollers, and side roller tracks for its products. Surveys of its dealers indicate that the majority of its doors are replacement purchases in the home remodeling segment of the residential housing market, with the balance of sales going to the new residential housing market and the commercial replacement garage door market.

Steel Door Technologies distributes its garage doors through 300 independent dealers that typically offer three different garage door manufacturer brands and 50

EXHIBIT 1

Steel Door Technologies Income Statement Projection:
For the Period Ending December 31, 2002

Net Sales	$9,200,000
Cost of Goods Sold	6,900,000
Gross Profit	$2,300,000
Selling, General & Administrative Expenses	1,840,000
Net Profit Before Income Tax	$ 460,000

This case was prepared by Professor Roger A. Kerin, of the Edwin L. Cox School of Business, Southern Methodist University, as a basis for class discussion and is not designed to illustrate effective or ineffective handling of an administrative situation. Certain names and data have been disguised. Copyright © 2002 by Roger A. Kerin. No part of this case may be reproduced without written permission of the copyright holder.

exclusive dealers that stock and sell only Steel Door garage doors. (Exclusive dealers often service competing brands of garage doors in their market area.) Combined, these 350 dealers service 150 markets in 11 western and Rocky Mountain states and parts of north and west Texas.[1] The exclusive dealers, however, are the sole Steel Door dealers in 50 markets. According to Hawly, this disparity in distribution policy and market coverage occurred as a result of the company's early history in gaining distribution. Hawly added, "Steel Door does not have a policy on exclusive versus nonexclusive dealers. As it so happens, the 50 exclusive dealers have been consistent performers for us. We have chosen not to distribute through other dealers in their markets given the mutually beneficial relationship we have enjoyed."

The 350 dealers that sell Steel Door garage doors engage in garage door sales, installation, and service. Most dealers operate from a single location. All stock and sell garage door openers and hardware. The two major garage door opener suppliers are Overhead Door, which also sells the Genie brand, and Chamberlain, which makes openers under its own label, as well as Craftsman and LiftMaster brands. All 350 Steel Door dealers are located in markets with populations of approximately 250,000 or less. All 150 markets are roughly equivalent in terms of population and housing units according to U.S. Census 2000 figures.

Steel Door operates two distribution centers. These distribution centers allow the company to maintain an inventory of garage doors and hardware near dealers for quick delivery. A distribution facility also operates at the company's manufacturing plant. Steel Door employs 10 technical sales representatives. Eight representatives call on independent (nonexclusive) dealers twice a month on average. Two representatives call on the 50 exclusive dealers.

■ THE RESIDENTIAL GARAGE DOOR INDUSTRY

The residential garage door industry in the United States was expected to post sales of $2 billion at manufacturer's prices in 2002. Steel garage doors account for 90 percent of industry sales. The home remodeling (replacement) market accounted for the bulk of steel garage door sales. Demand for replacement steel garage doors was driven by the continued aging of the housing stock in the United States and the conversion by homeowners from wood doors to lighter weight, easier-to-maintain steel doors. Also, product innovation such as insulated steel doors, new springing systems, and residential garage doors with improved safety features have made steel doors popular. Projected 2003 sales of residential garage doors to the home remodeling market were $2.05 billion, representing a 2.4 percent increase.

There are several large national manufacturers and many regional and local manufacturers in the U.S. residential garage store industry. The largest garage door manufacturer in the United States is the Clopay Corporation, with annual sales that exceed $400 million. Clopay Corporation markets its garage doors through a network of some 2,000 independent dealers and large home center chains, including Home Depot, Menards, and Lowe's Companies. Other large, well-known garage door manufacturers are Overhead Door Corporation, Wayne-Dalton Corporation, Amarr Garage Doors, and Roynor Garage Doors. Steel Door Technologies is considered to be one of the smaller regional garage door manufacturers in the industry.

---

[1] A "market" is defined by Steel Door Technologies as roughly equivalent to a U.S. Census-designated metropolitan statistical area (MSA). An MSA consists of (1) a city having a population of at least 50,000 or (2) an urbanized area with a population in excess of 50,000, with a total metropolitan population of at least 100,000. An MSA may include counties that have close economic and social ties to the central county. Examples of metropolitan statistical areas include the Modesto, California MSA, Pueblo, Colorado MSA, and the Cheyenne, Wyoming MSA.

EXHIBIT 2

Residential Garage Door Survey Results Summary: 2002

1. Residential garage door name awareness was very low. Just 10 percent of prospective buyers could provide a brand name when asked.

2. When asked what criteria they would use in buying a new residential garage door, price, quality, reliability of the installer, and aesthetic appeal of the door were mentioned most frequently in that order.

3. Friends, relatives, and neighbors were the principal sources identified when asked where they would look for information about residential garage doors. The Yellow Pages and newspaper advertisements were the next most frequently mentioned information sources. A company that may have installed or serviced a garage door opener or repaired an existing door also was considered an information source.

4. Thirty percent of prospective buyers expected to get at least two bids on a residential garage door installation. Virtually all expected to receive and review product literature, including warranty information, prior to installing a new door.

5. Fifteen percent of prospective buyers said they would install their own residential garage door when a replacement was needed.

6. Steel garage doors were preferred to wood garage doors by a nine to one margin.

In early 2002, Richard Hawly commissioned two studies on the residential garage door industry in the markets served by Steel Door Technologies. One study was a survey of 3,000 prospective residential garage door buyers in 25 cities that represented a cross section of the company's markets. A summary of the survey results is shown in Exhibit 2. A second study was commissioned to identify the number of dealers that installed residential and commercial steel garage doors in the 150 markets served by Steel Door Technologies and estimate their approximate sales volume. Telephone directories listing independent garage door sellers and installers were the primary data source for identifying the companies. Using industry data to adjust for sales of garage door openers, labor installation charges, garage door and opener maintenance and repair revenue, and the like, this study identified 3,002 independent garage door dealers with estimated 2002 steel garage door sales (at manufacturer prices after adjusting for markups) of $316.8 million. Replacement parts sold to dealers added another $31.7 million to the estimated garage door sales, bringing the total market size to $348.5 million in 2002. This research also reported that independent garage door dealers did not sell all brands of garage doors carried at an equal rate. As a rule, for dealers that sold three different manufacturer brands, the dominant brand accounted for 60 percent of their sales, the second brand, 30 percent of sales, and the third brand, 10 percent of sales. Commenting on the research, Hawly said, "These numbers indicate that our market share is 2.6 percent. I know we can do better than that. In fact, the ambitious sales goal of $12.5 million in 2003 is achievable given the potential existing in our present markets."

■ THE DISTRIBUTION STRATEGY ISSUE

The corporate planning process had affirmed the overall direction and performance of Steel Door's sales and marketing initiatives with good reason. The company recorded sales gains in each of the past 10 years that exceeded the industry growth rate and had added 50 dealers in the past decade. The $12.5 million sales goal for 2003 was driven principally by supply considerations. Senior company executives were of the firm belief that Steel Door had to attain a larger critical mass of sales volume to preserve its buying position with suppliers, particularly with respect to raw materials for its garage doors, namely, galvanized steel and insulated foam.

During the planning process, company executives agreed that additional investment in advertising and promotion dollars was necessary to achieve the ambitious sales goal. Accordingly, Hawly was able to increase his marketing budget by 20 percent for 2003. It was decided that this incremental expenditure should be directed at the 100 highest-potential markets currently served by Steel Door. These included the 50 markets served by exclusive dealers and 50 markets served by independent dealers, which had yet to be finalized. The remaining 50 markets and independent dealers would continue to receive the level of advertising and promotion support provided in 2002. This support was typically in the form of cooperative advertising allowances for Yellow Pages advertising, with additional incentives for featuring the Steel Door name, and product literature.

Hawly saw his charge as determining the characteristics, the number, and the locations of the dealers Steel Door would need to meet its sales goal of $12.5 million in 2003. Initially this would involve identifying the types of dealers that would work closely with Steel Door Technologies in meeting corporate objectives.

A number of different viewpoints had been voiced by Hawly's fellow executives. One viewpoint favored increasing the number of dealers in the markets currently served by the company. The reasoning behind this position was that it would be difficult for existing dealers to attain the sales goal specified in the corporate plan. Executives expressing this view noted that even with a 2.4 percent increase in sales following the industry trend, it would be necessary to add at least another 100 dealers. They said these dealers would likely be independent (nonexclusive) dealers located in the 100 markets not served by exclusive dealerships. Hawly believed that adding another 100 dealers in its present markets over the next year would not be easy and would require increasing the sales force that serviced nonexclusive dealers. Executives acknowledged that this plan had more merit in the long run of, say, three to four years. However, their idea had merit as a long-term distribution policy, they thought. The incremental direct cost of adding a sales representative was $80,000 per year.

A second viewpoint favored the development of a formal exclusive franchise program, since 27 nonexclusive dealers had posed such a possibility in the last year. Each of these dealers represented a different market, and each of these markets was considered to have high potential and be a candidate for the new advertising and promotion program. These dealers were prepared to sell off competing lines, most of which were supplied by regional and local garage door manufacturers. They would sell Steel Door garage doors exclusively in their market for a specified franchise fee. In exchange for the dealer's contractual obligation to stock, sell, install, and service the company's products in a specified manner consistent with Steel Door's policies, Steel Door would drop present dealers in their markets and not add new dealers. Furthermore, these dealers noted, the company's current contractual arrangements with its independent dealers allowed for cancellation by either party, without cause, with 90 days' advance notification. Thus, the program could be implemented during the traditionally slow first quarter of the upcoming year. If adopted, company executives believed the franchise program in these 27 markets could be served by the advertising and promotion program. The other 50 markets served by exclusive dealers would be unaffected, since the advertising and promotion program was already budgeted for these dealers. The remaining 73 markets would also be unaffected, except for increased advertising in 23 high-potential markets.

A third viewpoint called for a general reduction in the number of dealerships without granting any formal exclusive franchises. Executives supporting this approach cited a number of factors favoring it. First, analysis of dealers' sales indicated that 50 of Steel Door's dealers (all exclusive dealers) produced 70 percent of company sales. This success was achieved without a formal franchise program. Second, these executives believed that committing Steel Door to an exclusive franchise program could limit its flexibility in the future. And, third, an improvement in sales-force effort and possibly increased sales might result if more time were given to fewer dealers. Although a number had not been set, some consideration had been given to the idea of reducing the number of dealers in the 150 markets served by the company from 350 to 250. This would mean that the 50 exclusive dealers would be retained and 200 nonexclusive dealers would operate in the remaining 100 markets of which the top 50 would benefit from the additional marketing spending.

A fourth viewpoint voiced by several executives was not to change either the distribution strategy or the dealers. Rather, they believed that the company should do a better job with the current distribution policy and network. Moreover, they argued that because of slowed economic growth, this was not the time for major changes in distribution strategy and practices.

Masterton Carpet Mills, Inc.

In early July 2000, Suzanne Goldman was scheduled to meet with Robert Meadows, President of Masterton Carpet Mills, Inc. Goldman expected the meeting would relate to the recent board of directors meeting. In her position as Special Assistant to the President, or "troubleshooter," as she called herself, Goldman had noticed that such meetings often led to a project of some type. Her expectations were met, as Meadows began to describe what had happened at the board meeting.

> The directors were generally pleased with the present state of the industry and our performance last year. Even though we lagged behind industry sales growth, we recorded a profitable sales growth of 3.6 percent. Our net profit margin of 4 percent is respectable and our cash flow is more than sufficient to fund our present initiatives. Board members were quite complimentary in their comments about senior management and the recommended bonuses and raises were approved. You deserve the credit for pulling together a really professional packet of materials for the meeting.
>
> The possibility of establishing our own distribution centers or wholesale operation was raised, given the recent developments in the industry and our competitive position. We looked at this issue 10 years ago and concluded it wasn't strategically in our interest to do so. Besides we were too small and couldn't afford it. Would you examine such a program for me for fiscal 2001 and prepare a position paper for the October board meeting? Focus only on residential business, since we handle contract sales on a direct basis already, assume the same sales level as in fiscal 2000 to be conservative, and address both the strategic and economic aspects of a change in distribution practices. Remember that our policy is to finance programs from internal funds except for capital expansion. I know you'll do the same comprehensive job that you did on the advertising and sales program last year.

■ THE U.S. CARPET AND RUG INDUSTRY

U.S. consumers and businesses spend about $50 billion annually for floorcoverings. The largest category of floorcoverings is carpet and rugs, followed by resilient coverings (vinyl), hardwood, ceramic tile, and laminates.

Carpet and Rug Industry Sales and Trends

The U.S. carpet and rug industry recorded sales of $11.69 billion at manufacturer's prices in 1999.[1] Carpet and rug retail sales were estimated to be $17.9 billion. These figures represented about a 7 percent increase in sales from 1998. Industry sales are

---

[1]This overview is based on interviews with individuals knowledgeable about the carpet and rug industry and information contained in *The Tufted Carpet Industry History and Current Statistics* 2000 (Dalton, GA: The Carpet and Rug Institute, 2000); Kimberly Gavin, "Carpet: State of the Industry," *Floor Covering Weekly* (March 15, 1999): 1, 28; "The Focus Top 100," *Floor Focus* (May 2000): 19–25.

divided between "contract," or commercial, sales for institutions and businesses and residential sales for household replacement carpets. The residential segment accounted for about 74 percent of sales; the contract segment accounted for 26 percent of sales.

It is estimated that carpet and rugs commanded 68.1 percent of total U.S. floor-covering sales in 1999, down from 73.4 percent in 1995, and 82 percent in 1985. Resilient floorcoverings have shown a similar decline in market share while hardwood, ceramic tile, and laminate floorcoverings have grown (see Exhibit 1). In addition, U.S. carpet and rug manufacturers have experienced a decline in sales outside the United States. Since 1980, the export market for U.S.-made carpet and rugs has become highly competitive. In 1970 U.S. companies supplied 51 percent of the world's carpet; by 1999, this percentage had declined to 45 percent.

Some industry analysts claim that the carpet and rug industry itself is partially to blame for the present situation. Lack of marketing, particularly in the residential carpet and rug replacement segment, is an often-cited problem area. Even though manufacturers continue to improve the quality of their products and develop new patterns, critics say the industry has not communicated these value-added dimensions to consumers and differentiated carpet and rugs from other floorcoverings. They note that the industry as a whole spends 2.1 percent of its sales on consumer advertising. For comparison, other manufacturers of consumer durable products, such as household furniture and household appliances spend 4.2 percent and 2.5 percent of sales, respectively, for advertising. Instead, price had become the dominant marketing tool for much of the past decade and manufacturers focused attention on cost reduction and achieving economies of scale. A result of these efforts was an erratic upward trend in dollar sales over the past decade but marginal profitability for the industry as a whole.

Competitors

The U.S. carpet and rug industry is undergoing a period of consolidation begun in the mid-1980s. Mergers, acquisitions, and bankruptcies among manufacturers brought about by declining demand for carpet and rugs, excess manufacturing capacity, and dwindling profit margins reduced the number of carpet and rug manufacturers from more than 300 in the mid-1980s to about 100 companies in early 2000. This number includes 96 U.S.-based companies and 4 Canadian-based companies, most of which are privately held companies. Mergers and acquisitions since 1995 reflected a push to build further economies of scale in the production and distribution of carpet and rugs.

By 1999, it was estimated that 10 companies in the industry produced 91 percent of carpet and rug sales in the United States. The sales distribution in the residential segment was even more skewed. Three companies—Shaw Industries, Mohawk Indus-

EXHIBIT 1

U.S. Floorcovering Market Shares and Dollar Sales at Manufacturer Prices

Floorcovering Type	Market Share					
	1999	1998	1997	1996	1995	1994
Carpet and rug	68.1%	70.8%	71.1%	72.9%	73.4%	73.6%
Resilient/vinyl	10.5	11.6	12.5	13.5	14.5	14.5
Hardwood	8.0	7.6	7.5	6.9	6.4	6.1
Ceramic tile	9.4	7.0	6.7	5.0	4.6	5.0
Laminate	4.0	3.0	2.2	1.7	1.1	.8
	100.0%	100.0%	100.0%	100.0%	100.0%	100.0%
Total Mftr. sales ($ in millions)	$17,166	$15,436	$14,422	$13,893	$13,344	$13,509

tries, and Beaulieu of America—accounted for about 85 percent of U.S. residential carpet and rug sales.

The U.S. industry sales leader is Shaw Industries, with 1999 sales of $4.1 billion. The company also has the distinction of being the largest carpet and rug manufacturer in the world. Exhibit 2 lists the top 20 North American floorcovering manufacturers based on annual sales in 1998 and 1999.

Wholesale and Retail Distribution

Wholesale and retail distribution in the U.S. carpet and rug industry has undergone three distinct changes since the mid-1980s.

Mid-1980s: Direct Distribution In the mid-1980s, the largest carpet and rug manufacturers began to bypass floorcovering wholesalers (distributors) and sell directly to retailers in greater numbers. In many instances, direct distribution involved establishing sales offices located in manufacturer-operated distribution centers. The intent was to capture the margins paid to floorcovering wholesalers and offset declining and often negative manufacturer profit margins at the time. Lacking the capital to invest in distribution centers, smaller manufacturers continued to rely on floorcovering wholesalers that were increasingly expanding their product line to include ceramic, hardwood, and resilient floorcoverings. Although no statistics were available, it was believed that the majority of carpet and rug sales for residential use were distributed through company distribution

EXHIBIT 2

Sales of the Top 20 North American Floorcovering Manufacturers in 1998 and 1999

Manufacturer	Sales ($ in Millions, United States only)	
	1999	1998
1. Shaw Industries	$4,108	$3,542
2. Mohawk Industries	3,083	2,639
3. Armstrong World Industries[*]	2,221	2,075
4. Beaulieu of America	1,850	1,500
5. Interface Flooring	745	780
6. Mannington Mills[*]	532	475
7. Dal-Tile[*]	510	450
8. The Dixie Group	457	415
9. Lear Corporation	440	405
10. Burlington Industries	425	410
11. Milliken Carpets	315	290
12. C&A Floorcoverings	275	170
13. Congoleum[*]	246	259
14. Kraus Carpet	200	185
15. Royalty Carpet Mills	179	163
16. Springs Industries	167	155
17. Gulistan Carpet	163	155
18. Wilsonart[*]	130	95
19. J&J Industries	125	120
20. The Burruss Company[*]	102	93

[*]Manufacturer produces floorcoverings other than carpet and rugs or in addition to carpet and rugs.

Source: "The Focus 100 International" (*www.floordaily.com*).

centers to retailers by 1990. However, the majority of carpet and rug manufacturers still used floorcovering wholesalers.

Distribution through floorcovering wholesalers remained popular with the majority of carpet and rug manufacturers because of the retail distribution of residential carpet and rugs. In the mid-1980s, independent (and often small) floorcovering specialty stores were responsible for 58 percent of residential carpet and rug sales volume. Department stores and furniture stores accounted for 21 percent and 19 percent, respectively, of residential sales volume. Mass merchandisers, chain stores, and discount stores were relatively minor retail outlets for carpet and rugs until the early 1990s.

Early 1990s: Wholesale and Retail Consolidation   The early 1990s was marked by a second significant change in wholesale and retail distribution for residential carpet and rugs in the United States. Department stores, furniture outlets, and independent retail stores were being replaced by large mass-merchandise and discount stores (Kmart and Wal-Mart) and later by home centers such as Home Depot. The growing number of large retailers that were capturing an increasing share of residential carpet and rug sales spawned a new phenomenon in the retail floorcovering industry among specialty outlets: the buying group. A retail buying group is an organization of similar retailers that combine their purchases to obtain price (quantity) discounts from manufacturers. These pooled purchases allowed independent specialty floorcovering retailers to buy less inventory per order while still getting a lower price, which reduced their costs and pressure for markdowns caused by overordering. Lower carpet and rug cost plus an emphasis on service gave independent specialty floorcovering retailers a basis with which they could compete against their larger competitors. Logistical aspects of shipping and storing inventory varied from group to group. Some buying groups took physical custody of goods through a central warehouse which often replaced floorcovering wholesalers. Others simply requested manufacturers to deliver the goods directly to buying-group members from the manufacturer's mill or distribution center.

By 1995, three retail buying groups—CarpetMax, Carpet One, and Abby Carpets—registered $3 billion in floorcovering purchases. Another 10 smaller buying groups made another $1 billion in purchases. According to one industry observer, almost one-half of all U.S. residential carpet and rug sales volume was accounted for when buying group purchases were combined with those of large to medium-size carpet store chains (e.g., Carpet Exchange), mass merchandisers and discount stores, and home centers (e.g., Home Depot). Although estimates varied, about 40 percent of the roughly 23,000 retail outlets that carried carpet and rugs were members of buying groups, large mass-merchandise, discount, or home center chains. By 1999, CarpetMax, Carpet One, and Home Depot would account for 45 percent of total U.S. floorcovering sales.

Increased consolidation of retail purchasing evident in buying groups, chain stores, and large mass-merchandise, discount, and home center stores had either a positive or negative effect on manufacturers. Even with price discounting, and assuming the retail buying organization operated a central warehouse, it was easier and less expensive for a manufacturer to supply one location with large orders than to supply several separate retailers with smaller orders. On the other hand, if a buying organization flexed its buying power and persuaded manufacturers to take lower-than-normal margins (prices) and ship to diverse locations, a manufacturer risked seeing a lower dollar volume and profit.

Direct distribution by manufacturers in the mid-1980s followed by consolidated purchasing and warehousing by retailers in the early 1990s put many floorcovering wholesalers in a precarious position in the residential segment of the carpet and rug industry. Wholesalers that typically served small and medium-sized independent floorcovering specialty stores were particularly vulnerable to the ascension of retail buying groups that operated their own warehouse facility. These wholesalers advocated their role in distribution to both manufacturers and retailers. They argued that working with a buying group was worthwhile to a manufacturer only if the functions performed by the buying group were not only better than those offered by floorcovering wholesaler but also significant enough to justify the price discounts demanded by a buying group. Similarly, they argued that retailers benefited from wholesaling functions above and beyond the warehousing function. Nevertheless, the absolute number of floorcovering wholesalers had declined in recent years and was expected to decline further. The share of wholesaler floorcovering sales was projected to decline from 26 percent in 1995 to less than 23 percent in 2000.

Mid-1990s: Forward Integration into Retailing In late 1995, the carpet and rug industry watched as yet another change in distribution practices unfolded. On December 12, 1995, Shaw Industries, the largest carpet and rug manufacturer and sales leader, announced plans to engage itself directly in the residential and contract segments of the floorcovering industry. It would do this by operating its own retail stores and commercial dealer network. In announcing this initiative, Robert E. Shaw, the President and CEO of Shaw Industries, said:

> We have realized for some time that the manufacturer must become significantly involved in the retail environment to enhance the viability of our industry. Today, our industry offers products of exceptional quality and unsurpassed value, yet we continue to lose consumer dollars to other product groups. Moreover, because consumers have traditionally price-shopped our products, profits have stagnated for years, from fiber producer to manufacturer to retailer.
>
> Although our industry has matured considerably in recent years, the current structure cannot address many fundamental problems the industry is facing. A manufacturer-dealer affiliation was inevitable, since the only practical way to improve these adverse conditions is by consolidating the combined resources of the two. [2]

Shortly afterward, Shaw Industries announced that it had purchased a number of commercial carpet dealers and contractors and Carpetland USA, a retail chain of 55 stores.

In response to this initiative, Home Depot dropped Shaw Industries as a carpet and rug supplier and switched to Mohawk Industries. Carpet One and Abbey Carpets, two buying groups, asked their members not to do business with Shaw. Other carpet manufacturers courted floorcovering specialty stores with promises to support them with product and not to enter the retail market as competitors. Shaw Industries countered these actions by creating its own retail buying group—the Shaw Alignment Incentive Program—which operated 275 retail stores in 26 states with annual sales of $575 million by mid-1998. Then, in June 1998, Shaw Industries announced it would sell off its retail stores to the Maxim Group, the owner of CarpetMax floorcovering stores, for about $93 million. [3] In 1999, Home Depot was again carrying Shaw carpet.

■ THE COMPANY

Masterton Carpet Mills, Inc., is a privately held manufacturer of a full line of medium- to high-priced carpet primarily for the residential segment. The company markets its products under the Masterton and Chesterton brand names. Contract sales to institutions and businesses are also made but account for only 28 percent of company sales and occur principally in the southeastern United States. The company had no

---

[2]Quoted in "The North American Top 50 Carpet & Rug Manufacturers," *Carpet & Rug Industry* (April 1996): 12–13.

[3]"Shaw Industries to Sell Retail Arm to Maxim Group," *Wall Street Journal* (June 24, 1998): B11.

export sales. Total company sales in fiscal 2000 were $75 million, with a net profit before tax of $3 million. Exhibit 3 shows abbreviated company financial statements.

Masterton Carpet Mills currently distributes its line through seven floorcovering wholesalers located throughout the United States. These wholesalers, in turn, supplied 4,000 retail accounts, including department stores, furniture stores, and floorcovering specialty stores. Inspection of distribution records revealed that 80 percent of residential segment sales were made through 50 percent of its retail accounts. This relationship exists within all market areas served by Masterton Carpet Mills. Meadows believed these sales-per-account percentages indicated that at the retail level the company was gaining adequate coverage, if not overcoverage. The review of distribution records also indicated that it cost Masterton Carpet Mills 6 percent of its residential segment sales to service the seven floorcovering wholesalers.

Advertising by Masterton Carpet Mills appeared primarily in shelter magazines and newspapers. The emphasis in advertisements was on fiber type, colors, durability, and soil resistance. A cooperative advertising program with retailers had been expanded on the basis of Goldman's recommendation. According to Goldman, "The coop program is being well received and has brought us into closer contact with retail accounts." The company employed two regional sales coordinators, who acted as a liaison with wholesalers, assisted in managing the cooperative advertising program, and made periodic visits to large retail accounts. In addition, they were responsible for handling contract sales for institutions and businesses.

Floorcovering wholesalers played a major role in Masterton Carpet Mills' marketing strategy. Its seven wholesalers had long-term relationships with the company. Two had represented Masterton Carpet Mills products for over 30 years, four had been with the company for 20 to 25 years, and one had been with the company for 10 years. Masterton Carpet Mills' wholesalers maintained extensive sales organizations, with the average wholesaler employing 10 salespeople. On average, retail accounts received at least one sales call per month. Goldman's earlier evaluation of the sales program revealed that wholesaler sales representatives performed a variety of tasks, including

EXHIBIT 3

Masterton Carpet Mills, Inc. Financial Statements
(For the Fiscal Year Ending June 30, 2000)

Income Statement	
Net sales	$75,000,000
Less cost of goods sold	56,250,000
Gross margin	$18,750,000
Distribution expenses	$2,250,000
Selling and administrative expenses	11,250,000
Other expenses	2,250,000
Net income before tax	$ 3,000,000

Balance Sheet	
Current assets	$26,937,500
Fixed assets	24,000,000
Total assets	$50,937,500
Current liabilities	$10,312,500
Long-term debt and net worth	40,625,000
Total liabilities and net worth	$50,937,500

Source: Company records.

checking inventory and carpet samples, arranging point-of-purchase displays, handling retailer questions and complaints, and taking orders. About 25 percent of an average salesperson's time was spent on nonselling activities (preparing call reports, acting as a liaison with manufacturers, traveling, and so forth). About 40 percent of each one-hour sales call was devoted to selling Masterton Carpet Mills carpeting; 60 percent was devoted to selling noncompeting products. This finding disturbed company management, which felt that a full hour was necessary to represent the product line. In addition to making sales, wholesalers also stocked carpet inventory. Masterton Carpet Mills' wholesalers typically carried sufficient stock to keep the number of their inventory turnovers at five per year. Masterton Carpet Mills' executives felt that inventory levels sufficient for four turns per year were necessary to service retailers properly, however. Finally, wholesalers extended credit to retail accounts. In return for these services, wholesalers received a 20 percent margin on sales billed, at the price to retailers.

At a June 2000 meeting with its wholesalers, Masterton Carpet Mills executives were informed that several wholesalers were feeling increased pressure to shave their profit margins to accommodate retailer pricing demands. It seemed that an increasing number of their retail accounts had joined regional retail buying groups and were seeking price breaks comparable to those made possible through their group purchases. Subsequent probing on this topic led Masterton Carpet Mills executives to conclude that about 1,200 of the company's current retailers were members of buying groups; they represented about a third of the company's residential segment sales. The meeting concluded with Masterton Carpet Mills executives agreeing to consider a reduction in its price to wholesalers that could be passed on to retailers. At the same time, wholesalers agreed to consider a modest reduction in their margins as well. The "Margin Sharing" proposal, so named by a wholesaler, would be given top billing at the next meeting in January 2001. In the meantime, price accommodations would be made where and when it was necessary to meet the competition.

■ DIRECT DISTRIBUTION EXPERIENCE OF COMPETITORS

Following her meeting with Meadows, Goldman sought out information on competitors' experience with direct distribution. Despite conflicting information from trade publications and knowledgeable industry observers, she was able to arrive at several important conclusions. First, competitors with their own warehousing or direct distribution operations located them in or near seven metropolitan areas: Atlanta, Chicago, Dallas–Fort Worth, Denver, Los Angeles, New York City, and Philadelphia. Masterton Carpet Mills had wholesalers already operating in these metropolitan areas, except for Dallas–Fort Worth and Atlanta. The company serviced these two areas from wholesalers located in Houston, Texas, and Richmond, Virginia, respectively. Second, a minimum volume of approximately $5 million in wholesale sales was necessary to operate a warehouse operation economically. The average warehouse operation could be operated at an annual fixed cost (including rent, personnel, operations) of $700,000. Goldman was informed that suitable warehouse space was available in the metropolitan areas under consideration; therefore, the company would not have to embark on a building program. Third, salaries and expenses of highly qualified sales representatives would be about $70,000 each annually. One field sales manager would be needed to manage eight sales representatives. Salary and expenses would be approximately $80,000 per field sales manager per year. Sales administration costs (including fringe benefits) were typically 40 percent of the total sales force and management costs per year. Delivery and related transportation costs to retail accounts were estimated to be about 4 percent of sales, and inventory and accounts receivable carrying costs were 10 percent. Retail accounts receivable take about 90 days to collect, on average. Though these figures represented rough approximations, in Goldman's opinion and in the opinion of others with whom she conferred, they were the best estimates available.

In late September 2000, just as Goldman was about to draft her position paper for Robert Meadows, she received a disturbing telephone call from a long-time successful wholesaler of the company's products. The wholesaler told her that he and others were disappointed to hear of her inquiries about direct distribution possibilities given what transpired at the June meeting. Through innuendo, the wholesaler threatened a mass exodus from Masterton Carpet Mills once the first company warehouse operation was opened. He implied that plans were already under way to establish a trade agreement with a competitor. This conversation would have significant impact on her recommendation if direct distribution was deemed feasible. In short, a rollout by market area looked less likely. A rapid transition would be necessary, which would require sizable cash outlays and an aggressive sales force recruiting program.

CHAPTER 8

Pricing Strategy and Management

 Whether or not it is so recognized, pricing is one of the most crucial decision functions of a marketing manager. According to one marketing authority: "Pricing is an art, a game played for high stakes; for marketing strategists, it is the moment of truth. All of marketing comes to focus in the pricing decision."[1] To a large extent, pricing decisions determine the types of customers and competitors an organization will attract. Likewise, a single pricing error can effectively nullify all other marketing-mix activities. Despite its importance, price rarely serves as the focus of marketing strategy, in part because it is the easiest marketing-mix activity for the competition to imitate.

It can be easily demonstrated that price is a direct determinant of profits (or losses). This fact is apparent from the fundamental relationship

Profit = total revenue – total cost

Revenue is a direct result of unit price times quantity sold, and costs are indirectly influenced by quantity sold, which in turn is partially dependent on unit price. Hence, price simultaneously influences both revenues and costs.

Despite its importance, pricing remains one of the least understood marketing-mix activities. Both its effects on buying behavior and its determination continue to be the focus of intensive study and discussion.

■ PRICING CONSIDERATIONS

Although the respective structures of demand and cost obviously cannot be neglected, other factors must be considered in determining pricing objectives and strategies. Most important, the pricing objectives have to be consistent with an organization's overall marketing objectives. Treating the maximization of profits as the sole pricing objective not only is a gross oversimplification but also may under-mine the broader objectives of an organization. Other pricing objectives include enhancing product or brand image, providing customer value, obtaining an adequate return on investment or cash flow, and maintaining price stability in an industry or market. It is common for companies to state more than one pricing objective and prioritize the objectives.

EXHIBIT 8.1

Conceptual Orientation to Pricing

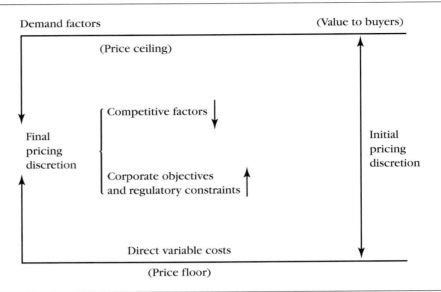

Source: Kent B. Monroe, *Pricing: Making Profitable Decisions*, 3rd ed. (Burr Ridge, IL: McGraw-Hill/Irwin, 2003) Reproduced with permission of McGraw-Hill/Irwin.

Exhibit 8.1 shows how numerous factors affect a marketing manager's pricing discretion. Demand for a product or service sets the price ceiling. Costs, particularly direct (variable) costs, determine the price floor. More broadly, consumer value perceptions and buyer price sensitivity will determine the maximum price(s) that can be charged. The Campbell Soup Company was recently reminded of this fact.[2] The company spent seven years and $55 million developing a line of Intelligent Quisine (IQ) food products. The 41 breakfasts, lunches, dinners, and snacks would be the first foods "scientifically proven to lower high levels of cholesterol, blood sugar, and blood pressure." After 15 months in test market, Campbell Soup yanked the entire IQ line. Consumers found the products too expensive and lacking in variety. On the other hand, the price(s) chosen must at least cover unit variable costs; otherwise, for each product sold or service provided, a loss will result. Some companies that sell products via the Internet have come to recognize that unit variable costs of a transaction (including order fulfillment and distribution expenses), often exceed the price of the products bought. The result? Increasing dollar sales and sizable financial losses.[3]

Although demand and cost structures set the upper and lower limit of prices, government regulations, the price of competitive offerings, and organizational objectives and policies narrow a manager's pricing discretion. Regulations prohibiting predatory pricing, the level of differentiation among competitive offerings, and the financial goals set by the organization are all factors that may affect the price range within broad demand and cost boundaries.

There are still other factors that must be considered in pricing a product or service. The life-cycle stage of the product or service is one factor—greater price discretion exists earlier in the life cycle than later. The effect of pricing decisions on profit margins of marketing channel members must be assessed. The prices of other products and services provided by the organization must be considered as well; that is, price differentials should exist among offerings such that buyers perceive distinct value differences.

Price As an Indicator of Value

In determining value, consumers often pair price with the perceived benefits derived from a product or service. Specifically, *value* can be defined as the ratio of perceived benefits to price:[4]

$$\text{Value} = \frac{\text{perceived benefits}}{\text{price}}$$

This relationship shows that for a given price, value increases as perceived benefits increase. Also, for a given price, value decreases as perceived benefits decrease. Seasoned marketers know that value is more than a low price. According to a Procter & Gamble executive, "Value is not just price, but is linked to the performance and meeting expectations of consumers."[5]

For some products, price alone influences consumers' perception of quality—and ultimately value. For example, in a *Better Homes and Gardens* survey of home furnishing buyers, 84 percent agreed with the statement "The higher the price, the higher the quality." For computer software, it has also been shown that consumers believe a low price implies poor quality.

Price also affects consumer perceptions of prestige so that as price increases, demand for the item may actually rise.[6] Rolls-Royce automobiles, Cartier jewelry, Chanel perfumes, fine china, Swiss watches, and Lalique crystal may sell worse at lower prices than at higher ones. The success of Swiss watchmaker TAG Heuer is an example. The company raised the average price of its watches from $250 to $1,000, and its sales volume increased sevenfold.

Consumer value assessments are often comparative. In such cases, determining value involves a judgment by a consumer as to the worth and desirability of a product or service relative to substitutes that satisfy the same need. A consumer's comparison of the costs and benefits of substitute items gives rise to a "reference value." Although Equal, a sugar substitute containing Nutrasweet, might be more expensive than sugar, some consumers value it more highly than sugar because it has no calories. Retailers have found that they should not price their store brands more than 20 to 25 percent below manufacturers' brands. When they do, consumers often view the lower price as signaling lower quality.[7]

Price Elasticity of Demand

An important concept used to characterize the nature of the price-quantity relationship is that of *price elasticity of demand*. The coefficient of price elasticity, *E*, is a measure of the relative responsiveness of the *quantity* of a product or service demanded to a change in the *price* of that product or service. In other words, the coefficient of price elasticity measures the ratio of the percentage change in the quantity purchased of a product or service to the underlying percentage change in the price of the product or service. This relationship can be expressed as follows:

$$E = \frac{\text{percentage change in quantity demanded}}{\text{percentage change in price}}$$

If the percentage change in quantity demanded is greater than the percentage change in price, demand is said to be *elastic*. In such cases, a small reduction in price will result in a large increase in the quantity purchased; thus, total revenue will rise. Conversely, if the percentage change in quantity demanded is less than the percentage change in price, demand is *inelastic*, and a price reduction will have less of an impact on revenues. Price elasticity of demand is an important factor, for example, in the setting of airline prices for business and leisure fares.[8] Business fares are less price elastic than leisure fares.

A number of factors influence the price elasticity of demand for a product or service. In general,

- The more *substitutes* a product or service has, the greater its price elasticity.
- The more *uses* a product or service has, the greater its price elasticity.
- The higher the *ratio* of the price of the product or service to the income of the buyer, the greater the price elasticity.

Product-Line Pricing

In practice, it is common to apply the concept of price elasticity simultaneously to more than one product or service. By computing the *cross-elasticity of demand* for product A and product B, it is possible to measure the responsiveness of the quantity demanded of product A to a price change in product B. A negative *cross-elasticity coefficient* indicates that the products are complementary; a positive coefficient indicates that they are substitutes. An understanding of the implications of cross-elasticity is especially important for successful implementation of product-line pricing, in which product demand is interrelated and the goal is to maximize revenue for the entire line and not just for individual products or services.

Consider a marketer of cameras and films (or of copying machines and paper, or of video game machines and video games). Should the marketer price cameras very low, perhaps close to or even below cost, in order to promote film sales? Film could then be marketed at relatively high prices. Or should an opposite strategy be employed—selling high-priced cameras but low-priced film? Examples of these alternative tie-in pricing strategies are readily available. For instance, Nintendo, a leader in video games, has traditionally priced its hardware at or near cost and made its profit on its software.[9] The important point is that in most organizations products are not priced in isolation. In certain instances, individual products may be sold at a loss merely to entice buyers or to ensure that the organization can offer potential buyers complete product lines. In such situations, the price may bear little relationship to the actual cost of a product.

In addition, product-line pricing involves determining (1) the lowest-priced product price, (2) the highest-priced product and price, and (3) price differentials for all other products in the line. The lowest- and highest-priced items in the product line play important roles. The highest-priced item is typically positioned as the premium item in quality and features. The lowest-priced item is the traffic builder designed to capture the attention of the hesitant or first-time buyer. Price differentials between items in the line should make sense to customers and reflect differences in their perceived value of the products offered. Behavioral research also suggests that the price differentials should get larger as one moves up the product line to more expensive items.[10]

Estimating the Profit Impact from Price Changes

In Chapter 2, the basic principles of break-even analysis and leverage were described. These same principles can be applied when assessing the effect of price changes on volume.[11]

The impact of price changes on profit can be determined by looking at cost, price, and volume data for individual products and services. Consider the data shown in the top half of Exhibit 8.2 for two products, alpha and beta. These products have identical prices ($10), unit volumes (1,000 units), and net profits ($2,000), but their cost structures differ. Product alpha has a unit variable cost of $7 and assignable fixed costs of $1,000. Product beta has a unit variable cost of $2 and assignable fixed costs of $6,000. The unit break-even volume for product alpha is 333.3 units ($1,000/$3). Product beta's unit break-even volume is 750 units ($6,000/$8).

EXHIBIT 8.2

Estimating the Effect of Price Changes

	Product Alpha	Product Beta
Cost, Volume, and Profit Data		
Unit sales volume	1,000	1,000
Unit selling price	$10	$10
Unit variable cost	$7	$2
Unit contribution (margin)	$3 (30%)	$8 (80%)
Fixed costs	$1,000	$6,000
Net profit	$2,000	$2,000
Break-Even Sales Change		
For a 5% price reduction	+20.0%	+6.7%
For a 10% price reduction	+50.0%	+14.3%
For a 20% price reduction	+200.0%	+33.3%
For a 5% price increase	-14.3%	-5.9%
For a 10% price increase	-25.0%	-11.1%
For a 20% price increase	-40.0%	-20.0%

The calculation for determining the unit volume necessary to break even on a price change is as follows (percentages expressed in whole numbers):

$$\begin{array}{l}\text{Percentage change} \\ \text{in unit volume to} \\ \text{break even on a} \\ \text{price change}\end{array} = \frac{-(\text{percentage price change})}{\left(\begin{array}{c}\text{original contribution} \\ \text{margin}\end{array}\right) + \left(\begin{array}{c}\text{percentage} \\ \text{price change}\end{array}\right)}$$

For example, if a product has a 20 percent contribution margin, a 5 percent price decrease will require a 33 percent increase in unit volume to break even:

$$+33 = \frac{-(-5)}{\left[20\right] + \left[-5\right]}$$

Alternatively, a product with the same contribution margin can absorb a 20 percent decline in unit volume if its price increases 5 percent without incurring a loss in profit:

$$-20 = \frac{-\left(+5\right)}{\left[20\right] + \left[+5\right]}$$

The lower half of Exhibit 8.2 illustrates the potential profit impact of price changes for products alpha and beta. For product alpha to profit from a 10 percent price cut, its unit volume would have to increase by 50 percent. In contrast, unit sales of product beta, with its larger contribution, would only have to increase by slightly more than 14 percent for a profit to be realized.

The same type of analysis can be applied to price increases. For example, if product alpha's price were increased 10 percent, its unit volume could decrease by 25 percent before profits would decline. On the other hand, product beta, with its higher contribution, could absorb only an 11 percent volume decline with a 10 percent price increase. Other price change effects are shown in Exhibit 8.2 for illustrative purposes.

■ PRICING STRATEGIES

Because of the difficulty of estimating demand, most pricing strategies have a decided reliance on cost as a basic foundation. To a great extent, price strategies can be termed either full-cost or variable-cost strategies. *Full-cost price strategies* are those that consider both variable and fixed costs (sometimes termed *direct* and *indirect costs*). *Variable-cost price strategies* take into account only the direct variable costs associated with offering a product or service.

Full-Cost Pricing

Full-cost pricing strategies generally take one of three forms: markup pricing, break-even pricing, and rate-of-return pricing. *Markup pricing* is a strategy in which the selling price of a product or service is determined simply by adding a fixed amount to the (total) cost of the product. The fixed amount is usually expressed as a percentage of either the cost or the price of the product. If it costs $4.60 to produce a product and the selling price is $6.35, the markup on *cost* would be 38 percent, and the markup on *price* would be 28 percent.

Markup pricing is frequently used in routine pricing situations, such as with grocery or clothing items, but it is also sometimes employed in pricing unique products or services—for example, military equipment or construction projects. Markup pricing may well be the most common type of pricing strategy. Although it possesses decided drawbacks (especially if a single percentage is applied across products without regard to their elasticities or competition), its simplicity, flexibility, and controllability make it highly popular.

As noted in Chapter 2 when discussing the financial aspects of marketing management, break-even analysis is a useful tool for determining how many units of a product or service must be sold at a specific price for an organization to cover its total costs (fixed plus variable costs). Through judicious use of break-even analysis, it is also possible to calculate the break-even price for a product or service. Specifically, the break-even price of a product or service equals the per-unit fixed costs plus the per-unit variable costs.

Rate-of-return pricing is slightly more sophisticated than either markup or break-even pricing. Still, it contains the basic ingredients of both of these strategies and can be viewed as an extension of them. In a *rate-of-return pricing strategy*, price is set so as to obtain a prespecified rate of return on investment (capital) for the organization. Since rate of return on investment (ROI) equals profit (Pr) divided by investment (I),

$$\text{ROI} = \text{Pr} / I = \frac{\text{revenues} - \text{cost}}{\text{investment}} = \frac{P \cdot Q - C \cdot Q}{I}$$

where P and C are, respectively, unit selling price and unit cost, and Q represents the quantity sold.

By working backward from a predetermined rate of return, it is possible to derive a selling price that will obtain that return rate. If an organization desires an ROI of 15 percent on an investment of $80,000, total costs per unit are estimated to be $0.175, and a demand of 20,000 units is forecast, then the necessary price will be

$$\frac{\left(\text{ROI}\right) \times I + CQ}{Q} = P = \frac{\left(0.15\right)\$80,000 + \$0.175 \times 20,000}{20,000} = 0.775$$

or roughly $0.78.

This pricing strategy, popularized by General Motors, is most commonly used by large firms and public utilities whose return rates are closely watched or are regulated by government agencies or commissions. Like other types of full-cost pricing strategies, rate-of-return pricing assumes a standard (linear) demand function and insensitivity of buyers to price. This assumption often holds true only for certain price ranges, however.

Variable-Cost Pricing

An alternative to full-cost pricing strategies is a variable-cost, or contribution pricing, strategy. This type of strategy is sometimes used when an organization is operating at less than full capacity and fixed costs constitute a great proportion of total unit costs. The basic idea underlying *variable-cost pricing* is that, in certain short-run pricing situations, the relevant costs to consider are the variable costs, not the total costs. Specifically, in this strategy, variable unit cost represents the minimum selling price at which the product or service can be marketed. Any price above this minimum represents a contribution to fixed costs and profits.

Variable-cost pricing is a form of demand-oriented pricing. As such, it can serve two different purposes: (1) stimulate demand and (2) shift demand. Since variable-cost prices are lower than full-cost prices, the assumption is that they will *stimulate demand* and increase revenues and, hence, will lead to economies of scale, lower unit costs, and greater profits. This is why airlines offer different classes of fares, hotels offer special weekend rates, and movie theaters have discounts for senior citizens. Variable-cost pricing also makes sense because fixed costs must be met no matter whether a product or service is sold—the airline must maintain its flight schedule whether or not there are any passengers; the hotel or movie theater has to remain open even if it is only partially filled—and the incremental (variable) costs of serving one more customer are minimal.

Consider a bus line making a daily run from Duluth to Minneapolis, Minnesota. The price of a one-way ticket is $30.00, and on an average trip the bus is 60 percent full. If unit fixed and variable costs are, respectively, $7.50 and $2.00, should the bus line offer a half-price fare for children under five years of age? Ignoring price elasticity and the like for the moment, the answer is yes, the reduced fare should be offered. The reduced fare ($15.00) covers the variable costs ($2.00) and makes a contribution of $13.00 to fixed costs. Since the bus line will make the trip regardless of how many passengers there are, in the short run every reduced-fare ticket sold contributes $13.00 to fixed expenses. Such a pricing approach always assumes that no more profitable use may be made of the revenue-generating activity.

In addition to stimulating demand, variable-cost pricing can be used to *shift demand* from one time period to another. Movie theaters sometimes have lower matinee ticket prices to encourage customers to switch from evening to afternoon attendance. Likewise, certain utilities (such as telephone companies) have different price schedules to shift demand away from peak load times and smooth it out over extended time periods.

New-Offering Pricing Strategies

Full- and variable-cost pricing strategies are *technical strategies* that can be used when an organization initially sets its prices or when it changes them. When pricing a new product or service, however, a manager also has to consider other, more *conceptual* strategies.

When introducing a new product or service to the marketplace, an organization can employ one of three alternative pricing strategies.[12] With a *skimming pricing strategy*, the price is set very high initially and is typically reduced over time. A skimming strategy may be appropriate for a new product or service if any of the following conditions hold:

1. Demand is likely to be price inelastic.
2. There are different price-market segments, thereby appealing first to buyers who have a higher range of acceptable prices.
3. The offering is unique enough to be protected from competition by patent, copyright, or trade secret.
4. Production or marketing costs are unknown.
5. A capacity constraint in producing the product or providing the service exists.
6. An organization wants to generate funds quickly to recover its investment or finance other developmental efforts.
7. There is a realistic perceived value in the product or service.

Many of these conditions were present when Gillette decided to price its innovative Mach3 shaving system 35 percent higher than its hugely successful SensorExcel shaving system introduced four years earlier. Mach3 posted $1.8 billion in annual worldwide sales in three years using this strategy in some 100 countries.[13]

At the other extreme, an organization may use a *penetration pricing strategy*, whereby a product or service is introduced at a low price. This strategy may be appropriate if any of the following conditions exist:

1. Demand is likely to be price elastic in the target market segments at which the product or service is aimed.
2. The offering is not unique or protected by patents, copyrights, or trade secrets.
3. Competitors are expected to enter the market quickly.
4. There are no distinct and separate price-market segments.
5. There is a possibility of large savings in production and marketing costs if a large sales volume can be generated.
6. The organization's major objective is to obtain a large market share.

Nintendo considered each of these factors and consciously chose a penetration strategy when it introduced its Gamecube video machine in 2001 with an introductory price of $199.95, which was $100.00 less than the list price for Microsoft's Xbox and Sony's Playstation 2 consoles.[14]

Between these two extremes is an *intermediate pricing strategy*. As might be expected, this type of strategy is the most prevalent in practice. The other two types of introductory pricing strategies are, so to speak, more flamboyant; given the vagaries of the marketplace, however, intermediate pricing is more likely to be used in the vast majority of initial pricing decisions.

Pricing and Competitive Interaction

No discussion of pricing strategy and management is complete without mention of competitive interaction.[15] Because price is the one element of the marketing mix that can be changed quickly and easily, competitive interaction is common. Competitive interaction in a pricing context refers to the sequential action and reaction of rival companies in setting and changing prices for their offering(s) and assessing likely outcomes, such as sales, unit volume, and profit for each company and an entire market. Competitive interaction is like playing chess. Those players who make moves one at a time, seeking to minimize immediate losses or to exploit immediate opportunities, invariably are beaten by those who can envision the game a few moves ahead.

Somewhat surprisingly, research and practice suggest that marketing managers infrequently look beyond an initial pricing decision to consider competitor countermoves, their own subsequent moves, and outcomes. Two remedies are often proposed to overcome this nearsightedness. First, managers are advised to focus less on short-term outcomes and attend more to longer-term consequences of actions. Competitive interactions are rarely confined to one period, that is, an action followed by a reaction.

Also, the consequences of actions and reactions are not always immediately observable. Therefore, managers are advised to "look forward and reason backward" by envisioning patterns of future pricing moves, competitor countermoves, and likely outcomes. Second, managers are advised to step into the shoes of rival managers or companies and answer a number of questions:

1. What are competitors' goals and objectives? How are they different from our goals and objectives?
2. What assumptions has the competitor made about itself, our company and offerings, and the marketplace? Are these assumptions different from ours?
3. What strengths does the competitor believe it has and what are its weaknesses? What might the competitor believe our strengths and weaknesses to be?

Failure to answer these questions can lead to misjudgments about the price(s) set or changed by competitors and misguide subsequent pricing moves and countermoves among competitors. Misreading the situation can result in price wars.

A *price war* involves successive price cutting by competitors to increase or maintain their unit sales or market share.[16] Over the past decade, price wars have broken out in a variety of industries: from personal computers to disposable diapers, from soft drinks to airlines, and from grocery retailing to long-distance telephone services. Price wars do not just happen. Managers expecting that a lower price will result in a larger market share, higher unit sales, and greater profit for their offering(s) often initiate them. This may indeed occur. However, if competitors match the lower price, other things being equal, the expected share, sales, and profit gain are lost. More importantly, the overall price level resulting from the lower price benefits none of the competitors. Marketing managers are advised to consider price cutting only when one or more conditions exist: (1) The company has a cost or technological advantage over its competitors, (2) primary demand for a product class will grow if prices are lowered, and (3) the price cut is confined to specific products or customers (as with airline tickets) and not across-the-board.

Certain industry settings tend to be prone to price wars. Exhibit 8.3 shows that the risk of price wars is higher or lower when an industry exhibits certain characteristics. For example, if a product or service supplied by the industry is undifferentiated, price tends to be an important buying factor. This situation increases the likelihood of price competition and price wars. A stable or declining market growth rate coupled with low capacity utilization by companies tends to result in corporate unit volume growth objectives, often promoted through price cutting. Clearly visible competitor prices, highly price sensitive buyers, and declining costs in an industry also increase the risk of price wars.

EXHIBIT 8.3

Industry Characteristics and the Risk of Price Wars

	Risk Level	
Industry Characteristics	*Higher*	*Lower*
Product/Service type	Undifferentiated	Differentiated
Market growth rate	Stable/Decreasing	Increasing
Price visibility to competitors	High	Low
Buyer price sensitivity	High	Low
Overall industry cost trend	Declining	Stable
Industry capacity utilization	Low	High
Number of competitors	Many	Few

NOTES

1. E. Raymond Corey, *Industrial Marketing: Cases and Concepts*, 4th ed. (Upper Saddle River, NJ: Prentice Hall, 1991): 256.

2. Vannessa O'Connell, "How Campbell Saw a Breakthrough Menu Turn into Leftovers," *Wall Street Journal* (October 6, 1998): A1, A12.

3. "Lessons of Cyber Survivors," *Business Week* (April 22, 2002): 42.

4. For a comprehensive review of the price-quality-value relationship, see Valarie A. Zeithaml, "Consumer Perceptions of Price, Quality, and Value," *Journal of Marketing* (July 1988): 2-22. Also see Rolf Leszinski and Michael V. Marn, "Setting Value, Not Price," *The McKinsey Quarterly* (Number 1, 1997): 98-115.

5. "Laundry Soap Marketers See the Value of 'Value'!" *Advertising Age* (September 21, 1992): 3, 56.

6. Jean-Noel Kapferer, "Managing Luxury Brands," *The Journal of Brand Management* (July 1997): 251-260; "Top of the Hour," *Fortune* (December 10, 2001): 283-284.

7. Jagmohan S. Raju, Raj Sethuraman, and Sanjay Dhar, "National Brand-Store Brand Price Differential and Store Brand Market Share," *Pricing Strategy and Practice*, Vol. 3, No. 2 (1995): 17-24.

8. "Business Fares Increase Even as Leisure Travel Keeps Getting Cheaper," *Wall Street Journal* (November 3, 1997): A1, A6.

9. "Console Wars," *The Economist* (June 22, 2002): 57-58.

10. Kent B. Monroe, *Pricing: Making Profitable Decisions*, 3rd ed. (Burr Ridge, IL: McGraw-Hill/Irwin, 2003): Chapter 15.

11. This discussion is based, in part, on Thomas T. Nagle and Reed K. Holden, *The Strategy and Tactics of Pricing*, 3rd ed. (Upper Saddle River, NJ: Prentice Hall, 2002): Chapter 3; George E. Cressman, Jr., "Snatching Defeat from the Jaws of Victory," *Marketing Management* (Summer 1997): 9-19.

12. The conditions favoring skimming versus penetration pricing are described in Monroe, *Pricing: Making Profitable Decisions*, 380-383.

13. "Gillette's Edge," *Brandweek* (May 28, 2001): 5.

14. "Nintendo Gamecube Set at Mass Market Price of $199.95," Nintendo of America, Inc. Press Release, May 21, 2001.

15. This discussion is based on Bruce Clark, "Managing Competitive Interactions," *Marketing Management* (Fall/Winter 1998): 9-20; Joe E. Urbany and David B. Montgomery, "Rational Strategic Reasoning: An Unnatural Act?" *Marketing Letters* (August 1998): 285-300.

16. The remaining discussion is based on Michael R. Baye, *Managerial Economics and Business Strategy*, 2nd ed. (Chicago: Richard D. Irwin, 1997); Chapters 9 and 10; Robert A. Garda and Michael V. Marn, "Price Wars," *The McKinsey Quarterly* (November 3, 1993); 87-100; Akshay R. Rao, Mark E. Burgen, and Scott Davis, "How to Fight a Price War," *Harvard Business Review* (March-April 2000): 1076-116; and "The Price Is Not Always Right, *Fortune* (May 14, 2001): 240.

Southwest Airlines

In late January 1995, Dave Ridley, Vice President–Marketing and Sales at Southwest Airlines, was preparing to join Joyce Rogge, Vice President–Advertising and Promotion, Keith Taylor, Vice President–Revenue Management, and Pete McGlade, Vice President–Schedule Planning, for their weekly "Tuesday meeting." The purpose of this regularly scheduled meeting was to exchange ideas, keep one another informed about external and internal developments pertaining to their areas of responsibility, and coordinate pricing and marketing activities. This informal gathering promoted communication among functional areas and fostered the team spirit that is an integral part of the Southwest corporate culture.

A recurrent "Tuesday meeting" topic during the past six months had been the changing competitive landscape for Southwest evident in the "Continental Lite" and "Shuttle By United" initiatives undertaken by Continental Airlines and United Airlines, respectively. Both initiatives represented targeted efforts by major carriers to match Southwest's price *and* service offering—a strategy that no major carrier had successfully implemented in the past. In early January 1995, Continental's effort was being scaled back due to operational difficulties and resulting financial losses.[1] However, United's initiative remained in effect. Launched on October 1, 1994, "Shuttle By United" was serving 14 routes in California and adjacent states by mid-January 1995, nine of which were in direct competition with Southwest. When "Shuttle By United" was announced, United's CEO predicted: "We're going to match them (Southwest) on price and exceed them on service."[2] In response to United's initiative, Southwest's Chairman Herb Kelleher said, the "United Shuttle is like an intercontinental ballistic missile targeted directly at Southwest."

Just as the meeting began, a staff member rushed in to tell the group that United had just made two changes in its "Shuttle By United" service and pricing. First, its service for the Oakland–Ontario, California, market would be discontinued effective April 2, 1995. This market had been among the most hotly contested routes among the nine where United and Southwest competed head-to-head and Southwest had lost market share on this route since October 1994. Second, the one-way walk-up first class and coach fare on all 14 "Shuttle By United" routes had just been increased by $10.00. "Shuttle By United" had previously matched Southwest's fare on the nine competitive routes and, as of mid-January 1995, had been increasing the number of flights on these routes and the five routes where they did not compete.

Changes in United's pricing and service for its shuttle operation caught Southwest executives by surprise. The original agenda for the "Tuesday meeting" was immediately

---

[1] Bridget O'Brian, "Continental's CALite Hits Some Turbulence in Battling Southwest," *Wall Street Journal* (January 10, 1995): A1, A5.

[2] Quoted in Jon Proctor, "Everyone Versus Southwest," *AIRWAYS Magazine* (November/December 1994): 6-13.

The cooperation of Southwest Airlines in the preparation of this case is gratefully acknowledged. This case was prepared by Professor Roger A. Kerin, of the Edwin L. Cox School of Business, Southern Methodist University, as a basis for class discussion and is not designed to illustrate effective or ineffective handling of an administrative situation. Certain information is disguised and not useful for research purposes. Copyright © 1996 by Roger A. Kerin. No part of this case may be reproduced without written permission of the copyright holder.

set aside. Attention focused on (1) what to make of these unexpected developments and (2) how Southwest might respond, if at all, to the new "Shuttle By United" initiatives.

■ THE U.S. PASSENGER AIRLINE INDUSTRY

The U.S. Department of Transportation classified U.S. passenger airlines into three categories on the basis of annual revenue.[3] A "major carrier" was an airline with more than $1 billion in annual revenue. A "national carrier" had annual revenues between $100 million and $1 billion, and a "regional and commuter airline" had annual revenues less than $100 million. Major carriers accounted for more than 95 percent of domestic passengers carried in 1994. Five carriers—American Airlines, Continental Airlines, Delta Airlines, Northwest Airlines, and United Airlines—accounted for over 80 percent of all major carrier domestic passenger traffic. Exhibit 1 shows major air carrier estimated market shares for 1994 in the United States.

Industry Background

The status of the U.S. passenger airline industry in early 1995 could be traced to 1978. Prior to 1978, and for 40 years, the U.S. airline industry was regulated by the federal government through the Civil Aeronautics Board (CAB). The CAB regulated airline fares, routes, and company mergers, and CAB approval was required before any changes in fares or route systems could be made. In this capacity, the CAB assured that individual airlines were awarded highly profitable and semi-exclusive routes necessary to subsidize less profitable routes which they were also assigned in the public interest. Price competition was suppressed, airline cost increases were routinely passed along to passengers, and the CAB allowed airlines to earn a reasonable rate of return on their investments. In 1978, the Airline Deregulation Act was passed. This act allowed airlines to set their own fares and enter or exit routes without CAB approvals. Jurisdiction for mergers was first transferred to the U.S. Department of Transportation and subsequently assigned to the U.S. Justice Department in 1988. The CAB was dissolved in 1985.

EXHIBIT 1

Estimated Market Shares for Major U.S. Carriers in 1994 Based on Revenue Passenger Miles Flown

Carrier	Market Share (%)	Carrier	Market Share (%)
1. United Airlines	22.1	6. USAir	7.8
2. American Airlines	20.2	7. Trans World Airlines	5.1
3. Delta Airlines	17.6	8. Southwest Airlines	4.4
4. Northwest Airlines	11.8	9. America West Airlines	2.5
5. Continental Airlines	8.5		

Source: Southwest Airlines company records. Figures rounded.

[3]This section is based on information provided in *FAA Aviation Forecasts* (Washington, D.C.: U.S. Department of Transportation, March 1995); *Standard & Poor's Industry Surveys* (New York: Standard & Poor's, January 1995); *U.S. Industrial Outlook* 1995 (Washington, D.C.: U.S. Department of Commerce, January 1995); Timothy K. Smith, "Why Air Travel Doesn't Work," *Fortune* (April 3, 1995): 42–56; and Jon Proctor, "Everyone Versus Southwest," *AIRWAYS Magazine* (November/December 1994): 6–13.

Deregulation and a Decade of Transition Public policy makers and industry analysts expected that deregulation would proceed in an orderly manner with multiple existing major carriers serving previously semi-exclusive routes, bringing about healthy price competition. However, the carriers responded to deregulation with unexpected changes in their operations that would have long-term effects on the industry.

Two changes in particular were noteworthy. First, major carriers turned their attention to serving nonstop "long-haul" routes anchored by densely populated metropolitan areas or city-pairs which had been highly profitable in a regulated environment. This meant that longer routes such as New York to Los Angeles and Chicago to Dallas were favored over "short-haul" routes between smaller city pairs such as Baltimore and Newark, New Jersey. As major carriers pruned or reduced service on these short-haul routes, existing regional carriers and new airlines filled the void. In 1978, the United States had 36 domestic carriers; by 1985 the number had grown to 100. Second, major carriers almost uniformly abandoned point-to-point route systems and adopted the hub-and-spoke route system. Point-to-point systems involved nonstop flights between city-pairs and often "shuttle" flights back and forth between city-pairs. The hub-and-spoke system featured "feeder flights" from outlying cities to a central hub city, where passengers would either continue their trip on the same plane or transfer to another plane operated by the same carrier to continue to their final destination. The key to this route system was to schedule numerous feeder flights into the hub airport to coincide with the more profitable long hauls, with each spoke adding passengers to the larger aircraft flying these longer distances. Potential increased revenue and some cost economies from flying more passengers longer distances, however, were offset by increased costs resulting from reduced utilization of aircraft as they waited to collect passengers, the capital investment in hub facilities, and the need for a larger ground staff.

Competition to survive and succeed intensified in the airline industry immediately following deregulation. Newly formed airlines and regional carriers, which had been permitted to serve only regional markets in a regulated environment, expanded both the number and length of their routes. These carriers typically retained the point-to-point route system which was more economical to operate than hubs. Absent the higher costs associated with the hub-and-spoke system and lower debt than older major carriers had assumed during the regulation era, these carriers had an immediate cost advantage. This advantage resulted in lower fares on both short- and long-haul routes. Price competition quickly erupted as all airlines scrambled to fill their seats. Price competition lowered the average fares paid on the formerly profitable long-haul routes serviced by major carriers while their operating costs remained high. The profit squeeze caused major carriers to cut their schedules and further reduce the number of short-haul routes.

Within five years after deregulation, the major carriers found themselves in a price-cost predicament best described by a senior airline executive: "Either we don't match (fares) and we lose customers, or we match and then because our costs are so high, we lose buckets of money."[4] This situation continued through the remainder of the 1980s as a price war of attrition was waged, ultimately resulting in a flurry of acquisitions by major carriers. Noteworthy acquisitions included Ozark Airlines by Trans World Airlines (TWA), Western Airlines by Delta, and Republic Airlines by Northwest in 1986. In 1987, AMR (American Airlines' parent company), acquired Air California and USAir acquired Pacific Southwest Airlines.

---

[4]William M. Carley, "Rough Flying: Some Major Airlines Are Being Threatened by Low-Cost Carriers," *Wall Street Journal* (October 12, 1983): 23.

Financial Calamity in the Early 1990s   Acquisition activity in the mid-1980s led industry analysts to believe the U.S. airline industry would soon evolve into an oligopoly with a few carriers capturing a disproportionate share of domestic traffic. By the late 1980s, eight airlines controlled 91 percent of U.S. traffic, but their financial condition was fragile due to a decade of marginal profitability.

Carrier bankruptcy and collapse marked the early 1990s due to a recession, a doubling of fuel prices during the Gulf War in 1991, and excess capacity in the industry. The U.S. airline industry recorded a cumulative deficit of $12 billion from 1990 through 1993. (See Exhibit 2, which plots U.S. air carrier operating revenues and expenses for fiscal years 1979 to 1994.) Between 1989 and 1992, Pan American Airlines (Pan Am), Continental Airlines, America West Airlines, Midway Airlines (a national carrier), Eastern Airlines, and TWA all filed for protection under Chapter 11 of the U.S. Bankruptcy Code. Eastern, Pan Am, and Midway ceased operations in 1991. Continental and TWA emerged from bankruptcy in 1993 as did America West in late 1994, and the industry as a whole recorded a modest operating profit in the 1994 fiscal year. Exhibit 3 shows 1994 financial and operating statistics for major U.S. carriers.

As existing airlines collapsed, new airlines were formed. The majority of new carriers, such as ValuJet, Reno Air, and Kiwi International Airlines, positioned themselves as "low-fare, low-frill" airlines. Benefiting from a cheap supply of aircraft grounded by major carriers from 1989 to 1993, the availability of furloughed airline personnel, and cost economies of point-to-point route systems, these new entrants had cost structures that were again significantly below most major carriers. For example, Kiwi was started by former Eastern and Pan Am personnel and was largely funded by its employees

EXHIBIT 2

U.S. Air Carrier Operating Revenues and Expenses, 1979–1994

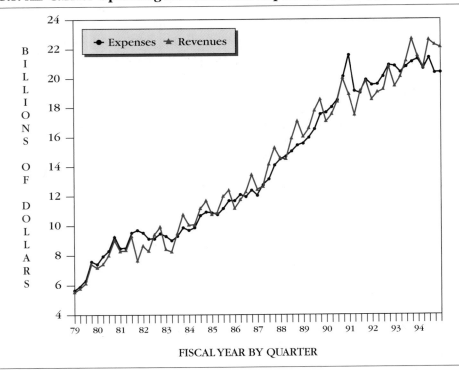

FISCAL YEAR BY QUARTER

Source: U.S. Department of Transportation.

EXHIBIT 3

1994 Financial and Operating Statistics for Major Carriers in the United States

	American Airlines (AMR)	America West Airlines	Continental Airlines	Delta Airlines	Northwest Airlines	Southwest Airlines	Trans World Airlines	United Airlines (UAL)	USAir
Financial Data ($ millions)									
Operating revenue	$14,895	$1,409	$5,670	$12,062	$8,343	$2,592	$3,408	$13,950	$6,997
Passenger	13,616	1,320	5,036	11,197	7,028	2,498	2,876	12,295	6,358
Freight/other	1,279	89	634	865	1,315	94	532	1,655	639
Operating expenses[a]	$14,309	$1,319	$5,921	$12,151	$7,879	$2,275	$3,883	$13,801	$7,773
Operating income	$586	$90	$(251)	$(89)	$464	$317	$(475)	$149	$(776)
Other income (expense)	$(593)	$2	$(399)	$(325)	$52	$(17)	$39	$22	$91
Net income before tax	$(7)	$92	$(650)	$(414)	$516	$300	$(436)	$171	$(685)
Operating Statistics									
Available seat miles (millions)	157,047[e]	18,060	65,861[f]	130,198	85,016	32,124	39,191	152,193	61,540
Revenue passenger miles (millions)	101,382	12,233	31,588	86,296	57,872	21,611	24,906	108,299	37,941
Load factor (%)	64.6	67.7	63.1	66.3	68.1	67.3	63.5	71.2	61.3
Yield (¢)[b]	13.40	10.79	11.44	12.97	12.14	11.56	11.31	11.35	16.76
Cost per available seat mile (¢)[c]	9.11	7.30	7.86	9.33	9.26	7.08	9.91	9.06	12.63
Labor productivity[d]	1,739	1,695	1,668	1,915	1,968	2,019	1,502	2,125	1,451

[a]Operating expenses include interest expense.

[b]Passenger revenue per revenue passenger mile.

[c]Operating expenses including interest expense per available seat mile.

[d]Thousands of available seat miles per employee.

[e]Includes the American Eagle commuter airline and transportation business only.

[f]Continental Airlines operating statistics are for jet operations only.

Source: Company annual reports. Data and calculations (all rounded) are useful for case analysis but not for research purposes. Revenue, expense, and operating statistics also include international operations.

(pilots paid $50,000 each to get jobs; other employees paid $5,000). These new "low-fare, low-frill" carriers reported combined revenues of about $1.4 billion in 1994 compared with $450 million in 1992. Although accounting for a small percentage of industry revenue, their pricing practices depressed fares on a growing number of routes also served by major carriers. In 1994, 92 percent of airline passengers bought their tickets at a discount, paying on average just 35 percent of the posted full fare.

Industry Economics and Carrier Performance

The financial performance of individual carriers and the U.S. airline industry as a whole could be attributed, in part, to the underlying economics of air travel. The majority of a carrier's costs (e.g., labor, fuel, facilities, planes) were fixed, regardless of the numbers of passengers served. The largest single cost to a carrier was people (salaries, wages, and benefits) followed by fuel. These two cost sources represented almost one-half of an airline's costs and were relatively fixed at a particular level of operating capacity. Fuel costs were uncontrollable and the industry had been periodically buffeted with skyrocketing fuel prices, most recently during the Gulf War in 1991. Fuel cost was expected to increase by 4.3 cents per gallon in late 1995 based on a tax imposed by the Revenue Reconciliation Act of 1993. Industry observers estimated that this tax would cost the U.S. airline industry an additional $500 million annually in fuel expense.

Labor cost, by comparison, was a controllable expense within limits, and more than 100,000 airline workers lost their jobs between 1989 and 1994. Recent efforts by major carriers to reduce labor cost included United Airlines, which completed an employee buyout of 55 percent of the company in exchange for $4.9 billion in labor concessions in the summer of 1994. In the spring of 1994, Delta Airlines announced a three-year plan to reduce operating expenses by $2 billion, which would involve 12,000 to 15,000 jobs being eliminated.

Carrier Operating Performance   Whereas the majority of a carrier's costs were fixed at a particular capacity level regardless of the number of passengers carried, a carrier's passenger revenues were linked to the number of passengers carried and the fare paid for a seat at a particular passenger capacity level. A carrier's passenger capacity is measured by the available seat miles (ASMs) it can transport given its airplane fleet, flight scheduling, and route length. An ASM is defined as one seat flown one mile whether the seat is occupied by a passenger or is empty. Carrier productivity is typically tracked by dividing a carrier's total operating cost by available seat miles. Carrier utilization is measured by what is termed a load factor. Load factor is computed by dividing a carrier's revenue passenger miles (RPMs) by its available seat miles. An RPM is defined as one seat flown one mile with a passenger in it and is a measure of a carrier's traffic. Yield is the measure of a carrier's passenger revenue-producing ability and is expressed as an average dollar amount received for flying one passenger one mile. Yield is calculated by dividing passenger revenue by revenue passenger miles.

The following expression shows how yield, load factor, and cost combine to determine the profitability of passenger operations for individual carriers, routes, and the industry:

$$\text{Operating income} = (\text{yield} \times \text{load factor}) - \text{cost, or}$$

$$\frac{\text{Operating income}}{\text{ASM}} = \left(\frac{\text{passenger revenue}}{\text{RPM}} \times \frac{\text{RPM}}{\text{ASM}} \right) - \frac{\text{operating cost}}{\text{ASM}}$$

By setting operating income to zero and monitoring yield and cost, individual carriers frequently computed a break-even load factor for passenger operations which was

EXHIBIT 4

Available Seat-miles, Revenue Passenger Miles, and Load Factors for All Certified U.S. Airlines, 1974–1994 Fiscal Years

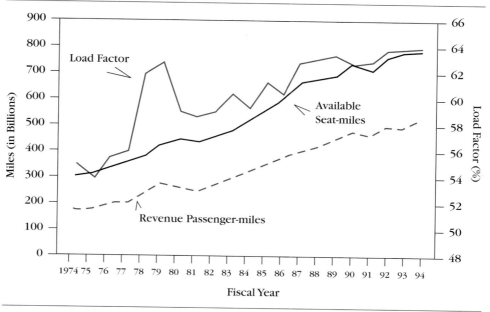

Source: U.S. Department of Transportation.

continually compared with actual load factors. Actual load factors higher than the break-even load factor produced an operating income for passenger operations; actual load factors below a break-even load factor resulted in an operating loss.

Industry Trends   Exhibit 4 charts available seat-miles, revenue passenger miles, and load factors for all FAA certified airlines for the 1974 fiscal year through the 1994 fiscal year. While revenue passenger miles and available seat miles for the industry have shown an upward trend, load factor fluctuated due to periodic imbalances between industry capacity and passenger demand. For example, domestic airline capacity (ASMs) increased by only 1.6 percent in fiscal year 1994 while revenue passenger miles increased 6.5 percent, producing a load factor of 64.3 percent. This figure represented the highest industry load factor ever achieved on domestic routes. Domestic passenger yields evidenced a long-term downward trend for 25 years in real (adjusted for inflation) dollars. In terms of real yield (discounting fares for inflation), fares in the years 1969 to 1971 produced an average yield of 21.4 cents in 1994 dollars. By 1994, the average industry yield was 12.73 cents.

Cost per available seat mile also exhibited a downward trend since 1978 despite periodic fluctuations in fuel prices. Nevertheless, labor cost reduction and productivity improvements coupled with the gradual addition of more fuel-efficient and lower cost maintenance planes by major carriers had not kept pace with the declining yields in the industry. Efforts by major carriers to reduce labor cost, described earlier, reflected the continuing attention to reducing the cost per available seat mile.

The Airline-Within-an-Airline Concept

Only Southwest Airlines, among the major carriers, appeared able to effectively navigate the economics of air travel and avoid the financial calamity that had befallen the airline industry in the early 1990s. Operating primarily short-haul, point-to-point routes, with minimal amenities, and able to make a fast turnaround of its aircraft between flights, Southwest had much lower operating costs than other major carriers. Lower operating costs were passed on to customers in the form of consistently low fares. From 1990 through 1994, Southwest more than doubled its operating revenues and almost quadrupled its operating income. Its operating practices and financial performance prompted a 1993 U.S. Department of Transportation study to conclude: "The dramatic growth of Southwest has become the principal driving force in changes occurring in the airline industry . . . As Southwest continues to expand, other airlines will be forced to develop low-cost service in short-haul markets."[5]

With Southwest's operating practices as a blueprint, several major carriers had already explored ways to implement a low-cost airline service in short-haul markets and produce a "clone" of Southwest. An outcome of this effort was the "airline-within-an-airline" concept. This concept involved operating a point-to-point, low-fare, short-haul, route system alongside a major carrier's hub-and-spoke route system.

Continental Lite   Continental was the first major carrier to implement this concept. Having just emerged from bankruptcy with lower operating costs and armed with a preponderance of consumer research showing that 75 percent of customers choose an airline on the basis of flight schedule and price, Continental unveiled what came to be known as "Continental Lite" on October 1, 1993. This service initially focused on Continental routes in the eastern and southeastern United States. By December 1994, Continental had converted about one-half of its 2,000 daily flights into low-fare, short-haul, point-to-point service, but was experiencing operating difficulties. In early January 1995, with operating difficulties resulting in a sizable financial loss, the "Continental Lite" initiative began folding back into Continental's hub-and-spoke system.

Shuttle By United   United, the world's largest airline in 1994, inaugurated its "airline-within-an-airline" on October 1, 1994. Branded "Shuttle By United," this initiative followed the United employee buyout in the summer of 1994 when employee wage cuts and more flexible work rules made possible a lower cost shuttle operation alongside the United hub-and-spoke route system. "Shuttle By United" was designed to be a high-frequency, low-fare, minimal amenity, short-haul flight operation initially serving destinations in California and adjacent states. If successful, United executives noted that the initiative could be expanded to 20 percent of United's domestic operations, and particularly to areas where the airline had a significant presence. One such area was the midwest, where United operated a large hub-and-spoke system out of Chicago's O'Hare Airport.

Beginning with eight routes, six of which involved United's San Francisco hub, "Shuttle By United" expanded to 14 routes by January 1995. Eight of the 14 routes involved point-to-point routes separate and apart from United's San Francisco hub. Nine of the routes competed directly with Southwest. In early December 1994, United executives reported that the initiative was exceeding expectations and some routes were profitable. "The Shuttle is working well," said its president, A. B. "Sky" Magary.[6]

[5]U.S. Department of Transportation press release, May 11, 1993.

[6]Quoted in Michael J. McCarty, "New Shuttle Incites a War Between Old Rivals," *Wall Street Journal* (December 1, 1994): B1, B5.

■ SOUTHWEST AIRLINES

Southwest Airlines was the eighth largest airline in the United States in 1994 based on the number of revenue passenger miles flown. Southwest recorded net income of $179.3 million on total operating revenue of $2.6 billion in 1994, thus marking 22 consecutive years of profitable operations—a feat unmatched in the U.S. airline industry over the past two decades. According to Southwest's Chairman, President, CEO, and co-founder, Herb Kelleher, Southwest's success formula could be succinctly described as, "Better quality plus lesser price equals value, plus spiritual attitude of our employees equals unbeatable."

The Southwest Model

Southwest began scheduled service on June 18, 1971, as a short-haul, point-to-point, low-fare, high-frequency airline committed to exceptional customer service. Beginning with three Boeing 737 aircraft serving three Texas cities—Dallas, Houston, and San Antonio—Southwest presently operates 199 Boeing 737 aircraft and provides service to 44 cities primarily in the midwestern, southwestern, and western regions of the United States. Fifty-nine percent of Southwest's capacity, measured in available seat miles flown, was deployed in the western United States, 22 percent in the southwest (Texas, Oklahoma, Arkansas, and Louisiana), and 19 percent in the midwest. Exhibit 5 shows the Southwest route map in early 1995.

EXHIBIT 5

Southwest Airlines Route Map in Early 1995

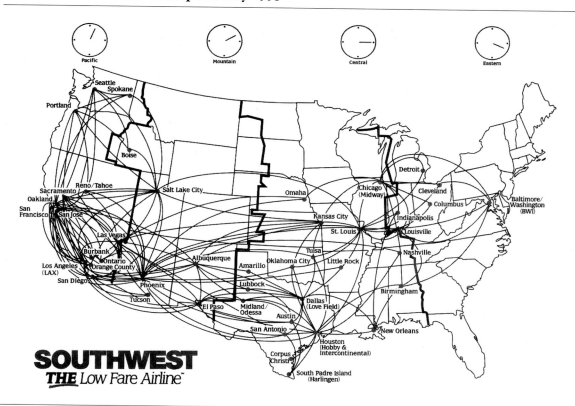

Source: Courtesy of Southwest Airlines.

Except for the acquisitions of Muse Air in 1985 and Morris Air in 1993, Southwest's management has steadfastly insisted on growing internally and refining and replicating what came to be known as the "Southwest Model" in the airline industry. This model was a mixture of a relentless attention to customer service and operations, creative marketing, and Southwest's commitment to its people. A healthy dose of fun was added for good measure.

Customer Service   Southwest's attention to customer service was embodied in the attitudes of its people. According to Herb Kelleher:

> What we are looking for, first and foremost, is a sense of humor. Then we are looking for people who have to excel to satisfy themselves and who work well in a collegial environment. We don't care that much about education and expertise, because we can train people to do whatever they have to do. We hire attitudes.[7]

A sense of humor, compassion for passengers and fellow workers, a desire to work, and a positive outlook manifested themselves in customer service at Southwest. Pilots could be found assisting at a boarding gate; ticket agents could be seen handling baggage. So important was the attention to customer service that Southwest chronicled legendary achievements in an internal publication titled *The BOOK on Service: What Positively Outrageous Service Looks Like at Southwest Airlines.*

The Southwest focus on customer service also produced tangible results. In 1994, Southwest won the annual unofficial "triple crown" of the airline industry for the third consecutive year by ranking first among major carriers in the areas of on-time performance, baggage handling, and overall customer satisfaction (see Exhibit 6). No other airline had ever won the "triple crown" for even a single month.

Operations   Southwest dedicated its efforts to delivering a short-haul, low-fare, point-to-point, high-frequency service to airline passengers. As a short-haul carrier with a point-to-point route system, it focused on local, not through or connecting, traffic that was common among carriers using a hub-and-spoke system. As a result, approximately

EXHIBIT 6

U.S. Department of Transportation Rankings of Major Air Carriers for 1994 by On-Time Performance, Baggage Handling, and Customer Satisfaction

On-Time Performance		*Baggage Handling*		*Customer Satisfaction*	
Southwest	1	Southwest	1	Southwest	1
Northwest	2	America West	2	Delta	2
Alaska	3	American	3	Alaska	3
United	4	Delta	4	Northwest	4
American	5	Alaska	5	American	5
America West	6	United	6	United	6
Delta	7	TWA	7	USAir	7
TWA	8	USAir	8	America West	8
USAir	9	Northwest	9	TWA	9
Continental	10	Continental	10	Continental	10

Source: U.S. Department of Transportation.

[7]Quoted in Kenneth Labich, "Is Herb Kelleher America's Best CEO?" *Fortune* (May 2, 1994): 28–35.

80 percent of its passengers flew nonstop. In 1994, the average passenger trip length was 506 miles and the average flight time was slightly over one hour. From its inception, Southwest executives recognized that flight schedules and frequency were important considerations for the short-haul traveler. This meant that Southwest aircraft had to "turn" quickly to maximize time in the air and minimize time on the ground. Turn referred to the elapsed time from the moment a plane arrived at the gate to the moment when it was "pushed back," indicating the beginning of another flight.[8] More than half of Southwest's planes were turned in 15 minutes or less while the remainder were scheduled to turn in 20 minutes. The U.S. airline industry turn time averaged around 55 minutes. A result of this difference was that Southwest planes made about ten flights per day, which was more than twice the industry average.

Southwest's operations differed from major carriers in other important ways. First, Southwest generally avoided major airline hubs in large cities. Instead, airports in smaller cities or less congested airports in larger cities were served. Midway Airport in Chicago, Illinois, and Love Field in Dallas, Texas, were examples of less congested airports in larger cities from which Southwest operated. Less congestion meant Southwest flights experienced less aircraft taxi time and less airport circling while awaiting landing permission. The practice of using secondary rather than hub airports also meant that Southwest did not transfer passenger baggage to other major airlines. In fact, Southwest did not coordinate baggage transfers with other airlines even in the few hub airports it served, such as Los Angeles International Airport (LAX).

Second, Southwest stood apart from other major carriers in terms of booking reservations and providing seat assignments. Rather than making reservations through computerized reservations systems, passengers and travel agents alike had to call Southwest. As a result, fewer than one-half of Southwest's seats were booked by travel agents. (Most airlines rely on travel agents to write up to 90 percent of their tickets.) Savings on travel agent commissions to Southwest amounted to about $30 million per year. Also, contrary to other major airlines, Southwest did not offer seat assignments. As Herb Kelleher said, "We still reserve your seat. We just don't tell you whether it's 2C or 38B!" Instead, reusable, numbered boarding passes identified passengers and determined boarding priority. The first 30 passengers checked in at the gate board first, then a second group of 30 (31–60) boarded, and so forth.

Third, only beverages and snacks were served on Southwest flights. The principal snack was peanuts, and 64 million bags of peanuts were served in 1994. Cookies were offered on longer flights.

Finally, Southwest flew only Boeing 737 jets in an all-coach configuration since no fare classes (first class, economy, business, etc.) existed. This practice differed from other major carriers which flew a variety of jet aircraft made by Airbus Industries, Boeing, and McDonnell Douglas, and reduced aircrat maintenance costs. Southwest's fleet was among the youngest of the major airlines at 7.6 years and had 25 new Boeing 737 aircraft scheduled for delivery in 1995. In 1994, less than one percent of Southwest flights were canceled or delayed due to mechanical incidents and Southwest was consistently ranked among the world's safest air carriers.

The combined effect of Southwest's operations was apparent in its cost structure. In 1994, Southwest's 7.08-cent cost per available seat mile was the lowest among major U.S. carriers.

Marketing Creative marketing was used to differentiate Southwest from other airlines since its beginning. As Herb Kelleher put it, "We defined a personality as well as a market niche. [We seek to] amuse, surprise and entertain."

---

[8]Numerous activities occurred during a turn's elapsed time. Passengers got on and off the plane and baggage was loaded and unloaded. The cabin and lavatories were tidied and the plane was refueled, inspected, and provisioned with snacks and beverages.

Southwest's marketing orientation was intertwined with its customer and operations orientation. In this regard, service, convenience, and price represented three pillars of Southwest's marketing effort. As with customer service and operations, Southwest's unique twist on marketing set it apart from other airlines. In the domain of pricing, for example, Southwest had always viewed the automobile as its primary competitor, not other airlines. According to Colleen Barrett, Southwest's Executive Vice President with responsibility for Customers:"We've always seen our competition as the car. We've got to offer better, more convenient service at a price that makes it worthwhile to leave your car at home and fly with us instead." In 1994, Southwest's average passenger fare was $58.44. Marketing communications continually conveyed the benefits to customers of flying Southwest. Advertising campaigns over the past 24 years featured Southwest service in "The Love Airline" campaign, convenience in "The Company Plane" campaign, and most recently, low price in "*The* Low Fare Airline" campaign (see Exhibit 7)

Southwest offered a frequent flyer program called "The Company Club," but again with a difference. Consistent with its focus on flight frequency and short-hauls, passengers received a free ticket to any city Southwest served with eight round-trips completed within 12 months. For 50 round-trips in a 12-month period, Southwest provided a companion pass valid for one year. Having no mileage or other qualifying airlines to track, the costs of "The Company Club" were minimal compared with other frequent flyer programs and rewarded the truly frequent traveler.

Southwest also flew uniquely painted planes that signified places on its route structure. Planes were painted to look like Shamu the Killer Whale to highlight Southwest's relationship with both Sea World of California and Texas. Other planes were painted to look like the Texas state flag and called "The Lone Star Over Texas." while others, such as "Arizona One," featured the Arizona state flag (see Exhibit 8 on page 450).

People Commitment   The bond between Southwest and its workers was generally regarded by the company as the most important element in the Southwest model. Herb Kelleher referred to this bond as "a patina of spirituality." He added:

> I feel that you have to be with your employees through all their difficulties, that you have to be interested in them personally. They may be disappointed in their country. Even their family might not be working out the way they wish it would. But I want them to know that Southwest will always be there for them.[9]

The close relationship among all Southwest employees contributed to Southwest's recent listing as one of the top ten best companies to work for in a recent study of U.S. firms. The study noted that the biggest plus at Southwest was that "it's a blast to work here"; the biggest minus was that "you may work your tail off."[10]

Southwest's commitment to its people was evident in a variety of forms. The company had little employee turnover compared with other major airlines and was the first U.S. airline to offer an employee profit-sharing plan. Through this plan, employees owned about 10 percent of Southwest stock. Eighty percent of promotions were internal and cross-training in different areas as well as team building were emphasized at Southwest's "People University."

---

[9]Quoted in Kenneth Labich, "Is Herb Kelleher America's Best CEO?" *Fortune* (May 2, 1994): 28–35.

[10]Robert Levering and Milton Mosckowitz, *The 100 Best Companies to Work for in America* (New York: Doubleday/Currency, 1993).

EXHIBIT 7

Representative Southwest Airlines Print Advertising Campaign

WHEN YOU WANT A LOW FARE, LOOK TO THE AIRLINE THAT OTHER AIRLINES LOOK TO.

Call your travel agent or **1-800-I-FLY-SWA**

Source: Courtesy of Southwest Airlines.

EXHIBIT 8

Southwest Airlines Aircraft

Source: Courtesy of Southwest Airlines.

Competitive and Financial Performance

Southwest's attention to customer service and efficient operations, creative marketing, and people commitment produced extraordinary competitive and financial results.

Competitive Performance   According to the U.S. Department of Transportation, Southwest carried more passengers than any other airline in the top 100 city-pair markets with the most passengers in the 48 contiguous United States.[11] These 100 markets represented about one-third of all domestic passengers. In its own top 100 city-pair markets, Southwest had an average 65 percent market share compared with about a 40 percent market share for other airlines in their own top 100 city-pair markets. Southwest consistently ranked first or second in market share in more than 90 percent of its top 50 city-pair markets. In Texas, where Southwest began operations in 1971, it ranked first in passenger boardings at 10 of the 11 Texas airports served and had an intra-Texas market share of 70.8 percent in mid-1994. Southwest recorded a market share of 56.4 percent in the intra-California market in mid-1994, compared with a market share of less than 3 percent in 1989.

Financial Performance   Southwest's average revenue and income growth rate and return on total assets and stockholders' equity were the highest of any U.S. air carrier during the 1990s. Exhibit 9 on page 452 provides a five-year consolidated financial and operating summary for Southwest Airlines.

Even though Southwest achieved record revenue and income levels in 1994, net income in the fourth quarter 1994 (October 1–December 31, 1994) fell 47 percent compared to the fourth quarter 1993. The last time Southwest reported quarterly earnings that were less than the same quarter a year earlier was in the third quarter of 1991. Fourth quarter 1994 operating revenues were up only three percent compared to the same period in 1993. This result was considerably less than the double-digit gains in operating revenues recorded in each of the preceding three quarters compared to 1993. Southwest's fourth quarter financial report sent the company's stock price reeling to close at a 52-week low of $15.75 in December 1994 in New York Stock Exchange composite trading, down from a record $39.00 in February 1994.

Southwest's fourth quarter 1994 earnings performance reflected the cumulative effect of numerous factors. These included the conversion of recently acquired Morris Air Corporation to Southwest's operations, competitors' persistent use of fare sales which Southwest often matched, and the airline-within-an-airline initiatives launched by Continental and United. Commenting on the fourth quarter financial and operating performance, Herb Kelleher said:

> While these short-term results will be disappointing to our shareholders, the recent investments made to strengthen Southwest Airlines are vitally important to our long-term success. We are prepared emotionally, spiritually and financially to meet our increased competition head-on with even lower costs and even better customer service.[12]

■ SOUTHWEST VS. SHUTTLE BY UNITED

The maiden flight for "Shuttle By United" departed Oakland International Airport for Los Angeles International Airport at 6:25 A.M. on Saturday, October 1, 1994. Later that morning, United's executive vice president of operations, who flew in from United's world headquarters near Chicago to mark the occasion, spoke to the media. He said:

> What we're doing is getting back into the market and getting our passengers back. We used to own Oakland and LA, and then Herb (Kelleher) came in. What we have to do is protect what's ours.[13]

---

[11]U.S. Department of Transportation press release, May 11, 1993.

[12]Quoted in Terry Maxon, "Southwest Forecasts Dip in Earnings," *The Dallas Morning News* (December 8, 1994): D1, D3.

[13]Quoted in Catherine A. Chriss, "United Shuttle Takes Wing," *The Dallas Morning News* (October 3, 1994): 1D, 4D.

EXHIBIT 9

Southwest Airlines Five-Year Financial and Operating Summary (Abridged)

Selected Consolidated Financial Data[a]

(In Thousands Except Per-Share Amounts)	1994	1993	1992	1991	1990
Operating revenues:					
Passenger	$2,497,765	$2,216,342	$1,623,828	$1,267,897	$1,1 44,421
Freight	54,419	42,897	33,088	26,428	22,196
Charter and other	39,749	37,434	146,063	84,961	70,659
Total operating revenues	2,591,933	2,296,673	1,802,979	1,379,286	1,237,276
Operating expenses	2,275,224	2,004,700	1,609,175	1,306,675	1,150,015
Operating income	316,709	291,973	193,804	72,611	87,261
Other expenses (income), net	17,186	32,336	36,361	18,725	(6,827)[f]
Income before income taxes	299,523	259,637	157,443	53,886	80,434
Provision for income taxes[c]	120,192	105,353	60,058	20,738	29,829
Net income[c]	$179,331	$154,284[d]	$97,385[e]	$33,148	$50,605
Total assets	$2,823,071	$2,576,037	$2,368,856	$1,854,331	$1,480,813
Long-term debt	$583,071	$639,136	$735,754	$617,434	$327,553
Stockholders' equity	$1,238,706	$1,054,019	$879,536	$635,793	$607,294

Consolidated Financial Ratios[a]

	1994	1993	1992	1991	1990
Return on average total assets	6.6%	6.2%[d]	4.6%[e]	2.0%	3.5%
Return on average stockholders' equity	15.6%	16.0%[d]	12.9%[e]	5.3%	8.4%
Debt as a percentage of invested capital	32.0%	37.7%	45.5%	49.3%	35.0%

Consolidated Operating Statistics[b]

	1994	1993	1992	1991	1990
Revenue passengers carried	42,742,602[g]	36,955,221[g]	27,839,284	22,669,942	19,830,941
RPMs (thousands)	21,611,266	18,827,288	13,787,005	11,296,183	9,958,940
ASMs (thousands)	32,123,974	27,511,000	21,366,642	18,491,003	16,411,115
Load factor	67.3%	68.4%	64.5%	61.1%	60.7%
Average length of passenger haul	506	509	495	498	502
Trips flown	624,476	546,297	438,184	382,752	338,108
Average passenger fare	$58.44	$59.97	$58.33	$55.93	$57.71
Passenger revenue per RPM	11.56¢	11.77¢	11.78¢	11.22¢	11.49¢
Operating revenue per ASM	8.07¢	8.35¢	7.89¢	7.10¢	7.23¢
Operating expenses per ASM	7.08¢	7.25¢[b]	7.03¢	6.76¢	6.73¢
Number of employees at year-end	16,818	15,175	11,397	9,778	8,620
Size of fleet at year-end[i]	199	178	141	124	106

[a] The Selected Consolidated Financial Data and Consolidated Financial Ratios for 1992 through 1989 have been restated to include the financial results of Morris.

[b] Prior to 1993, Morris operated as a charter carrier; therefore, no Morris statistics are included for these years.

[c] Pro forma assuming Morris, an S Corporation prior to 1993, was taxed at statutory rates.

[d] Excludes cumulative effect of accounting changes of $15.3 million ($.10 per share).

[e] Excludes cumulative effect of accounting change of $12.5 million ($.09 per share).

[f] Includes $2.6 million gains on sales of aircraft and $3.1 million from the sale of certain financial assets.

[g] Includes certain estimates for Morris.

[b] Excludes merger expenses of $10.8 million.

[i] Includes leased aircraft.

Source: Southwest Airlines 1994 Annual Report.

At the time, Dave Ridley believed that the Oakland flight had "symbolic significance" for two reasons. First, until the late 1980s, United was the dominant carrier at the Oakland airport, but left in the early 1990s following head-to-head competition with Southwest. Second, Oakland had become the main base of Southwest's Northern California operation and was the fastest growing of California's ten major airports in terms of air traffic.

Shuttle By United[14]

Created by a team of United Airlines managers and workers over the course of a year and code-named "U2" internally, "Shuttle By United" was designed to replicate many operational features of Southwest: point-to-point service, low fares, frequent flights, and minimal amenities. Lowering operating cost was a high priority since United's cost for shorter domestic routes (under 750 miles) was 10.5 cents per available seat mile. United's targeted cost per seat mile was 7.5 cents for its shuttle operation.

Like Southwest, "Shuttle By United" featured Boeing 737 jets with a seating capacity of 137 passengers, focused on achieving 20-minute aircraft turns, and offered only beverage and snack (peanuts and pretzels) service. Management and ground crews alike had attended "enculturalization" and motivational classes that emphasized teamwork and customer service. Unlike Southwest, "Shuttle By United" provided first-class (12 seats) and coach seating. Rather than boarding passengers in groups of 30 like Southwest, a boarding process—known as WILMA for windows, middle, and aisle seat—was used for seat assignments. Passengers assigned window seats boarded first, followed by middle seat travelers, and then aisle customers. United's "Mileage Plus" frequent flyer program was available to passengers, with an option that matched Southwest's offer of one free ticket for each eight shuttle round trips.

"Shuttle By United" was inaugurated with eight routes. Six of these were converted United routes involving the airline's San Francisco hub. Only three of the original eight routes competed directly with Southwest: San Francisco–San Diego, Oakland–Los Angeles, and Los Angeles–Sacramento. On these three routes, the "Shuttle By United" one-way, walk-up coach fare was identical to Southwest's $69.00 "California State Fare," which was Southwest's highest fare on all seats and flights within California.[15] One-way walk-up coach fares varied on the five noncompeting routes. Service from San Francisco to Burbank and to Ontario was priced at $104.00. Fares for the remaining San Francisco routes were $89.00 to Los Angeles, $99.00 to Las Vegas, and $139.00 to Seattle. The "Shuttle By United" first-class fare was typically $20.00 higher than its coach fare. "Shuttle By United" was advertised heavily using print and electronic media.

"Shuttle By United" soon expanded its route system to include six additional routes. All six routes competed directly with Southwest. Service out of Oakland included Oakland–Burbank, Oakland–Ontario, and Oakland–Seattle. Los Angeles to Phoenix and to Las Vegas and San Diego–Sacramento rounded out the new service. Except for the Oakland–Seattle route, all one-way walk-up coach fares were $69.00 for Southwest and "Shuttle By United." A one-way walk-up coach fare of $99.00 was charged on the Oakland–Seattle route by the two airlines. "Shuttle By United" also increased its flight frequency in 12 of 14 city-pair markets, primarily out of its San Francisco hub. Cities served by "Shuttle By United" appear in the map shown in Exhibit 10 on page 454.

---

[14]Portions of this discussion are based on Jesus Sanchez, "Shuttle Launch," *Los Angeles Times* (September 29, 1994): D1, D3; Randy Drummer, "The Not-So-Friendly Skies," *Daily Bulletin* (September 30, 1994): C1, C10; "United Brings Guns to Bear," *Airline Business* (November 1994): 10; Michael J. McCarthy, "New Shuttle Incites a War Between Old Rivals," *Wall Street Journal* (December 1, 1994): B1, B5.

[15]Walk-up fares refer to the fare available at any time, with no restrictions, no penalties, and no advance purchase requirements.

EXHIBIT 10

Cities Served by "Shuttle By United"

Note: The map is not drawn to scale.

In early December 1994, United reported that the cost per available seat mile of its shuttle operation had not yet achieved its targeted 7.5 cents. In an interview, "Sky" Magary said, "We're vaguely better than halfway there."[16]

Southwest Airlines

Southwest's planning for United's initiative began months before the "Shuttle By United" scheduled October 1 launch. In June 1994, a Southwest spokesperson said the airline would "vigorously fight to maintain our stronghold in California."

Prior to the launch of "Shuttle By United," Southwest committed additional aircraft to the California market to boost flight frequencies on competitive routes. By mid-January 1995, Southwest had deployed 16 percent of its total capacity (in terms

---

[16]Michael J. McCarthy, "New Shuttle Incites a War Between Old Rivals," *Wall Street Journal* (December 1, 1994): B1, B5.

of available seat miles flown) to the intra-California market. Thirteen percent of Southwest's total available seat-mile capacity overlapped with "Shuttle By United" by late January 1995.

Southwest also boosted its advertising and promotion budget for the intra-California market, with particular emphasis in city-pairs where "Shuttle By United" competed directly with Southwest. Southwest's "*The* Low Fare Airline" advertising campaign spearheaded this effort. Southwest's walk-up fare remained at $69.00 during the fourth quarter of 1994, unchanged from the fourth quarter of 1993. However, Southwest's 21-day advance fares and other discount fares were being heavily promoted. The effect of this pricing was that Southwest's average passenger fare in the markets also served by "Shuttle By United" (excluding Oakland–Seattle) was $44.00 during the fourth quarter of 1994 and into early January 1995, compared with $45.00 in the third quarter of 1994. The average 1994 fourth-quarter fare for the Oakland–Seattle route was $51.00, down from $60.00 in the third quarter of 1994. Dave Ridley estimated that the average passenger fare for "Shuttle By United" was five to ten percent higher than the average Southwest fare in the nine markets where it competed directly with Southwest, and about $20.00 higher than the average Southwest fare in the five markets served out of San Francisco where it did not compete directly with Southwest. The difference in average passenger fares between the airlines was due to first-class seating offered by "Shuttle By United" in competitive markets and generally higher fares in non-competitive markets.

■ THE TUESDAY MEETING

The original agenda for the "Tuesday meeting" in late January 1995 focused mostly on operational issues. For example, Southwest would begin scheduled service to Omaha, Nebraska, in March 1995, and advertising, sales, promotion, and scheduling matters still required attention. Southwest's "ticketless" travel system, or "electronic ticketing" was also on the agenda. This system, whereby travelers make reservations by telephone, give their credit card number and receive a confirmation number, but receive no ticket in the mail, was scheduled to go nationwide on January 31, 1995, after a successful regional test. Final details were to be discussed.

Dave Ridley also intended to apprise his colleagues of the competitive situation in California. A staff member had prepared a report showing fourth quarter load factors by route for Southwest and estimated load factors for "Shuttle By United." He wanted to share this information with the group (see Exhibit 11 on page 456), along with other recent developments. For example, a few days earlier, "Shuttle By United" had reduced its one-way walk-up coach fare on the San Francisco-Burbank route to $69.00. This fare was identical to the one charged on the Oakland-Burbank route by both airlines. In addition, Southwest's consolidated yield and load factor for January 1995 were tracking lower than the consolidated yield and load factor for January 1994. If present traffic patterns continued, Southwest's consolidated load factor would be about five points lower in January 1995 as compared to January 1994.

Unexpected news that "Shuttle By United" intended to discontinue some service and raise fares altered the original meeting agenda and posed a number of questions for Southwest executives. For instance, did the fare increase signify a major modification in United's "We're going to match Southwest" strategy? If so, what were the implications for Southwest? How might Southwest react to these changes, if at all? Should Southwest follow with a $10.00 fare increase of its own or continue with its present price and service strategy? What might be the profit impact of United's action and Southwest's reaction, if any, for each airline? And how, if at all, was United's pricing action linked to the announced withdrawal from the Oakland–Ontario market?

EXHIBIT 11

Daily Scheduled City-Pair Round Trips by Southwest Airlines and "Shuttle By United" and Quarterly Load Factor Estimates

Market (City-Pair)	Air Miles	Southwest Airlines Daily Round-Trip Flights		Shuttle By United Daily Round-Trip Flights		1994 4th-Quarter Load Factor		1994 3rd-Quarter Load Factor		1993 4th Quarter Load Factor	
		October–December 1994	Mid-January 1995	October–December 1994	Mid-January 1995	United	Southwest	United	Southwest	United	Southwest
San Francisco–Los Angeles	338	No Service →		31	40	66%	—	77%	—	68%	—
San Francisco–Burbank	359	No Service →		11	12	60%	—	70%	—	64%	—
San Francisco–Ontario	364	No Service →		11	12	47%	—	63%	—	64%	—
San Francisco–Las Vegas	417	No Service →		9	10	73%	—	85%	—	74%	—
San Francisco–Seattle	678	No Service →		13	16	74%	—	89%	—	77%	—
San Francisco–San Diego	417	12	12	10	12	77%	61%	87%	68%	84%	70%
Oakland–Los Angeles	338	19	25	10	15	62%	59%	—	74%	—	63%
Oakland–Burbank	326	13	16	7	11	40%	63%	—	80%	—	70%
Oakland–Ontario	362	12	14	7	7	32%	57%	—	68%	—	65%
Oakland–Seattle	671	4	7	4	5	52%	66%	—	77%	—	—
Los Angeles–Sacramento	374	5	6	5	6	81%	65%	73%	53%	67%	—
Los Angeles–Phoenix	366	25	23	9	10	48%	61%	—	60%	—	56%
Los Angeles–Las Vegas	241	13	19	10	12	61%	65%	—	73%	—	61%
San Diego–Sacramento	481	9	9	5	5	50%	68%	—	78%	—	67%

Source: Southwest Airlines company records. For analysis purposes, load factors can be applied to daily round-trip flights for both airlines on both legs of a round trip.

Superior Supermarkets
Everyday Low Pricing

In early April 2003, James Ellis was reviewing the first-quarter financial results for Superior Supermarkets. As Senior Vice President at Hall Consolidated and President of Superior Supermarkets, he was about to meet with the District Manager responsible for three Superior stores in Centralia, Missouri. Others in attendance would be Hall Consolidated's Vice President of Retail Operations and the Controller for Superior Supermarkets. The agenda for the first of four quarterly meetings scheduled for 2003 was to discuss the district's progress toward achieving planned goals and address any issues related to the District Manager's supermarkets.

In anticipation of the quarterly review, Randall Johnson, the District III Manager for Superior Supermarkets, had proposed that everyday low pricing be reconsidered for his three stores in Centralia.[1] He cited company research documenting Superior's relatively higher prices in Centralia and the growing price consciousness among Centralia shoppers. He also noted that Superior Supermarkets could lose market share in Centralia since store sales were below budgeted levels in this first quarter of 2003. He added that 2002 fourth-quarter sales revenue, which was normally a heavy sales period due to the Thanksgiving and Christmas holidays, was also lower than sales for the same period in 2001.

The everyday low pricing strategy option for Centralia had been discussed briefly in August 2002 as part of the annual planning process. However, a decision was made to continue Superior's current pricing strategy pending further study. James Ellis believed that the time had come to formally address the question in detail.

■ THE COMPANY

Superior Supermarkets is a division of Hall Consolidated, a privately owned wholesale and retail food distributor. Hall Consolidated was formed in 1959 and initially included a number of wholesale food operations and produce companies. The company's first retail grocery store chain was purchased in 1970. The Superior Supermarket chain was acquired in 1975. By 2002, Hall Consolidated distributed food and related products to some 150 company-owned supermarket units operating under three supermarket chain names through 12 wholesale distribution centers. These distribution centers also supplied about 1,100 independent grocery stores in the United States. Hall Consolidated sales in 2002 were $2.3 billion.

---

[1]With an everyday low price policy, a retailer charges a constant, lower everyday price for merchandise with few, if any, price discounts. This practice differs from a "Hi-Lo" price policy whereby a retailer charges higher prices on an everyday basis but then runs frequent promotions, sales, or specials in which selected merchandise prices are deeply discounted.

This case was prepared by Professor Roger A. Kerin, of the Edwin L. Cox School of Business, Southern Methodist University, as a basis for class discussion and is not designed to illustrate effective or ineffective handling of an administrative situation. Company names and data have been disguised. Copyright © 2003 by Roger A. Kerin. No part of this case may be reproduced without the permission of the copyright holder.

Superior is the smallest of the three supermarket chains owned by Hall Consolidated with sales of $192.2 million in 2002. Superior operates conventional supermarkets in trade areas that served small cities and towns in the South Central United States. The median size of a Superior Supermarket was 20,730 square feet, which is considered small by industry standards (the median size of a supermarket in the United States is about 44,000 square feet). Nevertheless, Superior was the number 1 or number 2 ranked supermarket chain in each of its trade markets as measured by market share.

■ COMPETITIVE ENVIRONMENT IN CENTRALIA, MISSOURI

Centralia is the primary trade area in Scott County, which is located in central Missouri. The Centralia trade area had total retail sales of $725 million in 2002. Food and beverage retail store sales were $62.3 million in 2002, which represented a 4.6 percent increase over 2001. There are 20 establishments in Centralia that sell food and beverages.

According to the U.S. Census 2000, Centralia has a total population of 41,000, including 13,500 households. The median age of the Centralia population was 35 years; the median household income was $36,000; and 80 percent of residents had a high school education or more. Slightly over one-half (51.5 percent) of Centralia's residents were employed by manufacturing, retail trade, and education, health, and social services establishments. Exhibit 1 shows the age and household income distribution of Centralia residents.

Major Competitors

Four grocery chain stores accounted for 85 percent of all food sales in Centralia in 2002 (see Exhibit 2). The remainder of the retail food business was shared primarily by two small independent grocery stores, several convenience stores, specialty food stores (bakeries, butcher shops) and a seasonal Farmers' Market. Three of the chains—Harrison's, Grand American, and Missouri Mart—operated one store in Centralia. Hall

EXHIBIT 1

Centralia Population Profile: Age and Household Income Distribution

Age Distribution		Household Income Distribution	
Category	*Percent*	*Category*	*Percent*
19 years and under	29.6	Less than $10,000	10.4
20 to 24 years	6.8	$10,000 to $14,999	7.5
25 to 34 years	13.8	$15,000 to $24,999	16.1
35 to 44 years	14.9	$25,000 to $34,999	14.5
45 to 54 years	12.9	$35,000 to $49,999	19.8
55 to 59 years	4.4	$50,000 to $74,999	19.8
60 to 64 years	3.5	$75,000 to $99,999	6.3
65 to 74 years	6.9	$100,000 to $149,999	3.8
75 years and over	7.3	$150,000 or more	1.9
	100.0		100.0

Source: U.S. Census 2000.

EXHIBIT 2

Estimated Share of Market for Supermarkets in Centralia

	1995	1996	1997	1998	1999	2000	2001	2002
Superior	24%	29%	27%	30%	31%	22%	23%	23%
Grand American	22	11	7	6	6	6	6	13
Missouri Mart	25	25	26	28	30	34	34	27
Harrison's	9	14	19	16	14	20	20	22
Others	20	21	21	20	19	18	17	15

Source: Company records.

Note: Share-of-market estimates were made by Hall Consolidated executives on the basis of information they considered reliable. The total market (100%) represents all food sales made in Centralia.

operated three Superior Supermarkets in Centralia. Each of the three Superior stores was smaller than the other chains' stores. Grand American, Harrison's, and Missouri Mart drew their customers from larger geographic areas than did Superior, including business from outside Centralia. Missouri Mart, in particular, enjoyed a sizable trade from outside Centralia. Store locations are shown in Exhibit 3 on page 460.

Harrison's   Harrison's supermarket on West Main Street was built in 1976, expanded in 1990, and remodeled in 1999. About 15 percent of the store's 50,000 square feet is devoted to an extensive assortment of general merchandise and a small pharmacy. Hall officials believe that Harrison's has captured most of the business of the middle- and upper-income groups in Centralia with annual household incomes in excess of $40,000. Harrison's supermarket has the second highest sales of all the major chain stores. It's store in Centralia is one of the company's 65 supermarkets located throughout Missouri and Illinois.

Harrison's is well managed, clean, orderly, and attractive. The décor is warm, the staff friendly, and the physical layout easy to shop. Its merchandising strength is a balanced variety of groceries, quality meats, and produce. The store is conveniently located, with excellent parking facilities. The store's principal promotion theme is everyday low prices, as evidenced by its advertising slogan, "Save on the Total." According to Hall executives, Harrison's has an extremely favorable customer image.

Grand American   The Grand American store, measuring 39,800 square feet, opened in mid-2001 and is located at the corner of Fairview and West Main. This store replaced an older, smaller facility located several blocks northeast of the new site. The Centralia store is one of 148 supermarkets operated by Grand American, a large regional food distributor and retailer. The Grand American store is the most modern store in Centralia and has the finest fixtures and décor. It has wide aisles and is relatively easy to shop.

Hall officials consider the Grand American store a secondary competitor. According to Hall executives, the store is highly regimented and lacks any innovative merchandising appeal. It has modest variety in meats, produce, and groceries, but its dairy department is highly regarded by Centralia shoppers. The store carries a skeleton variety of general merchandise and houses a small pharmacy. Grand American's weekly advertising emphasizes high-volume items and also attempts to create a low-price image by highlighting competitive prices on items listed in each ad. The store also offers double coupons and in-store "Manager's Specials." The store's customers come from residential areas similar to those of Harrison's customers; however, the annual household income of Grand American customers ranges from $20,000 to $35,000.

EXHIBIT 3

Location of Stores, Major Traffic Arteries, and Principal In-City Trade Areas of Major Supermarket Chain Stores in Centralia

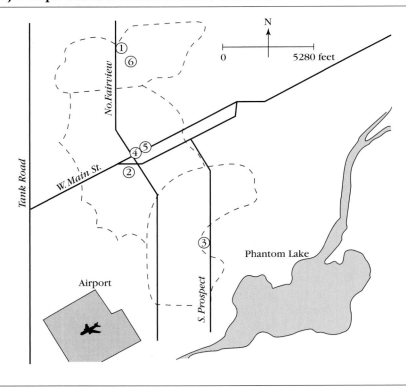

Key:

1. Superior (N. Fairview)   4. Grand American

2. Superior (W. Main St.)   5. Harrison's

3. Superior (S. Prospect)   6. Missouri Mart

Note: Trade area boundaries were drawn on the basis of personal interviews with customers in each Superior store. The address of each interviewee was then plotted on the map and boundaries drawn.

Missouri Mart According to Hall officials, Missouri Mart is the food sales volume leader in Centralia and is the principal competitor of Superior supermarkets. Approximately 32 percent of Superior customers shop Missouri Mart regularly. Most of Missouri Mart's customers are middle-aged and older families whose annual household incomes exceed $30,000. Sixty percent of the store's 120,000 square feet is allotted to general merchandise; 40 percent is devoted to food items. The store was remodeled in 2001. Managers of the three Superior stores maintain that "Missouri Mart's primary merchandising strength is in groceries and special purchase displays." One manager stated that "orderliness and cleanliness are sacrificed for production, and the store lacks the quality and freshness present in the other supermarkets in Centralia." Ads feature very low prices on particular items, which are displayed in large quantities at the ends of aisles in the grocery section of the store. Unlike Harrison's and Grand American, which are free-standing, the Missouri Mart store is part of a complex of other types of stores, including several service shops, a bakery, a drug store, and a furniture store. Missouri Mart, Inc., the regional chain that built the Centralia store and operated it for many years, recently franchised it to an independent businessperson who continues to operate the store under the Missouri Mart banner.

Superior Supermarkets   The three Superior Supermarkets in Centralia were generally older than those of its major competitors. Each of the stores anchored a strip shopping center (owned by Hall Consolidated) consisting of a Superior supermarket and a drugstore, plus two or three shops (e.g., a dry cleaner, a shoe repair shop, a barber shop, or a florist). Sales for the three stores had increased over the past three years reaching $14,326,700 in 2002 (see Exhibit 4). The overall gross profit margin for the three stores was 28.8 percent in 2002. By comparison, the median U.S. supermarket industry gross profit margin was 26.4 percent.

Sales of the three Superior stores were divided as follows: grocery (including dairy), 50 percent; fresh meat, poultry and seafood, 20 percent; produce, 18 percent; seasonal and general merchandise (including health and beauty care items), 7 percent; and bakery (including bread and baked goods) and deli (including self-serve and service deli), 5 percent. Gross profit margins in each of these departments were grocery (including dairy), 30 percent; fresh meat, poultry, and seafood, 18 percent; produce, 30 percent; general merchandise (including health and beauty items), 33 percent; and bakery and deli, 50 percent.

Company officials believed that Superior stores offered a more limited variety of merchandise than the major competitors but that Superior carried high-quality merchandise, particularly in grocery items and fresh produce. Officials recognized that the fresh meat, poultry, and seafood departments of the three stores varied in consumer acceptance.

Superior follows both Missouri Mart and Harrison's in terms of overall advertising exposure, measured in terms of newspaper advertising space, circulars, and newspaper inserts, radio spots, and outdoor. Grand American's advertising exposure is considerably less than Superior in these media. Superior features a value positioning in its advertising: Superior Supermarkets = Superior Value. In 2002, Superior spent $127,500 for advertising or .89 percent of its sales. Missouri Mart and Harrison's were spending the equivalent of about 1 percent of their sales on advertising, Hall officials believed. None of the food stores in Centralia advertise on television.

Superior is the highest-priced food store in the Centralia area, based on comparison market-basket studies of supermarket competitors. (Exhibit 5 on page 462 shows the dollar breakdown of products sold in Centralia supermarkets.) Nevertheless, Superior advertises high-volume items at deeply discounted prices and features "loss leaders"—items sold to the customer at or near their cost to the seller. Soft drinks, bread, eggs, and flour are popular loss leaders in the Centralia market.

North Fairview   Built in 1975, the North Fairview store is the oldest of the three Superior stores in Centralia. Improvements were made to the store in 1990 and 1995, including new checkstands and new freezers. The store is located less than two blocks from the shopping complex that houses Missouri Mart. About 20 percent of the North Fairview store's customers come from outside Centralia. Most of these customers live approximately three to four miles from the store.

EXHIBIT 4

Superior Supermarket Sales in Centralia: 2000–2002

Store	2000	2001	2002
North Fairview	$ 4,050,277	$ 4,287,686	$ 4,437,632
West Main	5,194,972	5,174,051	5,374,517
South Prospect	4,098,898	4,227,304	4,514,551
Total	$13,345,147	$13,689,041	$14,326,700

Source: Company records.

EXHIBIT 5

How $100 Is Spent in a Typical Centralia Supermarket

Perishables		$ 49.67
Fresh meat, poultry, and seafood	$ 14.32	
Produce	9.70	
Dairy	9.08	
Frozen foods	6.95	
Service deli	3.38	
Bread and baked goods	3.15	
In-store bakery	2.14	
Self-serve deli	0.77	
Floral	0.18	
Food grocery		$ 30.95
Beverages	10.71	
Main meal items	8.44	
Snack food	6.39	
Miscellaneous	5.41	
Non-food grocery		$ 8.77
Health and beauty care		3.72
General merchandise		3.45
Pharmacy		2.49
Unclassified		0.95
		$100.00

Source: Company records.

West Main Street   The Superior store on West Main Street was opened in 1977. Substantial improvements to the store were made in 1992, including an expansion of the frozen food and dairy departments and the addition of new checkstands. A "mini-deli" was added in 2000 as part of a modest renovation. The deli prepares items for sale on the premises and for delivery to and sale at the North Fairview and South Prospect stores.

Two competitors, Harrison's and Grand American, are situated across the street. Although both are strong competitors, Hall executives believe that the West Main Street store draws most of its customers from the area south of the store, and that Harrison's and Grand American draw fewer customers than Superior does from that area. Approximately 22 percent of the West Main store's sales come from people living beyond the city limits.

South Prospect   The South Prospect store was built in 1982 and substantially remodeled in 2000. No major competitors presently exist in the immediate vicinity of the store. The South Prospect store has the only on-premise "scratch" bakery among the three Superior stores. Deliveries are made to the other stores daily. Company executives believe that the bakery offers high-quality items but less variety than the typical retail bakery shop in Centralia. About 23 percent of the store's sales are to people who live outside Centralia.

■ CONSUMER RESEARCH INITIATIVES

In mid-2002, Hall commissioned an independent marketing research firm to conduct a series of studies for the three Superior stores in Centralia. Two objectives were outlined for these studies. First, Hall executives sought (1) to develop an updated profile of Superior shoppers and (2) to determine the shopping behavior of these customers. This information was to be used in making store merchandising and renovation decisions. Second, executives hoped that questioning shoppers about what they liked and disliked about the Superior stores would reveal what kind of retail image the stores projected. The question of store image had been a subject of discussion among corporate officials since 2000, when a retailing consultant to the company had concluded that the stores in Centralia failed to reach their full sales and profit potential because of the lack of a strong consumer image.

The first study consisted of a telephone survey of 400 Centralia residents, who were asked to comment on the principal strengths of the Superior stores, Missouri Mart, Grand American, and Harrison's. More than 30 percent of the interviewees considered Superior's prices "above average." In contrast, some 20 percent of the respondents thought the prices at Missouri Mart and at Grand American were below average. Harrison's was thought to have the lowest everyday prices. Additional results from this study appear in Exhibit 6.

A second study consisted of two focus groups recruited to discuss various aspects of food store choice and patronage in Centralia. A summary of their comments follows:

Price. Price is the most important store choice determinant. Focus group participants believe that for grocery items, in particular, Centralia stores carry the same national brands and the stores' private labels have similar quality. Harrison's is perceived as having the best overall prices.

Meat. Twenty of the 24 focus group participants stated that the quality of meat is the second-most important determinant of store choice and patronage. They like to see cleanliness in the meat department and bargains that are not simply poor cuts of

EXHIBIT 6

Association of Store Characteristics with Major Food Stores in Centralia

Characteristic	Grand American	Harrison's	Superior	Missouri Mart	Don't Know	Total
Most reasonable prices	11%	36%	7%	34%	12%	100%
Most convenient	18	21	35	25	1	100
Best-quality meat	20	27	18	11	24	100
Widest variety of meats	22	25	20	18	15	100
Best-quality produce	24	35	21	11	9	100
Widest variety of produce	24	30	14	18	14	100
Best store service	12	30	28	13	17	100
Quality of canned goods	12	24	14	14	26	100
Best overall variety	6	8	2	74	10	100
Best store layout	27	24	14	9	26	100
Best bakery	5	20	25	5	45	100
Best deli	5	9	9	2	75	100

Source: Company records.

meat. Meat display is also an important consideration. Harrison's was judged to have the best quality and variety of meat. Missouri Mart received the lowest marks on meat.

Produce. Produce quality, variety, and display follows meat as a major store choice and patronage determinant. Focus group participants tended to equate produce quality (and meat quality) with a quality store image. Harrison's is the "produce store" in Centralia. Missouri Mart rates lowest in produce quality, variety, and display.

Shopping Convenience. Focus group participants tended to lump together a host of factors that seem to represent a fourth major consideration in store choice and patronage. These factors tend to represent shopping convenience. Convenience includes ease of getting into and out of store parking lots, quick checkout, carry-out service, well-stocked and orderly shelves, and helpful store personnel. Closeness to home or work also seems important, particularly for last-minute shopping trips.

Stores in General. Focus group participants are generally pleased with their food shopping options. They shop for food twice a week on average. One trip is for major food purchases; the second trip is for fill-in items. They usually shop more than one store on a regular basis.

Missouri Mart. The typical comment made by focus group participants in reference to Missouri Mart was that "you can't stick to your budget if you shop at Missouri Mart because there are so many things to buy." However, they don't like the service at Missouri Mart, nor do they care for the quality of meat.

Grand American. Most remarks about Grand American were in a neutral or negative vein. Focus group participants stated that the store is often out of stock and that it usually overadvertises. Grand American-advertised specials are not in fact specials at all, according to some focus group participants.

Harrison's. Harrison's is winning the price competition with Missouri Mart in Centralia. Harrison's is recognized as having the best in price, courtesy, quality of merchandise, and service. Focus group participants believe Harrison's "Save on the Total" advertising.

Superior (combined stores). Superior appears to be the winner on shopping convenience. Focus group participants from all parts of Centralia considered Superior to be a good neighborhood store. The "Superior Supermarkets = Superior Value" advertising was questioned given the perceived higher grocery, meat, and produce prices.

A third study involved personal interviews with 587 Superior customers at the three store sites. Customers were asked to respond to questions asked by the interviewer and to comment on the store. Responses to questions are tabulated in Exhibit 7 for each store and for all three stores combined.

In commenting on Superior stores, shoppers emphasized that lower prices and greater variety were needed. Shoppers suggested that the dairy section be cleaner, the prices of meats be lower, the variety of goods in the bakery be greater, the out-of-stock situation in private labels be improved, and the quality and freshness of produce be enhanced. Questions concerning features of the Superior stores liked by shoppers generated a variety of responses. Appearance and cleanliness, friendliness, service, and convenient to home or work were liked most by shoppers.

■ THE QUARTERLY REVIEW MEETING

James Ellis convened the quarterly review meeting soon after pleasantries were exchanged among the participants. The performance of the 15 stores in Randall Johnson's District III were reviewed. Except for the three Superior Supermarkets in Centralia, Missouri, all met planned quarterly sales, gross profit margin, expense, and profit goals. The three stores in Centralia had posted a 1 percent negative variance on sales. Inspection of the store's sales mix, which evidenced an increase in the percentage sales among higher gross margin categories (grocery, general merchandise, and bakery/deli), had boosted the store's gross profit margin percent. The slightly higher gross

EXHIBIT 7

Superior Supermarket Shopper Interview Results

	S. Prospect	W. Main	N. Fairview	Superior, Combined
Age of customer (years):				
Over 65	7.5%	16.8%	9.7%	10.7%
64–50	13.7	25.5	28.0	21.6
49–35	33.0	35.8	33.1	33.8
34–25	18.9	15.3	24.0	19.7
24–18	21.2	6.6	4.0	11.6
Under 18 and no response	5.7	0	1.2	2.6
Average persons per household	2.6	1.9	1.9	2.1
Frequency of store visits:				
4 times a week	18.1%	11.7%	9.7%	13.4%
3 times a week	19.9	21.2	22.7	21.2
2 times a week	28.2	38.0	40.0	35.0
Once a week	10.6	11.2	9.2	10.3
3 times a month	0.9	1.7	5.4	2.6
2 times a month	6.0	4.5	7.0	5.9
Once a month	9.7	8.9	5.4	8.1
Other	6.5	2.8	0.5	3.5
Length of patronage:				
Less than 1 year	11.4%	10.0%	7.1%	7.6%
1–3 years	19.3	8.8	8.0	12.5
3 or more years	69.3	81.2	84.9	77.9
Proportion of total food needs purchased:				
Almost all	13.0%	12.4%	24.4%	17.0%
About ¾	18.8	14.1	13.3	15.0
About ½	50.0	58.2	47.2	51.7
About ¼ to ½	6.7	7.9	7.2	7.1
Less than ¼	11.5	7.3	7.8	9.2
Departments shopped:				
Grocery, meat, produce	22.5%	17.4%	30.2%	23.4%
Grocery, meat	10.7	10.4	13.6	11.5
Grocery, produce	11.2	7.3	5.4	8.2
Meat, produce	6.5	3.7	2.2	4.3
Grocery only	33.5	45.1	32.2	36.9
Meat only	1.4	2.4	4.3	2.7
Produce only	0.9	3.7	2.7	2.3
General Merchandise, including health/beauty items	15.2	9.2	7.5	10.9
Frozen foods	22.4	20.8	28.5	23.9
Dairy	39.6	37.6	49.7	42.3
Bakery and/or Deli	23.3	22.4	29.1	24.9

(continued on next page)

EXHIBIT 7   (continued)

	S. Prospect	W. Main	N. Fairview	Superior, Combined
Other stores shopped most regularly:				
Grand American	7.6%	7.8%	4.9%	6.8%
Harrison's	30.8	40.8	16.8	29.5
Missouri Mart	29.0	22.1	43.8	31.6
Superior	0.6	0.6	—	0.4
Independent 1	5.8	—	0.6	2.2
Independent 2	4.7	0.6	3.7	1.8
Other	3.5	3.0	0.1	3.4
None	18.0	15.0	30.1	14.3
Liked best about other regular store:				
Prices	33.8%	29.5%	19.5%	27.0%
Meat	8.8	22.7	7.8	11.6
Produce	10.3	9.1	6.5	8.5
Location	10.3	9.1	5.2	7.9
Other responses	36.8	29.6	61.0	45.0

(No one category accounted for more than 7% of the total.)

Source: Company records.

margin percent, coupled with lower operating expenses, resulted in the stores' net profit margin being slightly under 1 percent—just shy of the budgeted 1 percent net profit margin for the first quarter of 2003. In addition, customer counts at all three stores were higher than the first quarter of 2002. Over all, District III was performing according to plan.

Everyday Low Pricing Discussion

Following the District III quarterly performance review, the discussion turned to Randall Johnson's proposal to implement everyday low pricing in Centralia, Missouri. He reiterated the points made in an earlier memo to James Ellis: (1) Superior's prices were higher than the competition at a time of growing price consciousness among Centralia shoppers and (2) Superior could lose market share in Centralia due to the price differential. Sales in Centralia were already down 3 percent in the first quarter of 2003 compared with budgeted sales goals. This decline, following a slower than expected fourth quarter of 2002, "could indicate the beginning of a trend," Johnson said. He added, "We are running the risk of losing our hold as the second largest supermarket (based on market share) in Centralia."

Hall Consolidated had selectively employed everyday low pricing in well-defined market areas served by each of its three supermarket chains. According to Hall's Vice President of Retail Operations,

> Our success with everyday low pricing has been a mixed bag. We've learned that this pricing strategy tends to work better when it is part of a broader store positioning strategy and supported with advertising. We've also learned that for everyday low pricing to work, we don't have to be the lowest priced supermarket in the trade area.

James Ellis agreed with these observations and added:

> Everyday low pricing has to be used by all stores in a trade area, otherwise we'll only confuse our store image or positioning. In short, I think we need to take a hard look at our recent consumer research to see how we are positioned in Centralia and how everyday low pricing will change our image.

The Controller for Superior Supermarkets pointed out that everyday low pricing had the potential to reduce operating costs. He said:

> Everyday low pricing can lower our operating costs in two ways. It can reduce our inventory and handling costs due to more steady and predictable demand. It can also reduce our labor costs related to less frequent temporary price reductions. Our experience indicates that we can get an additional 50 basis points (.5 percent of sales) due to lower inventory and handling costs. The need to remark merchandise and shelf tags, including labor expense, costs us 60 basis points (0.6 percent of sales), which could be eliminated with everyday low pricing. Both savings could be added to our gross profit margin.

Randall Johnson injected, "Or we use the savings to bolster our advertising budget featuring our new everyday low pricing strategy." Everyone agreed that such an option existed.

Everyday Low Pricing Implementation Considerations

"Let's not rush to a conclusion on everyday low pricing yet," said James Ellis. "We still have a few things to consider, not the least of which are the knotty implementation questions."

All of the Hall executives acknowledged that Superior Supermarkets were "rightly perceived by supermarket shoppers as having the highest prices in Centralia." However, everyone agreed that few shoppers had specific product or brand price knowledge upon which to compare stores. To the extent that price knowledge existed, it tended to be category dependent. Prior company consumer research indicated that shoppers tended to have a relatively good idea of prices for products they purchased frequently. For example, new parents have a better price knowledge of baby foods and diapers. These price-knowledgeable shoppers also tended to recognize attractive (lower) and unattractive (higher) prices and were proficient at detecting a "good deal" when they saw it either in an ad or in the store.

"When we consider everyday low pricing, we have to consider whether or not we adopt this pricing strategy across-the-board for all our products or just certain categories," James Ellis said. Randall Johnson was in favor of the across-the-board approach noting that the impact on shopper perceptions would be greater. The Vice President of Retail Operations favored limiting everyday low pricing to grocery (including dairy items) and seasonal and general merchandise (including health and beauty care items) from an operational standpoint. The Controller agreed: "We are more likely to see cost savings due to everyday low pricing in these categories than in the others. These categories represent 57 percent of Superior's sales in Centralia and everyday low pricing there should convey the image we want to project."

James Ellis continued, "Another consideration is the pricing itself. How much should we lower our prices?" The market-basket studies of supermarket competitors consistently showed that Superior's everyday (nonpromotional) prices were about 10 percent higher than Harrison's prices and about 7 percent higher than Grand American and Missouri Mart. "That is, if there is such a thing as an everyday price at Grand American or Missouri Mart given their frantic discounting," said Randall Johnson. All of the Hall executives agreed that Superior could not "outprice" Harrison's and any suggestion that Superior intended to do that in Centralia would be unwise. "We are not about to start a price war in a market that has been profitable for us," said James Ellis. "Besides," said the Vice President for Retail Operations, "we offer greater convenience of shopping with our three stores and that is worth something."

At that moment, the telephone rang and James Ellis was told his scheduled meeting with the District II manager was running late. "Randy, I promised you that we would get closure on the everyday low pricing proposal while you are in town," said James Ellis. He concluded the meeting saying, "We've made some progress this morning, but I think the matter requires further attention. Let's all meet again tomorrow morning. In the meantime, all of us need to look hard at the Centralia situation, consider our present competitive position in the market, and agree on how we might proceed."

Burroughs Wellcome Company
Retrovir

"I think that Burroughs Wellcome is very interested in getting all their money back as soon as possible, because the sun won't shine forever."[1]

> Cofounder of Project Inform,
> an AIDS treatment information agency
> (1987)

"Once the drug is out on the marketplace, the company controls the pricing."[2]

> Dr. George Stanley,
> Food and Drug Administration (1987)

"To make AZT accessible to everyone who should be on it, Burroughs Wellcome has an obligation to give up a significant amount of money to allow people to get access."[3]

> Executive Director,
> National Gay and Lesbian Task Force
> (1989)

"There's no plan to make another price cut."[4]

> Sir Alfred Sheppard,
> Chairman of the Board, Wellcome PLC
> (1989)

In January 1990, Burroughs Wellcome executives were under continued pressure to reduce the price of Retrovir. Retrovir brand zidovudine is the trade name for a drug called azidothymidine (AZT), which had been found to be effective in the treatment of acquired immune deficiency syndrome (AIDS) and AIDS-related complex (ARC). AIDS is a disease caused by a virus that attacks the body's immune system and damages the system's ability to fight off other infections. Without a functioning immune system, a person becomes vulnerable to infection by bacteria, protozoa, fungi, viruses, and other malignant agents, which may cause life-threatening illnesses, such as pneumonia, meningitis, and cancer. AIDS is caused by HIV (human immunodeficiency virus), a human virus first discovered in 1983. AZT is classified as an antiviral drug that interferes with the replication of HIV. As such, AZT is a treatment, not a cure, for AIDS.

In 1987, Burroughs Wellcome obtained approval from the U.S. Food and Drug Administration to market Retrovir, the first and, as of 1990, the only drug authorized for the treatment of AIDS. Soon after Burroughs Wellcome made Retrovir available for prescription sales on March 19, 1987, the company became embroiled in controversy

---

[1]"The Unhealthy Profits of AZT," *The Nation* (October 17, 1987): 407.

[2]Ibid.

[3]"AZT Maker Expected to Reap Big Gain," *New York Times* (August 29, 1989): 8.

[4]"Wellcome Seeks Approval to Sell AZT to All Those Inflicted with AIDS Virus," *Wall Street Journal* (November 17, 1989): B4.

This case was prepared by Professor Roger A. Kerin, of the Edwin L. Cox School of Business, Southern Methodist University, with the assistance of Angela Bullard, graduate student, as a basis for class discussion and is not designed to illustrate effective or ineffective handling of an administrative situation. The case was prepared from published sources. Quotes, statistics, and published operating information are footnoted for reference purposes. Copyright © 1995 by Roger A. Kerin. No part of this case may be reproduced without the written permission of the copyright holder.

related to the price of the drug. Critics charged that Burroughs Wellcome, which sold the drug to wholesalers at a price of $188 for a hundred 100-milligram capsules, engaged in price gouging of a "highly vulnerable market." The company's President, T. E. Haigler, responded that the high price was due to the "uncertain market for the drug, the possible advent of new therapies, and profit margins customarily generated by significant new medicines."[5]

Nevertheless, the company reduced its price by 20 percent in December 1987, and again by 20 percent in September 1989. Prior to the 1989 price reduction, the Subcommittee on Health and the Environment of the U.S. House of Representatives had launched an investigation into possible "inappropriate" pricing of Retrovir. Soon after the announced price reduction in 1989, the chairman of the House subcommittee said that this was "a good first step. But I think the company can do better."[6] In November 1989, the Chairman of Wellcome PLC, the parent company of Burroughs Wellcome, was quoted as saying, "There's no plan to make another price cut."[7] However, pressure to again reduce the price continued.

■ ACQUIRED IMMUNE DEFICIENCY SYNDROME

Acquired immune deficiency syndrome can be traced to a blood sample taken and stored in the Central African nation of Zaire in 1959 (see Exhibit 1 for a chronology of important events). It was not until 1982, however, that the Centers for Disease Control and Prevention in Atlanta, Georgia, labeled the disease and warned that it

EXHIBIT 1

AIDS Chronology, 1959–1990

1959	Blood sample taken and stored in the Central African nation of Zaire. Retesting the sample in 1986, physicians discover it to be HIV-infected.
1978	Doctors determine that a child in New York died as a direct result of immune system breakdown.
1981	The Centers for Disease Control (CDC) reports breakdowns of the immune systems of several male homosexuals with the resulting occurrence of infectious diseases and cancers.
1982	CDC names the "mystery disease" acquired immune deficiency syndrome (AIDS) and warns that it may be spread by a virus in bodily fluids such as blood and semen.
1983	Scientists at the Pasteur Institute in Paris, France, isolate a suspected AIDS-causing virus.
1984	U.S. researchers identify an AIDS-causing virus as the same one isolated by the French scientists.
1985	A test is licensed to detect an AIDS-causing virus in blood.
1986	The AIDS-causing virus is named human immunodeficiency virus, or HIV.
1987	U.S. Food and Drug Administration permits sale of azidothymidine (AZT), which eases some of the symptoms of AIDS and AIDS-related complex (ARC).
1988–1990	AIDS fatalities continue to increase while the pharmaceutical industry searches for a cure.

[5]"The High-Cost AIDS Drug: Who Will Pay for It?" *Drug Topics* (April 6, 1987): 52.

[6]"How Much for a Reprieve from AIDS?" *Time* (October 2, 1989): 81.

[7]"Wellcome Seeks Approval to Sell AZT:," *Wall Street Journal* (November 17, 1989): B4.

might be spread by a virus in bodily fluids such as blood and semen. In 1983 and 1984, French and American scientists isolated a suspected AIDS-causing virus that was subsequently named human immunodeficiency virus, or HIV, in 1988. HIV is a retrovirus that can become an extra link in the genetic code, or DNA, of a cell. HIV inhibits and eventually destroys the T-4 cell, which is a key part of a person's immune system that attacks foreign germs. Without T-4 cells, people succumb to all manner of infections. The identification of HIV was a major breakthrough, especially since, prior to 1984, it was not established in the scientific community that retroviruses like HIV caused human diseases.

Incidence and Cost of HIV and AIDS

Efforts to track and forecast the incidence and cost of HIV and AIDS began in earnest in 1986. Research focused on identifying high-risk individuals, determining the geographical concentration of the disease, and arriving at estimates of the number of people afflicted with HIV and AIDS.[8] This research found that almost 90 percent of AIDS victims were homosexual men or intravenous drug users. One-half of all reported AIDS cases were in the San Francisco, Miami, New York City, Los Angeles, and Houston metropolitan areas.

Tracking and forecasting the incidence of AIDS cases and HIV infections proved to be more difficult. The CDCP reported 5,992 AIDS cases in 1984 and 35,198 cases in 1989. Estimates of HIV infections in 1990 ranged between 800,000 and 1,300,000 Americans, depending on the estimation procedure employed. The incidence of AIDS cases in the period 1981–1989 is charted in Exhibit 2 on page 472. The fatality rate for persons inflicted with AIDS was about 91 percent in 1981 and 46 percent in 1989.

Treating AIDS patients has proved to be extremely expensive. According to a 1987 study by the Rand Corporation, an internationally recognized research organization, the lifetime medical costs of an AIDS patient in his thirties were estimated to be between $70,000 and $141,000. For comparison, the lifetime cost of treating a person in his thirties with digestive tract cancer was $47,000; leukemia, $29,000; and a heart attack, $67,000.

An estimated 40 percent of persons with AIDS have received care under the Medicaid Program, which is administered by the Health Care Financing Administration and funded jointly by the federal government (55 percent) and individual states (45 percent). Estimated annual costs for AIDS care and treatment funded by Medicaid ranged between $700 million and $750 million in 1988. Medicaid spending for AIDS was estimated to reach $2.4 billion in 1992. In addition, private insurers paid $250 million annually in AIDS-related medical payments.

Anti-HIV Drug Treatment

The identification of HIV in the mid-1980s prompted numerous pharmaceutical companies to search for antiviral drugs. Burroughs Wellcome led the research effort in part because of its prior development of drugs that combat viral diseases. In addition to AZT supplied by Burroughs Wellcome, other compounds were in various stages of develop-

---

[8]Portions of this material are based on statistics reported in Brad Edmundson, "AIDS and Aging," *American Demographics* (March 1990): 28–34; Fred J. Hellinger, "Forecasting the Personal Medical Care Costs of AIDS from 1988 through 1991," *Public Health Reports* (May–June 1988): 309–319; William L. Roper and William Winkenwerder, "Making Fair Decisions about Financing Care for Persons with AIDS," *Public Health Reports* (May–June 1988): 305–308; Centers for Disease Control, "Human Immunodeficiency Virus Infection in the United States: A Review of Current Knowledge," *Morbidity and Mortality Weekly Report* (December 18, 1987): 2–3, 18–19; "Now That AIDS Is Treatable, Who'll Pay the Crushing Cost?" *Business Week* (September 11, 1989): 115–116; Centers for Disease Control, "HIV/AIDS Surveillance Report" (U.S. Department of Health and Human Services, Public Health Services: December 1990).

EXHIBIT 2

AIDS Cases, 1981–1989

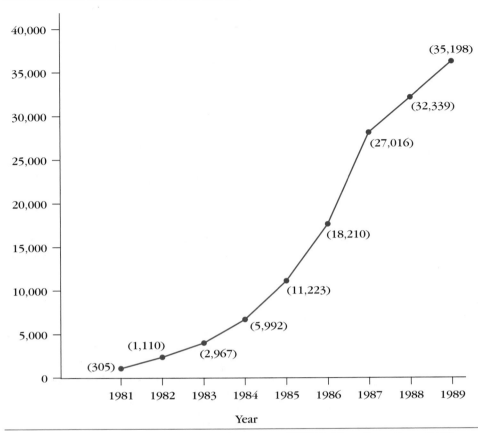

Source: Based on Centers for Disease Control and Prevention, "HIV/AIDS Surveillance Report" (U.S. Department of Health and Human Services, Public Health Services: December 1990).

ment and commercialization.[9] One antiviral drug has been given limited approval by the FDA and is available to patients who have a negative reaction to AZT. This drug, produced by Bristol Myers and called DDI, is an antiviral drug that appears to inhibit reproduction of HIV and slow the damage it causes. DDI was initially studied for AIDS use by the National Cancer Institute. Like AZT, it interferes with the ability of HIV-infected cells to produce new viruses and slows the progression of HIV infection, but does not eradicate or eliminate the infection. The principal advantage of DDI over AZT is that it appears to be less toxic. DDC, developed by Hoffman-LaRoche, was in clinical trials in 1989. Other drugs produced by Glaxo and Triton Biosciences, Inc. were being tested as well. Industry analysts believed that one or more of these drugs would obtain FDA approval for prescription sales by 1991.

[9]Portions of this material are based on "A Quiet Drug Maker Takes a Big Swing at AIDS," *Business Week* (October 6, 1986): 32; "There's No Magic Bullet, but a Shotgun Approach May Work," *Business Week* (September 11, 1989): 118.

■ BURROUGHS WELLCOME COMPANY

Burroughs Wellcome is the American subsidiary of Wellcome PLC, an English public limited company with headquarters in London.[10] Wellcome PLC is a multinational firm with manufacturing operations in 18 countries and employs 20,000 people. Approximately 18 percent of the company's employees are engaged in research and development efforts. The company's primary business, which accounts for 89 percent of its fiscal 1989 revenue, is human health care products, both ethical (prescription) and over the counter (nonprescription). Two ethical products account for 34 percent of its human health care revenue: Zovirax and Retrovir. Zovirax, which is used in the treatment of herpes infection, is the company's single largest-selling product with annual sales of $492 million in 1989. Retrovir is its second largest-selling product with sales of $225 million in fiscal 1989. In addition, the company markets Actifed and Sudafed, cough and cold preparations, as over-the-counter products. These two products combined account for annual sales of $253 million. Wellcome PLC had an animal health care business that accounted for about 11 percent of company revenue. This business was divested in late 1989.

North America represents the largest market for the products sold by Wellcome PLC, with annual sales of $997 million. Sales in the United States are roughly equivalent to 42 percent of Wellcome PLC's worldwide sales. The United Kingdom is the company's second largest market and accounts for about 10 percent of worldwide sales.

Wellcome PLC recorded total revenues of $1.75 billion and net profit before tax of $262.1 million in fiscal 1987. Total revenues for fiscal 1989 (fiscal year ended August 31, 1989) were $2.1 billion with net profit before taxes of $475 million.[11] Selected financial and operating ratios for Wellcome PLC for the fiscal years 1987–1989 are shown in Exhibit 3 on page 474. Exhibit 4 on page 475 presents comparative statistics for other major firms in the U.S. pharmaceutical industry. Percentage sales and the net income growth since fiscal 1985 for Wellcome PLC are shown below:

Fiscal Year	Sales Growth	Net Income Growth
1985–1986	0.2%	7.2%
1986–1987	12.6	47.3
1987–1988	10.4	35.1
1988–1989	12.6	42.9

■ DEVELOPMENT OF RETROVIR

Burroughs Wellcome's AIDS research program began in June 1984 with an extensive search for likely drug candidates. According to Philip Furman, head of virus research, "We looked at all our known antivirals on the off chance that one would work against retroviruses."[12]

---

[10]Much of this material is described in Wellcome PLC's 1989 and 1990 annual reports; "Burroughs Wellcome Company," Burroughs Wellcome news release, December 13, 1990; Brian O'Reilly, "The Inside Story of the AIDS Drug," *Fortune* (November 5, 1990): 112–29. Financial figures and percentages represent approximations, since information is reported in U.S. dollars and the British pound sterling. These figures are not useful for research purposes.

[11]These figures are based on the average exchange rate of $1.55 = £1 in 1987, and $1.68 = £1 in 1989 (*Welcome PLC 1990 Annual Report*).

[12]This material is based on "The Development of Retrovir," Burroughs Wellcome news release, June 1990; L. Wastila and L. Lasagna, "The History of Zidovudine (AZT)," *Journal of Clinical Research and Pharmacoepidemiology*, Vol. 4 (1990): 25–29; "The Inside Story of the AIDS Drug," *Fortune* (November 5, 1990): 112–129; "AIDS Research Stirs Bitter Fight over Use of Experimental Drugs," *Wall Street Journal* (June 18, 1986): 26.

EXHIBIT 3

Selected Financial and Operating Ratios of Wellcome PLC

	Fiscal Year*		
	1989	*1988*	*1987*
Financial Ratios			
Gross profit margin (gross profit/sales)	70.6%	68.1%	67.5%
Return on sales (net income before tax/sales)	20.0	17.7	14.9
Return on assets (net income before tax/total assets)	20.0	18.0	15.0
Return on equity (net income before tax/common equity)	35.0	36.0	32.0
Operating Ratios			
R&D expenditures/sales	13.4	13.1	12.6
Selling, general, and administration costs/sales	36.9	36.5	39.2

*Fiscal year ends August 31.

Source: Wellcome PLC annual reports.

Laboratory Testing

Burroughs Wellcome scientists examined hundreds of compounds over a period of five months, but none proved acceptable. In November 1984, AZT was found to inhibit animal viruses in a laboratory setting. AZT had been synthesized in 1964 by a researcher at the Michigan Cancer Foundation. It was hoped then that the drug would be useful in the treatment of cancer, but when investigated, it was found to have no potential as an anticancer agent. In the early 1980s, Burroughs Wellcome scientists resynthesized AZT in their exploration of compounds with possible effectiveness against bacterial infection. This research provided information about the spectrum of the drug's antibacterial activity and its toxicity and metabolism in laboratory animals, but intensive development was not pursued. The drug was not examined again until late 1984 when it showed promise as an AIDS treatment. (Exhibit 5 on page 476 details significant events in the development of Retrovir.)

Following *in vitro* demonstration of its potential by Burroughs Wellcome's scientists, 50 coded compounds including AZT were sent to Duke University, the National Cancer Institute (NCI), and the FDA for independent testing to assess their *in vitro* activity against the human retrovirus.[13] Early in 1985 these tests showed that AZT was, in fact, active against HIV in the test tube. The company then began extensive preclinical toxicologic and pharmacologic testing in the spring of 1985. At the same time, work began on scaling up synthesis of the drug in preparation for clinical testing in patients with HIV. On June 14, 1985, Burroughs Wellcome submitted an application to the FDA to obtain Investigational New Drug (IND) status for the compound, which would allow its use in a limited number of severely ill AIDS and ARC

---

[13]*In vitro*, a Latin phrase meaning "in glass," is used medically to mean to isolate from a living organism and artificially maintain in a test tube.

EXHIBIT 4

Selected Financial and Operating Ratios for Pharmaceutical Firms in the United States, 1989

	Pharmaceutical Firm					
	Schering-Merck & Co.	Pfizer, Inc.	Abbott Labs	Upjohn	Plough	Eli Lilly
Financial Ratios*						
Gross profit margin	76.3%	63.6%	52.5%	69.8%	73.8%	69.9%
Return on sales	34.8	16.2	22.2	15.8	20.4	31.9
Return on assets	33.8	11.0	24.6	14.2	17.9	22.7
Return on equity	64.9	20.2	43.8	26.5	33.0	35.4
Operating Ratios						
R&D/sales	11.5	9.4	9.3	14.0	10.3	14.5
SG&A/sales	30.7	37.2	20.5	40.3	42.3	27.5

* See Exhibit 3 for definitions of ratios.

Source: Company annual reports.

patients. A week later, the FDA notified Burroughs Wellcome that the submitted data were sufficient to allow clinical studies in humans to be initiated.

Human Testing

Retrovir was administered to patients for the first time on July 3, 1985, at the Clinical Center of the National Institutes of Health (NIH) in Bethesda, Maryland. This initial (Phase I) study, conducted under a protocol developed by Burroughs Wellcome in collaboration with scientists at the NCI, Duke University, the University of Miami, and UCLA, involved 40 patients infected with HIV. The purpose of Phase I testing was to determine how Retrovir acted in the body, the appropriate dosage, and potential adverse reactions or side effects. Initial results were encouraging. Some of the patients showed evidence of improvement, including an increased sense of well-being, weight gain, and positive changes in various measures of the immune system function. Extended treatment, however, lowered production of red blood cells and certain white blood cells in some patients who had taken high doses.

By early 1986, sufficient data on Retrovir were available to proceed with more extensive human testing. The need now was to prove that the drug could provide useful therapy for AIDS and ARC patients. More volunteers and an objective basis for comparison were essential to the conduct of the Phase II trial. A double-blind, placebo-controlled trial, conducted and financed by Burroughs Wellcome, began on February 18, 1986. A total of 281 patients participated. Safeguards built into the study provided for data to be reviewed periodically by a board of impartial experts convened under the auspices of the National Institute of Allergy and Infectious Diseases (NIAID). If either the placebo or the drug-treated group did either so poorly or so well that it would be unethical to continue the trial, the study would be stopped.

About this time, both the medical community and the general public had heard of the Phase II trial. As publicity about the trial gained momentum, AIDS patient-advocacy groups became impatient with what they perceived as an overly tedious and unnecessary process. They began accusing Burroughs Wellcome and the FDA of delaying the drug's availability. These critics argued that withholding potentially effective therapy

EXHIBIT 5

Retrovir Milestones, 1984–1990

June 1984	Burroughs Wellcome begins an AIDS research program to search for chemical compounds that might be effective against HIV.
November 1984	Burroughs Wellcome scientists identify AZT as potentially useful against AIDS.
Spring 1985	*In vitro* activity of AZT against HIV is confirmed by laboratories at Duke University, FDA, and NCI. This confirmatory work, requested by Burroughs Wellcome, is done on coded samples whose chemical identity is not revealed to the outside laboratories.
Spring 1985	Burroughs Wellcome continues toxicologic and pharmacologic testing of AZT. Work begins on scaling up synthesis of the drug, as the compound has never been produced beyond the few grams used for research purposes.
June 1985	FDA permits Burroughs Wellcome to begin clinical trials of AZT in humans.
July 1985	AZT is designated an "orphan drug" for the treatment of AIDS (a designation made when the affected population is less than 200,000).
July 1985	Burroughs Wellcome begins a collaborative Phase I study with NCI and Duke University to assess AZT's safety and tolerance in humans.
December 1985	Enrollment in the Phase I study, eventually involving 40 patients and investigators from NCI, Duke University, University of Miami, and UCLA, continues. Patient responses are encouraging.
February 1986	Burroughs Wellcome initiates and is the sole sponsor of a Phase II study at 12 academic centers, eventually involving 281 patients.
September 1986	The Phase II study is halted when an interim analysis by an independent data safety and monitoring board shows a significantly lower mortality rate in patients receiving AZT compared to those randomized to receive a placebo.
October 1986	Burroughs Wellcome, National Institutes of Health, and FDA establish a Treatment IND (Investigational New Drug) program as a means of providing wider access to AZT prior to FDA clearance.
December 1986	Burroughs Wellcome completes submission of a New Drug Application to FDA.
March 1987	The FDA clears Retrovir brand zidovudine (AZT) as a treatment for advanced ARC and AIDS.
February 1988	Burroughs Wellcome is issued a U.S. patent for the use of Retrovir as a treatment for AIDS and ARC based on the innovative work done by company scientists.
August 1989	Controlled clinical trials indicate that certain HIV-infected early symptomatic and asymptomatic persons can benefit from Retrovir with fewer or less severe side effects.
October 1989	Burroughs Wellcome establishes a Pediatric Treatment IND program, providing wider access to Retrovir for medically eligible children prior to FDA clearance.
January 1990	The FDA clears modified dosage guidelines for therapy with Retrovir patients with severe HIV infection.

Source: Abridged from a Burroughs Wellcome news release, "Retrovir Milestones," dated December 13, 1990.

from AIDS patients was inhumane and unethical, as was the use of a placebo. David Barry, Vice President and head of the research, medical, and development divisions, defended the trial process, asserting that, if placebo controls were removed, "it could destroy the most modern and rapid clinical research plans ever devised."[14]

In September 1986, the review board recommended that the administration of the placebo be terminated. Analysis of the data had shown a significantly lower mortality rate among those patients who had received Retrovir for an average period of six months. When the trial stopped, there had been 19 deaths among the 137 patients receiving the placebo and 1 death among those patients taking Retrovir. The group receiving Retrovir also had a decreased number of infections. In addition, the weight gain, improvements in the immune system, and ability to perform daily activities noted in the Phase I trial were confirmed. However, patients involved in the Phase II trial also experienced adverse reactions similar to those reported in the earlier trial. Since it was no longer appropriate to withhold drug treatment from placebo-treated patients, all patients who had formerly received the placebo were offered Retrovir treatment with the agreement of the FDA.

Expanded distribution of the drug meant that the company would have to obtain a larger supply of thymidine, a biological chemical first harvested from herring sperm and a key raw material in AZT. In 1986, the world's supply of thymidine was 25 pounds. Recognizing that this supply would be exhausted quickly, the head of technical development at Burroughs Wellcome began a worldwide search for a thymidine supplier, recognizing that it took months and 20 chemical reactions to produce this material. This search uncovered a small German subsidiary of Pfizer, Inc., a New York–based pharmaceutical firm, which had produced thymidine in the 1960s. This company was persuaded to produce thymidine by the ton.

In March 1987, the FDA released Retrovir for treatment for adult patients with symptomatic HIV infection, those patients for whom the drug had been shown to be beneficial in clinical trials. Although no hard figures were available, it was believed that about 50,000 individuals in the United States had symptomatic HIV infection. The recommended dosage for symptomatic HIV patients was 1,200 milligrams every day, administered in twelve 100-milligram capsules.

Research and Development Costs

The direct research and development costs associated with Retrovir were estimated to be about $50 million, according to industry analysts.[15] This cost was considered low, since the typical cost of developing a new drug in the United States is $125 million. Indeed, Wellcome PLC had spent $726 million for research and development on dozens of drugs in the five years preceding approval of Retrovir without producing a major commercial success. However, when the costs of new plant and equipment to produce Retrovir were also considered, total research and development cost estimates ranged from $80 million to $100 million. Furthermore, the company provided the equivalent of $10 million of the drug free to 4,500 AIDS patients and supplied free of charge a metric ton of AZT to the National Institutes of Health's AIDS Clinical Trials Group.

Burroughs Wellcome's research and development effort did benefit from AZT being designated as an "orphan drug" in 1985 under provisions of the Orphan Drug Act of 1983. This act, which applies to drugs useful in treating 200,000 or fewer people in the United States, confers special consideration to suppliers of these drugs. For

---

[14]David Barry, testimony before the House Committee on Government Operations Subcommittee on Intergovernmental Relations and Human Resources, July 1, 1987.

[15]Cost estimates have been made by industry analysts and have not been confirmed or denied by Burroughs Wellcome.

example, the orphan drug designation for Retrovir provided a seven-year marketing exclusivity after its commercial introduction, tax credits, and government subsidization of clinical trials.

■ MARKETING OF RETROVIR

Initial distribution of Retrovir was limited because of its short supply in March 1987. A special distribution system was set up to ensure availability of the drug to those patients who had been shown to benefit from its use. This system remained in place until September 1987, when supplies were adequate and broader distribution was possible.

The initial price set for Retrovir to drug wholesalers in March 1987 was $188 for a hundred 100-milligram capsules. This price represented an annual cost to AIDS patients ranging from $8,528 to $9,745 depending upon wholesaler and pharmacy margins, which combined ranged from 5 to 20 percent. An immediate controversy was created, with the public, media, and AIDS patient-advocacy groups seeking justification of the price for Retrovir, a decrease in its price, or federal subsidization. Critics pointed out that, for comparison, the annual cost of interferon, a cancer-fighting drug, was only $5,000. The cofounder of Project Inform, an AIDS treatment information agency, said, "I think that Burroughs Wellcome is very interested in getting all their money back as soon as possible, because the sun won't shine forever."[16] Congressional hearings resulted in the chairman of the House Subcommittee on Health and the Environment charging that Burroughs Wellcome's "expectation was that those people who want to buy the drug will come up with the money" and that the government would "step in" to subsidize those who could not.[17] Congress subsequently created a $30 million emergency fund for AIDS patients who were unable to afford the cost of AZT.[18]

Company officials acknowledged that the pricing decision was difficult to make. According to one official, "We didn't know the demand, how to produce it in large quantities, or what competing drugs would come out in the market. There was no way to find out." Another company official said, "I guess we assumed that the drug . . . would be paid in some manner by the patient himself out of his own pocket or by third-party payers. We really didn't get into a lot of calculation along those lines."[19]

On December 15, 1987, the capsule price of Retrovir was reduced by 20 percent. The company announced that the price reduction was made possible because of cost savings achieved in the production process and an improved supply of synthetically manufactured thymidine. The company continued its research on AZT throughout 1988 into 1989, including treatments for children with HIV infection. In August 1989, this research program indicated that Retrovir produced positive results in postponing the appearance of AIDS in HIV-infected people. This development expanded the potential users of the drug to between 600,000 and 1 million people. (However, industry sources believe that fewer than one-half of the people with HIV have been tested and told of their condition and would thus be seeking treatment.) FDA approval for marketing to this larger population was expected by March 1990.

Recognizing the expanded potential patient population and anticipated production economies, the capsule price of Retrovir was again reduced by 20 percent in September 1989. In reference to this price reduction, Burroughs Wellcome's *1989 Annual Report* noted:

[16]"The Unhealthy Profits of AZT," *The Nation* (October 17, 1987): 407.

[17]FDC Reports—the Pink Sheet 49 (11): 5, 1987.

[18]"Find the Cash or Die Sooner," *Time* (September 5, 1988): 27.

[19]"The Inside Story of the AIDS Drug," *Fortune* (November 5, 1990): 124–125.

EXHIBIT 6

Retrovir Sales Volume, Fiscal 1987–1989

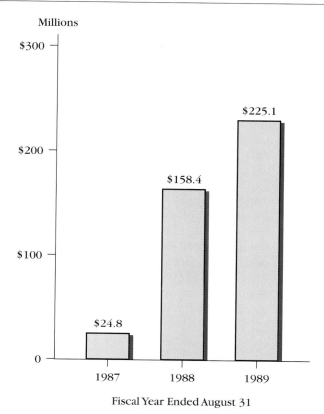

Millions

Fiscal Year Ended August 31

Note: U.S. dollar sales volume computed using average exchange rates £1 = $1.55 (1987), £1 = $1.76 (1988), and £1 = $1.68 (1989).

Source: Wellcome PLC, 1990 *Annual Report*.

In arriving at our decision to reduce the price, we carefully weighed a number of factors. These included our responsibility to patients and shareholders, the very real remaining uncertainties in the marketplace, and the vital need to fund our continuing research and development programmes.[20]

The new price to drug wholesalers was set at $120 for a hundred 100-milligram capsules. The retail price to users was about $150 for a hundred 100-milligram capsules. Industry analysts estimated that the direct cost of manufacturing and marketing Retrovir was 30 cents to 50 cents per capsule.[21]

Sales of Retrovir since its introduction are shown in Exhibit 6. Unit volume for Retrovir in fiscal 1990 was forecasted to be 53 percent higher than fiscal 1989 unit volume.

Patient-advocacy groups continued to criticize the pricing of Retrovir. AIDS activists chanted such slogans as "Be the first on your block to sell your Burroughs Wellcome stock" while picketing stock exchanges in London, New York, and San Francisco.

[20]Wellcome PLC 1989 *Annual Report*: 13.

[21]"How Much for a Reprieve from AIDS?" *Time* (October 2, 1989): 81.

The executive director of the National Gay and Lesbian Task Force said, "To make AZT accessible to everyone who should be on it, Burroughs Wellcome has an obligation to give up a significant amount of money to allow people to get access."[22] Members of Senator Edward Kennedy's staff began researching possible ways to nationalize the drug by invoking a law that allows the U.S. government to revoke exclusive licenses in the interest of national security. In addition, there were published reports that the American Civil Liberties Union was considering a suit against Burroughs Wellcome. The suit would challenge the 17-year-use patent awarded Burroughs Wellcome for Retrovir, arguing that government scientists discovered AZT's efficacy against HIV.[23] The Subcommittee on Health and the Environment of the U.S. House of Representatives, which had already launched an investigation into possible "inappropriate" pricing of the drug, continued its hearings. However, Sir Alfred Sheppard, the company's Chairman, remained firm, saying "There's no plan to make another price cut." Later in 1990, he added, "If we wrapped the drug in a £10 note and gave it away, people would say it cost too much."[24]

In January 1990, the FDA approved modified dosage guidelines for Retrovir. These guidelines reduced the recommended adult dosage to 500 milligrams per day for some symptomatic AIDS patients from the original recommended dosage of 1,200 milligrams per day established in 1987. However, some clinicians warned that lower dosages should be prescribed cautiously. Also in January, congressional lobbyists began a campaign to curb "excessive profits earned by the drug industry as a whole." Industry observers were speculating that the price of Retrovir might have to be cut again sometime in 1990 because of continued pressure from the U.S. Congress, the media, and AIDS patient-advocacy groups.[25]

[22]"AZT Maker to Reap Big Gain," *New York Times* (August 19, 1989): 8.

[23]"A Stitch in Time," *The Economist* (August 18, 1990): 21–22.

[24]"The Inside Story of the AIDS Drug," *Fortune* (November 5, 1990): 124–125.

[25]"Profiting from Disease," *The Economist* (January 27, 1990): 17–18.

Lieber Light

Alice Howell, President of the Lieber Light Division of Fraser Co., leaned forward at her desk in her bright, sunlit office and said, "In brief, our two options are either to price at a level that just covers our costs or to risk losing market leadership to those upstart Canadians at Vancouver Light. Are there no other options?" Tamara Chu, Lieber's marketing manager, and Sam Carney, the production manager, had no immediate reply.

Lieber Light, based in Seattle, Washington, had been the area's leading manufacturer of plastic moulded skylights for use in houses and offices for almost 15 years. However, two years earlier Vancouver Light, whose main plant was located in Vancouver, British Columbia, about 150 miles to the north of Seattle, had opened a sales office in the city and sought to gain business by pricing aggressively. Vancouver Light began by offering skylights at 20 percent below Lieber's price for large orders. Now, Vancouver Light had just announced a further price cut of 10 percent.

■ COMPANY BACKGROUND

The primary business of Fraser Co., which had recently celebrated its 50th anniversary, was the supply of metal and plastic fabricated parts for its well-known Seattle neighbor, Boeing Aircraft. Until the 1960s, Boeing had accounted for more than 80 percent of the company's volume, but Lieber then decided to diversify in order to protect itself against the boom- and-bust cycle that seemed to characterize the aircraft industry. Even now, Boeing still accounted for nearly half of Lieber's $50 million[1] in annual sales.

Lieber Light had been established to apply Fraser's plastic moulding skills in the construction industry. Its first products, which still accounted for nearly 30 percent of sales, included plastic garage doors, plastic gutters, and plastic covers for outdoor lights, all of which had proved to be popular among Seattle home builders. In 1968 Lieber began production of what was to be its most successful product, skylights for homes and offices. Skylights now accounted for 70 percent of Lieber's sales.

■ THE SKYLIGHT MARKET

Although skylights varied greatly in size, a typical one measured 1 meter × 1 meter and was installed in the ceiling of a kitchen, bathroom, or living room. It was made primarily of moulded plastic with an aluminum frame. Skylights were usually installed by home builders upon initial construction of a home or by professional contractors as part of a remodeling job. Because of the need to cut through the roof to install a skylight and to then seal the joint between the roof and skylight so that water would not

[1]All prices and costs are in U.S. dollars.

This case was prepared by Charles B. Weinberg, Presidents of SME Vancouver Professor of Marketing, University of British Columbia. Copyright © 2003 by Charles B. Weinberg. Used with permission.

leak through, only the most talented "do-it-yourselfer" would tackle this job on his or her own. At present, 70 percent of the market was in home and office buildings, 25 percent in professional remodeling, and 5 percent in the do-it-yourself market.

Skylights had become very popular. Homeowners found the natural light they brought to a room attractive and perceived skylights to be energy conserving. Although opinion was divided on whether the heat loss from a skylight was more than the light gained, the general perception was quite favorable. Home builders found that featuring a skylight in a kitchen or other room would be an important plus in attracting buyers and often included at least one skylight as a standard feature. Condominium builders found that their customers liked the openness that a skylight seemed to provide. Skylights were also a popular feature of the second homes that many people owned on Washington's lakes or in ski areas throughout the area.

In Lieber Light's primary market area of Washington, Oregon, Idaho, and Montana, sales of skylights had leveled off in recent years at about 45,000 units per year. Although Lieber would occasionally sell a large order to California home builders, such sales were made only to fill slack in the plant and, after including the cost of transportation, were break-even propositions at best. No sales were made to Canada.

Four home builders accounted for half the sales of skylights in the Pacific Northwest region of the United States. Another five midsized builders bought an average of 1,000 units each, and the remaining sales were split among more than 100 independent builders and remodelers. Some repackaged the product under their own brand name, and many purchased only a few dozen or fewer.

Lieber would ship directly only to builders who ordered at least 500 units per year, although it would subdivide the order into sections of one gross (144) for shipping. Most builders and remodelers bought their skylights from building supply dealers, hardware stores, and lumberyards. Lieber sold and shipped directly to these dealers, who typically marked up the product by 50 percent. Lieber's average factory price was $200 when Vancouver Light first entered the market two years ago.

Lieber maintained a sales force of three people, who contacted builders, remodelers, and retail outlets. The sales force was responsible for Lieber's complete line of products, which generally went through the same channels of distribution. The cost of maintaining the sales force, including necessary selling support and travel expense, was $90,000 annually.

Until the advent of Vancouver Light, there had been no significant local competition for Lieber. Several California manufacturers had small shares of the market, but Lieber had held a 70 percent market share until two years ago.

■ VANCOUVER LIGHT'S ENTRY

Vancouver Light was founded in the early 1970s by Jennifer McLaren, an engineer, Carl Garner, an architect, and several business associates in order to manufacture skylights. They believed there was a growing demand for skylights. Their assessment proved correct, and because there was no ready source of supply available in western Canada their business was successful.

Two years ago the Canadian company had announced the opening of a sales office in Seattle. Jennifer McLaren came to this office two days a week and devoted her attention to selling skylights to only the large-volume builders. Vancouver Light announced a price 20 percent below Lieber's with a minimum order size of 1,000 units, to be shipped all at one time. It quickly gained all the business of one large builder, True Homes, a Canadian-owned company. In the previous year that builder had ordered 6,000 skylights from Lieber.

A year later, one of Lieber's sales representatives was told by the purchasing manager of Chieftain Homes, a Seattle-based builder that had installed 7,000 skylights the previous year, that Chieftain would switch to Vancouver Light for most of its skylights unless Lieber were prepared to match Vancouver's price. Lieber then matched that price for orders above 2,500 units, guessing that smaller customers would value highly the local service that Lieber could provide. Chieftain then ordered 40 percent of its needs from Vancouver Light. During the same time, two midsized builders switched all their business to Vancouver Light as well, taking advantage of Vancouver Light's lower prices. Before Vancouver's latest price cut had been reported, Tamara Chu, Lieber's marketing manager, projected that Vancouver Light would sell about 11,000 units this year, compared to the 21,000 that Lieber was now selling.

Lieber had asked its lawyers to investigate whether Vancouver Light's sales could be halted on charges of export dumping, that is, selling below cost in a foreign market, but a quick investigation revealed that Vancouver Light's specialized production facility provided a 25 percent savings on variable cost, although a third of that was lost due to the additional costs involved in importing and transporting the skylights across the border from Canada to the United States.

■ THE IMMEDIATE CRISIS

Alice Howell and her two colleagues had reviewed the situation carefully. Sam Carney, the production manager, had presented the cost accounting data, which showed a total unit cost of $135 for Lieber's most popular skylight. Vancouver Light, he said, was selling a similar model at $144. The cost of $135 included $15 in manufacturing overheads directly attributable to skylights but not the cost of the sales force or the salaries, benefits, and overheads associated with the three executives in the room. General overheads, including the sales force and executives, amounted to $390,000 per year at present for Lieber as a whole.

Tamara Chu was becoming quite heated about Vancouver Light by this time. "Let's cut the price a further 10 percent to $130 and drive those Canadians right out of the market! That Jennifer McLaren started with those big builders and now she's after the whole market. We'll show her what competition really is!"

But Sam was shocked: "You mean we'll drive her *and us* out of business at the same time! We'll both lose money on every unit we sell. What has our sales force been doing all these years if not building customer loyalty for our product?"

"We may lose most of our sales to the big builders," cut in Alice Howell, "but surely most customers wouldn't be willing to rely on shipments from Canada. Maybe we should let Vancouver Light have the customers who want to buy on the basis of price. We can then make a tidy profit from customers who value service, need immediate supply, and have dealt with our company for years."

Augustine Medical, Inc.
The Bair Hugger® Patient Warming System

In July 1987, Augustine Medical, Inc., was incorporated as a Minnesota corporation to develop and market products for hospital operating rooms and postoperative recovery rooms. The first two products the company planned to produce and sell were a patented patient warming system designed to treat postoperative hypothermia in the recovery room and a tracheal intubation guide for use in the operating room and in emergency medicine.

By early 1988, company executives were actively engaged in finalizing the marketing program for the patient warming system named Bair Hugger® Patient Warming System. The principal question yet to be resolved was how to price this system.

■ THE BAIR HUGGER® PATIENT WARMING SYSTEM

The Bair Hugger® Patient Warming System is a device designed to control the body temperature of postoperative patients. Specifically, the device is designed to treat hypothermia (a condition defined as a body temperature of less than 36 degrees Centigrade or 96 degrees Fahrenheit) experienced by patients after operations.

Medical research indicates that 60 to 80 percent of all postoperative recovery room patients are clinically hypothermic. Several factors contribute to postoperative hypothermia. They are (1) a patient's exposure to cold operating room temperatures (which are maintained for the surgeons' comfort and for infection control), (2) heat loss due to evaporation of the fluids used to scrub patients, (3) evaporation from the exposed bowel, and (4) breathing of dry anesthetic gases.

The Bair Hugger® system consists of a heater/blower unit and a separate inflatable plastic/paper cover, or blanket. A photo of the system is shown in Exhibit 1. The heater/blower unit is a large, square, boxlike structure that heats, filters, and blows air through a plastic cover. An electric cord wraps around the back of the unit for storage, and the unit is mounted on wheels for easy transport. The blower tubing attaches to the warming cover through a simple cardboard connector strap and can be retracted into the top of the unit for storage. Temperature is set by a dial with four settings on the top of the unit. A top lid opens to a storage bin that holds 12 warming covers for easy access. The disposable warming covers come packaged in 18-inch-long tubes. When unrolled, the plastic/paper cover is flat and covers an average-sized patient from shoulders to ankles. The blanket consists of a layer of thin plastic and a

This case was prepared by Professor Roger A. Kerin, of the Edwin L. Cox School of Business, Southern Methodist University; Michael Gilbertson, of Augustine Medical, Inc.; and Professor William Rudelius, of University of Minnesota, as a basis for class discussion and is not designed to illustrate effective or ineffective handling of administrative situations. Certain names and data have been disguised. The assistance of graduate students Anne Christensen, Joanne Perty, and Laurel Wichman of the University of Minnesota is appreciated. The cooperation of Augustine Medical, Inc., in the preparation of the case is gratefully acknowledged. Copyright © 1993 by Roger A. Kerin. No part of this case may be reproduced without the written permission of the copyright holder.

EXHIBIT 1

Bair Hugger® Patient Warming System

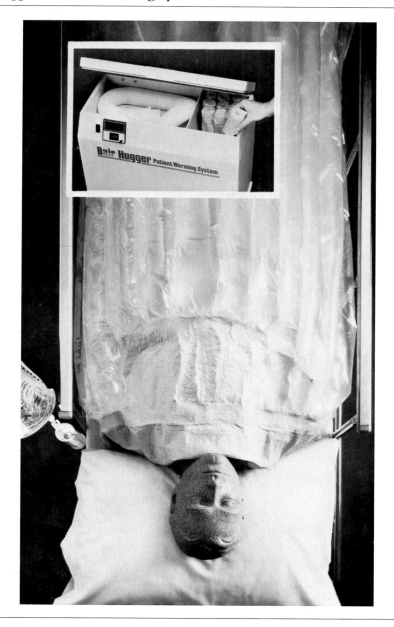

layer of plastic/paper material laminated into full-length channels. Small holes punctuate the inner surface of the cover. When inflated through a connection at the feet of the patient, the tubular structure arcs over the patient's body, creating an individual patient environment. The warm air exits through the slits on the inner surface of the blanket, creating a gentle flow of warm air over the patient. The warming time per patient is about two hours.

The plastic cover was patented in 1986; there is no patent protection for the heater/blower unit.

■ COMPETING TECHNOLOGIES

Many competing technologies are available for the prevention and treatment of hypothermia. These technologies generally fall into one of two broad types of patient warming: surface warming or internal warming.

Surface-Warming Technologies

Warmed hospital blankets are the most commonly used treatment for hypothermia in recovery rooms and elsewhere. An application of warmed hospital blankets consists of placing six to eight warmed blankets in succession on top of a patient. Almost all patients receive at least one application; it is estimated that 50 percent of the postoperative patients require more than one application. The advantages of warmed hospital blankets are that they are simple, safe, and relatively inexpensive. The main disadvantage is that they cool quickly, provide only insulation, and require the patient's own body heat for regenerating warmth.

Water-circulating blankets are the second most popular postoperative hypothermic treatment. Water-circulating blankets can be placed under a patient, over a patient, or both. If a blanket is placed just under the patient, only 15 percent of the body's surface area is affected. However, hospitals typically place water-circulating blankets either just over the patient or over and under the patient, forming an insulated environment that encloses 85 to 90 percent of the body's surface area. The disadvantages of water-circulating blankets are that they are heavy and expensive and can cause burns on pressure points. Moreover, although a widely used and accepted method of warming, especially for more severe cases of hypothermia, water-circulating blankets are considered only slightly to moderately effective.

Electric blankets are generally unacceptable as a hypothermic treatment because of the risk of burns to the patient and of explosion in areas where oxygen is in use.

Air-circulating blankets and mattresses are not in common use in the United States, although variations on this technology have been used in the past. This technology relies on warmed air flowing over the body to transfer heat to the patient. The advantages of warmed-air technology are that it is safe, lightweight, and theoretically more effective than warmed hospital blankets or water-circulating blankets. Products using this technology are not widely found in the U.S. market, however.

Thermal drapes, also known as reflective blankets, have recently been introduced and are gaining acceptance as a preventive measure used in the operating room. They consist of head covers, blankets, and leggings placed on the uninvolved portions of the patient's body. Their use is recommended when 60 percent of a patient's body surface can be covered. The advantages of this technology are that it is simple, safe, and inexpensive and has been shown to reduce heat loss. The disadvantage is that it merely insulates the patient and does not transfer heat to someone who is already hypothermic.

Infrared heating lamps are popular for infant use. When placed a safe distance from the body and shone on the skin, they radiate warmth to the patient. The advantages of heat lamps are that they are effective and illuminate the patient for observation or therapy. A disadvantage is that since the skin needs to be exposed, modesty prevents widespread use among adults. (They are, however, used in adult skin-graft operations.) Nurses dislike radiant heat lamps and panels because they tend to heat the entire recovery room and are uncomfortable to work under.

Partial warm-water immersion has been used in the past, especially in cases where a patient was deliberately cooled to slow down metabolism. With this method, the patient is placed in a bath of warm water and watched carefully. The advantages of this technology are that it transfers heat very effectively and it is simple. The disadvantages are that the system is inconvenient to set up and requires close monitoring of the patient, which increases labor costs. In addition, water baths must be carefully watched for bacterial growth, and they are very expensive to purchase and use.

Increasing room temperature is the most obvious way to prevent and treat hypothermia, but it is seldom used. The advantages of this method are that it is simple and relatively inexpensive and has been proven effective at temperatures of over 70 degrees Fahrenheit. The disadvantage is that warm room temperatures are not acceptable to the nurses and surgeons who must work in the environment. Furthermore, warm temperatures increase the risk of infection.

Internal-Warming Technologies

Inspiring *heated and humidified air* is a fairly effective internal-warming technique currently being used with intubated patients (those having a breathing tube in the trachea). However, delivery of heated and humidified air by mask or tent to nonintubated patients is not acceptable in postoperative situations, because mask or tent delivery would interfere with observation and communication and, in the case of a tent, might increase the chance of infection. The fact that the patient must be intubated is a disadvantage, since the vast majority of postoperative patients are not intubated.

Warmed intravenous (I.V.) fluids are used in more severe hypothermic cases to directly transfer heat to the circulatory system. Warmed I.V. fluids are very effective because they introduce warmth directly into the circulatory system. The disadvantages of this technology are that it requires very close monitoring of the patient's core temperature and high physician involvement.

Drug therapy diminishes the sensation of cold and reduces shivering but does not actually increase body temperature. Although drug therapy is convenient and makes patients feel more comfortable, it does not warm them and in fact slows their recovery from anesthesia and surgery.

■ COMPETITIVE PRODUCTS

A variety of competitive products that use the above-mentioned technologies are available (see Exhibit 2 on page 488). A review of competitors' sales materials and interviews with hospital personnel provided the following breakdown of competitive products.

Warmed Hospital Blankets

For treating adult hypothermia, hospitals use their own blankets, which they warm in large heating units. Many manufacturers produce heating units for hospital use. The cost of laundering six to eight two-pound hospital blankets averages $0.13 per pound. Laundering and heating costs are absorbed in hospital overhead.

Water-Circulating Blankets

Several manufacturers produce water-circulating mattresses and blankets, but Cincinnati Sub-Zero, Gaymar Industries, and Pharmaseal are the major suppliers. Prices of automatic control units that measure both blanket and patient temperatures range from $4,850 to $5,295. Manual control units are priced at about $3,000, although they appear to be discounted by as much as 40 percent in actual practice.

The average life of water-circulating control units is 15 years. Reusable blankets list at from $168 to $375, depending on quality. Disposable blankets list at from $20 to $26. Volume discounts for blankets can reduce the list price by almost 50 percent.

EXHIBIT 2

Representative Competitive Products and Prices

Product	List Price	Company	Estimated Size of Company (Sales, Employees)	Comments
Blanketrol 200	$2,995/manual unit; $4,895/automatic unit; $165–$305/reusable blanket; $20/disposable blanket	Cincinnati Sub-Zero	$10 million; 90 employees	Hypothermia equipment is a small part of its overall business.
MTA 4700	$4,735/unit; $139/reusable blanket; $24/disposable blanket	Gaymar Industries	$17 million; 150 employees	Hypothermia equipment seems to be a major part of its business.
Aquamatic	$4,479/unit	American Hamilton (division of American Hospital Supply)	$3.3 billion; 31,300 employees	Hypothermia equipment is a very minor part of American Hospital Supply's business.
Climator	$4,000/unit	Hosworth Air Engineering Ltd.	Not available	The company could begin distribution of hypothermia equipment in the United States in 1988.

Water-circulating blanket technology has changed little over the past 20 years except for the addition of solid state controls. There is little differentiation among the products of different firms.

Reflective Thermal Drapes

O.R. Concepts sells a product named the Thermadrape, which comes in both adult and pediatric sizes. Adult head covers list for $0.49 each; adult drapes list for $2.50 to $3.98, depending on size; leggings are priced at $1.50 each.

Air-Circulating Blankets and Mattresses

Two competitors are known to provide an air-circulating product like the Bair Hugger® Patient Warming System; however, neither is currently sold in the United States. The Sweetland Bed Warmer and Cast Dryer was in use 25 years ago but is no longer manufactured. This product consisted of a heater/blower unit that directed warm air through a hose placed under a patient's blanket. The Hosworth-Climator is an English-made product that provides a controlled-temperature microclimate by means of air flow from a mattress. The Climator comes in a variety of models for use in recovery rooms, intensive care units, burn units, general wards, and patients' homes. The model most suitable for postoperative recovery rooms is priced at $4,000. This product could be distributed in the United States sometime in 1988. A summary of representative competitor products and list prices is shown in Exhibit 2.

■ THE HOSPITAL MARKET

Approximately 21 million surgical operations are performed annually in the United States, or 84,000 operations per average eight-hour work day. Approximately 5,500 hospitals have operating rooms and postoperative recovery rooms.

Research commissioned by Augustine Medical, Inc., indicated that there are 31,365 postoperative recovery beds and 28,514 operating rooms in hospitals in the United States. An estimated breakdown of the number of postoperative hospital beds and the percentage of surgical operations is shown below:

Number of Postoperative Beds	Number of Hospitals	Estimated Percentage of Surgical Operations
0	1,608	0%
1–6	3,602	20
7–11	1,281	40
12–17	391	20
18–22	135	10
23–28	47	6
29–33	17	2
>33	17	2

Given the demand for postoperative recovery room beds, the research firm estimated that hospitals with fewer than seven beds would not be highly receptive to the Bair Hugger® Patient Warming System. The firm also projected that one system would be sold for every eight postoperative recovery room beds.

Interviews with physicians and nurses, followed by a demonstration of the system, yielded a variety of responses:

1. Respondents believed that the humanitarian ethic "to make the patient feel more comfortable" is important.

2. Respondents felt that the Bair Hugger® Patient Warming System would speed recovery for postop patients.

3. Respondents wanted to test the units under actual conditions in postoperative recovery rooms. They were reluctant to make any purchase commitments without testing. A typical comment was "No one today, in this market, ever buys a pig in a poke."

4. Respondents felt that the product was price-sensitive to alternative methods. Respondents were very receptive to the notion of using the heater/blower free of charge and only paying for the disposable blankets. Physicians wanted to confer with others who would be responsible for using the product to administer the warming treatment, however, such as the head nurse in postoperative recovery rooms and the chief anesthesiologist.

5. Respondents believed that the pressure to move patients through the operating room and out of postop is greater than in the past. Efficiency is the byword.

6. Capital expenditures in hospitals were subject to budget committee approval. Although the amounts varied, expenditures for equipment over $1,500 were typically subject to a formal review and decision process.

■ AUGUSTINE MEDICAL, INC.

Augustine Medical, Inc., was founded in 1987 by Dr. Scott Augustine, an anesthesiologist. His experience had convinced him that hospitals needed and desired a new approach to warming patients after surgery. His medical knowledge, coupled with a technical flair, prompted the development of the Bair Hugger® Patient Warming System.

The Bair Hugger® Patient Warming System has several advantages over water-circulating blankets. First, warm air makes patients feel warm and stop shivering. Second, the system cannot cause burns, and water leaks around electrical equipment are not a problem, as they are with water-circulating blankets. Third, the disposable

EXHIBIT 3

Sales Literature for the Bair Hugger® Patient Warming System

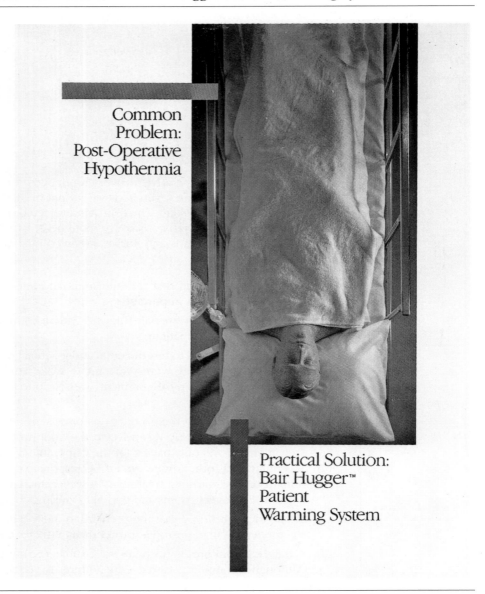

Common
Problem:
Post-Operative
Hypothermia

Practical Solution:
Bair Hugger™
Patient
Warming System

blankets eliminate the potential for cross-contamination among patients. Finally, the system does not require that the patient be lifted or rolled. Augustine's personal experience indicated that all of these features would be welcomed by nurses and patients alike. Features and benefits of the Bair Hugger® Patient Warming System are detailed in the company's sales literature, shown in Exhibit 3.

Investor interest in Augustine Medical and the medical technology it provided produced an initial capitalization of $500,000. These funds were to be used for further research and development, staff support, facilities, and marketing. It was believed that this initial investment would cover the fixed costs (including salaries, leased space, and promotional literature) of the company during its first year of operation. The company would subcontract the production of the heater/blower unit and would manufacture warming covers in-house using a proprietary machine. Only minor assembly would be performed by the company.

EXHIBIT 3 *(continued)*

A Warm Welcome for Your Recovery Room Patients

Augustine Medical, Inc.'s new Bair Hugger™ Patient Warming System is the most practical and comforting solution for post-operative hypothermia available today.

Every year more than 10,000,000 hospital patients experience the severe discomfort and vital signs instability associated with post-operative hypothermia. Years later, patients can still vividly recall this discomfort. Augustine Medical's new Patient Warming System is a warm and reliable solution to post-operative hypothermia.

A Practical Solution to Post-Operative Hypothermia

The Bair Hugger™ Patient Warming System consists of a Heat Source and a separate disposable Warming Cover that directs a gentle flow of warm air across the body and provides for safe and comfortable rewarming.

The Bair Hugger Heat Source uses a reliable, high efficiency blower, a sealed 400W heating element, and a microprocessor-based temperature control to create a continuous flow of warm air. There are no pumps, valves or compressors to maintain. Special features include built-in storage space for the air hose, power cord and a convenient supply of disposable Warming Covers. The Heat Source complies with all safety requirements for hospital equipment.

1. PATENTED SELF SUPPORTING DESIGN
   As the tubes fill with air, the Warming Cover naturally arches over the patient's body.

2. TISSUE PAPER UNDERLAYER
   The tissue paper underlayer of the Warming Cover is soft and comfortable against the patient's skin.

3. AIR SLITS
   Tiny slits in the underlayer allow warm air from the Heat Source to gently fill the space around the patient.

4. SHOULDER DRAPE
   The shoulder drape is designed to tuck under the chin and shoulders, trapping warm air under the cover and preventing air flow by the patient's face.

5. DISPOSABLE COVERS
   The disposable Covers prevent cross contamination and reduce laundry requirements.

EXHIBIT 3 (*continued*)

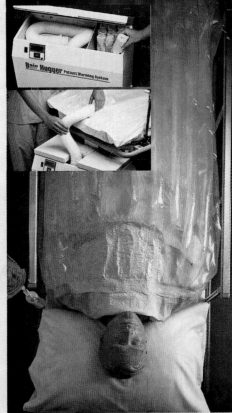

THE BAIR HUGGER™
PATIENT WARMING SYSTEM
IS SO EASY TO USE.
Remove a new Warming Cover
from the storage compartment
and unroll over the patient.

Connect the heater hose to the
inlet of the Warming Cover and
turn on the heater.

6. SIMPLE CONTROLS
A preprogrammed temperature range
and a preset high temperature limit of
110°F make the Bair Hugger safe and
simple to use.

7. INTERNAL WARMING COVER STORAGE
The storage compartment provides a
convenient supply of Warming Covers
ready for immediate use.

8. INTERNAL HOSE STORAGE
The hose retracts into its own
compartment for ready access.

9. LIGHTWEIGHT, COMPACT DESIGN
The Heat Source is designed for
convenience and portability. While in
use, it tucks under the foot of the gurney.
The unit's light weight and small size
make it simple to move and store.

10. BUILT-IN POWER CORD STORAGE
The power cord storage holds up to 12
feet of cord, making the Heat Source
portable and easy to store.

11. 5μ AIR FILTER
The air filter assures dust-free air
circulation through the Bair Hugger
Warming Cover. The filter is simple to
change when necessary.

The Bair Hugger™ Warming Cover:

The Warming Cover consists of a layer of plastic and a layer of tissue
paper laminate bonded together into long tubular channels. The
self-supporting Warming Cover is designed to arch over the patient's
body creating a warm, comfortable environment.

The Warming Cover is convenient to use because no straps, tapes or
other fasteners are required to stabilize the cover and the patient
does not have to be disturbed or moved.

When the Warming Cover is completely inflated, warm air from the
Heat Source exits the tubular channels through slits in the Cover's
soft underlayer, surrounding the patient with a gentle flow of warm air.

The Bair Hugger® Patient Warming System would be sold by and through medical
products distributor organizations in various regions around the country. These distributor organizations would call on hospitals, demonstrate the system, and maintain an
inventory of blankets. The margin paid to the distributors would be competitively set
at 30 percent of the delivered (that is, less discounts) selling price on the heater/blower
unit and 40 percent of the delivered (discounted if necessary) price on the blankets.

Preliminary estimates from subcontractors and a time-and-motion study on assembly indicated that the direct cost of the heater/blower unit would be $380. The cost of
materials, manufacturing, and packaging of the plastic disposable blankets was estimated
to be $0.85 per blanket.

EXHIBIT 3 *(continued)*

The central issue at this time was the determination of the list price to hospitals for the heater/blower unit and the plastic blankets, given the widespread incidence of price discounting. Immediate attention to the price question was important for at least three reasons. First, it was felt that the price set for the Bair Hugger® Patient Warming System would influence the rate at which prospective buyers would purchase the system. Second, price and volume together would influence the cash flow position of the company. Third, the company would soon have to prepare price literature for its distributor organizations and for a scheduled medical trade show, where the system would be shown for the first time.

Texas Instruments
Global Pricing in the Semiconductor Industry

Mr. John Szczsponik, Director of North American Distribution for Texas Instruments' Semiconductor Group, placed the phone back on its cradle after a long and grueling conversation with his key contact at Arrow, the largest distributor of Texas Instruments' semiconductors. With a market-leading 21.5 percent share of total U.S. electronic component distributor sales in 1994, Arrow was the most powerful distribution channel through which Texas Instruments' important semiconductor products flowed. It was also one of only two major American distributors active in the global distribution market.

Arrow's expanding international activities had made it increasingly interested in negotiating with its vendors a common global price for the semiconductors it sold around the world. In the past, semiconductors had been bought and sold at different price levels in different countries to reflect the various cost structures of the countries in which they were produced. Semiconductors made in European countries, for example, were usually more expensive than those made in Asia or North America, simply because it cost manufacturers more to operate in Europe than in the other two regions. Despite these differences, large distributors and some original equipment manufacturers were becoming insistent on buying their semiconductors at one worldwide price, and were pressuring vendors to negotiate global pricing terms. Szczsponik's telephone conversation with Arrow had been the third in the past month in which the distributor had pushed for price concessions based on international semiconductor rates:

> Yesterday they discovered that we're offering a lower price for a chip we make and sell in Singapore than for the same chip we manufacture here in Dallas for the North American market. They want us to give them the Singapore price on our American chips, even though they know our manufacturing costs are higher here than in the Far East. We can't give them that price without losing money!

In anticipation of increased pressure from Arrow and other large distributors, Szczsponik had organized a meeting with Mr. Kevin McGarity, Senior Vice President in the Semiconductor Group and Manager of Worldwide Marketing, to begin developing a cohesive pricing strategy. They were both to meet with Arrow executives in four days, on February 4, 1995, to discuss the establishment of common global pricing for the distributor.

Szczsponik knew that he needed to answer some basic questions before meeting with Arrow:

> Global pricing might make Arrow's job of planning and budgeting a lot easier, but our different cost structures in each region make it difficult for us to offer one price worldwide. How do we tell Arrow, our largest distributor, that we aren't prepared to

This case was developed by Profs. Per V. Jenster, CIMID, B. Jaworski, USC, and Michael Stanford as a basis for classroom discussion rather than to highlight effective or ineffective management of an administrative situation.

negotiate global pricing? Alternatively, how can we reorganize ourselves to make global pricing a realistic option? And what implications will a global pricing strategy have in relationship to other international customers?

With only two hours to go before his meeting with McGarity, Szczsponik wondered how they could respond to Arrow's request.

■ THE SEMICONDUCTOR INDUSTRY

Semiconductors were silicon chips which transmitted heat, light, and electrical charges and performed critical functions in virtually all electronic devices. They were a core technology in industrial robots, computers, office equipment, consumer electronics, the aerospace industry, telecommunications, the military, and the automobile industry. The majority of semiconductors consisted of integrated circuits made from monocrystalline silicon imprinted with complex electronic components and their interconnections (refer to Exhibit 1 for the key categories of semiconductors). The remainder of semiconductors were simpler discrete components that performed single functions.

EXHIBIT 1

Key Semiconductor Categories

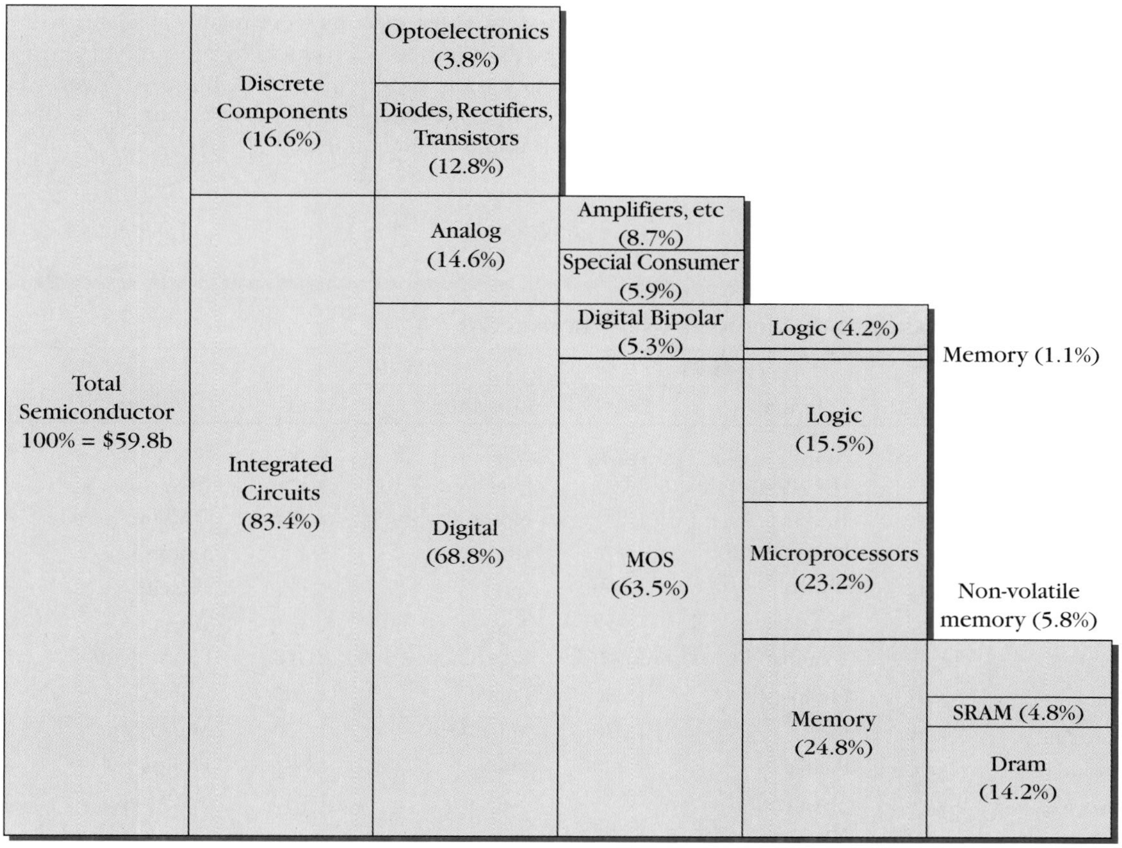

Total Semiconductor 100% = $59.8b

Discrete Components (16.6%)
- Optoelectronics (3.8%)
- Diodes, Rectifiers, Transistors (12.8%)

Integrated Circuits (83.4%)
- Analog (14.6%)
  - Amplifiers, etc (8.7%)
  - Special Consumer (5.9%)
- Digital (68.8%)
  - Digital Bipolar (5.3%)
    - Logic (4.2%)
    - Memory (1.1%)
  - MOS (63.5%)
    - Logic (15.5%)
    - Microprocessors (23.2%)
      - Non-volatile memory (5.8%)
    - Memory (24.8%)
      - SRAM (4.8%)
      - Dram (14.2%)

Source: Analysts' reports.

The pervasiveness of semiconductors in electronics resulted in rapidly growing sales and intense competition in the semiconductor industry. Market share in the industry had been fiercely contested since the early 1980s, when the once-dominant U.S. semiconductor industry lost its leadership position to Japanese manufacturers. There followed a series of trade battles in which American manufacturers charged their Japanese competitors with dumping and accused foreign markets of excessive protectionism. By 1994, after investing heavily in the semiconductor industry and embarking on programs to increase manufacturing efficiency and decrease production costs, American companies once again captured a dominant share of the market (refer to Exhibit 2 for the top ten semiconductor manufacturers).

In 1994, total shipments of semiconductors reached $99.9 billion, with market share divided among North America (33%), Japan (30%), Europe (18%), and Asia/Pacific (18%). The industry was expected to reach sales of $130 billion in 1995, and $200 billion by the year 2000. To capture growing demand in the industry, many semiconductor manufacturers were investing heavily in increased manufacturing capacity, although most industry analysts expected expanding capacity to reach rather than surpass demand. Combined with record low inventories in the industry and reduced cycle times and lead times, a balancing of supply and demand was causing semiconductor prices to be uncharacteristically stable. The last three quarters of 1994 had brought fewer fluctuations and less volatility in the prices of semiconductors (refer to Exhibit 3 for a history of semiconductor price stability) despite their history of dramatic price variations.

Regardless of price stability, most semiconductor manufacturers were looking for competitive advantage in further cost reduction programs, in developing closer relationships with their customers, and in creating differentiated semiconductors which could be sold at a premium price. Integrated circuits were readily available from suppliers worldwide and were treated as commodity products by most buyers. Any steps manufacturers could take to reduce their production costs, build stronger relationships with customers, or create unique products could protect them from the price wars usually associated with commodity merchandise.

EXHIBIT 2

Top Ten Semiconductor Manufacturers ($ in thousands)

1980		1985		1990		1992	
Company	Sales $	Company	Sales $	Company	Sales $	Company	Sales $
1. Texas Instruments	1,453	NEC	1,800	NEC	4,700	Intel	5,091
		Motorola	1,667	Toshiba	4,150	NEC	4,700
2. Motorola	1,130	Texas Instruments	1,661	Motorola	3,433	Toshiba	4,550
3. Philips	845			Hitachi	3,400	Motorola	4,475
4. NEC	800	Hitachi	1,560	Intel	3,171	Hitachi	3,600
5. National	745	National	1,435	Texas Instruments	2,518	Texas Instruments	3,150
6. Intel	630	Toshiba	1,400				
7. Hitachi	620	Philips	1,080	Fujitsu	2,300	Fujitsu	2,250
8. Fairchild	570	Intel	1,020	Mitsubishi	1,920	Mitsubishi	2,200
9. Toshiba	533	Fujitsu	800	Philips	1,883	Philips	2,041
10. Siemens	525	Advanced Micro Devices	795	National	1,730	Matsushita	1,900

Source: Analysts' reports.

EXHIBIT 3

History of Semiconductor Stability

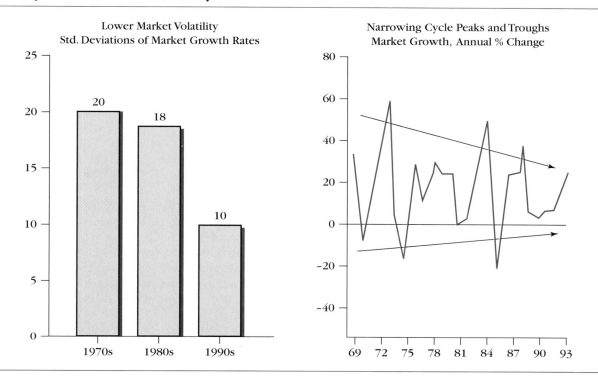

Lower Market Volatility
Std. Deviations of Market Growth Rates

Narrowing Cycle Peaks and Troughs
Market Growth, Annual % Change

■ TEXAS INSTRUMENTS INCORPORATED

Established in 1951 as an electronics company serving the American defense industry, by 1995 Texas Instruments was a leading manufacturer of semiconductors, defense electronics, software, personal productivity products and materials, and controls. Its 1994 sales of $10.3 billion, a 21% increase from the previous year, was split among components ($6.8 billion), defense electronics ($1.7 billion), digital products ($1.66 billion), and metallurgical materials ($177 million). 1994's profits of over $1 billion came almost entirely from its components business. Components made a profit of $1.1 billion, while defense electronics made $172 million (refer to Exhibit 4 on page 498 for income statements).

1994's performance was record-breaking for Texas Instruments. It marked the first time the company exceeded sales of $10 billion and over $1 billion in profit, and followed a history of volatile financial results. Although Texas Instruments was often considered the pioneer of the American electronics industry—it was one of the first companies to manufacture transistors and developed the first semiconductor integrated circuit in 1958—it struggled to maintain its position in the electronics industry through the intense competition of the 1980s. After receiving market attention with its development of such innovative consumer products as the pocket calculator and the electronic wrist watch, Texas Instruments lost its business in both markets to cheap Asian imports. Meanwhile, it struggled to keep up with orders for its mainstay business in semiconductors through the 1970s, only to see demand for its pioneer semiconductors shrink during the recession of the early 1980s. Faced with heavy losses in many of its core areas, Texas Instruments reorganized its businesses to foster

EXHIBIT 4

Income Statements

	Texas Instruments Key Financial Numbers				
	1994	*1993*	*1992*	*1991*	*1990*
Sales ($ millions)	10,200	8,523	7,049	6,628	6,395
Operating margin (%)	17.5	16.8	9.1	5.0	0.7
Net profit ($ millions)	715	459	254	169	0.7
Working capital ($ millions)	1,800	1,313	961	813	826
Long-term debt ($ millions)	800	694	909	896	715
Net worth ($ millions)	2,975	2,315	1,947	1,955	2,358

innovation and embarked on a program of cost-cutting. By 1985, the company had refocused its efforts on its strengths in semiconductors, relinquishing market dominance in favor of greater margins. While the company continued to grow its technological leadership, it also sought to build stronger relationships with its customers.

By 1995, Texas Instruments had developed a strong position in the electronics industry, despite its reputation as a technological leader rather than a skilled marketer of its products. The company continued to remain powerful in the semiconductor industry, in part because it was the only American company that continued to manufacture dynamic random access memory chips in the face of fierce Japanese competition in the 1980s. The company had manufacturing sites spread throughout North America, Asia, and Europe, and was pursuing its strategy of increasing manufacturing capacity and developing manufacturing excellence.

The Semiconductor Group

In 1958, Texas Instruments engineer Jack Kilby developed the first integrated circuit, a pivotal innovation in the electronics industry. Made of a single semiconductor material, the integrated circuit eliminated the need to solder circuit components together. Without wiring and soldering, components could be miniaturized and crowded together on a single chip. Only a few years after Kilby's invention, electronics manufacturers were demanding these integrated circuits, or chips, in smaller sizes and at lower costs, a move that led to unprecedented innovation in the electronics industry. Soon chips became a commodity, and chip manufacturers relied on high-volume, low-cost production of reliable chips for success. Only a few manufacturers had strong positions in the production of differentiated semiconductors.

Forty years after its discovery, Texas Instruments still remained dependent on its semiconductor sales, which fell primarily in integrated circuits. The Semiconductor Group, a part of the Components Division, had total sales of $2 billion in 1994, the third consecutive year in which Texas Instruments' semiconductor revenues grew faster than the industry. The company's return to financial success in the early 1990s was based on its strong performance in semiconductor sales and profits, both of which were at record levels in 1994. Management in the company expected semiconductor sales to continue to grow strongly and was planning heavy capital expenditures on new or expanded plants in the United States, Malaysia, and Italy to increase the company's capacity.

The Semiconductor Group divided its business into two segments: standard products and differentiated products. Standard semiconductors, which accounted for 90% of the Group's sales, included products which could be substituted by competitors. Standard semiconductors performed in the market much like other products for which substitutes were readily available. Texas Instruments, like its competitors, competed for market share in these commodity products based primarily on the price it offered to original equipment manufacturers and distributors. The remaining 10 percent of the company's semiconductor business came from differentiated products, of which Texas Instruments was the sole supplier. Because substitutes for these products were not available in the marketplace, differentiated products commanded higher margins than their standard counterparts and were receiving greater strategic emphasis on the part of Group management. While the company continued to hold a strong position in standard semiconductors, it was searching for a strategy that would allow it to achieve a higher return on development and manufacturing investments. Managers at Texas Instruments believed that higher returns were possible only by developing more successful differentiated semiconductors.

■ ELECTRONICS DISTRIBUTION MARKET

Texas Instruments sold its semiconductors through two channels: directly to original equipment manufacturers and through a network of electronics distributors. Szczsponik estimated that 70 percent of the Group's U.S. customers dealt directly with Texas Instruments. The remainder bought their semiconductors through one or more of the seven major semiconductor distributors that served the North American market (refer to Exhibit 5 for information on the top electronics distributors). Whether an original equipment manufacturer dealt directly with Texas Instruments or bought from a distributor depended on the manufacturer's size. The largest original equipment manufacturers were able to negotiate better prices from semiconductor manufacturers than were the distributors and therefore bought directly from the manufacturers. Because mid-sized and small original equipment manufacturers were fragmented, and thus more

EXHIBIT 5

Top Electronics Distributors

Company		1994	1993	1992	1991	1990
Arrow Electronics	Sales ($ billions)	3.973	2.536	1.622	1.044	.971
	Share (%)	21.5	17.4	14.8	11.0	10.2
Avnet	Sales ($ billions)	3.350	2.537	1.690	1.400	1.429
	Share (%)	18.1	17.4	15.4	14.8	15.0
Marshall Industries	Sales ($ billions)	.899	.747	.605	.563	.582
	Share (%)	4.8	5.1	5.5	6.0	6.1
Wyle Laboratories	Sales ($ billions)	.773	.606	.447	.360	.359
	Share (%)	4.2	4.2	4.1	3.8	3.8
Pioneer Standard	Sales ($ billions)	.747	.540	.405	.360	.343
	Share (%)	4.0	3.7	3.7	3.8	3.6
Anthem	Sales ($ billions)	.507	.663	.538	.420	.408
	Share (%)	2.7	4.6	4.9	4.4	4.3
Bell Industries	Sales ($ billions)	.395	.308	.282	.257	.239
	Share (%)	2.1	2.1	2.6	2.7	2.5

Source: Lehman Brothers, "Electronic Distribution Market," December 22, 1994.

difficult to serve, these customers were served more efficiently through the distribution channel. Szczsponik explained:

> The semiconductor market can be divided into three tiers. Fifty percent of our sales in semiconductors go to the top tier of perhaps 100 large electronics manufacturers who deal with us directly. The next 46 percent of sales come from 1,400 medium-sized companies at the next level, half of whom deal directly with us and half of whom buy through distributors. The remaining 4% of sales are to 150,000 smaller companies at the bottom tier in the market, who deal only through distributors. Distributors have a clearly defined role in servicing mid-sized and small buyers.

Distributors were considered to be clearinghouses for the semiconductor industry. Each distributor dealt with products from all the major semiconductor manufacturers. For example, Arrow Electronics sold semiconductors manufactured by Motorola and Intel as well as those made by Texas Instruments. The distributors specialized in handling logistics, material flows, sales and servicing for electronics manufacturers who were either too small to negotiate directly with the major semiconductor manufacturers or lacked sufficient expertise in logistics management. In addition, the distributors sometimes knitted packages of different products together for the smaller original electronics manufacturers as an added service. Some also performed varying scales of assembly operation.

The electronics distribution network had originally consisted of a large group of smaller companies. By 1995, however, industry consolidation had left almost 40 percent of the distribution market in the hands of its two largest competitors, Arrow Electronics and Avnet. The seven largest distributors captured 58 percent of sales in the market (refer to Exhibit 6 for the sales and market shares of the top distributors). This trend toward consolidation had had a major impact on the nature of the relationships among semiconductor manufacturers and the distributors through which they sold their products. According to Szczsponik:

> Fifteen years ago, 30 distributors were active in the industry and it was clear that the semiconductor manufacturers controlled the distribution network. With the consolidation of the distribution network into only 7 or 8 powerful players, however, power is shifting. It's hard to say if we are more important to them or they are more important to us.

Price Negotiations and Global Pricing Issues

Since the vast majority of semiconductors were considered commodity products, the buying decisions of distributors were based almost entirely on price. Distributors

EXHIBIT 6

Total Sales and Market Share of Top Distributors

		1994	*1993*	*1992*	*1991*	*1990*
Industry Total	Sales ($ billions)	16.22	12.95	10.18	9.06	9.17
Top 25	Sales ($ billions)	13.41	10.69	8.11	7.10	7.20
	Share (%)	82.7	82.5	79.7	78.4	78.5
Top 7	Sales ($ billions)	10.75	8.42	6.36	5.05	5.00
	Share (%)	58.0	57.9	57.9	53.5	52.5
Top 2	Sales ($ billions)	7.32	5.07	3.31	2.44	2.40
	Share (%)	39.6	34.8	30.2	25.8	25.2

Source: Lehman Brothers, "Electronic Distribution Market," December 22, 1994.

forecast the demand for the various semiconductor products they carried and nego-tiated with vendors for their prices. Since semiconductor prices were notoriously volatile, the price levels negotiated between manufacturers and distributors played a vital role in the distributors' profitability. The Semiconductor Group at Texas Instruments combined the practices of forward pricing and continuous price negoti-ations to set prices with its distributors.

Forward Pricing The cost of semiconductor manufacturing followed a generally predictable learning curve. When a manufacturer first began producing a new type of chip, it could expect only a small percentage of the chips it produced to function properly. As the manufacturer increased the volume of its production, it both decreased the costs of production and increased the percentage of functioning chips it could produce. This percentage, termed "yield" in the industry, and the standard learning curve of semiconductor manufacturing together had a large impact on the prices semiconductor manufacturers set for their products (refer to Exhibit 7 for the price curve of semiconductor products). This yield was important to TI; a 7 percent increase in overall yield was equivalent to the production of an entire Wafer Fab plant, an investment of $500 million.

According to Jim Huffhines, Manager of DSP Business Development in the Semi-conductor Group, managers could predict with considerable accuracy the production cost decreases and yield improvements they would experience as their production volumes increased:

> We know the manufacturing costs for any given volume of production. We also know that these costs will decrease a certain percentage and our yields will increase a cer-tain percentage each year. These predictions are the basis of the forward prices we set with both original equipment manufacturers and distributors.

Continuous Price Adjustments Production costs and yield rates were not the only contributing factors to price levels for standard semiconductors: market supply and demand also played a powerful role in establishing prices. As a result of volatile prices

EXHIBIT 7

Forward Pricing Curve

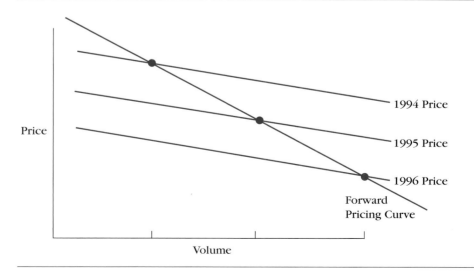

caused by shifts in supply and demand, distributors often held inventories of semiconductors that did not accurately reflect current market rates. To protect distributors from price fluctuations, most semiconductor manufacturers offered to reimburse distributors for their overvalued inventories. Szczsponik explained:

> Semiconductor prices have fallen by 15% over the past 9 months. If Arrow bought semiconductors from me for $1.00, nine months ago, they are worth only 85¢ now. Arrow is carrying a 15% "phantom" inventory. If Arrow sells those semiconductors now, we give it price protection by agreeing to reimburse it the 15¢ it has lost per semiconductor over the past three quarters.

At the same time, distributors had at their disposal sophisticated systems for monitoring semiconductor prices from each of the major manufacturers and were constantly in search of price adjustments from vendors when placing their orders. Szczsponik continued:

> Distributors have access to the prices of products from all the semiconductor manufacturers at any given time, and some anywhere in the world. The largest distributors have a staff of 20 to 30 people shopping around continuously for the best prices available for different types of semiconductors; add to this group a staff of accountants managing the price adjustment transactions. For example, they may call us to say that Motorola has quoted them a certain price for a semiconductor, and ask us if we can beat their price. In total, we get close to 150,000 of these calls requesting adjustments from distributors a year, and do over 10% of our sales through price adjustments. I have 10 people on my staff who negotiate price adjustments for distributors: 5 answer their calls, and 5 work with our product managers to make pricing decisions. These decisions are critical: if we make a mistake in our pricing, we lose market share in a day that can take us 3 months to recapture. At the same time, through our negotiations with distributors, we capture masses of data regarding the pricing levels of our competitors and the market performance of our different products. These data are critical to our ability to set prices.

As the distribution network consolidated into a small number of powerful companies, Szczsponik had begun to notice that his price negotiations were increasingly focused not only on beating the competition in North America, but on beating prices available around the world, including those of TI in other regions. With distributors becoming more active in the global market, they were more often exposed to semiconductor price levels from Europe and Asia. Industry analysts expected North American distributors to become more active in global markets as they pursued aggressive expansion campaigns in Europe and Asia. Although Texas Instruments' current contracts with its distributors prevented them from selling semiconductors outside of the region in which they were purchased, distributors were becoming insistent on access to freer global supplies and markets. While the concept may have appeared reasonable to the distributors, it was somewhat more complicated for Texas Instruments. Kevin McGarity elaborated:

> Because business is different everywhere in the world, our international distribution channels have evolved independently. They aren't subjected to the same costs, and don't operate under the same methods and calculation models. In the United States, for example, we offer a 30-day payment schedule for our customers. If they don't pay us within 30 days, we cut off their supply, no matter who they are. Italy operates under a 60-day schedule. Europeans include freight in their prices; we don't in North America. Finally, the cost of producing semiconductors varies by country. Europe tends to be more expensive than North America or Asia, simply because their infrastructure is more costly. So when one of our large distributors phones with the Singapore price for semiconductors manufactured in Düsseldorf, he is crossing boundaries that may be invisible to him but are very real to us.

Preparing for the Meeting with Arrow

With sales of almost $4 billion in 1994, Arrow Electronics was the largest semiconductor distributor in North America, of which TI products accounted for approximately 14 percent. Its aggressive growth had taken the company into global markets and had given it increased exposure to fluctuating price and exchange levels in different international markets. Seeking to minimize its costs, Arrow had begun to pressure semiconductor manufacturers to set standard global prices for each of their products. Motorola, one of Texas Instruments' largest competitors in the semiconductor industry, was rumored to be preparing for global pricing. Management at Texas Instruments, however, was unsure of the wisdom of moving toward global pricing. According to Szczsponik, the pros and cons of global pricing seem unevenly balanced:

> The large distributors want global pricing to reduce their costs and simplify their planning. But does it make sense for us? Right now our organization's calculation systems and costs in each country are too different for us to offer standard global prices. There are other things to consider as well. If we set global prices, we will no longer continue our price adjustment negotiations with the distributors. This may save us the cost of staffing our negotiations team, but it also takes away from us a powerful tool for gathering information on our customers' prices and our product performance. As soon as we stop negotiating price adjsutments, we lose our visibility in the market.

To prepare for his decision with McGarity and the forthcoming meeting with Arrow Electronics, Szczsponik knew TI had to make some fundamental decisions regarding global pricing. Who held the power in the relationships Texas Instruments had with its distributors? What was the source of the negotiating strength each party would bring to the meeting? Finally, what position should the Semiconductor Group take with its distributors regarding global pricing? And what organizational implications would such a decision imply?

CHAPTER 9

Marketing Strategy Reformulation: The Control Process

 Marketing strategies are rarely, if ever, timeless. As the environment changes, so must product-market and marketing-mix plans. Moreover, as organizations strive for gains in productivity, constant attention must be given to improving the efficiency of marketing efforts.

The marketing control process serves as the mechanism for achieving strategic adaptation to environmental change and operational adaptation to productivity needs. Marketing control consists of two complementary activities: strategic control, which is concerned with "doing the right things," and operations control, which focuses on "doing things right." *Strategic control* assesses the direction of the organization as evidenced by its implicit or explicit goals, objectives, strategies, and capacity to perform in the context of changing environments and competitive actions. The ever-present issue of defining the fit between an organization's capabilities and objectives and environmental threats and opportunities is at the core of strategic control. *Operations control* assesses how well the organization performs marketing activities as it seeks to achieve planned outcomes. It is implicitly assumed that the direction of the organization is correct and that only the organization's ability to perform specific tasks needs to be improved.

The distinction between strategic and operations control is important to grasp. It has been noted that a "poorly executed plan can produce undesirable results just as easily as a poorly conceived plan."[1] Though undesirable results (declining sales, eroding market share, or sagging profits) may be identical, remedial actions under the two types of control will differ. Remedial efforts drawn from an operations-control perspective focus on heightening the marketing effort or identifying ways to improve *efficiency*. Alternatively, remedial efforts based on a strategic-control orientation focus on improving the *effectiveness* of the organization in seeking opportunities and mitigating threats in its environment. Improper assessment of the need for strategic versus operations control can lead to a disastrous response in which an organization pours additional funds into an ill-conceived strategy, only to realize further declines in sales, market share, and profit.

■ STRATEGIC CHANGE

Strategic change is defined here as change in the environment that will affect the long-run well-being of the organization. Strategic change may represent opportunities or threats to an organization, depending on the organization's competitive posture. For example, the gradual aging of the U.S. population represents a potential threat to organizations catering to children, whereas this change represents an opportunity to organizations providing products for and services to the elderly.

Sources of Strategic Change

Strategic change can arise from a multitude of sources.[2] One source is *market evolution*, which results from changes in primary demand for a product class. For example, increased primary demand for calcium in the diets of children and adults prompted marketers of Tums antacid, Total Cereal, Nutri-Grain bars, and Minute Maid orange juice to promote the presence of calcium in their products. Similarly, consumer concerns about Internet privacy and security have created primary demand for software and computer systems that keep a consumer's personal data safe from abuse.

Technological innovation creates strategic change as newer technologies replace older technologies. The word-processing capabilities of personal computers pushed typewriters into decline. Compact discs did the same to cassette tapes in the prerecorded music industry. DVDs are quickly replacing videocassettes. Technological innovation also affects marketing practice, as evident by the impact of the Internet on marketing communications and marketing channels as described in Chapters 6 and 7.

Market redefinition is another source of strategic change. *Market redefinition* results from changes in the offering demanded by buyers or promoted by competitors. For example, firms that provided only automated teller machines (ATMs) for banks saw the market redefined to electronic funds transfer, with total systems rather than equipment alone being the offering purchased. Firms with systems capabilities, such as IBM, thus gained a competitive advantage in the redefined market.

Change in marketing channels is a third source of strategic change. The increasing role of Internet technology, the continuing focus on reducing distribution costs, and power shifts within marketing channels represent three opportunities or threats, depending on a marketer's relative position in a market. Strategic change, along these dimensions, is apparent in the distribution of automobiles in the United States.[3] Consumers today can price-comparison shop on the Internet without visiting dealers. The erosion in industry profit margins has caused manufacturers and dealers alike to look for cost-cutting opportunities, particularly in distribution costs, which represent 25 to 30 percent of the retail price of a new car.

Strategic Change: Threat or Opportunity?

Threat severity or opportunity potential is determined by the organization's business definition. In other words, does the threat or opportunity relate to the types of customers served by the organization, the needs of the customers, the means by which the organization satisfies these needs, or some combination of these factors?

The effects of strategic change are apparent in the transformation of the worldwide watchmaking industry.[4] Although Swiss watchmakers had dominated this industry for a century, market evolution, technological innovation, market redefinition, and marketing channel changes combined to spell disaster for the Swiss. While a technologically motivated market evolution changed the offering from jeweled watches to quartz and electronic watches, the primary marketing channel changed from select jewelry stores to mass merchandisers and supermarkets. Moreover, a redefinition of the term *watch* occurred. No longer was a watch defined solely in terms of craftsmanship or elegance as jewelry. Many people began to think of a watch as an economical and disposable timepiece. These changes, brought about by Timex and such Japanese firms as Seiko and Citizen, severely affected the Swiss watchmakers. Today, Swiss watchmakers have, for the most part, retreated to a highly specialized market niche, which can be identified as the prestige, luxury, artistry watch segment. For example, Swiss watches "tell you something about yourself" (Patek) and are "the most expensive in the world" (Piaget).

This example highlights how strategic change can affect an entire industry and its individual participants. In practice, several options exist for dealing with strategic change:

1. An organization can attempt to marshal the resources necessary to alter its technical and marketing capabilities to fit market-success requirements. (Swiss watchmakers did not do this but, rather, devoted modest research funds to perfecting the design of mechanical watches, in which they had a distinctive competency. Only Ebauches S.A. invested in electronic technology and pursued the marketing opportunity available for an inexpensive fashion watch—the Swatch. The Swatch Group is today the world's largest watchmaker, accounting for roughly one-quarter of global watch sales.)

2. An organization can shift its emphasis to product markets where the match between success requirements and the firm's distinctive competency is clear and can cut back efforts in those product markets where it has been out-flanked. (Many Swiss watchmakers chose this option.)

3. An organization can leave the industry. (Over 1,000 Swiss watchmakers selected this option, thereby eliminating more than 45,000 Swiss jobs.)

■ OPERATIONS CONTROL

The goal of operations control is to improve the productivity of marketing efforts. Because cost identification and allocation are central to the appraisal of marketing efforts and profitability, marketing-cost analysis is a fundamental aspect of operations control. This section provides an overview of marketing-cost analysis and selected examples of product–service mix control, sales control, and marketing-channel control.

Nature of Marketing-Cost Analysis

The purpose of *marketing-cost analysis* is to trace, assign, or allocate costs to a specified marketing activity or entity (hereafter referred to as a *segment*) in a manner that accurately displays the financial contribution of activities or entities to the organization. Marketing segments are typically defined on the basis of (1) elements of the product–service offering, (2) type or size of customers, (3) sales divisions, districts, or territories, and/or (4) marketing channels. Cost allocation is based on the principle that certain costs are directly or indirectly traceable or assignable to every marketing segment.[5]

Several issues arise in regard to the cost-allocation question:

1. *How should costs be allocated to separate marketing segments?* As a general rule, the manager should attempt to assign costs in accordance with an identifiable measure of application to an entity.

2. *What costs should be allocated?* Again, as a general rule, costs arising from the performance of a marketing activity or charged to that activity according to administrative policy are the costs that should be allocated.

3. *Should all costs be allocated to marketing segments?* The answer to this question will depend on whether the manager opts for a "whole equals the sum of

parts" income statement. If so, then all costs should be fully allocated. If it appears that certain costs have no identifiable measure of application to a segment or do not arise from one particular segment, however, these costs should not be allocated.

The manager should follow two guidelines in considering the cost-allocation question. First, when costs are allocated, fundamental distinctions between cost behavior patterns should be maintained. Second, the more joint costs there are (costs that have no identifiable basis for allocation or that arise from a variety of marketing segments), the less exact cost allocations will be. In general, greater detail in cost allocation or traceability will provide more useful information for remedial action.

Product–Service Mix Control

Proper control of the product-service mix involves two interrelated tasks. First, the manager must assess the performance of offerings in the relevant markets. Second, the manager must appraise the financial worth of product-service offerings.

Sales volume, as an index of performance, can be approached from two directions. Growth or decline in unit sales volume provides a quantitative indicator of the acceptance of offerings in their relevant markets. Equally important is the proportion of sales coming from individual offerings in the product-service mix and how this sales distribution affects profitability. Many firms experience the "80-20 rule"—80 percent of sales or profits come from 20 percent of the firm's offerings. For example, in the early 1990s, 20 percent of Kodak's products contributed more than 80 percent to the firm's sales. Such an imbalance in the mix can have a disastrous effect on overall profitability if sudden changes in competitive or market behavior threaten the viability of this 20 percent. This happened to Kodak when technological innovations such as digital imaging cameras began to redefine the photographic market. Also, Fuji proved to be an aggressive competitor in Kodak's traditional film and photographic markets.[6]

Market share complements sales volume as an indicator of performance. Market share offers a means for determining whether an organization is gaining or losing ground in comparison with competitors, provided it is used properly. Several questions must be considered when market share is used for control purposes. First, what is the market on which the market-share percentage is based, and has the market definition changed? Market share can be computed by geographic area, product type or model, customer or channel type, and so forth. In the Goodyear Tire and Rubber Company case in Chapter 7, the market share for tires was reported by geography (U.S. versus worldwide), product type (passenger car and truck), type of retail outlet (company-owned stores, discount tire stores, etc.), as well as by manufacturers' total sales. Second, is the market itself changing? For example, high market share by itself may be misleading, since overall sales in the market may be declining or growing. Finally, the unit of analysis—dollar sales or unit sales—must be considered. Because of price differentials, it is better to use unit rather than dollar volume in examining market share.

A second aspect of product-service control consists of appraising the financial contribution of market offerings. An important step in this process is to assign or trace costs to offerings in a manner that reflects their profitability. However, this step is difficult and often requires astute managerial judgment. Moreover, the definition of an offering is itself illusive. For example, a "red-eye" flight (early morning or late evening) scheduled by an airline might be viewed as an offering. The decision by McDonald's and Taco Bell to open for the breakfast trade can be viewed as a market offering, the costs of which include not only the cost of producing the menu items but also the cost of being open.

From a control perspective, the manager should examine the financial worth of market offerings using a *contribution-margin approach*, in which the relevant costs

EXHIBIT 9.1

Disaggregating Service Station Costs for Product–Service Mix Control (Thousands of Dollars)

	Total	Department Gasoline	General Merchandise	Automobile Service
Sales	$4,000	$2,000	$1,700	$300
Cost of goods sold and variable expenses	3,000	1,600	1,220	180
Contribution margin	1,000	400	480	120
Fixed expenses	900	500	310	90
Net income	$ 100	$ (100)	$ 170	$ 30

charged against an offering include direct costs and assignable overhead. The units by which these costs are broken down should be those that contribute most meaningfully to the analysis.

Consider the situation in which the owner of a chain of gasoline service stations is examining operating performance. Exhibit 9.1 shows the operating performance before and after cost allocation by department. Examination of the total yields little managerially relevant information. When costs are disaggregated and measured by department, however, it becomes apparent that gasoline operates at a net loss, whereas general merchandise and automobile service operate profitably. Fortunately, each department "contributes" to overhead; that is, each department's revenue exceeds its allocated variable costs.

This analysis serves a useful purpose in identifying potential trouble spots. Several alternatives exist for taking corrective action. If the owner decided to drop the unprofitable line and leave the selling space empty, then general merchandise and automobile service would have to cover the total fixed costs, which will continue. It is doubtful that this would occur. (Note that gasoline does contribute to the payment of fixed costs.) Another possibility is that the manager might expand the other departments to use the empty space. Estimates of market demand and forecasts of revenue would be needed for further consideration of this action. Moreover, a commitment of resources would have to occur that would in effect significantly alter the nature of the business.

Sales Control

Sales control directs a manager's attention to both the behavioral and the cost aspects of sales activity. The behavioral element consists of sales effort and allocation of selling time. The cost aspect consists of expenses arising from the performance and administration of the sales function.

Sales control is usually based on a performance analysis by sales territories or districts, size and type of customers or accounts, products, or some combination of these variables. Various measures used to assess sales performance include sales revenue, gross profit, sales call frequency, penetration of accounts in a sales territory, and selling and sales administration expenditures.

Consider a situation in which a district sales manager has requested a quarterly performance review of two sales personnel in a territory within the district. These individuals have failed to achieve their sales, gross profit, and profit quotas. Exhibit 9.2 on page 510 displays the representatives' performance according to customer-volume account categories. These categories were established by the national sales manager on the basis of industry norms, as were the following expected quarterly call frequencies:

EXHIBIT 9.2

Performance Summary for Two Sales Representatives

Account Category	(1) Potential Accounts in Sales District[a]	(2) Active Accounts[b]	(3) Sales Volume[c]	(4) Gross Profit[d]	(5) Total Calls[e]	(6) Selling Expenses[f]	(7) Sales Administration[g]
A	80	60	$ 48,000	$14,000	195	$18,400	
B	60	40	44,000	15,400	200	17,900	
C	40	10	25,000	12,250	50	11,250	
D	20	6	33,000	16,500	42	9,000	
Totals	200	116	$150,000	$58,550	487	$56,550	$10,000

[a] Based on marketing research data identifying potential users of company products.

[b] Current accounts.

[c] Based on invoices.

[d] Based on invoice price for full mix of products sold.

[e] Based on sales call reports cross-referenced by customer name.

[f] Direct costs of sales including allocated salaries of two sales representatives.

[g] Costs not assignable on a meaningful basis; includes office expense.

Account Definition	Expected Frequency of Quarterly Calls
A: $1,000 or less in sales	2
B: $1,000–$1,999 in sales	4
C: $2,000–$4,999 in sales	6
D: $5,000 or more in sales	8

Both representatives had an equal number of A, B, C, and D accounts.

Exhibit 9.3 shows various indices prepared by the district sales manager from the performance summary shown in Exhibit 9.2. Among the principal findings evident from Exhibit 9.3 are the following:

1. The representatives' account penetration varied inversely with the size of the account. Whereas representatives had penetrated 75 percent of the smaller A accounts, only 30 percent of the potentially large D accounts were listed as active buyers.

2. Part of the reason for this performance appears to lie in the call frequency of the representatives. The representatives exceeded the call norm on the A and B accounts, but fell short on call frequency on the C and D accounts. Moreover, their "effort" level appears questionable (487 calls ÷ 90 days ÷ 2 representatives = 2.7 calls per day).

3. The gross profit percentage derived from sales to smaller accounts was considerably lower than that derived from sales to the larger accounts, which in turn affected profitability.

4. When account sales volume is matched with gross profit and selling expenses, it becomes apparent that the smaller accounts actually produced a net contribution dollar loss.

The sales control process in this instance revealed that the two representatives were not actively calling on accounts (only 2.7 calls per day) and that their allocation of call activity focused on smaller-volume, less profitable accounts that were in fact contributing a *loss* to overhead. Redirection of effort is clearly called for in this situation.

EXHIBIT 9.3

Selected Operating Indices of Sales Performance

Sales Volume/ Active Account (Col. 3 ÷ Col. 4)	Gross Profit Active Account (Col. 4 ÷ Col. 2)	Selling Expenses/ Active Account (Col. 6 ÷ Col. 2)	Contribution to Sales Administration (Gross Profit – Selling Expenses)
A: $800	$240	$307	-$67
B: $1,100	$385	$448	-$63
C: $2,500	$1,225	$1,125	$100
D: $5,500	$2,750	$1,500	$1,250

Account Penetration (Col. 2 ÷ Col. 3)	Call Frequency/ Active Account (Col. 5 ÷ Col. 2)	Selling Expense per Call (Col. 6 ÷ Col. 5)	Gross Profit %/ Active Account (Col. 4 ÷ Col. 3)
A: 75%	3.25	$94.36	30%
B: 67	5.0	$89.50	35
C: 25	5.0	$225.00	49
D: 30	7.0	214.29	50

Marketing Channel Control

Marketing channel control consists of two complementary processes. The manager must first assess environmental and organizational factors that may alter the structure, conduct, and performance of marketing channels. These considerations were highlighted in Chapter 7. Second, the manager must evaluate the profitability of marketing channels.

Profitability analysis for marketing channels follows the general format outlined for product–service control. Cost identification and allocation differ, however. Two types of costs—order-getting and order-servicing costs—must be identified and traced to different marketing channels. *Order-getting costs* include sales expenses and advertising allowances. *Order-servicing expenditures* include packing and delivery costs, warehousing expenses, and billing costs.[7]

Consider a hypothetical marketer of furniture polishes, cleaners, and assorted furniture improvement products. This firm uses its own sales force to sell its products through three marketing channels: furniture stores, hardware stores, and home improvement stores. Exhibit 9.4 on page 512 shows income statements for all three channels combined, as well as individually (general and administration costs are not allocated or included). It is apparent that when costs and revenues are traced by channel, furniture store and hardware store channels generate equal sales revenue; however, furniture stores incur a sizable loss and hardware stores account for almost all of net income. Why are the returns so different?

Inspection of disaggregated costs suggests the following:

1. The gross margin percentage on the mix of products sold to hardware stores is 38 percent, whereas the gross margin percentage on products sold to furniture stores and home improvement stores is 30 percent. Thus, lower-margin products are being sold through furniture and home improvement stores on the average.

2. Order-getting costs (selling and advertising) run about 21 percent of sales for furniture stores, but only 7 percent for hardware stores and 16 percent for home improvement stores.

EXHIBIT 9.4

Disaggregated Costs of Furniture Improvement Products for Marketing Channel Control (Thousands of Dollars)

	Total	Marketing Channel		
		Furniture Stores	Hardware Stores	Home Improvement Stores
Sales	$12,000	$5,000	$5,000	$2,000
Cost of goods sold	8,000	3,500	3,100	1,400
Gross margin	4,000	1,500	1,900	600
Expenses				
Selling	1,000	617	216	167
Advertising	750	450	150	150
Packing and delivery	800	370	300	130
Warehousing	400	200	150	50
Billing	600	300	250	50
Total expenses	3,550	1,937	1,066	547
Net channel income (loss)	$ 450	$(437)	$ 834	$ 53

3. Order-servicing costs are 17 percent of sales for furniture stores, 14 percent for hardware stores, and about 12 percent for home improvement stores.

In short, a manager can conclude that the effort (reflected in costs) necessary to generate sales and service in the furniture store channel is much greater than that needed for hardware and home improvement stores. Moreover, furniture stores purchase products with a lower gross margin. Once these problems have been identified, efforts to remedy the situation can be explored in a more systematic fashion.

Some companies trace order-getting and order-servicing costs and revenues by individual customer in a marketing channel. The result of such analyses is often illuminating. For instance, LSI Logic, a high-tech semiconductor manufacturer, recently discovered that 90 percent of its profit arose from 10 percent of its customers. Moreover, the company was losing money on half of its customers![8]

■ CONSIDERATIONS IN MARKETING CONTROL

Proper implementation of strategic and operations control requires that the manager be aware of several pertinent considerations. Three of these considerations follow.

Problems Versus Symptoms

Effective control, whether at the strategic or the operations level, requires that the manager recognize the difference between root problems and surface symptoms. This means that the manager must develop causal relationships between occurrences. For example, if there is evidence of a sales decline or poor profit margins, the manager must "look behind" the numbers to identify the underlying causes of such performance and then attempt to remedy them. This diagnostic role is similar to that of a physician, who must first establish patient symptoms in order to identify the ailment.

Effectiveness Versus Efficiency

A second consideration is the dynamic tension that exists between effectiveness and efficiency. Effectiveness addresses the question of whether the organization is achieving its intended goals, given environmental opportunities and constraints and organizational capabilities. Efficiency relates to productivity—the levels of output, given a specified unit of input. Suppose a sales representative has a high call frequency per day and a low cost-per-call expense ratio. The individual might be viewed favorably from an efficiency perspective. If the emphasis of the organization is on customer service and problem solving, however, this person might be viewed as ineffective.

Data Versus Information

A third consideration is the qualitative difference between data and information. Data are essentially *reports* of activities, events, or performance. Information, on the other hand, may be viewed as a *classification* of activities, events, or performance designed to be interpretable and useful for decision making. The distinction between data and information was illustrated in the discussion of marketing-cost analysis techniques, where data were organized into meaningful classifications and operating ratios.

N O T E S

1. Thomas Bonoma, "Making Your Marketing Strategy Work," *Harvard Business Review* (March–April 1984): 68–76.

2. These concepts were drawn from Derek Abell, "Strategic Windows," *Journal of Marketing* (July 1978): 21–26.

3. Evan R. Hirsh et. al., "Changing Channels in the Automotive Industry: The Future of Automotive Marketing and Distribution," *Strategy & Business* (First Quarter 1999): 42–50; and "Click Here for a New Sedan! (Not Yet, Alas)," *Newsweek* (November 11, 2002): E-10–E-12.

4. David S. Landes, *Revolution in Time*, Revised Edition (Cambridge, MA: Harvard University Press, 2000); and Pete Yoo, "Innovate, Don't Downsize," *Wall Street Journal* (April 23, 2001): A22.

5. B. Ames and J. Hlavacek, "Vital Truths about Managing Your Costs," *Harvard Business Review* (January–February 1990): 140–47; and S. L. Mintz, "Two Steps Forward, One Step Back," *CFO* (December 1998): 21–25.

6. "Film vs. Digital: Can Kodak Build a Bridge?" *Business Week*, (August 2, 1999): 66–69; and "New Digital Camera Deals Kodak a Lesson in Microsoft's Ways," *Wall Street Journal* (July 2, 2001): A1, A6.

7. For an example of cost identification in marketing channels, see Robin Cooper and Robert S. Kaplan, "Profit Priorities from Activity-Based Costing," *Harvard Business Review* (May–June 1991): 130–137.

8. Bob Donath, "Fire Your Big Customers? Maybe You Should," *Marketing News* (June 21, 1999): 9.

Affiniscape, Inc.

". . . and a happy Groundhog Day to all of you," replied Adam Weedman as he locked the door to the Affiniscape office and walked to his pickup truck. Weedman, president of Affiniscape, Inc., had just finished an all-day planning meeting with the five other major shareholders of the company, and as he opened the door to his truck he could not help but ponder the issues that had been discussed at the meeting. The company had just closed the books on its second year of operation, and Weedman, along with the employees and other shareholders, was convinced that it was on the verge of a breakout year. Even so, given the financial performance of the firm in 2002, there was consensus that the strategic direction of the company had to be reassessed and certain operational decisions made in the near future. As he drove home, Weedman wondered whether the groundhog had seen its shadow.

■ THE COMPANY

Although several of the company's shareholders had thought about starting a company like Affiniscape for several years, it was not until January 2001 that the company formally came into existence. The strategic goal of Affiniscape was to serve as a virtual extension of the staffs of small (state, regional, or local) trade and professional associations. As a "virtual staff," Affiniscape would enhance the capabilities of the association's physical staff without increasing association costs. In particular, Affiniscape wanted to:

> Identify new ways to leverage client association resources through the use of technology, produce value-added programs that benefit both client associations and their members, and provide nondues revenue opportunities for client associations.

The operational goal of Affiniscape was to provide two general services for small, typically nonprofit, trade and professional associations—a comprehensive, easy-to-use Web site, and a portfolio of affinity programs. Each of Affiniscape's employees had been carefully selected to accomplish both the strategic and operational goal. Employee skills included computer programming, Web site and graphic design, in-depth knowledge of, and professional contacts with, associations, and knowledge of and experience in selling insurance. Collectively these individuals represented a very unique resource that Weedman thought could be leveraged to benefit a wide variety of associations.

Affiniscape's business model mandated that the company focus on annuity-type products and services. Thus, rather than focus on one-time purchases, the company emphasized long-term client relationships based on repeat purchases and an extensive service commitment. Weedman continually exhorted employees to refer to client associations as partners rather than customers, and to provide the best possible service: "I have always believed that Service, with a capital 'S,' is the key to any business and that if you truly provided good service, the business would follow."

Given Affiniscape's distinctive competencies and strategic goal, executives believed that the company could acquire 2,000 client associations by the end of is fourth year of operation. Moreover, on the day that the company was named, Weedman in particular was optimistic that the company would have at least 200 client associations by the end of its first year of operation and 500 by the end of the second year.

Product and Service Offerings

The first and principal product offering of Affiniscape was a branded, leading-edge, template-driven Web site that could be customized for an association. The Web site contained numerous features to facilitate the communication and administrative functions of an association. For example, the Web site contained a sophisticated online membership directory, a blast-email capability, online newsletter tools, event calendar, registration and dues payment capabilities, job bank and classified advertisements, various association administration tools, and a host of other useful features. Because an individual association member could personally customize certain aspects of his or her association's Web site, it could become that member's homepage and automatically link to a variety of other Web sites. One of the Web site's modules consisted of an online shopping mall of more than 100 companies. Each time a member of a client association purchased something from this mall through the association's Web site, the association and Affiniscape shared an affinity commission, thus providing the association with a source of nondues revenue and Affiniscape with "annuity revenue."

Consistent with its business model, Affiniscape did not offer its Web site at a one-time price. Unlike its competitors, which offered fixed-price Web site products at prices ranging from $10,000 to more than $100,000, Affiniscape licensed its Web site product to client associations at an annual targeted fee averaging about $3,000. For this fee, Affiniscape provided a branded Web site (i.e., the Web site would have only the client association's name on it; Affiniscape would not be listed on the Web site) and instructed the client association's staff on how to add and manage content as well as use other features and tools. Although Affiniscape would host the Web site on its servers, the client association was responsible for content maintenance and day-to-day upkeep after a training session conducted by an Affiniscape customer support representative.

Through a series of partners, Affiniscape also offered client associations discounted long-distance conference calling, selected software packages, and the like. A strategic objective of Affiniscape from its inception was to offer a variety of insurance products (e.g., life insurance, health insurance, long-term care insurance, and/or liability insurance), travel packages, credit card processing services, and Web development and hosting services for client associations. Although Affiniscape offered a limited insurance product, insurance had been extensively discussed at the Groundhog Day meeting. For example, questions had been raised regarding when and what additional insurance products should be introduced, whether the company should partner with an insurance company or broker, develop its own insurance products, or implement its own brokerage operation.

Marketing Approach

Marketing to trade and professional associations is simultaneously straightforward and challenging. Marketing is straightforward because, with sufficient resources, it is possible to identify potential client associations. There are directories of associations, and many associations are listed on various Web sites or have their own Web site. Thus, unlike much consumer marketing, it is possible, at least theoretically, to target specific, individual associations. However, because many associations have a Web site and often-times purchase decisions involve an association's board of directors due to limited financial resources and what might be termed political concerns, marketing to them can be quite time-consuming and challenging.

Affiniscape employs a variety of marketing approaches to reach potential client associations. Using e-mail addresses supplied by contract labor, sales representatives contact more than one thousand association executives each month. The e-mails direct recipients to the Affiniscape Web site or invite them to call the company. Approximately one percent of the e-mails results in a response. Weedman personally attends several conferences and trade shows every year, where he interacts with association executives and discusses the Affiniscape Web site offering. The company does virtually no advertising. From time-to-time it will provide complimentary Web sites to develop relationships. By far the most effective and efficient way of acquiring new client associations is to obtain referrals from existing clients. Because association executives, especially in a particular industry, know each other and work together on common problems, referrals tend to be powerful marketing levers.

Association executives who are interested in the Affiniscape Web site offering are given a one- to two-hour Web-based tour of a demonstration Web site and several active client association Web sites by one of Affiniscape's sales representatives. More than half of the executives touring the Affiniscape demonstration Web site purchase a license for their association. Affiniscape executives believe that once an association executive has viewed the Affiniscape Web site offering, the Web site "sells itself." As might be expected, sales representatives spend most of their working time on the telephone talking to potential client associations.

Company Performance

Affiniscape licensed its first client association, the Academy of Marketing Science, a professional association consisting of approximately 1,500 marketing educators, in March 2001. A second professional association was licensed the following April, and a third in May. Exhibit 1 presents the total number of client associations licensed in 2001 and 2002. Of the client associations represented in Exhibit 1, eight had received complimentary licenses in 2002, and four existing client associations had decided not to renew their licenses. In January 2003, 18 new associations were licensed.

Company revenues were approximately $150,000 in the first year of operation. In 2002, revenues were nearly $655,000. Exhibit 2 on page 518 contains an abbreviated profit and loss statement for 2002. The largest source of revenue was Web site licensing. The smallest source consisted of affinity commissions from merchants populating Affiniscape's shopping mall. Miscellaneous revenue came from activities not relating to client associations. The largest expense category was employee compensation. By the end of 2002, the company had grown to ten full-time and two part-time employees, with two full-time employees dedicated to selling (licensing) the company's Web site offering and an additional employee primarily selling ancillary products and services to associations once they became clients. The three sales representatives were each paid a base salary of $35,000; the two sales representatives selling the Web site offering were also paid a commission that averaged 15 percent of revenues generated on first-time licenses.

Although all three sales representatives were extremely capable, one of the two representatives selling the company's Web site offering had only been with the company since the summer of 2002 and just recently felt comfortable "closing" sales by himself.

EXHIBIT 1

Number of New Client Associations

Month	Number
2001	
March	1
April	1
May	1
June	6
July	2
August	0
September	10
October	8
November	6
December	14
2002	
January	16
February	20
March	20
April	14
May	20
June	16
July	24
August	26
September	30
October	20
November	10
December	16

Source: Company records (data disguised).

■ THE ASSOCIATION MARKET

Although no precise number exists, it has been estimated that more than 200,000 formal associations presently exist in the United States. These associations represent nearly every industry, profession, charity, hobby, cause, and interest imaginable. The *Encyclopedia of Associations* contains more than 129,000 local, state, and regional associations, 23,000 national associations, and 1,300 international associations headquartered in the United States. According to a 1998 study by the American Association of Retired Persons, nine out of ten adult Americans belong to at least one association, and one out of four adults belongs to four or more associations. Americans are forming as many as 1,000 new associations each year.

The Washington, D.C., area is home to more associations than any other metropolitan area in the United States (2,500), with New York City (1,900) and Chicago (1,500) respectively ranking second and third. Indeed, associations are the third largest industry in the Washington, D.C. metropolitan area, behind only government and tourism.

EXHIBIT 2

Affiniscape 2002 Abbreviated Profit and Loss Statement

Income	
Web site licenses	$601,200
Merchant commissions	800
Web site design	13,000
Software sales	8,400
Web site hosting	6,000
Domain names	5,200
Insurance commissions	5,200
Miscellaneous services	15,000
Total	$654,800
Expenses	
Payroll	$628,800
Employee benefits	44,000
Rent	31,000
Co-location fees	10,200
Computers and software	20,400
Domain names	2,400
Cost of goods sold	8,800
Internet services	4,600
Marketing	9,400
Professional fees	4,000
Association referral fees	9,200
Contract work	8,400
Telephone	18,400
Office supplies	4,400
Utilities	1,600
Total	$805,600
Profit (loss)	($150,800)

Source: Company records (data disguised)

Although some associations have millions of members, such as those that have consumers as members, a large proportion of associations, especially those that serve occupations or industries and are state, regional, or local associations, have less than 1,000 members. The five national associations with the largest memberships are

- American Automobile Association (43 million estimated members)
- American Association of Retired Persons (33 million estimated members)
- YMCA of the USA (17 million estimated members)
- National Geographic Society (9 million estimated members)
- National Congress of Parents and Teachers (6 million estimated members)

Associations are a major market for many products and services, either directly as end users or as intermediaries for their members. For example, it is estimated that associations spend more than $3 billion annually on printing magazines, newsletters, and so forth for their members, and another $4 billion on technology and communications. Associations dominate the meetings and convention industry; association members spend in excess of $75 billion each year traveling to and attending conventions, expositions, and meetings. Nearly $150 billion in insurance premiums annually pass through associations from members to insurance providers.

All formal trade and professional associations have some type of executive director and staff, and they usually have a board of trustees or directors. Oftentimes both the director and the staff are volunteers or part-time employees. There are even associations designed for association directors, with perhaps the most well known being the American Society of Association Executives (ASAE). Because more than 200 million people belong to associations represented by ASAE, it is an important gateway to reaching the trade and professional association community.

Target Markets

Affiniscape's initial target market consisted of small professional associations whose members were likely to be computer literate. Professional associations are defined as associations designed to serve individuals, usually in particular occupational categories, such as nurses, certified public accountants, teachers, and the like. Virtually every industry or professional occupation will have numerous associations ranging from national associations to regional, state, and even local associations. It is not unusual for a national association to have six regional chapters, 50 state chapters, and 300 local (metropolitan) chapters. Individuals join associations for a variety of reasons, including access to information and education (some associations offer certification programs), reduced insurance premiums, representation before legislative and regulatory bodies, and networking opportunities.

The initial strategy of Affiniscape was to target 20 different professional association categories. In alphabetical order, these association categories consisted of

Accountants	Lawyers
Architects	Librarians
Broadcasters	Music Educators
Counselors	Nurses
Court Reporters	Optometrists
Dentists	Pharmacists
Dieticians	Professional Administrators
Doctors	Psychologists
Engineers	Realtors
Insurance Agents	Teachers

At the beginning of 2003, approximately one-third of Affiniscape's client associations fell into one of these 20 categories.

Almost by accident Affiniscape began attracting small trade associations beginning in late 2001. Trade associations are defined as associations designed to serve organizations, such as businesses, and are found in virtually all industries. Among Affiniscape's initial trade association clients were home builders, magazine retailers, funeral homes, home care companies, and liquor stores. At the beginning of 2003, approximately 30 percent of Affiniscape's client associations were trade associations.

■ THE DECISION ARRAY

In the two weeks following the Groundhog Day meeting, Adam Weedman thought about the financial condition as well as the promise of Affiniscape almost daily. He knew that revenues had to increase in 2003, and he could feel the pressure from shareholders to get a better handle on expenses. A third year without a profit was not what the shareholders had expected when the company was founded. Should he dedicate resources to advertising and, if so, where and how would the resources be allocated? Should he add another sales representative to increase revenues or lay one off to reduce expenses? Or should he increase the price of initial license fees by 10 or 15 percent, or, perhaps, increase the price of license renewals by 10 or 15 percent? Although the year was just beginning to unfold, Weedman knew that Affiniscape needed to spend at least $50,000 on new servers, computers, and software, and a minimum of $20,000 on a new telephone system and communications infrastructure in the next few months just to support its present client base.

Pharmacia & Upjohn, Inc.
Rogaine Hair Regrowth Treatment

On February 9, 1996, the U.S. Food and Drug Administration (FDA) approved Rogaine Hair Regrowth Treatment for sale without a physician's prescription. Rogaine, the only medically proven hair regrowth treatment at the time for men and women with common hereditary hair loss, had been sold as a prescription drug in the United States since 1988. Cumulative sales of Rogaine in the United States since its introduction exceeded $700 million. Worldwide cumulative Rogaine sales exceeded $1 billion (see Exhibit 1 on page 522).[1]

With Rogaine's patent about to expire in four days, FDA approval of Rogaine as a nonprescription, or over-the-counter (OTC), drug was welcome news to Pharmacia & Upjohn, Inc., the manufacturer of the product. According to a company official, "We are pleased with the FDA's decision switching Rogaine from prescription to OTC sales. OTC availability of Rogaine is a welcome convenience for millions of men and women who experience common hair loss. We are pursuing an aggressive timetable to make Rogaine quickly and widely accessible to consumers."[2] The launch of nonprescription Rogaine was scheduled for April 1996. At that time, prescription-only Rogaine would be discontinued, since both prescription and nonprescription Rogaine had identical formulations. The company also requested the FDA to approve a three-year period of marketing exclusivity for nonprescription Rogaine under provisions of the Waxman-Hatch Amendment to the U.S. Food, Drug and Cosmetic Act. These provisions allow pharmaceutical companies to petition the FDA for a three-year marketing exclusivity if they pay for new research that is necessary to convert a prescription drug to nonprescription use. FDA response to this petition was expected in late March or April 1996.

In anticipation of FDA approval for nonprescription Rogaine following a positive recommendation by an FDA advisory committee in November 1995 and a favorable FDA response to the petition for a three-year marketing exclusivity, company officials had already outlined the marketing program for the brand scheduled for an April 1996 launch.[3] Rogaine would be targeted at men and women aged 25 to 49. The brand would be positioned as the only product available without a prescription that

---

[1] Sales figures are based on information provided in "Rogaine Will Be Sold Over-the-Counter," *PR Newswire*, February 12, 1996; estimates made by Bear, Stearns, & Company and Prudential Securities industry analysts; and data reported in "For Rogaine, No Miracle Cure—Yet," *Business Week* (June 4, 1990), p. 100, and "Blondes, Brunettes, Redheads, and Rogaine," *American Druggist* (June 1992), pp. 39–40.

[2] "Rogaine Will Be Sold Over-the-Counter," *PR Newswire*, February 12, 1996.

[3] This description is based on "Rogaine Will Be Sold Over-the-Counter," *PR Newswire*, February 12, 1996; Michael Wilke, "New Rivals Push Rogaine to Jump-Start Its OTC Ads," *Advertising Age* (April 15, 1996), p. 45; Michael Wilke, "Rogaine, Nicorette Seek Edge from FDA," *Advertising Age* (February 19, 1996), p. 4; "OTC Rogaine Receives FDA Advisory Committee Recommendation," *PR Newswire*, November 17, 1995; Sean Mehegan, "Hair Today," *BRANDWEEK* (April 8, 1996), pp. 1, 6.

This case was prepared by Professor Roger A. Kerin, of the Edwin L. Cox School of Business, Southern Methodist University, as a basis for class discussion and is not designed to illustrate effective or ineffective handling of an administrative situation. This case is based on published sources, including The Upjohn Company and Pharmacia & Upjohn, Inc. annual reports, news releases, and interviews with individuals knowledgeable about the industry. Quotes, statistics, and published information are footnoted for reference purposes. Copyright © 1996 Roger A. Kerin. No part of this case may be reproduced without written permission of the copyright holder.

E X H I B I T   1

Rogaine and Regaine Dollar Sales (Sales Reported Using Manufacturer Prices)

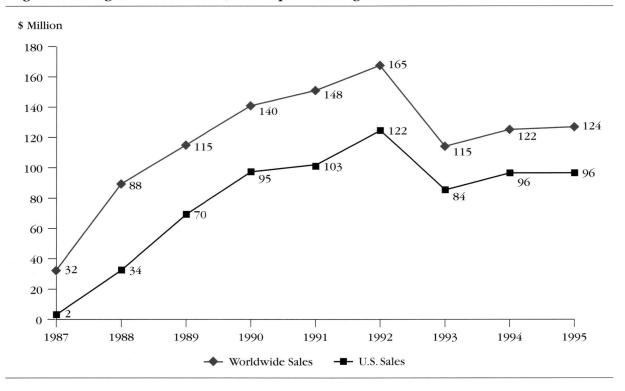

is medically proven to regrow hair. Separate packages—Rogaine for men and Rogaine for women—would be sold. Each package would feature labeling and include a brochure designed to help prospective users accurately identify themselves as Rogaine candidates. The suggested retail price for one bottle, which is equivalent to a one-month supply, would be $29.50. This price was approximately one-half the price of prescription Rogaine for a one-month supply. Distribution would be expanded to locate Rogaine in the pharmacy or hair-care section of food, drug, and mass-merchandise retail outlets. Marketing spending during the first six months of the brand introduction, estimated at $75 million, would support Rogaine and the company's relaunched nonprescription Progaine shampoo. More than half of the $75 million expenditure would be devoted to consumer advertising. The spending level represented the largest consumer and trade promotion campaign for a nonprescription product in the company's history. According to industry sources, company officials were telling retail store buyers of health and beauty aids that the brand had a retail sales potential of $250 million a year.

On April 5, 1996, the FDA notified Pharmacia & Upjohn, Inc. that its request for a three-year period of marketing exclusivity for nonprescription Rogaine had been denied.[4] In addition, by April 9, 1996, the FDA had approved three competing generic versions of Rogaine containing 2-percent solutions of minoxidil—the active chemical ingredient in Rogaine that stimulates hair regrowth—for sale without a prescription.

---

[4] This discussion is based on "Generic Versions of Rogaine Ok'd," *The Dallas Morning News* (April 9, 1996), p. 4D; "Pharmacia & Upjohn Files Lawsuit Over OTC Rogaine Exclusivity," *PR Newswire*, April 12, 1996; "Rogaine Awarded Temporary Restraining Order," *PR Newswire*, April 15, 1996.

Generic products, which are supposed to be medically equivalent to brand-name products, are typically priced 25 percent to 50 percent less than brand-name products and not advertised. On April 12, 1996, Pharmacia & Upjohn, Inc. filed a law suit against the FDA in Federal District Court in Grand Rapids, Michigan. The company asked the Court to reverse the FDA's ruling on the matter of market exclusivity for nonprescription Rogaine and to order the FDA to defer approval of competing nonprescription products containing minoxidil. On April 15, the Court issued a temporary restraining order prohibiting the FDA action. A preliminary hearing was set for April 30 to hear the Pharmacia & Upjohn, Inc. motion for a preliminary injunction which sought to extend injunctive relief until a full trial had been held.

The conversion of Rogaine from a prescription to nonprescription status and the FDA's possible denial of a three-year marketing exclusivity for Rogaine, along with approval of generic products, raised a variety of related market and marketing questions. First, what unit and dollar sales potential for the product category as a whole might be expected now that a minoxidil treatment for hair regrowth no longer required a prescription? Pharmacia & Upjohn, Inc. believed sales of $1 billion for Rogaine were possible over five years given its marketing program and assuming no competitive products. However, less optimistic views existed. One industry analyst believed "there is enough vanity out there, that a lot of people will try it, at least initially." However, another analyst noted that "those who are truly motivated have probably already tried it."[5]

Second, how might the loss of U.S. patent protection and marketing exclusivity that Rogaine had enjoyed since its introduction and competition from generic products affect sales of the Rogaine brand? There were no comparable situations to draw upon in the pharmaceutical industry to answer this question for a product like Rogaine.[6] For instance, pharmaceutical industry analysts estimate that it was common for patented prescription drugs to lose up to 60 percent of their volume within six months after their patent expired due to generic competition. However, this situation was typical of prescription drugs and not necessarily prescription drugs converting to a nonprescription status upon expiration of their patent. In another situation, Nicorette Gum, a smoking cessation product, lost its marketing exclusivity in June 1994. But with increased advertising and no direct branded or generic competition, except nicotine patches, the Nicorette brand saw dollar sales increase almost 6 percent in 1995. Unlike Nicorette Gum, if Rogaine lost its marketing exclusivity, it could face competition from generic or branded products with a 2-percent solution of minoxidil in 1996. These products were manufactured by Bausch & Lomb, Alpharma, and Lemmon Company, a division of Israeli-based Teva Pharmaceutical Industries. A Bausch & Lomb spokesperson said, "We do see a market for minoxidil as viable and would very much like to be a player." Lemmon Company manufactures generic drugs and private-label products and has announced that it intended to have generic and private-label versions of minoxidil available by mid-1996. The company has also initiated discussions with other companies to offer a branded product. In addition, Merck was testing its prostate medicine, Proscar, for hair growth which would be in pill form. This product could be submitted for FDA approval within a year and be on the market by 1999. Finally, would the U.S. marketing strategy developed for nonprescription Rogaine prior to the FDA's recent rulings need to be modified? If so, how? Nonprescription Rogaine was already being

[5] Laurie McGinley, "Baldness Drug Cleared for Sale Over Counter," *Wall Street Journal* (February 13, 1996), p. B3; Michael Wieke, "OTC Status Might Not Be Boon to Rogaine," *Advertising Age* (January 29, 1996), p. 10.

[6] The following discussion is based on Patricia Winters, "Prescription Drug Ads Up," *Advertising Age* (January 18, 1993), pp. 10, 50; "Rogaine, Nicorette Seek Edge from FDA," *Advertising Age* (February 19, 1996), p. 4; Sean Mehegan, "Hair Today," *BRANDWEEK* (April 8, 1996), pp. 1, 6.

shipped to retailers and the consumer advertising and sales promotion program was ready to be implemented.

■ TREATMENTS FOR BALDING

There are about 300,000 hairs on the scalp of a person considered to have a "full" head of hair.[7] The exact number of hairs on a person's head depends on the number of hair follicles, which is established before birth. On average, a person will shed 100 to 150 hairs per day from the scalp and a new hair begins to emerge from the follicle. However, many people experience permanent hair loss on the scalp. Called *androgenetic alopecia*, both men and women can have this condition. With male pattern baldness, the most common form of *alopecia*, normal hair is lost initially from the temples and crown, where it is replaced by fine, downy hair. The affected area gradually becomes wider as the line of normal hair recedes. This process of hair loss is inherited and the typical progression in men is shown in Exhibit 2. Women also experience hair loss, a condition referred to as diffuse hair loss. This condition is manifested by thinning hair all over the head, rather than the progression typical of male pattern baldness, although young women and women who have passed menopause occasionally exhibit this progression.

Survey research indicates that 38.6 percent of women say they would seek treatment if they were losing their hair, compared with 30.4 percent of men who say they would seek treatment.[8] However, this research also reported that at most 13.3 percent of surveyed women who were experiencing hair loss actually sought some form of treatment while at most 9.9 percent of men experiencing hair loss actually sought treatment. People with hair loss and who seek remedies have numerous options to treat this condition. The most popular treatments involve prescription and nonprescription hair shampoos, lotions, and conditioners. These hair-thickening products

EXHIBIT 2

Typical Progression of Male Pattern Baldness in Men

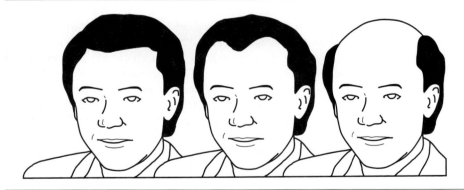

---

[7] This material is based on Charles B. Clayman, ed., *The American Medical Association Encyclopedia of Medicine* (New York: Random House, 1989), pp. 88, 504; William G. Flanagan and David Stix, "The Bald Truth," *Forbes* (July 22, 1991), pp. 309–310; "Baldness: Is There Hope?," *Consumer Reports* (September 1988), pp. 533–547; Gary Belsky, "Beating Hair Loss," *MONEY* (March 1996), pp. 152–155; "Hair Loss: Does Anything Really Help?," *Consumer Reports* (August 1996), pp. 62–63.

[8] Laurie Freeman, "Upjohn Takes a Shine to Balding Women," *Advertising Age* (February 27, 1989), p. S1. These statistics are based on a Gallup Organization survey of 1,000 adults in the United States.

EXHIBIT 3

The Amount U.S. Adults Are Willing to Spend for the Treatment of Balding

Amount	Men	Women
$1,000–$10,000	11.3%	11.1%
$600–$1,000	7.1	5.3
$300–$599	13.5	9.7
$100–$299	14.2	13.5
$99 or less	27.0	28.5
Don't know	26.9	31.9
	100%	100%

Source: Gallup Organization Survey of 1,000 U.S. adults commissioned by *Advertising Age*. Reported in Laurie Freeman, "Upjohn Takes a Shine to Balding Women," *Advertising Age* (February 27, 1989), p. S1. Reproduced with the permission of *Advertising Age*.

are often used to treat thinning hair. It is estimated that there are 40 million balding men and 20 million women with thinning hair in the United States and they spend over $300 million annually on these kinds of products. Exhibit 3 shows the amount of money men and women say they are willing to spend per year for the treatment of balding. Hairpieces or wigs, hair transplants, and drugs, such as minoxidil, can be used when hair loss is prominent. American consumers spend about $1.3 billion annually for these treatments. Another $100 million is spent for elixirs, teas, horse-hoof ointments and the like to treat hair loss.

Hairpieces or Wigs

Hairpieces (or toupees) and wigs are worn by over two million Americans. About $400 million is spent annually for these products, including periodic cleaning and styling. Hairpieces and wigs can be made from real human hair or from synthetic material, usually nylon. Hairpieces made from human hair usually last no more than one year. Synthetic hair will last up to two years. The cost of a small filler hairpiece made from human hair for a balding man's crown can be purchased for as little as $325; a full women's wig can cost $2,000 or more. A typical man's hairpiece made of human hair costs from $1,000 to $3,500. Synthetic hairpieces for men cost between $1,800 and $2,500. Hairpieces require maintenance every six to eight weeks with the average cost for adjusting, cleaning, and styling running between $50 and $100. Spirit gum or a double-faced tape is used to hold the hairpiece or wig on the scalp.

Hair Transplants

A hair transplant consists of a surgical cosmetic operation in which hairy sections of the scalp are removed and transplanted to hairless areas. One or a combination of the following procedures may be used. "Punch grafting" is the most common procedure. With this procedure, a punch is used to remove small areas of bald scalp (about one-fourth inch across), which are replaced with areas of hairy scalp. The grafts are taped into position until the natural healing process takes effect. "Strip grafting" is a procedure whereby strips of bald skin are removed from the scalp and replaced with strips of hairy scalp which are stitched into position. "Flap grafting" is similar to strip grafting, except that flaps of hairy skin are lifted from the scalp, swiveled, and stitched to replace areas of bald skin. This procedure is typically used to form a new hairline. "Male pattern baldness reduction" consists of cutting out areas of bald scalp and then stretching surrounding areas of hairy scalp to replace the bald area. Hair transplants, no matter how successful, do not last indefinitely. As time passes, transplanted areas become bald.

About $800 million is spent each year for hair transplants in the United States. Hair transplant procedures of the grafting variety cost patients $3,500 to $15,000. Male pattern baldness reduction often costs $2,000 to $3,500 per procedure plus the transplant fee. These procedures are usually not covered by medical insurance.

Drugs

Although many topical ointments and elixirs are promoted, only one product had been approved by the FDA as a drug to restore hair growth for men and women prior to April 1996. Rogaine Hair Regrowth Treatment, produced by Pharmacia & Upjohn, Inc., received FDA approval for use by men in the United States in August 1988 and for women in August 1991. Rogaine is a 2-percent solution of minoxidil that is applied twice daily to areas of the scalp that has thinning hair or no hair. Clinical tests conducted by the company indicated that hair growth appeared to be more pronounced for men under 30 years of age and those in the early stages of the male pattern baldness progression. An estimated 35 percent of men under 30 years of age experience hair loss. The properties of minoxidil and its use as a topical ointment for hair growth are such that if not applied twice daily, hair loss results. In other words, minoxidil is a lifetime treatment if its effects on hair growth and retention are to be permanent.

Until February 1996, treatment with Rogaine required a physician's prescription. A one-month supply of the product then cost a patient $50 to $60 and up to $125 if the product was used in high concentrations, or if mixed with other drugs such as Retin-A. In addition, periodic physician office fees raised the annual patient cost for treatment. Rogaine was not typically covered by medical insurance.

In February 1996, the FDA approved Rogaine as a nonprescription drug. This decision reversed a 1994 FDA ruling that denied nonprescription status for Rogaine. At that time, FDA officials testified that the drug was most effective when applied during the early stages of baldness, but that the drug was not a cure. The group leader of the FDA's dermatology group said Rogaine was a "marginal product" in curing baldness.[9] In approving Rogaine as a nonprescription drug in 1996, the FDA reported that Rogaine resulted in "meaningful" hair growth in 25 percent of men and 20 percent of women.[10] "Meaningful" hair growth was defined by the FDA as "new individual hairs that covered some or all of the thinning areas but weren't as close together as hairs on the rest of the head." A larger percentage of users saw "minimal" hair growth in which "some new hairs were seen but not enough to cover thinning areas."

In clinical tests conducted by Pharmacia & Upjohn, Inc., 26 percent of mostly white men between the ages of 18 and 49 with moderate hair loss reported moderate to dense hair regrowth and 33 percent reported minimal regrowth after using Rogaine for four months.[11] By comparison, 11 percent of men in the 18 to 49 age group who used a placebo (a liquid without a 2-percent solution of minoxidil) reported moderate to dense hair regrowth while 31 percent reported minimal regrowth after four months of treatment. Clinical tests with mostly white women aged 18 to 45 with mild to mod-

---

[9]"Upjohn's Rogaine Fails to Win Vote of FDA Panel in Nonprescription Bid," *Wall Street Journal* (July 28, 1994), p. A2.

[10]Laurie McGinley, "Baldness Drug Cleared for Sale Over Counter," *Wall Street Journal* (February 13, 1996), p. B3.

[11] Based on Rogaine product literature prepared by Pharmacia & Upjohn, Inc.

erate hair loss yielded different results. In these tests, 19 percent of women reported moderate hair regrowth and 40 percent reported minimal regrowth after using Rogaine for eight months. In a control group which received a placebo, 7 percent of women reported moderate regrowth and 33 percent had minimal regrowth after eight months of use.

According to a Rogaine marketing executive: "We have been very clear about what the drug delivers, that this is not a quick-fix product, that it needs the commitment to be used twice a day, every day, and it's a drug that must be used for four to six months—and for some individuals for up to a year before any results are seen."[12] Furthermore, Rogaine treated only male pattern baldness. This condition accounts for 95 percent of all hair loss cases among men and women in the United States. In addition, the drug is most likely to regrow hair on top of the head or crown, not on a receding frontal hairline.

■ PHARMACIA & UPJOHN, INC.

Pharmacia & Upjohn, Inc. was created with the merger of Pharmacia AB of Sweden and The Upjohn Company of the United States in November 1995.[13] The merger resulted in the new company becoming the world's ninth largest pharmaceutical firm. Pharmacia & Upjohn, Inc. reported net sales of $6.949 billion and net earnings of $924 million (excluding charges related to the merger) for the year ending December 31, 1995.

Pharmacia & Upjohn, Inc. is a provider of human health care products and related businesses, and operates on a global scale. Its corporate management center is located in London, England, with major research and manufacturing centers in the United States, Sweden, and Italy. Pharmaceutical products account for 90 percent of company sales; diagnostic and biotech/biosensor products produce 10 percent of company sales. Almost 70 percent of company sales are made outside of the United States.

The company's ongoing research and development effort, supported by a $1 billion annual budget, focused on developing new products and line extensions. In 1995, the company had 25 new products or line extensions expected to be submitted for regulatory approvals in the 1995–1997 period.

Human Health Care Business

With the merger, Pharmacia & Upjohn, Inc. announced its commitment to achieving and maintaining leading positions in a number of therapeutic areas. The largest of these were oncology, metabolic diseases, critical care, infectious diseases, central nervous system/neurology, women's health, and nutrition. Exhibit 4 on page 528 shows the company's net sales by major therapeutic group for 1994 and 1995.

Prescription Pharmaceutical Sales   About 84 percent of company pharmaceutical sales are for prescription products. These products are marketed directly to health care providers worldwide by technically trained representatives who call on physicians, pharmacists, hospital personnel, health maintenance organizations (HMOs) and other managed health care organizations and wholesale drug outlets. Product advertising literature and sales efforts for prescription pharmaceuticals are directed

---

[12] "Rogaine: Promises, Promises, Promises," *Advertising Age* (October 3, 1993), p. S14.

[13] This company overview is based on *The Upjohn Company Annual Report: 1994* and *Pharmacia & Upjohn, Inc. Annual Report 1995*.

EXHIBIT 4

Pharmacia & Upjohn, Inc. Year-to-Year Comparison of Consolidated Net Sales by Major Therapeutic Product Groups (U.S. $ in Millions)

Product Grouping	1995 Sales	% Change	1994 Sales
Infectious disease	$ 687.1	10.3%	$ 622.9
Metabolic disease	635.9	(2.1)	649.4
Critical care and thrombosis	579.7	12.8	514.1
Central nervous system	571.8	.3	570.3
Oncology	566.2	6.7	530.6
Women's health	541.2	6.1	509.9
Nutrition	399.0	8.1	369.0
Ophthalmology	296.0	5.3	281.0
Other prescription pharmaceuticals	957.7	(12.8)	1,098.1
Consumer health care	441.5	(2.1)	451.2
Animal health	383.1	14.0	336.2
Chemical and contract manufacturing	199.9	17.1	170.7
Total pharmaceuticals	6,259.1	2.6	6,103.4
Biotech/Biosensor	437.0	13.5	385.0
Diagnostics	253.0	17.1	216.0
Consolidated net sales	$6,949.1	3.6%	$6,704.4

Source: Pharmacia & Upjohn, Inc. Annual Report: 1995, p. 37.

mostly toward health care professionals. This practice is necessary because of long-standing FDA regulations that require virtually all prescription drug advertising to list all product use side effects and contraindications. Complete disclosure of such information for the great majority of prescription pharmaceutical products was often cost prohibitive for television and print advertisements directed at consumers due to time and space requirements and technical language.

In 1995, sales of infectious disease products were led by the Cleocin (Dalacin outside the United States) family of antibiotic products. Sales of metabolic disease products were led by Genotropin, a growth hormone. Critical care and thrombosis product sales were led by Solu-Medrol, an injectable steroid, and other Medrol products. Sales of central nervous system agents were led by Xanax, an anti-anxiety agent; Halcion, a sleep-inducing agent; and Sermion for senile dementia. Farmorubicin, which treats solid tumors and leukemias, and Adriamycin, a cancer drug, led sales of oncology products. Sales in the women's health product category were led by Depo-Provera, an injectable contraceptive. Sales of nutrition products were led by the non-U.S. sales of Intralipid, a fat emulsion for intravenous nutrient delivery, while Healon, for cataract surgery, led sales of ophthalmology products.

Nonprescription Pharmaceutical Sales Pharmacia & Upjohn, Inc. also manufactures and distributes many other familiar products which do not require a prescription, including Motrin IB tablets and caplets, used as an analgesic; Kaopectate products, for diarrhea; Cortaid products, which are anti-inflammatory topical products containing hydrocortisone; the family of Unicap vitamin products; Dramamine products which are anti–motion sickness medicines; Mycitracin, an antibiotic ointment for treatment of minor skin infections and burns; and nonprescription laxative products, Doxidan and Surfak. The company also manufactures Nicorette Gum, a smoking cessation product, which is marketed under a license to SmithKline Beecham.

Competition in the human health care business is intense. There are at least 50 competitors in the United States that market prescription and nonprescription pharmaceutical products. Companies compete on the basis of product development and their effectiveness in introducing new or improved products for the treatment and prevention of disease. Other competitive features include product quality, pricing to and through marketing channels, and the dissemination of technical information and medical support advice to health care professionals. Advertising and sales promotions directed at consumers and trade promotions provided to retailers are important in marketing nonprescription pharmaceutical products. For this reason, these products are often referred to as "advertised remedies."

Development of Rogaine Hair Regrowth Treatment[14]

The development of Rogaine can be traced to the mid-1960s, when researchers at The Upjohn Company observed that a drug, originally thought to be a possible antacid agent, lowered the blood pressure in laboratory animals. Subsequent research produced a drug, given the generic name minoxidil, which proved to be a potent agent for lowering high blood pressure in humans. Assigned the trade name Loniten, the drug was given FDA approval for marketing in 1979.

Clinical research on minoxidil as an antihypertensive drug led to an unexpected discovery in 1971 when investigators noticed unusual hair growth in some patients who were taking minoxidil orally. Then, in 1973, a patient taking minoxidil for hypertension began to grow hair on a previously bald spot on his head. Additional clinical trials of minoxidil and related studies were conducted between 1977 and 1982 with more than 4,000 patients. The primary clinical study at 27 different testing sites tracked 2,326 patients who were nearly all white men in good health, aged 18 to 49 and diagnosed as exhibiting a moderate degree of hair loss. This study concluded that a 2-percent minoxidil solution applied twice daily to the head offered the best safety and effectiveness profile for this group. The safety and effectiveness of this solution for people under 18 was not tested (Rogaine is not recommended for persons under 18 years of age). Some side effects of the drug included itching and skin irritation to the treated areas of the scalp. In terms of effectiveness, 48 percent of the patients said they had achieved moderate to dense hair growth after one year of use. Investigators at the time judged that 39 percent of the patients achieved moderate to dense hair growth after one year of use. These data were submitted to the FDA in 1985. The FDA approved the 39 percent moderate to dense hair growth claim. In 1986, The Upjohn Company began selling the 2-percent minoxidil solution outside the United States under the trade name Regaine. However, more stringent and time-consuming review procedures by the FDA slowed the approval process in the United States.

Continued study on minoxidil led company researchers to draw two basic conclusions:

> First, it was clear after four months that topical minoxidil could grow hair on some scalps. Second, efficacy seemed to be related in many cases to the age of the patient, the extent of his baldness and how long he had been bald. Younger men who were not as far into the balding process seemed to respond better to the drug. There are exceptions to this finding, however, and the correlation of age to efficacy has not been scientifically established.[15]

---

[14] This description is based on *The Upjohn Company Annual Report: 1988,* pp. 10–11; Steven W. Quickel, "Bald Spot," *Business Month* (November 1989), pp. 36–43; "Baldness: Is There Hope?" *Consumer Reports* (September 1988), pp. 533–547.

[15] *The Upjohn Company Annual Report: 1988,* p. 11.

In 1987, the Company established the Hairgrowth Research Unit to determine the mechanism of action of minoxidil, develop new and better minoxidil analogs, and investigate other agents that affect hair growth or loss. At the time, researchers could only theorize why minoxidil stimulated hair growth in some patients. According to the company's director of dermatology:

> The most plausible theory is that minoxidil somehow stimulates the matrix cell of the hair follicle to regrow when it is destined to turn off. It's an overcoming of the genetic propensity to shut down. But we don't know how minoxidil modifies the metabolic activity of that cell.[16]

Two noteworthy developments occurred in 1988. First, an eight-month clinical study on Rogaine use for female hair loss was completed. The study was submitted to the FDA and ultimately led to agency approval to market the minoxidil solution to women in August 1991. Pregnant women and nursing mothers were advised not to use Rogaine, however. Second, in August 1988, the FDA granted approval to market the solution to men in the United States. However, the Regaine name was replaced with the Rogaine name because an FDA official believed the Regaine name suggested that the minoxidil solution would result in complete hair growth. During this time, minoxidil had received considerable publicity in the consumer and marketing media and in the financial community as a miracle cure for baldness. For example, Wall Street financial analysts believed Rogaine's ability to reverse male pattern baldness in men would rapidly produce $400 to $500 million in annual sales.[17]

■ PRESCRIPTION DRUG MARKETING PROGRAM FOR ROGAINE HAIR REGROWTH TREATMENT

The initial marketing plan for prescription Rogaine for men in the United States was developed concurrently with the FDA approval process. The announced marketing objective for Rogaine was "to maximize sales of Rogaine in the new U.S. market."[18] Since Rogaine had FDA approval as a prescription drug, Upjohn's initial attention was placed on educating the members of its sales force who called on physicians, dermatologists, and other health care professionals. Rogaine was introduced to the medical community by its sales force and through advertisements in medical journals and periodicals. A company spokesperson said, "We couldn't begin marketing Rogaine to consumers until we felt the awareness level was adequate in the medical community."[19]

[16]"Baldness: Is There Hope?" *Consumer Reports* (September 1988), p. 544.

[17] "The Hottest Products: Baldness Treatment," *ADWEEK* (November 7, 1988), p. 6; "For Rogaine, No Miracle Cure—Yet," *Business Week* (June 4, 1990), p. 100. The Upjohn Company neither confirmed nor denied these sales projections.

[18] The Upjohn Company, annual report, 1988, p. 11. The following material is based on Stuart Elliott, "Upjohn Turns to Women to Increase Rogaine Sales," *Advertising Age* (January 2, 1992), p. 4; "Rogaine for Women Gets $20M in Support," *Advertising Age* (January 6, 1992), p. 1; "New Hope for the Hair-Impaired," *Business Week* (June 4, 1990), p. 100; "Britain Approves Upjohn Hair Drug," *New York Times* (April 6, 1990), p. 4; Laurie Freeman, "Can Rogaine Make Gains Via Ads?" *Advertising Age* (September 11, 1989), p. 4; Laurie Freeman, "Can Rogaine Make Gains Via Ads?" *Advertising Age* (September 11, 1989), p. 12; Stephen W. Quickel, "Bald Spot," *Business Month* (November 1989), pp. 36–37ff; Laurie Freeman, "Upjohn Takes a Shine to Balding Women," *Advertising Age* (February 27, 1989), p. S1; Patricia Winters and Laurie Freeman, "Nicorette, Rogaine Seek TV OK," *Advertising Age* (November 27, 1989), p. 31; "Minoxidil," *Vogue* (September 1989), p. 56; "Hair Today: Rogaine's Growing Pains," *New York* (October 30, 1990), p. 20; "Blondes, Brunettes, Redheads, and Rogaine," *American Druggist* (June 1992), pp. 39–40.

[19] Steven W. Quickel, "Bald Spot," *Business Month* (November 1989), p. 40.

Consumer Advertising Program

Consumer advertising for Rogaine, targeted at 25- to 49-year-old males, began in November 1988 (see Exhibit 5 on page 532 for an age and income summary for U.S. males and females). This start date, two months earlier than planned, was prompted by slow prescription sales due to low trial. The television campaign began on November 23, 1988. The print campaign featured advertisements in popular consumer magazines and newsstand business publications.

Television and print advertising messages emphasized a soft-sell that urged consumers to "see your doctor . . . if you're concerned about hair loss." These advertisements contained no mention of Rogaine since federal regulations at the time prohibited the use of brand names in prescription-drug advertising to consumers. However, The Upjohn Company name appeared in the advertisements. With a U.S. sales rate of $4 million per month for the first quarter of 1989, a decision was made to revamp the advertising campaign. The new campaign featured a bald man standing before his bathroom mirror. Like the earlier messages, viewers were again urged to see their doctor. Sales in the U.S. improved, reaching $70 million for 1989. A third advertising campaign was developed and launched in February 1990 with print advertisements featuring the Rogaine name for the first time with FDA approval. Advertisement copy emphasized that Rogaine was the only FDA-approved product for hair growth with the headline: "The good news is there's only one product that's proven to grow hair . . . Rogaine." Companion television advertising, however, did not mention Rogaine. Rogaine U.S. sales in 1990 totaled $95 million. This campaign continued in 1991; however, the Rogaine name now appeared in television advertisements with FDA approval. Year-end Rogaine sales totaled $103 million in 1991. Industry sources estimated that the amount spent on consumer-measured media advertising for Rogaine was $4,914,500 in 1989, $9,347,500 in 1990, and $3,443,000 in 1991.[20]

Price–Sales Promotion Program

A one-year supply of Rogaine could cost a user between $600 and $720 depending on pharmacist margins.[21] The total out-of-pocket cost to patients, including periodic physician office fees, could be as high as $800 to $900 per year, since patients were advised to visit their physicians twice per year after the initial consultation.

A variety of price incentives and sales promotion activities were also implemented to stimulate physician visits. For instance, rebates were offered to people who received a Rogaine prescription from their physician. The patient would either get a certificate worth $10 toward the purchase of the first bottle of Rogaine, or $20 for sending in the box tops from the first four bottles used. Selected barbershops and salons were also provided information packets to be given to customers worried about hair loss, including 150,000 copies of informational videos. Consumer advertising also included an 800 number to call to receive information about the product. By 1991, some one million calls had been made to The Upjohn Company. It has been estimated that The Upjohn Company spent between $40 and $50 million annually to market prescription Rogaine since its introduction through 1991. This cost included professional and consumer advertising, the price–sales promotion program, and selling expenses.

---

[20] *Measured media* refers to newspapers, consumer magazines and Sunday magazines, outdoor billboards, network, spot, syndicated and cable television, and network and spot radio. *Unmeasured media* include direct mail, co-op advertising, couponing, catalogs, and business publications.

[21] Although pharmacy margins varied, pharmacists typically obtained a gross profit margin of 10 percent based on the selling price to the consumer, based on "Blondes, Brunettes, Redheads, and Rogaine," *American Druggist* (June 1992), p. 40.

EXHIBIT 5

Age and Income of Persons in the United States

Age Category	Persons (millions)	Percent Distribution by Income Level							
		Less than $2,500	$2,500–$4,999	$5,000–$9,999	$10,000–$14,999	$15,000–$24,999	$25,000–$49,999	$50,000–$74,999	$75,000 or more
Males									
15–24	17.4	28.1	15.1	22.0	14.9	14.8	4.9	.3	—
25–34	21.3	3.1	3.7	10.0	13.8	28.6	34.4	4.7	1.7
35–44	19.0	2.6	2.8	6.5	8.3	20.1	41.8	11.8	6.0
45–54	12.4	3.0	2.4	6.3	8.5	18.4	39.3	13.9	8.1
55–64	10.2	3.1	4.1	10.8	11.2	21.1	33.1	10.1	6.4
65 and over	12.5	1.9	5.8	24.7	20.9	24.2	16.0	3.9	2.6
Total males	92.8								
Females									
15–24	17.5	31.0	19.7	22.8	13.1	10.5	2.7	.1	—
25–34	21.6	15.7	8.8	16.5	15.3	25.0	17.2	1.2	.4
35–44	19.6	14.9	7.6	14.8	13.8	23.0	22.2	2.7	1.0
45–54	13.3	14.7	7.9	15.3	14.2	21.7	22.2	3.0	1.0
55–64	11.2	17.0	14.8	20.4	14.5	17.0	13.0	2.5	.8
65 and over	17.5	5.0	19.4	37.0	16.7	13.8	6.8	.9	.5
Total females	100.7								

Source: U.S. Bureau of the Census, Current Population Reports.

In September 1991, the price–sales promotion program for Rogaine was the subject of a day-long Congressional hearing in Washington, D.C.[22] Several members of Congress expressed criticism of the practice of using consumer rebates and cash incentives to market a prescription drug. An FDA official said, "We are concerned about this kind of tactic." Commenting on prescription drug consumer advertising in general, FDA Commissioner Dr. David Kessler commented, "We believe the public, in general, is not well-served by ads for prescription drugs." An FDA spokesperson later said the agency ". . . will let [the current Rogaine campaign] continue as it is, though we are not going to tip our hand as to what might happen in the future."

Even though the FDA and some physicians did not favor prescription drug advertising, consumer response to prescription drug advertising was generally favorable. A survey of 2,000 adult U.S. consumers reported that 40 percent said they had talked to a physician because of an advertisement they had seen, 72 percent of consumers in the survey said the advertising was an educational tool, and 71 percent thought prescription drug advertising was worthwhile.[23]

Rogaine for Women[24]

FDA approval for Rogaine use by women was granted in August 1991 and the advertising and promotion program directed at women began in February 1992. The female-market entry plan mirrored the marketing program for males, including the same price and reference to the Rogaine name in advertisements. Extensive use of consumer print advertising appeared in *Cosmopolitan, People, US, Vogue*, and *Woman's Day*, as well as other magazines. The advertising copy for Rogaine advertising directed toward women differed from that used for men, however, because the topic of hair loss was discussed among men, but less often among women. According to an Upjohn Company official, women who suffer from hair loss "feel very much alone because no one talks about it."[25] This view materialized in the message conveyed in Rogaine print advertisements for women. For example, a woman in a Rogaine print advertisement said: "Finally I can do a lot more about my hair loss than just sit back and take it." The advertisement concluded by saying: "Take the control you've always wanted, and do it now." Television commercials also appeared in major U.S. metropolitan markets during daytime, early evening, and weekend programs on local stations and cable networks. In the television commercials, a woman portraying a news reporter says: "On this job, you cannot do a story until you get the facts. So when I heard about Rogaine with minoxidil, I wanted to get all the facts for myself."

The price–sales promotion program included a $10 incentive to visit a physician or dermatologist and an 800 number to call to receive an informational brochure about the product. Brochures were made available at drugstores and doctors' offices. An extensive professional effort evident in journal advertising, direct mail, and sales-staff support launched the product, including new print and video materials for pharmacists. The total marketing budget (including advertising) for the female market launch in 1992 was reported to be $20 million. U.S. sales of Rogaine in 1992 rose to

---

[22] Steven W. Colford and Pat Sloan, "Feds Take Aim at Rogaine Ads," *Advertising Age* (September 16, 1991), p. 47.

[23] "Upswing Seen in R$_X$ Drug Ads Aimed Directly At Consumer," *American Medical News* (June 1, 1990), pp. 13, 15.

[24] This discussion is based on "Blondes, Brunettes, Redheads, and Rogaine," *American Druggist* (June 1992), pp. 39–40; Steven W. Colford and Pat Sloan, "Feds Take Aim at Rogaine Ads," *Advertising Age* (September 16, 1991), p. 47; Stuart Elliott, "Upjohn Turns to Women to Increase Rogaine Sales," *Advertising Age* (January 2, 1992), p. 4.

[25] Stuart Elliott, "Upjohn Turns to Women to Increase Rogaine Sales," *Advertising Age* (January 2, 1992), p. 4.

$122 million due to the expanded customer base for the product. Total consumer advertising for Rogaine was $12,569,600 in 1992 according to industry sources.

Rogaine was marketed to both women and men as a prescription drug through 1995.[26] Two additional advertising campaigns directed at women appeared during this period and a new advertising campaign for men was launched. Advertising expenditures also increased. According to a company spokesperson, aggressive advertising that urged consumers to initiate a dialogue about hair loss with their physician was essential to maintaining sales of Rogaine. The spokesperson said: "A lot of physicians won't bring up the subject of hair loss in front of a patient."[27] Advertising in measured media was $34,579,800 in 1993, $32,404,000 in 1994, and $40 million in 1995 according to industry sources. With over $21 million spent on cable television alone in 1995, Rogaine was ranked as the fifth most-advertised brand in this medium in the United States. In addition, the company created the first-ever infomercial for a prescription drug in 1995. The 30-minute infomercial was targeted toward women and hosted by actress Cindy Williams, who interviewed a licensed dermatologist, a hair designer and stylist, and a company marketing executive. The company also established a World Wide Web site for the product, which was another industry first.

During this three-year period, company attention also was placed on building a Rogaine prospect and user database to support a relationship marketing program. This program proved to be useful for targeting prospects and users for direct mail and telemarketing. A result of this effort was that people who started the Rogaine treatment tended to stay with it for a longer period of time. Also, Rogaine's price-sales promotion program continued. Rogaine sales in the United States declined to $84 million in 1993, then rose and plateaued at $96 million in 1994 and 1995.

Product and Market Development

The company continued its product and market development efforts on Rogaine since its introduction in 1988. For example, a different concentration of minoxidil had been examined which would require only one application per day rather than two. This development could improve the product's convenience of use because, as one former company executive conceded, "It's hard to use something twice a day, come hell or high water."[28] Also, an easier-to-use gel was introduced to Europe. In early 1989, the nonprescription Progaine hair-thickener shampoo product line was introduced for use by men and women. These products did not promote hair growth, but served as a treatment for thinning hair. It was believed these products would benefit from the sound-alike name and be considered a companion to Rogaine. In December 1995, the company submitted a new drug application to the FDA for a Rogaine 5-percent minoxidil formulation to treat common hair loss. Marketing clearance for this prescription-only hair regrowth treatment was expected in late 1996.

Market development on a global scale also continued. By April 1996, Rogaine (Regaine in non-U.S. markets) was marketed in more than 80 countries and more than 3 million people had used the product. FDA approval of nonprescription Rogaine meant that the product was approved for sale without a prescription in 13 countries,

---

[26] This discussion is based on Emily DeNitto, "Rogaine Raises Women's Interest," *Advertising Age* (February 28, 1994), p. 12; "Rogaine: Promises, Promises, Promises," *Advertising Age* (October 3, 1993), p. S14; Emily DeNitto, "Rogaine Fashions New Ads for Women," *Advertising Age* (February 28, 1994), p. 12; Jeffrey D. Zbar, "Upjohn Database Rallies Rogaine," *Advertising Age* (January 23, 1995), p. 42; Joshua Levine, "Scalped," *Forbes* (November 6, 1995), p. 128; "Rogaine Opens New Category for Infomercials: Pharmaceuticals," *Advertising Age* (March 11, 1996), p. 10A; "Top 80 Brands on Cable TV," *Advertising Age* (March 25, 1996), p. 34.

[27] Yumiko Ono, "Prescription-Drug Makers Heighten Hard-Sell Tactics," *Wall Street Journal* (August 29, 1994), pp. B1, B7.

[28] "For Rogaine, No Miracle Cure—Yet," *Business Week* (June 4, 1990), p. 100.

including Denmark, the Netherlands, New Zealand, Spain, the United Kingdom, and the United States. Rogaine (Regaine) sales outside the U.S. were $30 million in 1995 in the face of competition from generic brands and substitute products in non-U.S. markets.

■ OVER-THE-COUNTER MARKETING PROGRAM FOR ROGAINE HAIR REGROWTH TREATMENT

The nonprescription drug marketing plan for Rogaine called for the prescription drug marketing program to be phased out by April 1996. Production, distribution, advertising, and promotion for prescription Rogaine had stopped by April 3, 1996.

Marketing Program for Nonprescription Rogaine

The marketing program planning process for nonprescription Rogaine had begun in late 1995. Its mission was to create a new product category called the "hair regrowth category." The reported expenditure for the marketing program was $75 million. More than half of this amount would be designated for consumer advertising to create awareness and trial of the product. Principal elements of the program are outlined below.[29]

Rogaine Targeting, Product Positioning, and Packaging Like the prescription drug marketing program, the target market for Rogaine would be men and women aged 25 to 49. Rogaine would be positioned as the only product medically proven to regrow hair.

Separate packaging for men and women would be prepared even though the product was identical. Rogaine For Men would be packaged in a light blue carton. Rogaine For Women would be packaged in a salmon-pink carton. Each carton would contain a brochure with gender-based instructions for use and address possible consumer questions. Single-packs with one 60-milliliter Rogaine bottle, twin-packs with two bottles, and triple-packs with three bottles would be sold. One bottle contained sufficient solution for one month's use. The bottles would be tamper-evident and child-resistant. Rogaine For Men would come with dropper and sprayer applicators. Rogaine For Women would have an extended sprayer for ease of application with longer hair.

Rogaine Advertising and Promotion A multipronged advertising and promotion program was designed for Rogaine. The advertising objectives for Rogaine were to raise consumer awareness of the brand's recently approved nonprescription status, encourage product trial, and communicate user expectations. Initially, one new 30-second television advertisement for Rogaine For Men and one 30-second television advertisement for Rogaine for Women would be created. According to a company spokesperson, "Men and women experience the physical and psychological effects of hair loss differently. Also, men and women respond differently to Rogaine. So Rogaine advertising, like Rogaine packaging, will address the gender-specific concerns of Rogaine users."[30] The brand manager for Rogaine added that advertising will take an educational slant, emphasizing the fact that "this is the only product medically proven to regrow hair."[31] The Rogaine For Men television commercial would air during evening

---

[29] This discussion is based on "Rogaine Will Be Sold Over-the-Counter," *PR Newswire* (February 12, 1996); "OTC Rogaine Introduced," *PR Newswire* (April 8, 1996); "New Rogaine TV Commercials Begin," *PR Newswire* (April 22, 1996); Sean Mehegan, "Hair Today," *BRANDWEEK* (April 8, 1996), pp. 1, 6; Sean Mehegan, "Rogaine/Progaine," *MEDIAWEEK* (April 8, 1996), p. 38; Michael Wilkie, "New Rivals Push Rogaine to Jumpstart Its OTC Ads," *Advertising Age* (April 15, 1996), p. 45.

[30] "New Rogaine TV Commercials Begin," *PR Newswire* (April 22, 1996).

[31] Sean Mehegan, "Hair Today," *BRANDWEEK* (April 8, 1996), p. 6.

prime time, sports, cable sports, late-night, and syndicated programs. The Rogaine For Women television commercial would air during evening prime time and day schedules on network, cable, and syndicated programs.

The planned media schedule for Rogaine was designed so that 92 percent of the target market would see Rogaine television advertisements seven times in a four-week period following the brand's introduction as a nonprescription drug. Print advertisements were scheduled to reach 77 percent of the target audience. The advertising agency executive responsible for Rogaine said, "If there still are consumers who don't know about Rogaine, how to apply it, how it works, and the fact that it is available without a prescription, this new ad campaign will take care of that."[32]

The advertising program for Rogaine would be complemented by an extensive consumer and trade promotion campaign. An estimated 40,000 physicians would receive a mailing announcing Rogaine's nonprescription status. More than 20,000 pharmacists would be mailed a Rogaine Pharmacy Kit. Items in the kit would include an educational brochure and video for pharmacists, consumer education brochures, and an announcement easel for the pharmacy counter. Free-standing inserts (FSIs), in-store circular ads, and coupons would comprise the consumer promotion program.

Direct marketing efforts would be employed with the objective of encouraging product compliance and repeat usage, and to reinforce user expectations. Planned periodic mailings to users would include money-saving coupons, a newsletter with hair care and styling suggestions, and comments from users, dermatologists, and other authorities. Consumers could join the direct marketing program by returning an enrollment card from the Rogaine package or by calling a Rogaine toll-free number.

Rogaine Distribution and Pricing   Planned distribution for Rogaine would include pharmacy or hair care sections of food, drug, and mass-merchandise retail outlets. This placement was based on Pharmacia & Upjohn, Inc. marketing research which indicated that consumers would look for and expect to find Rogaine in these sections.

Nonprescription Rogaine would be priced at about one-half of prescription Rogaine. A single-pack suggested retail price for Rogaine would be $29.50. Twin-packs would be priced at $55.00 and triple-packs would be available in some stores with a suggested retail price of $75.00. The retailer margin on Rogaine would be about 20 percent of the suggested retail price. Commenting on the expanded distribution and pricing, a senior company executive said: "The availability of OTC Rogaine is welcome news for the millions of men and women in this country who experience common hereditary hair loss. Instead of going to a doctor's office, they can simply walk into a food store, drug store, or mass merchandiser outlet and purchase Rogaine without a prescription at its full prescription strength. It's much more convenient and because the price is now lower, it's much more affordable."[33]

Hair Regrowth Category Development: Rogaine and Progaine

The launch of nonprescription Rogaine focused on creating a brand with $250 million-a-year in retail sales at the suggested retail prices in what Pharmacia & Upjohn, Inc. officials coined as the "hair regrowth category" of products. In this regard, the concurrent relaunch of Progaine shampoo represented an effort to synergize the Rogaine/Progaine brand names into a system of hair care. The Progaine relaunch involved a package redesign and a new formula with added proteins, conditioners, and hair-thickening agents. To bolster the linkage between Rogaine and Progaine,

---

[32]"New Rogaine TV Commercials Begin," *PR Newswire* (April 22, 1996).

[33]"OTC Rogaine Introduced," *PR Newswire* (April 8, 1996).

coupons for Progaine would be inserted in Rogaine cartons. The two products also would be located side-by-side in the hair-care aisle in retail stores. Progaine retail shampoo sales in 1995 were about $2 million. Total U.S. retail sales of shampoos in 1995 approached $1.5 billion.[34]

■ APRIL 30, 1996: THE FEDERAL DISTRICT COURT RULING

On April 30, 1996 the Federal District Court ruled in favor of the FDA.[35] This meant that Rogaine would not have a three-year marketing exclusivity and three competing generic products had approval for sale without a prescription in the United States.

This development raised a variety of issues related to the marketing opportunity for FDA-approved nonprescription hair regrowth products containing a 2-percent minoxidil solution, and the Rogaine brand in particular. For example, how might the unit and dollar sales potential of the hair regrowth category be affected? Pharmacia & Upjohn, Inc. believed sales of $1 billion were possible over five years for Rogaine when it was the only hair regrowth product containing a 2-percent minoxidil solution. Might this sales figure for the category as a whole need revision and by how much? A useful starting point might be to revisit the sales history of prescription Rogaine. This would involve simulating the trial and repeat purchase patterns for prescription Rogaine and determining how these patterns might have contributed to sales growth.

Relatedly, the absence of marketing exclusivity and the presence of generic products changed the competitive landscape for Rogaine. No longer would Rogaine hold a monopoly position as the sole supplier of a hair regrowth product with a 2-percent minoxidil solution. Rather, prospective users of this product could now try a competitive product and current Rogaine users could switch to another product. The effect on Rogaine sales required further attention.

Nonprescription hair regrowth product category sales and Rogaine's share of these sales would depend, in large measure, on the marketing program for nonprescription Rogaine. Developed in anticipation of a favorable FDA response to its petition for a three-year marketing exclusivity, this program was being currently executed. At issue at this time was how the marketing plan should be modified, if at all.

---

[34] Pat Sloan, "Brand Scorecard: Premium Products Lather Up Sales," *Advertising Age* (July 24, 1995), p. 24.

[35] "Court Allows Sale of Generic Forms of Rogaine," *New York Times* (May 1, 1996), p. 40.

The Circle K Corporation

The Circle K Corporation is one of the leading specialty retailers in the United States and is the nation's second largest operator and franchiser of convenience stores. From fiscal 1984 (year-end April 30), when it embarked on a significant growth strategy, to fiscal 1990, the company acquired 3,326 stores and built another 983 stores while closing 899 units. During this period, sales increased from $1 billion in fiscal 1984 to almost $3.7 billion in fiscal 1990.

On May 15, 1990, the company and its principal subsidiaries filed for protection under Chapter 11 of the United States Bankruptcy Code. This action was taken because of the company's deteriorating financial condition, due in part to increased competition, a heavy debt burden from the expansion program, and the negative effect of merchandise and price policies instituted in 1989. Shortly after the bankruptcy filing, Circle K president Robert A. Dearth, Jr., announced that he was determined to reposition the company so that it could return to profitability and pay its debt in fiscal 1991.[1] Key elements of the plan to revitalize Circle K included a change in merchandising practices, increased promotional efforts, and an aggressive pricing program, all of which were designed to improve customer service and increase sales. In addition, opportunities to close or sell unprofitable stores would be pursued. Circle K's planned turnaround strategy was scheduled for implementation in the summer of 1990. Of critical concern to Circle K management was consumer and competitive response and the profitability of the announced strategy.

■ THE COMPANY

The Circle K Corporation, which is headquartered in Phoenix, Arizona, is the 30th largest retailer in the United States according to *Fortune* magazine. The company's convenience store business was begun by Circle K Convenience Stores, Inc. in 1951. In 1980, this company became a subsidiary of the Circle K Corporation. The Circle K Corporation is a holding company, which, through wholly owned subsidiaries, operates 4,631 convenience stores in the United States and related facilities. In addition, the Circle K Corporation has approximately 1,400 licensed or joint-venture stores in 13 foreign countries.

Circle K recorded an average annual increase in sales of 25 percent since fiscal 1984. The number of stores operated by Circle K increased by 14 percent per year during the period 1984 through fiscal 1990. Most of the increase in stores came from acquisitions. In the four years prior to fiscal 1989, when Circle K incurred an operating loss

[1]"Circle K Squares Off with Its Creditors," *Wall Street Journal* (May 17, 1990): A4.

This case was prepared by Professor Roger A. Kerin, of the Edwin L. Cox School of Business, Southern Methodist University, as a basis for class discussion and is not designed to illustrate appropriate or inappropriate handling of administrative situations, or to be used for research purposes. The case is based on published sources, including the Circle K Corporation annual reports and 10-K Forms. The assistance of Angela Bullard and Deborah Ovitt, graduate students, in the preparation of this case is gratefully acknowledged. Copyright © 1995 by Roger A. Kerin. No part of this case may be reproduced without written permission of the copyright holder.

of $3.8 million, the company had recorded an average annual increase in operating profit of 25 percent. Exhibit 1 (below) and Exhibit 2 (on page 540) show the Circle K Corporation's consolidated financial statements for fiscal 1988 through fiscal 1990.

Stores and Unit Expansion

Circle K stores typically have 2,600 square feet of retail selling space. Most units are located on corner sites, have parking space on one or more sides, and are equipped with modern equipment, fixtures, and refrigeration. Nearly all the stores are open seven days a week, 24 hours a day. The 4,631 stores operated by Circle K are located in 32 states. However, about 84 percent of the stores are situated in Sun Belt states ranging from California to Florida. The primary concentration of stores is in Florida

EXHIBIT 1

The Circle K Corporation's Consolidated Statement of Earnings (Thousands of Dollars)

	For the Year Ending April 30		
	1990	1989	1988
Revenues:			
Sales	$3,686,314	$3,441,384	$2,613,843
Other	50,238	53,507	42,879
Gross revenues	3,736,552	3,494,891	2,656,722
Cost of sales and expenses:			
Cost of sales	2,796,559	2,580,398	1,893,058
Operating and administrative	865,602	729,306	561,894
Reorganization and restructuring charge[a]	639,310	—	—
Depreciation and amortization	127,652	93,033	65,659
Interest and debt expense	126,799	95,912	56,608
Total cost of sales and expenses	4,555,922	3,498,649	2,577,219
Operating profit (Loss)	(819,370)	(3,758)	79,503
Gain on sale of assets[b]	—	32,323	8,198
Equity loss on foreign joint ventures	(15,064)	(1,784)	—
Earnings (loss) before federal and state income taxes and cumulative effect of accounting change	(834,434)	26,781	87,701
Federal and state income tax (expense) benefit	61,565	(11,367)	(32,790)
Net earnings (loss) before cumulative effect of accounting change	(772,869)	15,414	54,911
Cumulative effect on prior years of change in accounting for income taxes	—	—	5,500
Net earnings (Loss)	($ 772,869)	$ 15,414	$ 60,411

[a]The company had been attempting a financial restructuring since October 1989. A review and assessment of operations by the Board of Directors resulted in a reorganization and restructuring charge of $639.3 million as of April 30, 1990. The charge includes (1) excess costs over acquired net assets and foreign investment; (2) abandonment, rejection, and reserves for fixed assets in nonperforming leased stores; (3) write-downs of real estate and other projects no longer under development, and (4) debt issuance and other costs.

[b]On October 31, 1988, the company sold all of its assets in connection with its manufacturing and distribution of fragmentary and block ice, sandwiches, and other fast foods. On October 27, 1987, the company sold a 50 percent interest in its wholly owned United Kingdom subsidiary.

Source: The Circle K Corporation, Form 10-K. Fiscal Year Ended April 30, 1990; The Circle K Corporation 1989 annual report. The statement of earnings information is accompanied by extensive explanations, which are an integral part of these consolidated financial statements.

EXHIBIT 2

The Circle K Corporation's Consolidated Balance Sheet, Abridged (Thousands of Dollars)

	April 30, 1990	April 30, 1989	April 30, 1988
Current assets:			
Cash and short-term investments	$ 50,205	$ 38,488	$ 44,216
Receivables	38,138	36,265	34,446
Inventories	175,308	239,916	191,000
Other current assets	39,865	94,341	109,851
Total current assets	303,516	409,010	379,513
Property, plant, and equipment (less accumulated depreciation and amortization)	836,123	1,068,489	708,314
Other assets	134,651	567,441	447,957
Total assets	$1,274,290	$2,044,940	$1,535,784
Current liabilities:			
Due to banks	$ —	$ 91,000	$60,000
Accounts payable	112,111	134,944	112,144
Other current liabilities	101,504	124,501	108,463
Total current liabilities	213,615	350,445	280,607
Liabilities subject to compromise	1,206,395	—	—
Long-term debt	54,651	1,158,563	844,065
Deferred income taxes	40,496	93,045	38,133
Other liabilities	130,915	45,359	17,191
Deferred revenue	32,285	19,632	24,767
Mandatory redeemable preferred stock	42,500	47,500	47,500
Stockholders' equity	(451,567)	330,396	283,521
Total liabilities and stockholders' equity	$1,274,290	$2,044,940	$1,535,784

Source: The Circle K Corporation, Form 10-K, Fiscal Year Ended April 30, 1990; Circle K Corporation 1989 annual report. Balance sheet information is accompanied by extensive explanations, which are an integral part of these consolidated financial statements.

(846 stores), Texas (735 stores), Arizona (679 stores), California (604 stores), and Louisiana (301 stores).

The present complement of stores was an outgrowth of an aggressive acquisition program begun in December 1983 with the purchase of the nearly 1,000-store UToteM chain. This acquisition was followed in October 1984 with the purchase of Little General Stores, consisting of 435 units. In February 1985, Circle K bought 21 Day-n-Nite stores, and in September 1985, it acquired the 449-unit Stop & Go chain. The company purchased 189 units from National Convenience Stores in March 1987 and three months later bought 63 franchised 7-Eleven units from the Southland Corporation. In late 1987, Circle K's director of public relations announced that the company intended to have 5,000 stores by 1990.[2]

[2] "Mergers of Convenience," *Progressive Grocer* (December 1987): 50–51; "Karl Eller's Big Thirst for Convenience Stores," *Business Week* (June 13, 1988): 86, 88; Circle K Corporation 1990 10-K Form.

In April 1988, Circle K purchased the assets of 473 convenience stores, 90 closed stores, convenience store sites, stores under construction, and related facilities from the Southland Corporation. The company's last major acquisition occurred on September 30, 1988, with the purchase of the Charter Marketing Group. This transaction resulted in the addition of 538 gasoline and convenience stores. Circle K did not acquire any stores in fiscal 1990 because of its deteriorating financial condition, which led to the company's Chapter 11 bankruptcy filings. However, negotiations concerning the sale of 375 stores in Hawaii and the Pacific Northwest were initiated.

Product-Service Mix

Circle K stores sell over 3,800 different products and services. Food items include groceries, dairy products, candies, bakery items, produce, meat, eggs, ice cream, frozen foods, soft drinks, and alcoholic beverages (beer, wine, and liquor) where permitted. Fast food items, including fountain drinks, doughnuts, sandwiches, and coffee, are also sold. Non-food items sold by Circle K include tobacco products, health and beauty aids, magazines, books, newspapers, household goods, giftware, and toys. Food and nonfood merchandise categories accounted for 50 percent of company revenue in fiscal 1990.

Circle K sells gasoline at 77.5 percent of its stores. Gasoline accounted for 48.6 percent of company revenue in fiscal 1990. In addition, the company provides a variety of consumer services. Consumer services include money orders, lottery tickets, game machines, and video cassette rentals. These services combined with interest income and royalty and licensing fees accounted for the remainder of company revenue.

Circle K had followed a program of continual testing and introduction of new products and services designed to appeal to a broader customer base and stimulate store traffic. According to the company's chairman of the board, Karl Eller, "We're a massive distribution system. Whatever we can push through that store, we will."[3] The addition of automated teller machines (ATMs) or debit card programs at 1,146 stores and leased space at certain locations for Federal Express drop-off package service are recent innovations indicative of this strategy.

Efforts to sell and promote high-profit-margin products while cutting back on popular, though less profitable, merchandise proved costly for Circle K in the summer of 1989. While the gross profit margin for merchandise sales increased, dollar sales decreased (see Exhibit 3 on page 542, which details sales and gross margins for merchandise and gasoline). Traditional customers did not want these products, according to Dearth, the company's president. An integral part of his merchandising plan for fiscal 1991 included tailoring product and service offerings to the particular ethnic or socioeconomic character of each store's clientele.[4] National Convenience Stores, Inc., with its Stop & Go stores, has adopted a similar program, matching its merchandise with the demographics of surrounding neighborhoods. Early results from this merchandise program indicate that dollar sales will increase 4 to 5 percent.[5]

Advertising and Promotion Program

Circle K has historically used media advertising and special promotions to attract customers. In fiscal 1989, the company spent $4 million on advertising. This figure was down 41.2 percent from the fiscal 1988 advertising expenditures. For comparison, National Convenience Stores, Inc. (with 1,100 Stop & Go stores), spends about $12

---

[3] Lisa Gubernick, "Stores for Our Times," *Forbes* (November 3, 1986): 40–42.

[4] "Circle K Squares Off with Its Creditors," p. A4.

[5] "Convenience Chains Pump for New Life," *Advertising Age* (April 23, 1990): 80.

EXHIBIT 3

The Circle K Corporation's Merchandise and Gasoline Sales and Gross Profit Percentage, Fiscal Years 1988–1990

Revenue Source	1990		1989		1988	
	Sales (Millions)	Gross Profit (Percentage)	Sales (Millions)	Gross Profit (Percentage)	Sales (Millions)	Gross Profit (Percentage)
Merchandise	$1,869.4	37.2%	$1,962.4	36.0%	$1,649.2	37.5%
Gasoline	1,817.0	10.8	1,479.0	10.5	964.6	10.6
Other*	50.2		53.5		42.9	
Total	$3,736.6		$3,494.9		$2,656.7	

*Other revenues consist of commissions on game machines and lottery tickets, money order fees, interest income, royalty and licensing fees, and other items.

Source: The Circle K Corporation, 1990 10-K Form, pp. 30-31.

million annually on advertising. Advertising as a percent-of-sales for the convenience store industry as a whole was 0.6 percent in 1989 and 0.3 percent in 1988 and 1987.

Circle K curtailed advertising in late fiscal 1990. "Circle K is not advertising and has not been," the company's national advertising manager said in April 1990. "We're going through bad times."[6] The company's most recent promotion was a "price-buster" campaign in Florida and Arizona. This campaign came to an end in the second quarter of fiscal 1990.

More aggressive advertising and promotion efforts were the second part of the turnaround strategy planned by Circle K. The company announced that a $100 million promotion would be launched in the summer of 1990.[7] The eight-week promotion would be centered on a "We're Driving Down Prices" game, which included some 180 million instant-winner, scratch-off tickets distributed to customers who made purchases at over 3,700 Circle K stores. Game tickets would feature instant-win merchandise discounts, theme park discounts, and grand prizes such as Jeep Wranglers, round-trip Continental Airline tickets, and Bayliner Capri 17-foot speed-boats.

The game would be publicized by in-store window banners, ceiling danglers, and tent cards located near checkout counters. Outdoor signage near gasoline pumps was also planned. In addition, the promotion would be supported by radio and outdoor advertising. The objective of the promotion was to communicate a change in store prices by providing Circle K customers "more value for their dollar," according to a company press release.

This new promotional program planned for the summer of 1990 would compete directly against a similar initiative launched by 7-Eleven in April 1990.[8] 7-Eleven's program involved giving away six-ounce samples of coffee, fountain drinks, and Slurpees. The company was also giving away a coupon book, valued at $250, with discounts on 7-Eleven products as well as merchandise from Sears, Roebuck and Company, Radio Shack, and Children's Place. 7-Eleven was promoting its program through television and radio advertising.

---

[6] *Ibid.*

[7] "Circle K Unveils $100 Million Promotion," *Convenience Store News* (August 27–September 23, 1990): 12.

[8] "Convenience Chains Pump for New Life," p. 80.

Pricing Policy

The third leg in the Circle K strategy involved an overall price cut of 10 percent to be implemented concurrently with the $100 million promotion and the change in merchandising practices. "Before, we had the attitude of gouging the customer for what we could get," said Dearth.[9] Historically, Circle K was able to charge premium prices for food and nonfood items because of convenience of location, longer hours, accessibility, and fast service without long checkout lines. Promotional pricing of high-traffic items such as cigarettes, beer, bread, soft drinks, milk, and gasoline also was used periodically. These pricing practices had provided Circle K with the highest gross-profit-margin percentages in the convenience store industry. However, due to increased competitive pressures and rising costs during fiscal 1989, the company's gross-profit-margin percentage slipped to 25 percent for the first time since fiscal 1984. In addition, the Circle K Corporation incurred its first operating loss since its incorporation in 1980.

At the beginning of the 1990 fiscal year, Circle K boosted store merchandise prices by about 6 to 7 percent. According to industry analysts, store merchandise sales volume declined 8 to 10 percent. Gasoline sales volume dropped between 1 and 6 percent.[10] In February 1990, Circle K reversed the price increases. Merchandise dollar sales for Circle K in fiscal 1990 were 4.7 percent below fiscal 1989 levels, and company gross profit dropped 3.3 percent.

■ THE CONVENIENCE STORE INDUSTRY

The convenience store industry has been one of the fastest-growing sectors of retailing over the past 20 years. Since 1977, the number of convenience stores has grown at an average annual rate of 6.5 percent. Sales volume grew at an average annual rate of 17 percent. However, sales and store growth declined in the latter half of the 1980s. In 1989, the convenience store industry generated sales of $67.7 billion through an estimated 70,200 stores nationwide.

Convenience store industry profitability has fluctuated during the past five years. The industry gross profit margin fell to its lowest level in 1989 as a result of narrowing margins on store merchandise. The industry net profit margin before income taxes decreased in each of the past five years reaching a low of 0.4 percent in 1989. Rising costs of leasing, building, equipping, insuring, and operating stores coupled with financing costs attributed to store expansion contributed to this decline, according to industry analysts. A summary of industry sales, unit growth, and profitability is shown in Exhibit 4 on page 544.

Competitors

The convenience store industry is highly fragmented. In 1989, 1,353 companies were listed as belonging to the National Association of Convenience Stores. According to Alex Brown and Sons, Inc., an investment banking firm, about 42 percent of total stores and 31 percent of industry sales were accounted for by convenience store chains with fewer than 50 stores.[11] The largest single convenience store chain is the Southland Corporation (7-Eleven). The largest U.S. convenience store operators in terms of sales and units are listed in Exhibit 5 on page 545.

---

[9] "Circle K Squares Off with Its Creditors," p. A4.

[10] *Ibid.*

[11] *The Convenience Store Industry* (Baltimore: Alex Brown & Sons, 1988).

EXHIBIT 4

Convenience Store Industry Summary: 1980–1989

	Year									
	1980	*1981*	*1982*	*1983*	*1984*	*1985*	*1986*	*1987*	*1988*	*1989*
Sales, Including Gasoline										
Total sales (billions of dollars)	24.5	31.2	35.9	41.6	45.6	51.4	53.9	59.6	61.2	67.7
Year-to-year change (%)	31.0	27.3	15.1	15.9	9.6	12.7	4.9	10.5	2.7	10.6
Sales, Excluding Gasoline										
Sales (billions of dollars)	17.7	21.6	23.7	25.8	29.3	33.3	36.0	39.1	39.2	40.6
Year-to-year change (%)	22.9	22.0	15.7	8.9	13.6	13.3	8.4	8.6	—	3.6
Store Data										
Total number of stores (thousands)	44.1	47.9	51.2	54.4	58.0	61.0	64.0	67.5	69.2	70.2
Year-to-year change (%)	10.0	8.6	6.9	6.3	6.6	5.2	4.9	5.5	2.5	1.4
Sales per store (thousands of dollars) (excluding gas)	394.0	450.0	463.0	474.0	511.0	544.0	564.0	579.2	567.0	578.0
Year-to-year change (%)	11.0	14.2	2.9	2.4	7.8	6.5	3.7	2.7	2.1	1.9
Profitability Data										
Gross profit margin (%)										
Merchandise						32.5	35.5	35.9	36.4	32.1
Gasoline						7.3	11.2	10.6	11.5	11.7
Total						22.8	25.1	24.4	26.2	21.8
Net profit margin before income taxes (%)						2.7	2.6	2.2	1.9	.4

Source: Based on *The Convenience Store Industry* (Baltimore: Alex Brown & Sons, 1988): 3; *The State of the Convenience Store Industry 1990* (Alexandria, VA: National Association of Convenience Stores, 1990).

Convenience store executives believe that their principal competitors are other convenience store chains, gas stations that sell food (g-stores), supermarkets, and fast food outlets. S. R. "Dick" Dole, an executive at the Southland Corporation, believed that competition for convenience stores depends on the product category:

> If you're talking about post-mix, coffee, and sandwiches, then our competition is the "fast feeders," like McDonald's and Burger King, and other convenience stores. If you're talking about beer and soft drinks, then our competition would be supermarkets, other convenience stores, and some g-stores, or a major oil company that operates a small convenience store with major emphasis on gasoline.[12]

Oil companies that operate g-stores engage in the most direct competition with convenience stores. Texaco, Chevron Corporation, Amoco Corporation, Atlantic Richfield Company, Coastal Corporation, Mobil Corporation, BP America, and Diamond Shamrock operate more than 600 g-stores each.[13] These well-capitalized companies, with the advantage of prime locations and newer stores, have become very aggressive in the creation of convenience-type stores. Although smaller than convenience stores in terms of retail selling space and number of items stocked (convenience stores stock 33 percent more items than g-stores), g-stores have focused on items traditionally viewed as convenience store staples—tobacco products, soft drinks, and beer.

---

[12]"A Conversation with S. R. 'Dick' Dole," *The Southland Family* (August 1986): 9.

[13]"Convenience Chains Pump for New Life," p. 80.

EXHIBIT 5

Largest U.S. Convenience Store Operators

Company	Key Chain(s)	Sales Volume (Millions of Dollars)	Number of Store Units (Approx.)
The Southland Corporation	7-Eleven, High's Dairy Stores, Quick Marts, Super 7	$7,950.3	7,200
The Circle K Corporation	Circle K	3,441.4	4,631
Emro Marketing Co.	Speedway, Gastown, Starvin Marvin, Bonded	1,250.0	1,673
National Convenience Stores, Inc.	Stop N Go	1,072.5	1,147
Convenient Food Mart, Inc.	Convenient Food Mart	875.0	1,258
Cumberland Farms, Inc.	Cumberland Farms	800.0	1,150

Source: Company annual reports and 10-K forms; *Convenience Store News Industry Report 1989* (New York: BMT Publications, 1989).

Supermarkets have also been aggressive in trying to attract the convenience shopper. In particular, supermarkets have targeted the "fill-in" shoppers who typically populate the "eight items and under" express counters by offering extended store hours and prepackaged foods. This segment represents about $45 billion in annual sales. Supermarkets also cater to consumers who desire prepared foods for off-premises consumption. Prepared foods sold by supermarkets now account for more than $2.4 billion in sales annually. Furthermore, industry research shows that supermarkets enjoy a better reputation among consumers for lower prices and higher-quality food than convenience stores.[14]

Convenience Store Customer and Purchase Behavior

About 90 percent of American adults (18 years or older) visit a convenience store at least once a year. Almost two-thirds of these shoppers visit a convenience store two to three times per month. The typical convenience store customer is a white male between the ages of 18 and 34 with a high school education who is employed in a blue-collar occupation. A profile of the convenience store customer is given in Exhibit 6 on page 546.

Convenience store executives are sensitive to the fact that a stereotypic convenience store customer exists. They also recognize that opportunities for future sales growth exist in attracting women generally and particularly employed women, older consumers of both sexes, and professional and white-collar workers. According to a 7-Eleven executive:

> Two important demographic groups for 7-Eleven are the increased numbers of older people and working women. The elderly, the fastest-growing segment of the population, generally are not convenience store customers. Also, working women now rep-

---

[14]"Convenience Store/Supermarket Market Segment Report," *Restaurant Business* (February 10, 1990): 125.

EXHIBIT 6

Profile of Convenience Store Customers on a Given Day

	Convenience Store Customers (Percentage)	United States Population (Percentage)
Sex		
Male	57%	48%
Female	43	52
Age		
18 to 24	21	15
25 to 34	31	24
35 to 49	25	25
50 and over	23	35
Education		
Did not finish high school	19	18
Graduated from high school	62	60
Attended college	19	22
Annual Household Income		
Less than $10,000	14	13
$10,000 to $14,999	11	10
$15,000 to $19,999	12	10
$20,000 and over	48	48
Unknown	15	19
Race		
White	83	87
Nonwhite	17	13

Source: The Gallup Organization. Used with permission.

resent 45 percent of the work force. By 1995, 80 percent of all women between the ages of 25 and 44 will be working. Right now, women represent less than one-third of our business. We must do a better job of attracting potential customers to our stores by developing programs that fit their needs.

The 24–45 age group is experiencing a tremendous growth in disposable income, which increases our need to upgrade our stores to meet their demands and tastes.[15]

Similarly, a Circle K executive said, "We feel we can appeal to other groups than the traditional blue-collar customer of the past. We'd like to skew more toward office workers and white-collar workers."[16]

Industry analysts also believe that a broadened customer base will be necessary if the convenience store industry is to prosper in the 1990s. They note that the U.S. population between the ages of 18 and 34 will actually shrink in the early 1990s. They also point out that the industry must expand its customer base to include more older, married, dual-income customers and women shoppers.

The principal purchases by the 643 customers who visit an average convenience store daily are gasoline, tobacco products, alcoholic beverages, prepared foods, and soft

[15] "A Conversation with S. R. 'Dick' Dole," pp. 9–10.

[16] "Convenience Store/Supermarket Market Segment Report," p. 134.

drinks. These five product categories account for almost 80 percent of convenience store sales. The average merchandise sale per customer visit was $2.29 in 1989.

Industry Trends and Concerns

Industry observers have identified several trends that are likely to affect convenience store industry growth and profitability prospects for the foreseeable future. These trends and their implications are outlined below.

The first trend relates to industry maturity and store saturation. Industry analysts cite several developments, some of which are documented in Exhibit 4.

1. Industry sales growth has slowed in recent years compared with growth rates in the 1970s and early 1980s. Similarly, the number of new stores being opened has leveled off, and consolidation is occurring as firms have elected to grow through acquisition.

2. Industry profitability has declined in recent years. The downward spiral in net profit margins has hampered the ability of firms to reinvest in their operations.

3. Store saturation is present in many geographic markets. Potentially overstored areas include the southwestern, southeastern, and western United States. Industry forecasters predict that the demand for convenience stores is such that the market can only support 400 to 500 new stores per year in the period 1990–1995.

A second concern is the lack of differentiation among convenience store competitors. According to a 7-Eleven executive, "The thing to overcome is the battle of sameness."[17] The lack of differentiation has often produced costly price competition in selected markets, most notably in Florida and Texas. Efforts at differentiation reflected in new products and services have often been met with an immediate response. "We are the worst thieves around," said a Circle K executive. "As soon as one of us finds something that works, the copycats go to work."[18]

A third trend is the changing sales mix between merchandise and gasoline. In the late 1970s, roughly 82 percent of convenience store sales were merchandise. By 1989, 60 percent of sales were merchandise. The increase in gasoline sales as a percentage of total revenue has affected industry profitability because of gasoline's lower gross profit margin and often higher equipment cost. Moreover, some industry watchers believe that oil company g-stores are better equipped to deal with the lower margins. These "low-price, high-volume" g-stores, with about 80 percent of their sales coming from gasoline, and supermarkets, with a growing commitment to serving the convenience-oriented consumer, have left convenience stores "stuck in the middle," say industry analysts.[19]

■ STRATEGY CONSIDERATIONS FOR FISCAL 1991

One week prior to the announced bankruptcy filing, Karl Eller resigned as chairman, chief executive officer, and board director of the Circle K Corporation. He did so to pursue personal business opportunities and to give the company's board of directors "the latitude to establish new objectives for the future."[20]

---

[17] "Convenience Chains Pump for New Life," p. 80.

[18] "Stores for Our Times," p. 41.

[19] "Recent Events Show Plight of C-Store Chains," *National Petroleum News* (May 1990): 10.

[20] "Karl Eller Resigns as Circle K Chairman, CEO," *Wall Street Journal and Dow Jones News Wire* (May 7, 1990).

The principal elements of the announced strategy to revitalize the Circle K Corporation included (1) an overall price reduction of 10 percent, (2) a change in merchandise practices so that individual stores could stock items reflective of the socioeconomic characteristics of their trade areas, and (3) a $100 million advertising and promotion program. As the architect of the strategy, Dearth, Circle K's president, expressed no intention of downsizing the company or laying off any of the company's 27,000 employees when the bankruptcy filing was announced.

The initial reaction to the announced strategy was mixed. According to one of Circle K's bank creditors, "We would encourage any plan that generates income. We believe this [marketing] plan probably will."[21] However, industry analysts were skeptical. Some believed that the company's troubles would force it to sell about 10 percent of its stores. By August 1990, Circle K had terminated 400 leases on stores that had been shut down. These 400 leases were estimated to cost Circle K $1 million to $1.5 million per month. Furthermore, 201 unprofitable stores were scheduled to close in August 1990. In addition, the company had deals to sell 375 stores in Hawaii and the Pacific Northwest before its bankruptcy filing. These deals were delayed pending approval by the bankruptcy court. Savings from store closings, costs associated with terminating leases, and the potential gain on the sale of stores had yet to be determined.[22]

Industry analysts also expressed doubts about the financial viability of specific elements of Circle K's turnaround strategy. Lower prices might attract customers and increase store traffic. However, gross profit margins would suffer. Furthermore, efforts to modify the merchandise mix would involve a substantial change in inventories, and the advertising and promotion program was expensive. According to a convenience store analyst, "I don't know where they will get the money."[23]

In affidavits filed with the Securities and Exchange Commission, Circle K management stated that it "believes, but has no assurances, that this plan will succeed in improving operating results." Moreover, the company "expects to continue to incur operating losses until the business plan is fully implemented and refined."[24] The question yet to be answered was "Could the announced strategy return Circle K to profitability as envisioned by its president?"

[21] "Circle K Squares Off with Its Creditors," p. A4.

[22] "Circle K Begins Closing 201 Unprofitable Stores," *Wall Street Journal and Dow Jones News Wire* (August 21, 1990).

[23] "Circle K Squares Off with Its Creditors," p. A4.

[24] The Circle K Corporation, Form 10-K, for the fiscal year ended April 1990, "Management's Discussion and Analysis of Financial Condition and Results of Operations," pp. 26, 30.

3M Telecom Systems Division

Fibrlok™ Splice

It was early 1996. Dr. Dennis W. (Denny) Hamill sat back in his chair and stared at the stacks of documents in front of him on his desk. "Okay," he thought to himself, "I need to start someplace, so I might as well begin by reviewing the Fibrlok™ Splice history."

Hamill held the title of Business Director in the Telecom Systems Division of 3M Corporation, and it was his responsibility to review the performance of one of the division's most vaunted products, the Fibrlok™ Splice, a device used by telecommunications firms ("telecoms") to splice optical fibers when providing telephone service to households. Although the splice had initially exceeded the company's sales expectations, in recent years sales had leveled off, and it was Hamill's responsibility to determine if, and how, sales could be stimulated.

■ THE COMPANY

Minnesota Mining and Manufacturing Company, or 3M as it prefers to be called, is one of the best-known and most respected corporations in the world. 3M, whose stock price forms part of the Dow Jones Industrial Average, routinely makes the annual *Fortune* top-ten listing of the most admired U.S. companies, and recently it was rated as one of the best companies to work for. In 1995, 3M received the National Medal of Technology® from President Clinton in recognition of its technological achievements over the past 90 years. It is, without question, a world-class corporation, one that employs 71,000 individuals in nearly 200 countries. Ranked 62nd in the *Fortune* 500 listing of the largest U.S. corporations in 1995, 3M's net revenue was nearly $13.5 billion. Exhibit 1 on page 550 contains selected financial and operating data for the company for the period 1993–1995. More than half (54 percent) of the company's revenue stream in 1995 was derived from international operations.

3M consists of 50 product divisions, subsidiaries, and departments organized into two major business sectors: Industrial and Consumer, and Life Sciences. About 62 percent of firm revenues are derived from the Industrial and Consumer sector. It is primarily a manufacturing company that produces in excess of 60,000 different products. These products range from adhesives, roofing granules, pharmaceuticals, overhead projectors, heart-lung machines, and coated abrasives to surgical drapery. 3M is unique among large corporations in that it does not focus on a single strategic core competency. Rather, 3M builds on some 30 core technologies in which it has acquired unique competencies. As such, the company follows a very decentralized management philosophy. In fact, the company can perhaps best be viewed as a community of smaller business units that tend to focus on niche markets with niche products. The emphasis

This case was prepared by Professor Robert A. Peterson, The University of Texas at Austin, as a basis for class discussion and is not designed to illustrate effective or ineffective handling of an administrative situation. Certain information is disguised. Consequently, the case is not useful for research purposes. Copyright © 1997 Robert A. Peterson.

EXHIBIT 1

Selected 3M Operating Results, 1993–1995 (Millions of Dollars)

	1993	1994	1995
Net sales (millions)	$11,053	$12,148	$13,460
Cost of goods sold	6,344	6,839	7,713
Gross profit	4,709	5,309	5,747
Operating expenses			
Selling, general, and administrative expenses	2,918	3,219	3,446
Research and development	794	828	883
Other expenses (income)	(266)	(60)	442
Net income	1,263	1,322	976

Source: Annual reports of company.

on "smallness" and "community" is illustrated by the fact that the average 3M factory has only 400 employees.

Company Beginning

Minnesota Mining and Manufacturing was founded in 1902 by a physician, an attorney, a merchant, and two railroad executives in Two Harbors, Minnesota, a small community on the north shore of Lake Superior. Its charter was to mine a very hard mineral, corundum, that was used in grinding wheels. When that business foundered, the company headquarters was moved to Duluth, Minnesota, with the intent of manufacturing sandpaper and abrasive wheels. In 1910, the company moved to St. Paul, Minnesota, where today it occupies a 425-acre campus with some two dozen buildings.

In 1907, William McKnight joined the company as bookkeeper. Less than seven years later he was named general manager. McKnight became the spiritual leader of the company and eventually served as chairman for more than 40 years. When he died at age 90 in 1976, McKnight was still serving on the 3M board of directors. In a 1944 speech, McKnight set forth what was to become the guiding principle of 3M: "Management that is destructively critical when mistakes are made kills initiative, and it's essential that we have many people with initiative if we are to continue to grow." This principle has been steadfastly adhered to and is embraced by the 3M corporate culture that emphasizes risk taking, teamwork, innovation, and entrepreneurship.

3M Products

One of the enduring characteristics of 3M is its continual focus on new and useful products. Consequently, 3M is legendary for the products it has pioneered. Perhaps the best-known 3M consumer products are its Scotch™-brand tapes, of which there are now hundreds of varieties. 3M also developed the first commercially viable magnetic recording tape. Other well-known 3M brands include Scotchgard™ Fabric Protector, Scotchlike™ Reflective Sheetings (for highway signs and clothing), O-Cel-O™ Stay Fresh™ Sponges, and Thinsulate™ Insulation for winter clothing. Exhibit 2 shows a breakdown of 3M's sales by general product grouping.

Bootlegging Time and Venture Teams

One of 3M's financial goals is to obtain at least 30 percent of sales every year from products less than four years old at every level in the company. Needless to say, this

EXHIBIT 2

3M Revenue by General Product Grouping (Millions of Dollars)

	Year		
Product Line	*1993*	*1994*	*1995*
Tape products	$1,617	$1,801	$2,042
Abrasive products	1,002	1,117	1,220
Automotive and chemical products	1,176	1,195	1,328
Connecting and insulating products	1,252	1,362	1,470
Consumer and office products	1,844	2,069	2,272
Health care products	1,876	2,002	2,221
Safety and personal care products	974	1,067	1,220
All other	1,312	1,535	1,687

Source: Annual reports.

goal has fostered innovation and entrepreneurship throughout the company, from top managers to rank-and-file employees. In fact, to encourage innovation, the company has a formal policy that allows technical and engineering staff members to spend up to 15 percent of their time (termed "bootlegging time") on projects of their own choosing. One of the most celebrated consequences of bootlegging is the Post-it® Note Pad. The note pad was developed by Art Fry, a company scientist who was searching for a solution to stop book marks from falling out of his hymnal during church services. Working on his bootlegging time, Fry found an adhesive that another 3M scientist, Spence Silver, had created but abandoned because it was not very sticky. Fry brushed the adhesive on some paper and created a product line that now annually generates sales in the hundreds of millions of dollars. Post-it® Notes currently come in 18 colors, 27 sizes, 56 standard shapes, and 20 fragrances.

In addition to providing bootlegging time, 3M fosters innovation by allowing the formation of both formal and informal new venture teams. A new venture team is essentially a task force with very special characteristics. Team members are volunteers on full-time, indefinite assignment from their normal task. They come from disciplines that include manufacturing, engineering, and marketing, and have the ability to stay together if a product proves to be successful. In such instances, the product may form the nucleus of a new business unit. In keeping with the corporate spirit of entrepreneurship, venture teams are encouraged to "make a little, sell a little," which is interpreted at 3M to mean start small, learn how a business works, and then expand.

■ TELECOM SYSTEMS DIVISION

The Telecom Systems Division is a typical division at 3M. It has a 30-year history of selling products, first to telephone companies and now communication companies, all over the world. About 60 percent of the division's sales originate outside of the United States. The division has grown by concentrating first on products that help technicians and craft people (the "craft") in telephone companies splice copper cable and then protect those splices from the elements using closures and various kinds of cabinets. Over time the division built on these competencies by first adding testing equipment for copper wire and then by adding new technologies as the craft moved into fiber optics, coaxial cable, and wireless communications. Telecom Systems

Division is part of the Electrical and Communications Markets Group, which in turn is part of the Industrial and Consumer Sector.

Since a large percentage of the Telecom Systems Division's sales are direct to large customers, it does not depend heavily on advertising for communicating its product offerings. Instead, the communication budget is focused on direct communication with customers, on trade shows, on press releases and success stories, and on technical articles emphasizing the benefits of the division's products. Advertising that is done (see Exhibit 3) is in very specific industry-focused trade publications.

Scotchlok™ Connector

In 1959, 3M introduced the Scotchlok™ Connector, a device for splicing copper wires used in telephone lines. This device allowed telecom technicians to splice two wires together by just inserting the wires into a connector (without stripping the insulation) and, through the use of a simple tool, snapping the connector together to make a connection between the wires that protects them from the environment. The Scotchlok™ Connector was an instant success and literally millions have been sold since its introduction. Indeed, it ultimately became the industry standard.

About 1969 3M introduced modular splicing, called MS^2, for splicing copper wire. MS^2 was a major innovation in that it allowed the telecom technician to splice 25 pairs of copper wires at a time in a single connector. Indeed, modular splicing was so popular that it has been credited with helping the telecommunications industry grow significantly over the last 20 years. At the present time, 3M sells a two-wire Scotchlok™ Connector for about 5 cents; MS^2 sells for about $2, but it allows splicing 50 wires together very quickly, thereby improving craft productivity substantially. Presently, there are about 10 billion copper splices produced per year globally by 3M and its competitors.

By the mid-1980s, however, fiber optic cable was replacing copper wire in telephone lines at an increasingly rapid pace. There was a concerted effort by telecoms to replace coaxial copper wire with fiber optic cable for the "backbone" of telephone networks, that is, the "long haul" or major lines that were used to transmit long-distance telephone calls from one major point to another. Copper wire trunk lines, telephone lines that originate from a backbone and lead into a particular limited geographic location (such as a neighborhood), were also being replaced by fiber optic cable. There was considerable speculation that the major telecoms or RBOCs, as they are called (i.e., the regional operating companies resulting from the breakup of AT&T, such as Pacific Telesys and U.S. West), would soon be replacing the copper loops—the telephone lines linking a neighborhood location to a single home—with fiber optic cable.

3M's Telecom Systems Division estimated that about eight times more optical fiber would be required to replace the copper loops than was used for the backbone and trunk telephone lines. Moreover, the division estimated that the number of splices required to bring fiber optic cable into homes would be approximately 20 times greater on a per mile basis than that necessary for the backbone and trunk lines. In particular, it was expected that there would be between five and ten splices (spliced points) between a central telephone office and a home. Realizing the enormity of the task of bringing optical fiber into individual homes, telecom companies began to search for ways to minimize the expenditures required for installing, testing, and maintaining fiber optic cables to the home. These companies were joined in this quest by cable television operators, one of which estimated that the cost of running fiber to homes could be as high as $2,000 per home.

EXHIBIT 3

Typical Telecom Systems Division Trade Advertisement

From copper to fiber, you can count on 3M.

For more than 25 years, people requiring innovative solutions to their telephony or network problems have turned to 3M for answers.

3M Telecom Systems Division is a global leader in the supply of materials, components, products and services that ensure signal integrity while helping you effectively maintain the outside plant network and achieve your goals of fewer service interruptions and minimal downtime.

Copper or fiber, you can count on 3M for connections with tapes, jumpers, cable assemblies, fault finders, test sets, closures, cabinets and terminals. In fact, 3M offers thousands of products to keep your network operating day and night. And by offering this innovative blend of knowledge, hardware and skill, 3M is working to be your First Choice In Outside Plant.™

To learn more, contact your local 3M representative, fax us at 512-984-5811, or visit our Web site at www.mmm.com/telecom

3M Telecommunications

©3M

Source: 3M.

■ OPTICAL FIBER

Optical fibers are hair-thin strands of ultra-pure glass (often referred to as "light pipes") that digitally transmit voice, video, and computer data at the speed of light. A single fiber can transport up to 48 broadcast-quality video channels, whereas a 144-fiber cable can handle millions of simultaneous two-way telephone calls. Transmission is accomplished by means of light pulses through a glass fiber that has a diameter less than that of a human hair. In general, a fiber optic link consists of a light source (transmitter), fiber optic cables with connectors and/or splices, and a detector (receiver). More specifically, a fiber optic communication system consists of a transmitter that takes an electric signal, typically digital, and changes it into photons of light that are transmitted through the fiber. At various distances along the fiber are devices that amplify the light pulse. When the light pulse reaches its destination, it is detected and changed back into an electrical signal for reception. Light pulses are transmitted by total internal reflection. Consequently, the optical fibers are coated with a low refractive-index transparent material such as glass or plastic of a different type than that used in the fiber. This coating not only protects the internal reflecting surface of the fiber but also insulates adjacent fibers in a bundle.

Optical fiber was perfected in 1970 by scientists at Corning Glass Works (renamed Corning, Inc. in 1989). However, it was not until 1982 that the demand for fiber optic cable took off, spurred in part by the deregulation of the telecommunications industry. As of 1995, more than 60 million miles of optical fiber had been installed worldwide. In 1995, Corning alone produced more than 5.2 million miles of optical fiber.

There are more than 1,000 suppliers of fiber optic equipment in the world. Corning, Inc., with a global market share of 32 percent, and AT&T Network Cable Systems dominate worldwide production of optical fiber. In general, the fiber optic equipment market is fiercely competitive, with firms from all over the globe competing.

Fusion Versus Mechanical Splices

Properly splicing fiber optic cables is a very exacting task that requires great precision. If the splice does not result in the fiber optic cable being exactly aligned, the performance of the cable will be degraded substantially. Oversimplifying somewhat, there are two types of splicing, construction splicing and restoration splicing. The primary requirements for splices used in constructing fiber optic networks are that they be permanent and provide high performance. Cost is of secondary importance. The primary requirements for splices used in restoring (repairing) fiber optic networks are that they are easy and fast to install so that service can be restored as soon as possible.

There are essentially two methods for joining optical fiber: fusion and mechanical. Both methods of splicing accomplish the same goal in that they bring together two optical fibers and hold them in such a fashion that a light pulse can pass through the splice unhindered. Fusion splicers are a type of equipment that brings two or more optical fibers together and melts them to form a single strand. Mechanical splicers are devices that join optical fibers by aligning them and then maintaining them in alignment through the use of adhesives or epoxies or what is called elastomeric material. This material deforms under compression and can accommodate minor differences in the outside diameters of spliced fibers.

The instrument used for fusion splicing can be relatively expensive. Typical prices vary from $5,000 to $30,000 or more, and the instrument can be somewhat cumbersome when used in constrained quarters (e.g., in tunnels or false ceilings in buildings). Although a mechanical splicer does not require the large capital outlay of a fusion splicer, on average the total cost of each splice is between $7 and $20 because of the physical connector required (there is no physical connector in fusion splicing). Hence, from a cost perspective, if only a few splices are required, a mechanical splicer may be preferred. However, if many splices are to be made, a fusion splicer may be more cost effective. Moreover, fusion splicing requires highly trained technicians, whereas technicians can be easily trained to make mechanical splices. According to industry sources, the fusion splice has been widely accepted in applications requiring high volume (continuous) splicing. The mechanical splice is widely used in installations requiring relatively few splices at a time.

■ THE FIBRLOK™ SPLICE

In early 1987, Dick Patterson, a research scientist in the Telecom Systems Division, was using his bootleg time to develop a better way to splice fiber optic cable. Because he had worked on Scotchlok™ connectors, Patterson was convinced that a huge market existed for a mechanical fiber optic splice that was reasonably priced, easy to install, and resulted in high performance.

By April 1987, Patterson had formed a new venture team. The team consisted of himself as leader and Don Larson, an engineering specialist, Wes Raider, a senior design engineer, Jim Carpenter, a senior engineer, Barbara Birrell, an advanced physicist, and Al Lindh, a sales and marketing manager. As Patterson later noted, "We had a cross-functional team without knowing it." In November 1987, the team successfully tested a working optical fiber lock splice design.

The team worked literally day and night testing the mechanical splice, modifying the design, testing the modified mechanical splice, and so on. A working prototype was constructed and subjected to a myriad of engineering tests at the same time that reactions were obtained from potential customers in attempts to judge market responsiveness.

In August 1988, the Fibrlok™ Splice was introduced at a trade show in Chicago; all of the telecoms sent representatives. The splice was an inch and a half long, a quarter-inch high, and one-sixth of an inch wide. It contained a grooved aluminum element inside a plastic body with a plastic cap in the middle. A technician connecting two optical fibers would cleave and slide the ends of the fibers to be spliced into the device until they met in the center. By pressing down on the cap, the fibers would be locked into a perfectly aligned permanent splice. While the technology was complex (partly because of the high quality standards required), using the splice was easy, and telecom construction and repair workers could be taught how to use it in a short period of time. In fact, splicing could be accomplished in 30 seconds using only a simple hand-operated tool once the two ends of the fiber had been properly prepared (i.e., cleaned and cleaved), a task that would take an experienced technician one to two minutes.

Exhibit 4 on page 556 contains two diagrams of the fiber optic splice. One diagram shows the size of the splice, whereas the other shows an "exploded" schematic view of the splice. Technically, the Fibrlok™ Splice was developed to facilitate permanent splicing of standard single and multi-mode optical fibers that have 125-, 250-, or 900-micron diameters. Because any failure of the splice could have enormous loss potential for the telecom (revenue streams in the hundreds of thousands of dollars per minute can pass through a fiber optic cable) as well as 3M, great caution was observed in manufacturing and testing the Fibrlok™ Splice.

Initially, the Fibrlok™ Splice was packaged in units of five in individually sealed compartments in thermal-formed packages. Three different (color-coded) splices were available, depending on the size of the two optical fibers to be joined. To use the Fibrlok™ Splice required an assembly tool. Plans were made to market a Fibrlok™ Splice kit that included an assembly tool and 55 splices.

EXHIBIT 4

Fibrlok™ Splice Schematics

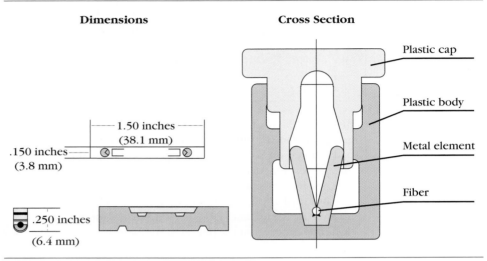

Source: Company documents.

Similar to other Telecom Systems Division products, it was expected that the division's largest customers, such as Bell South, would buy Fibrlok™ Splices directly from 3M on a contracted price that would be negotiated. This meant that about 80 companies in the United States would buy Fibrlok™ Splices directly from 3M. The rest of the industry, literally thousands of companies, was expected to purchase Fibrlok™ Splices from 3M distributors including Anixter, Graybar, GTE Supply, and North Supply. 3M decided to price the Fibrlok™ Splice about the same regardless of whether it was sold to a distributor or to a large customer directly. Exhibit 5 contains selected information about the initial Fibrlok™ Splice offering.

The Fibrlok™ market introduction was extremely successful, with sales far exceeding projections. In October 1988, only six weeks after its introduction, sales forecasts were revised. Sales were initially estimated to be approximately 85,000 units in 1989, but the early success led 3M to increase the forecast to 240,000 units. Because of the

EXHIBIT 5

Initial Order Information and Pricing for the Fibrlok™ Splice

		Price $	
	Units/Case	*Trade*	*Distributor*
Fibrlok™ Optical Fiber Splice 250 × 250	50	16	12
Fibrlok™ Optical Fiber Splice 250 × 900	50	16	12
Fibrlok™ Optical Fiber Splice 900 × 900	50	16	12
Fibrlok™ Optical Fiber Splice Kit 250 × 250	1 each	975	755
Fibrlok™ Optical Fiber Splice Kit 250 × 900	1 each	975	755
Fibrlok™ Optical Fiber Splice Kit 900 × 900	1 each	975	755
Fibrlok™ Splice Assembly Tool	1 each	125	96.16

Source: Company records.

labor-intensive nature of the initial manufacturing process, a factory cost of about 50 percent of the price of each Fibrlok™ Splice was anticipated. However, it was also anticipated that significant per unit cost reductions would be achieved once manufacturing was appropriately ramped up to handle the increased demand. Exhibit 6 contains an advertisement for the Fibrlok™ Splice.

In 1995, Telecom Systems Division introduced a multi-fiber Fibrlok™ Splice. Although not much larger than the original single-fiber Fibrlok™ Splice, this new splice allowed technicians to connect up to twelve fibers at a time in a single splice. This improved craft productivity considerably. However, because taking a single fiber

EXHIBIT 6

Advertisement for Fibrlok™ Splice

Take a closer look at the future of mass fiber splicing.

Signal Integrity

Fibrlok Multi-Fiber Splicing Assembly Tool

Mass fiber splicing will never be the same. With our Fibrlok Multi-Fiber Optical Splicing System, it's strip, cleave and splice – up to twelve fibers at a time. A completed splice can be assembled in less than five minutes, making the Fibrlok Multi-Fiber Splice ideal for both new construction and cable restoration applications.

Splice performance is comparable to our original Fibrlok Splice, delivering low insertion loss, low reflectance and superior thermal stability. Splicing is fast, efficient and permanent.

The Fibrlok Multi-Fiber Splice is easy to use and accommodates single-mode or multimode 125 micron fibers (individual and ribbon). The splice is available in 4-, 6-, 8-, 10- and 12-fiber configurations.

The low cost assembly tool is lightweight and portable, perfect for most real world applications.

To learn more, talk to an authorized 3M Telecom Systems distributor or your 3M representative. Or contact 3M Telecom Systems Division at 800/745 7459 or via fax at 512/984 5811.

3M *Innovation*

Source: 3M

to the home does not necessarily require multi-fiber splicing (multi-fiber splicing occurs at points farther back in the network, such as in trunk lines where multiple fibers are in the same cable), sales of Fibrlok™ Splices did not increase substantially following the introduction of the multi-fiber Fibrlok™ Splice. Consequently, there have not been significant improvements in factory costs, and the price per fiber splice has remained fairly constant over time.

At the beginning of 1996, about 5 million single-fiber mechanical splices were being sold globally per year, with 3M's Fibrlok™ Splice holding about a 30 percent market share. Although the market for mechanical splices grew rapidly for the first three years after the Fibrlok™ Splice was introduced, in the last seven years or so it has been relatively flat. Fusion splices still outnumber mechanical splices by about 8 to 1.

■ JANUARY 1996

With a doctorate in physics, Hamill was known for his keen analytical ability, and his tenure in the company had provided him with considerable expertise in many areas. Even so, Hamill enjoyed working with marketing-related issues because of their generally challenging nature.

As Hamill finished going through the piles of reports in front of him, he leaned back in his chair and rested his hands on his head. He thought about the division's forecast for the Fibrlok™ Splice nearly 10 years ago. Back in 1987, expectations were that within 5 to 10 years every household, at least in the United States, would either be served with fiber optic cable or have fiber "right to the curb." "Strange," he muttered to himself, "that same forecast holds today. Nothing seems to have changed. The same forecast, but it just seems to move out a year every year." Hamill was intimately familiar with the history of the Fibrlok™ Splice since one of the original venture team members, Al Lindh, indirectly reported to him.

At the beginning of 1996, there were in excess of 600 million identifiable telephone lines in the world, of which roughly one quarter were in the United States. Only a negligible proportion of these telephone lines incorporated fiber optic cable. Of the households that did have fiber optic cable, virtually all were in Japan, where the giant telecom NTT operated.

From the market research reports that he had read, Hamill calculated that new construction of telephone lines globally was running about eight percent a year (using as a base the 600 million existing telephone lines). For planning purposes Hamill assumed that three annual copper wire-to-optical fiber conversion or change-out rates were possible over the next few years—2 percent, 6 percent and 10 percent. He assigned a .65 probability of occurrence to the two percent rate, a .25 probability to the 6 percent rate, and a .10 probability to the 10 percent rate.

Three Scenarios

Just as Hamill was finishing his musings, Steve Webster walked into his office. Hamill decided to bounce a couple of ideas off of Webster. "Steve, I have been thinking about the Fibrlok™ marketing strategy for 1996 and 1997, and there are three possibilities that occur to me. The first is that the market will grow very slowly. If this is the case, are we properly positioned with our existing splices, pricing, and communications to maintain the market share that we currently have without changing our current strategy?"

"But, what if we see significantly higher growth in penetration of fiber to the home? If this happens, are we still properly positioned with respect to product, price, and market support to keep our share and to be able to grow with the growing market?" Hamill paused and thought for a moment. "Finally, is it possible that we could, through significant product redesign, different pricing and cost structures, and different marketing communications or other kinds of market support, position ourselves to actually drive market growth by offering improved productivity in fiber optic mechanical splicing? What do you think, Steve?"

Webster paced the room for a few minutes before returning to his seat. "Denny," he began, "you know as well as I do that a part of the uncertainty in predicting the rate of penetration of fiber to the home is the constant change in the preferences of consumers regarding services that they want and are willing to pay for. At the same time, since copper is already installed, telephone and cable companies are increasingly finding new ways to add electronic enhancements such as ISDN, ADSL, and so on to upgrade the copper line. These enhancements allow the lines to handle more data faster. Remember, much of what is going on in the home is being driven by the Internet, fax machines, and even e-mail. Telecoms are trading off installing fiber against the cost of electronics to enhance the capability of in-place copper."

"If the last kilometer of the network remains copper to the home, enhanced by electronics, then the present model of fiber to the neighborhood will provide continued growth for fiber splicing. This growth, though, will not be the explosive growth that would occur if we can improve installation productivity by driving down the cost of splicing. Remember, telecom technicians operate at a loaded labor rate of $60 per hour. You know, Denny, without a real breakthrough in fiber splicing costs, say to under 50¢ per splice, even wireless local loop, fed by fiber to the last kilometer, moves ahead of fiber to the home."

"Well, Steve," responded Hamill, "how can we cover all options in this uncertain market? Should we invest in major cost reduction and design strategies and attempt to drive the market? Should we partner with a major end user of fiber like NTT to reduce our risk? Or should we be satisfied with a small but profitable market?"

Macon Museum of Art

In early 2003, Ashley Mercer, Director of Development and Community Affairs, and Donald Pate, Director of Finance and Administration, of the Macon Museum of Art, met to discuss what had transpired at a meeting the previous afternoon. The meeting, attended by the senior staff of the museum and several members of the Board of Trustees, had focused on the financial status of the museum. The Macon Museum recorded its third consecutive annual loss in 2002, and Mercer and Pate were assigned responsibility for making recommendations that would reverse the situation.

■ MACON MUSEUM OF ART

The Macon Museum of Art (MMA) is a not-for-profit corporation located in Universal City, a large metropolitan area in the western United States. Founded in 1925, the museum was originally chartered as the Fannel County Museum of Fine Arts and funded by an annual appropriation from Fannel County. In 1998, the name was changed to the Jonathon A. Macon Museum of Art to recognize the museum's major benefactor, Jonathon A. Macon. Macon, a wealthy local landowner and philanthropist, had provided the museum with a sizable endowment. According to the terms of a $25 million gift given to the museum upon his death, the museum's charter was revised and its name changed. The charter of the museum stated that its purpose was

> To provide an inviting setting for the appreciation of art in its historical and cultural contexts for the benefit of this and successive generations of Fannel County citizens and visitors.

Randall Brent III, the Museum Director, noted that this charter differentiated the MMA from other art museums. He said:

> Our charter gives us both an opportunity and a challenge. By spanning both art and history, the museum offers a unique perspective on both. On the other hand, a person can only truly appreciate what we have here if they are willing to become historically literate—that is our challenge.

In 1995, the MMA benefited from a $28 million county bond election, which led to the construction of a new and expanded facility in the central business district of Universal City, the county seat of Fannel County. The location, six blocks from the museum's previous site, had extensive parking availability and access through public transportation. The site was made available for $1.00 from Jonathon Macon's real estate holdings. At the dedication of the MMA in January 1998, Brent said:

> I will always believe that the greatest strength of our new museum is that it was publicly mandated. The citizens of Fannel County and the vision and generosity of Jonathon Macon have provided the setting for the appreciation of art and its historical

This case was prepared by Professor Roger A. Kerin, of the Edwin L. Cox School of Business, Southern Methodist University, as a basis for class discussion and is not designed to illustrate effective or ineffective handling of an administrative situation. The museum name and certain operating data are disguised and not useful for research purposes. Copyright © 2003 by Roger A. Kerin. No part of this case may be reproduced without the written permission of the copyright holder.

and cultural contexts. As stewards of this public trust, the Macon Museum can now focus on collecting significant works of art, encouraging scholarship and education, and decoding the history and culture of art.

■ MUSEUM COLLECTION AND DISPLAY

The MMA has over 15,000 works of art in its permanent collection. However, as with most museums, MMA does not display all of its collection at the same time because of space limitations. Artworks in the collection are rotated, with some periodically loaned to other museums.

The MMA collection includes pre-Columbian, African, and Depression-era art, as well as European and American decorative arts. The art is displayed in different portions of the museum, where the building architecture accents the display. For example, Depression-era art is displayed in an Art Deco setting of the 1920s and 1930s; decorative and architectural art of the late nineteenth century is displayed in the Art Nouveau wing. In addition, museum docents provide a historical context for the art-works during tours.

The MMA collection is open for viewing Monday through Saturday from 10:00 A.M. to 6:00 P.M. and Thursday evenings until 8:00 P.M. Sunday hours are from 12:00 noon to 6:00 P.M. There is no charge for viewing the permanent collection; however, a modest fee of $3.00 to $5.00 is charged for special exhibitions. The MMA is also available for private showings and is often used for corporate, foundation, and various fund-raising events during weekday and weekend evenings. Exhibit 1 shows museum attendance for the period 1994–2002.

Museum Organization

The MMA is organized by function: (1) Collections and Exhibitions, (2) Development and Community Affairs, and (3) Finance and Administration. Each function is headed by a director who reports to the Museum Director, Randall Brent III. The museum has a staff of 185 employees. In addition, 475 volunteers work at the museum in a variety of capacities.

EXHIBIT 1

Museum Attendance

Year	Total Museum Attendance	Special Exhibitions [a]	
		Attendance	Proportion of Total Attendance
1994	269,786	N/A	N/A
1995	247,799	N/A	N/A
1996	303,456	N/A	N/A
1997	247,379	N/A	N/A
1998	667,949	220,867	0.33
1999	486,009	140,425	0.29
2000	527,091	227,770	0.43
2001	468,100	203,800	0.44
2002	628,472	284,865	0.45

[a] Special exhibitions attendance includes attendance at private corporation, foundation, and fund-raising events held at the museum.

The Collections and Exhibitions staff, headed by Thomas Crane, oversees the MMA's art collections, arranges special exhibits, is responsible for educational programming, and provides personnel and administrative support for museum operations that directly involve the artwork. The Finance and Administration staff, headed by Donald Pate, is responsible for the daily operation of the museum. The MMA's profit centers (the Skyline Buffet restaurant, parking, gift shop, and special exhibitions events) are also managed by this function. The Development and Community Affairs staff, under the direction of Ashley Mercer, is responsible for marketing, public relations, membership, and grants. This function engages in fund raising for the museum, which provides supplemental funds for general operating support, endowment, and acquisitions. This function also handles all applications for foundation, federal, state, and local grants.

Museum Finances

Exhibit 2 shows the financial condition of the MMA for the period 2000–2002. Total revenues and expenses during this period are shown below:

	2002	*2001*	*2000*
Total revenue	$10,794,110	$7,783,712	$8,694,121
Total expenses	11,177,825	7,967,530	8,920,674
Net income (loss)	($ 383,715)	($ 183,818)	($ 226,533)

The three consecutive years of losses followed seven consecutive years of either break-even or profitable status. The cumulative loss of $794,066 had depleted the MMA's financial reserves.

During a recent Board of Trustees meeting, several observations and projections were made that indicated that the MMA's financial condition needed attention:

1. The appropriation from Fannel County would decline. Whereas the county appropriated about $2 million annually to the MMA, the museum could expect no more than $1.6 million in county appropriations in 2003 and for the foreseeable future.

2. Low interest rates in 2001 and 2002 indicated that earnings from the MMA endowment and investments would probably remain flat or decline.

3. Income from grants and other contributions in 2002 were extraordinary, and it was unlikely that the same amounts would be forthcoming in 2003.

4. Membership revenues were down for the fifth consecutive year. Membership represented the single largest source of revenue for the museum.

5. Income from auxiliary activities—those that were intended to produce a profit—continued to show a positive contribution to museum operations.

Special exhibitions and events were very profitable. Nevertheless, limited availability of special exhibitions in 2003, a declining number of scheduled events, and rising costs (for insurance as an example) indicated that the revenues from such activities would probably decline and costs increase in 2003. The Skyline Buffet restaurant, gift shop and parking, and the Museum Association were operating at about break-even.

■ MUSEUM MARKETING

As Director of Development and Community Affairs, Ashley Mercer was responsible for marketing at the MMA. Her specific responsibilities related to enhancing the image of the museum, increasing museum visitation, and building museum memberships. Reflecting on her responsibilities, she said:

EXHIBIT 2

Summary of Income and Expenses, 2000–2002

Operations	Year Ending December 31		
	2002	2001	2000
Income			
Appropriations by Fannel County	$1,786,929	$1,699,882	$1,971,999
Memberships	2,917,325	2,956,746	3,134,082
Contributions	338,664	221,282	42,244
Grants	763,581	281,164	645,853
Investment income	27,878	28,537	32,205
Earnings from endowment	673,805	693,625	583,612
Other	149,462	128,628	196,195
Total revenue	$6,657,644	$6,009,864	$6,606,190
Expenses			
Personnel	$1,973,218	$1,086,177	$1,681,653
Memberships	854,461	869,043	906,314
Publications/public information	594,067	404,364	441,710
Education	616,828	519,805	542,076
Administration*	3,777,042	3,345,153	3,389,124
Total expenses	$7,815,616	$6,224,542	$6,960,877
Operating income	($1,157,972)	($ 214,678)	($ 354,687)
Auxiliary Activities			
Revenue from auxiliary			
Special exhibitions	$1,655,200	$ 510,415	$ 451,347
Museum gift shop	1,596,775	606,503	810,123
Skyline Buffet	515,843	305,952	418,960
Museum parking	131,512	45,068	64,651
Museum Association	337,136	305,910	342,850
Revenue from auxiliary	4,236,466	1,773,848	2,087,931
Expenses from auxiliary			
Special exhibitions	814,741	313,057	137,680
Museum gift shop	1,679,294	662,685	990,090
Skyline Buffet	592,051	457,841	462,475
Museum parking	31,168	16,528	16,536
Museum Association	344,955	292,877	353,016
Expenses from auxiliary	3,462,209	1,742,988	1,959,797
Profit from auxiliary activities	$ 774,257	$ 30,860	$ 128,134
Net income	($ 383,715)	($ 183,818)	($ 226,553)

*Administration expenses included mostly overhead costs, such as insurance, maintenance, utilities, equipment lease agreements, and so forth.

In reality, museum image, visitation, and membership are intermingled. Image influences visitation and membership. Visitation is driven somewhat by membership, but membership seems to also drive visitation and, in a subtle way, affects the image of the museum.

Museum Image

Interest in the public image of the MMA began soon after the new facility was dedicated. The new four-story building, situated downtown adjacent to skyscrapers, was occasionally referred to as the "marble box" by its critics, since the building facade contained Italian marble. When asked about the image of the MMA, Brent commented:

> It is basically correct to say that, in the mind of the public, the MMA has no image. There is nothing about this [building] that says, "I'm a museum," or "Come in." There are a lot of people that are not interested in high culture and think this is a drive-in bank or an office building.
>
> Most art museums in America have a problem with image. One of the things that makes me mad is that people think there is something wrong with the museum. The MMA is one of the most public in the country, and more heavily dependent on the membership contribution than any other [museum]. Like most, it is underendowed and underfunded from reliable public funds. In fact, the American Association of Museums reports that only about 60 percent of America's 2000-plus art museums have enough income from their endowment to cover their operating costs. Nevertheless, this institution has chosen to be public, with free access, and this is very noble. It is wonderful that the museum has decided not to belong to an agglomeration of very rich people.
>
> This museum has more character than it thinks it has. It has the best balanced collection between Western and non-Western art of any museum in the country. We have not chosen to sell or promote the unique aspects of this collection or the museum's emphasis on historical context. What we have are the makings of an institution that is very different from other museums, and we ought to be able to make that into an advantage rather than apologize for it.

Other staff members believed either that an image existed but was different for the various publics the museum served or that the MMA had not made a sufficient effort to create an image for itself. According to Ashley Mercer:

> Based on our marketing research, I think there are two distinctly different images. One is a non-image. People don't know what the museum is. They also don't know what we have to offer in the way of lunch, dinner, brunch, shopping, movies, etc. They are not familiar with our collections. They are probably proud, however, that their community has a beautiful art museum.
>
> The other image is that we are only for specific people. This image is probably based on our membership. About 85 percent of members are college-educated (compared to 70 percent of the county population of 2.5 million), 60 percent have household incomes in excess of $70,000 (compared to 20 percent of the county population), half are over 40 years old (compared to 25 percent of the county population), and 98 percent are white (compared to 75 percent of the county population).

Janet Blake, Staff Assistant in charge of membership, noted:

> Among our membership, the MMA is viewed as a community organization that has a cachet of class. It is exciting, educational, convenient, and inviting. It is a great place to bring visitors to our city for an afternoon of lunch and browsing.

A critic of the MMA said:

> The MMA has a definite image in my opinion. It's a great place to have lunch or brunch, buy an art or history book for the coffee table, and see a few things if time permits. Its parking facility is strategically located to allow its members to park conveniently for downtown shopping, particularly during the Christmas holidays.

Museum Visitation

Because there is a general belief that increased numbers of visitors lead to increased membership, Mercer's staff has historically focused its efforts on increasing the traffic through the museum. "Social, cultural, and educational activity in the museum is a major goal, and is not exclusive to the viewing of art," said Mercer. These efforts can be separated into general and outreach programs and programs involving special exhibitions and events.

Press Relations   The MMA continually promotes its special exhibitions and activities by sending out press releases, and it maintains a close relationship with the local media. Stories about art and history, public programs, and human interest issues are often featured in the local media. A five-year anniversary party was held at the museum in early 2002, designed as a free special event aimed to involve the general public with the museum.

Education and Outreach   The MMA has many programs directed toward educating the public. Among these are public programs such as adult tours, school tours, lectures, art films, and feature films. The MMA engages in programming to create community involvement and lends performing space to local performing arts organizations.

Special Exhibitions   Public service announcements written by the museum are aired on local radio stations to promote special exhibitions. Advertisements are run in local newspapers in a five-county area for special exhibitions. For major special exhibitions, advertising is usually sponsored by a local corporation.

Ashley Mercer believed that these efforts increased museum attendance. For example, periodic visitor surveys indicate that on a typical day when only the permanent collection was available for viewing, 85 percent of visitors were non-MMA members. She added that even though less than 1 percent of nonmembers actually applied for membership during a visit, this exposure helped in the annual membership solicitation.

Museum Membership

According to Mercer:

> Museum membership and the revenue earned from membership play significant roles in the success and daily operations of the MMA. The museum and its members have a symbiotic relationship. Members provide the museum with a volunteer base, without which our cost of operation would be astronomical. Member volunteers provide tours, assist at the information desk, help in the gift shop and the Skyline Buffet, and are invaluable in recruiting new members and renewing existing members.
>
> The Museum Association was created to encourage membership involvement in the MMA. The Association, with some 1,000 members, makes our volunteer effort possible—95 percent of our 475 volunteers are Association members. The Association's assistance in fund raising is critical, and we appreciate what its members have done for the MMA. Last year alone, the Association was directly responsible for raising almost $350,000. In return, the MMA sponsors social events for Association members, offers them lectures by authorities on art and history, and provides various other privileges not available to the general membership.

Member Categories, Benefits, and Costs   The MMA has two distinct memberships: (1) personal and (2) corporate. These two memberships are further divided into categories based on dollar contributions and benefits received. There are six categories of personal membership ranging from $50 per year to $5,000 per year. Corporate memberships are divided into four categories ranging from $1,000 per year to $10,000 per year. These categories and participation levels were created in 1998 with the move to the new building. In 2002, there were 17,429 personal memberships and 205 corporate memberships.

Exhibit 3 shows the benefits received by each personal membership category. Exhibit 4 provides a breakdown of personal memberships by category and the revenue generated by each category over the past five years. In 2002, personal memberships accounted for almost 80 percent of membership revenue.

Corporate memberships provide many of the same benefits as the $500 or higher personal memberships. In addition, corporate members are given "Employee Memberships" depending on their category. For example, corporate members that fall into the $1,000 category are given 25 Employee Memberships; those in the $10,000 category are given 250 such memberships.

The direct cost of benefits provided by the MMA to personal and corporate members was estimated by the museum's accounting firm. The MMA was required to do this because of income tax laws that limited the deductibility of membership to the difference between the direct cost of membership and the value of the benefits received. The estimated total cost of member benefits provided exceeded $1 million each year since 1998.[1] An itemized summary of benefit costs by category in 2002 follows.

EXHIBIT 3

Membership Benefits by Membership Categories

Benefits	Membership Category					
	$50	$100	$250	$500	$1,500	$5,000
Invitations to special previews/events	*	*	*	*	*	*
Free limited parking	*	*	*	*	*	*
Free admission to special exhibits	*	*	*	*	*	*
15% discount at Skyline Buffet and gift shop	*	*	*	*	*	*
Monthly calender	*	*	*	*	*	*
Discounts on films/lectures	*	*	*	*	*	*
Reciprocal membership in other museums		*	*	*	*	*
Invitations to distinguished lectures			*	*	*	*
Listing in annual report			*	*	*	*
Personal tours of exhibition areas				*	*	*
Invitations to exclusive previews/events					*	*
Free unlimited parking					*	*
Unique travel opportunities					*	*
Recognition on plaques in the museum					*	*
First views of new acquisitions					*	*
Priority on all museum trips						*
Dinner with the Director						*

---

[1]The estimated cost of benefits exceeds the membership expense shown in Exhibit 2 because the cost of publications and other items is included in this estimate. These costs are allocated across several different items in Exhibit 2.

EXHIBIT 4

Personal Membership Categories and Revenues by Year, 1998–2002

Membership Category	Amount	Number of Members				
		2002	2001	2000	1999	1998
Regular	$ 50	13,672	12,248	13,483	16,353	17,758
Associate	$ 100	2,596	2,433	2,548	2,576	2,465
Collector	$ 250	364	325	397	461	454
Patron	$ 500	102	85	65	0	0
Partner	$1,500	604	638	679	741	882
Director's Club	$5,000	91	86	98	0	0
Total membership		17,429	15,815	17,370	20,131	21,559

		Membership Revenue[a]				
		2002	2001	2000	1999	1998
Regular	$ 50	$ 639,664	$ 556,120	$ 611,864	$ 600,188	$ 662,631
Associate	$ 100	234,871	232,398	249,317	244,961	242,981
Collector	$ 250	81,415	76,987	97,474	108,432	105,840
Patron	$ 500	48,100	44,293	35,500	0	0
Partner	$1,500	815,666	958,419	968,239	1,187,728	1,041,898
Director's Club	$5,000	406,673	405,016	458,938	282,219	0
Total membership revenue[b]		$2,298,449	$2,334,583	$2,485,352	$2,451,638	$2,079,330

[a]The number of memberships times the dollar value does not equal the amounts given as the membership revenue, since some memberships are given gratis.

[b]The inconsistency between these figures and the figures shown on the income and expense statement is due to memberships given gratis.

Category	Benefit Cost
Regular ($50)	$ 631,016
Associate ($100)	81,903
Collector ($250)	64,135
Patron ($500)	39,628
Partner ($1,500)	99,567
Director's Club ($5,000)	15,975
Corporate (all categories)	125,576
Total cost	$1,057,800

The principal cost items in each category were (1) free admissions to exhibits, (2) parking, (3) the monthly calendar of museum activities, exhibits, and events, and (4) discounts at the Skyline Buffet restaurant and gift shop.

Member Recruiting and Renewals   "Recruiting new members and renewing existing members is a major undertaking," said Mercer. While some recruiting and renewals occur at the museum during visitation, the recruitment effort mostly revolves around mail, telephone, and personal solicitations. Mail and telephone solicitations focus primarily on recruiting and renewing personal memberships in the $50 to $250 categories. Personal solicitations by the Museum Association are used to recruit and renew personal memberships in the $500 to $5,000 categories and corporate memberships.

The MMA uses mailing and telephone lists obtained from other cultural organizations and list agencies. These lists are culled to target zip codes and telephone prefix numbers. Mail solicitations include a letter from the Museum Director, a brochure describing the museum, and a membership application form. Telephone solicitations include a follow-up brochure and application form.

The economics of direct mail solicitation are illustrated below, based on an August 2002 mailing considered typical by Mercer.

Total mail solicitations	148,530
Total memberships obtained	1,532
Response rate	1.03%
Total membership revenue	$84,280.00
Total direct mail costs	$66,488.80

Two direct mail solicitations of this magnitude are conducted each year.

The solicitation process for personal memberships in larger dollar categories and corporate memberships relies on personal contact by MMA volunteers and corporate member executives. Prospective members are identified on the basis of personal contacts and from the lapsed membership roster, the society page, other organizations' membership lists, and lower-membership-level lists. Once identified, these prospects are approached on a one-to-one basis. An initial letter is sent introducing the prospect to the museum. This first letter is followed by a personal telephone call or another letter inviting the prospect to an informal gathering at the museum. At the gathering, the prospect is introduced to other members and is asked directly to become a member.

Renewal efforts also include mail and telephone solicitation. In addition, membership parties, special previews, and special inserts in the monthly calendar of MMA activities are used.

Museum records indicate that 70 percent of the $50 members do not renew their membership after the first year. Among those that do, 50 percent renew in each successive year. Members in the $100 to $500 categories have a renewal rate of 60 percent, and members in the $1,500 and $5,000 categories have a renewal rate of 85 percent. Mercer believed that less than 10 percent of personal members who do renew their membership increase the dollar value of their membership. Renewal rates among corporate members is about 75 percent, regardless of category.

■ CONSIDERATIONS FOR 2003

Ashley Mercer and Donald Pate met to discuss measures they might recommend to the Board of Trustees to reverse the deteriorating financial condition of the MMA. Pate noted that at an earlier meeting with his staff, personnel reductions were discussed. Specifically, he felt that a 10 percent reduction in personnel and administration costs was possible. Furthermore, his staff estimated that the appropriation from Fannel County, contributions, grants, investment income, endowment earnings, and other income would be 15 percent below 2002 levels. A "best guess" estimate from the Director of Collections and Exhibitions indicated that special exhibitions and events would generate revenues of $1.2 million and cost $675,000 in 2003. Parking revenues and expenses resulting from nonmember visitors would remain unchanged from 2002. Rough budgets for education programs indicated that an expenditure of $500,000 for 2003 was realistic, given planned efforts. Pate said that changes in other auxiliary activities for which he was responsible, namely the Skyline Buffet restaurant and gift shop, were not planned.

Mercer was impressed with the attention Pate had already given to the museum's situation. She too had given consideration to matters of museum image, visitation, and membership prior to the meeting. Unfortunately, an earlier meeting with her staff had raised more issues than hard-and-fast recommendations. Staff suggestions ranged from implementing an admission fee of $1.00 per adult (with no charge for children under 12 years old) to instituting student (ages 13 to 22) and senior citizen (60 and older) memberships at $30. The need for institutional advertising was raised, since the MMA had only been promoting special exhibitions and events. Other staff members said that the benefits given to members needed to be enhanced. For example, raising discounts at the Skyline Buffet and gift shop to 20 percent was suggested. Another possibility raised was commissioning a "coffee table" book featuring major artwork at the MMA to be given with personal memberships of $500 or more.

Mercer listened to these suggestions, knowing that some were unlikely to receive Board of Trustee approval. These included any proposal to increase expenses for Publications/Public Information (for example, new books and paid institutional advertising). She had already been informed that expenses for such activities could not exceed the 2002 expenditure. Improving the member benefit package seemed like a good idea. Increasing restaurant and gift shop discounts, even though 65 percent of the business for both was already on discount, seemed like a good idea, at least at the margin. Pate said that he would give this suggestion consideration, but asked that Mercer think further about it in the context of the overall member-benefit package. Charging a nominal admission fee for nonmembers also seemed reasonable. Visitor surveys had shown that 50 percent of nonmember visitors said that they would be willing to pay a $1.00 admission fee for viewing the permanent collection (access to special exhibitions would continue to have admission fees). Furthermore, members could then be given an additional benefit, that is, free admission. However, Pate noted that the MMA had always prided itself on free access, and he wondered how the Board of Trustees would view this suggestion. Additional membership categories below $50 and for students and senior citizens also seemed to provide new opportunities to attract segments of the population that had not typically yielded members.

Mercer and Pate believed that their initial meeting had produced some good ideas, but both thought that they had to give these matters further thought. They agreed to meet again and begin to prepare an integrated plan of action and a pro forma income statement for 2003.

CHAPTER **10**

Comprehensive Marketing Programs

 An organization's comprehensive marketing program integrates the choice of which product or service markets to pursue with the choice of which marketing mix to use to reach target markets and, ultimately, create value for customers. The process of formulating and implementing a comprehensive marketing program encompasses all the concepts, tools, and perspectives described in previous chapters.

The challenge facing the manager responsible for formulating and implementing a comprehensive marketing program divides into three related decisions and actions.[1] First, the manager must decide *where to compete*. Product-market choice determines the organization's customers and competitors. This decision is often based on the organization's business definition and opportunity and target market analysis. In this regard, the manager has multiple options, ranging from concentrated marketing with a focus on a single product market to differentiated marketing, whereby multiple product markets are pursued simultaneously. Second, the manager must decide *how to compete*. The means a manager has available reside in the marketing-mix elements or activities. Multiple options again exist. In a simple situation with two alternatives for each of the four marketing-mix elements, 16 different marketing-mix combinations are possible. Third, the manager must determine *when to compete*. This decision relates to timing. For example, some organizations adopt a "first-to-market" posture, while others take a "wait-and-see" stance concerning market-entry decisions. Four issues are central to the design and execution of comprehensive marketing programs. First, a marketing manager must consider issues of *fit* with the market, the organization, and competition. Second, marketing-mix *sensitivities* and *interactions* must be considered as they relate to target markets. Third, issues of *implementation* must be addressed. Fourth, *organizational* issues must be taken into account. Each of these topics is discussed in this chapter.

■ MARKETING PROGRAM FIT

A successful comprehensive marketing program must effectively stimulate target markets to buy, must be consistent with organizational capabilities, and must outmaneuver competitors.[2] The fit of a program to a market is determined by the extent to which the marketing mix satisfies the unique needs and buyer requirements of a chosen target market. The fit of a program to an organization depends on the match between an organization's marketing skills and financial position, on the one hand, and the marketing mix being considered, on the other. Finally, the fit of a program to the competition relates to the strengths, weaknesses, and marketing mixes of competitors who are serving the target markets under consideration.

Establishing a program-market fit can be a daunting task. For over 20 years, DuPont explored applications for Kevlar, a synthetic fiber with five times the tensile strength of steel on an equal-weight basis. The chosen target market for Kevlar was tire makers that produced steel-belted radials. Despite Kevlar's unique qualities and $600 million of development and marketing costs, DuPont's marketing program did not persuade tire makers that Kevlar adequately satisfied their needs. DuPont's CEO subsequently announced that the company should focus "more intensely on customer needs." Today, Kevlar is successfully marketed as bullet-resistant personal body armor to the military, a composite used in hockey sticks, airplane construction, and boats, along with numerous other applications, each with a separate marketing program.[3]

A comprehensive marketing program must be symbiotic with the organization implementing the program. Successful marketing programs build on an organization's strengths and distinctive competencies and avoid stressing organizational weaknesses. Failure to do this can have serious consequences. For example, Continental Airlines launched a comprehensive marketing program dubbed "Continental Lite," which centered on replicating Southwest Airlines' successful low-fare, short-flight, and point-to-point route system. However, Continental's higher operating costs and its inability to manage a short-flight, point-to-point route system produced a financial loss of almost $600 million over 15 months. The "Continental Lite" initiative was abandoned largely because it stressed organizational shortcomings rather than strengths and competencies.[4]

Finally, a successful marketing program fits the competitive realities of the marketplace. As described in Chapter 9, marketing strategies are rarely timeless. As the competitive environment changes, so must marketing programs. This was the case in the recently deregulated U.S. telecommunications industry. The Telecommunications Act of 1996 allowed long-distance telephone companies (e.g., AT&T, Sprint) to compete for local telephone service with regional telephone companies such as Bell Atlantic, U.S. West, and Nynex. It also paved the way for the merging of telephone, cellular, paging, and Internet communication technologies and services and the formation of new competitor alliances, each vying to satisfy the complete communication needs of businesses and households. These developments made obsolete marketing programs created in a near monopoly environment. Marketing programs that focused on a single communication technology (e.g., cellular) and service and high prices made possible by regulation were replaced with marketing programs that focused on bundling communication technologies and services with lower prices.[5]

■ MARKETING-MIX SENSITIVITIES AND INTERACTIONS

Many of the case analyses thus far have implicitly or explicitly focused on target-market sensitivity to one or more elements of the marketing mix. The Jones • Blair Company case in Chapter 4 is an example. When company management embarked on a planning effort, several views on how best to stimulate sales were voiced. One executive favored an increase of $350,000 in corporate brand advertising. Another argued for a 20 percent price reduction, and still another recommended hiring additional salespeople. Each of these executives implicitly suggested that the target market was most sensitive to the marketing-mix element he recommended.

In reality, however, the options are generally broader, and interaction effects between two or more marketing-mix elements must be considered. For instance, what would be the effect on sales of increasing corporate brand advertising *and* introducing a 20 percent price reduction? Would this action be more or less effective in stimulating sales than changing only one element of the marketing mix?

Although simultaneous consideration of marketing-mix sensitivities and interactions is a complex process, it is a necessity for the marketing manager. Consider the situation faced by John Murray, the marketing manager for DuPont's Sontara, a polyester fabric used for disposable surgical gowns and drapes used in hospital operating rooms.[6] Murray's charge was to prepare a comprehensive marketing program that would meet two objectives for Sontara: (1) maintain market share and (2) persuade garment makers that DuPont could support them in promoting Sontara to end users and would remain a strong force in the disposable fabric business.

Murray thought that if sales-force/maintenance expenditures were raised from the proposed level of $450,000 to a maximum reasonable level of $550,000 while other spending was held to proposed levels, market share could reach 35 percent of the total market. Similarly, if the other mix elements were increased to their maximum reasonable levels while the remaining expenditures were held at their proposed levels, market-share increases would be likely as well, although they would not be as dramatic. Specifically, he thought:

- If instead of spending nothing on sales-force/missionary expenses, management spent $200,000, market share would increase to 33 percent.
- If trade support/maintenance expenses were increased to $100,000, a 33 percent market share would result.
- If $100,000 were spent on trade support/missionary expenses, market share would be 33 percent.
- If advertising to intermediate users were increased to $50,000, the net effect would be a 1 percent increase in market share.
- An increase to $300,000 in advertising to end users would also result in a 1 percent share gain.

Reductions in spending were thought to have the opposite effect. Reducing sales-force/maintenance expenditures to zero while holding other spending at the proposed level was thought likely to reduce Sontara's share to 22 percent of the total market during the next 12 months. Similarly, reductions to zero spending for sales-force/missionary expenditures, trade support/maintenance, trade support/missionary, advertising to intermediaries, or advertising to end users were thought likely to reduce expected market share to 32, 27, 32, 31, or 28 percent, respectively.

As a validity check on the above estimates, Murray described what he thought would happen if all mix elements were raised simultaneously to their maximum reasonable expenditure levels or if all support was withdrawn from the product. He thought that with maximum effort a 39 percent share could be realized, although he was not sure how viable such an aggressive strategy would be for the long run. If all support was withdrawn, he estimated that market share would drop to 22 percent in the next 12 months and then decline further.

This example demonstrates the complex relationships that exist among marketing-mix elements. It also illustrates the role of assumptions and judgment in considering marketing-mix sensitivities and interactions.

Increasingly, marketing managers are turning to carefully designed market tests designed to measure marketing-mix sensitivities and interactions. By experimentally manipulating the amount and type of advertising and promotion and price levels in test markets, quantitative estimates of marketing-mix elasticities and relationships can be determined for individual products and services. For example, one consistent finding from these tests is that television advertising intensity has a far greater effect on sales volume growth for new consumer products than for products already established in the marketplace.[7] Market tests help to qualify assumptions made by marketing managers; however, they are not a substitute for judgment acquired through experience.

■ MARKETING IMPLEMENTATION

Implementation is the third leg in developing a comprehensive marketing program. Marketing managers have come to realize that poor implementation can hamper the success of an otherwise brilliantly conceived program. More succinctly, "The best strategy for any company is a strategy it can implement."[8]

Among the wide variety of subtle factors that can make or break a marketing program is timing. Failure to execute a marketing program when a window of opportunity opens can lead to failure or reduce the likelihood of success. For example, some industry observers believe that the failure of Matilda Bay Wine Cooler, introduced by the Miller Brewing Company, was due to poor timing on two counts. First, the popularity of wine coolers was declining. Second, the product was launched in the fall, typically a slow selling season.[9]

A second factor that can hamper implementation is not considering logistical aspects of a marketing program. When Holly Farms test-marketed a roasted chicken for distribution through supermarkets, consumer response was favorable. Holly Farms soon realized, however, that the roasted chicken was edible for only 18 days and it took 9 days to get the chicken from the production plant to supermarkets. As supermarkets could not be expected to sell the chicken within 9 days, Holly Farms had to halt its planned national introduction of roasted chicken.[10]

Poor implementation is often marked by a failure to synchronize marketing-mix activities. The experience of Iridium LLC is an example.[11] The company's $5 billion global satellite telephone system was intended to revolutionize telecommunications by allowing phone calls anytime, anywhere. Iridium's $100 million international marketing plan, anchored by a worldwide advertising campaign, generated over one million inquiries from potential customers. However, with no marketing channels and few salespeople in place, and a short supply of phones for demonstration, orders failed to materialize. The company subsequently filed for bankruptcy.

Formulating a comprehensive marketing program is a formidable task that demands rigorous analysis and judgment, often without the benefit of complete information. At the same time, program planning and design cannot be separated from implementation issues. "What should we do?" cannot be separated from "How do we do it?" By assigning equal attention to program formulation and program implementation, marketing managers increase the likelihood that their comprehensive marketing programs will succeed.[12]

■ MARKETING ORGANIZATION

Emphasis on marketing implementation focuses attention on organizational structure. It is often said that strategy determines structure and that organizational structure, in turn, determines whether a marketing strategy is effective and efficiently designed and implemented.[13]

A central issue in creating an effective and efficient marketing organization is finding the proper balance between centralization and decentralization of marketing activities, including strategy formulation and implementation. The strategy of regional marketing, whereby firms attempt to satisfy unique customer needs and meet competitive demands in limited geographical areas, has prompted increased decentralization of strategic marketing decisions and practices. For example, regional marketing groups at Frito-Lay design and implement region-specific marketing programs, including pricing practices and sales promotion activities. They also manage 30 percent of the company's advertising and promotion budget.[14] Efforts to "glocalize" marketing programs in the international arena have created elastic organizational structures that simultaneously strive for efficiencies through scale economies in product development and manufacturing, and for effectiveness through customization of advertising, promotion, pricing, and distribution in separate countries. As an example, Coca-Cola's concentrate formula and advertising theme are standardized worldwide, but the artificial sweetener and packaging differ across countries as do sales and distribution programs.[15] The relative emphasis on standardization versus customization in marketing strategy planning and execution ultimately manifests itself in organizational structure. For Frito-Lay and Coca-Cola, and an increasingly large number of other firms, the notion of "coordinated centralization" has produced domestic and global organizational structures that seek to foster adaptability to local conditions while preserving centralized direction in the pursuit of market opportunities and implementation of comprehensive marketing programs.

NOTES

1. This discussion is based on Subhash C. Jain, *Marketing Planning and Strategy*, 6th ed. (Cincinnati, OH: Southwestern Publishing Co., 2000):24.

2. Benson P. Shapiro, "Rejuvenating the Marketing Mix," *Harvard Business Review* (September–October 1985): 28–34.

3. Scott McMurry, "Changing a Culture: DuPont Tries to Make Its Research Wizardry Serve the Bottom Line," *Wall Street Journal* (March 27, 1992): A1, A4; and "What's New," Kevlar.com.

4. Bridget O'Brien, "Continental's CALite Hits Some Turbulence in Battling Southwest," *Wall Street Journal* (January 10, 1995): A1, A5; "Familiar Flight Plan," *Dallas Morning News* (August 10, 1996): 1F, 11F.

5. "Telecommunications," *Wall Street Journal* (September 16, 1996): R1–R26.

6. *E. I. DuPont de NeMours & Co.: Marketing Planning for Sontara and Tyvek* (Charlottesville, VA: University of Virginia, Darden School of Business Administration).

7. For a description of this research and additional research, see Demetrios Vakratsas and Tim Ambler, "How Advertising Works: What Do We Really Know?" *Journal of Marketing* (January 1999): 26–43.

8. Claudio Aspesi and Dev Vardan, "Brilliant Strategy, But Can You Execute?" *The McKinsey Quarterly* (Number 1, 1999): 88–99.

9. "Miller Jumps into Cooler Cooler Market," *Business Week* (October 26, 1987): 36–38.

10. "Holly Farms' Marketing Error: The Chicken That Laid an Egg," *Wall Street Journal* (February 9, 1988): 36.

11. Eric M. Olson, Stanley F. Slater, and Andrew J. Czaplewski, "The Iridium Story: A Marketing Disconnect?" *Marketing Management* (Summer 2000): 54–57.

12. For a discussion on marketing strategy implementation, see Charles H. Noble and Michael P. Mokwa, "Implementing Marketing Strategies: Developing and Testing a Managerial Theory," *Journal of Marketing* (October 1999): 57–73.

13. Bill Donaldson and Tom O'Toole, *Strategic Marketing Relationships: From Strategy to Implementation* (New York: John Wiley & Sons, 2002).

14. S. McKenna, *The Complete Guide to Regional Marketing* (Homewood, IL: Richard D. Irwin, 1992).

15. Philip R. Cateora and John L. Graham, *International Marketing*, 11th ed. (Burr Ridge, IL: McGraw-Hill/Irwin, 2002).

Nintendo
The Launch of Game Boy Color

■ INTRODUCTION

In June 1998, Peter MacDougall, president of Nintendo Canada, was looking forward to November 23, 1998, when a color version of Nintendo's Game Boy would be released simultaneously in North America and Europe. It would be one of the most important launches in Nintendo's history. Both Game Boy hardware and software sales had declined steadily from 1992 to 1996 on a worldwide basis (see Exhibit 1). They had recovered somewhat in 1997 as a result of increased marketing effort, but without significant new products the recovery was unlikely to be a sustained one. Game Boy was arguably the most successful gaming platform in history, boasting sales of more than 70 million units during its almost 10-year life in a highly fickle and competitive market. By the end of 1997, Game Boy had sold more than 1.6 million units in Canada (see Exhibit 2 on page 578). In the United States, Game Boy products claimed nearly 10 percent of category revenues in 1997.

MacDougall was responsible for ensuring that the Canadian launch was successful. Although he hoped to leverage elements of the U.S. launch, he recognized that the Canadian market situation, and Game Boy's competitive position in Canada, might require the Canadian launch strategy to be different in significant ways.

■ NINTENDO

Game Boy was manufactured by Nintendo Co. Ltd. of Kyoto, Japan (see Exhibit 3 on page 579 for a summary of Nintendo's financial results from 1994 to 1998). Nintendo was the leader in the worldwide US$15 billion retail video game industry. The company manufactured and marketed hardware and software for home game systems, including the 16-bit Super Nintendo Entertainment System, the 64-bit Nintendo 64, as well as Game Boy. Nintendo of America, Inc., based in Redmond, Washington, served as headquarters for Nintendo's operations in the Western Hemisphere. In 1997, more than 40 percent of U.S. households owned a Nintendo game system.

Professors Robert Fisher and Adrian Ryans prepared this case solely to provide material for class discussion. The authors do not intend to illustrate either effective or ineffective handling of a managerial situation. The authors may have disguised certain names and other identifying information to protect confidentiality.

E X H I B I T 1

Worldwide Game Boy Sales

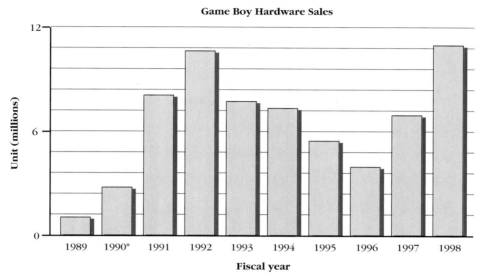

Game Boy Hardware Sales

* 7 months to reflect change in fiscal year

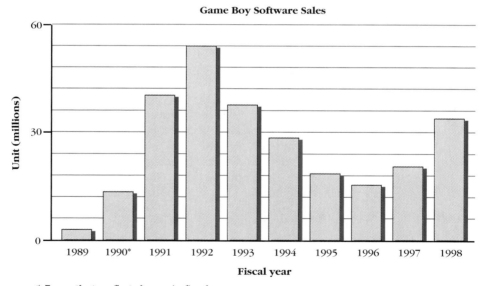

Game Boy Software Sales

* 7 months to reflect change in fiscal year

Source: Nintendo Co., Ltd. 1998 Annual Report (year ending March 1998).

EXHIBIT 2

Canadian Game Boy Hardware Sales

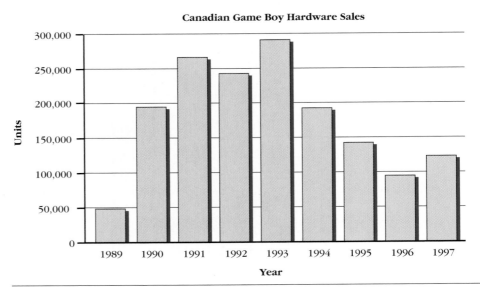

Source: Company files.

Nintendo 64 had been launched with heavy support in 1996 and it rapidly became the hottest product on the market. Fights sometimes broke out in retail stores as customers competed to take the product off the shelf. Nintendo 64 was named *Time Magazine's* "Machine of the Year" for 1996. One of the historical strengths of Nintendo had been its control of the games that ran on its game machines. Nintendo produced 10 to 15 of its own games each year, but it relied to a significant degree on third-party software providers for the rest of its game product line. Nintendo kept these third-party software providers under tight control. Nintendo built a security chip into the console and then licensed certain third-party developers to develop specific games for Nintendo. These suppliers came up with game concepts, which Nintendo either accepted or rejected. If Nintendo accepted the concept, the developer began the software development with Nintendo reviewing the new product at several points. If the final product was approved, then Nintendo would manufacture the cartridges for the developer to take advantage of Nintendo's economies of scale in purchasing and production. This allowed Nintendo to leverage the expertise of particular developers. For example, Electronic Arts had a real competence in the development of sports games.

In 1997, sales of Nintendo consoles and games were very strong, but in 1998 Nintendo began to lose momentum as some of the third-party developers began focusing more of their development effort on Sony Playstation. They viewed the Sony Playstation as an easier platform on which to develop games, as well as viewing the Sony business model as being a more profitable one for them. With the slowdown in the Nintendo 64 business, Nintendo became more dependent than ever on the Game Boy business. In North America, the total handheld games market was only about 10 percent of the total market for Nintendo with console sales of hardware and software accounting for the other 90 percent. But with its dominant position in the handheld games segment, Game Boy was a very significant profit generator for Nintendo in both

EXHIBIT 3

Five-Year Summary

			¥ millions		
Years ended March 31	*1998*	*1997*	*1996*	*1995*	*1994*
For the period					
Net sales	¥534,325	¥417,593	¥353,754	¥415,240	¥485,612
Income before income taxes and equity earning	171,753	115,491	133,283	85,704	104,411
Net income	83,697	65,482	59,871	41,661	52,653
At the period-end					
Total assets	848,607	735,620	649,841	578,662	591,227
Property, plant and equipment—net	59,746	60,667	60,076	69,507	61,856
Shareholders' equity	633,083	563,718	512,523	464,784	444,193

			¥		
Years ended March 31	*1998*	*1997*	*1996*	*1995*	*1994*
Amounts per share					
Net income	¥590.80	¥462.22	¥422.61	¥294.09	¥371.72
Cash dividends	120	100	100	70	70

			$ U.S. thousands		
Years ended March 31	*1998*	*1997*	*1996*	*1995*	*1994*
For the period					
Net sales	$4,047,916	$3,163,585	$2,679,954	$3,145,759	$3,678,875
Income before income taxes and equity earning	1,301,160	874,928	1,009,719	649,274	790,994
Net income	634,068	496,073	453,566	315,613	398,889
At the period-end					
Total assets	6,428,839	5,572,881	4,923,035	4,383,805	4,478,994
Property, plant and equipment—net	452,614	459,597	455,120	526,571	468,609
Shareholders' equity	4,796,087	4,270,598	3,882,760	3,521,092	3,365,100

			$ U.S. Dollars		
Years ended March 31	*1998*	*1997*	*1996*	*1995*	*1994*
Amounts per share					
Net income	$4.48	$3.50	$3.20	$2.23	$2.82
Cash dividends	0.91	0.76	0.76	0.53	0.53

Source: Nintendo Co., Ltd. 1998 Annual Report (year ending March 1998).

the United States and Canada. By 1998, support of third-party developers for Game Boy was waning. Many viewed it as a "spent force" in the market and were reluctant to invest the US$200,000 to US$300,000 to develop a new Game Boy cartridge, when there were more attractive opportunities in the much larger console market.

In some respects, Game Boy was less successful in Canada than the United States. Partly because of the sheer size of the U.S. market, Nintendo had been able to develop a more demographically balanced set of users for Game Boy. For example, Nintendo in the United States had developed some adult-oriented Game Boy advertising that had helped nurture the development of this market segment. The overall result was that Game Boy in the United States was significantly stronger in the teen and adult segments of the market. Another factor impacting Game Boy in Canada was Sega. Sega had been much more aggressive in promoting its console business in Canada than in the United States. This had forced Nintendo Canada to focus more of its resources on its consoles to the detriment of Game Boy. One result of these differences between the U.S. and Canadian markets was that by the late 1990s only 6 percent of Nintendo Canada's sales came from Game Boy hardware and software versus 10 percent in the United States.

Globally, Nintendo first-party software (that is, software developed by Nintendo itself) accounted for a little more than a quarter of the Game Boy software. However, in Canada, Nintendo first-party software accounted for about 50 percent of the Game Boy software sold. This was largely a result of the third-party developers spending fewer marketing dollars in Canada due to the relatively small size of the Canadian market. Canada represented only about 3 percent of the global Game Boy software market, whereas the United Sates accounted for between 35 percent to 40 percent.

■ THE EVOLVING GAME BOY PRODUCT

The original Game Boy was introduced in Canada in 1989 with a suggested retail price of Cdn$139.95 for the hardware and *Tetris*, which became an extremely popular game on Game Boy. During the 1990s, Nintendo introduced a number of upgrades to the original Game Boy, as well as adding several accessories. In 1993, the original Game Boy was made available in several different color cases. Game Boy Pocket, which was 50 percent smaller than the original Game Boy and 30 percent lighter, was launched at Cdn$64.95 (the price of the original Game Boy had been steadily reduced over the years, so that the basic hardware had a suggested retail price of Cdn$59.95 by 1992). Game Boy Pocket also had sharper black and white graphics than the original Game Boy.

In 1994, an add-on for the Super Nintendo Entertainment System was launched, enabling gamers to play Game Boy games on that system. This move was meant to broaden the appeal of the Game Boy by allowing gamers to use its games on either system.

In 1996, Game Boy was relaunched in a slimmer housing with further improvements in screen clarity. In 1997, Game Boy Pocket was introduced in six new colors (see Exhibit 4). Cumulative sales through the end of 1997 were 1.65 million in Canada.

Game Boy Camera and Game Boy Printer were scheduled to be released in July 1998. Game Boy Camera was a cartridge with a swiveling lens that fitted into any Nintendo Game Boy, turning it into a low-cost, simple-to-use digital camera. Game Boy Printer could be attached to any Game Boy and allowed the user to print photo stickers for kids to collect and trade. The camera could store up to 30 digital pictures that could be manipulated on the screen. The two products allowed kids to photograph and insert their own faces as stars of games or print off stickers.

EXHIBIT 4

November 1997 Print Ad for Game Boy

Source: Leo Burnett U.S.A., November 1997.

■ MARKETING OF GAME BOY IN CANADA

The marketing of Game Boy in Canada and the United States was quite similar in many respects, but there were some important differences due to the size of the U.S. market and to cultural and other differences between Canada and the United States.

Distribution of Game Boy in Canada

During the 1990s, the distribution of Game Boy in Canada had become increasingly concentrated in about 20 large direct accounts, such as Wal-Mart, Zellers, Future Shop, and Toys "R" Us. These types of accounts represented more than 1,000 retail outlets and accounted for 80 percent of Game Boy sales. Distributors served smaller retail accounts, such as specialty electronics stores. The biggest distributors were Beamscope and Fidelity. These distributors would sell Game Boy hardware, software, and accessories to approximately 500 outlets across the country. The distributors typically carried a wide variety of products. Beamscope, for example, distributed brand-name home office products, home computer hardware, software, video gaming and digital entertainment products. It used both inside sales and field representatives to call on accounts to encourage them to prebook products. It also used its historical sales information to advise retailers on what types of products were likely to be popular in their area. For example, games based on winter sports, such as hockey, sold particularly well across the country. Soccer was popular in Toronto, and American football was relatively unpopular in Quebec. Distributors also carried inventory and could efficiently fill small orders on short notice. They also promoted Nintendo's point-of-purchase materials to retailers.

Game Boy's position in the market was deteriorating during the mid to late 1990s. As sales velocity slowed, retailers shifted more of their shelf space to Nintendo consoles and competing platforms and reduced their advertising and promotional support for Game Boy. This contributed to a downward spiral in Game Boy sales.

Nintendo had basically the same pricing structure for the large direct accounts and the distributors. The distributors passed on most of the margin to their retailers, retaining perhaps 2 percent of the margin on the hardware, which basically covered their shipping and handling costs. The distributors made the bulk of their margin on Game Boy from the margin they earned by distributing third-party games for the Game Boy. In the late 1990s, a number of specialty stores had delisted Game Boy because they felt that they were not achieving competitive returns on their sales of Game Boy hardware and software.

A major challenge in dealing with the large retailers was to get them to commit their "open to buy" dollars to Game Boy. The retailers' buyers for gaming hardware and software had budgets and had to decide how much of their budget to invest in Game Boy, Nintendo 64, Sony Playstation, and competing gaming platforms. These "open to buy" dollars could be shifted around during the year to support the "hot" products, but there was often a lag before this occurred. If a new product failed to get much initial support from the large direct accounts, the product didn't get much retail visibility, and it became a real uphill battle to achieve high sales. With some of its largest accounts, Nintendo Canada shipped direct-to-store based on an automatic replenishment system. Based on historical data, each store within a chain was placed in a certain size category. Maximum and minimum inventory levels were established for each Nintendo stock-keeping unit (SKU) by the buyer working with the Nintendo staff. The sales of each SKU would then be monitored and Nintendo would make a shipment weekly to bring each SKU up to its maximum level.

Marketing Communications

The marketing communications budget for Nintendo in Canada was only a small fraction of the Nintendo budget in the United States. In fact, Nintendo in the United States spent more money on developing its advertisements than Nintendo Canada spent on buying media time. In a typical year, Nintendo would develop 15 to 20 television advertisements in the United States. In order to make as effective use as possible of its advertising dollars, Nintendo Canada selected its ads from the pool developed by Nintendo in the United States. Only for the Quebec market did it develop its own ads, and even these tried to leverage the advertisement development work done in the United States.

Nintendo Canada has historically done more grassroots marketing than its counterpart in the United States. At one point, in the 1990s Nintendo had permanent Nintendo demonstration centers in Toronto, Montreal, and Vancouver, where people could try out the latest Nintendo hardware and games. Nintendo periodically had tours across Canada, where people again had access to the latest hardware and games. Nintendo also worked closely with partners, such as McDonald's and Famous Players Theatres, to promote its products.

Pricing

When the original Game Boy was launched in 1989, it had been priced slightly higher in Canada than the United States. Given that disposable income was substantially lower in Canada, especially among kids/"tweens" (8- to 14-year-olds) and teens, MacDougall attributed Game Boy's proportionately greater sales in the United States partly to this pricing decision.

Competition

Over the years, a number of competitors to Game Boy had appeared. An early competitor for Game Boy was the Atari Lynx, which was the world's first color handheld video game system. It was launched in 1989 and had a backlit screen. A second-generation Lynx model was introduced in the early 1990s. It was slightly smaller and lighter than the original model and had about 15 percent longer battery life. However, even with this improvement in battery life, a set of batteries lasted less than four hours. Atari experienced significant difficulties during the 1990s and had essentially gone out of business by 1998.

The TurboExpress was a handheld with 16-bit graphics and a 6.6-centimeter (approximately 2.5 inches) active-matrix color liquid crystal display (LCD) screen. The TurboExpress was capable of playing the same software as the NEC's full-size TurboGrafx 16. Sega's Game Gear and the Atari Lynx had 8-bit graphics chips and inferior passive-matrix color screens. The passive-matrix screens were cheaper and consumed less power, but fast motion on screen tended to blur, and the colors were lacking in contrast. By comparison, the active-matrix screen of the TurboExpress, although smaller, was crisp and vibrant. Battery life was extremely short (six alkaline AA batteries lasted a scant three hours). However, there were several rechargeable battery packs that were compatible with it, and the backlit screen automatically deactivated itself after a period of inactivity to conserve power.

Perhaps the strongest early competitor was Sega's Game Gear, which was introduced in April 1991. It had a 32-color backlit LCD screen. Because it did not rely on ambient light, it could be used under all lighting conditions. Sega's handheld product was judged by industry observers to be a good product except that it drained batteries very quickly. The other reason that Sega and others had failed to dent Game Boy's early market dominance was the lack of new exciting software. Because Sega viewed its console business as its main platform and Sega Game Gear as a spinoff, it seemed to think it was sufficient to "port" over two-year-old software from its console product. Handheld users seemed to want exciting, current software. At its peak, Sega Game Gear sold approximately 18 percent of all handheld units in Canada.

In October 1995, Sega introduced the Nomad, its first portable 16-bit video game system. Priced at less than US$200, the Nomad had an 8.25-centimeter (approximately 3 inches) full-color screen and, most importantly, was compatible with the 600 game cartridges developed for the Sega Genisys (Sega's console product). However, battery life was still a major issue, since six AA batteries lasted for less than three hours.

Therefore, despite all this competitive activity in the color handheld arena, the almost decade-old, black and white Game Boy continued to dominate the handheld video game market in 1998.

■ COLOR GAME BOY

The New Product

The new Game Boy Color units were similar in size to the existing black and white units, but the color version contained new technology that would display sharp and vivid color graphics. In contrast to the technology used by the Sega, Atari, and TurboExpress color game handhelds, Game Boy Color's screen was not backlit and required an external light source (the brighter the ambient light, the better the color). However, by using an external light source, two AA batteries would last about 12 hours. A new reflective screen allowed the units to be used either indoors or outdoors. Game Boy Color would be able to display up to 56 colors with a very low power drain resulting in long battery life. Game Boy Color would be backwards compatible, allowing users to run any of the 1,000 games written for Game Boy since its launch in 1989. These games would show colors in a range of hues from a 10-palette selection chosen by the user. Six new games, specifically developed to take advantage of the 56-color palette on Game Boy Color, were expected to be available at the launch date.

Launching Game Boy Color

As he prepared for the launch of Game Boy Color in November 1998, MacDougall knew that he had a number of important decisions to make in such areas as target segments, positioning, marketing communications, pricing, and products.

Target Markets and Positioning   MacDougall believed that picking the right targets and the right positioning was going to be an important decision. He knew that his counterparts in the United States were planning to target Game Boy Color at new users as well as existing kids/tweens and teen users. The marketing people in the United States were even developing print advertisements for Game Boy Color targeted at adult users. MacDougall knew that the younger the audience he targeted the less likely it was to already own a Game Boy product. Game Boys were typically purchased for kids and tweens by their parents as gifts. As a result, peak sales tended to occur in November and December for holiday gift giving, and in June as a graduation or "great report card" present. The teen market was more sophisticated in a variety of ways. First, many in this segment already had a black and white Game Boy and a library of five or six games. As a result, they viewed the product as "old technology." Many teens appeared to have moved past the handheld machines to consoles, which offered greater speed and game complexity. Also, teens tended to purchase machines with their own money. Their purchases occurred year-round, in contrast to the purchases related to kids and tweens. Approximately 75 percent of all Game Boy users were male.

MacDougall wondered if he should target more narrowly in Canada than Nintendo was planning to do in the United States, perhaps by focusing first on either teens, who were more likely to already own a Game Boy, or on new kid/tween users. If Nintendo Canada targeted teens that had used Game Boy in the past, they might view the Game Boy as a product that was great when they were younger but not sophisticated enough to meet their current gaming needs. Getting them to adopt Game Boy Color might be a challenge, albeit not an impossible one. If he were successful in getting teens to adopt, this might spur sales among kids and particularly tweens, who often aspired to use the same products as teens. On the other hand, if Nintendo targeted teens and was unsuccessful with them because Game Boy was something "I had when I was a kid," then perhaps kids and tweens would avoid it as well.

Alternatively, if Nintendo targeted kids and tweens and was able to convince kids/tween nonusers of Game Boy that Game Boy Color was a "cool" product, it could become a "gotta have" for the younger set. But the difference between being cool or not cool with the younger set was a very fine line. Furthermore, if he focused on the kids and tweens, it might turn off the teens because Game Boy Color was "a kid's toy." He saw significant risks associated with each option, and he felt it essential that Nintendo have a quick success to ensure retail interest in the product and gain retail momentum. The size of the different demographic segments is shown in Exhibit 5.

Marketing Communications   Marketing communications was a closely related and key decision area. MacDougall was tentatively planning to spend Cdn$3 million on corporate advertising for Game Boy Color in the first year, rising to perhaps Cdn$7 million in the second and third years. In addition, Nintendo Canada typically supported its retailers' advertising efforts with a 2 percent cooperative advertising allowance.

It appeared that Nintendo Canada would have access to a broad selection of ads from the United States that could appeal to all the target segments he was considering. A major decision in the advertising area would be the selection of media vehicles, so that the ads could reach the target audience. MacDougall planned to spend approximately 80 percent of the Game Boy corporate advertising budget on television with the balance on print and out of home. Nintendo believed that Cdn$500,000 of advertising targeted at kids and tweens (8- to 14-year-olds) over a four-week period would

EXHIBIT 5

Population of Canada by Sex and Age (1996)

	Both Sexes	Male	Female	Both Sexes	Male	Female
	Number (in thousands)			% of total population		
All ages	29,963.6	14,845.0	15,118.6	100.0	100.0	100.0
0–4	1,960.9	1,005.9	955.0	6.5	6.8	6.3
5–9	2,015.8	1,031.3	984.5	6.7	6.9	6.5
10–14	2,019.6	1,031.9	987.7	6.7	7.0	6.5
15–19	2,002.9	1,026.3	976.5	6.7	6.9	6.5

Source: Statistics Canada.

generate about 100 gross rating points (GRPs).[1] There were a number of important tactical issues that needed to be resolved, including the relative emphasis on hardware and software in the advertising.

In the merchandising area, MacDougall planned to spend Cdn$400,000 in the first year and Cdn$800,000 in each subsequent year on point-of-sale materials. In addition, he would need Cdn$1,100,000 in the launch year and Cdn$2,500,000 in years two and three to cover the cost of sales promotions. This spending would be for contests and cross promotions with manufacturers of other products purchased by Game Boy Color's target market.

Ron Bertram, Nintendo Canada's director of communications and consumer support, felt a crucial factor contributing to Game Boy Color's success would be the consumer sampling program. Three major sampling approaches were being considered. The first approach was to place a low-cost interactive display in high-volume retail outlets (gaming specialty retailers, department stores, or mass merchandisers). Teens might visit these stores alone, but kids and tweens would often visit these stores as part of a shopping trip with their parents. Bertram estimated that retail interactive displays would be in use approximately 20 percent of store hours for an average of three minutes per use. No sales support was expected for the displays, as most sales clerks knew little about Game Boy Color hardware or software. Each interactive display included one Game Boy Color unit and game and cost Cdn$250. Bertram estimated that there were 1,000 potential outlets and that Nintendo could achieve an 80 percent placement rate.

Also considered was a sampling strategy called Mall Tours. Here, Nintendo representatives would visit major malls and set up kiosks that would be decorated with banners and would feature dramatic interactive displays and product information. A Mall Tour kiosk would feature two display units, each with six Game Boy Colors and a sampling of games. Nintendo representatives, who were highly knowledgeable gamers, would show game insights and tricks that kiosk visitors could use to improve their scores on popular games. Mall Tour visitors could also enter contests for Nintendo products, and would receive a temporary Nintendo tattoo when they left. Each mall visit lasted one week and cost about Cdn$10,000 per mall visited. Nintendo had the capacity to run up to 25 mall tours per year. It was expected that the interactive displays would be used approximately 60 percent of the time with each visitor contact typically lasting six to eight minutes.

Finally, there was the option of a cross-Canada tour, which would cost Cdn$150,000 per year for major regional or national events, such as the CNE, Klondike Days, and the Calgary Stampede. These events took place in the summer months. The approach would be the same as the Mall Tours but with larger kiosks and with more freedom to promote in a bold manner. The usage levels, because of the high volume of people at such events, would be highest at 80 percent.

A final element of the marketing communications strategy was public relations. Bertram planned to have Nintendo marketing representatives take the new hardware and software to leading gaming magazine and Web publications such as *Electronic Gaming Monthly*, *Next Generation*, and *Computer Gaming World*. The representatives would visit each publication about three months before launch and let the writers play with the new product for five or six hours. The objective was to get favorable

---

[1]GRPs are a measure of advertising weight that is equal to the reach times the frequency of a campaign during (typically) a four-week period. Reach is defined as the percentage of an advertiser's target audience that is exposed to at least one advertisement within the designated time. Frequency is the number of times, on average, that members of the target audience are exposed. For example, 100 GRPs could be achieved by exposing 50 percent of the target audience to an average of two ads or 25 percent of the target audience to four ads during the period.

coverage and the front cover of the magazine two months before launch. The combined monthly circulation of the top seven magazines was 110,000 Canadian readers. Also important was coverage in *Nintendo Power*, a magazine published by Nintendo with a Canadian circulation base of 60,000 readers (monthly).

Price All Game Boy Color units would be manufactured in Japan and Nintendo Canada would be charged on a per unit basis.

Price was a particularly tricky issue for Nintendo Canada. Nintendo of America had decided to price Game Boy Color at US$79.95. At mid-1998 exchange rates this translated into Cdn$120. The software was expected to retail at an average price of Cdn$43 with a retail margin of 20 percent. MacDougall expected Nintendo Canada would achieve its normal 40 percent margin on Game Boy Color cartridges. However, he was concerned that the hardware price would be too high to drive high-volume sales in the Canadian market, particularly if Nintendo Canada decided to focus on the kid/tweens market. However, if he recommended a price under Cdn$100, say Cdn$99, this would be the lowest Game Boy Color price in the world, and there would be the potential for such a portable product to be exported to other markets. He knew that this would be an issue with Nintendo of America executives. In addition, at such a low price, Nintendo Canada's gross margin would be only about 5 percent if Nintendo gave retailers their normal 6 percent margin (in addition the retailers received the 2 percent cooperative advertising allowance). He also wondered if the resulting retail margin dollars would be sufficient to motivate Nintendo retailers to carry and aggressively push Game Boy Color. Since retailers often discounted the hardware, actual margins for hardware were often less than 6 percent. However, retailers could make good returns per square metre, if they achieved good retail turns.

Product Two product-related issues remained. First, should Nintendo continue to offer the black and white version of the product? If it were to continue to offer this option, MacDougall was concerned about the profitability of doing so and the potential for cannibalizing sales of Game Boy Color. If Nintendo Canada retained the old version of Game Boy, he believed that the retail price could not be set higher than Cdn$49. At this price, the black and white version would not generate any profit. On the plus side, the backward compatibility of Game Boy Color games meant that consumers could buy the black and white version and then trade up at a later date without making their games obsolete. A second issue was whether Nintendo Canada should bundle a game cartridge with Game Boy Color at launch.

■ DECISION TIME

MacDougall knew that he had to immediately start making some tough decisions if Nintendo Canada was to have a detailed marketing plan in place to support the November 23, 1998 launch of Game Boy Color. He hoped to be able to sell 150,000 to 200,000 units in the 1999 fiscal year (which ended on March 31, 1999). In the second and third fiscal years, under an optimistic scenario sales might be as high as 500,000 units if Game Boy Color achieved retail and consumer momentum. If it didn't, they might plateau at 200,000 units per year. He expected that on average, over the first three years, approximately three Nintendo first-party game cartridges would be sold for each Game Boy Color unit. He was determined to develop a launch plan that would generate the highest possible level of profitability for Nintendo.

Show Circuit Frozen Dog Dinner

Executives of Tyler Pet Foods (TPF), Inc. looked forward to their meeting with representatives of Marketing Ventures Unlimited, a marketing and advertising consulting firm. The purpose of the meeting was to review the program for TPF's entry into the household dog food market in the Boston, Massachusetts, metropolitan area. TPF had sought out the consulting firm's services after discussions with food brokers who cited the tremendous potential for TPF in the household dog food market. These brokers had become aware that frozen dog food was being sold in the freezer section of selected supermarkets in a few cities in the southwestern United States. They believed these limited efforts represented a market opportunity for frozen dog food in Boston-area supermarkets.

■ THE COMPANY AND THE PRODUCT

Tyler Pet Foods, Inc. is a major distributor of dog food for show-dog kennels in the United States. TPF has prospered as a supplier of a unique dog food for show dogs called Show Circuit Frozen Dog Dinner. Show Circuit was originally formulated by a mink rancher as a means of improving the coats of his minks. After several years of research, he perfected the formula for a specially prepared food and began feeding his preparation to his stock on a regular basis. After a short period of time, he noticed that their coats showed a marked improvement. Shortly thereafter, a nearby kennel owner noticed the improvement and asked to use some of the food to feed his dogs. The dogs' coats improved dramatically, and a business was born.

Show Circuit contains federally inspected beef by-products, beef, liver, and chicken. Fresh meat constitutes 85 percent of the product's volume, and the highest-quality cereal accounts for the remaining 15 percent. The ingredients are packaged frozen to prevent spoilage of the fresh uncooked meat.

■ PACKAGING AND DISTRIBUTION MODIFICATIONS

TPF executives recognized that modifications in the packaging of Show Circuit would be necessary to make the transition from the kennel market to the household dog food market. After some discussion, it was decided that Show Circuit would be packaged in a 15-ounce plastic tub, with 12 tubs per case. The cost of production, freight, and packaging of the meal was $6.37 per case, which represented total variable costs.

The discussions with food brokers indicated that distribution through supermarkets would be best for Show Circuit because of the need for refrigeration. Food brokers

The cooperation of Tyler Pet Foods, Inc. in the preparation of this case is gratefully acknowledged. This case was prepared by Professor Roger A. Kerin, of the Edwin L. Cox School of Business, Southern Methodist University, as a basis for class discussion and is not designed to illustrate effective or ineffective handling of an administrative situation. Certain names have been disguised. Copyright © 2002 by Roger A. Kerin. No part of this case may be reproduced without written permission of the copyright holder.

would represent Show Circuit to supermarkets and would receive for their services a 7 percent commission based on the suggested price to retailers, which had yet to be determined. Supermarkets typically receive a gross margin of 22 percent of their selling price for dog foods.

■ THE MEETING

TPF executives listened attentively to the presentation made by representatives from Marketing Ventures Unlimited. Excerpts from their presentation follow.

During the course of the meeting, TPF executives raised a number of questions. The questions were primarily designed to clarify certain aspects of the program. One question that was never asked but that plagued TPF executives was "Will this program establish a place in the market for Show Circuit?" This direct question implied several subissues:

1. Was the market itself adequately defined and segmented?
2. What position would Show Circuit seek in the market? Should the program be targeted toward all dog food buyers or toward specific segments?
3. Could the food brokers get distribution in supermarkets given the sales program?
4. What should be TPF's recommended selling list price to the consumer for Show Circuit?
5. Could TPF at least break even in the introductory year and achieve a 15 percent return on sales in subsequent years?

TPF executives realized that they had to answer these questions and others before they accepted the proposal. The cost of the proposed plan could be $400,000 to $600,000, exclusive of slotting fees, which TPF executives considered reasonable, although it would stretch their promotional budget.

■ PROPOSAL OF MARKETING VENTURES UNLIMITED

The following is an excerpted version of the proposal presented to TPF.

The Situation

Our goal is to introduce and promote effectively the sale of Show Circuit dog food in the Boston market area. Show Circuit is among the costliest dog foods to prepare and will be available through supermarkets.

Show Circuit is a completely balanced frozen dog food. It is of the finest quality and has been used and recommended by professional show-dog owners for years.

Yet, in spite of this history, Show Circuit is essentially a new product and is unknown to the general public. The fact that Show Circuit will be the only dog food located right next to "people food" in the frozen food section of the supermarket is an advantage that must be capitalized upon. Show Circuit's history of blue-ribbon winners is another plus. So, in essence, to market Show Circuit successfully, we must accomplish two objectives:

• Make the public aware of the brand name of Show Circuit, what the packaging looks like, and the fact that Show Circuit is a high-quality dog food.
• Direct dog owners to shop for dog food in the frozen food section of supermarkets.

The Environment

Sales of dog food will total about $6.08 billion this year at manufacturers' prices. Still, fewer than half of the dogs in the United States are regularly fed prepared dog food, which means the dog food industry has yet to tap its full potential.

Four trends indicate that this optimism is well founded. First, the dog food industry has benefited from increasing dog ownership. The U.S. dog population of 53 million, spurred on by the owners' desire for companionship or need for protection, is growing steadily and is expected to continue growing. Second, the trend toward using convenience foods in the household contributes to a lack of table scraps to be served to the dog, a fact that will only improve the prospects for selling prepared dog foods. A third important trend is that pet owners continue to invest their animal companions with human qualities and view them as members of the family. For example, a study conducted by the advertising agency, Bates USA, reported: "A person who owns a dog actually identifies with the pet, assigning human characteristics to the dog such as language, thoughts, feelings, and needs."[1] Not surprisingly, one-half of dog owners consider themselves "Mom and Dad" to their animal companions and 95 percent pet and hug their dog every day.[2] Therefore, it comes as no surprise that dog owners spend more than $15 billion annually for veterinarian fees; medication for dogs; and dog toys, clothing, accessories, and furniture. A fourth trend is the growth in premium and superpremium dog foods. These higher-quality–higher-priced dog foods have fueled the growth in dog food sales along with the increase in dog ownership.[3]

The choice of supermarket distribution focuses on the single dominant retail channel for dog food. Supermarkets (and grocery stores) dispense 51 percent of all dog food sold in the United States, which represents $3.1 billion in sales at manufacturers' prices. The other 49 percent is sold by mass merchandisers such as Wal-Mart (20%), pet superstores such as Petco and Petsmart (15%), warehouse clubs (3%), farm/feed stores (3%), and veterinarians, Internet retailers, and independent pet stores (8%). These percentages also apply to the greater Boston market.

Finally, the Boston market is an ideal area for launching a new dog food. We estimate that the greater Boston area has 1.2 percent of the U.S. population (and 1.2 percent of the dog population since dog and human populations are highly correlated). Also, expenditures for pet products in the greater Boston area approximate the national average.[4]

The Competition

There are about 50 dog food manufacturers and 350 dog food brands in the United States. However, in 2001, five companies—Ralston Purina, Kal-Kan Foods (a subsidiary of Mars, Inc.), H. J. Heinz, Nestlé USA, and Nabisco—accounted for 83 percent of supermarket dog food sales in early 2002. (Note: Nestlé acquired Ralston Purina in early 2002). Exhibit 1 shows the estimated supermarket share of the major dog food manufacturers along with their most well-known brand. Private label dog food accounted for about 10 percent of supermarket dog food sales.

In addition to market share, competitor advertising spending and forms of advertising used will be major considerations in planning Show Circuit's introductory marketing strategy. Total spending for advertising in the dog food industry is about 2 percent of sales. Ralston Purina is the leading national advertiser of dog food, spending about $470 million per year, exclusive of major new product launches.[5]

---

[1]*Pet Food Market Gets a Touch of the Good Life* (New York: Bates, USA, 1995): 3.

[2]"Man's Best Friend," *American Demographics* (January 2002): 7.

[3]"Tail of the Pampered Pooch," *U.S. News & World Report* (May 17, 1999): 46–47.

[4]"Pet Places," *American Demographics* (September 1998): 38–39.

[5]"100 Leading National Advertisers, 2001 Edition," *Advertising Age* (September 24, 2001): S 43.

EXHIBIT 1

Market Share of Dog Food Manufacturers in Supermarkets

Rank	Company	Estimated Market Share	Principal Brand
1	Ralston Purina	30.0%	Purina
2	Kal-Kan Foods	19.0	Pedigree
3	H.J. Heinz	17.9	Ken-L-Ration
4	Nestlé USA	12.0	Alpo
5	Nabisco	4.3	Milk-Bone
	Other (including private labels)	16.8	
		100.0%	

The Problems and Opportunities

Introducing a New Dog Food in a New Form This is an opportunity to educate the consumer. Until Show Circuit's program breaks, dog foods fall into four categories: canned, dry, semimoist, and snack-type (dog biscuits and treats), as shown in Exhibit 2 on page 592.

Canned dog foods average about 75 percent moisture and 25 percent solid materials. They are marketed either as complete foods or as supplementary foods.

Dry dog foods are usually produced as flakes, small pellets, or large chunks containing about 10 percent moisture and 90 percent solids. They are chewy, usually well rounded, and more economical than canned or moist foods.

Semimoist dog foods come in chunk or patty form and are about 25 percent moisture and 75 percent solids. They require no refrigeration and are made to look tempting to humans.

Dog biscuits and treats have a wide variety of ingredients and, while tasty, are not recommended as a complete food.

All these product forms are typically marketed in the same area of the store. The consumer must now be taught to shop for dog food in another part of the store—the frozen-food section. Fortunately, some of the pioneering work has been done already. A few Boston-area supermarkets carry a frozen dog treat called Frosty Paws, which sells for $1.89 for 14 fluid ounces. This product is often placed near ice cream.

Overcoming Objections to Frozen Dog Food An objection must be anticipated regarding the requirement for thawing time and freezer space. Therefore, we should state on the container the thawing time, suggestions for quick thawing, how long the food will keep in the refrigerator, plus a gentle reminder to pull that container out of the freezer in the morning. Microwave instructions are a possibility.

Lack of Appeal of Frozen Dog Food We can quickly turn this problem into an asset in our advertising ("the first dog food made to appeal only to dogs").

Pricing We have considerable latitude in pricing as shown in Exhibit 3 on page 593. Furthermore, while dog owners in general are price sensitive, they are also concerned about the health and welfare of their animal companion. Show Circuit's quality suggests a premium price. This view is supported by the food brokers who first recognized the opportunity for Show Circuit. They report that Bil Jac, a frozen dog food sold in selected supermarkets in Dallas, Texas, carried a retail price of $2.29 for a two-pound package and $4.19 for a five-pound package.

EXHIBIT 2

Top Companies in Four Major Dog Food Categories

Category	Category Share of Total Dog Food	Dog Food Company Category Share	
		Company	*Category Share*
Dry	59%	Ralston Purina	43.9%
		Kal-Kan Foods	16.1
		H. J. Heinz	15.0
		Nestlé USA	6.8
		Private Label	9.3
		Others	8.9
			100.0%
Canned	24%	Kal-Kan Foods	37.7%
		Nestlé USA	30.8
		H. J. Heinz	20.0
		Private Label	8.6
		Others	2.9
			100.0%
Semimoist	2%	Ralston Purina	67.5%
		H. J. Heinz	14.4
		Private Label	15.8
		Others	2.3
			100.0%
Biscuits/Treats	15%	Nabisco	27.9%
		H. J. Heinz	26.4
		Ralston Purina	17.5
		Nestlé USA	4.9
		Kal-Kan Foods	4.3
		Private Label	13.3
		Others	5.7
			100.0%

Summary of Opportunities   We see Show Circuit seizing upon three opportunities:

1. The opportunity to be first to tap the vast market potential of a complete frozen dog food in supermarkets
2. The opportunity to be among the first to claim to produce an organic dog food (Ralston Purina has introduced Nature's Course, a dry dog food positioned as "organic")
3. The opportunity to lay the groundwork for entering the frozen cat food business

Creative Strategies

Positioning   Show Circuit will be positioned as the finest dog food available at any price and the only thing you will want to feed a dog that is truly a member of the family.

Target Market   We believe Show Circuit advertising should be targeted at singles and marrieds between the ages of 21 and 54 with a household income greater than

EXHIBIT 3

**Representative Dog Food Brand Prices and Package Sizes
in Boston-Area Supermarkets by Product Form**

Canned Foods		Dry Foods	
Mighty Dog	$.59/5.5 oz.	Dog Chow	$9.79/22 lbs.
Cycle	$.69/13.2 oz.	Gravy Train	$8.79/17.6 lbs.
Alpo	$.69/13.2 oz.	Purina O•N•E	$9.99/8 lbs.
Semimoist Foods		Biscuits/Treats	
Moist & Meaty	$10.69/13.5 lbs.	Milk-Bone	$2.79/24 oz.
Butcher's Burger	$3.39/3.375 lbs.	Jerky Treats	$3.19/7.5 oz.

$25,000. The reason is that single adults and married couples, with and without children, and roommate households regard their dogs as part of the family. The dog sleeps on the bed and has free run of the house or apartment. Industry research indicates that 79 percent of parents with school-age children buy pet food and supplies, compared with 71 percent of parents with younger or older children, 72 percent of roommate households, and 73 percent of young, childless couples. Income also plays a role in pet spending. Only 48 percent of households with annual incomes of less than $12,000 spend money to keep a pet. However, over 63 percent of households with incomes greater than $25,000 invest in pet food, supplies, and care according to research by the American Veterinary Medical Association. We see little initial opportunity in targeting older households. Only 30 percent of older singles and 41 percent of retired couples spend money on pets.

Concepts   Because Show Circuit is such a unique product, there are a variety of concepts that can easily be applied, each with adequate justification:

1. The luxurious fur coat
2. The world's finest dog food
3. The guilt concept (shouldn't your dog eat as well as you do?)
4. Now your dog can eat what show champions have been eating for years

All these will be touched on as the campaign progresses.

Creative Directions   Initially, the campaign will focus attention on product identification and an introductory coupon offer.

Newspapers will supply a smaller, more retentive audience with facts to justify all claims. They will also supply the coupon, proven crucial to a successful introduction in the pet food market. The container and coupon will be prominently displayed, and the copy will emphasize Show Circuit's quality. Special-interest ads will appear in the society, sports, television, and dining-out sections. This unusual media placement is warranted by the product's unique qualities. Also, placement in these sections will pull a relatively low promotional budget out of the mass of food-section advertising.

Radio and television will provide access to a mass audience. Prime objectives are to register the brand name and the package design in the viewer's or listener's memory. Because of the proven qualities of these media, an imaginative and all-important emotional approach will be taken.

Geographical Directions   The entire campaign has been designed to accommodate product introduction outside the Boston market area. When the product goes national, the television spot will be ready, the introductory ads will be ready, the radio spots will be ready, and the immediate follow-up will be ready.

Sales Packet

The sales packet given to brokers should include, in the most persuasive form possible, the following categories of information:

1. Profits available in the dog food category
2. Chain store acceptance of dog food
3. Market potential
4. Suggested manufacturer's list price to consumers and quantity discount schedule
5. Information about Show Circuit
6. Information about the container
7. User endorsements
8. Promotional schedule
9. Order information
10. Reprint of ads and TV storyboard
11. Sample shelf strip

The packet should be designed to persuade the supermarket frozen-food buyer to provide freezer space to Show Circuit. Two major problems have to be overcome. Because of the organizational modes of supermarket buying departments, we will not be dealing with the regular pet food buyer. Instead, it will be necessary to persuade the frozen-food buyer to stock Show Circuit. The other major problem involves the usual higher margin for frozen foods. It will be necessary to persuade the buyer that greater product turnover will compensate for a potentially lower margin for Show Circuit.

The task will not be easy. Some 15 percent of new products introduced to supermarkets each year are aimed at the freezer case. Eighty percent of these products fail. It is highly likely Tyler Pet Foods will need to budget about $30,000 for slotting fees paid to supermarkets to buy freezer space.

Creative Strategy by Media

Creative strategies will differ by media. Print media will be utilized to position the product against its competition by comparing it to canned, dry, and semimoist categories. The print campaign will open with an attention-getting ad with a brief product history.

Television will carry the brunt of the attack. The most pressing problem is seen as the difficulty of finding the food in the supermarket, so the TV spot will emphasize location.

In order to give the campaign continuity, each ad will show the container. At the top of each of the ads designed to position the competition, the artwork reproduced on the container will be used.

No single breed of dog will be associated with the product. Both the container and the ads will show a variety of breeds from show dogs to mongrels.

The myth/fact format in newspapers will be utilized to take advantage of the current publicity dealing with the nutritional value of all-meat dog food and the continued trend toward more natural foods (see Exhibit 4).

The copy block dealing with Show Circuit will turn the problem of Show Circuit's being frozen into a product advantage.

E X H I B I T 4

Show Circuit Print Advertisement

Media Plan

Because dog food is heavily advertised, TPF must follow suit to compete.

General Media Strategy Advertising objectives are as follows:

1. Create awareness of new brand
2. Obtain distribution through grocery outlets
3. Motivate trial through coupon redemption
4. Motivate trial through emotional impact of television

Collateral Advertising Accomplishment of objective 2, getting distribution in grocery stores, is the main purpose of collateral advertising. The sales packet, containing fact sheets, shelf strips, the TV storyboard, and testimonial letters, gives the food broker an impressive story to tell to the supermarket buyer. This is recognized as the critical stage of the campaign, for without sufficient distribution, consumer advertising will be delayed.

Newspaper/Magazine The primary purpose of newspaper advertising is distribution of coupons into the market. This will be accomplished by half-page ads in major Boston newspapers. As a secondary means of distribution, full-page ads will be placed in *Better Homes and Gardens* and *Dog Fancy* magazine for distribution throughout most of the Boston market area (see Exhibit 5 on page 596). We expect that one out of ten sales will involve a coupon redemption.

EXHIBIT 5

Show Circuit Print Advertisement

The second phase of coupon distribution will be effected through 30-inch ads in the same newspapers. A final coupon distribution will be made through a 30-inch ad midway through the campaign. Newspaper insertion will be coordinated with TV flights.

Television   The bulk of the budget will be placed in TV production and time. A sizable portion of the time budget will be spent on "The Late Show with David Letterman." Fixed space will be purchased within the first half-hour of the program. The remainder of the budget will reach daytime and nighttime audiences. Each flight will begin on a Monday, and newspaper advertising will be placed on Thursday of the following week.

Two basic approaches can be used for 30-second TV spots. The first approach capitalizes on the love of pet owners for their dogs. A somewhat frowzy, middle-aged, semigreedy woman is shown enjoying a steak dinner—in contrast to an unappetizing cylinder of canned dog food. The spot ends on a close-up of the product. The storyboard for this spot is shown in Exhibit 6.

A second TV spot will emphasize location of the food in the supermarket. A description of the video and audio characteristics of this spot is as follows:

Video	*Audio*
Supermarket—long establishing shot of small boy with bulge under jacket	Announcer: There are many things to remember about new Show Circuit Frozen Dog Dinner.
Close-up of boy, as puppy pops out of top of jacket	Remember, although it's new to you, champion dogs have eaten it for years.
Manager walks by, boy hides dog, looks relieved	Remember, it contains all the vitamins your dog needs.
Close-up of sign indicating pet foods	Remember, Show Circuit is a perfectly balanced diet of meat and cereal. Remember, it doesn't come in a can.
Dolly shot of boy looking at competitive brands	
Close-up of boy and dog (sync)	Boy: I don't see it anywhere, Sparky.
Boy walks out of store past frozen-food compartment	Announcer: But most important, remember you find Show Circuit in the frozen (bark) food section, where you shop for other members of your family.
People turn to stare	
Tilt down and zoom in on product	

EXHIBIT 6

Show Circuit Television Spot

Program Budget   The budget for the program described can be either $400,000 or $600,000 (Exhibit 7). We see this expense and the $30,000 slotting fee as being the only incremental cost associated with the launch in the Boston market.

We believe that this expenditure is reasonable, since most major established brands are spending $7 million to $8 million annually for ongoing nationwide media promotion. For a new product, a higher initial expense is necessary. For instance, Heinz Pet Products spent $30 million to introduce Reward, a premium canned dog food. Ralston Purina spent $34 million on television and print advertising to introduce Beneful, a premium dry dog food. A line extension, Alpo Lite, with 25 fewer calories than regular Alpo, was launched with a $10 million advertising effort.

EXHIBIT 7

Alternative Advertising and Trade Promotion Expenditure Levels for Show Circuit Frozen Dog Dinner

	Budget Levels	
Item	*$400,000*	*$600,000*
Television[a]	$259,000	$429,000
Newspapers/Magazines[b]	100,500	130,500
Collateral (sales pack)	9,750	9,750
Miscellaneous	5,250	5,250
Agency fees	25,500	25,500
Total	$400,000	$600,000

[a] The difference in television cost is due to the production of a second commercial and larger television schedule.

[b] The difference in newspaper/magazine cost is due to a larger number of insertions in *Better Homes and Gardens* and *Dog Fancy* magazines.

Unilever Canada
Becel Margarine

In early January 2000, Ross Hugessen, Brand Manager at Unilever Canada, reflected on the last several months of managing Becel Margarine, one of the company's most important brands. Becel had just been awarded a CASSIE[1] for advertising effectiveness, and it appeared as though Becel would end the year with a record market share in the $450-million margarine/butter category. It seemed as though things had never been better for the business. Ross knew, however, that he would soon be faced with some important issues regarding the brand's future.

For some time, Becel had been a very strong player in the market, having grown substantially in its relatively short history. But while Becel was still growing, the growth trend was below that of prior years—and well below what senior management had come to expect. Positioned as the "best margarine for your heart's health," Becel had a compelling point of differentiation that seemed to be one of the key reasons the brand had done so well. However, this positioning had been attracting several new competitors at a price point considerably below the premium price Becel had built its business on. In addition, the margarine category had some very tight regulations (for example, margarine in Quebec had to be white, not butter colored, and no dairy ingredients could be added), which limited the potential for margarine brands like Becel to come forward with much innovation.

Ross had to evaluate the brand from all angles to determine the best strategic plan to deliver both the short- and long-term significant growth that was expected by Unilever. Even though the brand had met with a record share, the rate of growth had fallen below what was expected for 1999. Becel had been built by targeting older, educated, and affluent adults, but Ross began to question the ability to attract any higher proportion of this target market. Furthermore, although the Becel communication strategy had been very successful, it didn't seem to be driving the rates of growth it had initially, even though advertising had been clearly proven to drive sales. The advertising campaign had been running for many years and had been developed by his boss. Ross knew he would be challenged to keep the level of advertising spending on his brand if the returns were less than before, especially as other brands in the company were vying for the budget.

He wondered if the brand team could determine a convincing strategy that would shape the future success of Becel margarine and maintain its share leadership and growth momentum.

---

[1]The CASSIE awards are given biannually to recognize significant achievements by Canadian advertisers.

This case was written by Phil Connell and Peggy Cunningham. We gratefully acknowledge the support of Mr. Ross Hugessen and Ms. Jan Mollenhauer of Unilever Canada. Some information in the case has been disguised in the interest of confidentiality. This case is used herein with permission, but may not otherwise be reproduced without the express consent of Queen's University School of Business or Unilever Canada. Copyright, Queen's University School of Business 2001.

■ UNILEVER CANADA

Unilever Canada, a division of the international Unilever group, is headed by two parent companies, Unilever NV and Unilever PLC, headquartered in Rotterdam and London, respectively. Unilever was formed in 1930 when the British soapmaker Lever Brothers merged with the Dutch company Margarine Unie. This allowed both companies to benefit from many raw materials and resources that they had in common. Today, Unilever is one of the world's largest consumer products companies.

In 1999, Becel Margarine fell under the Foods division, Lipton. In addition to having a category-leading position in the margarine market with more than eight brands, each of which was managed separately, Lipton also sold products in the tea, soup, packaged side dish, and pasta sauce markets. Unilever's other major division was Home Care and Personal Products, marketing such products as Dove, Sunlight Detergent, Salon Selectives, and Degree. The Personal Products brands often took priority for marketing budgets due to the competitive nature of their markets.

■ BECEL MARGARINE

A History of the Becel Brand

Becel Margarine was launched in 1978 as a premium-priced product, positioned as the heart-healthy margarine choice. Lipton's intention at the time was to create a brand that helped consumers meet their needs for heart health, as had been the position in Europe for 20 years prior to the Canadian introduction. Becel entered the market using very direct communication about the health advantages of the product.

Over the years, as Becel began to gain some success with its positioning, it increasingly attracted competitive attention. Nabisco, with its Fleischmann's brand, was most threatened, since it was the leader in the health segment of the market. Kraft also responded as it realized that the health-segment growth was taking share away from mainstream brands like Parkay. Also, the Dairy Bureau (butter) increased its marketing and advertising support; the target market for Becel and butter seemed to be the same. Furthermore, private-label brands launched their own products using "me-too" positioning strategies at significantly reduced prices.

Despite the uniqueness of the positioning, Becel struggled for many years. By 1991, the brand had managed to establish only an 8.1 percent share of the market, and had very limited growth at only 1 to 2 percent per year. Furthermore, as a result of new legislative guidelines, many of the direct, rational messages about Becel's heart health benefits could no longer be used. By 1991, Lipton knew it had to take the brand in a new direction or risk discontinuing the brand.

The company considered several options for growing the Becel brand. Lipton considered a price decrease, to increase volume; however, health brands in other categories typically had large price premiums that successfully delivered strong profits and communicated a price/quality relationship. The company also thought about repositioning the product—maybe not enough Canadians were concerned with heart health. Finally, Lipton considered dramatic increases in advertising support for Becel, but getting approval for heavy investment in a brand with poor volume was not really an option. Management decided that the only viable alternative was to try to grow the brand through a new break-through communication strategy without any change in expenditure. Any advertising budget would have to support the margarine, as well as the newly launched line of cooking oil and spoonable dressings.

In 1991, Lipton was able to devise a strategy that would eventually make Becel the leading brand of margarine in Canada. It decided to develop a communication strategy that would revolve around the notion of "living a life that is young at heart." This strategy allowed Lipton to communicate a simple message that became the emotional benefit of consuming Becel.

Becel's "Young at Heart" advertising campaign depicted the benefits of being young at heart through consumers' hope and optimism as expressed in the tagline "Becel takes your health to heart." The ads featured active, fit, outgoing seniors enjoying life to the fullest while enjoying a heart-healthy diet—which included the consumption of Becel. Seniors were used to create an association between Becel and living life to the fullest at a time in life that is often associated with health deterioration. The TV campaign, featuring the famous Jimmy Durante song "Young at Heart," focused on the emotional benefits of Becel, while a comprehensive print campaign delivered the rational heart-health messages (see Exhibit 1A/1B on pages 602-603 for sample Becel print ads). This communication strategy provided consumers with a powerful reason to believe in the product. Becel was ready to embrace mass consumption.

In addition, Becel started to educate consumers and health professionals about the dietary benefits of margarine through the Becel Heart Health Information Bureau. The Becel Heart Health Information Bureau sought to disseminate key brand messages based on sound scientific principles, while maintaining its objectivity and credibility. With increased marketing spending directed to health professionals, Becel built a solid reputation as a leader in heart health and nutrition education.

In 1998, Becel continued to develop the communication strategy even further and launched an interactive Web site (*www.becelcanada.com*). The Web site was an extension of the Becel Heart Health Information Bureau and provided information on meal planning, cooking recipes, the basics of heart health, and, of course, product information on the Becel lineup. In addition, there was a portion of the site dedicated exclusively to healthcare professionals.

Becel Today

Brand Performance As a result of the comprehensive Becel communication strategy, the brand went from being a small player to being the market leader within a relatively short time frame. In 1992, when the "Young at Heart" campaign was launched, Becel had a 17.7 percent dollar share of the market. By early 1997, the dollar share had increased to 28.4 percent. Sustained growth and impressive market share results had been achieved while Becel had commanded the highest price premium of any brand in its category. This price premium helped to provide a justification for advertising spending (see Exhibits 2A/B on page 604 for a description of the market share data and Exhibit 3 on page 605 for a profit/loss statement; Exhibit 4 on page 605 shows media costs).

Brand Awareness, Trial, and Advertising Awareness The success of this communication and positioning strategy was even further realized in the consumers' awareness of Becel in the market. Brand awareness of Becel increased substantially from 1992 onward. In addition to consumer brand awareness, the number of consumers in the market who had tried Becel had also increased substantially. Even more impressive was that Becel had the highest consumer loyalty of any brand in the category, at 50 percent—this in a category where brand switching was very high.

Given that brand awareness, brand trial, an advertising awareness were so high, it is not surprising that consumers also had a very good understanding of Becel's position in the marketplace. It was very clear that Becel's heart health message was getting through; substantial portions of the market believed that Becel was the heart health expert. Over all, there was no question that Lipton had developed a successful strategy for a strong product (see Exhibit 5 on page 606 for a summary).

The Spreads Category

Competitive Environment By 1999, the health segment of the margarine market had become very competitive, with many brands attracted by the success of Becel and consumer interest in healthy products. Even with the health segment growing, Becel's most formidable competitor was butter. Butter had just over 50 percent of the market in

EXHIBIT 1A

Sample Becel Print Ads

MARION IRVINE IS ON THE RIGHT PATH.

Making the choice to pursue a heart healthy lifestyle is important. Staying on that path is equally important.

Perhaps that's why so many choose Becel. It's low in saturated fat and non-hydrogenated (and therefore contains virtually no trans fat). No wonder more doctors and dietitians recommend Becel than any other margarine.

And to help you on the path to heart health, Becel is proud to support and make available the Heart and Stroke Foundation's booklet: "Heart Healthy Eating On the Go."

takes your health to heart.

Please write to us for your free copy:

Becel Heart Health Information Bureau
PO Box 12073, Saint John, NB, E2L 5E7

www.becelcanada.com

EXHIBIT 1B

THE BEST PART

ABOUT BEING OVER 70

IS STEALING THE GOLD

FROM AN UPSTART

58-YEAR-OLD.

The Canada Senior Games are what being young at heart is all about. That's why Becel is a major partner. For 20 years, we've educated Canadians about the rewards of choosing a balanced diet as part of a heart healthy lifestyle. And for many, that choice includes Becel. So here's to all the athletes – and everyone else who is young at heart.

BECEL IS A PROUD SPONSOR OF THE 1998 CANADA SENIOR GAMES.

Becel takes your health to heart.

EXHIBIT 2

A. Volume and Dollar Market Share for Becel

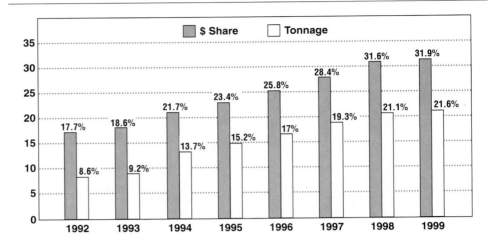

B. Market Share Data Analysis: Margarine

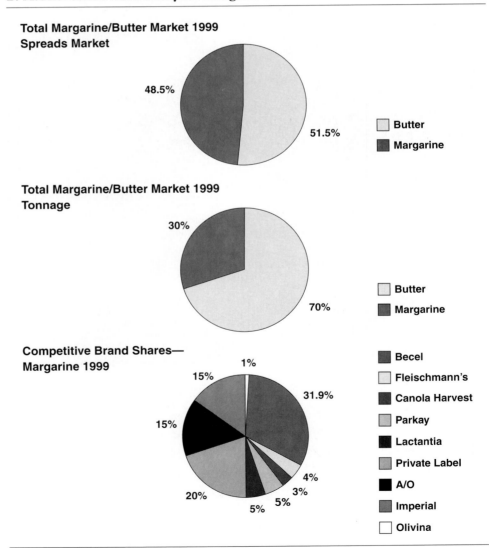

Total Margarine/Butter Market 1999
Spreads Market

48.5%   51.5%

Butter
Margarine

Total Margarine/Butter Market 1999
Tonnage

30%   70%

Butter
Margarine

Competitive Brand Shares—
Margarine 1999

1%   15%   31.9%   15%   20%   5%   5%   4%   3%

Becel
Fleischmann's
Canola Harvest
Parkay
Lactantia
Private Label
A/O
Imperial
Olivina

EXHIBIT 3

Becel Profit/Loss Statement

	Actual 1998 (000s)	Actual 1999 (000s)
Standard Cases	1,537	1,562
Gross Sales	$55,629	$58,746
Total Direct Costs	36,567	39,947
Gross Profit	$19,062	$18,799
Market Expenditure	5,200	3,800
Advertising	3,200	1,800
Promotion	2,000	2,000
Profit before Indirects	$13,862	$14,999

Canada, and Ross knew that for Becel to grow it had to make further inroads with butter consumers. The Dairy Bureau (which markets butter on behalf of Canadian dairy farmers) was very aggressive with positioning butter on its primary benefit of taste and naturalness. The campaign highlighted the "naturalness" of dairy over the perceived "processed food" reputation of margarine. The butter industry led the category in advertising spending with over a 50 percent share of voice, with about $7 million in spend-

EXHIBIT 4

Media and Advertising Cost Estimates

Primetime Television Commercial Rates (30 seconds)[a]

Network	Number of Stations	Basic Average Cost
Atlantic TV Network	1	$ 90
ATV	4	$ 650
CBC		
Atlantic	5	$1,000
Central/Quebec	15	$6,000
Western	12	$2,500
Pacific	6	$1,000
Global	1	$7,000
MITV	2	$ 500
BBS Ontario	8	$5,000

Cost of Production: one commercial $300

Newspaper Advertising[b]

Newspaper	Cost of Advertisement	Cost per 1,000 People Reached (CPM)
Toronto Star	$11,340	$2,438
Globe and Mail	$16,938	$5,314
Toronto Sun	$ 5,463	$2,366

Cost of Production: one ad $25

[a] "Estimated Cost of Network Commercials" *Media Digest* 1999–2000 ed., p. 22.

[b] Tuckwell, Keith J., *Canadian Advertising in Action*, 5th ed., (Prentice Hall: Scarborough, 2000), p. 332.

EXHIBIT 5

Brand Awareness, Brand Trial, and Advertising Awareness

Brand Awareness

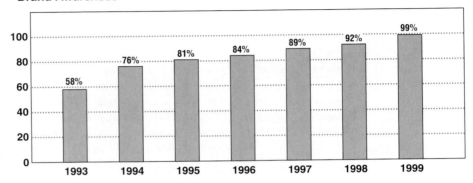

Brand Trial

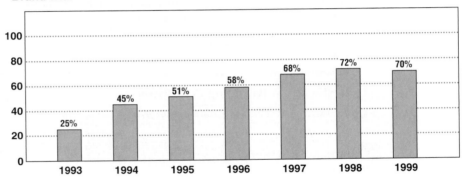

Advertising Awareness

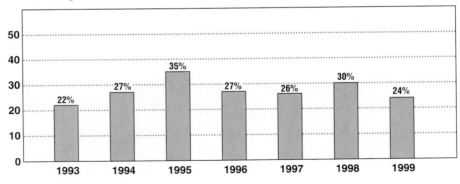

ing every year in television and print. Further, Parmalat, a large producer of butter, had recently begun to promote its Lactantia margarine brand of products. Using a positioning that leveraged the association with butter—"the makers of great tasting butter now bring you great tasting margarine"—Parmalat had only a small portion of the margarine market share, but it was increasing off a smaller base at a rate faster than Becel. Ross could not ignore the potential threat posed by this brand.

Finally, there were two other brands that were growing that Ross knew he had to keep an eye on. Canola Harvest was a product that had a small share of the national market, with its strongest market being in western Canada. This product was positioned as the margarine with the best taste and best health because it contains canola oil. Retailers liked the product because it seemed to offer many of the same benefits of Becel but at a much cheaper price. The other product was Olivina, which was positioned using a "Mediterranean diet" association. This product had secured only about 0.6 percent of the national market, but was showing strong growth. Ross knew that health professionals were starting to favor recommending olive oil over margarine. Ross also knew about the growing interest in olive oil, since Unilever had recently bought the Bertolli brand. This caused Ross to wonder if he had the right range of products (Exhibit 6).

Examining the Marketing Mix

Targeting the Market   The demographics of the margarine and butter category are quite diverse, although they do identify some interesting trends in the consumers that Becel and its competitors attract. Specifically, there is an interesting dichotomy between the types of consumers who purchase margarine versus those who purchase

EXHIBIT 6

Becel's Lineup of Products, 1999

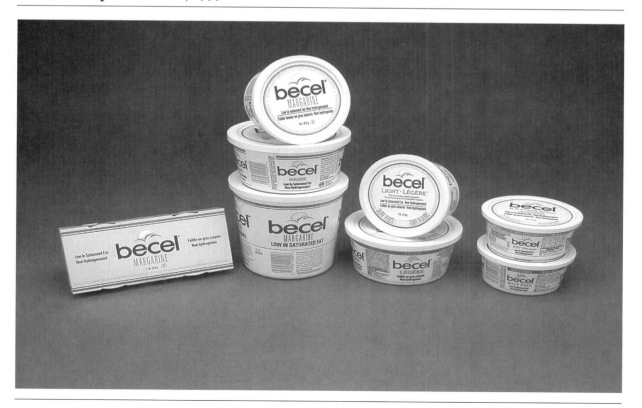

butter. A substantial portion of the volume of margarine purchased is by people with large families, particularly ones with four or five members, and who tend to have lower than average incomes (Exhibit 7).

Conversely, the total volume of butter consumed was disproportionately weighted toward families without children and families with older children. Furthermore, a large portion of butter consumers tended to be over 55 years of age, and the most affluent buyers. The target market for Becel tended to be very close to that of butter. However, most households bought both margarine and butter. Ross knew that the reasons people bought butter were quite different from the reasons they bought a health margarine.

These data made Ross's job more difficult. The demographics showed that Becel had been doing exactly what it was intended to do, serving the needs of those pursuing heart-healthy lifestyles. In addition, they had secured very high customer loyalty. Those who purchased Becel satisfied almost half of their margarine volume requirements with Becel. Most brands did not have remotely close to this degree of loyalty. Yet the rate of growth for Becel was beginning to slow down. Ross wondered why.

He had a look at some market data that showed what consumers tend to look for when purchasing margarine (Exhibit 8). The data showed that individuals who purchase margarine exclusively on the basis of taste seemed to account for the lowest volume of margarine purchased. Those who purchase exclusively on the basis of health or price reasons accounted for almost the same percentage of volume of margarine sold. However, this was really just scratching the surface. For the most part, consumers purchase products for a variety of reasons, and margarine is no exception. Thus, the data further showed what percentage of margarine consumption was based on the interaction among taste, health, and price. Apparently individuals considering all three attributes purchased the largest percentage volume of margarine. Looking at these data, Ross realized that he would have to consider the complex interaction of taste, health, and price in deciding his go-forward recommendation.

Pricing Considerations   Becel's price has remained relatively consistent over time, but since its inception Becel has been priced at a premium to other margarines to reflect the premium quality formulation (see Exhibit 9 on page 610 for pricing information).

EXHIBIT 7

Consumer Household Profiles

Margarine Households

• 4+ members

• head of household 45+

• strongest in lower income households

• families/empty nesters and childless couples (<$70,000)

Butter Households

• 3+ members

• head of household 45+

• strongest in high income households (>$70,000)

• strongest with empty nesters

Becel Households

• strongest with empty nesters

• 65+

• affluent with high income

Source: Nielsen Homescan.

EXHIBIT 8

Margarine Buyer Considerations

Taste Versus Health Versus Price
Homescan – National

	Buyers (000's)	% Buyers	Volume	% Volume
Taste or Health or Price	9,776	100.0	239,253	100.0
Excellent Health	1,644	16.8	27,646	11.6
Excellent Taste	1,333	13.6	21,118	8.8
Excellent Price	1,359	13.9	28,765	12.0
Health & Taste	1,176	12.0	27,842	11.6
Health & Price	711	7.3	17,925	7.5
Price & Taste	1,766	18.1	52,685	22.0
Taste and Health and Price	1,786	18.3	63,271	26.4

Taste Versus Health Versus Price
1999—Buyer Interaction—100%
Total Margarine

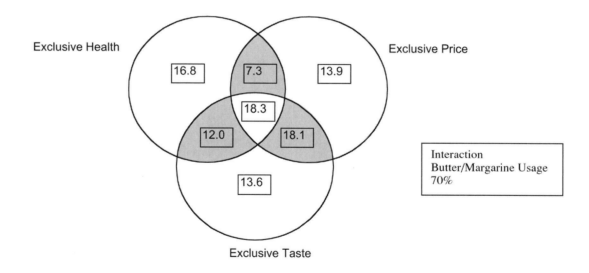

Exclusive Health

Exclusive Price

16.8   7.3   13.9

18.3

12.0   18.1

13.6

Exclusive Taste

Interaction
Butter/Margarine Usage
70%

EXHIBIT 9

Spreads Category Pricing Information

Product	Average Retail Price per Lb.
General Butter	$3.08
General Margarine	$1.45
Health Margarines	$2.09
Taste Margarines	$1.51
Price Margarines	$0.98
Becel	$2.10

Interestingly, though, all margarines are priced lower than butter. Butter was the highest-priced spread in the category and had the ability to demand a premium price because of its strong heritage and loyal user base. Butter had always been the gold standard for taste and best for baking. Margarine had always been considered a cheaper alternative to butter and so the largest share of the margarine market was held by more price-driven brands. In fact, in consumer surveys, price/value was the biggest reason for buying margarine over butter. The pricing strategy was an important area Ross had to give more consideration to if he wanted to grow volume.

Channel Considerations   The channels of distribution for packaged goods are quite broad: grocery stores (Loblaws, Sobeys), convenience stores (Becker's), discount super stores (Wal-Mart, Zellers) and club stores (Costco) are just a few examples of where packaged goods are sold. However, the dominant force in these channels is the grocery channel. Throughout Canada in the last decade, the grocery industry has seen intense consolidation and increased growth of private-label products. In 1999, the consolidation became even greater as Canada's biggest grocery chain, Loblaws, acquired Quebec's Provigo chain. Historically, Quebec had been the biggest market for butter and the weakest market for Becel.

■ THE FUTURE OF BECEL[2]

Ross glanced out his office window as he considered the various strategies that Becel could follow. Becel was an important business and any strategy taken also got lots of attention from the European head office. In fact, the Europeans were strongly considering using the Canadian advertising idea, which his boss was very proud of. Ross needed to carefully review what he saw to be some of his major alternatives before proceeding with a decision that would reinvigorate the expected growth for Becel.

Ross began to prepare his recommendation on the long-term vision for Becel, which was due within a month. As he considered a number of options, he got a call from his new advertising agency telling him about some new butter print advertising that was challenging the health benefits of the product. The ad actually made a specific reference to the ingredients for Becel, paralleling butter as "Nothing but Good Stuff."

---

[2]Note: Becel, Lipton, Sunlight, Salon Selectives, Dove, Degree, and Fleischmann's are all trademarks of Unilever Canada.

Frito-Lay, Inc.

Sun Chips™ Multigrain Snacks

In mid-1990, Dr. Dwight R. Riskey, Vice President of Marketing Research and New Business at Frito-Lay, Inc., assembled the product management team responsible for Sun Chips™ Multigrain Snacks. The purpose of the all-day meeting was to prepare a presentation to senior Frito-Lay executives on future action pertaining to the brand.

Sun Chips™ Multigrain Snacks is a crispy, textured snack chip consisting of a special blend of whole wheat, corn, rice, and oat flours with a lightly salty multigrain taste and a slightly sweet aftertaste. The product contains less sodium than most snack chips and is made with canola or sunflower oil. The chip is approximately 50 percent lower in saturated fats than chips made with other cooking oils and is cholesterol-free. According to a Frito-Lay executive, it is "a thoughtful, upscale classy chip."

The product had been in test market for 10 months in the Minneapolis-St. Paul, Minnesota, metropolitan area. Even though it appeared consumer response was extremely favorable, Riskey and his associates knew their presentation to senior Frito-Lay executives would have to be persuasive. In addition to presenting a thorough assessment of test-market data, Riskey added:

> We will have to do heavy-duty selling [to top executives] because Sun Chips™ Multigrain Snacks required a new manufacturing process, carried a new brand name, and pioneered a new snack chip category. There is a huge capital investment and a huge marketing investment that could be financially justified only with a product that could be sustainable for an extended time period.

■ FRITO-LAY, INC.

Frito-Lay, Inc. is a division of PepsiCo, Inc., a New York–based diversified consumer goods and services firm. Other PepsiCo, Inc. divisions include Pizza Hut, Inc., Taco Bell Corporation, Pepsi-Cola Company, Kentucky Fried Chicken, and PepsiCo Foods International. PepsiCo, Inc. recorded net income of $1.077 billion on net sales of $17.8 billion in 1990.

Company Background

Frito-Lay, Inc. is a worldwide leader in the manufacturing and marketing of snack chips. Well-known brands include Lay's® brand and Ruffles® brand potato chips, Fritos® brand corn chips, Doritos® brand, Tostitos® brand, and Santitas® brand tortilla chips, Chee•tos® brand cheese-flavored snacks, and Rold Gold® brand pretzels. The com-

The cooperation of Frito-Lay, Inc. in the preparation of this case is gratefully acknowledged. This case was prepared by Professor Roger A. Kerin, of the Edwin L. Cox School of Business. Southern Methodist University, and Kenneth R. Lukaska, Product Manager, Frito-Lay, Inc., as a basis for class discussion and is not designed to illustrate effective or ineffective handling of an administrative situation. Certain company information is disguised and not useful for research purposes. Copyright © 1995 by Roger A. Kerin. No part of this case may be reproduced without written permission of the copyright holder.

pany's major brands are shown in Exhibit 1 along with estimated worldwide retail sales. Other well-known Frito-Lay products include Baken-Ets® brand fried pork skins, Munchos® brand potato crisps, and Funyuns® brand onion-flavored snacks. In addition, the company markets a line of dips, nuts, peanut butter crackers, processed beef sticks, Smartfood® brand ready-to-eat popcorn, and Grandma's® brand cookies.

Frito-Lay, Inc. accounts for 13 percent of sales in the United States snack-food industry, which includes candy, cookies, crackers, nuts, snack chips, and assorted other items. The company is the leading manufacturer of snack chips in the United States, capturing nearly one-half of the retail sales in this category. Eight of Frito-Lay's snack chips are among the top ten best-selling snack chip items in U.S. supermarkets (see Exhibit 2). Doritos® brand tortilla chips and Ruffles® brand potato chips have the distinction of being the only snack chips with $1 billion in retail sales in the world.

Frito-Lay's snack-food business spans every aspect of snack-food production, from agriculture to stacking supermarket shelves. During 1990 in the United States alone, Frito-Lay used 1.6 billion pounds of potatoes, 600 million pounds of corn, and 55 million pounds of seasonings. The company has 39 manufacturing plants, more than 1,600 distribution facilities, and a 10,000-person route-sales team that calls on more than 400,000 retail store customers each week in the United States. Frito-Lay, Inc., recorded U.S. sales of $3.5 billion in 1990.

EXHIBIT 1

Frito-Lay, Inc.: Major Brands

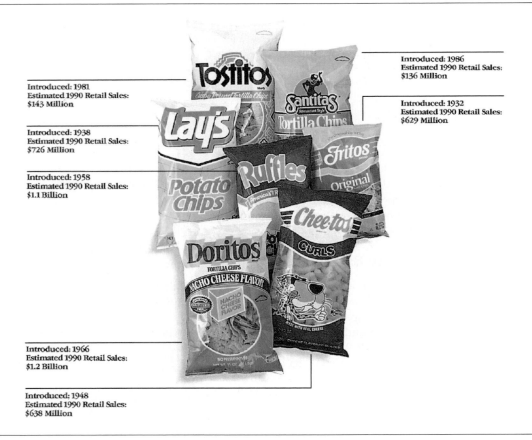

Introduced: 1981
Estimated 1990 Retail Sales:
$143 Million

Introduced: 1938
Estimated 1990 Retail Sales:
$726 Million

Introduced: 1958
Estimated 1990 Retail Sales:
$1.1 Billion

Introduced: 1966
Estimated 1990 Retail Sales:
$1.2 Billion

Introduced: 1948
Estimated 1990 Retail Sales:
$638 Million

Introduced: 1986
Estimated 1990 Retail Sales:
$136 Million

Introduced: 1932
Estimated 1990 Retail Sales:
$629 Million

Source: 1990 PepsiCo, Inc. Annual Report

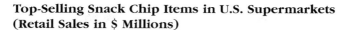

EXHIBIT 2

**Top-Selling Snack Chip Items in U.S. Supermarkets
(Retail Sales in $ Millions)**

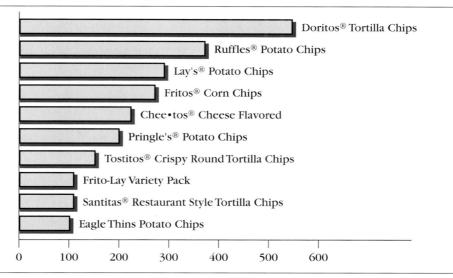

Source: 1990 PepsiCo, Inc. Annual Report.

Product-Marketing Strategies

Frito-Lay pursues growth opportunities through four product-marketing strategies.

1. *Grow established Frito-Lay brands through line extension.* Recognizing that consumers seek variety in snack tastes and sizes without compromising quality, Frito-Lay marketing executives use line extensions to satisfy these wants. Recent examples of line extension include Tostitos® brand bite-sized tortilla chips and Chee•tos® brand Flamin' Hot Cheese Flavored Snacks.

2. *Create new products to meet changing consumer preferences and needs.* Continuous marketing research at Frito-Lay is designed to uncover changing snacking needs of customers. A recent result of these efforts is evident in the launch of a low-oil light line of snack chips.

3. *Develop products for fast-growing snack-food categories.* Recognizing that snack-food categories experience different growth rates, Frito-Lay marketing executives continually monitor consumption patterns to identify new opportunities. For example, Frito-Lay acquired Smartfood® brand popcorn in 1989. In 1990, this brand became the number one ready-to-eat popcorn brand in the United States.

4. *Reproduce Frito-Lay successes in the international market.* Initiatives pursued in the United States often produce opportunities in the international arena. Primary emphasis has been placed in large, well-developed snack markets such as Mexico, Canada, Spain, and the United Kingdom. Innovative marketing coupled with product development efforts produced $1.6 billion in international snack-food sales in 1990.

■ THE SNACK CHIP CATEGORY

The United States snack-food industry recorded retail sales of $37 billion in 1990, representing a 5 percent increase over 1989. Dollar retail sales of snack chips consisting of potato, corn, and tortilla chips, pretzels, and ready-to-eat popcorn were estimated to be $9.8 billion—a 5 percent increase over 1989. A major source of growth in the snack chip category results from increased per capita consumption. In 1990, consumers in the United States bought 3.5 billion pounds of snack chips, or nearly 14 pounds per person; in 1986, snack chip per capita consumption was slightly less than 12 pounds.

Competitors

Three types of competitors serve the snack chip category: (1) national brand firms, (2) regional brand firms, and (3) private brand firms. National brand firms, which distribute products nationwide, include Frito-Lay, Borden (Guys brand potato and corn chips, and Wise brand potato chips, cheese puffs, and pretzels), Procter and Gamble (Pringles® brand potato chips), RJR Nabisco (several products sold under the Nabisco name as well as Planter's brand pretzels, cheese puffs, and corn and tortilla chips), Keebler Company (O'Boisies brand potato chips), and Eagle Snacks (a division of Anheuser-Busch Companies, Inc., which sells Eagle brand pretzels and potato and corn chips). A second category of competitors consists of regional brand firms, which distribute products in only certain parts of the United States. Representative firms include Snyder's, Mike Sells, and Charles Chips. Private brands are produced by regional or local manufacturers on a contractual basis for major supermarket chains (for example, Kroger and Safeway).

Competition

The snack chip category is very competitive. As many as 650 snack chip products are introduced each year by national and regional brand companies. Most of the products are new flavors for existing snack chips. The new-product failure rate for snack chips is high, and industry sources report that fewer than 1 percent of new products generate more than $25 million in first-year sales.

Snack chip competitors rely heavily on electronic and print media advertising, consumer promotions, and trade allowances to stimulate sales and retain shelf space in supermarkets. Pricing is very competitive, and snack chip manufacturers often rely on price deals to attract customers. The nature of the technology used to produce snack chips allows snack chip manufacturers to react swiftly to new product (flavor) introductions by competitors. Extensive sales and distribution systems employed by national brand competitors, in particular, allow them to monitor new product and promotion activities and place competing products quickly in supermarkets.

■ DEVELOPMENT OF SUN CHIPS™ MULTIGRAIN SNACKS

Sun Chips™ Multigrain Snacks resulted from Frito-Lay's ongoing marketing research and product development program. However, its taste and name heritage can be traced to the early 1970s.

Product Heritage

Frito-Lay product development personnel first explored the possibility of a multigrain product in the early 1970s when corporate marketing research studies indicated

consumers were looking for nutritious snacks. A multigrain snack chip called Prontos®
was introduced in 1974 with the following positioning statement: "The different, delicious new snack made from nature's own corn, oats, and whole grain wheat all rolled
into one special recipe, together in a snack for the first time from Frito-Lay." The product was only mildly successful despite advertising and merchandising support. The
product was subsequently withdrawn from national distribution in 1978 due to
declining sales and manufacturing difficulties. According to Frito-Lay executives, the
demise of Prontos® in 1978 was driven by "noncommittal" copy, a confusing name, and
a product that generated appeal among too narrow a target market. Reflecting on this
experience, Riskey added, "I'm not sure there were dramatic things wrong with the
product design so much as difficulty with the manufacturing process. It may have
been invented and introduced before its time."

The brand name for the product had an equally arduous past. The Sun Chips™
name was originally assigned to a line of corn chips, potato chips, and puffed corn
snacks in the early 1970s. In 1976, the brand name was given to a line of corn chips, but
by 1985, this line was also withdrawn from distribution due to poor sales performance.

Product Development: The "Harvest" Project

Early 1980s   Interest in a multigrain snack was revisited in the early 1980s when Frito-
Lay marketing executives began to worry whether the aging baby boomers (people
born between 1946 and 1964) would continue to eat salty snacks such as potato, corn,
and tortilla chips. According to Riskey:

> The aging baby boomers were a significant factor [in our thinking]. We were looking
> for new products that would allow them to snack. But we were looking for "better-for-
> you" aspects in products and pushing against that demographic shift.

In 1981, Frito-Lay marketing research and product development personnel instituted
the "Harvest" project with an objective of coming up with a multigrain snack that would
have consumer appeal. After several product concept tests and in-home product use
tests failed to generate any consumer excitement, it was concluded that the market for
wholesome snacks was not yet fully developed to accept such products. Other evidence seemed to support this view. In 1983, Frito-Lay test marketed O'Grady's™ brand
potato chips. The results had been phenomenal. Projections based on test market performance indicated the brand would produce $100 million in annual sales, which it did
in 1984 and 1985.

Mid-1980s   The "Harvest" project continued in the mid-1980s, albeit at a slower pace
due to staff changes and other responsibilities of project team members. At about this
time, a change in top management and corporate objectives focused product development efforts on traditional snacks with an emphasis on flavor line extensions for
established Frito-Lay brands (for example, Cool Ranch Doritos® brand tortilla chips)
and low-fat versions of its potato, corn, and tortilla chips. In addition, attention was
placed on cost-containment measures coupled with continuous quality-improvement
initiatives using existing manufacturing facilities and existing product and process
snack chip technology.

Late 1980s   Development efforts on a multigrain product were renewed in early
1988. Over the following 13 months, different product formulations (for example, low
oil vs. regular oil; salt content; chip shape), alternative positionings, and branding
options (extension of an existing Frito-Lay brand vs. a new brand name) were extensively studied using consumer taste tests and product concept tests. The combined
results of these tests yielded a multigrain rectangular chip with ridges and an exceptional taste. Further testing of brand names and flavors revealed consumer preferences

for two names (one of which was Sun Chips™) and three flavors (original/natural, French onion, and mild cheddar).

Further consumer research revealed that the multigrain product concept and assorted flavors were perceived as a "healthier product." This research also indicated that consumer expectations prior to use (that is, before initial trial of the product) were that the product would not be an "everyday snack" item. Consumers who tried the product, however, perceived the multigrain product to be an "everyday snack," at least for the natural and French onion flavors. Exhibit 3 shows a plot of pretrial consumer expectations and postuse perceptions of different flavors and representative snack

EXHIBIT 3

Consumer Expectations and Perceptions of Snack Chips and Multigrain Snacks

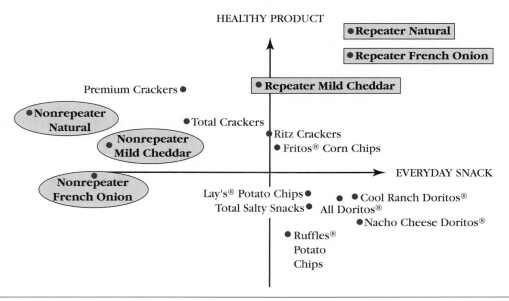

chip brands and crackers. Concurrent research on brand names indicated a decided preference for the Sun Chips™ name. The name evoked positive consumer imagery and attributes of "wholesomeness, great taste, light and distinctive, and fun," according to a Frito-Lay executive.

Premarket Test

Positive consumer response to the product concept and brand name prompted an initial assessment of the commercial potential of Sun Chips™ Multigrain Snacks. A simulated test market or premarket test (PMT) was commissioned in April 1989 and conducted by an independent marketing research firm.

A PMT involves interviewing consumers about attitudes and usage behavior concerning a product category (for example, snack chips). Consumers would be exposed to a product concept using product descriptions or mock-ups of advertisements, and their responses would be assessed (see Exhibit 4 on page 618). These consumers would then be given an opportunity to receive the product if interested. After an in-home usage period of several weeks, they would be contacted by telephone and asked about their attitude toward the product, use of the product, and intention to repurchase. These data would be incorporated into computer models that would include elements of the product's marketing plan (price, advertising, distribution coverage). The output provided by the PMT would include estimates of household trial rates, repeat rates, average number of units purchased on the initial trial and subsequent repeats in the first year, product cannibalism, and first-year sales volume.[1]

The product concept tested in the PMT was priced at parity with Doritos® brand tortilla chips. Planned distribution coverage was set at levels comparable for Frito-Lay potato, corn, and tortilla chips. Two-flavor combinations (natural and French onion and natural and mild cheddar) and three advertising and merchandising expenditure levels ($11 million, $17 million, and $22 million) were tested.[2]

Results from the PMT indicated that Sun Chips™ Multigrain Snacks would produce a most likely first-year sales volume of $113 million at manufacturer's prices given the marketing plan set for the product, including a $22 million advertising and merchandising expenditure. The estimated first-year sales volume exceeded the $100 million Frito-Lay sales goal for new products. The natural and French onion flavor combination produced the lowest cannibalization (42 percent) of other Frito-Lay brands. Summary statistics for the simulated test market are shown in Exhibit 5 on page 619.

■ TEST MARKET

Positive results from consumer research and the simulated test market led to a recommendation to proceed with Sun Chips™ Multigrain Snacks and implement a test market under Dwight Riskey's direction. The Minneapolis–St. Paul, Minnesota metropolitan area was chosen as the test site because Frito-Lay executives were confident it had a social and economic profile representative of the United States. Furthermore, Minneapolis–St. Paul, in general, represented a typical competitive environment in which to test consumer acceptance and competitive behavior. The Minneapolis–St. Paul metropolitan area contained 1.98 million households that were identified as users of snack chips, or 2.2 percent of the 90 million snack chip user households in

---

[1]Published validation data on premarket test models indicate that 75 percent of the time they are plus or minus 10 percent of actual performance when a product was introduced (see, for example, A. Shocker and W. Hall, "Pretest Market Models: A Critical Evaluation," *Journal of Product Innovation Management* 3, (1986): 86–107.

[2]Advertising and merchandising expenditures included electronic and print media advertising, consumer promotions, and trade allowances.

EXHIBIT 4

Concept Board for the Premarket Test

Introducing new SUN CHIPS™ multigrain snacks from Frito-Lay®

The great tasting snack chip for people who care about what they eat.

More and more people care about what they eat because they know that eating habits affect overall health and fitness. SUN CHIPS™ are a special blend of whole wheat, golden corn and other natural great tasting grains. These wholesome grains combined make a uniquely delicious chip with the golden goodness of corn and the nut-like flavor of wheat. They're cooked 'till lightly crisp and crunchy. Then they're lightly salted to let all that naturally good flavor come through. SUN CHIPS™ are a unique combination of great taste, great crunch, and natural goodness, all rolled into one remarkable chip.

So, try new SUN CHIPS™, the chip with the uniquely delicious taste for people who care about what they eat.

Available in these two delicious flavors:
● Natural   ● French Onion

the United States. Discussion among Frito-Lay marketing, sales, distribution, and manufacturing executives and the company's advertising agency indicated that the test market could begin October 9, 1989. Accordingly, a test-market plan and budget were finalized. The test market was scheduled to run for 12 months, with periodic reviews scheduled throughout the test.

Snack-food industry analysts became aware of Frito-Lay's development efforts on a multigrain snack chip soon after the company began preparation for the test market. According to one industry analyst:

EXHIBIT 5

Simulated Test-Market Results (Selected Statistics)

	Product and Promotion Strategy[a]			
	Natural & Mild Cheddar Combination		Natural & French Onion Combination	
	A&M Budget $17 million	A&M Budget $22 million	A&M Budget $17 million	A&M Budget $22 million
Purchase Dynamics				
Brand awareness (% of households)	40	48	40	48
Cumulative first-year trial rate (%)[b]	23	27	21	25
Cumulative first year repeat rate (%)[c]	61		57	
Number of purchases in first-year per repeating household	5.9		6.2	
Volume Projections ($ millions)				
Pessimistic	87	102	86	102
Most likely	96	113	95	113
Optimistic	106	125	106	125
Incremental annual volume (%)	50		58	
Cannibalized pound volume (%) (from Frito-Lay products)	50		42	

[a] The $11 million advertising and merchandising (A&M) budget for the two flavor combinations produced lower figures than those shown. For example, brand awareness was 35 percent and the cumulative first-year trial rate was 19 percent regardless of flavor combination.

[b] *Cumulative first-year trial* refers to the percentage of households that would try the product.

[c] *Cumulative first-year repeat* refers to the percentage of trier households that repurchased the product.

This is a departure from corn or potatoes. Wheat is different. Remember they departed from corn and potatoes a few years ago with Rumbles®, Stuffers®, and Toppels®, and it was a distasteful business. I'm sure they will take their time and really test it. It's not like they don't have other products, so there's no hurry.[3]

Test-Market Plan

Product Strategy Frito-Lay executives decided to introduce both the natural and French onion flavors given consumer research and simulated test-market results. Sun Chips™ Multigrain Snacks would be packaged in two sizes: a 7-ounce package and an 11-ounce package. These package sizes were identical to Doritos® brand tortilla chips. A 2¼-ounce trial package would be used as well.

Package design was considered to be extremely important. According to a Frito-Lay executive, "We wanted distinctive, contemporary graphics which would communicate new, different and fun amidst positive images—sun and a sprig of wheat." This view materialized in a metalized flex bag with primary colors of black (natural flavor) and green (French onion flavor). Exhibit 6 on pages 620-621 shows the packages used in the test market.

---

[3] "New Multigrain Chip Being Readied for Test," *Advertising Age* (June 26, 1989): 4. The products referred to were Stuffers® cheese-filled snacks, Rumbles® granola nuggets, and Toppels® cheese-topped crackers. These products were introduced in the mid-1980s, failed to meet sales expectations, and were subsequently withdrawn from the market.

EXHIBIT 6

Sun Chips™ Multigrain Snacks Packaging: Original Flavor

EXHIBIT 6 *(continued)*

Sun Chips™ Multigrain Snacks Packaging: French Onion Flavor

EXHIBIT 7

Sun Chips™ Multigrain Snacks Price List

Package Size	Suggested Retail Price	Frito-Lay Selling Price to Retailer
2¼ ounce	$0.69	$0.385
7 ounce	$1.69	$1.240
11 ounce	$2.39	$1.732

Pricing Strategy   Sun Chips™ Multigrain Snacks would have the same suggested retail prices as Doritos® brand tortilla chips. Research indicated these price points were consistent with consumer reference prices for snack chips and represented a good value. Suggested retail prices and Frito-Lay's selling prices to retailers are shown in Exhibit 7.

Advertising and Merchandising Strategy   The primary audience for Sun Chips™ Multigrain Snacks television advertising was adults between the ages of 18 and 34, since this target audience is the principal purchasers and heavy users of snack chips. A secondary audience expanded the age bracket to 49 years of age, since 34- to 49-year-olds appeared to be receptive to healthier snacks. Household members under 18 years of age would be exposed to the product through in-home usage. The advertising message would convey subtle messages, including wholesomeness, fun, and simplicity. One of the television commercials to be shown in the test market is reproduced in Exhibit 8. In addition to television advertising, the brand would be supported by in-store displays and free-standing inserts (FSIs) in newspapers (see Exhibit 9 on page 624).

Coupons placed in newspaper FSIs were to be used during the test market to stimulate trial and repeat sales. In addition, free samples would be distributed in supermarkets. Trade allowances were provided to retailers as well.

Distribution and Sales Strategy   Distribution and sales of Sun Chips™ Multigrain Snacks would be handled through Frito-Lay's store-door delivery system, in which the duties of a delivery person and a salesperson are combined. Under this system, a delivery/salesperson solicits orders, stocks shelves, and introduces merchandising programs to retail store personnel. Sun Chips™ Multigrain Snacks would be sold through supermarkets, grocery stores, convenience stores, and other retail accounts that already stocked Frito-Lay's snack products.

Manufacturing Considerations   Frito-Lay manufacturing personnel worked concurrently with marketing personnel on matters related to mass production of a multigrain product. While prototypes were easily developed in limited quantities, large-scale manufacturing would require a production line capable of delivering an adequate product for a market test. Since a multigrain product required different product and process technology than corn or potato products, an investment in one new production line would be necessary. Approval was granted to create a production line to produce and package 1 million pounds of the multigrain snack per year at full theoretical capacity. The production line could be in operation to ship the product in two flavors and three package sizes for the test market in September 1989.

Test-Market Budget

The advertising and merchandising budget for the test market was equivalent to a $22 million expenditure on a nationwide distribution basis. Approximately 70 percent of the budget would be spent during the first six months of the test market.

EXHIBIT 8

Sun Chips™ Multigrain Snacks Television Commercial

LEVINE, HUNTLEY, SCHMIDT
& BEAVER, INC.
CLIENT: FRITO-LAY, INC.
PRODUCT: SUNCHIPS

TITLE: "POLLY"
LENGTH: 30 Seconds
COMM'L NO.: PESU–9013

(Music under) GUY: Polly want one?

AVO: It seems everyone who tries new SUNCHIPS feels smarter eating them.

POLLY: Polly wants another one.

AVO: Smarter because they're multigrain.

POLLY: Polly wants you to fill her water cup.

AVO: Smarter because of the taste.

POLLY: Polly thinks you should paint this room and this time pick a better color.

AVO: Smarter because they're naturally delicious.

POLLY: Polly wants to know why one species feels it's OK to imprison another

purely for its own entertainment.

AVO: New SUNCHIPS.

You'll feel smarter eating them.

Test-Market Results

Consumer response was monitored by an independent research firm from the beginning of the test market. Data gathered by the research firm were submitted to Frito-Lay monthly and consisted of the types of purchases, the incidence of trial and repeat-purchase behavior, and product cannibalization in the test market.

Type of Purchase   Data supplied by the research firm indicated that the coupon program had a major impact on trial activity and approximately 90 percent of purchases were made in supermarkets and convenience stores. After 10 months in test market,

EXHIBIT 9

Sun Chips™ Multigrain Snacks Free-Standing Insert (FSI)

the 2¼-ounce package accounted for 15 percent of purchases, the 7-ounce package accounted for 47 percent of purchases, and the 11-ounce package accounted for 38 percent of purchases. Fifty-five percent of purchases were for the French onion flavor; 45 percent of purchases were for the natural flavor.

Trial and Repeat Rates Of critical concern to Frito-Lay executives were the incidences of household trial and repeat-purchase behavior for Sun Chips™ Multigrain Snacks. Exhibit 10 shows the cumulative trial and repeat rates for both flavors combined during the first 10 months of the test market. Almost one in five households in the test market had tried the product, and 41.8 percent of these trier households had repurchased the product at least once over the 10-month period.

Equally important to Frito-Lay executives were the "depth of repeat" data supplied by the research firm. *Depth of repeat* is the number of times a repeat purchaser buys a product after an initial repeat purchase. Repeater purchasers of Sun Chips™ Multigrain Snacks purchased the product an average of 2.9 times. An estimated average purchase amount for triers was 6 ounces. Initial repeat and repeater households purchased an average of 13 ounces per purchase occasion.

Product Cannibalization The independent research firm also identified the incidence of product cannibalization. The research firm's tracking data indicated that 30 percent of Sun Chips™ Multigrain Snack pound volume resulted from consumers switching from Frito-Lay's potato, tortilla, and corn snack chips. About one-third of the cannibalized volume from Frito-Lay's products came from Doritos® brand tortilla chips.

The 30 percent cannibalism rate was not uncommon in new product introductions in the snack food industry. For example, when Frito-Lay introduced O'Grady's™ brand potato chips, one-third of its pound volume came from its Ruffles® brand and Lay's® brand potato chips. Even though cannibalization was an issue to be considered in evaluating test-market performance, Frito-Lay executives noted that the gross profit for Sun Chips™ Multigrain Snacks was higher than that for its other snack chips.[4] (*Case writer note*: Footnote 4 contains important information for case analysis purposes.)

EXHIBIT 10

Household Trial and Repeat Rates for Sun Chips™ Multigrain Snacks

	Tracking (4-week Period)									
	1	*2*	*3*	*4*	*5*	*6*	*7*	*8*	*9*	*10*
Cumulative trial[a] (%)	4.7	8.2	9.8	11.3	14.1	15.7	16.5	17.4	19.5	19.9
Cumulative repeat[b] (%)	8.0	22.5	27.1	31.0	32.7	36.5	39.0	39.7	41.8	41.8

[a]*Trial* refers to the percentage of households that tried the product.

[b]*Repeat* refers to the percentage of trier households that repurchased the product.

[4]Frito-Lay, Inc. does not divulge profitability data on individual products and product lines. However, for case analysis and class discussion purposes, a multigrain snack chip can be assumed to have a gross profit of $1.30 per pound, while other snack chips (potato, tortilla, and corn) can be assumed to have a gross profit of $1.05 per pound. Gross profit is the difference between selling price and the cost of materials and manufacturing (ingredients, packaging/cartons, direct labor, other assignable manufacturing expenses, and equipment depreciation).

■ TEST-MARKET REVIEW

Riskey's presentation to senior Frito-Lay executives would conclude with his recommendation for the future marketing of Sun Chips™ Multigrain Snacks. He could recommend that the test be continued for another six months, or be expanded to other geographical areas with the same introductory strategy or some modification. Alternatively, he could recommend that Sun Chips™ Multigrain Snacks be readied for a national introduction with the strategy used in the test market or some modification in the strategy.

Planning Considerations

Numerous topics were raised in his meeting with the product management team responsible for Sun Chips™ Multigrain Snacks. Timing and competitive reaction were important issues. Riskey believed that national and regional competitors were monitoring Frito-Lay's test market. There was also a high probability that these competitors were examining the chip with the intention of developing their own version. Timing was a concern for a variety of reasons. First, if Riskey continued testing the product, a competitor might launch a similar product nationally or regionally and upstage Frito-Lay. The opportunity to be first-to-market would be lost. Second, if an expanded test market or a national introduction was considered, a decision would be needed quickly to assure adequate manufacturing capacity was in place and operating efficiently. Manufacturing capacity expansion would require a significant capital investment. Although preliminary figures represented rough estimates, manufacturing capacity capable of serving 25 percent and 50 percent of snack chip households in the United States would involve a capital expenditure recommendation of $5 million and $10 million, respectively. A full-scale national introduction would require a capital expenditure of $20 million.

Recommendations related to manufacturing capacity expansion would require a justification of the magnitude and sustainability of Sun Chips™ Multigrain Snacks sales over time. Accordingly, Riskey requested marketing research personnel to supply him with comparative brand awareness and cumulative household trial and repeat rate data for O'Grady's™ brand potato chips, since this brand was the most recent Frito-Lay product introduction to achieve $100 million in first-year sales.

Brand-awareness studies on the two brands indicated that O'Grady's™ brand potato chips achieved brand awareness among 28 percent of snack chip households during its market test compared with 33 percent for Sun Chips™ Multigrain Snacks. Exhibit 11 charts trial and repeat data for comparable test-market periods for Sun Chips™ Multigrain Snacks and O'Grady's™ brand potato chips. His interest in the sustainability of sales over time prompted a request for additional data on depth of repeat statistics for the two brands. The depth of repeat, or "repeats per repeater" for O'Grady's™ brand potato chips was 1.9 times, or about twice on an annual basis, compared with 2.9 times for Sun Chips™ Multigrain Snacks, or about three times on an annual basis.

Strategy Considerations

Several strategy options were also discussed. Some product management team members advocated increased advertising and merchandising spending if the brand was tested further or launched nationally. They believed that brand awareness would increase with additional spending and felt that spending the national introduction equivalent of $30 million could stimulate brand trial as well. Others interpreted the purchase data to mean that additional volume was possible by introducing a larger package size (for example, a 15-ounce package). They believed that a fourth, larger

EXHIBIT 11

Cumulative Trial and Repeat Rates for O'Grady's™ Potato Chips and Sun Chips™ Multigrain Snacks: 40-Week Test Market

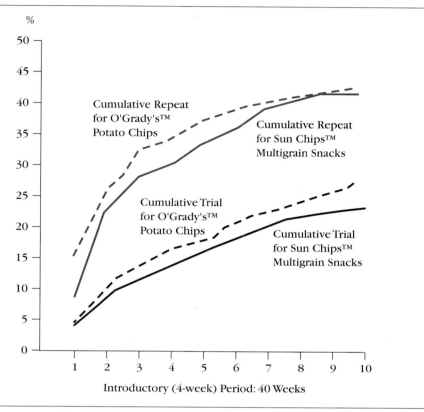

package could add about one-half ounce to the average annual purchase amount per repeat (and repeater) purchase occasion. Priced at the same price per ounce as the 11-ounce size, this action would not have a material effect on the brand's gross profit per pound. Others believed that another package size made more sense after the brand was established in the marketplace. Furthermore, the manufacturing and marketing of four sizes could stretch the production capacity, increase inventory, and challenge Frito-Lay sales personnel to get retailer shelf and display space.

Some discussion was also directed toward building the household repeat and depth of repeat business. For example, a flavor extension (for example, mild cheddar) was proposed. An advocate of this approach suggested that a flavor extension could increase the "repeats per repeater" to an average of 3½ times per year given greater variety for consumers. However, the addition of another flavor could increase the cannibalization rate to 35 percent, some thought. Also, the mild cheddar flavor still needed to be perfected in large-scale production. Others noted that if a larger package and a flavor extension were simultaneously pursued, the number of stock-keeping units would double from six (2 flavors × 3 sizes) to twelve (3 flavors × 4 sizes). It was agreed by everyone that this action would cause severe manufacturing difficulties, since the multigrain snack process technology was still untested.

Cima Mountaineering, Inc.

"What a great hike," exclaimed Anthony Simon as he tossed his Summit HX 350 hiking boots into his car. He had just finished hiking the challenging Cascade Canyon Trail in the Tetons north of Jackson, Wyoming. Anthony hiked often because it was a great way to test the hiking boots made by Cima Mountaineering, Inc., the business he inherited from his parents and owned with his sister, Margaret. As he drove back to Jackson, he began thinking about next week's meeting with Margaret, the President of Cima. During the past month they had been discussing marketing strategies for increasing the sales and profits of the company. No decisions had been made, but the preferences of each owner were becoming clear.

As illustrated in Table 1, sales and profits had grown steadily for Cima and by most measures the company was successful. However, growth was beginning to slow as a result of foreign competition and a changing market. Margaret observed that the market had shifted to a more casual, stylish hiking boot that appealed to hikers interested in a boot for a variety of uses. She favored a strategy of diversifying the company by marketing a new line of boots for the less experienced, weekend hiker. Anthony also recognized that the market had changed, but he supported expanding the existing lines of boots for mountaineers and hikers. The company had been successful with these boots, and Anthony had some ideas about how to extend the lines and expand distribution. "This is a better way to grow," he thought. "I'm concerned about the risk in Margaret's recommendation. If we move to a more casual boot, then we have to resolve a new set of marketing and competitive issues and finance a new line. I'm not sure we can do it."

When he returned to Jackson that evening, Anthony stopped by his office to check his messages. The financial statements shown in Table 2 (page 629) and in Table 3 (page 630) were on his desk along with a marketing study from a Denver consulting firm. Harris Fleming, Vice President of Marketing, had commissioned a study of the hiking boot market several months earlier to help the company plan for the future. As

Table 1
Cima Mountaineering, Inc. Revenues and Net Income, 1990–1995

Year	Revenues	Net Income	Profit Margin (%)
1995	$20,091,450	$857,134	4.27
1994	18,738,529	809,505	4.32
1993	17,281,683	838,162	4.85
1992	15,614,803	776,056	4.97
1991	14,221,132	602,976	4.24
1990	13,034,562	522,606	4.01

Lawrence M. Lamont is Professor of Management at Washington and Lee University. Eva Cid and Wade Drew Hammond were seniors in the class of 1995 at Washington and Lee, majoring in Management and Accounting, respectively.

Table 2

Cima Mountaineering, Inc. Income Statement (Years Ended December 31, 1995 and December 31, 1994)

	1995	1994
Net sales	$20,091,450	$18,738,529
Cost of goods sold	14,381,460	13,426,156
Gross margin	5,709,990	5,312,373
Selling and admin. expenses	4,285,730	3,973,419
Operating income	1,424,260	1,338,954
Other income (expenses)		
Interest expense	(160,733)	(131,170)
Interest income	35,161	18,739
Total other income (net)	(125,572)	(112,431)
Earnings before income taxes	1,298,688	1,226,523
Income taxes	441,554	417,018
Net income	$ 857,134	$ 809,505

Anthony paged through the report, two figures caught his eye. One was a segmentation of the hiking boot market (see Exhibit 1 on page 631) and the other was a summary of market competition (see Exhibit 2 on page 632). "This is interesting," he mused. "I hope Margaret reads it before our meeting."

■ HISTORY OF CIMA MOUNTAINEERING

As children, Anthony and Margaret Simon watched their parents make western boots at the Hoback Boot Company, a small business they owned in Jackson, Wyoming. They learned the craft as they grew up and joined the company after college.

In the late 1960s, the demand for western boots began to decline and the Hoback Boot Company struggled to survive. By 1975, the parents were close to retirement and they seemed content to close the business, but Margaret and Anthony decided to try to salvage the company. Margaret, the older, became president and Anthony became the executive vice president. By the end of 1976, sales had declined to $1.5 million and the company earned profits of only $45,000. It became clear that to survive, the business would have to be refocused on products with a more promising future.

Refocusing the Business

As a college student, Anthony attended a mountaineering school north of Jackson in Teton National Park. As he learned to climb and hike, he became aware of the growing popularity of the sport and the boots being used. Because of his experience with western boots, he also noticed their limitations. Although the boots had good traction, they were heavy, uncomfortable, and had little resistance to the snow and water always present in the mountains. He convinced Margaret that Hoback should explore the possibility of developing boots for mountaineering and hiking.

In 1977, Anthony and Margaret began 12 months of marketing research. They investigated the market, the competition, and the extent to which Hoback's existing equipment could be used to produce the new boots. By the summer of 1978, Hoback had developed a mountaineering and a hiking boot that were ready for testing. Several instructors from the mountaineering school tested the boots and gave them excellent reviews.

Table 3
Cima Mountaineering, Inc. Balance Sheet (Years Ending December 31, 1995 and December 31, 1994)

	1995	1994
Assets		
Current assets		
Cash and equivalents	$ 1,571,441	$ 1,228,296
Accounts receivable	4,696,260	3,976,608
Inventory	6,195,450	5,327,733
Other	270,938	276,367
Total	12,734,089	10,809,004
Fixed assets		
Property, plant and equipment	3,899,568	2,961,667
Less: accumulated depreciation	(1,117,937)	(858,210)
Total fixed assets (net)	2,781,631	2,103,457
Other assets		
Intangibles	379,313	568,087
Other long-term assets	2,167,504	1,873,151
Total fixed assets (net)	$18,062,537	$15,353,699
Liabilities and shareholder equity		
Current liabilities:		
Accounts payable	$ 4,280,821	$ 4,097,595
Notes payable	1,083,752	951,929
Current maturities of long-term debt	496,720	303,236
Accrued liabilities		
Expenses	2,754,537	2,360,631
Salaries and wages	1,408,878	1,259,003
Other	1,137,940	991,235
Total current liabilities	11,162,648	9,963,629
Long-term liabilities		
Long-term debt	3,070,631	2,303,055
Lease obligations	90,313	31,629
Total long-term liabilities	3,702,820	2,334,684
Other liabilities		
Deferred taxes	36,125	92,122
Other noncurrent liabilities	312,326	429,904
Total liabilities	14,672,043	12,820,339
Owner's equity		
Retained earnings	3,390,494	2,533,360
Total liabilities and owner's equity	$18,062,537	$15,353,699

The Transition

By 1981, Hoback was ready to enter the market with two styles of boots: one for the mountaineer who wanted a boot for all-weather climbing, and the other for men and women who were advanced hikers. Both styles were made of water-repellent leather uppers and cleated soles for superior traction. Distribution was secured through mountaineering shops in Wyoming and Colorado.

EXHIBIT 1

Segmentation of the Hiking Boot Market

	Mountaineers	Serious Hikers	Weekenders	Practical Users	Children	Fashion Seekers
Benefits	Durability/Ruggedness Stability/Support Dryness/Warmth Grip/Traction	Stability Durability Traction Comfort/Protection	Lightweight Comfort Durability Versatility	Lightweight Durability Good value Versatility	Durability Protection Lightweight Traction	Fashion/Style Appearance Lightweight Inexpensive
Demographics	Young Primarily male Shops in specialty stores and specialized catalogs	Young, middle aged Male and female Shops in specialty stores and outdoor catalogs	Young, middle aged Male and female Shops in shoe retailers, sporting goods stores, and mail-order catalogs	Young, middle aged Primarily male Shops in shoe retailers and department stores	Young marrieds Male and female Shops in department stores and outdoor catalogs	Young Male and female Shops in shoe retailers, department stores and catalogs
Lifestyle	Adventuresome Independent Risk taker Enjoys challenge	Nature lover Outdoorsman Sportsman Backpacker	Recreational hiker Social, spends time with family and friends Enjoys the outdoors	Practical Sociable Outdoors for work and recreation	Enjoys family activities Enjoys outdoors and hiking Children are active and play outdoors Parents are value conscious	Materialistic Trendy Socially conscious Nonhikers Brand name shoppers Price conscious
Examples of brands	Asolo Cliff Raichle Mt. Blanc Salomon Adventure 9	Raichle Explorer Vasque Clarion Tecnica Pegasus Dry Hi-Tec Piramide	Reebok R-Evolution Timberland Topozoic Merrell Acadia Nike Air Mada, Zion Vasque Alpha	Merrell Eagle Nike Air Khyber Tecnica Volcano	Vasque Kids Klimber Nike Merrell Caribou	Nike Espirit Reebok Telos Hi-Tec Magnum
Estimated market share	5% Slow growth	17% Moderate growth	25% High growth	20% Stable growth	5% Slow growth	28% At peak of rapid growth cycle
Price range	$210-$450	$120-$215	$70-$125	$40-$80	Will pay up to $40	$65-$100

EXHIBIT 2

Summary of Competitors

Company	Location	Mountaineering (Styles)	Hiking (Styles)	Men's	Women's	Children's	Price Range
Raichle	Switzerland	Yes (7)	Yes (16)	Yes	Yes	Yes	High
Salomon	France	Yes (1)	Yes (9)	Yes	Yes	No	Mid
Asolo	Italy	Yes (4)	Yes (26)	Yes	Yes	No	High
Tecnica	Italy	Yes (3)	Yes (9)	Yes	Yes	No	Mid/High
Hi-Tec	U.K.	Yes (2)	Yes (29)	Yes	Yes	Yes	Mid/Low
Vasque	Minnesota	Yes (4)	Yes (18)	Yes	Yes	Yes	Mid/High
Merrell	Vermont	Yes (5)	Yes (31)	Yes	Yes	Yes	Mid
Timberland	New Hampshire	No	Yes (4)	Yes	No	No	Mid
Nike	Oregon	No	Yes (5)	Yes	Yes	Yes	Low
Reebok	Massachusetts	No	Yes (3)	Yes	Yes	Yes	Low
Cima	Wyoming	Yes (3)	Yes (5)	Yes	Yes	No	High

Source: Published literature and company product brochures, 1995.

Hoback continued to manufacture western boots for its loyal customers, but Margaret planned to phase them out as the hiking boot business developed. However, because they did not completely understand the needs of the market, they hired Harris Fleming, a mountaineering instructor to help them with product design and marketing.

A New Company

During the 1980s, Hoback prospered as the market expanded along with the popularity of outdoor recreation. The company slowly increased its product line and achieved success by focusing on classic boots that were relatively insensitive to fashion trends. By 1986, sales of Hoback Boots had reached $3.5 million.

Over the next several years, distribution was steadily expanded. In 1987, Hoback employed independent sales representatives to handle the sales and service. Before long, Hoback boots were sold throughout Wyoming, Colorado, and Montana by retailers specializing in mountaineering and hiking equipment. Margaret decided to discontinue western boots to make room for the growing hiking boot business. To reflect the new direction of the company, the name was changed to Cima Mountaineering, Inc.

Cima Boots "Take Off"

The late 1980s were a period of exceptional growth. Demand for Cima boots grew quickly as consumers caught the trend toward healthy, active lifestyles. The company expanded its line for advanced hikers and improved the performance of its boots. By 1990, sales had reached $13 million and the company earned profits of $522,606. Margaret was satisfied with the growth, but she was concerned about low profitability as a result of foreign competition. She challenged the company to find new ways to design and manufacture boots at lower cost.

Growth and Innovation

The next five years were marked by growth, innovation, and increasing foreign and domestic competition. Market growth continued as hiking boots became popular for casual wear in addition to hiking in mountains and on trails. Cima and its competitors began to make boots with molded footbeds and utilize materials that reduced weight.[1] Fashion also became a factor, and companies like Nike and Reebok marketed lightweight boots in a variety of materials and colors to meet the demand for styling in addition to performance. Cima implemented a computer-aided design (CAD) system in 1993 to shorten product development and devote more attention to design. Late in 1994, Cima restructured its facilities and implemented a modular approach to manufacturing. The company switched from a production line to a system in which a work team applied multiple processes to each pair of boots. Significant cost savings were achieved as the new approach improved the profit and quality of the company's boots.

The Situation in 1995

As the company ended 1995, sales had grown to $20.0 million, up 7.2 percent from the previous year. Employment was at 425, and the facility was operating at 85 percent of capacity, producing several styles of mountaineering and hiking boots. Time-saving innovations and cost reduction had also worked, and profits reached an all-time high. Margaret, now 57, was still president, and Anthony remained executive vice president.

■ CIMA MARKETING STRATEGY

According to estimates, 1994 was a record year for sales of hiking and mountaineering boots in the United States. Retail sales exceeded $600 million, and about 15 million pairs of boots were sold. Consumers wore the boots for activities ranging from mountaineering to casual social events. In recent years, changes were beginning to occur in the market. Inexpensive, lightweight hiking boots were becoming increasingly popular for day hikes and trail walking and a new category of comfortable, light "trekking" shoes were being marketed by the manufacturers of athletic shoes.

Only a part of the market was targeted by Cima. Most of its customers were serious outdoor enthusiasts. They included mountaineers who climbed in rugged terrain and advanced hikers who used the boots on challenging trails and extended backpacking trips. The demand for Cima boots was seasonal, and most of the purchases were made during the summer months when the mountains and trails were most accessible.

Positioning

Cima boots were positioned as the best available for their intended purpose. Consumers saw them as durable and comfortable with exceptional performance. Retailers viewed the company as quick to adopt innovative construction techniques but conservative in styling. Cima intentionally used traditional styling to avoid fashion obsolescence and the need for frequent design changes. Some of the most popular styles had been in the market for several years without any significant modifications. The Glacier MX 350 shown in Exhibit 3 and the Summit HX 350 boot shown in Exhibit 4 on page 634 are good examples. The MX 350, priced at $219.00, was positioned as a classic boot for men with a unique tread design for beginning mountaineers. The Summit HX 350 was priced at $159.00 and was a boot for men and women hiking rough trails. Exhibit 5 on page 635 describes the items in the mountaineering and hiking boot lines, and Table 4 on page 635 provides a sales history for Cima boots.

---

[1]Two processes are used to attach the uppers to the soles of boots. In classic welt construction, the uppers and soles are stitched. In the more contemporary method, a molded polyurethane footbed (including a one-piece heel and sole) is cemented to the upper with a waterproof adhesive. Many mountaineering boots use classic welt construction because it provides outstanding stability, while the contemporary method is often used with hiking boots to achieve lightweight construction. Cima used the classic method of construction for mountaineering boots and the contemporary method for hiking boots.

EXHIBIT 3

The Glacier MX 350 Mountaineering Boot

Product Lines

Corporate branding was used and "Cima" was embossed into the leather on the side of the boot to enhance consumer recognition. Product lines were also branded, and alphabetic letters and numbers were used to differentiate items in the line. Each line had different styles and features to cover many of the important uses in the market.

EXHIBIT 4

The Summit HX 350 Hiking Boot

EXHIBIT 5

Cima Mountaineering, Inc. Mountaineering and Hiking Boot Lines

Product Line	Description
Glacier	
MX 550	For expert mountaineers climbing challenging mountains. Made for use on rocks, ice, and snow. Features welt construction, superior stability and support, reinforced heel and toe, padded ankle and tongue, step-in crampon insert, thermal insulation, and waterproof inner liner. Retails for $299.
MX 450	For proficient mountaineers engaging in rigorous, high-altitude hiking. Offers long-term comfort and stability on rough terrain. Features welt construction, deep cleated soles and heels, reinforced heel and toe, padded ankle and tongue, step-in crampon insert, and waterproof inner liner. Retails for $249.
MX 350	For beginning mountaineers climbing in moderate terrain and temperate climates. Features welt construction, unique tread design for traction, padded ankle and tongue, good stability and support, and a quick-dry lining. Retails for $219.
Summit	
HX 550	For experienced hikers who require uncompromising performance. Features nylon shank for stability and rigidity, waterproof inner liner, cushioned midsole, high-traction outsole, and padded ankle and tongue. Retails for $197.
HX 450	For backpackers who carry heavy loads on extended trips. Features thermal insulation, cushioned midsole, waterproof inner liner, excellent foot protection, and high-traction outsole. Retails for $179.
HX 350	For hikers who travel rough trails and a variety of backcountry terrain. Features extra cushioning, good stability and support, waterproof inner liner, and high-traction outsole for good grip in muddy and sloping surfaces. Retails for $159.
HX 250	For hikers who hike developed trails. Made with only the necessary technical features, including cushioning, foot and ankle support, waterproof inner liner, and high-traction outsole. Retails for $139.
HX 150	For individuals taking more than day and weekend hikes. Versatile boot for all kinds of excursions. Features cushioning, good support, waterproof inner liner, and high-traction outsole for use on a variety of surfaces. Retails for $129.

However, all boots had features that the company believed were essential to positioning. Standard features included water-repellent leather uppers and high-traction soles and heels. The hardware for the boots was plated steel, and the laces were tough, durable nylon. Quality was emphasized throughout the product lines.

Glacier Boots for Mountaineering

The Glacier line featured three boots for men. The MX 550 was designed for expert all-weather climbers looking for the ultimate in traction, protection, and warmth. The

Table 4
Cima Mountaineering, Inc. Product Line Sales

	Unit Sales (%)		Sales Revenue (%)	
Year	Mountaineering	Hiking	Mountaineering	Hiking
1995	15.00	85.00	21.74	78.26
1994	15.90	84.10	22.93	77.07
1993	17.20	82.80	24.64	75.36
1992	18.00	82.00	25.68	74.32
1991	18.80	81.20	26.71	73.29
1990	19.70	80.30	27.86	72.14

MX 450 was for experienced climbers taking extended excursions, while the MX 350 met the needs of less-skilled individuals beginning climbing in moderate terrain and climates.

Summit Boots for Hiking

The Summit line featured five styles for men and women. The HX 550 was preferred by experienced hikers who demanded the best possible performance. The boot featured water-repellent leather uppers, a waterproof inner liner, a cushioned midsole, a nylon shank for rigidity, and a sole designed for high traction. It was available in gray and brown with different types of leather.[2] The Summit HX 150 was the least expensive boot in the line, designed for individuals who were beginning to hike more than the occasional "weekend hike." It was a versatile boot for all kinds of excursions and featured a water-repellent leather upper, a cushioned midsole, and excellent traction. The HX 150 was popular as an entry-level boot for outdoor enthusiasts.

Distribution

Cima boots were distributed in Arizona, California, Colorado, Idaho, Montana, Nevada, New Mexico, Oregon, Washington, Wyoming, and western Canada through specialty retailers selling mountaineering, backpacking, and hiking equipment. Occasionally, Cima was approached by mail-order catalog companies and chain sporting goods stores offering to sell their boots. The company considered the proposals, but had not used these channels.

Promotion

The Cima sales and marketing office was located in Jackson. It was managed by Harris Fleming and staffed with several marketing personnel. Promotion was an important aspect of the marketing strategy, and advertising, personal selling, and sales promotion were used to gain exposure for Cima branded boots. Promotion was directed to consumers and to the retailers that stocked Cima mountaineering and hiking boots.

Personal Selling

Cima used 10 independent sales representatives to sell its boots in the western states and Canada. Representatives did not sell competing boots, but they sold complementary products such as outdoor apparel and equipment for mountaineering, hiking, and backpacking. They were paid a commission and handled customer service in addition to sales. Management was also involved in personal selling. Harris Fleming trained the independent sales representatives and often accompanied them on sales calls.

Advertising and Sales Promotion

Advertising and sales promotion were also important promotional methods. Print advertising was used to increase brand awareness and assist retailers with promotion.

---

[2]Different types of leather are used to make hiking boots. *Full Grain*: High-quality, durable, upper layer of the hide. It has a natural finish, and is strong and breatheable. *Split Grain*: Underside of the hide after the full-grain leather has been removed from the top. Lightweight and comfort are the primary characteristics. *Suede*: A very fine split-grain leather. *Nubuk*: Brushed full-grain leather. *Waxed*: A process in which leather is coated with wax to help shed water. Most Cima boots were available in two or more types of leather.

Mountaineering and hiking boots are made water repellent by treating the uppers with wax or chemical coatings. To make the boots waterproof, a fabric inner liner is built into the boot to provide waterproof protection and breatheability. All Cima boots were water repellent, but only those styles with an inner liner were waterproof.

Advertising was placed in leading magazines such as *Summit*, *Outside*, and *Backpacker* to reach mountaineers and hikers with the message that Cima boots were functional and durable with classic styling. In addition, cooperative advertising was offered to encourage retailers to advertise Cima boots and identify their locations.

Sales promotion was an important part of the promotion program. Along with the focus on brand name recognition, Cima provided product literature and point-of-sale display materials to assist retailers in promoting the boots. In addition, the company regularly exhibited at industry trade shows. The exhibits, staffed by marketing personnel and the company's independent sales representatives, were effective for maintaining relationships with retailers and presenting the company's products.

Pricing

Cima selling prices to retailers ranged from $64.50 to $149.50 a pair depending on the style. Mountaineering boots were more expensive because of their construction and features, while hiking boots were priced lower. Retailers were encouraged to take a 50 percent margin on the retail selling price, so retail prices shown in Exhibit 5 should be divided by two to get the Cima selling price. Cima priced its boots higher than competitors, supporting the positioning of the boots as the top quality product at each price point. Payment terms were net 30 days (similar to competitors), and boots were shipped to retailers from a warehouse located in Jackson, Wyoming.

■ SEGMENTATION OF THE HIKING BOOT MARKET

As Anthony reviewed the marketing study commissioned by Harris Fleming, his attention focused on the market segmentation shown in Exhibit 1. It was interesting, because management had never seriously thought about the segmentation in the market. Of course, Anthony was aware that not everyone was a potential customer for Cima boots, but he was surprised to see how well the product lines met the needs of mountaineers and serious hikers. As he reviewed the market segmentation, he read the descriptions for mountaineers, serious hikers, and weekenders carefully because Cima was trying to decide which of these segments to target for expansion.

Mountaineers

Mountain climbers and high-altitude hikers are in this segment. They are serious about climbing and enjoy risk and adventure. Because mountaineers' safety may often depend on their boots, they need maximum stability and support, traction for a variety of climbing conditions, and protection from wet and cold weather.

Serious Hikers

Outdoorsmen, who love nature and have a strong interest in health and fitness, comprise the serious hikers. They hike rough trails and take extended backpacking or hiking excursions. Serious hikers are brand conscious and look for durable, high-performance boots with good support, comfortable fit, and good traction.

Weekenders

Consumers in this segment are recreational hikers who enjoy casual weekend and day hikes with family and friends. They are interested in light, comfortable boots that provide good fit, protection, and traction on a variety of surfaces. Weekenders prefer versatile boots that can be worn for a variety of activities.

■ FOREIGN AND DOMESTIC COMPETITION

The second part of the marketing study that caught Anthony's attention was the analysis of competition. Although Anthony and Margaret were aware that competition had increased, they had overlooked the extent to which foreign bootmakers had entered the market. Apparently, foreign competitors had noticed the market growth and they were aggressively exporting their boots into the United States. They had established sales offices and independent sales agents to compete for the customers served by Cima. The leading foreign brands such as Asolo, Hi-Tec, Salomon, and Raichle were marketed on performance and reputation, usually to the mountaineering, serious hiker, and weekender segments of the market.

The study also summarized the most important domestic competitors. Vasque and Merrell marketed boots that competed with Cima, but others were offering products for segments of the market where the prospects for growth were better. As Anthony examined Exhibit 2, he realized that the entry of Reebok and Nike into the hiking boot market was quite logical. They had entered the market as consumer preference shifted from wearing athletic shoes for casual outdoor activities to a more rugged shoe. Each was marketing footwear that combined the appearance and durability of hiking boots with the lightness and fit of athletic shoes. The result was a line of fashionable hiking boots that appealed to brand- and style-conscious teens and young adults. Both firms were expanding their product lines and moving into segments of the market that demanded lower levels of performance.

■ MARGARET AND ANTHONY DISCUSS MARKETING STRATEGY

A few days after hiking in Cascade Canyon, Anthony met with Margaret and Harris Fleming to discuss marketing strategy. Each had read the consultant's report and studied the market segmentation and competitive summary. As the meeting opened, the conversation developed as follows:

MARGARET: It looks like we will have another record year. The economy is growing, and consumers seem confident and eager to buy. Yet, I'm concerned about the future. The foreign bootmakers are providing some stiff competition. Their boots have outstanding performance and attractive prices. The improvements we made in manufacturing helped to control costs and maintain margins, but it looks like the competition and slow growth in our markets will make it difficult to improve profits. We need to be thinking about new opportunities.

HARRIS: I agree, Margaret. Just this past week we lost Rocky Mountain Sports in Boulder, Colorado. John Kline, the sales manager, decided to drop us and pick up Asolo. We were doing $70,000 a year with them and they carried our entire line. We also lost Great Western Outfitters in Colorado Springs. They replaced us with Merrell. The sales manager said that the college students there had been asking for the lower-priced Merrell boots. They bought $60,000 last year.

ANTHONY: Rocky Mountain and Great Western were good customers. I guess I'm not surprised though. Our Glacier line needs another boot, and the Summit line is just not deep enough to cover the price points. We need to have some styles at lower prices to compete with Merrell and Asolo. I'm in favor of extending our existing lines to broaden their market appeal. It seems to me that the best way to compete is to stick with what we do best, making boots for mountaineers and serious hikers.

MARGARET: Not so fast, Anthony. The problem is that our markets are small and not growing fast enough to support the foreign competitors who have entered with excellent products. We can probably hold our own, but I doubt if we can do much better. I think the future of this company is to move with the market. Consumers are demanding more style, lower prices, and a lightweight hiking boot that can be worn for a variety of uses. Look at the segmentation again. The "Weekender" segment is large and it's growing. That's where we need to go with some stylish new boots that depart from our classic leather lines.

ANTHONY: Maybe so, but we don't have much experience working with the leather and nylon combinations that are being used in these lighter boots. Besides, I'm not sure we can finance the product development and marketing for a new market that already has plenty of competition. And I'm concerned about the brand image that we have worked so hard to establish over the past 20 years. A line of inexpensive, casual boots just doesn't seem to fit with the perception consumers have of our products.

HARRIS: I can see advantages to each strategy. I do know that we don't have the time and resources to do both, so we had better make a thoughtful choice. Also, I think we should reconsider selling to the mail-order catalog companies that specialize in mountaineering and hiking equipment. Last week, I received another call from REI requesting us to sell them some of the boots in our Summit line for the 1997 season. This might be a good source of revenue and a way of expanding our geographic market.

MARGARET: You're right, Harris. We need to rethink our position on the mail-order companies. Most of them have good market penetration in the East where we don't have distribution. I noticed that Gander Mountain is carrying some of the Timberland line and that L.L. Bean is carrying some Vasque styles along with its own line of branded boots.

ANTHONY: I agree. Why don't we each put together a proposal that summarizes our recommendations and then we can get back together to continue the discussion.

HARRIS: Good idea. Eventually we will need a sales forecast and some cost data. Send me your proposals and I'll call the consulting firm and have them prepare some forecasts. I think we already have some cost information. Give me a few days and then we can get together again.

■ THE MEETING TO REVIEW THE PROPOSALS

The following week, the discussion continued. Margaret presented her proposal, which is summarized in Exhibit 6 on page 640. She proposed moving Cima into the "Weekender" segment by marketing two new hiking boots. Anthony countered with the proposal summarized in Exhibit 7 on pages 640-641. He favored extending the existing lines by adding a new mountaineering boot and two new Summit hiking boots at lower price points. Harris presented sales forecasts for each proposal and after some discussion and modification, they were finalized as shown in Table 5 on page 642. Cost information was gathered by Harris from the Vice President of Manufacturing and is presented in Table 6 on page 643. Following a lengthy discussion, in which Margaret and Anthony were unable to agree on a course of action, Harris Fleming suggested that each proposal be explored further by conducting marketing research. He proposed the formation of teams from the Cima marketing staff to research each proposal and present it to Margaret and Anthony at a later date. Harris presented his directions to the teams in the memorandum shown in Exhibit 8 on pages 675 and 676.

EXHIBIT 6

Margaret's Marketing Proposal

MEMORANDUM

TO: Anthony Simon, Executive Vice President
         Harris Fleming, Vice President of Marketing

FROM: Margaret Simon, President

RE: Marketing Proposal

I believe we have an excellent opportunity to expand the sales and profits of Cima by entering the "Weekender" segment of the hiking boot market. The segment's estimated share of the market is 25 percent and according to the consultant's report it is growing quite rapidly. I propose that we begin immediately to develop two new products and prepare a marketing strategy as discussed below.

Target Market and Positioning

Male and female recreational hikers looking for a comfortable, lightweight boot that is attractively priced and acceptable for short hikes and casual wear. Weekenders enjoy the outdoors and a day or weekend hike with family and friends.

The new boots would be positioned with magazine advertising as hiking boots that deliver performance and style for the demands of light hiking and casual outdoor wear.

Product

Two boots in men's and women's sizes. The boots would be constructed of leather and nylon uppers with a molded rubber outsole. A new branded line would be created to meet the needs of the market segment. The boots (designated WX 550 and WX 450) would have the following features:

	WX 550	WX 450
Leather and nylon uppers	X	X
Molded rubber outsole	X	X
Cushioned midsole	X	X
Padded collar and tongue	X	X
Durable hardware and laces	X	X
Waterproof inner liner	X	

Uppers: To be designed. Options include brown full-grain, split-grain, or suede leather combined with durable nylon in two of the following colors: beige, black, blue, gray, green, and slate.

Boot design and brand name: To be decided.

Retail Outlets

Specialty shoe retailers carrying hiking boots and casual shoes and sporting goods stores. Eventually mail order catalogs carrying outdoor apparel and hiking, backpacking, and camping equipment.

Promotion

Independent sales representatives	Point-of-sale display materials
Magazine advertising	Product brochures
Co-op advertising	Trade shows

Suggested Retail Pricing

WX 550: $89.00

WX 450: $69.00

Competitors

Timberland, Hi-Tec, Vasque, Merrell, Asolo, Nike, and Reebok.

Product Development and Required Investment

We should allow about one year for the necessary product development and testing. I estimate these costs to be $350,000. Additionally, we will need to make a capital expenditure of $150,000 for new equipment.

E X H I B I T   7

Anthony's Marketing Proposal

MEMORANDUM

TO: Margaret Simon, President

          Harris Fleming, Vice President of Marketing

FROM: Anthony Simon, Executive Vice President

RE: Marketing Proposal

We have been successful with boots for mountaineers and serious hikers for years, and this is where our strengths seem to be. I recommend extending our Glacier and Summit lines instead of venturing into a new, unfamiliar market. My recommendations are summarized below:

Product Development

Introduce two new boots in the Summit line (designated HX 100 and HX 50) and market the Glacier MX 350 in a style for women with the same features as the boot for men. The new women's Glacier boot would have a suggested retail price of $219.99, while the suggested retail prices for the HX 100 and the HX 50 would be $119.00 and $89.00 respectively to provide price points at the low end of the line. The new Summit boots for men and women would be the first in the line to have leather and nylon uppers as well as the following features:

	HX 100	*HX 50*
Leather and nylon uppers	X	X
Molded rubber outsole	X	X
Cushioned midsole	X	X
Padded collar and tongue	X	X
Quick-dry lining	X	X
Waterproof inner liner	X	

The leather used in the uppers will have to be determined. We should consider full-grain, suede and nubuck since they are all popular with users in this segment. We need to select one for the initial introduction. The nylon fabric for the uppers should be available in two colors, selected from among the following: beige, brown, green, slate, maroon, and navy blue. Additional colors can be offered as sales develop and we gain a better understanding of consumer preferences.

Product Development and Required Investment

Product design and development costs of $400,000 for the MX 350, HX 100 and HX 50 styles and a capital investment of $150,000 to acquire equipment to cut and stitch the nylon/leather uppers. One year will be needed for product development and testing.

Positioning

The additions to the Summit line will be positioned as boots for serious hikers who want a quality hiking boot at a reasonable price. The boots will also be attractive to casual hikers who are looking to move up to a better boot as they gain experience in hiking and outdoor activity.

Retail Outlets

We can use our existing retail outlets. Additionally, the lower price points on the new styles will make these boots attractive to catalog shoppers. I recommend that we consider making the Summit boots available to consumers through mail order catalog companies.

Promotion

We will need to revise our product brochures and develop new advertising for the additions to the Summit line. The balance of the promotion program should remain as it exists since it is working quite well. I believe the sales representatives and retailers selling our lines will welcome the new boots since they broaden the consumer appeal of our lines.

EXHIBIT 7 *(continued)*

Suggested Retail Pricing

MX 350 for women: $219.00

HX 100: $119.00

HX 50: $89.00

Competitors

Asolo, Hi-Tec, Merrell, Raichle, Salomon, Tecnica, Vasque

The discussion between Margaret and Anthony continued as follows:

MARGARET: Once the marketing research is completed and we can read the reports and listen to the presentations, we should have a better idea of which strategy makes the best sense. Hopefully, a clear direction will emerge and we can move ahead with one of the proposals. In either case, I'm still intrigued with the possibility of moving into the mail order catalogs, since we really haven't developed these companies as customers. I just wish we knew how much business we could expect from them.

ANTHONY: We should seriously consider them, Margaret. Companies like L.L. Bean, Gander Mountain, and REI have been carrying a selection of hiking boots for several years. However, there may be a problem for us. Eventually the catalog companies expect their boot suppliers to make them a private brand. I'm not sure this is something we want to do since we built the company on a strategy of marketing our own brands that are made in the U.S.A. Also, I'm concerned about the reaction of our retailers when they discover we are selling to the catalog companies. It could create some problems.

HARRIS: That is a strategy issue we will have to address. However, I'm not even sure what percentage of sales the typical footwear company makes through the mail-order catalogs. If we were to solicit the catalog business, we would need an answer to this question to avoid exceeding our capacity. In the proposals, I asked each of the teams to provide an estimate for us. I have to catch an early flight to Denver in the morning. It's 6:30; why don't we call it a day.

The meeting was adjourned at 6:35 P.M. Soon thereafter, the marketing teams were formed with a leader assigned to each team.

Table 5

Cima Mountaineering, Inc. Sales Forecasts for Proposed New Products (Pairs of Boots)

	Project 1		*Project 2*		
Year	*WX 550*	*WX 450*	*MX 350*	*HX 100*	*HX 50*
2001–02	16,420	24,590	2,249	15,420	12,897
2000–01	14,104	21,115	1,778	13,285	11,733
1999–00	8,420	12,605	897	10,078	9,169
1998–99	5,590	8,430	538	5,470	5,049
1997–98	4,050	6,160	414	4,049	3,813

Note: Sales forecasts are expected values derived from minimum and maximum estimates.

Some cannibalization of existing boots will occur when the new styles are introduced. The sales forecasts provided above have taken into account the impact of sales losses on existing boots. No additional adjustments need to be made.

Forecasts for WX 550, WX 450, HX 100, and HX 50 include sales of both men's and women's boots.

Table 6

Cima Mountaineering, Inc. Cost Information for Mountaineering and Hiking Boots

	Inner Liner	*No Inner Liner*
Retail margin	50%	50%
Marketing and Manufacturing Costs		
Sales commissions	10	10
Advertising and sales promotion	5	5
Materials	42	35
Labor, overhead, and transportation	28	35

Cost information for 1997–1998 only. Sales commissions, advertising and sales promotion, materials, labor, overhead, and transportation costs are based on Cima selling prices. After 1997–1998, annual increases of 3.0 percent apply to marketing and manufacturing costs and 4.0 percent apply to Cima selling prices.

EXHIBIT 8

Harris Fleming's Memorandum to the Marketing Staff

MEMORANDUM

TO: Marketing Staff

CC: Margaret Simon, President
            Anthony Simon, Executive Vice President

FROM: Harris Fleming, Vice President of Marketing

SUBJECT: Marketing Research Projects

Attached to this memorandum are two marketing proposals (see case Exhibits 6 and 7) under consideration by our company. Each proposal is a guide for additional marketing research. You have been selected to serve on a project team to investigate one of the proposals and report your conclusions and recommendations to management. At your earliest convenience, please complete the following.

Project Team 1: Proposal to enter the "Weekender" segment of the hiking boot market.

Review the market segmentation and summary of competition in Exhibits 1 and 2. Identify consumers that would match the profile described in the market segment and conduct field research using a focus group, a survey, or both. You may also visit retailers carrying hiking boots to examine displays and product brochures. Using the information in the proposal, supplemented with your research, prepare the following:

1. A design for the hiking boots (WX 550 and WX 450). Please prepare a sketch that shows the styling for the uppers. We propose to use the same design for each boot, the only difference being the waterproof inner liner on the WX 550 boot. On your design, list the features that your proposed boot would have, considering additions or deletions to those listed in the proposal.

2. Recommend a type of leather (from among those proposed) and two colors for the nylon to be used in the panels of the uppers. We plan to make two styles, one in each color for each boot.

3. Recommend a brand name for the product line. Include a rationale for your choice.

4. Verify the acceptability of the suggested retail pricing.

5. Prepare a magazine advertisement for the hiking boot. Provide a rationale for the advertisement in the report.

6. Convert the suggested retail prices *in the proposal* to the Cima selling price and use the sales forecasts and costs (shown in Tables 5 and 6) to prepare an estimate of before-tax profits for the new product line covering a five-year period starting in 1997–98.

Assume annual cost increases of 3.0 percent and price increases of 4.0 percent beginning in 1998–99. Discount the future profits to present value using a cost of capital of 15.0 percent. Use 1996–97 as the base year for all discounting.

7. Determine the payback period for the proposal. Assume product development and investment occurs in 1996–97.

8. Provide your conclusions on the attractiveness of these styles to mail order catalog companies and their customers. You may wish to review current mail order catalogs to observe the hiking boots featured. Assuming Cima is successful selling to mail order catalog companies, estimate the percentage of our sales that could be expected from these customers.

9. Prepare a report that summarizes the recommendations of your project team, including the advantages and disadvantages of the proposal. Be prepared to present your product design, branding, pro-forma projections, payback period and recommendations to management shortly after completion of this assignment.

10. Summarize your research and list the sources of information used to prepare the report.

Project Team 2: Proposal to extend the existing lines of boots for mountaineers and hikers.

Review the market segmentation and summary of competition in Exhibits 1 and 2. Identify consumers that match the profile described in the market segment and conduct field research using a focus group, a survey, or both. You may also visit retailers carrying hiking boots to examine displays and product brochures. Using the information in the proposal, supplemented with your research, prepare the following.

1. Designs for the hiking boots (HX 100 and HX 50). Please prepare sketches showing the styling for the uppers. We propose to use a different design for each boot, so you should provide a sketch for each. On each sketch, list the features that your proposed boots would have, considering additions or deletions to those listed in the proposal. No sketch is necessary for the mountaineering boot, MX 350, since we will use the same design as the men's boot and build it on a women's last.

2. Recommend one type of leather (from among those proposed) and two colors for the nylon to be used in the panels of the uppers. We plan to make two styles, one in each color for each boot.

3. Verify the market acceptability of the suggested retail pricing.

4. Prepare a magazine advertisement for your hiking boots. Include a rationale for the advertisement in the report.

5. Using the suggested retail prices *in the proposal*, convert them to the Cima selling prices and use the sales forecasts and costs (shown in Tables 5 and 6) to prepare an estimate of before-tax profits for the new products covering a five-year period starting in 1997–98. Assume annual cost increases of 3.0 percent and price increases of 4.0 percent beginning in 1998–99. Discount the profits to present value using a cost of capital of 15.0 percent. Use 1996–97 as the base year for all discounting.

6. Determine the payback period for the proposal. Assume product development and investment occurs in 1996–97.

7. Provide your conclusions on the attractiveness of these styles to mail order catalog companies and their customers. You may wish to review current mail order catalogs to observe the hiking boots featured. Assuming Cima is successful selling to mail order catalog companies, estimate the percentage of our sales that could be expected from these customers.

8. Prepare a report that summarizes the recommendations of your project team, including the advantages and disadvantages of the proposal. Be prepared to present your product design, pro-forma projections, payback period and recommendations to management shortly after completion of this assignment.

9. Summarize your research and list the sources of information used to prepare the report.

Blair Water Purifiers India

"A pity I couldn't have stayed for Diwali," thought Rahul Chatterjee. "But anyway it was great to be back home in Calcutta." The Diwali holiday and its festivities would begin in early November 1996, some two weeks after Chatterjee had returned to the United States. Chatterjee worked as an international market liaison for Blair Company, Inc. This was his eighth year with Blair Company and easily his favorite. "Your challenge will be in moving us from just dabbling in less developed countries (LDCs) to our thriving in them," his boss had said when Chatterjee was promoted to the job last January. Chatterjee had agreed and was thrilled when asked to visit Bombay and New Delhi in April. His purpose on that trip was to gather background data on the possibility of Blair Company entering the Indian market for home water purification devices. Initial results were encouraging and prompted the second trip.

Chatterjee had used his second trip primarily to study Indian consumers in Calcutta and Bangalore and to gather information on possible competitors. The two cities represented quite different metropolitan areas in terms of location, size, language, and infrastructure—yet both suffered from similar problems in terms of water supplied to their residents. These problems could be found in many LDCs and were favorable to home water purification.

Information gathered on both visits would be used to make a recommendation on market entry and on elements of an entry strategy. Executives at Blair Company would compare Chatterjee's recommendation to those from two other Blair Company liaisons who were focusing their efforts on Argentina, Brazil, and Indonesia.

■ INDIAN MARKET FOR HOME WATER FILTRATION AND PURIFICATION

Like most aspects of India, the market for home water filtration and purification took a good deal of effort to understand. Yet despite expending this effort, Chatterjee realized that much remained either unknown or in conflict. For example, the market seemed clearly a mature one, with four or five established Indian competitors fighting for market share. Or was it? Another view portrayed the market as a fragmented one, with no large competitor having a national presence and perhaps 100 small, regional manufacturers, each competing in just one or two of India's 25 states. Indeed, the market could be in its early growth stages, as reflected by the large number of product designs, materials, and performances. Perhaps with a next generation product and a world-class marketing effort, Blair Company could consolidate the market and stimulate tremendous growth—much like the situation in the Indian market for automobiles.

This case was written by Professor James E. Nelson, University of Colorado at Boulder. He thanks students in the Class of 1996 (Batch 31), Indian Institute of Management, Calcutta, for their invaluable help in collecting all data needed to write this case. He also thanks Professor Roger Kerin, Southern Methodist University, for his helpful comments in writing this case. The case is intended for educational purposes rather than to illustrate either effective or ineffective decision making. Some data as well as the identity of the company are disguised. Copyright © 1997 by James E. Nelson. Used with permission.

Such uncertainty made it difficult to estimate market potential. However, Chatterjee had collected unit sales estimates for a 10-year period for three similar product categories—vacuum cleaners, sewing machines, and color televisions. In addition, a Delhi-based research firm had provided him with estimates of unit sales for Aquaguard, the largest selling water purifier in several Indian states. Chatterjee had used the data in two forecasting models available at Blair Company along with three subjective scenarios—realistic, optimistic, and pessimistic—to arrive at the estimates and forecasts for water purifiers shown in Exhibit 1. "If anything," Chatterjee had explained to his boss, "my forecasts are conservative because they describe only first-time sales, not any replacement sales over the 10-year forecast horizon." He also pointed out that his forecasts applied only to industry sales in larger urban areas, which was the present industry focus.

One thing that seemed certain was that many Indians felt the need for improved water quality. Folklore, newspapers, consumer activists, and government officials regularly reinforced this need by describing the poor quality of Indian water. Quality suffered particularly during the monsoons because of highly polluted water entering treatment plants and because of numerous leaks and unauthorized withdrawals from water systems. Such leaks and withdrawals often polluted clean water after it had left the plants. Politicians running for national, state, and local government offices also reinforced the need for improved water quality through election campaign promises. Governments at these levels set standards for water quality, took measurements at thousands of locations throughout the nation, and advised consumers when water became unsafe.

During periods of poor water quality, many Indian consumers had little choice but to consume the water as they found it. However, better educated, wealthier, and more health-conscious consumers took steps to safeguard their family's health and often

EXHIBIT 1

Industry Sales Estimates and Forecasts for Water Purifiers in India 1990–2005 (Thousands of Units)

	Unit Sales	Unit Sales Forecast Under . . .		
Year	Estimates	Realistic Scenario	Optimistic Scenario	Pessimistic Scenario
1990	60			
1991	90			
1992	150			
1993	200			
1994	220			
1995	240			
1996		250	250	250
1997		320	370	300
1998		430	540	400
1999		570	800	550
2000		800	1,200	750
2001		1,000	1,500	850
2002		1,300	1,900	900
2003		1,500	2,100	750
2004		1,600	2,100	580
2005		1,500	1,900	420

continued these steps year around. A good estimate of the number of such households, Chatterjee thought, would be around 40 million. These consumers were similar in many respects to consumers in middle- and upper-middle-class households in the United States and the European Union. They valued comfort and product choice. They saw consumption of material goods as a means to a higher quality of life. They liked foreign brands and would pay a higher price for such brands, as long as purchased products outperformed competing Indian products. Chatterjee had identified as his target market these 40 million households plus those in another four million households who had similar values and lifestyles, but as yet took little effort to improve water quality in their homes.

Traditional Method for Home Water Purification

The traditional method of water purification in the target market relied not on any commercially supplied product but instead on boiling. Each day or several times a day, a cook, maid, or family member would boil two to five liters of water for 10 minutes, allow it to cool, and then transfer it to containers for storage (often in a refrigerator). Chatterjee estimated that about 50 percent of the target market used this procedure. Boiling was seen by consumers as inexpensive, effective in terms of eliminating dangerous bacteria, and entrenched in a traditional sense. Many consumers who used this method considered it more effective than any product on the market. However, boiling affected the palatability of water, leaving the purified product somewhat "flat" to the taste. Boiling also was cumbersome, time consuming, and ineffective in removing physical impurities and unpleasant odors. Consequently, about 10 percent of the target market took a second step by filtering their boiled water through "candle filters" before storage. Many consumers who took this action did so despite knowing that water could become recontaminated during handling and storage.

Mechanical Methods for Home Water Filtration and Purification

About 40 percent of the target market used a mechanical device to improve their water quality. Half of this group used candle filters, primarily because of their low price and ease of use. The typical candle filter comprised two containers, one resting on top of the other. The upper container held one or more porous ceramic cylinders (candles) which strained the water as gravity drew it into the lower container. Containers were made of either plastic, porcelain, or stainless steel and typically stored between 15 and 25 liters of filtered water. Purchase costs depended on materials and capacities, ranging from Rs.350 for a small plastic model to Rs.1,100 for a large stainless steel model.[1] Candle filters were slow, producing 15 liters (one candle) to 45 liters (3 candles) of filtered water each 24 hours. To maintain this productivity, candles regularly needed to be removed, cleaned, and boiled for 20 minutes. Most manufacturers recommended that consumers replace candles (Rs.40 each) either once a year or more frequently, depending on sediment levels.

The other half of this group used "water purifiers," devices that were considerably more sophisticated than candle filters. Water purifiers typically employed three water processing stages. The first removed sediments, the second objectionable odors and colors, and the third harmful bacteria and viruses. Engineers at Blair Company were skeptical that most purifiers claiming the latter benefit actually could deliver on their promise. However, all purifiers did a better job here than candle filters. Candle filters

---

[1]In 1996, 35 Indian Rupees (Rs.) were equivalent to U.S.$1.00.

were totally ineffective in eliminating bacteria and viruses (and might even increase this type of contamination), despite advertising claims to the contrary. Water purifiers generally used stainless steel containers and sold at prices ranging from Rs.2,000 to Rs.7,000, depending on manufacturers, features, and capacities. Common flow rates were one to two liters of purified water per minute. Simple service activities could be performed on water purifiers by consumers as needed. However, more complicated service required units to be taken to a nearby dealer or an in-home visit from a skilled technician.

The remaining 10 percent of the target market owned neither a filter nor a purifier and seldom boiled their water. Many consumers in this group were unaware of water problems and thought their water quality acceptable. However, a few consumers in this group refused to pay for products that they believed were mostly ineffective. Overall, Chatterjee believed that only a few consumers in this group could be induced to change their habits and become customers. The most attractive segments consisted of the 90 percent of households in the target market who either boiled, boiled and filtered, only filtered, or purified their water.

All segments in the target market showed a good deal of similarity in terms of what they thought important in the purchase of a water purifier. According to Chatterjee's research, the most important factor was product performance in terms of sediment removal, bacteria and virus removal, capacity (either in the form of storage or flow rate), safety, and "footprint" space. Purchase price also was an important concern among consumers who boiled, boiled and filtered, or only filtered their water. The next most important factor was ease of intallation and service, with style and appearance rated almost as important. The least important factor was warranty and availability of financing for purchase. Finally, all segments expected a water purifier to be warranted against defective operation for 18 to 24 months and to perform trouble free for five to ten years.

■ FOREIGN INVESTMENT IN INDIA

India appeared attractive to many foreign investors because of government actions begun in the 1980s during the administration of Prime Minister Rajiv Gandhi. The broad label applied to these actions was "liberalization." Liberalization had opened the Indian economy to foreign investors, stemming from recognition that protectionist policies had not worked very well and that western economies and technologies— seen against the collapse of the Soviet Union—did. Liberalization had meant major changes in approval requirements for new commercial projects, investment policies, taxation procedures, and, most importantly, attitudes of government officials. These changes had stayed in place through the two national governments that followed Gandhi's assassination in 1991.

If Blair Company entered the Indian market, it would do so in one of three ways: (1) joint working arrangement, (2) joint venture company, or (3) acquisition. In a joint working arrangement, Blair Company would supply key purifier components to an Indian company which would manufacture and market the assembled product. License fees would be remitted to Blair Company on a per unit basis over the term of the agreement (typically five years, with an option to renew for three more). A joint venture agreement would have Blair Company partnering with an existing Indian company expressly for the purpose of manufacturing and marketing water purifiers. Profits from the joint venture operation would be split between the two parties per the agreement, which usually contained a clause describing buy/sell procedures available to the two parties after a minimum time period. An acquisition entry would have Blair Company purchasing an existing Indian company whose operations then would be expanded to include the water purifier. Profits from the acquisition would belong to Blair Company.

Beyond understanding these basic entry possibilities, Chatterjee acknowledged that he was no expert in legal aspects attending the project. However, two days spent with a Calcutta consulting firm had produced the following information. Blair Company must apply for market entry to the Foreign Investment Promotion Board, Secretariat for Industrial Approvals, Ministry of Industries. The proposal would go before the Board for an assessment of the relevant technology and India's need for the technology. If approved by the Board, the proposal then would go to the Reserve Bank of India, Ministry of Finance, for approvals of any royalties and fees, remittances of dividends and interest (if any), repatriations of profits and invested capital, and repayment of foreign loans. While the process sounded cumbersome and time consuming, the consultant assured Chatterjee that the government usually would complete its deliberations in less than six months and that his consulting firm could "virtually guarantee" final approval.

Trademarks and patents were protected by law in India. Trademarks were protected for seven years and could be renewed on payment of a prescribed fee. Patents lasted for 14 years. On balance, Chatterjee had told his boss that Blair Company would have "no more problem protecting its intellectual property rights in India than in the United States—as long as we stay out of court." Chatterjee went on to explain that litigation in India was expensive and protracted. Litigation problems were compounded by an appeal process that could extend a case for easily a generation. Consequently, many foreign companies preferred arbitration, as India was a party to the Geneva Convention covering Foreign Arbitral Awards.

Foreign companies were taxed on income arising from Indian operations. They also paid taxes on any interest, dividends, and royalties received, and on any capital gains received from a sale of assets. The government offered a wide range of tax concessions to foreign investors, including liberal depreciation allowances and generous deductions. The government offered even more favorable tax treatment if foreign investors would locate in one of India's six Free Trade Zones. Overall, Chatterjee thought that corporate tax rates in India probably were somewhat higher than in the United States. However, so were profits—the average return on assets for all Indian corporations in recent years was almost 18 percent, compared to about 11 percent for United States corporations.

Approval by the Reserve Bank of India was needed for repatriation of ordinary profits. However, approval should be obtained easily if Blair Company could show that repatriated profits were being paid out of export earnings of hard currencies. Chatterjee thought that export earnings would not be difficult to realize, given India's extremely low wage rates and its central location to wealthier South Asian countries. "Profit repatriation was really not much of an issue, anyway," he thought. Three years might pass before profits of any magnitude could be realized; at least five years would pass before substantial profits would be available for repatriation. Approval of repatriation by the Reserve Bank might not be required at this time, given liberalization trends. Finally, if repatriation remained difficult, Blair Company could undertake crosstrading or other actions to unblock profits.

Overall, investment and trade regulations in India in 1996 meant that business could be conducted much easier than ever before. Hundreds of companies from the European Union, Japan, Korea, and the United States were entering India in all sectors of the country's economy. In the home appliance market, Chatterjee could identify 11 such firms—Carrier, Electrolux, General Electric, Goldstar, Matsushita, Singer, Samsung, Sanyo, Sharp, Toshiba, and Whirlpool. Many of these firms had yet to realize substantial profits, but all saw the promise of a huge market developing over the next few years.

■ BLAIR COMPANY, INC.

Blair Company was founded in 1975 by Eugene Blair, after he left his position in research and development at Culligan International Company. Blair Company's first product was a desalinator used by mobile home parks in Florida to remove salts from brackish well water supplied to residents. The product was a huge success, and markets quickly expanded to include nearby municipalities, smaller businesses, hospitals, and bottlers of water for sale to consumers. Geographic markets also expanded, first to other coastal regions near the company's headquarters in Tampa, Florida, and then to desert areas in the southwestern United States. New products were added rapidly as well and, by 1996, the product line included desalinators, particle filters, ozonators, ion exchange resins, and purifiers. Industry experts generally regarded the product line as superior in terms of performance and quality, with prices higher than those of many competitors.

Blair Company sales revenues for 1996 would be almost $400 million, with an expected profit close to $50 million. Annual growth in sales revenues averaged 12 percent for the past five years. Blair Company employed over 4,000 people, with 380 having technical backgrounds and responsibilities.

Export sales of desalinators and related products began at Blair Company in 1980. Units were sold first to resorts in Mexico and Belize and later to water bottlers in Germany. Export sales grew rapidly, and Blair Company found it necessary to organize its International Division in 1985. Sales in the International Division also grew rapidly and would reach almost $140 million in 1996. About $70 million would come from countries in Latin and South America, $30 million from Europe (including shipments to Africa), and $40 million from South Asia and Australia. The International Division had sales offices, small assembly areas, and distribution facilities in Frankfurt, Germany; Tokyo, Japan; and Singapore.

The Frankfurt office had been the impetus in 1990 for development and marketing of Blair Company's first product targeted exclusively to consumer households—a home water filter. Sales engineers at the Frankfurt office began receiving consumer and distributor requests for a home water filter soon after the fall of the Berlin wall in 1989. By late 1991, two models had been designed in the United States and introduced in Germany (particularly to the eastern regions), Poland, Hungary, Romania, the Czech Republic, and Slovakia.

Blair Company executives watched the success of the two water filters with great interest. The market for clean water in LDCs was huge, profitable, and attractive in a socially responsible sense. However, the quality of water in many LDCs was such that a water filter usually would not be satisfactory. Consequently, in late 1994, executives had directed the development of a water purifier that could be added to the product line. Engineers had given the final design in the project the brand name "Delight." For the time being, Chatterjee and the other market analysts had accepted the name, not knowing if it might infringe on any existing brand in India or in the other countries under study.

■ DELIGHT PURIFIER

The Delight purifier used a combination of technologies to remove four types of contaminants found in potable water—sediments, organic and inorganic chemicals, microbials, or cysts, and objectionable tastes and odors. The technologies were effective as long as contaminants in the water were present at "reasonable" levels. Engineers at Blair Company had interpreted "reasonable" as levels described in several

World Health Organization (WHO) reports on potable water and had combined the technologies to purify water to a level beyond WHO standards. Engineers had repeatedly assured Chatterjee that Delight's design in terms of technologies should not be a concern. Ten units operating in the company's testing laboratory showed no signs of failure or performance deterioration after some 5,000 hours of continuous use. "Still," Chatterjee thought, "we will undertake a good bit of field testing in India before entering. The risks of failure are too large to ignore. And, besides, results of our testing would be useful in convincing consumers and retailers to buy."

Chatterjee and the other market analysts still faced major design issues in configuring technologies into physical products. For example, a "point of entry" design would place the product immediately after water entry to the home, treating all water before it flowed to all water outlets. In contrast, a "point of use" design would place the product on a countertop, wall, or at the end of a faucet and treat only water arriving at that location. Based on cost estimates, designs of competing products, and his understanding of Indian consumers, Chatterjee would direct engineers to proceed only with "point of use" designs for the market.

Other technical details were yet to be worked out. For example, Chatterjee had to provide engineers with suggestions for filter flow rates, storage capacities (if any), unit layout and overall dimensions, plus a number of special features. One such feature was the possibility of a small battery to operate the filter for several hours in case of a power failure (a common occurrence in India and many other LDCs). Another might be one or two "bells or whistles" to tell cooks, maids, and family members that the unit indeed was working properly. Yet another might be an "additive" feature, permitting users to add fluoride, vitamins, or even flavorings to their water.

Chatterjee knew that the Indian market would eventually require a number of models. However, at the outset of market entry, he probably could get by with just two—one with a larger capacity for houses and bungalows and the other a smaller capacity model for flats. He thought that model styling and specific appearances should reflect a western, high-technology school of design in order to distinguish the Delight purifier from competitors' products. To that end, he had instructed a graphics artist to develop two ideas that he had used to gauge consumer reactions on his last visit (see Exhibit 2 on page 652). Consumers liked both models but preferred the countertop design over the wallmount design.

■ COMPETITORS

Upwards of 100 companies competed in the Indian market for home water filters and purifiers. While information on most of these companies was difficult to obtain, Chatterjee and the Indian research agencies were able to develop descriptions of three major competitors and brief profiles of several others.

Eureka Forbes

The most established competitor in the water purifier market was Eureka Forbes, a joint venture company established in 1982 between Electrolux (Sweden) and Forbes Campbell (India). The company marketed a broad line of "modern lifestyle products" including water purifiers, vacuum cleaners, and mixers/grinders. The brand name used for its water purifiers was "Aquaguard," a name so well established that many consumers mistakenly used it to refer to other water purifiers or to the entire product category. Aquaguard, with its 10-year market history, was clearly the market leader and came close to being India's only national brand. However, Eureka Forbes had recently

EXHIBIT 2

Delight Water Purifier Wallmount and Countertop Designs

Wallmount Design	*Countertop Design*

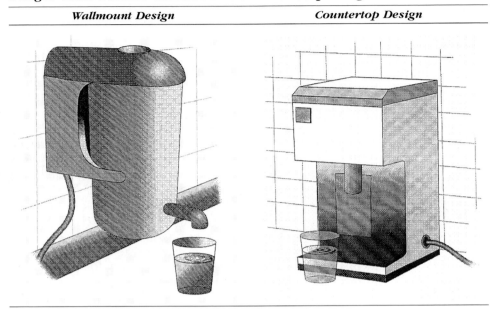

introduced a second brand of water purifier called "PureSip." The PureSip model was similar to Aquaguard except for its third stage process, which used a polyiodide resin instead of ultraviolet rays to kill bacteria and viruses. This meant that water from a PureSip purifier could be stored safely for later usage. Also in contrast to Aquaguard, the PureSip model needed no electricity for its operation.

However, the biggest difference between the two products was how they were sold. Aquaguard was sold exclusively by a 2,500 person salesforce that called directly on households. In contrast, PureSip was sold by independent dealers of smaller home appliances. Unit prices to consumers for Aquaguard and PureSip in 1996 were approximately Rs.5,500 and Rs.2,000, respectively. Chatterjee believed that unit sales of PureSip were much smaller than unit sales for Aquaguard but growing at a much faster rate.

An Aquaguard unit typically was mounted on a kitchen wall, with plumbing required to bring water to the purifier's inlet. A two-meter-long power cord was connected to a 230-volt AC electrical outlet—the Indian standard. If the power supply were to drop to 190 volts or lower, the unit would stop functioning. Other limits of the product included a smallish amount of activated carbon that could eliminate only weak organic odors. It could not remove strong odors or inorganic solutes like nitrates and iron compounds. The unit had no storage capacity and its flow rate of one liter per minute seemed slow to some consumers. Removing water for storage or connecting the unit to a reservoir tank could affect water quality, like a candle filter.

Aquaguard's promotion strategy emphasized personal selling. Each salesman was assigned to a specific neighborhood and was monitored by a group leader who, in turn, was monitored by a supervisor. Each salesman was expected to canvass his neighborhood, select prospective households (e.g., those with annual incomes exceeding Rs.70,000), demonstrate the product, and make an intensive effort to sell the product. Repeated sales calls helped to educate consumers about their water quality and to reassure them that Aquaguard service was readily available. Television commercials and advertisements in magazines and newspapers (see Exhibit 3) supported

EXHIBIT 3

Aquaguard Newspaper Advertisement

DON'T JUST GUARD YOUR FAMILY THIS MONSOON.

AQUAGUARD IT.

The monsoons bring a welcome relief from the long hot summer. But they also bring along some of the most dangerous water-borne diseases. Like cholera, dysentry, gastro-enteritis and jaundice. Which is why you need an Aquaguard Water Purifier, to safeguard your family.

Today, Aquaguard is synonymous with clean, pure and safe drinking water.

 Aquaguard is a 3 stage water purification system using the latest Ultra Violet technology, which destroys disease causing bacteria and virus in the water. It also has a unique

Electronic Monitoring System which stops water flow automatically if the purification level falls below pre-determined standards.

In addition, with Aquaguard you have the Eureka Forbes guarantee of After-Sales-Service at your doorstep.

So install an Aquaguard today. And help your family enjoy the monsoons better.

For a free demonstration at your home call the friendly man from Eureka Forbes or write to us at the addresses given below

Aquaguard
EUREKA FORBES LTD.

Calcutta: Mani Tower, Block Uttara, 1st Flr., 31/41 Vinoba Bhave Rd., Calcutta - 700 038. Tel: 4766845/5444. * 27 A, Lal Mohan Bhattacharjee Rd., 2nd Flr., Calcutta - 700 014. Tel: 2451548/2325. * 12 D, Chakraberia Rd. (North), Calcutta - 700 020. Tel: 746411/5326. * 177, Raja Dinendra Street, Opp. Desbandhu Park, Shyam Bazar, Calcutta - 700 004. Tel: 5545729/7248. * 21 G, Deodar Street, Calcutta - 700 019. * Guwahati: G.N.B.Rd., Silpukhuri, Above Jungle Travels, Near Goswami Service Station, Guwahati - 781 003. Tel: 31574. * Howrah: 105/106 A Panchsheel Apt., 1st Flr., 493, B.G.T. Road (South), Howrah - 711 102. Tel: 6606042. * Siliguri: 521 Swamiji Sarani, 1st Flr., Hakimpara P.O. Siliguri, Dist. Darjeeling. Tel: 26332.

the personal selling efforts. Chatterjee estimated that Eureka Forbes would spend about Rs.120 million on all sales activities in 1996 or roughly 11 percent of its sales revenues. He estimated that about Rs.100 million of the Rs.120 million would be spent in the form of sales commissions. Chatterjee thought the company's total advertising expenditures for the year would be only about Rs.1 million.

Eureka Forbes was a formidable competitor. The salesforce was huge, highly motivated, and well managed. Moreover, Aquaguard was the first product to enter the water purifier market and the name had tremendous brand equity. The product itself was probably the weakest strategic component—but it would take much to convince consumers of this. And, while the salesforce offered a huge competitive advantage, it represented an enormous fixed cost and essentially limited sales efforts to large urban areas. More than 80 percent of India's population lived in rural areas, where water quality was even lower.

Ion Exchange

Ion Exchange was the premier water treatment company in India, specializing in treatments of water, processed liquids, and waste water in industrial markets. The company began operations in 1964 as a wholly owned subsidiary of British Permutit. Permutit divested its holdings in 1985 and Ion Exchange became a wholly owned Indian company. The company presently served customers in a diverse group of industries, including nuclear and thermal power stations, fertilizers, petrochemical refineries, textiles, automobiles, and home water purifiers. Its home water purifiers carried the family brand name, ZERO-B (Zero-Bacteria).

ZERO-B purifiers used a halogenated resin technology as part of a three-stage purification process. The first stage removed suspended impurities via filter pads, the second eliminated bad odors and taste with activated carbon, and the third killed bacteria using trace quantities of polyiodide (iodine). The latter feature was attractive because it helped prevent iodine deficiency diseases and permitted purified water to be stored up to eight hours without fear of recontamination.

The basic purifier product for the home carried the name "Puristore." A Puristore unit typically sat on a kitchen counter near the tap, with no electricity or plumbing hookup needed for its operation. The unit stored 20 liters of purified water. It sold to consumers for Rs.2,000. Each year the user must replace the halogenated resin at a cost of Rs.200.

Chatterjee estimated that ZERO-B captured about 7 percent of the Indian water purifier market. Probably the biggest reason for the small share was a lack of consumer awareness. ZERO-B purifiers had been on the market for less than three years. They were not advertised heavily nor did they enjoy the sales effort intensity of Aquaguard. Distribution, too, was limited. During Chatterjee's visit, he could find only five dealers in Calcutta carrying ZERO-B products and none in Bangalore. Dealers that he contacted were of the opinion that ZERO-B's marketing efforts soon would intensify—two had heard rumors that a door-to-door salesforce was planned and that consumer advertising was about to begin.

Chatterjee had confirmed the latter point with a visit to a Calcutta advertising agency. A modest number of 10-second TV commercials soon would be aired on Zee TV and DD metro channels. The advertisements would focus on educating consumers with the position, "It is not a filter." Instead, ZERO-B is a water purifier and much more effective than a candle filter in preventing health problems. Apart from this advertising effort, the only other form of promotion used was a point of sale brochure that dealers could give to prospective customers (see Exhibit 4).

On balance, Chatterjee thought that Ion Exchange could be a major player in the market. The company had over 30 years' experience in the field of water purification and devoted upwards of Rs.10 million each year to corporate research and development. "In fact," he thought, "all Ion Exchange really needs to do is to recognize the market's potential and to make it a priority within the company." However, this might be difficult to do, given the company's prominent emphasis on industrial markets. Chatterjee estimated that ZERO-B products would account for less than two percent

EXHIBIT 4

ZERO-B Sales Brochure

of Ion Exchange's 1996 total sales, estimated at Rs.1,000 million. He thought the total marketing expenditures for ZERO-B would be around Rs.3 million.

Singer

The newest competitor to enter the Indian water purifier market was Singer India Ltd. Originally, Singer India was a subsidiary of The Singer Company, located in the United States, but a minority share (49 percent) was sold to Indian investors in 1982. The change in ownership had led to construction of manufacturing facilities in India for sewing machines in 1983. The facilities were expanded in 1991 to produce a broad line of home appliances. Sales revenues for 1996 for the entire product line—sewing machines, food processors, irons, mixers, toaster, water heaters, ceiling fans, cooking ranges, and color televisions—would be about Rs.900 million.

During Chatterjee's time in Calcutta, he had visited a Singer Company showroom on Park Street. Initially he had hoped that Singer might be a suitable partner to manufacture and distribute the Delight purifier. However, much to his surprise, he was told that Singer now had its own brand on the market, "Aquarius." The product was not yet available in Calcutta but was being sold in Bombay and Delhi.

A marketing research agency in Delhi was able to gather some information on the Singer purifier. The product contained nine stages (!) and sold to consumers for Rs.4,000. It removed sediments, heavy metals, bad tastes, odors, and colors. It also killed bacteria and viruses, fungi, and nematodes. The purifier required water pressure (8 PSI minimum) to operate but needed no electricity. It came in a single countertop model that could be moved from one room to another. Life of the device at a flow rate of 3.8 liters per minute was listed as 40,000 liters—about four to six years of use in the typical Indian household. The product's life could be extended to 70,000 liters at a somewhat slower flow rate. However, at 70,000 liters, the product must be discarded. The agency reported a heavy advertising blitz accompanying the introduction in Delhi—emphasizing TV and newspaper advertising, plus outdoor and transit advertising as support. All 10 Singer showrooms in Delhi offered vivid demonstrations of the product's operation.

Chatterjee had to admit that photos of the Aquarius purifier shown in the Calcutta showroom looked appealing. And a trade article he found had described the product as "state of the art" in comparison to the "primitive" products now on the market. Chatterjee and Blair Company engineers tended to agree—the disinfecting resin used in Aquarius had been developed by the United States government's National Aeronautics and Space Administration (NASA) and was proven to be 100 percent effective against bacteria and viruses. "If only I could have brought a unit back with me," he thought. "We could have some test results and see just how good it is." The trade article also mentioned that Singer hoped to sell 40,000 units over the next two years.

Chatterjee knew that Singer was a well-known and respected brand name in India. Further, Singer's distribution channels were superior to those of any competitor in the market, including those of Eureka Forbes. Most prominent of Singer's three distribution channels were the 210 company-owned showrooms located in major urban areas around the country. Each sold and serviced the entire line of Singer products. Each was very well kept and staffed by knowledgeable personnel. Singer products also were sold throughout India by over 3,000 independent dealers, who received inventory from an estimated 70 Singer-appointed distributors. According to the marketing research agency in Delhi, distributors earned margins of 12 percent of the retail price for Aquarius while dealers earned margins of five percent. Finally, Singer employed over 400 salesmen who sold sewing machines and food processors door-to-door. Like Eureka Forbes, the direct salesforce sold products primarily in large urban markets.

■ OTHER COMPETITORS

Chatterjee was aware of several other water purifiers on the Indian market. The Delta brand from S & S Industries in Madras seemed a carbon copy of Aquaguard, except for a more eye-pleasing, countertop design. According to promotion literature, Delta offered a line of water-related products—purifiers, water softeners, iron removers, desalinators, and ozonators. Another competitor was Alfa Water Purifiers, Bombay. The company offered four purifier models at prices from Rs.4,300 to Rs.6,500, depending on capacity. Symphony's Spectrum brand sold well around Bombay at Rs.4,000 each but removed only suspended sediments, not heavy metals or bacteria. The Sam Group in Coimbatore recently had launched its "Water Doctor" purifier at Rs.5,200. The device used a third stage ozonator to kill bacteria and viruses and came in two attractive countertop models, 6- and 12-liter storage. Batliboi was mentioned by the Delhi research agency as yet another competitor, although Chatterjee knew nothing else about the brand. Taken all together, unit sales of all purifiers at these companies plus ZERO-B and Singer probably would account for around 60,000 units in 1996. The remaining 190,000 units would be Aquaguards and PureSips.

At least 100 Indian companies made and marketed candle filters. The largest of these probably was Bajaj Electrical Division, whose product line also included water heaters, irons, electric light bulbs, toasters, mixers, and grillers. Bajaj's candle filters were sold by a large number of dealers who carried the entire product line. Candle filters produced by other manufacturers were sold mostly through dealers who specialized in small household appliances and general hardware. Probably no single manufacturer of candle filters had more than 5 percent of any regional market in the country. No manufacturer attempted to satisfy a national market. Still, the candle filters market deserved serious consideration—perhaps Delight's entry strategy would attempt to "trade-up" users of candle filters to a better, safer product.

Finally, Chatterjee knew that sales of almost all purifiers in 1996 in India came from large urban areas. No manufacturer targeted rural or smaller urban areas and at best, Chatterjee had calculated, existing manufacturers were reaching only ten to fifteen percent of the entire Indian population. An explosion in sales would come if the right product could be sold outside metropolitan areas.

■ RECOMMENDATIONS

Chatterjee decided that an Indian market entry for Blair Company was subject to three "givens," as he called them. First, he thought that a strategic focus on rural or smaller urban areas would not be wise, at least at the start. The lack of adequate distribution and communication infrastructure in rural India meant that any market entry would begin with larger Indian cities, most likely on the west coast.

Second, market entry would require manufacturing units in India. Because the cost of skilled labor in India was around Rs.20 to Rs.25 per hour (compared to $20 to $25 per hour in the United States), importing complete units was out of the question. However, importing a few key components would be necessary at the start of operation.

Third, Blair Company should find an Indian partner. Chatterjee's visits had produced a number of promising partners: Polar Industries, Calcutta; Milton Plastics, Bombay; Videocon Appliances, Aurangabad; BPL Sanyo Utilities and Appliances, Bangalore; Onida Savak, Delhi; Hawkins India, Bombay; and Voltas, Bombay. All companies manufactured and marketed a line of high-quality household appliances, possessed one or more strong brand names, and had established dealer networks (minimum of 10,000 dealers). All were involved to greater or lesser degrees with international partners. All were medium-sized firms—not too large that a partnership with Blair Company would be one-sided, not too small that they would lack managerial talent and other resources. Finally, all were profitable (15 to 27 percent return on assets in 1995) and looking to grow. However, Chatterjee had no idea if any company would find the Delight purifier and Blair Company attractive or if they might be persuaded to sell part or all of their operations as an acquisition.

Field Testing and Product Recommendations

The most immediate decision Chatterjee faced was whether or not he should recommend a field test. The test would cost about $25,000, placing 20 units in Indian homes in three cities and monitoring their performance for three to six months. The decision to test really was more than it seemed—Chatterjee's boss had explained that a decision to test was really a decision to enter. It made no sense to spend this kind of time and money if India were not an attractive opportunity. The testing period also would give Blair Company representatives time to identify a suitable Indian company as either a licensee, joint venture partner, or acquisition.

Fundamental to market entry was product design. Engineers at Blair Company had taken the position that purification technologies planned for Delight could be "packaged in almost any fashion as long as we have electricity." Electricity was needed to operate the product's ozonator as well as to indicate to users that the unit was functioning properly (or improperly, as the case might be). Beyond this requirement, anything was possible.

Chatterjee thought that a modular approach would be best. The basic module would be a countertop unit much like that shown in Exhibit 2. The module would outperform anything now on the market in terms of flow rate, palatability, durability, and reliability, and would store two liters of purified water. Two additional modules would remove iron, calcium, and other metallic contaminants that were peculiar to particular regions. For example, Calcutta and much of the surrounding area suffered from iron contamination, which no filter or purifier now on the Indian market could remove to a satisfactory level. Water supplies in other areas in the country were known to contain objectionable concentrations of calcium, salt, arsenic, lead, or sulfur. Most Indian consumers would need neither of the additional modules, some would need one or the other, but very few would need both.

Market Entry and Marketing Planning Recommendations

Assuming that Chatterjee recommended proceeding with the field test, he would need to make a recommendation concerning mode of market entry. In addition, his recommendation should include an outline of a marketing plan.

Licensee Considerations   If market entry were in the form of a joint working arrangement with a licensee, Blair Company financial investment would be minimal. Chatterjee thought that Blair Company might risk as little as $30,000 in capital for production facilities and equipment, plus another $5,000 for office facilities and equipment. These investments would be completely offset by the licensee's payment to Blair Company for technology transfer and personnel training. Annual fixed costs to Blair Company should not exceed $40,000 at the outset and would decrease to $15,000 as soon as an Indian national could be hired, trained, and left in charge. Duties of this individual would be to work with Blair Company personnel in the United States and with management at the licensee to see that units were produced per Blair Company's specifications. Apart from this activity, Blair Company would have no control over the licensee's operations. Chatterjee expected that the licensee would pay royalties to Blair Company of about Rs.280 for each unit sold in the domestic market and Rs.450 for each unit that was exported. The average royalty probably would be around Rs.300.

Joint Venture/Acquisition Considerations   If entry were in the form of either a joint venture or an acquisition, financial investment and annual fixed costs would be much higher and depend greatly on the scope of operations. Chatterjee had roughed out some estimates for a joint venture entry, based on three levels of scope (see Exhibit 5). His estimates reflected what he thought were reasonable assumptions for all needed investments plus annual fixed expenses for sales activities, general administrative overhead, research and development, insurance, and depreciation. His estimates allowed for the Delight purifier to be sold either through dealers or through a direct, door-to-door salesforce. Chatterjee thought that estimates of annual fixed expenses for market entry via acquisition would be identical to those for a joint venture. However, estimates for the investment (purchase) might be considerably higher, the same, or lower. It depended on what was purchased.

Chatterjee's estimates of Delight's unit contribution margins reflected a number of assumptions—expected economies of scale, experience curve effects, costs of Indian labor and raw materials, and competitors' pricing strategies. However, the most important assumption was Delight's pricing strategy. If a skimming strategy were used

EXHIBIT 5

Investments and Fixed Costs for a Joint Venture Market Entry

	Operational Scope		
	Two Regions	Four Regions	National Market
1998 Market potential (units)	55,000	110,000	430,000
Initial investment (Rs.000)	4,000	8,000	30,000
Annual fixed overhead expenses (Rs.000)			
Using dealer channels	4,000	7,000	40,000
Using direct salesforce	7,200	14,000	88,000

and the product sold through a dealer channel, the basic module would be priced to dealers at Rs.5,500 and to consumers at Rs.5,900. "This would give us about a Rs.650 unit contribution, once we got production flowing smoothly," he thought. In contrast, if a penetration strategy were used and the product sold through a dealer channel, the basic module would be priced to dealers at Rs.4,100, to consumers at Rs.4,400, and yield a unit contribution of Rs.300. For simplicity's sake, Chatterjee assumed that the two additional modules would be priced to dealers at Rs.800, to consumers at Rs.1,000, and would yield a unit contribution of Rs.100. Finally, he assumed that all products sold to dealers would go directly from Blair Company to the dealers (no distributors would be used).

If a direct salesforce were employed instead of dealers, Chatterjee thought that prices charged to consumers would not change from those listed above. However, sales commissions would have to be paid in addition to the fixed costs necessary to maintain and manage the salesforce. Under a skimming price strategy, the sales commission would be Rs.550 per unit and the unit contribution would be Rs.500. Under a penetration price strategy, the sales commission would be Rs.400 per unit and the unit contribution would be Rs.200. These financial estimates, he would explain in his report, would apply to 1998 or 1999, the expected first year of operation.

Skimming versus penetration was more than just a pricing strategy. Product design for the skimming strategy would be noticeably superior, with higher performance and quality, a longer warranty period, more features, and a more attractive appearance than the design for the penetration strategy. Positioning, too, most likely would be different. Chatterjee recognized several positioning possibilities: performance and taste, value for the money/low price, safety, health, convenience, attractive styling, avoiding diseases and health-related bills, and superior American technology. The only position he considered "taken" in the market was that occupied by Aquaguard—protect family health and service at your doorstep. While other competitors had claimed certain positions for their products, none had devoted financial resources of a degree that Delight could not dislodge them. Chatterjee believed that considerable advertising and promotion expenditures would be necessary to communicate Delight's positioning. He would need estimates of these expenditures in his recommendation.

"If we go ahead with Delight, we'll have to move quickly," thought Chatterjee. "The window of opportunity is open but if Singer's product is as good as they claim, we'll be in for a fight. Still, Aquarius seems vulnerable on the water pressure requirement and on price. We'll need a product category 'killer' to win."

Preparing a Written Case Analysis

 Chapter 3 outlined an approach to marketing decision making and case analysis. The purpose of this appendix is to provide a more detailed description of what is involved in a thorough written case analysis through the use of an example. The following case—Republic National Bank of Dallas: NOW Accounts—describes an actual problem encountered by bank executives. The case is accompanied by a student analysis in the format described in Chapter 3. The student analysis shows how to organize a written case and the nature and scope of the analysis, which includes both qualitative and quantitative analyses. You should read and analyze the case before examining the student analysis.

Republic National Bank of Dallas
NOW Accounts

■ INTRODUCTION

In early 1977, Ruth Krusen, marketing officer for Republic National Bank of Dallas (RNB), was asked to assess the impact on Republic Bank of offering NOW (negotiable order of withdrawal) accounts if they became legal nationwide. Specifically, she was asked to:

1. Determine the impact on profits that Republic National Bank could anticipate from NOW accounts

2. Recommend a NOW account marketing strategy

The cooperation of Republic National Bank of Dallas in the preparation of this case is gratefully acknowledged. This case was prepared by Professor Roger A. Kerin, of the Edwin L. Cox School of Business, Southern Methodist University, as a basis for class discussion and is not designed to illustrate effective or ineffective handling of an administrative situation. Certain data have been disguised.

NOW accounts, which are effectively interest-bearing checking accounts, have been in use since 1972 in New England. In early 1977, however, a bill was introduced into Congress that would allow commercial banks and thrift institutions in all 50 states to provide this service.[1] Despite opposition in Congress, observers were of the opinion that legislation enabling NOW accounts would be passed by the first quarter of 1978 and would become effective January 1979.

■ BANKING IN TEXAS

Texas is a "unit banking" state. This means that individual banks cannot operate branch banks. The regulation that limits a bank to a single location was specified in the state constitution of 1876. In 1971, however, amendments to the Bank Holding Act allowed individual banks to acquire smaller institutions if the identity of the acquired bank was maintained. Since 1971, large banks in Texas have formed holding companies to improve their lending capability in order to better serve large commercial accounts. By 1977, 33 bank holding companies were operating in Texas. Holding companies owned 250 of the state's 1,360 banks and held about 55 percent of the state's total bank deposits in 1977.

Three of the largest bank holding companies in Texas are based in Dallas. Each operates its largest bank in downtown Dallas. First International Bancshares, which operates First National Bank, is the largest bank holding company in Texas. Republic of Texas Corporation operates the Republic National Bank of Dallas and is the second-largest holding company. Mercantile Texas Corporation operates Mercantile National Bank and is the fifth-largest bank holding company in terms of total assets.

Banking activity in Texas generally corresponds to pockets of urban and commercial growth. Accordingly, banking activity is concentrated in the Dallas–Fort Worth and Houston metropolitan areas. The San Antonio metropolitan area has shown a dramatic increase in banking activity due in part to population growth and increased economic growth.

■ COMPETITIVE SITUATION IN DALLAS

The Dallas banking market consists of 57 banks in the city of Dallas and an additional 43 banks in Dallas County. At the end of 1976, the 57 banks in the city of Dallas recorded total deposits of $13.27 billion. The 43 banks in Dallas County recorded deposits of about $1.25 billion.

Three large downtown banks dominate the Dallas banking market. At the end of 1976, Republic National Bank, First National Bank, and the Mercantile National Bank accounted for approximately 78 percent of total bank deposits in the city of Dallas and 71 percent of Dallas County bank deposits. Republic National Bank was the leader with approximately $4.6 billion in deposits, followed closely by First National Bank with $4.4 billion. Mercantile National Bank recorded total deposits of about $1.3 billion at the end of 1976. These three banks are located within walking distance of one another, as well as of some 12 other banks.

---

[1] Thrift institutions include mutual savings banks, cooperative banks, credit unions, and savings and loan associations. Thrift institutions differ from commercial banks in that only banks have the authority to accept demand deposits or checking accounts or offer commercial loans.

Competitive activities of Dallas banks have historically focused on retail (consumer) or wholesale (business) bank account development. Banks located in suburban areas typically emphasized the retail business, whereas downtown banks emphasized the wholesale business. Nevertheless, the Dallas competitive environment in recent years has been characterized by aggressive bank marketing efforts on both fronts. According to one observer of the Dallas banking scene:

> The competitive marketing furor is fierce, and it's not just the catchy advertising themes. . . . There's a scramble going on to repackage consumer services, put forth new services, cross-sell services, and woo corporate customers. There's Saturday banking, extended hours banking, 24-hour tellers, foreign currency sales, cash machines, no-charge checking package deals, automatic payroll deposits, pension fund management services, computer billing services, specially arranged travel tours, traveler's checks to spend on travel tours, equipment leasing, credit card loans, loan syndications, lock boxes, and on and on. First National Bank in Dallas alone lists more than 400 different bank "products" in its inventory of services.[2]

Krusen confirmed the observation that the Dallas banking market was competitive. She noted that RNB continues to be competitive in banking services, but "the question of how aggressive we should be has not been resolved at least as regards retail account marketing." RNB has at least as many bank services for customers as competitors do, if not more services than are offered by the vast majority of commercial banks in Dallas.

In addition to commercial banks, savings and loan association (S&Ls) also compete for passbook savings accounts among Dallas County residents. At the end of 1976, deposits of the 22 Dallas County-based savings and loan associations were $2.85 billion. Dallas Federal Savings was the largest savings and loan association with about $909.6 million in deposits, or about 32 percent of total deposits. Texas Federal Savings and First Texas Savings combined accounted for approximately $992 million in deposits, or 35 percent of total deposits. Dallas-based savings and loan associations operated approximately 150 offices in Dallas County. Savings and loan associations based outside Dallas County also operated about 50 officers in the county.

Savings and loan associations have aggressively sought deposits in recent years. Dallas-based associations have historically outpaced the national average for savings and loan deposit volume growth. Savings associations have emphasized two competitive advantages in their passbook savings marketing programs. First, they could pay $5\frac{1}{4}$ percent on passbook savings, whereas commercial banks were limited by law to 5 percent on passbook savings. Second, they could develop branch operations with a common name, whereas commercial banks were limited to a single location in Texas.

Savings and loan associations have placed greater emphasis on consumer, or installment, loans in recent years. Texas is unique among states in that it allows savings associations to provide installment loans, and some associations have used this opportunity to attract deposit volume. According to an industry observer, "S&Ls have historically attracted older customers. Installment loans are a useful service to bring in younger customers, introduce them to S&Ls, and get them to open a passbook savings account."

Credit unions also represent a competitive force in the Dallas market. By the end of 1976, 218 credit unions were located in the city of Dallas and its immediate environs. These credit unions operated 232 officers. Combined, credit unions held over $666 million in assets and served almost one-half million members.

Credit unions compete effectively in the Dallas market in three ways. First, they offer consumer, or installment, loans to their members at competitive interest rates. They hold a significant share of the automobile loans in the Dallas market. Second,

---

[2] Dave Clark, "A Big Pitch for Bucks," *Dallas-Fort Worth Business Quarterly* 1, no. 2.

credit unions hold substantial funds in member savings accounts. Third, credit unions provide share drafts to their members. A *share draft* is a withdrawal document that permits credit union members to make payments from interest-bearing savings accounts. These drafts resemble checks but are actually drafts drawn on a credit union and payable through a bank.

■ REPUBLIC NATIONAL BANK

Republic National Bank was founded in 1920. At that time, the bank was called Guaranty Bank and Trust, and it held a state banking charter. After several name changes, the present name was adopted in 1937, and RNB obtained a national bank charter. Today, RNB is the largest member of the Republic of Texas Corporation bank holding-company system. By the end of 1977, RNB would be ranked twenty-first in the United States in total assets and deposits and would be the largest bank in Texas and the South in terms of total assets, deposits, loans, and equity capital. Also by the end of 1977, RNB would be ranked 150th among the 500 largest banks in the non-Communist world, according to *American Banker* magazine. RNB had total assets exceeding $6 billion and a net income of approximately $36.3 million by that time.

Retail Account Marketing

Although figures are not available for competing banks, RNB is considered to have one of the largest, if not the largest, retail account bases in the Dallas area. According to Krusen, this occurred as a result of RNB's historic position of "taking chances on the little guy and community service." It was estimated that about 55 percent of RNB's retail checking accounts in 1977 were under $500. Exhibit 1 shows the distribution of accounts by account size.

EXHIBIT 1

Estimated Distribution of Personal Checking Account Balances in Early 1977

Account size	Percentage of Accounts	Percentage of Total Checking Account Deposits
Under $200	32%	3%
$200– $499	23	3
$500– $999	14	4
$1,000– $4,999	18	13
$5,000– $9,999	7	11
$10,000– $24,999	3	13
$25,000– $100,000	2	20
Over $100,000	1	33
	100%	100%

Number of Personal checking accounts: 45,000

Personal checking account deposits: $150 million

Note: Figures reported in this exhibit reflect approximations drawn from 1977 *District Bank Averages: Functional Cost Analysis* (Dallas: Federal Reserve Bank of Dallas, 1977).

This philosophy is communicated in RNB advertising. Beginning in the late 1960s with its "Silver Star Service" campaign and continuing with the "Star Treatment" advertising campaign, RNB communicated to present and potential customers that they were special and that RNB had a number of special services to provide them. In early 1977 the "Republic National Bank *Is* Dallas" campaign was launched, with Orson Welles narrating television and radio advertising spots and the Dallas Symphony playing the theme music. This campaign was designed to reflect the mutual traditions of RNB and Dallas residents as progressive and growth-oriented, as well as emphasize the interdependence of banking leadership and service with the prosperity and quality of Dallas life. Marketing research has shown that RNB has had the highest "top-of-mind awareness" of any bank in the Dallas area since 1975.

Retail Account Services

RNB retail account marketing efforts have resulted in a variety of traditional as well as innovative bank services for its customers. For example, RNB provides its Teller 24® Service, which is an automatic bank teller/cash machine. This service operates 24 hours a day at 26 locations around the city of Dallas and in six other Texas cities. Another innovation, the *Starpak* Account, is a complete package of banking services provided to customers for a fixed monthly fee of $3. Exhibit 2 gives a description of this service. RNB personal checking is highly competitive in the Dallas market, with no service charge for accounts that maintain a minimum monthly balance of $400. A $1 charge accrues to accounts with a minimum monthly balance of $300, a $2 charge with a minimum monthly balance of $200, and a $3 charge with no minimum balance requirement.

Retail Checking Account Revenue and Cost Estimates

In the course of preparing her report, Krusen contacted the RNB Controllers Division to obtain revenue and cost data on retail checking accounts. The Controllers Division report, based largely on Federal Reserve statistics, indicated that approximately 85 percent of retail checking account deposits were investable. In other words, about 15 percent of checking account deposits must be held in reserve. Ninety-six percent of savings accounts balances were investable.

The Controllers Division also indicated that RNB would realize an average yield on loans and securities of about 7.5 percent in 1977. Krusen noted that this figure was the lowest experienced by RNB in recent years. In 1974 RNB had realized an average yield of 10.59 percent. Other figures obtained directly from Federal Reserve statistical averages for commercial banks with total deposits of over $200 million were as follows:

Service and handling charge revenue per account per month:	$1.56
Account cost per month (including checks, deposits, and other assignable overhead):	$5.24

■ NOW ACCOUNTS

NOW accounts came into being as the result of the attempt of a Massachusetts mutual savings bank to circumvent the prohibition against thrift institutions' offering checking accounts. After a two-year regulatory and legal battle, Consumer Savings Bank of Worcester, Massachusetts, won its case and in June 1972 began to offer a savings account on which checklike instruments called negotiable orders of withdrawal could be written. Other mutuals in Massachusetts and New Hampshire soon followed suit.

EXHIBIT 2

Components of Republic National Bank's Starpak Account

1. *Unlimited Checking* —There's no minimum balance requirement, no per check charge, and no limit on the number of checks you write when you have a Starpak personal checking account.

2. *Free Personal Checks*—They're prenumbered and personalized with your name, address, and phone number, and you can order as many as you need any time you need them.

3. *Reduced Loan Rates*—With this feature alone, many people make Starpak pay for itself. At the end of the loan period, we'll refund 10 percent of the total interest you paid on installment loans of $1,000 or more, when the loan has been repaid as agreed. Of course, your loan is subject to normal credit approval.

4. *No Bank Charge for Traveler's Checks*—Or for Money Orders or Cashier's Checks when you show us your Starpak Account Card.

5. *Free Safe Deposit Box*—We'll give you the $5 size free. Or take $5 off the rent for a larger size.

6. *Combined Monthly Statement*—Your monthly statement can include status reports on any or all of the accounts you and your spouse have at Republic. You select the accounts you want the Combined Statement to cover. We can include your checking, savings, personal certificates of deposit, and even personal loans. Yes, you'll also receive separate regular statements on each of your Republic accounts you include in the Combined Statement.

7. *Numerical Check Listing*—Your Monthly statement will report each check in the order written. That makes it much easier to reconcile your statement each month.

8. *Automatic Overdraft Protection*—This optional service gives you additional peace of mind and the opportunity to take advantage of an exceptional bargain. It works this way. If the checks you write exceed your balance, we'll cover the overdrafts up to the limit of your Republic Master Charge or VISA Credit. Finance charges for deferred payment will apply at the normal rate. Repayment will be through your monthly Master Charge or VISA account payment.

9. *Teller 24® Service*—You can get cash from your Starpak Checking Account, or your Republic Master Charge or VISA Card, at any of 26 Teller 24 machines located in Dallas and six other Texas cities, and at 12,000 banks nationwide. With Teller 24 your money is available 24 hours a day, 7 days a week.

10. *Automatic Loan Repayment*—If you have an installment loan at Republic, we will, at your request, withdraw your monthly loan payment from your Starpak Checking Account. It's a good way to make sure you can take advantage of the 10 percent interest refund.

11. *Automatic Savings Account Deposits*—If you've never been able to save before, this plan solves the problem. Just tell us how much and on what day of the month. On the date you specify, we'll automatically transfer the amount you select from your checking to your savings account. Then, to help your savings grow even faster, we'll pay the highest interest rates allowable.

12. *Starpak Account Card*—It identifies you as a preferred customer of Republic National Bank, entitled to the privileges and special savings available with your Starpak Account.

13. *No Separate Charges*—All these Starpak services are available for the flat monthly fee of $3. There's no separate charge.

Plus these other services available to all Republic National Bank customers—We pay postage both ways when you bank by mail. We'll validate your in-bank parking stub when you bank. And you'll have a personal banker assigned to your accounts so that you can call for advice or assistance with any banking need.

Source: Bank brochure.

Although regulatory authorities persist in regarding the NOW account as a savings account on which checks can be written, from a consumer point of view (and from an operational point of view) it is a checking account that pays interest. As consumers gradually became educated about NOWs, commercial banks began to lose customers to this attractive type of account, with which they were unable to compete. In response, federal and state laws were passed permitting commercial banks as well as mutuals and S&Ls in Massachusetts and New Hampshire to offer NOW accounts starting in January 1974. As of March 1976, financial institutions in the other New England states were granted the same powers. In two of the states (Connecticut and Maine), state-chartered thrifts had been empowered to offer checking accounts a few months earlier.

In New England, NOW accounts may be offered to individuals and to nonprofit organizations (except that in Connecticut, thrifts can offer NOWs only to individuals).[3] A uniform rate ceiling of 5 percent applies to all institutions. Excerpts from a report prepared by the RNB Marketing Division on the development of NOW accounts in New England are presented in the appendix at the end of this case.

■ NOW ACCOUNT MARKETING STRATEGY

The task facing Krusen was difficult for a number of reasons. First, the only NOW account information available pertained to the New England experience. Although this information would be useful in gauging the rate of adoption of NOW accounts, it was not entirely clear how the Dallas-area banks and thrift institutions would react. Second, several contingency plans would have to be charted. If NOW accounts were not deemed appropriate for RNB by top management, then Krusen would have to recommend a strategy to maintain the RNB customer base. This strategy would depend on whether a "free" NOW account program became popular in the Dallas area or a more conservative approach was adopted by competitors. If the NOW account was adopted by RNB, she realized, the NOW account package (separate account or part of an existing bank service) and the price (service charges, if any) would have to be defined. The package and price would be, in part, determined by the competitive environment that developed and the cost of NOW accounts.

Timing was a third consideration. Should RNB be a leader and set the competitive tenor in the market or take a "wait and see" stance? Finally, if RNB decided to adopt the NOW account, then a question of communications would arise. For example, should RNB quietly inform present customers of NOW account availability or actively communicate availability to the Dallas market as a whole via an advertising program?

■ APPENDIX: NOW ACCOUNTS IN NEW ENGLAND, A REPORT PREPARED BY THE MARKETING DIVISION OF REPUBLIC NATIONAL BANK OF DALLAS

The objectives of this investigation of NOW accounts in New England were

1. To learn the speed and magnitude of NOW account impact as a basis for estimating the impact on RNB
2. To identify and evaluate various marketing strategies and their possible relevance to our own market

---

[3]At the time of this case and for analysis purposes, only retail (personal and nonprofit) checking accounts were affected by NOW accounts in the Dallas area.

EXHIBIT A.1

NOW Account Adoption in New England as of August 1976

| | Percentage of Institutions Offering | | Commercial Bank's Share of NOW Market | |
	Thrifts	Commercial Banks	Percentage of Accounts	Percentage of Balances
Massachusetts	94[a]	72	32	52
New Hampshire	81[a]	64	43	62
Connecticut	69	53	35	74
Maine	32	40	68	81
Vermont	23	29	89	93
Rhode Island[b]	25	75	83	85

[a]Mutual savings banks only; in each state two-thirds of the savings and loans also offer NOWs.

[b]Rhode Island has a unique situation of affiliated mutual savings banks and commercial banks. Figures in exhibit refer only to unaffiliated thrifts and commercial banks. NOWs are offered by 66 percent of the affiliated group.

Penetration of NOWs

Reaction of New England financial institutions given the power to offer NOWs is shown in Exhibit A.1. It indicates the percentages of thrifts and commercial banks that were offering NOWs by August 1976 and the market shares of commercial banks. By August 1976 mutual savings banks in Massachusetts and New Hampshire had been able to offer NOWs for 50 months, commercial banks for 30 months. In the other states, all institutions had been able to offer them for only 6 months.

Despite the resistance of commercial banks in Massachusetts and New Hampshire to offering NOWs, Exhibit A.1 shows that a substantial majority are now providing them. In the other New England states, commercial banks have moved more quickly to adopt NOW accounts. This is one of the reasons that they have a larger share of NOW accounts and balances than do commercial banks in Massachusetts and New Hampshire. Nevertheless, even in the latter states, commercial banks have captured more of the total NOW balances than have thrifts.

One conclusion supported by the data is that the competitiveness of financial institutions is directly related to the degree to which the state's population is concentrated in large urban markets.

The additional data on Massachusetts and New Hampshire shown in Exhibit A.2 indicate the substantial impact of NOWs in the personal payment account market.

EXHIBIT A.2

Personal Payment Accounts, August 1976

| | Personal Payment Balances | |
	Percentage in NOWs	Percentage in Thrifts
New Hampshire	72%	27%
Massachusetts	44	21

Note: Personal payment accounts consist of all checking balances plus 80 percent of NOW balances. The 20 percent of NOW balances estimated to have come from savings accounts have been deducted.

Exhibit A.2 shows that after four years, 72 percent of checking account balances in New Hampshire have been converted to NOWs and 44 percent have been converted in Massachusetts. Thrifts have captured 27 percent of this market in New Hampshire and 21 percent in Massachusetts.

Marketing Strategies

Massachusetts and New Hampshire   As simple as the concept of an interest-bearing checking account appears to be, NOW account introduction in New England produced an initial confusion of positioning, pricing, and marketing strategies.

Positioning   For a variety of reasons, thrifts initially positioned NOWs as savings accounts with a special convenience feature in getting access to funds. Consumers who opened them did not regard them as checking accounts and there was relatively low account activity. Adding to the confusion, when banks began to offer NOWs, some of them were very negative in their presentations. They told customers, in effect, "We have NOW accounts, but you don't really want to spend your savings, do you?"

In time, thrifts and then banks became more daring in presenting NOWs as accounts that were identical in function to checking accounts but paid interest. NOWs are by now recognized as a substitute for checking accounts, are opened instead of checking accounts (or an existing checking account is closed when it is realized that it is no longer needed), and have virtually the same level of activity as checking accounts.

Pricing.   Pricing was initially fairly conservative. In New Hampshire, NOWs were usually offered at a lower rate of interest than savings account, while in Massachusetts per-item charges were prevalent. Then a price war began and increasing numbers of institutions offered free NOWs—that is, maximum rate of interest, no service or item charges, and no minimum balance requirements.

The proportion of institutions offering free NOWs increased until mid-1975, but since then the trend has been reversed, largely because late entrants into the field have offered less generous terms. It has also been true that some institutions that previously offered free NOWs have imposed charges or minimum balance requirements.

The free NOW resulted from a variety of causes and motives:

1. At the time of introduction, money market rates were so high that the cost of NOW funds might still allow a margin of profit.
2. Thrifts were inexperienced in the costs involved in servicing checking accounts.
3. Some thrifts were determined to establish a good market share early, regardless of short-run lack of profitability.
4. In the major market areas, there was a free checking environment.

Price and Service Package   Pricing structures on NOWs in New England are as varied as checking account charges have historically been. The possibility of competing through the interest rate paid is the only new element. When NOW accounts are not free, some variant of the following occurs:

1. *Interest rates.* Initially, some institutions paid less than the maximum rate on savings accounts. However, under competitive pressure, rates rose to the 5 percent ceiling in all major markets. However, some institutions do not pay on a day-of-deposit to day-of-withdrawal basis. While very few now pay only on collected balances, several large banks are contemplating going in that direction. A few banks pay only on minimum balances.

2. *Balance requirements.* Balances above which the NOW account is "free" range from $200 to $1,000. In most cases, this is the minimum balance, although one large bank, Shawmut, has an average balance requirement.

   What happens when the balance that goes below the minimum varies?

   In some cases, no interest is paid; in others, a transaction or service fee is imposed; and in some cases, both. In some isolated markets, fees are imposed on all accounts, but in competitive major markets, NOWs become free at some balance level.

3. *Transaction charges.* Charges per check range from 10 to 25 cents. Usually, the charge is levied on all checks if the balance is below the required level. In some cases, a certain number of checks are free (5 to 15 per month), and in some other cases the number of free checks is related to balances (for example, 5 checks per $100 of average balance).

4. *Service charge.* Some banks charge flat fees rather than per-transaction charges. Fees generally are $1 or $2.

Other New England States   By the time NOW accounts were authorized in the other New England states, both thrifts and commercials had the opportunity to assess the cost and competitive impact of NOWs in the two original states, and money market conditions had changed. These facts are reflected in the response of financial institutions in offering NOWs. Commercial banks have moved more rapidly than they did in Massachusetts and New Hampshire. At the same time, both thrifts and commercial banks have been more conservative in pricing.

Connecticut.   Thrifts have moved aggressively to offer both checking accounts and NOWs. Although free checking prevails in major Connecticut markets and although about one-third of the thrifts offer free NOWs, large Connecticut banks have offered NOWs on conservative terms (high minimum balances with transaction charges for lower-balance accounts). The effect of this strategy is reflected in the high average balances of commercial bank NOWs—over $4,000.

Rhode Island.   The financial market is highly concentrated in a very few institutions. Six months after NOWs became legal, six of the nine commercial banks affiliated with thrift institutions, six of the eight unaffiliated banks, and one of the four unaffiliated thrifts were offering NOWs. None of them offered free NOWs. As in the checking account market in this state, relatively high minimum balances are required. It should be noted that because of the thrift-commercial bank affiliations, a majority of thrifts have in effect been able to offer checking accounts to their customers.

Maine.   Thrifts have concentrated harder on selling checking accounts than on offering NOWs. Neither thrifts nor commercial banks have moved very fast to offer NOWs. Few offer them free.

Vermont.   This state shows the slowest gain in institutions offering NOWs. None offers them free.

Republic National Bank of Dallas

NOW Accounts

■ STRATEGIC ISSUES AND PROBLEMS

Ruth Krusen, marketing officer for RNB, has been given responsibility for (1) determining the profit impact RNB could anticipate from NOW accounts and (2) recommending a contingency plan for a NOW account marketing strategy. Her task involves a number of important factors. She must assess the likelihood that the Dallas competitive environment will be liberal or conservative in its marketing of NOW accounts. An important consideration is RNB's role in affecting this environment, given its dominant position in the Dallas market and its posture regarding aggressiveness in retail account marketing. Ultimately, she must make a "go–no go" decision. A "go" decision requires a recommendation on the form of the service, its target market, its price reflected in service charges, and promotion. A "no go" decision must take into consideration RNB's competitive position without NOW accounts and measures to minimize their impact. The problem facing RNB is how to retain its dominant competitive position given an environmental threat (NOW accounts) while at the same time preserving profitability and its customer base.

■ INSIGHTS FROM THE NEW ENGLAND EXPERIENCE

The NOW account experience, based on the data in the report of the marketing division, reveals the following:

1. The faster commercial banks move to adopt NOW accounts, the larger their share of NOW accounts and NOW account balances.

2. Cannibalization of checking accounts occurs when NOW accounts are available; 72 percent of checking account balances in New Hampshire have been converted to NOW accounts, and 44 percent of checking accounts in Massachusetts have been converted to NOWs. These figures developed over 50 months (four years) after the NOW introduction (see Exhibit A.2.).

3. Exhibit 1 in the case provides some evidence that NOW account balances are high. This could mean that those individuals with high checking account balances are more likely to switch to NOWs. Alternatively, the Connecticut experience would indicate that minimum balance requirements increase NOW account balances. Data for Massachusetts and New Hampshire—both of which experienced "free NOWs"—would tend to support the point that individuals with high account balances convert to NOWs.

4. NOW account usage activity approaches checking account activity; hence checking account costs are merely transferred to managing NOW accounts.

5. Competitive activity, reflected in the NOW package provided, reveals that "free NOWs" were initially provided. Financial institutions subsequently offered less generous terms, however.

6. NOW account packages differ greatly with respect to minimum balances, service charges, and positioning against checking and savings accounts.

Results from the New England experience suggest that three scenarios are possible in the Dallas market.

Environment	*Environment Description*
No NOW adoption:	Financial institutions refrain from adoption.
Liberal NOW adoption:	NOWs are adopted with no minimum balance, service charges, 5 percent interest, an active promotion/communication program.
Conservative NOW adoption:	NOWs are adopted with some form of minimum service charges, less than 5 percent interest, little promotion or communication.

Numerous factors will affect the likelihood of each environment's developing in the Dallas market.

Factors in favor of a no-NOW environment:

1. The New England experience suggests that a no-win possibility exists for all financial institutions. For example, banks will have to pay interest on previously interest-free funds, and S&Ls and credit unions will incur costs not previously encountered.

2. Money market rates are quite low at present, suggesting little spread to make an adequate profit margin.

Factors in favor of a NOW environment:

1. The New England experience suggests that where NOWs are legalized, they are adopted in some form, by someone.

2. If the Dallas market is competitive *and* various financial institutions are vying for deposits, then NOWs offer a means to attract deposits. Moreover, the New England experience suggests that "getting in first" is crucial. "Followership" is not rewarded.

3. S&Ls are poised to take some advantage of NOWs in that their interest rate paid on deposits will fall from 5¼ percent to 5 percent, assuming a 5 percent ceiling level.

Factors in favor of a liberal NOW environment:

1. Thrifts might view NOWs as a way of gaining deposits quickly.

2. S&Ls will benefit from NOWs even if 5 per cent interest is offered on NOW accounts, since they are currently paying 5¼ percent on savings.

3. Share drafts provided by credit unions have characteristics similar to those of NOWs; NOW accounts would seem like a logical extension.

Factors in favor of a conservative NOW environment:

1. This appears to be the trend in New England states.

2. Dallas banks do not generally offer free checking.

3. Money market rates are low.

It would seem that a potential determinant of how the NOW environment evolves will be the decision of RNB, given its dominance in the Dallas banking market. RNB's dominant position would seem to affect the environment *only* if RNB acts immediately with a well thought out NOW account program. NOWs are probably inevitable—that is, the no-NOW environment seems unlikely. The question, then, is whether a liberal or a conservative NOW environment will develop. The environment could be influenced by RNB.

■ REPUBLIC NATIONAL BANK

RNB dominates the Dallas financial market. Its assets alone ($6 billion) are almost ten times *total* assets of all credit unions ($666 million). RNB's deposits ($4.6 billion) exceed the total for *all* S&Ls ($2.85 billion). RNB has the largest deposit base of all Dallas banks *and* the largest retail account deposit base in Dallas.

Nevertheless, RNB management apparently has not resolved how aggressive the bank should be in retail account marketing efforts. The aggressiveness issue would seem to be related to the bank's emphasis on the wholesale rather than the retail business.

Exhibit 1 in the case indicates that about 55 percent of RNB's checking accounts are under $500. However, 96 percent of total checking account balances are accounted for by accounts of $500 and up, and 53 percent of total deposits are accounted for by accounts of over $25,000. The average account size is $3,333 ($150 million in deposits divided by 45,000 accounts). A profitability analysis of checking account sizes reveals that RNB loses money on accounts that are less than $500 on an annual basis (see Exhibit 1 in this analysis). This profitability analysis indicates that accounts below $500 produce a *loss* of $519,210 annually:

Accounts under $200:   14,400 accounts × ($24.24) = ($349,056)

Accounts $200–$499:   10,350 accounts × ($16.44) = ($170,154)

Loss   = ($519,210)

More important, this analysis provides important data on the pricing of NOW accounts and the form of the service, as will be discussed later.

■ PLAN OF ACTION

There are two primary alternatives open to RNB: to offer NOWs or not to offer NOWs. If NOWs are considered, then the form, price, and promotion must be determined. The alternatives are:

1. Do not offer NOW accounts.

2. Offer NOW accounts with no conditions and promote them heavily or modestly.

3. Offer NOW accounts with conditions and promote them heavily or modestly.

The advantages and disadvantages of the options available to RNB can be outlined as follows:

1. Not offering NOW accounts:

   Advantages

   • RNB is dominant and has the resources to wait and see what will happen.

   • The impact on revenue of offering NOWs would be too server. Assuming that *all accounts* are cannibalized by NOWs and the interest yield drops

EXHIBIT 1

RNB Retail Account Profit Analysis (Based on Exhibit 1 in the Case)

Account Size	Average Interest Revenue per Account[a]	+	Average Service/ Handling Revenue per Account[b]	=	Average Revenue per Account	−	Account Cost[b]	=	Profit/ (Loss)
Less than $200	$19.92		$18.72		$38.64		$62.88		$(24.24)
$200–$499	27.72		18.72		46.44		62.88		(16.44)
$500–$999	60.71		18.72		79.43		62.88		16.55
$1,000–$4,999	153.47		18.72		172.19		62.88		109.31
$5,000–$9,999	333.93		18.72		352.65		62.88		289.77
$10,000–$24,999	920.83		18.72		939.55		62.88		876.67
$25,000–$100,000	2,125.00		18.72		2,143.72		62.88		2,080.84
Greater than $100,000	7,083.00		18.72		7,101.72		62.88		7,038.84

[a] Computed as follows: $\dfrac{\text{Account size deposit volume}}{\text{Number of accounts in category}} \times 85\% \times 0.075$.

For an account size of $200, using Exhibit 1 data: $\dfrac{\$4.5 \text{ million}}{14,400} \times 0.85 \times 0.075 = \$19.92$

[b] Annualized average account revenue and cost given in the case where service/handling charge revenue per account per month = $1.56; account cost per month = $5.24.

from 7½ percent to 2½ percent because of 5 percent interest on NOWs, the interest revenue lost will be about $6.0 million.

Checking Deposits		Percent Investable		Investable Deposits
$150 million	×	85%	=	$127.5 million
				Interest Revenue
$127.5 million	×	0.075	=	$9,562,500
$144 million	×	0.025	=	−3,600,000
Interest revenue lost				$5,962,500

Note that NOW accounts are viewed as savings accounts, and 96 percent of deposits are investable.

Disadvantages

- RNB will lose an opportunity to be an innovator or the "first to market," which has been shown in New England to be advantageous.

- Erosion of accounts may occur, as individuals switch to institutions offering NOW accounts. This factor is particularly important if *large* accounts switch, and they are most likely to do so, since they stand to benefit most from NOW accounts.

2. Offering NOW accounts with no conditions:

Advantages

- Nonconditional NOWs will have a dramatic impact on the Dallas banking market. Banks offering them will most likely attract deposits and accounts in great numbers, particularly since they are a better deal than checking accounts with minimum balances or service charges, *plus* they give interest!

- Nonconditional NOW accounts will set the competitive tenor of the market; retail banks not offering them may be unable to compete.
- By offering nonconditional NOWs, RNB will keep current account from being attracted to competitors (preemptive cannibalism).

Disadvantages

- This strategy could be very expensive. As noted earlier, in addition to the account costs, a loss of interest of $6 million is possible.
- This strategy will cannibalize checking accounts almost totally.

3. Offering NOW accounts with conditions:

Advantages

- A minimum-balance condition would allow RNB to accept only those accounts on which it can make money.
- A service/handling charge condition would also result in greater account selectivity.
- A break-even analysis shows how RNB can determine a minimum balance given current service charge and account costs per year. The break-even point is the point at which total (interest plus handling/service charges) minus total costs (account cost per month) equals zero. Since RNB will net 2.5 percent in account interest revenue, has an $18.72 handling and service revenue per account per year ($1.56 × 12 months), and has an annual account cost of $62.88 ($5.24 × 12 months), solving for the minimum account balance reveals the following:

$$\text{Profit} = \frac{\text{acct. interest}}{\text{revenue}} + \frac{\text{handling/}}{\text{service charge}} - \frac{\text{acct.}}{\text{cost}}$$

$$0 = 0.025X + \$18.72 - \$62.88$$

$$\$44.16 = 0.025X$$

$$\$1{,}766.40 = X$$

Thus, RNB breaks even at an account balance of $1,766.40, given existing handling/service revenue per account and account maintenance costs. This minimum balance level would be a condition that from 80 percent to 90 percent of RNB's accounts could meet (see Exhibit 1 in the case).

Disadvantages

- This strategy leaves RNB open to being undercut by competitors if conditions are too stringent.
- Overly complex conditions and the likelihood of customers' being unexpectedly hit with service charges could hurt goodwill, particularly among larger balance account holders.

■ RECOMMENDED NOW ACCOUNT MARKETING STRATEGY

The previous analysis indicates that RNB can shape the NOW account environment in Dallas. The following NOW account marketing strategy will ensure that this will happen.

Goals and Objectives

1. RNB should pioneer NOW accounts in the Dallas market to set the competitive tone and create a "rational" NOW environment.

2. RNB should focus on achieving 85percent customer retention.

3. RNB should break even on NOW accounts.

Target Market

The target market for NOW accounts should be current customers with large account balances. Specifically, current customers with a minimum account size of $1,800.00 is the primary target market. This market represents almost all of RNB's current accounts. There is little to gain from attracting new customers for NOW accounts.

Marketing Mix

Product Strategy   NOW accounts will be included with an existing service bundle—the Starpak Account. It is expected that NOW accounts will cannibalize existing accounts. RNB's focus on current customers is a form of preemptive cannibalism necessary to retain existing customers.

Price Strategy   NOW accounts should carry a service charge. The recommended charge is $18.75 per account. This service charge, given the account cost, account interest revenue, and an account interest revenue, will allow RNB to break even on estimated annual minimum account balance of $1,766.40.

Distribution and Sales   NOW accounts will be provided at all locations by the New Account staff. Training for the New Account RNB staff should begin immediately. Documentation for the Starpak Account should be immediately modified to incorporate NOW accounts.

Advertising and Promotion   A modest advertising and promotion (A&P) program is recommended for NOW accounts. The A&P program should focus on current customers via a direct mail program and specifically inserts in monthly statements. Starpak print and TV advertising should incorporate reference to NOW accounts.

Advertising opportunity. Conditions suggesting that a product or services would benefit from advertising. They are (1) favorable primary demand for the product or service category, (2) the product or service to be advertised can be significantly differentiated from its competitors, (3) the product or service has hidden qualities or benefits that can be portrayed effectively through advertising, and (4) there are strong emotional buying motives for the product or service.

Brand equity. The added value a brand name bestows on a product or service beyond the functional benefits provided.

Brand extension strategy. The practice of using a current brand name to enter a completely different product class.

Break-even analysis. The unit or dollar sales volume at which an organization neither makes a profit nor incurs a loss. The formula for determining the number of units required to break even is: unit break-even = total dollar fixed costs ÷ (unit selling price-unit variable costs).

Bundling. The practice of marketing two or more product or service items in a singe "package" with one price.

Business mission. Describes the organization's purpose with reference to its customers, products or services, markets, philosophy, and technology.

Cannibalism. The process whereby the sales of a new product or service come at the expense of existing products (services) already marketed by the firm.

Chain ratio method. A technique for estimating market sales potential that involves multiplying a base number by several adjusting factors that are believed to influence market sales potential.

Channel captain. A member of a marketing channel with the power to influence the behavior of other channel members.

Channel conflict. A situation that arises when one channel member believes another channel member is engaged in behavior that is preventing it from achieving its goals.

Co-branding. The pairing of two brand names of two manufacturers on a single product.

Contribution. The difference between total sales revenue and total variable costs, or, on a per-unit basis, the difference between unit selling price and unit variable cost. Contribution can be expressed in percentage terms (contribution margin) or dollar terms (contribution per unit).

Cost of goods sold. Material, labor, and factory overhead applied directly to production.

Cross-elasticity of demand. The percentage responsiveness of the quantity demanded of one product or service to a percentage price change in another product of service.

Discounted cash flows. Future cash flows expressed in terms of their present value.

Disintermediation. The elimination of traditional intermediaries and direct distribution, often through electronic marketing channels.

Distinctive competency. An organization's unique strengths or qualities, including skills, technologies, or resources that distinguish it from other organizations. These competencies are imperfectly imitable by competitors and provide superior customer value.

Diversification. A product-market strategy that involves the development or acquisition of offerings new to the organization and the introduction of those offerings to publics (markets) not previously served by the organization.

Dual distribution. The practice of distributing products or services through two or more different marketing channels that may or may not compete for similar buyers.

Effective demand. The situation when prospective buyers have both the willingness and ability to purchase an organization's offerings.

Electronic marketing channels. Marketing channels that employ some form of electronic communication, including the Internet, to make products and services available for consumption or use by consumers and industrial users.

Exclusive distribution. A distribution strategy whereby a producer sells its products or services in only one retail outlet in a specific geographical area.

Fighting brand strategy. The practice of adding a new brand whose sole purpose is to confront competitive brands in a product class being served by an organization.

Fixed cost. Expenses that do not fluctuate with output volume within a relevant time period (usually defined as a budget year), but become progressively smaller per unit of output as volume increases. Fixed costs divide into programmed costs, which result from attempts to generate sales volume, and committed costs, which are those required to maintain the organization.

Flanker brand strategy. The practice of adding new brands on the high or low end of a product line based on a price-quality continuum.

Full-cost price strategies. Those that consider both variable and fixed cost (total cost) in the pricing of a product or service.

Gross margin (or gross profit). The difference between total sales revenue and total cost of goods sold, or, on a per-unit basis, the difference between unit selling price and unit cost of goods sold. Gross margin can be expressed in dollar or percentage terms.

Harvesting. The practice of reducing the investment in a business entity (division, product) to cut costs or improve cash flow.

Integrated marketing communications. The practice of blending different elements of the communication mix in mutually reinforcing ways.

Intensive distribution. A distribution strategy whereby a producer sells its products or services in as many retail outlets as possible in a geographical area.

Life cycle. The plot of sales of a single product or brand or service or a class of products or services over time.

Market. Prospective buyers (individuals or organizations) who are willing and able to purchase the existing or potential offering (product or service) of an organization.

Market-development strategy. A product-market strategy whereby an organization introduces its offerings to markets other than those it is currently serving. In global marketing, this strategy can be implemented through exportation, licensing, joint ventures, or direct investment.

Market evolution. Changes in primary demand for a product class.

Market-penetration strategy. A product-market strategy whereby an organization seeks to gain greater dominance in a market in which it already has an offering. This strategy often means capturing a larger share of an existing market.

Market redefinition. Changes in the offering demanded by buyers or promoted by competitors.

Market sales potential. The maximum level of sales that might be available to all organizations serving a defined market in a specific time period given (1) the marketing-mix activities and effort of all organizations, and (2) a set of environmental conditions.

Market segmentation. The breaking down or building up of potential buyers into groups on the basis of some sort of homogeneous characteristic(s) (e.g., age, income, geography) relating to purchase or consumption behavior.

Market share. Sales of a firm, product or brand divided by the sales of the served "market."

Market targeting (or target marketing). The specification of the particular market segment(s) the organization wishes to pursue. Differentiated marketing means that an organization simultaneously pursues several different market segments, usually with a different strategy for segments, usually with a different strategy for each. Concentrated marketing means that only a single market segment is pursued.

Marketing audit. A comprehensive, systematic, independent, and periodic examination of a company's or business unit's marketing environment, objectives, strategies, and activities with a view of determining problem areas and opportunities and recommending a plan of action to improve the company's marketing performance.

Marketing channel. Individuals and firms involved in the process of making a product or service available for consumption or use by consumers and industrial users.

Marketing-cost analysis. The practice of assigning or allocating costs to a specified marketing activity or entity in a manner that accurately displays the financial contribution of activities or entities to the organization.

Marketing mix. Those activities controllable by the organization that include the product, service, or idea offered, the manner in which the offering will be communicated to customers, the method for distributing or delivering the offering, and the price to be charged for the offering.

Mass customization. Tailoring product and services to the tastes and preferences of individual buyers in high volumes and at a relatively low cost.

Multi-channel marketing. The blending of an electronic marketing channel and a traditional channel in ways that are mutually reinforcing in attracting, retaining, and building relationships with customers.

New-brand strategy. The development of a new brand and often a new offering for a product class that has not been previously served by the organization.

Net profit margin (before taxes). The remainder after cost of goods sold, other variable costs, and fixed costs have been subtracted from sales revenue, or simply, total revenue minus total cost. Net profit margin can be expressed in dollar or percentage terms.

Offering. The sum total of benefits or satisfaction provided to target markets by an organization. An offering consists of a tangible product or service plus related services, warranties or guarantees, packaging, etc.

Offering mix or portfolio. The totality of an organization's offering (products and services).

Operating leverage. The extent to which fixed costs and variable costs are used in the production and marketing of products and services.

Operations control. The practice of assessing how well an organization performs marketing activities as it seeks to achieve planned outcomes.

Opportunity analysis. The process of identifying opportunities, matching the opportunity to the organization, and evaluating the opportunity.

Opportunity cost. Alternative uses of resources that are given up when pursuing one alternative rather than another. Sometimes referred to as the benefits not obtained from not choosing an alternative.

Payback period. The number of years required for an organization to recapture its initial investment in an offering.

Penetration pricing strategy. Setting a relatively low initial price for a new product or service.

Positioning. The act of designing an organization's offering and image so that it occupies a distinct and valued place in the target customer's mind relative to competitive offerings. A product or service can be positioned by (1) attribute or benefit, (2) use or application, (3) product or service user, (4) product or service class, (5) competitors, and (6) price and quality.

Price elasticity of demand. The percentage change in quantity demanded relative to a percentage change in price for a product or service.

Product-development strategy. A product-market strategy whereby an organization creates new offerings for existing markets through product innovation, product augmentation, or product line extensions.

Pro forma income statement. An income statement containing projected revenues, budgeted (variable and fixed) expenses, and estimated net profit for an organization, product, or service during a specific planning period, usually a year.

Product-line pricing. The setting of prices for all items in a product line. It involves determining (1) the lowest-priced product price, (2) the highest-priced product, and (3) price differentials for all other products in the line.

Pull communication strategy. The practice of creating initial interest for an offering among potential buyers, who in turn demand the offering from intermediaries, ultimately "pulling" the offering through the channel. The principal emphasis is on consumer advertising and consumer promotions.

Push communication strategy. The practice of "pushing" an offering through a marketing channel in a sequential fashion, with each channel representing a distinct target market. The principal emphasis is on personal selling and trade promotions directed toward wholesalers and retailers.

Regional marketing. The practice of using different marketing mixes to accommodate unique preferences and competitive conditions in different geographical areas.

Relevant cost. Expenditures that (1) are expected to occur in the future as a result of some marketing action and (2) differ among marketing alternatives being considered.

Sales forecast. The level of sales a single organization expects to achieve based on a chosen marketing strategy and an assumed competitive environment.

Selective distribution. A distribution strategy whereby a producer sells its products or services in a few retail outlets in a specific geographical area.

Situation analysis. The appraisal of operations to determine the reasons for the gap between what was or is expected and what has happened or will happen.

Skimming pricing strategy. Setting a relatively high initial price for a new product or service.

Strategic change. Environmental change that will affect the long-run well-being of the organization.

Strategic control. The practice of assessing the direction of the organizations as evidenced by its implicit or explicit goals, objectives, strategies, and capacity to perform in the context of changing environments and competitive actions.

Strategic marketing management. The analytical process of (1) defining the organization's business, mission, and goals; (2) identifying and framing organizational opportunities; (3) formulating product-market strategies; (4) budgeting marketing, financial, and production resources; and (5) developing reformulation and recovery strategies.

Sub-branding. The practice of combining a family brand with a new brand when introducing new product or service offerings.

Success requirements. The basic tasks that must be performed by an organization in a market or industry to compete successfully. These are sometimes "key success factors," or simply KSFs.

Sunk cost. Past expenditures for a given activity that are typically irrelevant in whole or in part to future decisions. The "sunk cost fallacy" is an attempt to recoup spent dollars by spending still more dollars in the future.

SWOT analysis. A formal framework for identifying and framing organizational growth opportunities. SWOT is an acronym for an organization's Strengths and Weaknesses and external Opportunities and Threats.

Trade margin. The difference between unit sales price and unit cost at each level of a marketing channel. Trade margin is usually expressed in percentage terms.

Trading down. The process of reducing the number of features or quality of an offering and lowering the purchase price.

Trading up. The practice of improving an offering by adding new features and higher quality materials or augmenting products with services and raising the purchase price.

Value. The ratio of perceived benefits to price for a product or service.

Variable cost. Expenses that are uniform per unit of output within a relevant time period (usually defined as a budget year); total variable costs fluctuate in direct proportion to the output volume of units produced. Variable costs includes cost of goods sold and other variable costs such as sales commissions.

Variable-cost price strategies. Those that consider only direct (variable) costs associated with the offering in pricing a product or service.

Viral marketing. An Internet/Web-enabled promotion strategy that encourages individuals to forward marketer-initiated messages to others via e-mail.

Working capital. The dollar value of an organization's current assets (such as cash, accounts receivable, prepaid expenses, inventory) *minus* the dollar value of current liabilities (such as short-term accounts payable for goods and services, income taxes).

Subject Index

Locators with n indicate note.

Company and Brand Index